Handbook For Teaching Introductory Psychology

Volume Two

Edited by

Michelle R. Hebl
Rice University

Charles L. Brewer
Furman University

Ludy T. Benjamin, Jr.
Texas A&M University

LEA LAWRENCE ERLBAUM ASSOCIATES, PUBLISHERS
2000 Mahwah, New Jersey   London

Lawrence Erlbaum Associates, Inc., Publishers
10 Industrial Avenue
Mahwah, New Jersey 07430

Library of Congress Cataloging-in-Publication Data

Handbook for teaching introductory psychology.
  Bibliography: p.
  Includes index.
  1. Psychology—Study and teaching (Higher)
I. Benjamin, Ludy T., 1945–   . II. Daniel, Robert S.
III. Brewer, Charles L.
BF77.H26 1985   150′.7   85-6758
ISBN 0-89859-561-4 (volume 1)
ISBN 0-8058-3654-3 (volume 2)

Printed in the United States of America
10 9 8 7 6 5 4 3 2 1

TABLE OF CONTENTS

Preface

Section I. Issues and Approaches in Teaching Introductory Psychology

1. **Structure of the Introductory Course**
   Improving textbook selection. *Steven P. Chatman and Ernest T. Goetz* 3
   Introductory course content and goals. *Benjamin Miller and Barbara F. Gentile* 5

2. **Approaches to the Introductory Course: Techniques**
   Teaching introductory psychology at a distance by two-way interactive video. *Emir-Anne Andrews, Verena F. Gosse, Rennie S. Gaulton, and Richard I. Maddigan* 14
   Personalization and active learning in the large introductory psychology class. *Ludy T. Benjamin, Jr.* 17
   The vital role of psychology's history in introductory courses: An interview with Ludy T. Benjamin, Jr. *C. James Goodwin* 24
   "Giving psychology away": Some experiences teaching undergraduates practical psychology. *Anthony F. Grasha* 27
   A rotational format for team teaching introductory psychology. *Henry C. Morlock, William P. Gaeddert, Naomi B. McCormick, Matthew R. Merrens, Lary C. Shaffer, and Taher Zandi* 31
   A method for teaching name mnemonics. *Steven M. Smith* 32
   How I kicked the lecture habit: Inquiry teaching in psychology. *William H. Zachry* 34

3. **Approaches to the Introductory Course: Content**
   Integrating research ethics into the introductory psychology course curriculum. *Celia B. Fisher and Tara L. Kuther* 38
   Incorporating evolutionary theory into the teaching of psychology. *Peter Gray* 42

4. **Examinations and Grading**
   Practice versus review exams and final exam performance. *William R. Balch* 50
   Holistic grading of written work in introductory psychology: Reliability, validity, and efficiency. *Robert J. Madigan and James J. Brosamer* 54
   Rating class participation: The prof/peer method. *Kenneth B. Melvin* 57
   Study strategy portfolio: A project to enhance study skills and time management. *Gabriele B. Sweidel* 59

5. **Students' Interests, Perceptions, and Motives**
   Student expectations of course and instructor. *Angela H. Becker, Stephen F. Davis, Loretta Neal, and Cathy A. Grover* 62
   The semantic profile technique for measuring students' impressions of psychology courses. *William B. Davidson, William J. House, and O. Joseph Harm* 64
   Motivation in the college classroom: What students tell us. *Edmund J. Sass* 67
   Introductory psychology from the standpoint of the consumer. *Mary Lou Zanich and David E. Grover* 68

6. **Enhancing Student Interest**
   The create-a-game exam: A method to facilitate student interest and learning. *Joy L. Berrenberg and Ann Prosser* 71
   A method for enhancing student interest in large introductory classes. *William Buskist and Devin Wylie* 73
   Motivating students to read journal articles. *David M. Carkenord* 75

7. **Discussion Exercises and Group Activities**
   Consider the opposite: Opening minds through in-class debates on course-related controversies. *Thomas Lee Budesheim and Arlene R. Lundquist* 78
   Cooperative learning and critical thinking. *James L. Cooper* 82
   In-class collaborative learning: Practical suggestions from the teaching trenches. *Peter J. Giordano and Elizabeth Yost Hammer* 84

Case study pedagogy to advance critical thinking. *Sharon A. McDade*   86
Writing to discuss: Use of a clustering technique. *Deborah G. Ventis*   87

8. **Diversity in the Introductory Classroom**
Suggestions on teaching international students: Advice for psychology instructors. *Dave S. Collingridge*   90
On teaching about the cultural relativism of psychological constructs. *Carolyn Zerbe Enns*   92
Confronting heterosexism in the teaching of psychology. *Jane M. Simoni*   98
Infusing black psychology into the introductory psychology course. *Lisa A. Whitten*   104

9. **Teaching Critical Thinking**
Using riddles and interactive computer games to teach problem solving skills. *John H. Doolittle*   113
Engaging students' intellects: The immersion approach to critical thinking in psychology instruction. *Peter Gray*   115
Inquiring minds really do want to know: Using questioning to teach critical thinking. *Alison King*   122
Using writing to develop and assess critical thinking. *Carole Wade*   126

10. **Writing to Learn, Learning to Write**
Novels as case-study materials for psychology students. *Joan C. Chrisler*   130
Critiquing articles cited in the introductory textbook: A writing assignment. *Karen C. Gareis*   131
Improving the writing skills of students in introductory psychology. *Robert Madigan and James Brosamer*   134
The psychology portfolio: Promoting writing and critical thinking about psychology. *Cheryl A. Rickabaugh*   137
Effective feedback on written assignments. *Daniel B. Willingham*   139

11. **Computers in the Introductory Course**
Psychology on a disk: Then what? *Thomas Brothen*   143
Developing visual displays for lecture-based courses. *Michael A. Seaman*   146
Developing a web-assisted class: An interview with Mark Mitchell. *Jeanne M. Slattery*   150
Computer-assisted instruction as a supplement to lectures in an introductory psychology class. *Everett L. Worthington, Jr., Josephine A. Welsh, C. Ray Archer, Erica J. Mindes, and Donelson R. Forsyth*   154

*Section II. **Demonstrations and Activities in Introductory Psychology***

12. **General**
Invertebrates in the classroom. *Charles I. Abramson*   163
In-class poster sessions. *Brian N. Baird*   168
The science fair: A supplement to the lecture technique. *Thomas A. Fish and Ian H. Fraser*   171
Rap singing as an icebreaker for large classes. *E. Rae Harcum*   173
Integrating disability awareness into psychology courses: Applications in abnormal psychology and perception. *Stephen A. Wurst and Karen Wolford*   174
Combining the use of progressive writing techniques and popular movies in introductory psychology. *Scott H. Hemenover, Jeffrey B. Caster, and Ayumi Mizumoto*   177

13. **Research Methods and Statistics**
From the laboratory to the headlines: Teaching critical evaluation of press reports of research. *Patricia A. Connor-Greene*   180
A sweet way to teach students about the sampling distribution of the mean. *Jennifer L. Dyck and Nancy R. Gee*   182
"The eye of the beholder": A classroom demonstration of observer bias. *Miriam D. Goldstein, J. Roy Hopkins, and Michael J. Strube*   185
A "handy" way to introduce research methods. *David E. Johnson*   188
Publication bias: A computer-assisted demonstration of excluding nonsignificant results from research interpretation. *Todd C. Riniolo*   190

14. **Biopsychology**
Propagation of action potentials: An active participation exercise. *Gary Felsten*   194
Some simple classroom experiments on cerebral lateralization. *Ernest D. Kemble, Terri Filipi, and Linda Gravlin*   196
Classroom demonstration of behavioral effects of the split-brain operation. *Edward J. Morris*   199
Neural coding and synaptic transmission: Participation exercises for introductory psychology. *Richard Reardon, Francis T. Durso, and Donald A. Wilson*   201

15. **Developmental Psychology**

"Dear Mom and Dad": Using personal letters to enhance students' understanding of developmental issues. *Ellen N. Junn* — 205

Using biographies of adults over 65 years of age to understand life-span developmental psychology. *Joan M. Neysmith-Roy and Carmel L. Kleisinger* — 208

Create-a-children's game: An exercise for developmental psychology classes. *Georgia N. Nigro* — 211

Dr. Kohlberg goes to Washington: Using congressional debates to teach moral development. *Johnna K. Shapiro* — 212

16. **Sensation and Perception**

The garbage-can illusion as a teaching demonstration. *Robert Cavalier and Richard Wesp* — 215

Demonstrations of color perception and the importance of contours. *David T. Horner* — 216

A teaching demonstration involving perceived lunar size. *Mark A. Kunkel* — 218

17. **Learning**

Classical-conditioning demonstrations for elementary and advanced courses. *Charles I. Abramson, Tim Onstott, Shawn Edwards, and Kathy Bowe* — 221

Preparing for an important event: Demonstrating the modern view of classical conditioning. *Art Kohn and James W. Kalat* — 225

Demonstrating classical conditioning in introductory psychology: Needles do not always make balloons pop! *Mark W. Vernoy* — 228

18. **Memory and Cognition**

Demonstrating the influence of cognition on emotion and behavior. *Jerry L. Deffenbacher* — 229

Using a videotape clip to demonstrate the fallibility of eyewitness testimony. *Nancy R. Gee and Jennifer L. Dyck* — 232

Memory and the Seven Dwarfs. *Marianne Miserandino* — 234

Mnemopoly: Board games and mnemonics. *Lawrence M. Schoen* — 236

19. **Psychological Disorders**

Exploring mental illness through a poetry-writing assignment. *Joan C. Chrisler* — 239

The disordered monologue: A classroom demonstration of the symptoms of schizophrenia. *Timothy M. Osberg* — 240

20. **Social Psychology and Personality**

Defining aggression: An exercise for classroom discussion. *Ludy T. Benjamin, Jr.* — 242

The power of stereotypes: A labeling exercise. *Susan B. Goldstein* — 244

Unveiling positions of privilege: A hands-on approach to understanding racism. *Sandra M. Lawrence* — 246

Freudian principles in everyday life. *Marianne Miserandino* — 248

21. **Sex and Gender**

Gender bias in leader selection. *Michelle R. Hebl* — 252

Defining normal sexual behavior: A classroom exercise. *Mary E. Kite* — 254

Using science fiction to teach the psychology of sex and gender. *Hilary M. Lips* — 256

We dream, you do: "Great" grandmothers teach a lesson in women's changing roles. *Elizabeth C. Vozzola* — 257

22. **Industrial/Organizational Psychology**

Promoting human factors psychology thinking through design assignments. *David M. Carkenord* — 260

Consumer behavior classroom exercises that really work. *Allan J. Kimmel* — 262

Subject Index — 266

Appendix — 269

PREFACE

Introductory psychology is one of the most popular courses for college and high school students in the United States. Several recent events highlight the importance of this course. First, the National Conference on Enhancing the Quality of Undergraduate Education held at St. Mary's College of Maryland in June 1991 stressed the centrality of introductory psychology in the undergraduate curriculum (see McGovern, 1993). Because the introductory course may be the only formal study of psychology for most students, it "should provide a survey of psychological topics and methodological approaches that reflect breadth of the field, including various concepts, theories, and subspecialties" (Brewer et al., 1993, p. 172). Second, the Educational Testing Service developed an Advanced Placement (AP) Examination in Psychology for high school students. In 1992, approximately 4,000 students throughout the country took the first AP psychology exam, and the number has increased dramatically every year since. More than 28,000 students took the exam in 1999. Third, Teachers of Psychology in Secondary Schools (TOPSS) was established as part of the Education Directorate of the American Psychological Association (APA) in 1993 and is now an APA continuing committee. Fourth, TOPSS was instrumental in developing an important document, *National Standards for the Teaching of High School Psychology* (Brewer, 1999), which was officially approved by the APA Council of Representatives in August 1999. These developments illustrate the significance of introductory psychology and indicate widespread concern for how it is taught. Recommendations from the St. Mary's Conference on the college curriculum, along with the high school *Standards*, provided important guidance in selecting articles for Volume 2 of this *Handbook*.

Teaching of Psychology (*ToP*), the official journal of the Society for the Teaching of Psychology (Division 2 of the APA), is recognized as one of the foremost pedagogical journals across all academic disciplines (see Weimer, 1993). Volume 1 of the *Handbook for Teaching Introductory Psychology* included 89 articles that appeared in *ToP* between 1974 and 1984 (Benjamin, Daniel, & Brewer, 1985). Many instructors used these articles to improve the quality of teaching and learning in their courses; they were especially enthusiastic about the effective demonstrations and activities.

In preparing Volume 2, we examined articles published in *ToP* from 1985 through the first three issues of 1999 and found a plethora of useful materials, which made selecting articles difficult but gratifying. Volume 2 contains 85 completely new articles presented in two main sections. Section I, Issues and Approaches in Teaching Introductory Psychology, consists of 44 articles in the following subsections: Structure of the Introductory Course; Approaches to the Introductory Course: Techniques; Approaches to the Introductory Course: Content; Examinations and Grading; Students' Interests, Perceptions, and Motives; Enhancing Student Interest; Discussion Exercises and Group Activities; Diversity in the Introductory Classroom; Teaching Critical Thinking; Writing to Learn, Learning to Write;

and Computers in the Introductory Course. Articles in Section I cover a wide array of topics, such as course goals and content, student participation in large classes, team teaching, alternatives to the lecture, engaging and maintaining students' interest, active and collaborative learning, incorporating material about diversity, improving students' writing and critical-thinking skills, and using computers. Section II, Demonstrations and Activities in Introductory Psychology, consists of 41 articles in subsections titled General, Research Methods and Statistics, Biopsychology, Developmental Psychology, Sensation and Perception, Learning, Memory and Cognition, Psychological Disorders, Social Psychology and Personality, Sex and Gender, and Industrial/Organizational Psychology. Articles in Section II present numerous demonstrations, class and laboratory projects, and other techniques to enhance teaching and learning. Most articles in both major sections relate to themes stressed by the St. Mary's Conference (see McGovern, 1993) and in the high school *Standards* (Brewer, 1999). Also, Volume 2 covers emphases not included in Volume 1. For example, we have added subsections on diversity issues, computers, sex and gender, and I/O psychology. Because all articles in Volume 2 are new and reflect how psychology continues to evolve, they will enliven introductory psychology for teachers and students in colleges and high schools everywhere.

Like Volume 1, this book contains work by many diligent and dedicated teachers who have enriched the lives of countless students. We praise their work and thank them for sharing it with others. The pedagogical pearls in this volume indicate that John Maynard Keynes, the eminent economist, was wrong when he described education as "the inculcation of the incomprehensible into the indifferent by the incompetent."

All royalties from this book will go directly to The Society for the Teaching of Psychology to promote its laudable activities for improving the teaching of psychology in all educational settings. If this collection of articles increases the passion and effectiveness with which introductory psychology is taught and learned, then we will have been richly rewarded.

Michelle R. Hebl
Charles L. Brewer
Ludy T. Benjamin, Jr.

References

Brewer, C. L. (Ed.). (1999). *National standards for the teaching of high school psychology*. Washington, DC: American Psychological Association.

Brewer, C. L., Hopkins, J. R., Kimble, G. A., Matlin, M. W., McCann, L. I., McNeil, O. V., Nodine, B. F., Quinn, V. N., & Saundra. (1993). Curriculum. In T. V. McGovern (Ed.), *Handbook for enhancing undergraduate education in psychology* (pp.

161–182). Washington, DC: American Psychological Association.

Benjamin, L. T., Jr., Daniel, R. S., & Brewer, C. L. (Eds.). (1985). *Handbook for teaching introductory psychology*. Hillsdale, NJ: Lawrence Erlbaum Associates, Inc.

McGovern, T. V. (Ed.). (1993). *Handbook for enhancing undergraduate education in psychology*. Washington, DC: American Psychological Association.

Weimer, M. (1993, November/December). The disciplinary journals on pedagogy. *Change*, 44–51.

Section I
Issues and Approaches in
Teaching Introductory Psychology

1. STRUCTURE OF THE INTRODUCTORY COURSE

Improving Textbook Selection

Steven P. Chatman
Ernest T. Goetz

One of the most important decisions an instructor makes is the selection of a textbook. A well chosen textbook allows the instructor to elaborate on or reinforce what students have read, rather than contradict or correct it. It can also reduce the time and effort required to design and coordinate other instructional materials and activities to be used in the course (Morris, 1977).

Given that textbook selection is crucial, the method of textbook selection should be comprehensive, reliable, and responsive to learner characteristics and course objectives. Because of the large number of textbooks available, the selection method must be efficient to permit consideration of even a representative sample of textbooks in introductory college courses. Recent examinations of introductory psychology and educational psychology textbooks demonstrate the problem. In their content analysis of introductory psychology textbooks, Quereshi and Sackett (1977) examined 60 books published between 1968 and 1975. Examinations of educational psychology textbooks by Roweton and Roweton (1980) and Goetz and Chatman (1985) were based on a total of 64 textbooks published between 1969 and 1983. Although these lists are not exhaustive, they clearly illustrate the tremendous task facing a textbook evaluation committee or an individual faculty member attempting to select a textbook for an introductory course.

Many instructors are aware of the need for systematic and objective means of evaluating texts to supplement their subjective impressions. The problem has been that existing metrics, which might be applied in textbook selection, are often inherently subjective, too cumbersome for wide use, or inappropriate in terms of information provided. For example, touchstones or self-directed questions (e.g., Glenn & Lewis, 1982; Warming & Baber, 1980) prompt broad subjective evaluations, such as, "Is the book written for the level of the students to be taught?" or "Does the text recommend related sources to foster students' reading interests?" (Warming & Baber, 1980, p. 694). Although they are the simplest of the weighted formula approaches (e.g., Quereshi, 1981), touchstone methods, properly applied, require time consuming, in-depth text analysis that limits the likelihood of their use in the selection process.

Readability formulas, in their various forms (Flesch, 1948; Fry, 1977; Gray & Leary, 1935; Lorge, 1939; Raygor, 1977), yield simple numerical indices of text complexity based on easily countable features of the text such as word length and sentence length. Although intended to predict the difficulty that students at different levels will have reading text, readability formulas are imperfect reflections of comprehensibility. For example, the readability formulas do not consider concept difficulty; quality of the writing; or student background, interest, and motivation (Klare, 1976). Further, they are ill-suited to subject areas that are not heavily verbal (e.g., trigonometry) and yield the same measure of difficulty when words are scrambled (Warming & Baber, 1980).

Recently, Gagne and Bell (1981) proposed a theoretically motivated alternative to readability formulas. Gagne and Bell drew on Kintsch and van Dijk's (1978) theory of text comprehension and recent information processing research to define assessment procedures for 15 important text aspects in 4 categories. Gagne and Bell's approach represents a largely objective method that goes beyond readability indices and is consistent with recent advances in information processing. The time and effort required by the use of these techniques, however, are implied by their use of fewer than 4 chapters in 3 textbooks and suggest that, like other approaches, this method of evaluation is not likely to be useful in the evaluation of 20 or more textbooks. However, their approach would probably be useful in text development and in final textbook selection decisions.

A similar but more limited approach to textbook evaluation was developed by Schallert, Alexander, and Goetz (1984) as part of a project that examined the use of textbooks in college classes. Schallert et al. examined text samples at the beginning, middle, and end of randomly selected chapters in introductory psychology and biology textbooks. They counted the number of strategy cues that might prompt the student to process the text in a manner that is consistent with important comprehension functions (e.g., relating the text to prior knowledge, identifying important information, organizing information presented). The analysis was objective, proved very reliable (interrater reliability was above 0.95), and revealed interesting differences between disciplines and among texts. The procedure, however, is too time consuming to be applied to a large potential selection pool and too narrow in focus to serve as the sole selection criterion.

Student ratings (e.g., Jacobs, 1983; Meredith, 1980) are a potentially valuable source of information for the textbook adopter. Students can be asked to list strong points and weak points, assign the texts a letter grade (Jacobs, 1983), or rate the text on several scales (Meredith, 1980). One obvious concern with student ratings is the ability of students to judge the adequacy of textbook coverage of content within the field. Further, the time and effort required to evaluate textbooks limit the number of textbooks that can be reviewed, the depth of the review, and/or the number of students completing the task. Given these limitations, student evaluations should probably be a part of an in-depth evaluation, but are probably not a useful method of evaluating a large group of textbooks.

Although there are some conceptual limitations of textbook evaluation methods described above, their major limitation in attempting the evaluation of a large number of textbooks is the amount of time and effort required. A method is needed that facilitates the selection of a subgroup of textbooks that possess predefined traits. This subgroup can then be more thoroughly analyzed in accordance with other more time consuming procedures.

In his discussion of textbook selection, Morris (1977) briefly describes a procedure that appears sufficiently streamlined to permit use on large numbers of texts. Recent book reviews in *Contemporary Psychology* and *Teaching of Psychology* were used to identify an initial textbook pool. General descriptors of the texts that appeared in the reviews were then used to identify appropriate texts from the initial pool. Although the process certainly appears time-efficient, its reliability depends on the availability and accuracy of the reviews. Further, the descriptors used for textbook selection (e.g., survey-eclectic and behavioral) appear too general to provide adequate information about what the textbooks actually cover.

An alternative approach was developed by Goetz and Chatman (1985) in an analysis of introductory educational psychology textbooks' treatment of cognitive psychology theory and research. Goetz and Chatman's technique consists of three steps. First, major theorists and key concepts are identified. Second, reference lists and subject indexes are examined to determine the extent to which major theorists and key concepts are represented. Third, a subset of textbooks for further analysis can then be determined through analysis of the extent of coverage.

Goetz and Chatman (1985) identified major theorists through postal questionnaires to journal editorial board members of 4 major journals devoted to research in educational psychology, and key concepts through an examination of the indexes of graduate level texts. Other sources could be used for this purpose, including: (a) recent reviews of major developments such as those found in *Annual Review of Psychology*, *Psychological Review*, and *American Psychologist*; (b) lists developed by a panel of instructors; or (c) carefully articulated syllabi or course notes. The preparation of these lists may take some time and effort but, once the lists are prepared, textbooks can be quickly evaluated. Because the index counts are objective and straightforward, students and clerical personnel could perform this task.

In their examination of educational psychology texts, Goetz and Chatman (1985) found that the textbooks varied widely; the number of theorists indexed ranged from 5 to 21 and the number of concepts ranged from 1 to 11. This variability suggests that a simple tally of major theorists referenced and key concepts included in the subject index will probably be adequate to discriminate among texts on the extent to which subject areas are represented. For example, only 3 of the 24 textbooks examined referenced 14 or more major theorists and 7 or more key concepts. When this procedure is additionally applied to other major concept areas,

a composite score for each text can be computed from the application of weights to reflect course content. The few texts so selected can then be subjected to more in-depth treatments.

This textbook search reduction technique is limited by the assumption that the extent of coverage in a subject area can be measured by the number of major theorists and key concepts in a subject area included in the respective indices. In order to check the validity of index searches, Goetz and Chatman (1985) conducted a more thorough examination of six textbooks, one selected at random from each publication year. They reported that the validity of index-based measures was supported by an examination of suggested readings, reference lists, major headings, subheadings, words in italic print, margin notes, and glossaries.

Of course, the idea of examining textbook indexes to assess the content of textbook coverage is not new. For example, Quereshi and Sackett (1977) performed a content analysis of introductory psychology texts in 2,484 terms found in the subject indexes of at least 2 of the 60 books. Factor analysis techniques revealed 10 principal components that replicated factors identified in a previous study (Quereshi & Zulli, 1975), proved readily interpretable, and correlated with external variables (e.g., number of pages of text, human interest measures). Quereshi and Sackett addressed the issue of textbook selection and concluded that their results could be used to identify five "reasonably disparate and identifiable groups of textbooks" (p. 29), based on factor loadings on five empirically and conceptually linked pairs of factors. Although this analysis was clearly objective and comprehensive, the time and effort required for such factor analytic treatment of nearly all index entries far exceed that required for a simple tally of selected entries, as done by Goetz and Chatman (1985). At the same time, the level of analysis of the resulting 10 factors appears closer to that advocated by Morris (1977) than the textbook search reduction technique of Goetz and Chatman.

In conclusion, the textbook search reduction technique appears to be a useful one that can easily be applied to large numbers of textbooks. By using this objective technique to limit the initial pool of textbooks, the evaluator can focus more effort and apply in-depth analysis on a small subset of the textbooks available. It should be repeated that this technique is not proposed as a method of final evaluation and that further examinations of additional subject areas and other disciplines are needed before the method's limitations will be adequately known. The technique has been applied to the initial screening of textbooks for possible adoption in introductory educational psychology by the second author and it seemed to work well. His subjective estimate of the validity of the technique was increased by the fact that the index counts tended to match his impressions from previous inspections of the texts.

As we now think of it, the text selection procedure should incorporate three stages. First, a quick, inexpensive, objective screening procedure such as the textbook search reduction procedure (Goetz & Chatman, 1985), survey reviews (Morris, 1977), or content analysis (Quereshi & Sackett, 1977) are used to identify a small subset for further consideration from all available textbooks. Second, the texts identified are subjected to more intensive and time consuming analysis such as readability calculations, examination of text features (e.g., Gagne & Bell, 1981; Schallert et al., 1984), and student ratings. Finally, based on these two initial stages, the textbook adopter should then carefully examine the remaining textbooks. As Morris (1977) argued, the selection of a textbook is too important of a decision to make without spending some time with the text itself. The bottom line is that the instructor should read the textbook before adopting it. With a carefully planned, multi-stage selection procedure, however, an instructor may make the decision without reading *every* available textbook, or feeling guilty for failing to do so.

References

Flesch, R. (1948). A new readability yardstick. *Journal of Applied Psychology, 32,* 221–233.

Fry, E. (1977). Fry's readability graph: Clarifications, validity, and extensions to level 17. *Journal of Reading, 21,* 242–252.

Gagne, E. D., & Bell, M. S. (1981). The use of cognitive psychology in the development and evaluation of textbooks. *Educational Psychologist, 16,* 83–100.

Glenn, A. D., & Lewis, V. J. (1982). Analyzing the textbook to improve student reading and learning. *Reading World, 21,* 293–298.

Goetz, E. T., & Chatman, S. P. (1985). Coverage of cognitive psychology in educational psychology textbooks. *Educational Psychologist, 20,* 41–46.

Gray, W. S., & Leary, B. E. (1935). *What makes a book readable?* Chicago, IL: University of Chicago Press.

Jacobs, K. W. (1983). Textbook evaluations by students. *Teaching of Psychology, 10,* 183–184.

Kintsch, W., & van Dijk, T. A. (1978). Toward a model of text comprehension and production. *Psychological Review, 85,* 407–413.

Klare, G. R. (1976). A second look at the validity of readability formulas. *Journal of Reading Behavior, 8,* 129–152.

Lorge, I. I. (1939). *The Lorge formula for estimating difficulty of reading materials.* New York: Bureau of Publications, Teachers College, Columbia University.

Meredith, G. M. (1980). Brief scale for measuring the impact of a textbook. *Perceptual and Motor Skills, 51,* 370.

Morris, C. J. (1977). Choosing a text for the introductory course. *Teaching of Psychology, 4,* 21–24.

Quereshi, M. Y. (1981). Analytic procedures for selecting a general psychology textbook. *Teaching of Psychology, 8,* 143–147.

Quereshi, M. Y., & Sackett, P. R. (1977). An updated content analysis of introductory psychology textbooks. *Teaching of Psychology, 4,* 25–30.

Quereshi, M. Y., & Zulli, M. R. (1975). A content analysis of introductory psychology textbooks. *Teaching of Psychology, 2,* 60–65.

Raygor, A. L. (1977). The Raygor readability estimate: A quick and easy way to determine difficulty. In P. D. Pearson (Ed.), *Reading: Theory, research, and practice—The Twenty-sixth Yearbook of the National Reading Conference* (pp. 259–263). Clemson, SC: National Reading Conference, Inc.

Roweton, W. E., & Roweton, M. S. (1980). Introductory educational psychology's core literature: A reference survey approach. *JAS Catalog of Selected Documents in Psychology, 10,* 44 (Ms. No. 2057).

Schallert, D. L., Alexander, P. A., & Goetz, E. T. (1984, October). *Implicit instruction of strategies for learning from text.* Paper presented at an invitational conference, Learning and study strategies: Issues in assessment, instruction, and evaluation. College Station, TX: Texas A&M University.

Warming, E. O., & Baber, E. C. (1980). Touchstones for textbook selection. *Phi Delta Kappan, 61,* 694–695.

Note

A version of this paper was presented in M. J. Ash (Chair), *Trivializing undergraduate educational psychology through text content.* Symposium conducted at the meeting of the American Psychological Association, Anaheim, CA, August, 1983.

Introductory Course Content and Goals

Benjamin Miller
Barbara F. Gentile

In 1908, the American Psychological Association (APA) established its first committee to study the introductory psychology course. As part of the committee's efforts, E. C. Sanford (1910) surveyed instructors of psychology and identified the chief hindrances to teaching the introductory course as

> inconveniently large classes . . . lack of equipment or inconvenience in quarters . . . students ill-prepared . . . the mixed and uneven character of the classes . . . the student's unwillingness to work, or his overinterest in the practical aspects

of the science . . . lack of a first-rate text book . . . and insufficient time in the program of studies. (p. 60)

Wolfle (1942) remarked that "these reports make discouraging reading. Now, 30-odd years later, we are still debating many of the same issues and being embarrassed by the same difficulties. Many of the recommendations considered necessary in 1909 are still necessary in 1942" (p. 686).

Virtually all colleges (97% in 1992–1993; Cooney & Griffith, 1994) offer an introductory psychology course, and vast numbers of students take it. Scheirer and Rogers (1985) pointed out that because 27% of full-time students take the course each year, most take the course at some point in their careers. They do so for many reasons. Some are considering majoring in psychology; others are meeting another major's requirement, satisfying a general education requirement, or taking an elective. Sanford (1910) mentioned the same variety of reasons for enrolling and pointed out that "we have . . . a student group whose major interests are in other directions and who make the course in psychology incidental to the main trend of their studies" (p. 58). Cooney and Griffith reported that 94% of departments offering introductory psychology said that the course has a general audience. Indeed, Kulik (1973) reported that majors constitute only 6% of introductory students. This diversity of needs and interests presents challenges to those teaching the course.

The variety of pedagogical goals instructors have for the course mirrors the variety of student reasons for taking it. Wolfle (1942) described the results of Gilliland's (1932) survey and others' anecdotal reports dealing with instructors' objectives for the elementary course and identified what he believed to be the three most important objectives:

1. To teach the facts, technical vocabulary, and principles of psychology, and to instill critical habits of thought.
2. To train students in the scientific method as it applies to the study of human behavior.
3. To help students develop the ability to understand and to cope with the personal problems of daily life.

Wolfle rejected the objectives of attracting students to the field and preparing them for a psychology major, arguing that instead the course should be taught

> as if none of the students would ever take another course in psychology . . . attainment of these objectives [above] will constitute good preparation for advanced work in psychology, while at the same time doing the much more important job of helping to prepare the student for the role of an educated member of society. (p. 690)

Half a century later, the question of goals for the introductory course is still important. We wanted to know what instructors' pedagogical goals are and how they are reflected in the structure and content of the course.

No theme is more long standing or consistent in the literature than a pair of complaints about introductory texts: They are too big and too similar. The monster textbook may seem a recent affliction, but the Wolfle Committee called on textbook authors to leave out some topics and to integrate better those they did include (Buxton et al., 1952). Weiten and Wight (1992) described the appearance of encyclopedic texts in the 1950s and of homogeneous texts in the 1970s. Paul (1987) identified the enrollment surge of the 1960s as the beginning of an increasing homogenization of all science textbooks. In addition to limiting instructors' choices, other authors pointed out that this trend perpetuates error (Blumenthal, 1991; Gould, 1988; Paul, 1987). Finally, today's texts are often written from a research rather than a teaching perspective (Blumenthal, 1991) and tend to include the latest findings and give comparatively little attention to the way material, new or old, is presented. We wanted to know more about the role of the textbook in the introductory course.

A conservative estimate (based on Cooney & Griffith's 1994 data) suggests that over one million students take introductory psychology every year in North America. Despite its importance in the undergraduate curriculum, there have been no recent comprehensive studies of the course. Irion (1976) raised a number of issues, but his account of the course seems to be based more on a limited number of interviews than on his survey. Discussions of the psychology curriculum as a whole have given varying amounts of attention to the introductory course (Buxton et al., 1952; Cooney & Griffith, 1994; Henry, 1938; Kulik, 1973; McGovern, Furumoto, Halpern, Kimble, & McKeachie, 1991; McKeachie & Milholland, 1961; Sanford & Fleishman, 1950; Scheirer & Rogers, 1985). For historical accounts of this work, see Brewer et al. (1993), Goodwin (1992), Lloyd and Brewer (1992), McGovern (1992, 1993), and Nelson and Stricker (1992).

Much has changed in psychology, but it is not apparent that the first-course problem has been solved. To assess the state of the course, we surveyed instructors of introductory psychology, asking about the structure and content of their courses, their goals for the course, how well they think students achieve those goals, and about perceptions of their students' expectations of the course. We also asked students about their expectations of the introductory course and, later, about their experience in the course.

Faculty Survey

Method

Participants

We sent questionnaires to all 1,190 departments of psychology at institutions in the United States enrolling at least 300 undergraduate students and offering a baccalaureate degree in psychology. We addressed the mailing to the chair, requesting that all people teaching the introductory course complete the questionnaire.

Faculty at 490 different colleges and universities returned a total of 761 surveys (41% of the institutions surveyed returned at least one completed questionnaire). The 490 schools that responded represented a good sample of the original 1,190 schools with respect to all important institutional variables: size, public or private, secular or religious, coed or single sex, and geographical region.[1]

Questionnaire

The three-page questionnaire contained 17 questions in four categories.

Instructor's background. These questions asked about rank, gender, area of expertise, full- or part-time status, and number of years teaching the course.

---

[1]Here, and in analyses that follow, we have summarized large quantities of data. We will provide more detailed information on request.

Course structure and content. We asked about enrollment, course length, class activities, and reading and writing assignments. We were particularly interested in several aspects of textbook use and asked about which topics were assigned and how important it was that various topics be included.

Course goals and outcomes. We asked instructors to rate the importance of each of nine goals, the degree to which they believed the structure of their courses reflected each goal, and the degree to which they believed students achieved each goal.

Perceptions of student expectations. We asked instructors to check up to 6 of 13 possible student expectations.

Results and Discussion

Instructors

Most (65%) introductory psychology instructors were men. Most (90%) were full-time faculty; 36% were full professors, 25% associate, 27% assistant, 5% instructors, 4% graduate students, and 3% other. Men were more likely than women to be full time (93% and 85%, respectively; $z = 4.87, p < .0001$) and were overrepresented in the full and associate professor ranks and underrepresented in the lower ranks. Seventy-four percent of respondents had taught the course for 4 or more years (M = 12.2 years); 25% for 20 or more years.

Structure and Content

The typical course lasted one semester (89%) and had 50 or fewer students (57%). The instructor used a textbook (98%) and assigned most of the topics (M = 17). There was little additional reading (56% assigned none), particularly in larger classes. Students did some writing, most often a short paper (46%) or essay exam (39%).

The textbook. Twenty-five textbook topics[2] were listed in the questionnaire. Figure 1 shows the proportion of respondents who assigned each topic. One indication of the stability and uniformity of the introductory course is the absence of differences among instructors in the assignment of readings in the textbook. Differences due to rank, gender, and area of expertise were small and nonsystematic.

Instructors assigned what they believed was important or believed that what they assigned was important ($r = .97$). Figure 1 also shows the percentage of respondents who rated high (4 or 5 on a 5-point scale ranging from 1 [*should not be included*] to 5 [*should be included*]) the importance of including each topic. Only 4 topics (cross-cultural, psychology of women, applied psychology, industrial/organizational) were assigned by a smaller proportion of respondents than rated those topics important, likely because these topics do not appear in most textbooks. The other 21 topics were assigned

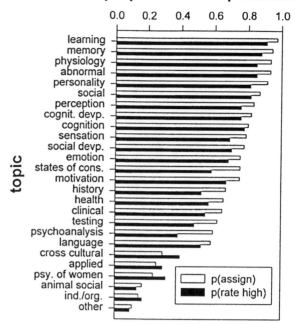

proportion of respondents

Figure 1. Proportion of respondents who assigned each textbook topic and who rated each topic as important for inclusion in the course.

by a larger proportion of respondents than rated them important, and the overall rate of assignment (64%) was higher than the overall rate of importance judgments (57%); $t(25) = 4.65, p = .0001$. This discrepancy may reflect the ease of including textbook material (or the difficulty of excluding it) or a sense that these topics are part of a traditional introductory course.

Beyond the textbook. Unlike patterns of textbook use, additional readings,[3] written assignments,[4] and classroom activities[5] varied from school to school and instructor to instructor in systematic ways. Relations among course content variables and institution and instructor variables are summarized in Table 1. These relations are interesting, but a different glimpse of the state of introductory psychology comes from looking at the data in absolute rather than relative terms. Students at one kind of school may have done more reading beyond the textbook than did students at another kind of school, but we think it is more important that more than half of our respondents assigned no such reading.

---

[2]Textbook topics were not necessarily the names of chapters. We selected topics to reflect the range of substantive material in contemporary introductory psychology textbooks.

[3]Reading assignments were journal articles, articles from science magazines, other articles, collections of readings, case histories, and other books.

[4]Writing assignments were short papers, term papers, take-home exams, in-class essay exams, journals, workbooks, lab reports, and other.

[5]Class activities were guest speakers, field trips, examples from current events, activities that illustrate phenomena, dream analysis, psychological testing, experiments, demonstrations with human participants, demonstrations with animal subjects, student presentations, role playing, surveys, Socratic problem solving, and deception.

Table 1. Course Content Variables by Instructor and Institution Variables

	Reading[a]	Writing[b]	Activities[c]
Institution characteristics			
Private or Public			
Private	52	85	4.2
Public	33	72	3.7
Religious or secular			
Religious	52	85	4.3
Secular	39	76	3.8
Class size[d]			
Small	52	86	4.3
Large	24	61	3.3
Institution size[e]			
Small	57	88	4.3
Large	33	70	3.6
Instructor characteristics			
Gender			
Women	51	88	4.4
Men	40	75	3.8
Full- or part-time	No difference	No difference	No difference
Years teaching introductory psychology	No systematic difference	No systematic difference	No systematic difference
Rank[f]			
Graduate	59	91	4.7
Assistant	45	85	4.4
Associate	53	81	3.9
Professor	35	74	3.6
Area of expertise			
Clinical	46	77	4.0
Individual	46	84	4.0
Experimental	44	77	3.9
Biopsychology	42	82	4.0
Applied	36	81	4.5

Note. With the exception of activities by area of expertise, differences were statistically significant ($p \leq .05$). [a]Percentage of respondents who assign any kind of reading beyond the textbook. [b]Percentage of respondents who assign any kind of writing. [c]Mean number of activities used. [d]Small: ≤ 50; large: ≥ 101. [e]Small: $< 1,735$; large $> 3,218$. [f]The relation between rank and the course content variables may be partly accounted for by the fact that only 52% of full professors teach small (≤ 50) classes, as compared with 58% of graduate students and 65% of associate and assistant professors.

Goals

Respondents rated nine goals (see Table 2) in terms of importance, the degree to which course structure reflected each goal (reflection), and the degree to which they believed students achieved each goal (achievement). For each of the three ratings of the nine goals, we looked at summary statistics, relations to the other two ratings, and relations to instructor and course variables. Because these analyses required many comparisons and cross-tabulations, the probability of false positive significance tests was high. To avoid unwarranted claims about the data, instead of reporting many *p* values reflecting discrete relations among specific variables, we give a more global account of our results in terms of broad patterns of relatedness among the variables. Specifically, we report points of convergence among four distinct analytic approaches:

1. Percentages of respondents who gave the highest rating to each goal, broken down by all appropriate independent variables, to give an indication of how these variables are related to the ratings.
2. Interpolated medians of the ratings, broken down by all appropriate independent variables, indicating the central tendency of the rating distributions.
3. Cross-tabulations of independent variables with the rating variables, permitting computation of χ^2 as a test of independence and τ_b as a measure of association.
4. Ordered logit models of the data to evaluate the predictive relation between independent variables and the ratings.

We do not report results unique to a particular method of analysis. The following synthesis represents those relations among variables and patterns of responses that most strongly emerged from the analyses.

Table 2. Goals for the Introductory Course

Goal	Short Name
Help students understand people and relationships	People
Engage students in scientific inquiry about psychological processes	Engage
Provide a comprehensive survey of the field	Survey
Teach students to think like psychologists	Think
Make students aware of and/or more knowledgeable about important social issues	Social
Provide students with knowledge that could help them in their personal and professional lives	Personal
Introduce students to the different approaches psychologists take	Approaches
Convince students that psychology is a science	Science
Encourage students to major in psychology	Major

Note. The goals appear in the order and wording used in the questionnaire.

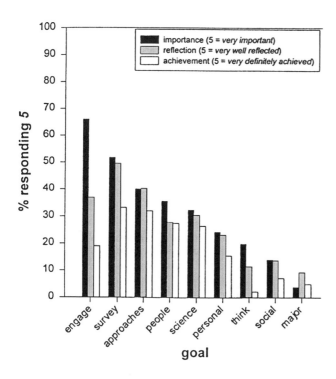

Figure 2. Percentage of respondents who gave a rating of 5 to each goal based on a 5-point scale.

Overall ratings. Figure 2 shows the percentage of instructors who gave the highest rating (5) to the importance, reflection, and achievement of the goals; median ratings of the goals show the same patterns as the percentages. Instructors who rated a goal high in importance were likely to rate that goal high in reflection and achievement. An important exception was *engage*, which was rated very high in importance but lower in reflection and lower still in perceived student achievement. Other goals rated high in importance were *survey* and *approaches*; these remained high in reflection and reasonably high in achievement. Four others (*people, science, personal,* and *social*) were less important and were consistent across the three ratings. The two remaining goals (*think* and *major*) were not rated consistently.

Although instructors rated the goal of engage as most important, what instructors believed their courses did best was to provide a "comprehensive survey of the field" and an introduction to the "different approaches psychologists take."

When we compared the importance rating of each goal with the importance rating of each of the other eight, an interesting pattern emerged. Four of the goals—engage, think, approaches, and science—were consistently related to one another. All four concern learning about the field of psychology, appreciating its scientific nature, and understanding its different models and paradigms. Another four goals, not related to the goals in the first group, were consistently related to one another: people, social, personal, and major. Except for the last, all of these involve using psychology in ways that are personally rewarding or socially useful. The fact that the goals formed these clusters suggests that instructors, although sharing most of the same goals, valued one set of goals more than the other. The last goal, survey, did not fall into either cluster but tended to be positively re-

lated to all goals. Ratings of reflection and achievement showed the same pattern, but in much muted form.

Activities and assignments. To understand the relation between instructors' goals and what instructors do in class, we looked at differences in goal ratings between those who included particular assignments or activities and those who did not.

Because engage received the highest importance ratings, we were particularly interested in determining which activities and assignments were associated with it. Instructors who rated this goal high were more likely than others to include in-class experiments, and demonstrations with humans and, to a lesser extent, animals in their courses. Those who gave high importance ratings to science were more likely than others to use demonstrations with humans. Instructors who placed particular importance on engage and think were more likely than others to assign lab reports.

We might expect instructors who gave high importance ratings to the goals associated with the nature of psychological inquiry to be more likely to assign journal articles or other scientific readings, but this was not the case. In fact, although the ratings of goal importance did predict the likelihood of including some class activities and written assignments, they did not predict anything about the assignment of reading beyond the textbook. This was also true of ratings of reflection and achievement. Instructors who believed that the goals related to the nature of psychological inquiry were reflected in their courses and achieved by their students were more likely than others to include in-class experiments and lab reports but were not more likely to assign journal articles or other scientific readings.

Instructors who valued the three goals related to providing students with personally and socially useful knowledge and who believed that these goals were reflected in their courses and achieved by their students were more likely than others to use surveys, role playing, psychological tests, and current examples, and to assign short papers.

Instructors' responses to survey were related to a number of course characteristics. For example, instructors who rated high the importance of survey were less likely than others to use any kind of reading assignment beyond the text. Similarly, high reflection and achievement ratings of survey were negatively related to most kinds of reading. Those who gave essay exams rated survey lower in importance, reflection, and achievement than did other instructors. Of the classroom activities, more were negatively related to survey than to any of the other goals. These results are consistent with aspects of the widely held stereotype of the survey course: no writing, multiple-choice exams, shallow coverage of many topics, and near-complete reliance on the textbook. Indeed, there was a positive relation ($r = .33$) between ratings of the importance of survey and the number of textbook topics assigned.

Perceptions of Student Expectations

Discussion of instructors' responses to the question about student expectations appears with the results of the student survey.

Method

Participants

We surveyed students enrolled in introductory psychology courses at four private colleges in Massachusetts in the spring semester of 1994. Two were women's colleges, and there were more women than men in the introductory courses at the two coeducational colleges. Instructors administered the questionnaire on the 1st day of class ($n = 497$) and again at the end of the semester ($n = 414$). Sixty-six percent of the pretest respondents and 68% of the posttest respondents were women. Fifty-four percent of the students surveyed were 1st-year students, 28% sophomores, 10% juniors, and 8% seniors. Percentages of students in the four classes were nearly identical in the pretests and posttests.

Questionnaires

The pretest questionnaire students indicated which of the 14 expectations shown in Table 3 they had for the course. In the posttest, students completed a version of the questionnaire in which the same items appeared as statements rather than expectations. Students indicated which statements best described the course they had just finished. In both the pretest and posttest we asked them to check no more than six items, to check one of four possible reasons for taking the course (considering a major, requirement for another major, all-college requirement, elective), and to tell us their sex, age, and class standing. On the posttest we also asked whether, at the end of the semester, they were majoring in, or considering majoring in, psychology. Because the questionnaires asked for no identifying information, we had no way to match a student's pretest and posttest questionnaires.

Results and Discussion

Pretest Results

Reasons for taking the course. Thirty-three percent of the students said they were taking the course because they were considering majoring in psychology, 14% for another major, 18% to meet an all-college requirement, and 35% as an elective. There was little difference between the pretest and posttest distributions of responses to this question.

Forty-eight percent of the 1st-year women and 49% of the 1st-year men were considering majoring in psychology. The comparable figures for sophomore women and men were 20% and 18%.

Overall results. The expectations students cited most often had to do with acquiring general knowledge or skills (e.g., understanding people and relationships, gaining knowledge useful in personal or professional life, and learning to think critically). Students did not expect to be helped with serious personal problems, to learn to think like psychologists, or to find the course easy. Table 3 shows the

Table 3. Student and Instructor Responses to Student Expectation Items

Item	Pretest %[a]	Posttest %[b]	Change Pretest–Posttest	Instructor %[c]	Short Name of Goal
To learn what you need to go on in psychology	36	38	+2	59	Go on
That it will be an easy course	8	12	+4*	36	Easy
To increase your understanding of people and relationships	86	72	−14*	85	People
To be entertained, amazed, and surprised	43	38	−5	29	Amaze
To learn to think critically about ideas and data	53	38	−15*	14	Critical
To learn of bizarre and aberrant behavior	31	35	+4	60	Bizarre
To be exposed to a comprehensive survey of the field	48	69	+21*	51	Survey
To be helped with serious personal problems	5	2	−3*	27	Problems
To gain knowledge that could help you in your personal and professional	65	45	−20*	76	Personal
To increase your awareness of and/or knowledge about important social issues	51	37	−14*	15	Social
To contribute your own knowledge and experience to class discussions	15	10	−5*	10	Discuss
To be challenged intellectually	37	27	−10*	18	Challenge
To learn to think like a psychologist	16	14	−2	9	Think
Other	1	3	+2*	—	Other

Note. Items appear in the order and wording of the student pretest questionnaire.
[a]$n = 497$. [b]$n = 414$. [c]$n = 761$.
*$p < .05$.

percentage of students who checked each of the 14 expectations at the beginning of the semester.

Group differences. Students enrolling as prospective psychology majors were more likely than others to expect that the course would prepare them to go on in psychology ($z = 21.51$, $p < .0001$) and teach them to think like psychologists ($z = 6.86$, $p < .0001$). Students taking the course for another major were more likely than others to expect that the course would help them in their personal and professional lives ($z = 1.90$, $p = .03$) and less likely than others to expect that the course would be a survey ($z = -2.41$, $p = .008$). Male upperclassmen, almost all of whom were taking the course as an elective, were most likely to expect that it would be easy ($z = 4.02$, $p < .0001$).

Item clusters. To look for patterns of expectations, we submitted our data to BMDP's (1991) cluster analysis. Included were 13 of the questionnaire items (all but *other*) plus 2 additional variables derived from the question about the student's reason for taking the course: considering a major in psychology and not considering a major in psychology.

Cluster 1 (*major, go on, think*) has to do with considering a psychology major and preparing for it. Cluster 2 (*people, personal, social, critical*) concerns ideas and skills that can be of use in a student's life. Cluster 3 (*not major, easy, amaze, bizarre*) has to do with not majoring in psychology and with the belief that the course will be fun, exciting, and easy. Cluster 4 (*challenge, discuss*), if it is describable, seems to be about the student's academic participation and involvement in the course. Two questionnaire items—*problems* and *survey*—were not part of any cluster.

Posttest Results

Group differences. Students considering a major in psychology were more likely than others to believe that the course provided what they needed to go on in psychology ($z = 11.33$, $p < .0001$). Students taking the course to meet the requirements of another major were the least likely to describe the course as a survey ($z = -4.58$, $p < .0001$). Students taking the course as prospective majors or to satisfy a requirement of another major were more likely than others to describe the course as intellectually challenging ($z = 4.76$, $p < .0001$). These students may have been more involved in the course and, therefore, more likely to identify its intellectual challenges.

Item clusters. Cluster analysis of the posttest data used 13 questionnaire items (all but *other*) and two additional variables: considering and not considering a major in psychology. The latter variables came from responses to a question added to the posttest that asked students if they were majoring in (or planning to major in) psychology. Because students agreed more about what the course was like than about their expectations of it, there were not the same clear clusters of responses in the posttest data as there were in the pretest data. Survey remained apart from the other items, and items related to the psychology major remained together.

Pretest and posttest differences. Students' descriptions of the introductory course at the end of the semester were different from their expectations at the beginning (see Table 3). The most widely held expectations (people, personal, critical, and social) were less likely to be checked on the posttest than on the pretest. Few expected the course to be easy, but more found that it was; more than a third expected an intellectual challenge, but fewer found it. The biggest change between pretest and posttest was in the proportion of students who expected a comprehensive survey. Forty-eight percent had this expectation at the beginning of the course, but 69% described the course this way at the end.

Students agreed more at the end of the semester about what the course was like than they had at the beginning about what to expect. For example, in the pretest, those considering a major in psychology had been much more likely than those taking the course for any other reason to say that they expected to learn what they needed to go on in psychology, but in the posttest, the prospective majors were less likely than they had been, and others more likely, to check this item. This convergence offers some validation of the description of the course that emerges from the posttest data.

Although we have been careful to maintain the distinction between expectation and hope, the fact remains that most items were checked more often in the pretest (i.e., as expectations) than in the posttest (i.e., as descriptions), and it is hard to avoid the suspicion that students experienced these unfulfilled expectations as disappointments more often than as pleasant surprises. Nevertheless, most students (69%) who enrolled in introductory psychology planning to major in the field were undeterred at the end of the course.

Instructor Perceptions and Student Expectations

In our faculty survey, we gave instructors the same list of expectations that appeared in our student questionnaire and asked them to check up to six expectations they thought their students had for the course.

Student and instructor data cannot be directly compared. On the one hand, we have the percentage of students to whom a particular expectation was one of the six most salient, and on the other, the percentage of instructors who perceived that a majority of their students held a particular expectation. A sizable difference between the two in either direction, however, indicates a misperception on the part of instructors.

The percentage of students who checked each expectation and the percentage of instructors who believed their students had each expectation appear in Figure 3. Sometimes instructors' perceptions were accurate: Most believed that people and personal were common student expectations, and they were. Similarly, most instructors believed that discuss and think were not common expectations, and they were not. On the other hand, most instructors imagined that go on and bizarre were widely held expectations, but they were not. Conversely, few instructors said that social and critical were widely held expectations, but they were.

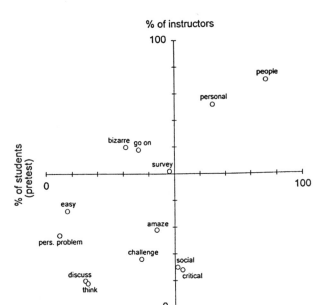

Figure 3. Relation of student expectations to instructor perceptions of student expectations.

The four expectations most often checked by students were the same four that formed Cluster 3 in the student pretest data, having to do with the acquisition of skills and general knowledge (people, personal, critical, and social). Instructors perceived the importance to students of the first two, both of which are related to interpersonal knowledge and skills, but not of the latter two, more intellectual and outer-directed expectations.

Most instructors believed that a majority of students come to the introductory course expecting to learn what they need to go on in psychology, but only a third had that expectation. Because it was primarily students considering a major in psychology who held this expectation, instructors' error may have been one of overestimating the proportion of their students who were considering a psychology major. If so, we may expect instructors' other perceptions of student expectations to have been closer to those of prospective majors, but curiously this was not so.

Summary

These data provide a useful picture of the state of the introductory course. Several points stand out. First, introductory psychology courses are quite uniform. For the most part, course content and structure variables interact with institution and instructor variables in unsurprising ways. Differences among institutions and instructors with respect to the nature of the introductory psychology course are few. Second, the course is centered on a textbook, and, despite differing goals for and expectations of the course, instructors and students agree that it winds up being a survey. Third, instructors' most important goal is to engage students in scientific inquiry about psychological processes, but few believe they achieve this goal. Taken together, these findings suggest that the first-course problem is still with us.

References

Blumenthal, A. L. (1991). The introductory psychology textbook. *The International Journal of Social Education, 5,* 11–28.

BMDP [Computer software]. (1991). Los Angeles: BMDP Statistical Software.

Brewer, C. L., Hopkins, J. R., Kimble, G. A., Matlin, M. W., McCann, L. I., McNeil, O. V., Nodine, B. F., Quinn, V. N., & Saundra. (1993). Curriculum. In T. V. McGovern (Ed.), *Handbook for enhancing undergraduate education in psychology* (pp. 161–182). Washington, DC: American Psychological Association.

Buxton, C. E., Cofer, C. N., Gustad, J. W., MacLeod, R. B., McKeachie, W. J., & Wolfle, D. (1952). *Improving undergraduate instruction in psychology.* New York: Macmillan.

Cooney, B. R., & Griffith, D. M. (1994). *The 1992–1993 undergraduate department survey.* Washington, DC: American Psychological Association.

Gilliland, A. R. (1932). The nature and aims of the introductory course in psychology. *Journal of Applied Psychology, 16,* 614–622.

Goodwin, C. J. (1992). The American Psychological Association and the teaching of psychology, 1892–1945. In A. E. Puente, J. R. Matthews, & C. L. Brewer (Eds.), *Teaching psychology in America: A history* (pp. 329–343). Washington, DC: American Psychological Association.

Gould, S. J. (1988, January). The case of the creeping fox terrier clone. *Natural History, 97,* 16–24.

Henry, E. R. (1938). A survey of courses in psychology offered by undergraduate colleges of liberal arts. *Psychological Bulletin, 35,* 430–435.

Irion, A. L (1976). A survey of the introductory course in psychology. *Teaching of Psychology, 3,* 3–8.

Kulik, J. A. (1973). *Undergraduate education in psychology.* Washington, DC: American Psychological Association.

Lloyd, M. A., & Brewer, C. L. (1992). National conferences on undergraduate psychology. In A. E. Puente, J. R. Matthews, & C. L Brewer (Eds.), *Teaching psychology in America: A history* (pp. 263–284). Washington, DC: American Psychological Association.

McGovern, T. V. (1992). Evolution of undergraduate curricula in psychology, 1892–1992. In A. E. Puente, J. R. Matthews, & C. L. Brewer (Eds.), *Teaching psychology in America: A history* (pp. 13–38). Washington, DC: American Psychological Association.

McGovern, T. V. (1993). Introduction. In T. V. McGovern (Ed.), *Handbook for enhancing undergraduate education in psychology* (pp. 3–15). Washington, DC: American Psychological Association.

McGovern, T. V., Furumoto, L., Halpern, D. F., Kimble, G. A., & McKeachie, W. J. (1991). Liberal education, study in depth, and the arts and sciences major—Psychology. *American Psychologist, 46,* 598–605.

McKeachie, W. J., & Milholland, J. E. (1961). *Undergraduate curricula in psychology.* Chicago: Scott, Foresman.

Nelson, P. D., & Stricker, G. (1992). Advancing the teaching of psychology: Contributions of the American Psychological Association, 1946–1992. In A. E. Puente, J. R. Matthews, & C. L. Brewer (Eds.), *Teaching psychology in America: A history* (pp. 345–364). Washington, DC: American Psychological Association.

Paul, D. B. (1987, May/June). The nine lives of discredited data. *The Sciences, 27,* 26–30.

Sanford, E. C. (1910). The teaching of elementary psychology in colleges and universities with laboratories. *Psychological Monographs, 12,* 54–71.

Sanford, F. H., & Fleishman, E. A. (1950). A survey of undergraduate psychology courses in American colleges and universities. *American Psychologist, 5,* 33–37.

Scheirer, C. J., & Rogers, A. M. (1985). *The undergraduate psychology curriculum: 1984*. Washington, DC: American Psychological Association.

Weiten, W., & Wight, R. D. (1992). Portraits of a discipline: An examination of introductory psychology textbooks in America. In A. E. Puente, J. R. Matthews, & C. L. Brewer (Eds.), *Teaching psychology in America: A history* (pp. 453–504). Washington, DC: American Psychological Association.

Wolfle, D. (1942). The first course in psychology. *Psychological Bulletin, 39*, 685–712.

Notes

1. This research was supported by Grant 364 from the Simmons College Fund for Research.

2. We thank our colleagues at Harvard University, College of the Holy Cross, and Mount Holyoke College for their help in collecting the student data, and Susan Regan for her assistance with the cluster analyses. We thank the editor and three anonymous reviewers, especially the one with the red pen, for their comments on an earlier draft.

2. APPROACHES TO THE INTRODUCTORY COURSE: TECHNIQUES

Teaching Introductory Psychology at a Distance by Two-Way Interactive Video

Emir-Anne Andrews
Verena F. Gosse
Rennie S. Gaulton
Richard I. Maddigan

Alternate means of course delivery have become the exploratory focus of much research. Distance education is established in virtually all levels of education because of its ability to serve increased numbers of students, especially in remote areas (Brown, 1988; Miller, McKenna, & Ramsey, 1993). Additionally, the rapid expansion of sophisticated electronic technology and its incorporation in distance delivery systems have further enhanced the ability to reach site-bound students (Farr & Muscarella, 1991). Foremost on this scene has been the emergence of interactive video, a medium whose potential is increasingly being recognized, especially for distance education, by both educational leaders and technologists (Ely, 1989). Two-way interactive video allows linkage of traditional (on campus) classes with nontraditional (remote) classes and has the additional advantage of preserving real-time interaction between students and instructor. Against a backdrop of shifting demographics, economic conditions, and the history of using Introductory Psychology as a "testing ground" for new teaching techniques (distance education, personalized system of instruction, videotaped instruction, computer assisted learning, etc.), the Psychology Department of Memorial University of Newfoundland recently participated in evaluating the feasibility of two-way interactive video in the Newfoundland environment.

Whenever new technology is applied to educational settings, questions arise regarding its academic effectiveness. Although two-way interactive video is relatively new, there have been some program evaluations. They have not, however, always been well controlled. By necessity they have had to use comparisons between groups already assigned to different instructional conditions (usually live vs. some variation of remote instruction) with few controls. Results have generally been mixed. Parkinson and Parkinson (1988) found no significant difference between the exam scores of nursing students in a live lecture group and those in an interactive remote group, whereas course perceptions were considerably less favorable for the remote condition than for the live condition. Baker and Hansford (1990) evaluated the perceptions of college students and staff in a 2-week teaching trial using interactive video technology in a variety of courses and found that, although students were generally satisfied, staff were guarded in their responses.

A small number of studies have been designed to ensure that all participating students experience both the traditional instructional method and the interactive video method. These results, too, have been mixed. Miller et al. (1993) evaluated 51 students enrolled in graduate-level education courses, with each student exposed to both teaching conditions. They found that exam results were lower and that both the students' perceptions of content mastery and their feeling of belonging were less favorable under the interactive video condition. Using the same model as Miller et al., Johnson, O'Connor, and Rossing (1984) found no significant difference in achievement and no negative attitude associated with either mode of instruction. In a related study with undergraduate courses, Kolomeychuk and Peltz (1992) found students' responses to be positive both to interactive sessions and to technology.

Other issues and problems associated with alternate methods of instruction have also been studied. Farr and Muscarella (1991) compared interactivity in three settings presenting psychology to undergraduate students. They found that in both face-to-face and two-way interaction conditions, student interactions were mostly questions, whereas in the audio-teleconferencing condition interactions were mostly comments. In a related study, Dillon, Hengst, and Zoller (1989) interviewed faculty regarding methods used in televised distance courses. These faculty indicated that they perceived television to be a valuable tool for distance education. However, they continued to lecture and indicated that they would choose not to use television.

Problems associated with two-way interactive video instruction include technical difficulties (e.g., television-style production, signal transmission, and discomfort with microphones; Denton, Clark, Rossing, & O'Connor, 1985) and problems related to the students' subjective experience. This latter category of problems is most likely to be reported by remote students and includes lack of perceived belonging (Kolomeychuk & Peltz, 1992; Miller et al., 1993), impersonal passive learning (Brown, 1988; Parkinson & Parkinson, 1988), perceived pressure to perform, and expectations of video instruction being easier (Miller et al., 1993).

Suggestions for increasing the effectiveness of interactive video have included multimedia coverage of content (Miller et al., 1993), more active teaching (Johnson et al., 1984), and enhancing student receptivity via instructor visits and training sessions (for both student and instructor) prior to course onset (Dillon et al., 1989; Kromholz & Johnson, 1988). According to Parkinson and Parkinson (1988), success increased if the instructor was committed to the media format, had additional preparation time, and was prepared to accept less face-to-face interaction.

Hence, although a case can be made for the use of two-way interactive video, we conclude that producers should develop appropriate teaching strategies and address technical challenges. Our project's objective was to add to the existing literature by reporting our experiences using two-way interactive video in the Newfoundland environment.

Method

In the Spring of 1994, the Division of Educational Technology (ETV) at Memorial University of Newfoundland, St. John's, asked the Psychology Department and the Clarenville campus of the Eastern Community College to collaborate in a pilot study using two-way interactive video to bridge the distance (approximately 200 km) between the main Memorial University of Newfoundland campus in St. John's (studio) and the Clarenville site (remote). The purpose was to compare these sites on the achievement and attitudes of students after taking one or both of Psychology 1000 and Psychology 1001 (two sequential one-semester courses in Introductory Psychology) by various methods of course delivery. As part of the ETV request, one group was in the studio on the main campus with one remote group receiving simultaneous transmission of the same lecture. A second remote group received the same lecture (at a different time) but without a studio class present.

Participants

All participants in this study were 1st-year students, with an average age of approximately 18 years old. Students at Memorial University of Newfoundland register for each semester separately. Therefore, students in the Fall 1994 Psychology 1000 classes were not necessarily the same students as those in the Winter 1995 Psychology 1001 classes. In the Fall 1994 semester there were 27 students in the studio group and 62 at the remote site. In the Winter 1995 semester there were 30 students in the studio group and 47 at the remote site.

Classroom Equipment

For each course the studio classroom contained three cameras: one dedicated to graphics and two (at different angles) focused on the chalkboard and the studio students (where appropriate). Also in the studio were three television monitors, one allowing the studio group to see the remote students and two dedicated to graphics. The classroom at the remote site contained one camera, allowing the studio to see the remote students, and two television monitors, allowing the remote group to see the instructor and the studio students (where appropriate).

Communication was via bidirectional transmission of audio and video across multiple telephone lines. Thus, two-way video and audio (by teleconference microphones) allowed students at both sites to participate.

The telephone company promptly rectified any transmission problems. During the remote site classes, a teaching assistant supervised students, operated equipment, and performed clerical tasks.

Procedure

The instructor delivered lectures to three classes. These classes received the same course content, but differed with respect to course delivery. Thus, for each of the courses, three classes participated:

1. A class taught in the ETV studio on campus (shown live to a remote class). This studio class could watch their instructor, see a televised screen image of the remote students, and participate.
2. A remote class that received the same lecture (via television) as the class in the campus studio (described previously). This class could see and hear the instructor, see a televised image of the studio class, and participate.
3. A second remote class that received a live lecture delivered from the ETV studio, but with no class in the studio. This class could see and hear the instructor and participate.

Remote site classes had access to supplementary contact with the instructor via electronic mail or audio-teleconferencing equipment (2 hr a week). The studio group had access to regularly scheduled office hours.

Assessment of the effectiveness of instructional conditions included students' final grades and a questionnaire regarding their attitudes toward various aspects of course delivery. Assessment also included interviews (conducted at the end of the project) with instructors and production staff.

Results

Tables 1 and 2 contain students' academic performance in each semester. A one-way ANOVA revealed no significant difference among the final grades obtained by any of the three classes during the fall semester, $F(2, 86) = 0.51$, $p > .05$, or during the winter semester, $F(2, 74) = 0.66$, $p > .05$.

A questionnaire assessing students' attitudes toward various aspects of course delivery yielded response rates of over 75% in the fall and 65% in the winter semesters. The attitudes expressed were largely favorable, with those of the winter semester essentially paralleling those of the fall semester. Typical were items such as, "Do you find it difficult

Table 1. Psychology 1000 Performance Measure, Fall 1994

Group	Final Grade
Studio	
M	66.11
SD	17.70
n	27
Remote/studio	
M	62.14
SD	13.28
n	21
Remote/no studio	
M	62.44
SD	16.47
n	41

Table 2. Psychology 1001 Performance Measure, Winter 1995

Group	Final Grade
Studio	
M	70.17
SD	13.38
n	30
Remote/studio	
M	65.00
SD	17.20
n	12
Remote/no studio	
M	69.43
SD	11.45
n	35

Table 3. Problems and Solutions From Instructors and Production Staff

Problem	Solutions
Where to gaze?	Consciously allocate eye contact with specific groups
	Lecture and ignore equipment
Student participation	Encourage involvement
	Transparencies
	Pose question and await response
	Handouts increase interaction
	Camera close-ups and more eye contact
	Precourse orientation for all
Microphone push buttons	Install open microphones
Focus time: chalkboard	Longer camera focus time
Legibility: chalkboard	More transparencies
Preproduction work	More lead time

to remain attentive to the professor during a two-way video teleconference class?", "Do you feel intimidated by the technology involved in a two-way video teleconference?", and "Would you enroll in another course using the two-way video teleconference technology?" Most students from all three groups in both semesters answered "no" (69%), "no" (95%), and "yes" (87%), respectively. One item, "The use of two-way video teleconferencing as a method of instruction is just as effective as having the professor physically present in the classroom," involved ranking responses on a 5-point scale ranging from 1 (*strongly disagree*) to 5 (*strongly agree*). Answers to this item were favorable (70%), although responses from students at the remote site were marginally less so (64%).

Students in all conditions rarely utilized the available supplementary contact with the instructor, even though students in the winter semester were encouraged to prepare specific questions. When queried as to this lack of use, remote students said that they knew, and so could help, each other (as they were from the same small geographic area).

Instructors and production staff identified a number of concerns and offered possible solutions (outlined in Table 3). Both noted that they as well as students required more preparation and orientation prior to course onset.

Discussion

These findings are not unlike those of previous researchers. For example, Johnson et al. (1984) found similarity in student achievement and positive attitude across instructional conditions. Parkinson and Parkinson (1988) also found similarity in academic performance across conditions. However, they found students' perceptions of the remote condition to be less positive than of the live condition. The need for extra preparation and for orientation prior to course onset (for all parties) identified in our study were also noted by Parkinson and Parkinson (1988) and Dillon et al. (1989), respectively. This last result is in line with others' thinking on the matter. For example, Roberts and Keough (1995) discussed the use of the information highway within the context of distance education and lifelong learning. Also, see Haughey's (1995) thoughts on the notion of presence and student participation and McKinnon's (1995) view on the necessity of orientation for students, teachers, and administrators.

In summary, the results of this study (performance and attitude) showed that, for our particular circumstances, the two-way interactive video method was an acceptable technique for teaching introductory psychology at a distance. Although this method of course delivery is not without its unique problems (live-lecture format preventing utilization of the full technical potential of the television medium), remote site students performed just as well as on-campus students and rated the classes positively.

References

Baker, R. A., & Hansford, B. C. (1990). *An evaluation of a two-week teaching trial using interactive video technology: Perceptions of students and staff.* Armidale, New South Wales: University of New England. (ERIC Document Reproduction Service No. ED 339 354)

Brown, C. (1988). The live video teleconference in distance learning. *Lifelong-Learning: An Omnibus of Practice and Research, 11*(5), 8–10.

Denton, J. J., Clark, F. E., Rossing, R. G., & O'Connor, M. J. (1985). Assessing instructional strategies and resulting student attitudes regarding two-way television instruction. *Journal of Educational Technology Systems, 13,* 281–298.

Dillon, C., Hengst, H., & Zoller, D. (1989). Instructional strategies, distance education, and student involvement. In University of Wisconsin, Madison, School of Education, Department of Continuing and Vocational Education (sponsors), *Helping learners learn at a distance: Fifth annual conference on teaching at a distance* (pp. 163–167). Madison: University of Wisconsin.

Farr, C. W., & Muscarella, D. (1991). *Is video really necessary? A study comparing interactivity in video and audio classrooms.* Laramie: University of Wyoming. (ERIC Document Reproduction Service No. ED 350 984)

Haughey, M. (1995). Distinctions in distance: Is distance education an obsolete term? In J. M. Roberts & E. M. Keough (Eds.), *Why the information highway? Lessons from open and distance learning* (pp. 2–14). Toronto, Canada: Trifolium Books.

Johnson, K. A., O'Connor, M. J., & Rossing, R. G. (1984). Interactive two-way television versus person-teaching. *Journal of Education Technology Systems, 12,* 265–272.

Kolomeychuk, T., & Peltz, D. P. (1992, May). Assessing effectiveness of interactive compressed video at University of Minnesota. *Educational Technology, 32*(5), 61–62.

Kromholz, S. F., & Johnson, S. M. (1988). A practical application to training instructional television faculty and students. *Lifelong-Learning: An Omnibus of Practice and Research, 11*(8), 15–16.

McKinnon, N. C. (1995). Distance education and the transformation of elementary/secondary education. In J. M. Roberts & E. M. Keough (Eds.), *Why the information highway? Lessons from open and distance learning* (pp. 60–76). Toronto, Canada: Trifolium Books.

Miller, J. W., McKenna, M. C., & Ramsey, P. (1993). Evaluation of student content-learning and affective perceptions of a two-way interactive video-learning experience. *Educational Technology, 33*(6), 51–55.

Parkinson, C. F., & Parkinson, S. B. (1988). Comparative study between interactive television and traditional lecture course offerings in nursing students. *Nursing and Health Care, 10,* 499–502.

Roberts, J. M., & Keough, E. M. (Eds.). (1995). *Why the information highway? Lessons from open and distance learning.* Toronto, Canada: Trifolium Books.

Notes

1. Funding for this project was provided by the Human Resources Development Agreement, Department of Education; The Atlantic Canada Opportunities Agency; Memorial University of Newfoundland; and Eastern Community College, Clarenville Campus.
2. R. Gaulton and R. Maddigan taught the courses; E. Andrews and V. Gosse conducted the research and reporting.
3. We acknowledge and thank the section editor and anonymous reviewers for their suggestions and useful comments on earlier drafts of this article. We also thank Virginia Grant for her helpful review of the last version of this article.

Personalization and Active Learning in the Large Introductory Psychology Class

Ludy T. Benjamin, Jr.

This article discusses issues inherent in teaching large sections of introductory psychology and strategies for dealing with them. Specifically, I (a) discuss the importance of personalizing the large class, (b) describe ways to make large classes into small classes to facilitate active learning, and (c) describe strategies to promote active learning in the large class.

A few observations about class size set the stage. First, the average undergraduate class size has increased steadily in this century, especially during the last several decades (Carnegie Foundation for the Advancement of Education, 1986). Although most professors and students prefer small classes, economic realities indicate that large classes are here to stay (Gleason, 1986; McKeachie, 1986).

Second, large classes are now found in small colleges as well as in large universities. Pressures to increase enrollment without adding faculty and to expand the curriculum contribute to larger classes. Curriculum expansion is often accomplished by combining many small sections of the same course into one huge class to make room for another course in the teaching schedule (Carnegie Foundation for the Advancement of Education, 1986; Krabill, 1981).

Third, concern with possible adverse effects of large classes is not a recent phenomenon. McKeachie (1980) suggested that class size was probably the first issue of college teaching to be subjected to educational research (e.g., Edmonson & Mulder, 1924; Hudelson, 1928). That interest in class size continues and is supported by the nearly 200 relevant citations found in a search of the literature since 1960. This field of study is so well established that it bears its own acronym—LGI or large-group instruction.

I do not propose to survey that literature in detail. Interested readers are referred to Klein (1985), Lewis and Woodward (1984), McKeachie (1980, 1986), and Williams, Cook, Quinn, and Jensen (1985) for more comprehensive treatments. However, a brief summary of the research on class size sets the stage for the discussion that follows.

Even restricting this summary to the studies on college classes, conflicting results still abound. These contradictions arise for several reasons, including differences in outcome measures, length of study, and the confounding of numerous variables, such as teaching method and instructor experience.

Part of the difficulty in making sense of LGI literature begins with the definition of what constitutes a large class. Some studies have compared small classes of 7 students with large classes of 40; others have compared small classes of 40 students with large classes of 300. Although agreement is not universal, recent literature seems to have settled on a figure of 100 or more for defining the large class.

Small and large classes have been compared and contrasted with respect to many variables, such as these important ones: performance on exams, long-term retention of the course material, student attitudes toward the discipline, student attitudes toward the instructor, student ability, instructional methods, course objectives, course management, and testing methods. McKeachie (1980) summarized this literature, and his conclusions have not been altered by an additional decade of research. He wrote:

> . . . large lectures are not generally inferior to smaller lecture classes when traditional achievement tests are used as a criterion. When other objectives are measured, large lectures are on shakier ground. Goals of higher level thinking, application, motivation, and attitudinal change are most likely to be achieved in small classes. Moreover, both students and faculty members feel that teaching is more effective in small classes. . . . In general, large classes are simply not as effective as small classes for retention of knowledge, critical thinking, and attitude change. (pp. 26–27)

Although McKeachie's general conclusions are still accurate, at least one study can be cited to cast doubt on each of his claims for the superiority of small classes.

Like most teachers and students, I believe that small is better. In small classes, course management is easier, interaction with students is facilitated, options for teaching techniques are greater, and more methods for evaluating student learning are feasible. Perhaps in an ideal world there would be no large classes. However, economic considerations guarantee their continued existence in higher education, especially in the absence of evidence suggesting that they are ineffective. Some instructors have wondered if, rather than trying to improve teaching large classes, "we might be better off just using our energy to fight against teaching under these conditions" (Silverstein, 1982, p. 155). However, Silverstein rejected that strategy and accepted the challenge of teaching large classes well. I reluctantly acknowledge this reality and try to improve the educational experience for students in my large classes.

Large introductory psychology classes are not a recent phenomenon. At the University of Leipzig in the 1880s, Wilhelm Wundt's introductory psychology class contained approximately 300 students. Edward Bradford Titchener's description of Wundt's class, written when he was a student at Leipzig in 1890, sounds familiar. Titchener told us that with the room filled, Wundt walked to the front of the class, leaned on the podium, his notes resting between his elbows, and lectured for 1 hr, after which he gathered up his notes and left the room (Baldwin, 1921).

Class size may be similar today, but staffing large classes is different. At the turn of this century, the beginning course in psychology was commonly taught by the senior faculty member—Titchener, William James, and G. Stanley Hall, to name a few. Today that class is often taught by graduate students or new faculty members. Attracting senior faculty to this course has become increasingly difficult (Griggs, Lange, & Meyer, 1988). In some institutions, teaching the introductory course is a mark of low status, which disturbs me. The introductory course is the most important course in the undergraduate curriculum. It is also the most difficult course to teach well. Giving full responsibility for that course to graduate students and beginning faculty members serves neither well, nor does it do justice to the undergraduate students. And assigning beginning teachers to large classes only compounds the problems (Weimer, 1987). A procedure that partially addresses this issue and calls for a fairer use of graduate teaching assistants (TAs) is described later.

Large classes are essentially lecture courses. Studies using in-class observers report that the lecture occupies 80% to 95% of class time, with less than 5% involving student participation (Lewis & Woodward, 1984). In fact, the larger the class size, the more likely it is that class time will be filled exclusively with lectures (Lewis, 1982).

When lecturers ask questions in large classes, their questions are usually rhetorical or procedural. An example of the latter is, "Does everyone know the reading assignment for tomorrow?" Such questions are not meant to engage students in active learning. Although some students enjoy the anonymity provided by large classes, more students complain about the impersonal nature of those classes (Lewis & Woodward, 1984; Wulff, Nyquist, & Abbott, 1987). The remainder of this article addresses two related issues—depersonalization and the perceived lack of opportunities for active learning.

Personalizing the Large Class

Depersonalization can affect students' interest in and enjoyment of the course, both of which are likely to affect how much a student learns (Gleason, 1986; McConnell & Sosin, 1984; Wulff et al., 1987). Personalizing the class starts with the instructor knowing the students' names. Yet as class enrollments mushroom beyond 150 students, this ideal ceases to be attainable for most instructors. One of my colleagues uses mnemonics to learn the names of his class of 250 students (see Smith, 1985). Another professor I know takes Polaroid photographs of his 100 students the first day of class and successfully matches all names and faces by the second week.

I am either lazier or less gifted in learning the names of the 250 students in my class. I try to learn most of their names by the end of the course by studying a seating chart, especially while they are taking exams. By the time of the first exam, I know many of their faces, at least those in the first few rows, so I spend exam time matching names with those faces. I learn about one third of the names at that time and can later direct questions to students by name or call some of them by name when their hands are raised. Some students are shocked that I know their names, and I try to give the impression that I know all their names.

Some instructors teach sections of 1,200 students, and it seems unlikely that any procedure would be effective for them. However, my advice is that you try to learn your students' names. Do not take the attitude that having a large class excuses you from that responsibility.

I also use the seating chart to record attendance each day. I do this partly because my university requires such records, although what faculty members do with attendance data is their business. There is another reason to record attendance, even if you do not require it. Pearson (1986) reported that "students feel more obligated to go to class when the instructor knows if they are present" (p. 9).

Another device for combating depersonalization is the autobiographical sheet that I distribute during the first week of class. Students fill it out in class and turn it in before leaving. I ask them to list their hometown, year in college, and major. I ask them why they are taking the course and what they hope to get out of it. Some students share Shakespeare's belief about the "soul of wit," and they answer: "It's required" and "An A." I ask them about their job (if they work) and about what they like to do when they are not being students. I also ask them if there is anything they would like to ask me or anything else they would like for me to know about them.

I read those autobiographies, usually in an evening, taking notes about items I want to use in class. Throughout the course, I try to use some of that material. For example, an aerospace engineering student told me she was taking the course because she wanted something totally unrelated to her major. Because of that comment, I used several occasions in class to talk about why aerospace engineers might be interested in such psychological topics as human factors, pilot selection and training, flight crew compatibility, and decision making regarding shuttle launches.

I try to answer all questions, either in class or by note to the student, and try to let them know that I read what they wrote by commenting in class. I avoid personal information and would not knowingly say anything to embarrass a student. I will use a student's name when appropriate, perhaps by saying something like, "I got a most interesting question from Ms. Gloria Ortiz." I may even ask her to raise her hand so I and other members of the class can know who she is, after which I answer the question. Students' questions can be used throughout the course as relevant topics appear.

Having traveled around Texas enough to know something about many of my students' hometowns, I may comment in class about a particularly good pit barbecue restaurant or an attractive courthouse located there. Sometimes I tease them, for example: "Mr. Randall Martin, where are you? I see that you graduated from San Antonio Brackenridge High School. They defeated us in football when I was in high school, and I have never forgotten it. As a result, the best grade you can hope for in this class is a C." I say it all with a straight face and smile only after the rest of the class laughs. The important purpose of this approach is to let students know that I took the time to read what they wrote and was interested enough to comment on some of it.

The University of Nebraska at Lincoln has a more formal program for giving instructors of large classes information about their students (Wright & Bond, 1985). From information in official records, each student is described in terms of 149 demographic and attitudinal variables. These data are provided in summary form to the LGI faculty. Faculty members can meet with an educational consultant to discuss the results of the class analysis and how they might be used to promote student achievement.

All these procedures allow instructors to learn something about the people who occupy the chairs in their classrooms. The knowledge teachers gain may influence their selection of lectures, activities, or examples, matching them to specific student interests. Good teachers know their audience. For other ideas on personalizing large classes, see Aronson (1987), Gleason (1986), and Rosenkoetter (1984).

Lecturing Versus Active Learning

Many instructors probably chose the teaching profession because they enjoy talking more than listening. As one of my students described it, "Professors love to profess." Maybe that is why the lecture is the dominant teaching mode regardless of class size (Eble, 1988). Some of us may even believe that students are incapable of learning unless the truth goes from our mouths to their ears. We are reluctant to give up valued lecture time to other teaching techniques or to students.

I believe that we lecture so much because it is easier and safer than other teaching techniques. Other methods usually require more preparation, such as assembling equipment for demonstrations, meeting with groups of students outside class to prepare for simulations, and preparing handouts for in-class exercises that have to be read and analyzed for class feedback. After you have taught introductory psychology for a few years, preparing a lecture probably takes less time than many other things you might do in class. It may also be the case that less can go wrong with a lecture; thus, its reliability adds to its attractiveness.

As noted earlier, some students enjoy the anonymity of the large lecture class that leaves them with little responsibility other than taking notes. Students report feeling less pressure in lecture classes, and the larger the class the less pressure they feel (Weimer, 1987). Even if every student felt that way, I would object to a course that allowed complete passivity.

Fortunately, many students resent being viewed as empty vessels to be filled by their professor. They want a more active role, and the large class should not prevent that involvement. Think about the students who take the beginning course in psychology. This course in the science of behavior is not their first exposure to behavior. They have been observing and thinking about behavior all of their lives. Insights will occur to them while they are reading their textbook and when you are lecturing. When will they have the opportunity to express those insights to you? Most students hesitate to comment in a large lecture, even when told that it is okay to interrupt the instructor.

Barbara Nodine (personal communication, September 1, 1989) suggested using informal, ungraded writing activities during the lecture to make student participation more active and more personal. Stopping the lecture and asking students to write an answer to a discussion question and then proceeding with a lecture–discussion that includes student reactions will be much more interactive. Asking students to record their thoughts will make each one of them (not just those who speak during the class) more interested in what you say. As you make points, you could ask students to raise their hands if they had a similar idea. Or you can tell students to exchange their summaries or answers with the persons next to them. Thus, in a short time, you can create an occasion for every student to have a dialogue with someone about the lecture material.

You might ask students to come to class with personal anecdotes illustrating points from lecture or their textbooks that they would be willing to share. Exchanging anecdotes with the people seated next to them and perhaps submitting a few unusual ones to be read to the entire class is an effective means of engaging students personally and actively with the course material. For a description of other ungraded "writing to learn" exercises, see Maimon, Nodine, Hearn, and Haney-Peritz (1990).

Although some instructors will be uncomfortable with such interruptions, there are compelling reasons to supplement the lecture. If only the lecture is used, how can students be taught about perceptual adaptation to displaced vision, the difficulties of mirror tracing, the nature of polarization in group decisions, the application of mnemonics, or the nature of propositional reasoning? These phenomena, and many others in psychology, are better understood by active learning.

The educational literature is filled with studies supporting the advantages of *active learning*, a term used to describe a broad array of learning situations in which students enjoy hands-on and minds-on experiences (e.g., Brothen, 1986; Frederick, 1987; Michaelsen, 1983; Wittrock, 1984). Students learn through simulations, games, demonstrations, discussions, debates, problem solving, interactive lectures, and the kinds of writing exercises described earlier.

How important is active learning? The National Institute of Education's 1984 report, *Involvement in Learning: Realizing the Potential of American Higher Education*, identified active learning as the Number 1 priority in American higher education today. That report emphasized the special importance of such learning experiences for the development of higher cognitive abilities and for affective development. But how can active learning be accomplished in large classes? The short answer is—not easily. The best answer is to turn your large-class swords into small-class plowshares.

Turning Large Classes Into Small Ones

One teaching model divides some of the large-class hours into small-group classes to facilitate active learning. With movable chairs, one can create small groups within the large classroom, but many large classrooms do not permit that. One popular alternative is to schedule the small groups at different times and places (Mendenhall & Burr, 1983; Michaelsen, 1983; Silverstein, 1982; Weaver, 1983). My approach involves dividing a class of 250 into groups of about 30 each. The large class meets twice a week, and the small groups meet once each week. At some universities, the ratio is reversed with students meeting in their small groups twice each week (Silverstein, 1982). The small groups in my course are led by two graduate TAs, each with responsibility for four groups per week.

We do things in the smaller groups that we cannot do in the large class. Thus, we do not show films or use demonstrations and exercises that could be used as effectively for a large group. Lecturing is kept to the minimum needed for the day's activity, usually in the form of giving instructions about the exercise.

Small-group activities are coordinated each week with the content of the text and the large class. I meet weekly with the TAs to plan the activity for the coming week, typically rehearsing those parts that we can. Activities are planned to involve all students; for many of our exercises, everyone in the class has a role to play.

Students spend the entire first period getting to know one another and their TA. We use the autobiographical sheets described earlier to accomplish that. I usually attend all of the small-group classes during the first week because it gives me a head start on getting to know my students. I also attend other meetings of the small groups throughout the semester.

The exercises in these small classes are planned with specific educational goals in mind. They typically involve considerable structure, but we also try to include some activities that encourage students to explore their own interests. In these small classes, students practice deep muscle relaxation, often used in anxiety therapies; construct their own personality test, administer it to subjects outside the class, and collect, analyze, and discuss their data (Benjamin, 1983); wear prism displacement goggles until adaptation has occurred, discovering why the adaptation represents a motor change and not a visual one and experiencing the brief exasperation of readaptation (Benjamin, 1981); discuss the concept of aggression in a critical thinking exercise using data collected from their own small group (Benjamin, 1985); try to identify a "murderer" by using a number of measures such as galvanic skin responses, word associations, response latencies, and nonverbal cues; and transport themselves back in time via a simulated first-grade class that allows them to learn how to read all over again and to understand what books look like to those who cannot read. After years of refinement, we now have exercises that score high on measures of learning and satisfaction.

The teaching experience is usually gratifying for the TA who prepares a lesson once each week and practices it four times. The duties are considerable, but far less demanding than having full responsibility for a lecture course. Too often graduate students are given little or no preparation for teaching. Part of the value of our approach is the diversity of teaching techniques used in the small classes. The TA gains familiarity with such methods as simulations, discussion exercises, role-playing, and demonstrations. Coupled with some guest lectures in the large class, leading the small groups is an excellent apprenticeship for TAs who might later have full responsibility for a course.

For the instructor, these classes are always a lot of work, despite using many of the same exercises each year. That is partly because TAs change every two or three semesters, so there are always new people to train. I often think how much easier it would be just to lecture for that third hour, but then I read the course evaluations that indicate how highly students rate the small classes. At my university of 42,000 students, this class of 30 may be the smallest a student will have all year. Some regularly make that comment in their evaluations. Many remark about actually being able to express their own ideas in a class. Some talk about how it helps them to meet other people in the class. One couple who met in a small group announced their wedding to the group on the final day of the course. However, matchmaking is not one of my course objectives.

I have used this approach for 10 consecutive years. I continue to use it because of the active learning opportunities for the students, their obvious enjoyment of the exercises, and the close contact it provides me with my TAs.

I think the best solution to the large class is to create small classes within it. Some of you may say that you cannot use the model I have described or one of its variants because you do not have graduate TAs available. My reply is that undergraduate students can serve the same function. I taught for 8 years at Nebraska Wesleyan University, a 4-year liberal arts college of approximately 1,200 students. We used junior and senior psychology majors to assist in a number of classes and laboratories, and many of them served with distinction. There is considerable literature on peer teaching by undergraduates and on programs that combine undergraduate and graduate TAs, such as pyramid plans (McKeachie, 1986). This literature generally rates performance of student teachers quite highly. (For some of the variations using undergraduate TAs in psychology courses, see Gnagey, 1979; Kohn & Brill, 1981; Mendenhall & Burr, 1983; White & Kolber, 1978; Wortman & Hillis, 1976.)

Some colleges and universities use so many TAs that they divide large classes into small groups of 5 to 7. These small-group formats require more work from the supervising teacher, but the rewards are worth the extra effort. If the small-group class is not something you can or will try and if you acknowledge the value of active learning, what can you do to facilitate it in the large class?

Active Learning in the Large Class

If you ask professors what they like about small classes, many will say "the opportunity for discussion," even when no discussion occurs. These same professors often say that discussion is impossible in large classes, and they conclude that the only alternative is to lecture.

I do not denigrate the lecture method. It has dominated the educational scene for centuries, and its survival is not due solely to tradition or inertia. The lecture has many advantages, perhaps the greatest of which is its ability to impart a large amount of information in a short time. However, lectures usually relegate students to a completely passive role in the learning process. Involving students in active learning necessarily reduces the amount of information that can be presented in class. The quantitative loss often allows for a qualitative gain. I am not asking you to stop giving lectures. I am asking you to replace some lectures with active learning exercises for your large class.

If you do not use active learning exercises in your large class, you might experiment by adding a few throughout the course. If you already use several favorite exercises, you might consider expanding your repertoire. One reasonable goal would be to include an active learning activity in every class period except on review and examination days. Some of these exercises might require the entire period; others might be used for only a few minutes. Good exercises will increase students' interest and motivation. Students will ex-

pect to have some direct involvement in the class instead of just taking notes from a lecture.

Most teachers of introductory psychology use a textbook. These books tend to be encyclopedic, averaging 600 to 900 pages, and there are many good ones from which to choose. After examining these books, I must admit that almost everything I want students to know about psychology is in their textbook. I assume that college students can read and understand these books on their own. Given that assumption, what is my role as a teacher? I can lecture from the book, which will bore those who have read and understood their assignments. Instead, I lecture on topics not in the book or expand on some that are.

I am not obligated to cover the text material at all, unless I believe that some psychological phenomenon is either poorly explained or wrongly interpreted. Therefore, I can rely on the text to accomplish one very important course objective: to provide the basic content of psychology. That frees me to pursue other objectives in my lectures.

I might want my students to become familiar with the scientific method and how a scientific attitude can be used in everyday life, to recognize the relevance of psychology to current events, to learn some problem-solving strategies, to think critically, to develop some social skills, to apply the information learned in their text, or to learn about some psychological phenomena that are largely experiential in nature. Some of those goals can be accomplished by the lecture, but others can be achieved only by involving students in active learning.

As noted earlier, these active learning exercises can be part of the large class every day, either alone or in conjunction with the lecture method. They can also be conducted as homework assignments by students working individually or together. The in-class exercises offer the opportunity for direct interaction with the instructor and perhaps with a number of other students in the class.

Here are some exercises that can be used in the large class. Many other appropriate exercises are described fully in Division Two's journal, *Teaching of Psychology,* in the several teaching activities handbooks published by the American Psychological Association, and in the instructor's manuals that accompany introductory psychology textbooks.

Demonstrations constitute one kind of active learning, but not all demonstrations qualify. For example, using a student volunteer to wear prism goggles in front of your class while engaging in selected motor tasks is an excellent active learning experience for that student. Demonstrating discrimination learning by showing a rat in an operant chamber to your class is a good active learning experience for the rat. But neither demonstration provides any active involvement for the rest of the class. I am not arguing against the use of these demonstrations; I am only noting that they do not constitute active learning.

The kinds of demonstrations I have in mind require entire class participation. Some demonstrations are quite simple, such as having the class watch you take their picture with a flash camera and then asking them to manipulate the size of the afterimage they experience by projecting it on different surfaces within the room, such as their desk top, their hand, or a distant wall. Emmert's law can be much more meaningful in that context.

In a lecture on depth perception, you can help students understand the binocular cue of convergence by having them fully extend one of their arms in front of them, give a thumbs up sign, and then stare at their thumb with both eyes as they bring it slowly toward their nose, reminding them to pay attention to the muscle tension they feel in their eyes.

Although these simple demonstrations are not innovative, they offer a nice change of pace from standard lectures. They also allow students to experience the phenomena in a situation that allows the instructor to reinforce reading or lecture. These two examples illustrate (a) how simple some active learning demonstrations are, (b) how little time some of them require, and (c) that you already know how to do them.

Other demonstrations are more complicated, such as a mnemonic system using interacting images. I use such a demonstration to illustrate the ease with which many mnemonic systems can be learned and used and to show the importance of imagery in memory. I write the numbers 1 through 12 on the chalkboard, one at a time. As I write each number, I give it its associated peg word: 1 is a *wand*, 2 is a *swan* (looks like a swan), 3 is a *three-leaf clover*, 4 is a *four-legged table*, 5 is a *five-pointed star*, 6 is an *elephant's trunk in a curled up position*, 7 is a *flag*, 8 is an *hourglass*, 9 is a *smoking pipe* (laying on its side), 10 is a *ball and bat*, 11 is a *very small portion of spaghetti*, and 12 is a *clock* (hands pointing to midnight). I leave those numbers and words on the board while I describe how students are to use those words to form interactive images to remember new material in a particular order. I then tell students that I am going to call out 12 new words in a random order, giving each word a number. Students are told that these are the words they are to remember and be able to recall later by number. Then I begin: 6 is *Volkswagen*, 11 is *mountain*, 2 is *ambition*, and so forth. During this part of the exercise, students listen and concentrate on creating their mental images without taking notes. After calling out the 12 new words, I erase the associated words on the board and tell students to number a piece of scratch paper from 1 to 12 and write down the words I just called out. After students finish writing, I lead the class in a unison recitation of the words. I say the number, and they say the word. Their response is impressive because more than 200 people say the correct word in response to my number. I then ask for a show of hands of how many got them all right; typically, two thirds of the class responds. Next I ask them to volunteer some of their associations, reminding them that this class is a "family show." One student describes how she pictured an ugly duckling with an ambition to become a beautiful swan. Another says he pictured an elephant with a Volkswagen wrapped up in its trunk, and many students nod their heads. Another student says she pictured a Volkswagen whose trunk looked like an elephant's trunk. The entire demonstration takes from 15 to 20 min, depending on how long I let the student comments continue.

To reinforce the text information on forgetting, I repeat the recitation part of the demonstration several weeks later. I ask students to remember the 12 words I called out to them, and I begin by saying the numbers. Their responses are quite different. The number of students responding is considerably smaller than before, perhaps reduced by 75% or more. The quieter response is a cacophony, produced by students saying a number of different words (see Shimamura, 1984).

Again, many demonstrations like this take very little class time, involve everyone in the class, prompt student comments, and require the instructor to do very little preparation or data analysis. You could collect the student responses in the mnemonic demonstration, analyze the data sheets, and report the results to the class at a later time. Yet, the recitation by students makes the point quite nicely and timely.

Many other good demonstrations require students to generate data. I use an aggression questionnaire intended as a critical thinking exercise in the small groups (Benjamin, 1985), but it is easily adapted to the large class. The one-page questionnaire is given to the students in one class period and requires 3 min to complete. The questionnaires are collected, the data analyzed, and the questionnaire and results given back to the students in the next class period, setting the stage for a lecture and discussion of the data, drawing heavily on student comments. Students always seem more interested in their data than they are in hearing about data collected on others. One-page questionnaires are easily generated. For example, I use another one that asks students questions about their sleep and dreaming. Discussion of the data from these questionnaires provides a good supplement to lecture and probably increases students' motivation to learn.

Active learning techniques for large classes involve writing and discussion. In one format, the class is divided into pairs of students to discuss a particular issue or to solve a problem. For example, I might ask them to write an answer to the following question, "Human infants cannot be tested on the visual cliff until they are able to crawl, around 6 months of age, because movement off the runway is the dependent variable. Can you think of another dependent variable that could be used in human newborns to determine whether they can perceive differences between the shallow and deep sides?" After committing their thoughts to writing and then spending 5 to 10 min engaged in dyadic discussion, students can be asked to volunteer their proposed solutions. This approach is a variant of what is known as a *learning cell*, which is a form of the student dyad in the classroom.

In this final section, I have not discussed several active learning formats for large classes, including out-of-class exercises, interactive lectures, debates, and class simulations. However, I have described some forms of active learning that you might use in large classes.

Summary

In this article, I shared some personal philosophies and observations about teaching large classes. I emphasized the importance of personalizing the course and stated my belief that a large class does not fully exempt the instructor from that responsibility. I stressed the importance of active learning. If you were not already a convert, I hope I convinced you that active learning is possible in the large class. I hope I have encouraged you to make active learning more prominent in your own classes, large or small.

References

Aronson, J. R. (1987). Six keys to effective instruction in large classes: Advice from a practitioner. In M. G. Weimer (Ed.), *Teaching large classes well* (pp. 31–37). San Francisco: Jossey-Bass.

Baldwin, B. T. (1921). In memory of Wilhelm Wundt. *Psychological Review, 28,* 153–188.

Benjamin, L. T., Jr. (1981). Adaptation to displaced vision. In L. T. Benjamin, Jr. & K. D. Lowman (Eds.), *Activities handbook for the teaching of psychology* (Vol. 1, pp. 51–53). Washington, DC: American Psychological Association.

Benjamin, L. T., Jr. (1983). A class exercise in personality and psychological assessment. *Teaching of Psychology, 10,* 94–95.

Benjamin, L. T., Jr. (1985). Defining aggression: An exercise for class discussion. *Teaching of Psychology, 12,* 40–42.

Brothen, T. F. (1986). Using active learning in large classes. In S. F. Schomberg (Ed.), *Strategies for active teaching and learning in university classrooms* (pp. 40–46). Minneapolis: University of Minnesota Teaching Center.

Carnegie Foundation for the Advancement of Education. (1986). *College: The undergraduate experience.* New York: Carnegie Foundation.

Eble, K. E. (1988). *The craft of teaching: A guide to mastering the professor's art* (2nd ed.). San Francisco: Jossey-Bass.

Edmonson, J. B., & Mulder, F. J. (1924). Size of class as a factor in university instruction. *Journal of Educational Research, 9,* 1–12.

Frederick, P. J. (1987). Student involvement: Active learning in large classes. In M. G. Weimer (Ed.), *Teaching large classes well* (pp. 45–56). San Francisco: Jossey-Bass.

Gleason, M. (1986). Better communication in large courses. *College Teaching, 34,* 20–24.

Gnagey, W. J. (1979). Peer leadership of small research teams in two introductory psychology classes. *Teaching of Psychology, 6,* 80–82.

Griggs, R. A., Lange, S. K., & Meyer, M. E. (1988). Staffing the introductory psychology course in graduate departments. *Teaching of Psychology, 15,* 124–127.

Hudelson, E. (1928). *Class size at the college level.* Minneapolis: University of Minnesota Press.

Klein, K. (1985). The research on class size. *Phi Delta Kappan, 66,* 578–580.

Kohn, A., & Brill, M. (1981). An introductory demonstration laboratory produced entirely by undergraduates. *Teaching of Psychology, 8,* 133–138.

Krabill, E. K. (1981, February). Some deleterious consequences of increased enrollments. *Engineering Education,* pp. 333–335.

Lewis, K. G. (1982). *The large class analysis project* (Final report). Austin: University of Texas, Center for Teaching Effectiveness.

Lewis, K. G., & Woodward, P. J. (1984). *What really happens in large university classes?* Paper presented at the 1984 meeting of the American Educational Research Association. (ERIC Document Reproduction Service No. ED 245 590)

Maimon, E. P., Nodine, B. F., Hearn, G. W., & Haney-Peritz, J. (1990). Beaver College. In T. Fulwiler & A. Young (Eds.), *Programs that work: Models and methods for writing across the curriculum* (pp. 1–26). Portsmouth, NH: Boynton-Cook.

McConnell, C. R., & Sosin, K. (1984). Some determinants of student attitudes toward large classes. *Journal of Economic Education, 15,* 181–190.

McKeachie, W. J. (1980). Class size, large classes, and multiple sections. *Academe, 66,* 24–27.

McKeachie, W. J. (1986). *Teaching tips: A guidebook for the beginning college teacher* (8th ed.). Lexington, MA: Heath.

Mendenhall, M., & Burr, W. R. (1983). Enlarging the role of the undergraduate teaching assistant. *Teaching of Psychology, 10,* 184–185.

Michaelsen, L. K. (1983). Team learning in large classes. In C. Bouton & R. Y. Garth (Eds.), *Learning in groups* (pp. 13–22). San Francisco: Jossey-Bass.

National Institute of Education. (1984). *Involvement in learning: Realizing the potential of American higher education.* Washington, DC: U.S. Department of Education.

Pearson, J. C. (1986). *Teaching a large lecture interpersonal communication course.* Paper presented at the 1986 meeting of the Speech Communication Association. (ERIC Document Reproduction Service No. ED 278 071)

Rosenkoetter, J. S. (1984). Teaching psychology to large classes: Videotapes, PSI, and lecturing. *Teaching of Psychology, 11,* 85–87.

Shimamura, A. P. (1984). A guide for teaching mnemonic skills. *Teaching of Psychology, 11,* 162–166.

Silverstein, B. (1982). Teaching a large lecture course in psychology: Turning defeat into victory. *Teaching of Psychology, 9,* 150–155.

Smith, S. M. (1985). A method for teaching name mnemonics. *Teaching of Psychology, 12,* 156–158.

Weaver, R. L. (1983, Fall). The small class group in large classes. *The Educational Forum,* pp. 65–73.

Weimer, M. G. (Ed.). (1987). *Teaching large classes well.* San Francisco: Jossey-Bass.

White, K. M., & Kolber, R. G. (1978). Undergraduate and graduate students as discussion section leaders. *Teaching of Psychology, 5,* 6–9.

Williams, D. D., Cook, P. F., Quinn, B., & Jensen, R. P. (1985). University class size: Is smaller better? *Research in Higher Education, 23,* 307–318.

Wittrock, M. C. (1984). Learning as a generative process. *Educational Psychologist, 11,* 87–95.

Wortman, C. B., & Hillis, J. W. (1976). Undergraduate-taught "minicourses" in conjunction with an introductory lecture course. *Teaching of Psychology, 3,* 69–72.

Wright, D. L., & Bond, S. C. (1985). *Quantitative assessments of student differences: A faculty development approach for teachers of large classes.* Paper presented at the 1985 meeting of the American Educational Research Association. (ERIC Document Reproduction Service No. ED 255 112)

Wulff, D. H., Nyquist, J. D., & Abbott, R. D. (1987). Students' perceptions of large classes. In M. G. Weimer (Ed.), *Teaching large classes well* (pp. 17–30). San Francisco: Jossey-Bass.

Notes

1. This article is adapted from a G. Stanley Hall Lecture presented at the 1989 meeting of the American Psychological Association, New Orleans, LA.

2. I thank Barbara F. Nodine, Jack R. Nation, and Jeffry Simpson for their help in preparing this article.

The Vital Role of Psychology's History in Introductory Courses: An Interview With Ludy T. Benjamin, Jr.

C. James Goodwin

CJG: From your observations of the structure of textbooks in general psychology, how is psychology's history currently being taught in the introductory course?

LTB: I make no claims to a broad knowledge of current introductory psychology textbooks. I have been using the same book for several editions now and consequently have not looked much at other books. Nevertheless, my impression is that most introductory psychology textbooks offer very little coverage of the history of psychology, typically no more than five to six pages in the introductory chapter.

CJG: Have you noticed any trends or changes, for better or worse, within the past 20 years?

LTB: I have been teaching the beginning course for 25 years now, and I can't say that I have seen much change in the way psychology's history is presented. Mostly, it is a modern history that begins with Wundt and then moves to a chronology of the "schools" of psychology in America. Typically, those schools are used as a lead-in to a discussion of theoretical perspectives in contemporary psychology, for example, behaviorism, psychoanalysis. I haven't seen much of a change in the past 25 years other than the fact that most introductory psychology textbook authors have learned that Titchener was not Wundt's clone in America.

CJG: Are there any exceptions to this standard pattern?

LTB: Les Sdorow's (1995) introductory psychology textbook has a much more thorough treatment of psychology's history in its opening chapter, and he has spread historical material throughout most of the other chapters in his book as well. In addition, Henry Gleitman's (1995) book contains a more thorough historical treatment of psychology throughout his chapters, and he treats other historical topics as well. I am particularly fond of his frequent use of art history in his text.

CJG: In her G. Stanley Hall lecture, Laurel Furumoto (1989) urged instructors in the history course to shift from teaching it in the traditional way, with an emphasis on great people, great events, and great ideas, to a "new history," which places events and people in the appropriate historical context and is a critical rather than a ceremonial history. Although her remarks were aimed at those teaching the course in history and systems, how might her message improve introductory psychology texts and classes?

LTB: I consider Laurel's Hall Lecture an articulate statement of the new scholarship in the history of psy-

chology, but it is not a message that has reached most introductory textbook authors nor teachers of introductory psychology. As you note, Laurel's message was for teachers of the history of psychology and authors of history of psychology textbooks. I can't tell you if it has affected the teaching of the history of psychology, but it does seem to me that history of psychology textbooks are moving in the direction she espoused, albeit slowly. It is probably too much to expect that introductory textbook authors and introductory psychology teachers would find much value in the kind of history that Laurel is advocating. That kind of externalist history means providing a context for understanding and appreciation that is beyond the survey nature of the typical textbook and course. It argues for depth instead of breadth, an argument that seems to have already been decided in favor of the latter in most introductory psychology courses. However, I could envision a psychology text that wove psychology into the broader cultural, political, social, and economic fabric of which it was a part.

CJG: Could you give some examples of how adding some historical context might enrich the introductory course?

LTB: An instructor could talk about the relationship of research on leadership styles and obedience to authority to fascism and the Holocaust; or the growth of a profession of psychology to issues of urbanization, immigration, and industrialization; or developmental research tied to the women's movement of the 1970s and the graying of America's population. Those are just a few of the many examples that could be cited for an introductory psychology course that would place the development of psychology as science and practice into the larger historical picture of which it is a part. Such courses, however, await such textbooks, and those won't appear until a publisher is willing to take a chance on a book that truly deviates from the standard fare of the introductory market. And, historically, few publishers have been willing to take such chances.

CJG: Could you elaborate on the meaning of the concept of "critical history"? It can be taken several ways.

LTB: As defined by Laurel Furumoto and several others, it calls for a history that critically examines the givens and myths of psychology; a greater use of archival records; avoidance of errors of historical interpretation, such as presentism; and the writing of externalist histories that place psychology in the broader sociocultural context of which it is a part.

In recent years, however, the label "critical history" has too often been associated with a very narrow approach that finds value only in deconstructionism. That approach often dismisses the validity of textual material as written, searching instead for the hidden "truths" the author intended, or, worse, arguing that there is no validity to such writings, that meaning is only in the eye of the beholder, and thus, there are infinite meanings. Should that approach become synonymous with critical history, then critical history will be reduced in scholarly reputation in the same way that psychohistory has suffered from an exclusive identity with psychodynamic interpretations.

CJG: Those unfamiliar with research in history might not recognize the problem posed by "presentism." And most introductory psychology texts give the clear impression of an uninterrupted march of progress from the simplistic understanding of human behavior and mental processes held by psychologists 100 years ago and that held by more "enlightened" modern psychologists. Could you make the concept of presentism clear to our readers?

LTB: Okay. Presentism speaks to the issue of objectivity, and that's a concern both in historical work and in the science of psychology. As an error in historical interpretation, presentism has been discussed among historians for more than 60 years. Yet, it is still too commonplace. Presentism, like it sounds, means interpreting the past in the context of the present. It is often found in accounts that judge the individuals or events of the past in terms of contemporary attitudes, values, or understanding. Or in a second form, presentism means selecting out those aspects of the past that are most consonant with the present and then glorifying and validating the present in terms of that selective past. Presentism is an easy error to make, and one could argue that history is never really free of it. The best historians can do is to immerse themselves in the times they are studying so as to portray those events in that context. Of course, that is exactly the task that psychologists face as well in trying to explain behavior. We have to try to minimize our own biases of observation and interpretation and try to account for behavior in its setting, drawing on the historical, personal, and situational variables at work.

CJG: Could you comment on how an understanding of presentism might enhance the introductory psychology course?

LTB: Well, students often are dismayed to discover that great minds of the 18th and 19th centuries could have believed, for example, that the liver governed emotion or that bleeding a person could cure mental illness. They just can't fathom how smart people could have believed such "silly" notions. They assume that, clearly, these people were not as smart as we are today. Such judgments are arguably the most blatant examples of presentism, and in that

sense they are easy to deal with. Making students aware of why such thinking is problematic gives them a better understanding of history, and it may even teach them some humility about their own views and how those views may be regarded by students or scholars 100 years from now.

CJG: Some instructors without a strong appreciation for history might say to you: "As it is now, I can barely get through three quarters of the chapters in my intro text during the semester. How can you expect me to introduce students to modern psychology and on top of that, tell them about psychology's history as well?"

LTB: I think this response is a reasonable one. Unlike introductory courses in the natural sciences that are taught as 2-semester courses with a required laboratory, social science courses, like psychology, are mostly 1-semester offerings. The American Psychological Association has evidence from 35 years of national curriculum surveys that the number of 2-semester introductory psychology courses at American colleges and universities has declined to about 7%. Introductory psychology textbook authors are pressured to include more material about cross-cultural research, about applied psychology, about ethnic minorities, about gerontology, about expanding psychological subfields (such as sport psychology, psychopharmacology), and so forth. The demand for such broader coverage is not an unreasonable one, but at the same time the books are not increasing in size, and in many cases are required to get smaller. Again, the debate over breadth versus depth has largely been won by those favoring the former. It means that for the average introductory psychology instructor covering human development, if you are discussing infancy at 10:05, you had better be talking about adolescence by 10:35 if you want to finish the subject. To answer more directly the question you raised, teachers can only be expected to teach history if they leave out a lot of the other standard fare of the introductory course.

CJG: One response to the overwhelming amount of material found in modern introductory textbooks is to emphasize process over content by trying to shape critical thinking in students taking their first psychology course. How can the way introductory students are taught about history become an exercise in critical thinking rather than a memorization episode?

LTB: The approach that you suggest is the one I take in teaching introductory psychology. That is, the emphasis in the course is on how psychologists ask questions and how they attempt to answer those questions. The process focus is intended to improve critical thinking skills in my students, to send them out of my class as a more sophisticated processor of information as a worker, employer, spouse, parent, television viewer, medical patient, newspaper reader, and so forth. Material from history, including the history of psychology, provides excellent examples for teaching critical thinking.

CJG: Could you give an example or two of how that works in your class?

LTB: First, in the material on biopsychology I describe the 19th century debate on cortical localization of function and the physiological studies using ablation (e.g., the work of Flourens) and why that work failed to recognize cortical specialization. I use that work to make a methodological point in contemporary biopsychology. I want students to understand that behavioral changes produced by lesion studies that destroy certain cell groups or pathways do not necessarily show us the functions of those anatomical sites, but instead that they show us how the organism behaves in the absence of the damaged neuroanatomy. Second, in my coverage of psychological disorders and their treatments, I give examples of 19th century treatments for mental disorders, such as spinning chairs, bleeding, and surprise baths. We discuss both the nature of the treatment and the supposed etiology that gave rise to the treatment, with a focus on the evidence used in support of the treatment's efficacy. I use that discussion to lead into a discussion on the nature of contemporary research on psychotherapy, especially the efficacy of therapy.

CJG: You have contributed significantly to the literature on how to teach the history of psychology course. Are any of the exercises or techniques that you use in your history course appropriate for the general psychology course?

LTB: Although there is a strong active learning emphasis in my introductory psychology course, which means a number of demonstrations, discussions, simulations, and experiments, I do not use many of the history exercises because those tend to take more time than I can make for them in the introductory course. I do use a few, however, for example, using students in a reaction-time chain, on simple- and choice-reaction time trials, to illustrate how reaction-time measures were used by Wundt, Cattell, and others in the late 19th century to measure the speed of mental processes, and to relate that early work to mental chronometry research by contemporary cognitive psychologists. I have used a portion of Army Alpha to introduce the development of psychological testing, testing my students in much the same way that the World War I American military recruits were examined. In addition, I have used classical perceptual demonstrations like the phi phenomenon, the spiral aftereffect, and the Pulfrich effect as a lead into contemporary work on the perception of movement.

CJG: Most teachers of psychology learned their history from texts based on Boring's version of history and have a conception of psychology's past that is mostly a history of experimental psychology, emphasizing various so-called "schools" of psychology. That is, they see modern psychology as emerging from the debate among those advocating different theories about human nature that took the labels structuralism, functionalism, behaviorism, and so

on. What are some of the more important ways in which our understanding of psychology's history and our writing about it have changed in the past 20 years?

LTB: A quick response to your question is to return to Laurel Furumoto's G. Stanley Hall address on the "new history" of psychology and the components of critical history that I named earlier. As a specialty area of research within psychology, history of psychology is only about 30 years old. As you know, 1965 was the founding date for the Archives of the History of American Psychology at the University of Akron, the founding year for the *Journal of the History of the Behavioral Sciences,* and the founding of Division 26 (APA's division on the history of psychology). In the past 30 years historical research in psychology has improved considerably, stimulated by historians who share their craft with psychologists and by psychologists who brought a strong social science perspective to historical research. In the tradition of Boring, history of psychology was too often limited to the history of experimental psychology, which largely meant a history of learning, perception, and biopsychology. Recent scholarship has broadened the scope of psychology to include other fields such as social psychology, developmental psychology, and applied work in such areas as clinical psychology, school psychology, and industrial psychology. Further, there has been an emphasis on social history, at least American social history, that has helped us understand psychology as part of that history. There is considerable new historical research that speaks to the role of women in the history of psychology and to psychology in this century as it shaped and was shaped by gender issues.

CJG: What changes have transpired in how historical research is conducted?

LTB: Historians of psychology today are more likely to use primary sources rather than relying on secondary treatments or translations, to search out archival records, and to seek out multiple strains of evidence for the claims they make. I would say that the most significant change in historical scholarship in the past 20 years has been the shift from internal to external histories that have given us a much richer understanding of psychology as one of many players on the historical stage. The eminent British historian Edward Carr has argued that history is a "study of causes." For too long psychology looked only within itself for those causes. External histories have greatly broadened our list of possible causes, providing us with a significantly richer understanding of our field.

CJG: Psychologists seem to be unique among scientists in being interested in the history of their discipline.

LTB: In psychology we have long been interested in the history of our field, an interest not typically shared by the other sciences. History of psychology courses have been part of the curriculum in American colleges since at least the early 1920s. The reason for this, I think, is that the fields of history and psychology are actually quite similar. Historians and psychologists are interested in explaining the human mind, in being able to generalize beyond the characteristics of a single event to other individuals and other events, and to be able to answer the "why" of human behavior in terms of motivation, personality, past experience, expectations, and so forth. And so, as psychologists or students of psychology, we are not moving very far from our own field of interest when we study the history of psychology.

CJG: In my discussions with you and in the talks that I have heard you give, I have always been impressed by your passion for psychology's history and your belief that an education in psychology is necessarily incomplete without history.

LTB: Well, I believe that, and I join some pretty good company in advocating such a belief, for example, George Santayana and Edwin G. Boring. In my opinion, an understanding of psychology's history is important for a lot of reasons. History provides an integrative framework that connects disparate ideas in psychology with one another and with the broader sociocultural context of which psychology is a part. History helps us understand and appreciate contemporary psychology. In essence, I think that historical understanding grounds us; it ties us to our roots. Some will view that as constraining, but I see it as providing us the foundation that we need to appreciate the complexities of the world. Returning to your observation about my passion for history, I would like to comment on the oft-heard remark that history is boring. I have even

seen articles in this journal that offer suggestions about taking the "ho-hum" out of history of psychology courses. Well, I have never seen boredom in my students. As one whose scholarly interests are in the history of psychology, I feel very fortunate that my vocation and avocation are one and the same. Like many teachers I am passionate about my work, which happens to be history. And, with no effort at all, I take that passion into my classes. History frames much of my thinking and my teaching. And my experience of 25 years in the classroom has shown me how eager students are to embrace such an approach. Students find history exciting, and they recognize its value for their understanding of psychology. Observing their enthusiasm and their self-discovery is a very rewarding experience for me. And that's why I am excited about going to class every day.

Resources

Benjamin, L. T., Jr. (Ed.). (1992). The history of American psychology [Special issue]. *American Psychologist, 47*(2).

Benjamin, L. T., Jr. (1993). *A history of psychology in letters.* Madison, WI: Brown & Benchmark.

Buckley, K. W. (1989). *Mechanical man: John Broadus Watson and the beginnings of behaviorism.* New York: Guilford.

Fancher, R. E. (1996). *Pioneers of psychology* (3rd ed.). New York: Norton.

Furumoto, L. (1989). A new history of psychology. In I. S. Cohen (Ed.), *The G. Stanley Hall Lecture Series: Vol. 9* (pp. 5–34). Washington, DC: American Psychological Association.

Gleitman, H. (1995). *Psychology* (4th ed.). New York: Norton.

Sdorow, L. M. (1995). *Psychology* (2nd ed.). Madison, WI: Brown & Benchmark.

"Giving Psychology Away": Some Experiences Teaching Undergraduates Practical Psychology

Anthony F. Grasha

In recent years, a good deal of discussion regarding the significance of psychology and the need to make psychological principles and methods more generally available has occurred (cf. Anastasi, 1972: Bartz, 1970; Miller, 1969, 1970). My personal bias was to integrate the above thinking into the content of a traditional undergraduate psychology curriculum.

Several factors motivated this decision. I believe that if psychology is to have a wider impact on the problems of human existence, then the thousands of undergraduates who major in psychology each year represent an excellent population for teaching skills applicable to such problems. With

the exception of research method courses, undergraduates seldom have the opportunity to learn psychological skills and principles that they can use. There is a tendency in the field to guard the "psychological treasure chest" of applied methods and principles for graduate study. While we probably need to do some guarding of skills (e.g., psychological testing and therapy skills), I suspect that we have overdone it. There is much in the broad areas of psychology beyond therapy and testing skills that are usable in the daily lives of people. Discussions with colleagues show an unwillingness in many to directly teach undergraduates how to apply principles from the major areas of psychology. I find that this attitude represents both a distrust of the capabilities of undergraduates and a feeling that we don't know enough to teach application. The distrust reflects a parental-protective model of education which results in the majority of our psychology majors placed into a job market with little in the way of usable psychological skills. Not knowing enough represents the caution of the empirical researcher who wants additional data before recommending action. What is never clear is how much additional data is needed. A major problem I see is that the data supporting the use of principles cannot come from the laboratory. In the first analysis, success in application will tell us how useful the principles are.

What happens at the undergraduate level is that we tend to concentrate on teaching basic terminology, a few research skills and some of the theoretical controversies in the field. This certainly helps the small percentage of our graduates who go on to graduate school and such students have a right to decent preparation. However, this should not be at the expense of the majority who never continue beyond the B.A. We probably need more balance in our undergraduate offerings with both groups getting something useful out of the experiences. To do this, we need to do a better job of integrating the usable aspects of psychology into our undergraduate curriculum. To lecture or otherwise tell people about how they can use certain principles is *not enough*. We need to provide opportunities for them to *learn and practice* using principles.

With the above considerations in mind, I designed a two quarter course in practical psychology for the Evening College of the University of Cincinnati. My general goals were: (a) to teach psychological principles which were usable in daily life employing an active participatory classroom model, (b) to teach students how to synthesize principles from existing theoretical data, and (c) to establish a learning climate where students gained experience employing many of the principles covered.

Course Design

Students. Each student in the class of 30 had taken at least a course in general psychology. Their ages ranged from 18 to 51 with a mean of 29. A variety of occupations was represented including housewife, lab technician, personnel supervisor, appliance store owner, shoe salesman, sales clerk, bank teller, nurse, police officer, secretary, life insurance underwriter, school teacher, factory worker, and a military non-commissioned officer. While not representative of the entire population, there was an interesting mix of everyday vocations in the class.

Topics Covered. Table 1 presents the major topic areas covered in the course. Topics were selected from data obtained by a questionnaire given to a sample of 30 undergraduates six months before the course began, from ideas suggested by colleagues and a few of my personal biases. An attempt was made to select areas of psychology that had principles that were generally applicable across situations. This was done in order to avoid the problem of the insurance salesman expecting to learn sales principles and the

housewife expecting to have the course concentrate on child rearing. I knew that this would be somewhat unsatisfactory for some students. Therefore, during the second quarter, each student also picked a personal area of interest (child rearing, advertising, salesmanship), read relevant articles and books, and then developed and used principles that were applicable to that area.

Class Sessions. The format for the class session consisted of meeting one evening a week for two academic quarters (18 weeks), three hours per night. Each topic area took at least two evening sessions to cover. A typical sequence of events for each topic consisted of an initial one hour lecture on a general overview of the theoretical aspects of the area. This was followed by a listing of 8–14 principles that the instructor derived from the work in that area. The principles were then clarified and discussed with the students for 30-40 minutes. Next the class participated in 1–3 experiential exercises which were designed to illustrate the principles covered. For example, several communication principles were presented employing a 1 way/2 way communication exercise and a paraphrase exercise (cf. Pfeiffer & Jones, 1969). Learning principles were illustrated with an instructor-designed mnemonic and study habit exercise. Immediately following such experiences, the class was divided into either trios or quartets to process what occurred and discuss how various principles operated.

To facilitate the use of principles in their daily lives, I designed a Principle Application Diary Format (PADF). A

Table 1. General Topic Areas Covered in the Course

1. Attitude change
   a. General theory
   b. Persuasion designs based on theory
   c. Persuasive communication
2. Group processes
   a. General theory
   b. Group development processes
   c. Communication processes in groups
   d. Decision making processes in groups
   e. Leadership
   f. Organizational behavior
3. Interpersonal communication
   a. General theory
   b. 1 way versus 2 way communication skills
   c. Paraphrasing and listening skills
   d. Conflict management
4. Learning
   a. General theory
   b. Behavior modification
   c. Study habits
   d. Goal and objective setting
5. Personal characteristics and motivation
   a. General theory
   b. Individual differences in behavior
   c. Student teaming styles
   d. Competitive versus collaborative behavioral styles
   e. Need achievement and power motives
6. Problem Solving
   a. General theory
   b. Problem solving in groups
   c. Planning processes for groups
   d. Individual problem solving
   e. Career planning

Table 2. Principle Application Diary Format

1. *Situation:* Describe the situation that you will attempt to use the principle(s) in. Be sure to indicate the nature of the interactions involved or any other special characteristics of the situation. What is the problem that you are trying to apply principles to in this situation?

2. *Principle(s):* From the list of principles covered on the topic under discussion select from 1–3 that you think will be useful in the situation described above. Briefly indicate why you feel each principle is relevant to that situation.

3. *Action Plan:* Describe the specific way that you will employ each principle(s). What goals do you have for the use of each principle(s)? What criteria will you use to know if you are successful?

4. *Timing:* Indicate the frequency of usage of each principle and the approximate dates and time of day that they were used.

5. *Outcomes:* For each week that you used the principles answer the following:
   a. Throughout the week, what changes if any did you notice in the situation?
   b. What reactions did you or others have to the application of principles?
   c. How well do you feel you were able to achieve your application goals? What are the criteria you used to make this decision? Be as specific as possible.
   d. If more than one principle was used in the same situation, which one seemed to work best? Which one seemed to work less well?
   e. If you were unsuccessful, what do you attribute your lack of success to?

6. *Future:* If you were to use the principle(s) again, what would you do differently to try and insure a more effective application?

copy of the PADF sequence appears in Table 2. The purpose of the PADF was to provide each student with a common base to plan, use and evaluate the application of principles. It also allowed me to monitor the application of principles for 30 students. After discussing the exercise, students worked on the first three parts individually for 20–30 minutes. Students were asked to select from 1–3 principles that *they* felt were relevant to a situation in their lives. They then shared their plan with two other students. Students provided helpful suggestions to each other and I acted as a consultant when called upon. Students then used the principles they selected for a minimum of two weeks. After the first week of use, they gave a progress report to the other members of their trio and turned in a copy of the report to me. Modifications were often made based on the feedback they received. A completed PADF for each assignment was turned in at the end of the quarter.

To help insure that they honestly reported what happened, and to facilitate their learning, I assured them that *success in application was not a criterion for a grade.* Rather, everyone received an A provided that they completed each PADF assignment, participated in class, and completed a synthesis of principles assignment as discussed below.

Principle Synthesis Requirement. Since psychological principles are not generally spelled out in ways suggesting application in articles and books, students were asked to synthesize principles and to suggest ways that they could be employed. Synthesis is a skill, and over the two quarters I asked students to do two things to help promote the development of this skill. One was to synthesize 10 principles from each half of a reading book (Wertheimer, 1970). The

second requirement was for them to work in groups of four on one section of the book. Each group was to select three important principles and to design an experience for a smaller portion of the rest of the class illustrating the principles. The latter assignment was made after the topic on group planning and problem solving was covered in class. Thus, they were also able to apply some of the principles in this topic on the synthesis assignment.

Course Outcomes

Student Experiences. The situations in which students used the principles were quite varied. Data derived from the PADF's and interviews with individual students showed that the overall reported success in application of all principles covered was 70%. Several of the more interesting uses of principles were:

1. A police officer was experiencing difficulty obtaining reliable data for a drug abuse program he was running. Based on several communication principles, he made attempts to personalize his communication with juveniles when seeking information. This included attempts to de-emphasize his status in communicating, the use of paraphrasing to insure better listening and attempts to take a more active interest in the people he was talking to. He reports that over time he began to receive more useful information.

2. A housewife who sells books at her church's book stand decided to try several persuasive communication and motivation principles in her selling. She advertised specials and placed the marriage, dating and sexual relationship books out front and attempted to take a more active interest in her customer's needs. She reports an increase in sales of 40% over her base period.

3. A military training NCO used learning principles and communication principles discussed in class to improve the training atmosphere in his reserve unit. His efforts earned him a commendation from his commanding officer.

4. A department store personnel supervisor took principles derived from interpersonal relationships, organizational behavior and learning and initiated a training program to increase job satisfaction by cross training people in jobs and rotating them to increase their satisfaction with working conditions.

Several other personally satisfying outcomes for the students were the use of principles to improve their study habits, to toilet train their children, to obtain a better understanding of the effects of their behavior on others, being able to run meetings more effectively, improved relationships with their close personal friends, and becoming more skillful at planning and seeking solutions to personal and group problems.

In two quarters of having students employ principles, no drastic unsuccessful experiences occurred. The worst thing that happened was the inability for everyone to get principles to work all the time. However, the unsuccessful attempts led to useful discussions regarding the need for careful planning in application, the role of individual differences in receptivity to principles and the problems inherent in going from theory to practice. The 30% failure rate in the use of principles was rather evenly distributed across the topic areas covered.

Ninety percent of the students reported that they used a minimum of five principles that were not part of specific assignments. I suspect that once given a structure to use principles and some experience with application, students will continue to use them in the absence of that structure.

A final outcome from the students' point of view was the ability of the classroom procedures to influence their learning styles (Grasha, 1972). Student data showed that compared to their other classes, the methods and procedures of the current class encouraged fewer competitive student behaviors and encouraged participatory and collaborative classroom learning style orientations.

Instructor Experiences. I kept a weekly diary regarding class related experiences. The data from this diary and the PADF's suggests the following problems were associated with attempts at application only during the first 4–5 weeks of the course.

There was a tendency for 30% of the students occasionally to deny that they encountered situations where the principles were useful, or to avoid helping someone else with their problem. Through discussions with students I sensed that this initial avoidance was due to a failure to admit to their problems; personal apprehensions regarding the possibility of failure in applying principles; and to a lack of experience in application. As one student told me in disbelief, "you're really serious about us using principles."

A second issue early in the first quarter was a tendency for 60% of the students to work uphill by picking situations that were too broad and unmanageable. An interesting example was a student who had a "deal" with his friend and his friend's wife to "wife swap." One problem was his wife's refusal to participate. I recommended that he pick another problem. A more usual example of working uphill was the student who wanted to increase interpersonal communication among 20 people in her office within one week. The difficulties the students encountered showed them the necessity for picking smaller, more manageable problems.

Third, everyone in class had problems with the PADF during the first quarter. These difficulties centered around setting criteria for assessing the success of their application interventions. A session on setting objectives for tangible and intangible goals (cf. Mager, 1972) proved to be helpful for their goal and criteria setting behaviors.

Fourth, a master key approach was noted early in the course. This was a tendency on the part of 20% of the students to assume that a given principle would work across the board. A good example of this was the teacher who asked his 4th grade students to "just call me Jim." While it might help to de-emphasize titles to promote better communication in some interpersonal situations, it did not work well with the 4th graders in that particular school.

Finally, a recurring problem early in the first quarter was the tendency for 20% of the students to treat the application as an experiment. This was particularly evident with the communication principles. Some students tended to treat principles as a variable they were laying on a group of subjects. In not making it part of themselves, they appeared phony. This was readily picked up by those on whom the principles were being applied and an unsuccessful application resulted.

In all, I was satisfied with the first pass through the course. The fact that these students were eventually able to learn how to use principles of psychology and found it useful and satisfying suggests that more integration of application into our undergraduate offerings is possible and desirable. My experiences also suggest that application opportunities need to be programmed into the course design. It is unreasonable to lecture about application and expect that it will occur on a wide basis. Students need support and advice from their peers and the instructor when attempting to apply what they are learning outside the university. With the many problems confronting us today, giving our undergraduates some of the psychological tools to deal with everyday problems is a socially responsible action that psychologists are capable of taking now.

References

Anastasi, A. The cultivation of diversity. *American Psychologist*, 1972, 27, 1091–1099.

Bartz, W. R. While psychologists doze on. *American Psychologist*, 1970, 25, 500–503.

Grasha, A. F. Observations on relating teaching goals to student response styles and classroom methods. *American Psychologist*, 1972, 27, 144–147.

Mager, R. R. *Goal analysis.* Belmont, California: Fearon, 1972.

Miller, G. A. Psychology as a means of promoting human welfare. *American Psychologist*, 1969, 24, 1063–1075.

Miller, G. A. Assessment of psychotechnology. *American Psychologist*, 1970, 25, 991–1001.

Pfeiffer, J. W., & Jones, J. E. *A handbook of structured experiences for human relations training.* Iowa City, Iowa: University Associates Press, 1969.

Wertheimer, M. *Confrontation: Psychology and the problems of today.* Glenview, Illinois: Scott, Foresman, 1970.

Note

This article is based on remarks presented at the American Psychological Association Meetings, Division 2, Montreal, 1973.

A Rotational Format for Team Teaching Introductory Psychology

Henry C. Morlock
William P. Gaeddert
Naomi B. McCormick
Matthew R. Merrens
Lary C. Shaffer
Taher Zandi

Introductory psychology at the State University College at Plattsburgh is a one-semester survey of the major areas of contemporary psychology. Until recently, the chairperson drafted seven or eight instructors to teach sections of 60 to 80 students. Students in the different sections received quite different introductions. We developed the method described in this article to decrease heterogeneity, facilitate the inclusion of current perspectives, and attract faculty to teach the course.

One approach to team teaching consists of having instructors teach all sections but only during one portion of the term (Ware, Gardner, & Murphy, 1978). Another approach is having all instructors participate throughout the term (Flanagan & Ralston, 1983; Levine, 1977). Our version uses some aspects of both.

Description of the Approach

Instructors lecture on their areas of expertise to one section of the course. After giving an exam, they move to another section, where they repeat their presentations. Usually the semester is divided into quarters with four instructors repeating their parts four times.

Presently, instructors in our rotating form (RF) of team teaching represent the following areas in psychology: biological, social, developmental, and clinical. They are responsible for covering material in their areas of expertise. Topical units for the semester are: (a) basic processes, (b) social and methods, (c) cognition and development, and (d) personality and abnormal. Topic order is the same across sections, but sections begin at different points in the order. Specifically, the order for Section A is a, b, c, d; Section B, d, a, b, c; Section C, c, d, a, b; and Section D, b, c, d, a. Instructors follow each other consistently, allowing smooth transitions from one topic to the next.

Most students in the course are freshmen (85%); 55% are women, which is the same as the college population. The majority (55%) are in professionally oriented programs (e.g., nursing, education, and business). About 30% have not declared a major, and only 5% are psychology majors. Sections may be as large as 140 in the Fall and 60 in the Spring.

Each section has two undergraduate teaching assistants (TAs), who earn three credits in Teaching Practicum. The TAs lecture, grade homework, hold review sessions, and tu-

tor. Others have noted that undergraduate TAs can be very effective (Mendenhall & Burr, 1983; White & Kolber, 1978; Wortman & Hillis, 1976). A faculty coordinator and a graduate assistant manage administrative components of the course such as recording test scores and assigning midterm and final grades.

We use Kottke's (1985) method for handling makeup exams. A comprehensive final exam is optional; if a student takes it, the score, properly weighted, is substituted for a missing exam or one on which the student obtained a lower score. Each semester, about half of the students take the final, usually to improve a score on a previous exam.

Evaluation

The instructors have been enthusiastic about the RF; two of the original four have taught in it for nine consecutive semesters. Student evaluations of the instructors and the course have been conducted frequently. At the end of each instructor's block, a seven-question evaluation form is distributed by the TAs. Instructors combine the four evaluations into one at semester's end. Near the end of each semester, students also complete a course evaluation in which they rate their agreement with statements such as: "The rotating format is a good idea."

Approximately 75% of the students have agreed that the format is a good idea. Table 1 shows the responses to this statement for three representative semesters. In their open-ended comments, students have often indicated that changing the instructors made the course stimulating.

In one early evaluation, we tried to determine whether the rotating form had detrimental effects on academic performance. All students took the final exam, and those in the RF sections did significantly better, $p < .05$, than those in a traditional section. We also failed to find significant relationships between section and either final grade or satisfaction with the format.

These indications were encouraging, but the evaluations did reveal some disadvantages of the RF.

1. Each semester, some students complained about adjusting to the frequent changes of instructor. In one course evaluation, 7% of the students indicated they had difficulty each time the instructors were changed, and 30% indicated they had trouble about half the time.

Table 1. Responses (%) to "The Rotating Format Was a Good Idea"

Semester	Agree Strongly	Agree	No Opinion	Disagree	Disagree Strongly
Fall 1985[a]	38.2	35.1	9.1	10.2	7.2
Spring 1986[b]	37.7	44.7	6.1	7.9	3.5
Fall 1986[c]	37.3	38.5	13.2	7.1	3.9

[a]N = 361. [b]N = 114. [c]N = 410.

2. Instructors rarely became well acquainted with students.
3. We expended time and effort to train, select, and supervise TAs.

To assist students who have anticipated that they would have difficulty with the RF, the department has always offered a section taught by a single instructor. During the first week of the semester, students can change sections readily; there has been little switching between sections. Moreover, the number of students who withdrew from the RF sections at later points in the semester has been very low. College policy allows students to withdraw without penalty until midterm. The number of people withdrawing from the RF sections each semester has remained at about 2.5%, which is below the mean (7%) for all courses in the department.

Recommendations

We have used the RF as the principal method for teaching introductory psychology for the last nine semesters. To those who wish to try the RF we suggest that:

1. Instructors be chosen who can work well as a team.
2. The coordinator be actively involved in all details of the course.
3. The TAs be encouraged to take an active role in class meetings.
4. A text be selected that can be easily divided into areas of the faculty's expertise.
5. Participants try the format for at least two semesters. (It took us a semester to learn how to work with each other, the text, and the TAs.)

Although we continue to make improvements, the RF may never be as well integrated or as personal as a course taught by a single instructor. But, as Irion (1976) suggested,

format may be less important than the motivation of the instructors. In that case, the RF may have a strong advantage over sections led by single instructors drafted into taking their turn at introductory psychology.

References

Flanagan, M. F., & Ralston, D. A. (1983). Intra-coordinated team teaching: Benefits for both students and instructors. *Teaching of Psychology, 10,* 116–117.

Irion, A. L. (1976). A survey of the introductory course in psychology. *Teaching of Psychology, 3,* 3–8.

Kottke, J. L. (1985). Using a comprehensive makeup exam to replace a missed exam. *Teaching of Psychology, 12,* 51–52.

Levine, R. V. (1977). An interdisciplinary approach to the introductory psychology course. *Teaching of Psychology, 4,* 132–134.

Mendenhall, M., & Burr, W. R. (1983). Enlarging the role of the undergraduate teaching assistant. *Teaching of Psychology, 10,* 184–185.

Ware, M. E., Gardner, L. E., & Murphy, D. P. (1978). Team teaching introductory psychology as pedagogy and for faculty development. *Teaching of Psychology, 5,* 127–130.

White, K. M., & Kolber, R. G. (1978). Undergraduate and graduate students as discussion section leaders. *Teaching of Psychology, 5,* 6–9.

Wortman, C. B., & Hillis, J. W. (1976). Undergraduate-taught "minicourses" in conjunction with an introductory lecture course. *Teaching of Psychology, 3,* 69–72.

Notes

1. Portions of this article were presented at a conference on teaching psychology, State University of New York at Farmingdale, 1987.
2. We gratefully acknowledge the help of Margaret Anderson, Michael Becker, W. Raney Ellis, III, Peter Hornby, and Patricia Jarvis in planning and teaching sections of the course and anonymous reviewers for comments on previous drafts.

A Method for Teaching Name Mnemonics

Steven M. Smith

When people meet me for the first time, they can't help noticing my bushy *beard*. This may remind them of the man with the beard on packages of *Smith* Brothers cough drops.

Now, if you need cough drops for your cough or cold, you may also have a stuffy nose; if so, you should remember that in an emergency, one's *sleeve* may be substituted for a missing handkerchief. Because sleeve rhymes with *Steve,* you can remember my entire name simply by seeing me, face to (bearded) face: The *beard* leads to *Smith* brothers cough drops, which leads to *sleeve,* which rhymes with *Steve.*

This is an example of a name mnemonic, a mental device for remembering names that works surprisingly well, even for novices. The mnemonic associates a person's appearance and name, using imagery and rhymes. Teaching name mnemonics on the first day of class in introductory psychology, cognition, memory, or experimental psychology can demonstrate the power of cognition via a firsthand experience. Within a short period of time, not only can it be demonstrated that "psychology really works," but students will be impressed with their own untapped mental abilities. The exercise teaches about mnemonics, the use of interacting imagery and rhymes to achieve useful associations in memory (see Shimamura, 1984). Students will also get experience with group creative problem solving as small groups try to think divergently in order to create name mnemonics for each group member. Finally, and perhaps most important, the exercise helps to ensure that everyone in the class (including the teacher) will know everyone else's name, a situation likely to facilitate any class where frequent and open discussions are encouraged.

Method

The exercise should begin with a brief discussion on the importance of knowing others' names in a variety of social and professional situations. Students can be given the opportunity at this time to testify as to how difficult it is for them to remember names, and how that difficulty may have caused some of them considerable embarrassment.

At this time the teacher should come to the rescue with the name mnemonic, which one can use either to remember others' names, or to ensure that others will remember one's own name. The name mnemonic technique could be described (see Bellezza, 1982) with the aid of the teacher's own name mnemonic as an example. Briefly, a mnemonic is a mental device that helps memory, often creating associations via the creation of interacting mental images that link or integrate the items to be associated, or creating associations via acoustic properties (such as rhymes) which the to-be-associated items have in common. Generally, names are needed when the person in question is seen; hence, the name mnemonic should begin with an image of the person's appearance (or with some real or imagined component of the person's appearance), and should link that image with an image related to the sound of the person's name (or related to the sound of part of the name).

The teacher might throw out a few other examples of both good and poor name mnemonics. For a good example, my burly former teaching assistant named Rodney Flanary could be easily imagined as a football player who had a knee injury; hence the *rod* in his *knee—Rodney.* Benched for the injury, he kept warm by wearing *flannel—Flanary.* This example makes use of a physical cue (burliness) that immediately evokes an image, and the components of the image are acoustically related to the name. Mnemonics that fail to use a physical appearance cue or imagery associations, or that

use obscure personal characteristics unknown to the learner (e.g., "I like to read science fiction") are typically less memorable.

At this time the teacher should inform the students that their task for the next few minutes will be to convene in small groups (2 to 4 students per group) and create name mnemonics for each member of the group. Students will ultimately be responsible for their own name mnemonic, but the groups greatly facilitate this creative process. Assign students to the small groups, and recommend that they first appoint a secretary to write down the name of each member of the group. Also, recommend that each student try to come up with a mnemonic for at least one of their names, but preferably for both names.

Briefly monitor the groups, one at a time. Ask about current progress and make a few suggestions to groups that seem to be totally stuck. Encourage them to be as creative and free-wheeling as possible, as it will help them get ideas. Teachers familiar with brainstorming or other group techniques devoted to divergent thinking should make suggestions along those lines. Briefly, brainstorming has four basic rules: (a) avoid criticism of ideas, at all costs; (b) the wilder the idea, the better; (c) the more ideas, the better; and (d) combine and modify ideas. For a further discussion of brainstorming, see Osborn (1957).

After 5 or 10 minutes, have the students reassemble into the original large group. One at a time, each student should go to the chalkboard, legibly print his or her name, speak the name aloud, clearly enough to satisfy everyone in the room, and give the mnemonic for his or her name. It is also helpful if, while at the chalkboard, students briefly mention a bit of personal data, such as where they are from, why they are taking the course, or what their hobbies are. Such information helps to enrich and elaborate learning, making it more memorable. After giving all information, each student should erase his or her name before returning to be seated. If names are left on the board, confusion about which name belongs to which student is bound to result.

Finally, when all the name mnemonics have been given, the teacher should call on two "volunteers" from the class to recite every name in the class. Students are rarely impressed with a psychology teacher who can use mnemonics, but they are greatly impressed when they can use the mnemonics successfully. The volunteer should select students in any order he or she wishes, looking at each one for a visual cue, and recalling each name aloud. When a volunteer falters on a name, the class should prompt the student with a hint about the mnemonic in question. After the first student has finished, a second volunteer should say the names again. This procedure will assure that nearly everyone will know nearly everyone's name in the class.

Once students' names have been learned with this mnemonic, there is likely to be a considerable amount of repetition of names throughout the semester and names are not likely to be forgotten. Even without such repetition, however, the instructor can demonstrate later in the semester that the mnemonics can endure the test of time by giving a pop quiz over the names of class members. Performance should remain at a high level.

This method for teaching name mnemonics may be limited by class size, but possibly not so much as one might think. The largest class for which I have used this technique had 64 students, and both student volunteers got more than 50 names correct even without prompts from class members.

Another limitation that may concern teachers is the anticipated difficulty with very unusual or "foreign" names. My experience has been that such names are no harder than more common "American" names and occasionally such names are easier than others because of their distinctiveness. Memorable examples are "Bahardoust," who said her name might be "the hardest," or "Sinha," who had us imagine that he looked like a "sinner."

Should the learner be advised to use bizarre imagery rather than more common images? There is no clear consensus on this question, as the relative usefulness of bizarreness appears to depend on such factors as number of learning trials, type of test (free or cued recall), and delay between learning and testing (see O'Brien & Wolford, 1982; Wollen & Cox, 1981).

One final problem may be in the mnemonic "decoding" stage. That is, sometimes learners recall the mnemonic device, but cannot remember the correct name that goes with it. For example, Rodney Flanary (rod-knee-flannel) might be remembered as Rodney Flannigan, or Steve Smith (sleeve-cough drops) might be remembered as Steve Vicks. The remedy for such difficulty is fairly simple; one or two practice trials will usually solve the entire decoding problem.

References

Bellezza, F. S. (1982). *Improve your memory skills*. Englewood Cliffs, NJ: Prentice-Hall.

O'Brien, E. J., & Wolford, C. R. (1982). Effect of delay in testing on retention of plausible versus bizarre mental images. *Journal of Experimental Psychology: Learning, Memory, and Cognition, 8,* 148–152.

Osborn, A. (1957). *Applied imagination*. New York: Charles Scribner's.

Shimamura, A. P. (1984). A guide for teaching mnemonic skills. *Teaching of Psychology, 11,* 162–166.

Wollen, K. A., & Cox, S. D. (1981). Sentence cuing and the effectiveness of bizarre imagery. *Journal of Experimental Pschology: Human Learning and Memory, 7,* 386–392.

How I Kicked the Lecture Habit: Inquiry Teaching in Psychology

William H. Zachry

Everyone complains about the lecture method, but no one does anything about it. Or so it seemed to me for 15 years. Then I found a way to kick the lecture habit.

Wrightsman (1972) cited Calisher's perceptive comment: "The habit of the lectern instills the habit of knowing; the habit of writing instills the habit of finding out" (p. xx). She was right about the lectern. The essence of lecturing was captured in a cartoon in which an instructor told her students, "OK class, my job is to talk and your job is to listen. If you finish first, please let me know." Teachers who rely solely on lecturing cast themselves in the role of omniscient source and the students in the role of passive audience. Preparation for a lecture is largely a matter of organizing information and clearing your throat. The student who attends the lecture needs only to possess good auditory perception, short-term memory, and fine motor coordination—or a dependable cassette recorder.

Psychologists label as "higher mental processes" the skills of abstracting, hypothesizing, and problem solving. Surely we might expect to find the higher thought processes somewhere in higher education. Unfortunately these abilities usually appear, if at all, as content to be memorized rather than as skills to be used. From the viewpoint of the student in a lecture class, Calisher's aphorism might be restated: "Lecturing instills the habit of speed writing; testing instills the habit of cramming." These habits do not require high-level cognitive skills, and they are certainly no challenge to the ordinary college student. If many students are "finishing first" in the lecture hour, it may not be due to lack of interest. They may be simply bored with the low level of mental activity they are called upon to display.

Inquiry Teaching

Inquiry teaching is a method that aims to engage the student's full range of cognitive abilities. A species of what is sometimes termed "discovery learning," inquiry teaching requires the student to engage in hypothesis formation, collection and evaluation of evidence, and the drawing of logical conclusions. Beyer (1979), in his book entitled *Teaching Thinking in Social Studies*, states:

> Inquiry teaching involves creating, conducting and evaluating learning experiences that require students to go through the same processes and develop or employ the same knowledge and attitudes they would use if engaged in independent rational inquiry. Inquiry teaching involves students in learning situations in which they must make hypothetical assertions and test assertions against a variety of evidence. (p. 84)

In addition to increasing the use of higher cognitive skills, inquiry teaching aims to create in the student attitudes of curiosity, open-mindedness, and tolerance for ambiguity. These attitudes are of course standard equipment for the scientific investigator. They are also among the first casualties of many lecture courses.

As outlined by Beyer (1979), inquiry teaching is a five-step process. It amounts to basing an entire course on the steps of the scientific method. Step 1 is to define a problem. This may be accomplished by the instructor's presenting a general problem, which is then refined by discussion to one or more specific questions. Step 2 is to develop hypotheses, tentative answers to the stated question. These also are derived from discussion, although students may work out individual hypotheses before meeting as a group. The instructor tries to create a "brainstorming" atmosphere in which divergent thinking is encouraged and helps word final statements to make them testable. Step 3 is to search for evidence by which hypotheses may be tested. This may entail a wide-open library search or assigned readings, films, mini-lectures or demonstrations that bear on the stated hypotheses. Oral reports are a good way for students to share their findings while learning how to summarize research procedures and results. Step 4 is to draw conclusions by evaluating hypotheses in light of collected evidence. The list of hypotheses is subjected to deletion, addition, or alteration, and the modified result is stated as an answer to the original problem (Step 1). Finally, Step 5 is to test the adequacy of the conclusion by applying it to new evidence. The inquiry process may then end with a general statement of findings, or it may cycle back to Step 2 and be repeated as many times as needed to achieve the desired depth of investigation of the original problem.

Although the inquiry approach may have some utility in large classes, it seems best suited to the small group or discussion section in which face-to-face interaction is feasible. My best results so far have come in a small honors section of General Psychology (enrollment was limited to 15 students).

Prerequisite Skills

Learning by inquiry demands two skills that many students either lack or do not use often. One is combinatorial logic (in the sense of Piaget's formal operational thought), the ability to identify all potential causal variables in a situation and to design a controlled experiment to isolate the effect of each factor. The other is the ability to retrieve information from published literature in order to test hypotheses and conclusions. Both deficiencies need to be addressed before inquiry can proceed.

To deal with the first problem, I recommend using exercises from the fascinating volume, *Rival Hypotheses: Alternative Interpretations of Data Based Conclusions* (Huck & Sandler, 1979). The authors constructed 100 brief summaries of published research and other articles in which the methods or assumptions leave room for alternative explanations. The reader is challenged to identify the plausible "rival hypotheses," then to turn to the back of the book for the authors' solutions. Mystery mixed with light humor makes the topic of experimental design fun to study. After my class had cut their teeth on several of these case exercises, they

much improved their combinatorial thinking. They did well on an examination in which they were asked to critique a new *Rival Hypotheses* case (on the effects of hypnosis on biofeedback) and to redesign the study.

To deal with the second deficiency—that of library research skills—I recommend a brief introduction to the use of *Psychological Abstracts*. Library staff may provide this service, or the instructor may put together a handout based on the American Psychological Association booklet entitled *Library Use: A Handbook for Psychology* (Reed & Baxter, 1983). Another useful resource is the APA's cassette–slide kit, *A Guide to Psychological Abstracts* (Westwood Productions, 1980). I find that one hour invested in learning library research skills pays off later in the successful data gathering that is essential to inquiry. It is also satisfying, if not amazing, to see a freshman negotiate the triple hazards of thesaurus, index, and abstract and come up grinning with exactly the right primary source.

Examples From the Classroom

The value of inquiry teaching is best conveyed by example. Two instances from a recent offering of honors General Psychology serve to illustrate the five steps in inquiry. The first instance deals with defining the term "intelligence," and the second concerns the problem of bystander nonintervention in emergencies.

To initiate Step 1 (Problem Definition) in a unit on intelligence, I posed the question: "What does it mean to be an intelligent person?" Class members gave the following responses: "Someone who has knowledge"; "Someone with common sense"; "One who can apply knowledge"; "A person who can reason"; "Someone who can solve problems"; "One who is motivated." One student shared her feelings about being elected "Most Intelligent" in high school; she felt that another girl, "a real brain," deserved the title. To move the focus away from school, I asked for examples of an intelligent act in other settings: mountain climbing, NFL quarterbacking, nuclear reactor control. Finally, after much discussion, the class was asked to condense their ideas to one general statement or hypothesis (Step 2, Hypothesis Formation). After a pause, one student, in a moment of real insight, offered the following: "An intelligent person is one who does the right thing at the right time." I should have left such a clear statement alone, but I offered the restatement that intelligence, broadly conceived, is the ability to adapt successfully to a current situation. The class accepted this "broad definition" as a working hypothesis for the best meaning of intelligence.

In Step 3 (Hypothesis Testing), students were assigned a textbook chapter on intelligence; they were to use the chapter as a source of data. At the next class meeting, they discussed the material and focused especially on the multifactor models of Thurstone and Guilford. A consensus was reached that the broad definition of intelligence was supported by the theories and other data contained in the text. Thus the tentative hypothesis was accepted as a conclusion (Step 4, Conclusion Formation).

Finally, in Step 5 (Conclusion Testing), the conclusion of a broadly defined, multifactor model of intelligence was tested against new data. I assigned Wechsler's (1975) short article, "Intelligence Defined and Undefined: A Relativistic Appraisal." Students were expected to find the article on their own, read it, and relate it to the conclusion drawn in class. In this article Wechsler emphasized "nonintellective factors of intelligence" such as drive, attitude, and value. He concluded that intelligence tests measure "the capacity of an individual to understand the world about him and his resourcefulness to cope with its challenges" (p. 139). My students quickly saw that Wechsler's views supported and enhanced their broad conception of intelligence. Their conclusion was confirmed.

In this case, the original hypothesis stood the test of repeated examination and emerged as the final conclusion. The inquiry process developed differently when applied to "bystander intervention." Inquiry was now initiated with a question: "Why do bystanders help (or not help) in emergencies?" Students were asked to develop tentative hypotheses on this question (Step 2). After writing down hypotheses, each student was assigned to search a different annual index of *Psychological Abstracts* and find and read a primary source article on the topic. The motivating effect of inquiry was soon demonstrated. Within 24 hours one frustrated student came to the office with a complaint: Out of 20 annual index entries on bystander intervention, only one article could be found in the library. How often does a freshman come to us with such a problem?

At the next class meeting, the inquiry question was quickly amended to: "Why *don't* people help?" Five hypotheses were suggested: fear of personal injury, fear of hurting someone, fear of embarrassment, not wanting to take responsibility, and peer pressure. The article abstracts were summarized and presented orally as a means of testing the tentative hypotheses (Step 3). Most articles were found to be related to the stated hypotheses; one or two were on other aspects of altruism; one seemed to contradict the "bystander effect." The latter was due to a misreading of the article. The class concluded (Step 4) that all five hypotheses were supported.

I opened the following class meeting by reviewing the inquiry process and by pointing out that we were now at Step 5—applying our conclusions to new data. We would view the film *When Will People Help?* (Bobker & Vision Associates, 1976), which was based on the experiments of Latane and Darley (1970). Afterwards, we would decide whether to alter or leave unchanged the five hypotheses. The film was then shown. As a result of obtaining new evidence, the class added a sixth hypothesis concerning task load (being in a hurry). They also changed "fear of hurting someone" to "risk of a lawsuit." Finally, the students arrived at two general conclusions by condensing three hypotheses into a factor of "cost to oneself" and three others into "social pressure." I then drew on Latane and Darley's (1970) five-step helping sequence to summarize the topic and to suggest means of increasing bystander intervention.

Comparison with Lecture Method

As the preceding examples show, a class based on inquiry differs significantly from a lecture class. The most obvious contrast is in student involvement. Active participation, both during and outside class, is required in inquiry. A student who must be prepared to discuss the material during each class meeting is a motivated student. Many lecture classes, however, limit participation to a few questions—usually by the same small core of front-row dwellers. The silent majority of the class remains silent for several weeks—before an exam requires any solid evidence of mental activity.

A bit of confirming evidence on this point comes from an objective course evaluation form administered to two of my General Psychology classes in the same term, one a small honors section ($N = 8$) taught by inquiry and the other a larger lecture section ($N = 26$). The answer choices on the form ranged from 1 (*strongly disagree*) to 5 (*strongly agree*). In rating the item, "The instructor made students feel free to ask questions and express their ideas," the lecture class median was 4.5, and the inquiry class median was significantly higher at 5.0, $\chi^2(1, N = 34) = 4.09$, $p < .05$. Likewise, on the item, "The instructor tried to stimulate students to think for themselves," the lecture class median was 4.1, and the inquiry class median was 5.0, $\chi^2(1, N = 34) = 8.01$, $p < .01$. Because of the variation in class size and ability levels, this course cannot be considered a controlled comparison. Nevertheless, these are two items that should show a difference if inquiry teaching is successful. And it is very pleasant, as well as rare, to get straight As on any evaluation item.

Another contrast between the two methods is in the number of topics covered versus the depth of coverage. The first time I tried inquiry teaching, I made a valiant but futile effort to cover the entire General Psychology syllabus. It can't be done. The five-step inquiry process seems to require a bare minimum of three class meetings to explore any one topic; five or six hours is preferable. Even the limited studies of intelligence and bystander intervention each took one week. The instructor who uses inquiry teaching must give up some breadth of coverage to buy the time students need to hypothesize, collect evidence, and evaluate results.

The inquiry method is flexible and may be adapted to a variety of class situations. It seems especially well suited for the in-depth study of selected topics, study that characterizes upper-division and graduate courses. Only in very large classes without discussion opportunities would the five-step sequence be hard to complete. In such cases the instructor might still adopt the "inquiry attitude" by opening each new topic with a problem statement, by offering several hypotheses, and by orienting students to read their assignments in an active effort to evaluate the hypotheses. If the class is too large to hear even a few oral responses, students could turn in their conclusions in writing. These need not be graded, but they should be checked and used as feedback to guide the lecturer.

Conclusion

The inquiry approach has proved itself to me as a way of achieving certain goals in teaching. Chief among these goals are increased classroom participation and a deeper level of intellectual involvement with course material. The method demands more of students, gets more from them, and even gets them to like the inquiry attitude.

Fifteen-year addictions don't die easily. The old lectures still rise to my lips every time I enter a classroom, see a lectern, or feel the texture of new chalk in my fingers. Like all recovered addicts, I hope to be strong enough to lecture in moderation without losing control. At least I now have a choice, even if in the long run I go cold turkey.

References

Beyer, B. K. (1979). *Teaching thinking in social studies: Using inquiry in the classroom* (rev. ed.). Columbus, OH: Merrill.

Bobker, L. R., & Vision Associates (Producer). (1976). *When will people help? The social psychology of bystander intervention* [Film]. New York: Harcourt Brace Jovanovich.

Huck, S. W., & Sandler, H. M. (1979). *Rival hypotheses: Alternative interpretations of data based conclusions.* New York: Harper & Row.

Latane, B., & Darley, J. M. (1970). *The unresponsive bystander: Why doesn't he help?* New York: Appleton-Century-Crofts.

Reed, J. G., & Baxter, P. M. (1983). *Library use: A handbook for psychology.* Washington, DC: American Psychological Association.

Wechsler, D. (1975). Intelligence defined and undefined: A relativistic appraisal. *American Psychologist, 30,* 135–139.

Westwood Productions (Producer). (1980). *A guide to Psychological Abstracts* [Cassette-Slide Kit]. Washington, DC: American Psychological Association.

Wrightsman, L. S. (1972). *Social psychology in the seventies.* Belmont CA: Wadsworth.

Note

I thank Clifton F. Conrad of the University of Arizona for introducing me to inquiry teaching.

Integrating Research Ethics Into the Introductory Psychology Course Curriculum

Celia B. Fisher
Tara L. Kuther

Psychology faculty have long recognized the importance of integrating ethics into the early education of college students as an effective means of fostering the values and standards that guide responsible scientific practice and of encouraging critical thinking about ethical issues for those who will become research psychologists or who will continue to be consumers of knowledge generated by psychological science (American Psychological Association [APA], 1992; Association of American Colleges, 1985; Baum et al., 1993; Hobbs, 1948; McGovern, 1988). However, surveys of psychology course offerings and reading materials suggest that there are major gaps in the coverage of research ethics in introductory psychology textbooks (e.g., Korn, 1984; Matthews, 1991; Warwick, 1980). For example, although we found mention of research ethics in 100% of 14 introductory psychology textbooks published between 1990 and 1994, these mentions were restricted to an average of 3 pages (range = 1–8 pp.) appearing at the end of chapters covering research methodology and Milgram's (1963) classic obedience study. Thus, discussion of research ethics in introductory textbooks remains tangential to presentation of core material, and introductory psychology instructors have little guidance in how to integrate the teaching of ethical issues into the course. The broad educational goal of the project described later was to develop and evaluate didactic materials that would help introductory psychology instructors teach students to identify ethical issues in human and animal research, consider moral ambiguities that arise within various experimental contexts, and to generate alternative ethical approaches to specific research designs.

The report of the National Commission for the Protection of Human Subjects of Biomedical and Behavioral Research (NCPHSBBR; 1978), known as the Belmont Report, identified three fundamental ethical principles as relevant to research with human participants: (a) beneficence (promotion of welfare and avoidance of harm), (b) respect for persons (protection of privacy and self-determination), and (c) justice (fair and equal treatment). These principles also are reflected in the APA's (1992) ethical standards related to research with human and animal participants. However, the complexity of issues examined by research psychologists often gives rise to situations for which the Belmont Report principles and APA ethical standards appear ambiguous or

contradictory when applied to specific situations (e.g., Fisher, Hoagwood, & Jensen, 1996; Fisher & Tryon, 1990; Kitchener, 1986; Sieber, 1992). Accordingly, Celia B. Fisher developed six ethics cases and accompanying student focus questions to encourage introductory psychology students to recognize and critically evaluate ethical issues in experimentation with human and animal participants and to consider multiple bases and alternative perspectives on ethical problems posed by different scientific approaches to psychological issues (Jonsen & Toulmin, 1988; Whitbeck, 1987, 1992).

Curriculum

Case Studies

The curriculum consisted of six case study teaching modules based on a broad sample of "classic" empirical studies cited in a majority of introductory psychology textbooks (e.g., McConnell & Gorenflo, 1989). The case study format complements the instructor's pedagogical goals by being suitable for both coverage of ethical issues and extended discussion of research design and the topical domain addressed by the study. The first case study asked students to consider whether harm can come to participants or to society when social psychologists stage crises in public places (Piliavin & Piliavin, 1972). This was followed by case presentations on animal experimentation (Hubel, 1959) and the use of aversive procedures with human participants (Watson & Rayner, 1920). Two additional cases required critical thinking about ethical issues in socially sensitive (Scarr & Weinberg, 1976) and deception research (Schacter & Singer, 1962). The last case study drew attention to ethical issues associated with randomized clinical trials (RCT) research with participants with psychological disorders (Elkin et al., 1989).

Critical Thinking Questions

Students received a workbook that included (a) a brief abstract of each study; (b) a more detailed description of each experiment including the purpose of the study, primary hypothesis, participants, procedure, results, and conclusions (Fisher & Fyrberg, 1994); and (c) homework assignments composed of four sets of focus questions requiring students to critically evaluate ethical issues derived from the Belmont Report (NCPHSBBR, 1978) and the APA Ethics Code (1992). The first set of questions focused on the scientific validity and social value of the study. This was followed by questions highlighting potential research risks within the context of the need for experimental control. The third set of questions targeted protections and threats to participant autonomy and privacy. The final set of questions addressed the tension between the investigator's dual responsibility to conduct well-controlled experiments and protect participant welfare.

Instructor's Manual

An instructor's guide for leading class discussions and grading student homework assignments included summaries of ethical issues specifically relevant to the particular experiment under study, a list of additional readings, standards relevant to research with human and animal participants from the APA's Ethics Code (1992), and three test questions and guides for grading. Piloting, student focus groups, and faculty workshops contributed to the final set of case summaries, student focus questions, and test questions.

Method

Participants

The initial sample consisted of 585 students enrolled in a total of 24 introductory psychology sections taught during fall and spring semesters at Fordham University, New York and Loyola University, Chicago. Half of the sections received the ethics-enhanced instruction and half the sections received standard ethics instruction. Although all instructors using the ethics curriculum assigned the student focus questions as homework assignments and led student discussions, the amount of time allotted to each ethics module varied as a function of differences in class size (range = 17–75 students) and teaching format (primary focus in small laboratory sections or a portion of the main lecture). Standard ethics instruction typically included a brief overview of informed consent requirements and the ethical issues associated with Milgram's (1963) use of deception in his classic obedience study. Both the enhanced and standard instructional groups received pretest and posttest questionnaires.

Instruments and Procedure

Pretest and posttest research ethics vignettes. The three test vignettes included a deception study using a Milgram-like procedure with school-aged children (Shanab & Yahya, 1977), an animal aversive conditioning study (Routtenberg & Lindy, 1965), and an RCT study with a nursing home population (Langer, 1983). For each vignette students answered two questions.

The first question (Part A) asked students to describe three ethical procedures or modifications they would use to protect the welfare and rights of the research participants in the study. Scores were on a 4-point scale ranging from 0 (*no credit*) to 3 (*full credit*) for inclusion of ethical procedures specific to the study design and population (e.g., forewarning and dehoaxing, proper care and housing of animals, health monitoring and provision of postexperimental treatment). The second question (Part B) asked students to give ethical reasons for why they would or would not conduct the study in its original form or with their modifications. A full-credit (2 points) response required articulation of the tension between a psychologist's responsibility to conduct well-controlled scientifically valuable studies and the obligation to protect the rights and welfare of research participants. Mention of only one side of this issue merited a score of 1; failure to address the moral dimensions of conducting research (e.g., simply a reiteration of the results of the study) received no credit.

Students received an explanation of the project at the beginning of the semester and either a grade or extra credit (at the discretion of their instructors) for their performance on the posttest exam. Consequently, some students chose not to take the tests, to answer only some of the questions, or failed to distinguish between Parts A and B of their answers. To ensure reliability of scoring we rated only essays of students who answered all portions of both the pre- and posttests (182 and 131 for the ethics-enhanced and standard instructional sections, respectively). Raters were blind to the instructional group. (Interrater reliability calculated on half of pretests and posttests yielded κ = .84; Cohen, 1968).

Student and faculty curriculum evaluations. At the end of the semester, students (*n* = 332) and instructors (*n* = 7) participating in the enhanced ethics instruction classes completed a 14-item evaluation questionnaire on the clarity, value, and difficulty of course material, and how well the ethics modules fit in the introductory psychology curriculum.

Curriculum Evaluation

We evaluated the impact of the curriculum in three different ways: scores on student essays, student course evaluations, and instructor curriculum evaluations. The major results of this project were derived through planned comparison tests on student essay scores following the significant Test × Condition interaction, $F(1, 305) = 16.49$, $p < .04$, derived from a 5-factor analysis of variance (ANOVA) on pretest–posttest, instructional condition, vignette, semester, and university. As predicted, significant posttest improvement emerged only for students who received the ethics-enhanced instruction (critical diff. = .28, $p < .01$; effect sizes for pretest–posttest differences were d = .44 and .05 for the enhanced and standard instructional conditions, respectively; see Table 1). Significant Instructional Class ×

Table 1. Student Scores and Standard Deviations on Pretest and Posttest Essays With Respect to Knowledge of Specific Ethical Procedures (Part A), Ability to Weigh Scientific Responsibility and Participant Rights and Welfare (Part B), and the Combined Score

| | Enhanced Ethics Instruction | | | | Standard Instruction | | | |
| | Pretest | | Posttest | | Pretest | | Posttest | |
Test Component	Scores	SD	Scores	SD	Scores	SD	Scores	SD
Part A (range = 0–3)	.91	.72	1.26	.73	.88	.70	1.02	.70
Part B (range = 0–2)	.80	.61	.87	.61	.84	.54	.76	.62
Full test (range = 0–5)	1.69	1.00	2.13	1.03	1.72	.92	1.79	1.20

Table 2. Means and Standard Deviations for Student and Teacher Evaluations of the Enhanced Ethics Instructional Modules

| | Student Evaluations[a] | | Instructor Evaluations[b] | |
Curriculum Features	M	SD	M	SD
Difficulty				
Brief summaries	3.13	.70	2.86	1.07
Extended summaries	3.08	.56	3.14	0.69
Student focus questions	3.19	.68	3.43	0.53
Value				
Extended summaries	2.74	.88	2.00	0.58
Student focus questions	2.70	.88	2.57	1.13
Class discussions	2.43	.94	2.14	0.90
Instructor's guide for grading homework	—	—	2.71	1.11
Instructor's guide for grading homework	—	—	2.25	0.96
Workload compared to other courses	2.82	.61	2.29	0.76
Additional Topics				
Relevance of exam questions	2.17	.60	1.71	0.49
Compatibility	2.13	.65	2.00	0.00
Increased interest in psychological research	2.32	.76	—	—
Increased interest in scientific ethics	2.36	.73	—	—
Consider using modules in future	—	—	1.00	1.00
Consider using modules on practice	—	—	1.86	0.69

Note. Judgments were made using 5-point scales for difficulty, ranging from 1 (*very elementary*) to 5 (*very difficult*); value, ranging from 1 (*excellent*) to 5 (*poor*); and workload, ranging from 1 (*much heavier*) to 5 (*much lighter*). Judgments on additional topics were made using a 4-point scale ranging from 1 (*strongly agree*) to 4 (*strongly disagree*).
[a]n = 332. [b]n = 7.

Test interactions also emerged from 5-factor ANOVAs used to separately examine student knowledge of specific ethical procedures (Part A) and their ability to weigh scientific responsibility and participant welfare (Part B), $F(1, 305) = 12.07, p < .001$, and $F(1, 305) = 6.23, p < .02$. Although the mean scores for each part suggested posttest improvement for the ethics-enhanced instruction group, this pattern was significant only for Part A when Scheffé tests were applied (critical diff. = .31, $p < .01$; effect sizes for differences between pretest and posttest performance for Parts A and B were $d = .48$ and .12, respectively). A perusal of the means for Part A responses to the deceptive research posttest vignette written by students in the standard instructional classes suggests that the presence of ethics coverage on the Milgram (1963) experiment in a majority of introductory psychology textbooks also enhances knowledge of ethical issues and procedures related to deception research.

As illustrated in Table 2, students and faculty participants in the ethics-enhanced classes responded favorably toward the curriculum and judged the instructional and testing materials to be appropriate for introductory psychology students. Faculty agreed that the ethics modules complemented and enhanced the introductory psychology curriculum and strongly agreed that they would use the modules in the future. Perhaps most importantly, students agreed that the topics discussed increased their interest in scientific ethics and research aspects of psychology.

Concluding Comments

Our findings demonstrate that expanded instruction in the ethics of scientific psychology using the case study method can be easily incorporated into introductory psychology classes. Ethics-enhanced instruction increased student awareness of particular ethical procedures used to protect participant's rights and welfare and to a lesser extent increased student sensitivity to the importance of considering both scientific responsibility and participant welfare in ethical decision making. The small gain in the ability to move beyond a single fixed approach to an ethical problem toward the construction of ethical resolutions that connect alternative views reflected in posttest scores on Part B is consistent with evidence indicating that although college experiences can produce gains in moral judgments (Rest & Narvaez, 1994), immersion in ethics education may be required to change college students' epistemic assumptions and reflective judgments (King & Kitchener, 1994).

In addition to enhancing introductory students' awareness of ethical guidelines and ethical decision-making skills for research with animal and human participants, this project demonstrated that the case study approach can increase students' interest in research ethics and in scientific psychology. In the future, case study instructional formats for introductory psychology classes should be used as pedagogical tools for broadening students' understanding and sensitivity not only to research ethics but also to the full spectrum of professional and scientific ethical challenges confronting psychologists.

References

American Psychological Association. (1992). Ethical principles of psychologists and code of conduct. *American Psychologist, 47,* 1597–1611.

Association of American Colleges. (1985). *Integrity in the college curriculum: A report to the academic community.* Washington, DC: Author.

Baum, C., Benjamin, L. T., Bernstein, D., Crider, A., Halonen, J., Hopkins, R., McGovern, T., McKeachie., W., Nodine, B., Reid, P., Suinn, R., & Wade, C. (1993). Principles for quality undergraduate psychology programs. In T. V. McGovern (Ed.), *Handbook for enhancing undergraduate education in psychology* (pp. 17–20). Washington, DC: American Psychological Association.

Cohen, J. (1968). Weighted kappa: Nominal scale agreement with provision for scaled disagreement or partial credit. *Psychological Bulletin, 70,* 213–220.

Elkin, I., Shea, M. T., Watkins, J. T., Imber, S. D., Sotsky, S., Collins, J. F., Glass, D. R., Pilkonis, P., Leber, W. R., Docherty, J. P., Fiester, S. J., & Parloff, M. B. (1989). National Institute of Mental Health treatment of depression collaborative research program. *Archives of General Psychiatry, 46,* 971–983.

Fisher, C. B., & Fyrberg, D. (1994). Participant partners: College students weigh the costs and benefits of deceptive research. *American Psychologist, 49,* 417–427.

Fisher, C. B., Hoagwood, K., & Jensen, P. S. (1996). Casebook on ethical issues in research with children and adolescents with mental disorders. In K. Hoagwood, P. S. Jensen, & C. B. Fisher (Eds.), *Ethical issues in mental health research with children and adolescents* (pp. 135–238). Mahwah, NJ: Lawrence Erlbaum Associates, Inc.

Fisher, C. B., & Tryon, W. W. (1990). *Ethics in applied developmental psychology: Emerging issues in an emerging field.* Norwood, NJ: Ablex.

Hobbs, N. (1948). The development of a code of ethical standards for psychology. *American Psychologist, 3,* 80–84.

Hubel, D. H. (1959). Single unit activity in striate cortex of unrestrained cats. *Journal of Physiology, 147,* 226–238.

Jonsen, A. R., & Toulmin, S. (1988). *The abuse of casuistry: A history of moral reasoning.* Berkeley: University of California Press.

King, P. M., & Kitchener, K. S. (1994). *Developing reflective judgment.* San Francisco: Jossey-Bass.

Kitchener, K. S. (1986). Intuition, critical evaluation and ethical principles: The foundation for ethical decision in counseling psychology. *Counseling Psychologist, 12,* 43–55.

Korn, J. H. (1984). Coverage of research ethics in introductory and social psychology textbooks. *Teaching of Psychology, 11,* 146–149.

Langer, E. J. (1983). *The psychology of control.* Beverly Hills, CA: Sage.

Matthews, J. R. (1991). The teaching of ethics and the ethics of teaching. *Teaching of Psychology, 18,* 80–85.

McConnell, J. V., & Gorenflo, D. W. (1989). *Classic readings in psychology.* New York: Holt, Rinehart & Winston.

McGovern, T. V. (1988). Teaching the ethical principles of psychology. *Teaching of Psychology, 15,* 22–26.

Milgram, S. (1963). Behavioral study of obedience. *Journal of Abnormal and Social Psychology, 67,* 371–378.

National Commission for the Protection of Human Subjects of Biomedical and Behavioral Research. (1978). *The Belmont Report: Ethical principles and guidelines for the protection of human subjects* (DHEW Publication No. OS 78–0012). Washington, DC: U.S. Government Printing Office.

Piliavin, J. A., & Piliavin, I. M. (1972). Effect of blood on reactions to a victim. *Journal of Personality and Social Psychology, 23,* 353–361.

Rest, J. R., & Narvaez, D. (1994). *Moral development in the professions: Psychology and applied ethics.* Hillsdale, NJ: Lawrence Erlbaum Associates, Inc.

Routtenberg, A., & Lindy, J. (1965). Effects of the availability of rewarding septal and hypothalamic stimulation on bar pressing for food under conditions of deprivation. *Journal of Comparative and Physiological Psychology, 60,* 158–161.

Scarr, S., & Weinberg, R. (1976). IQ test performance of black children adopted by white families. *American Psychologist, 31,* 726–739.

Schacter, S., & Singer, J. E. (1962). Cognitive, social, and physiological determinants of emotional state. *Psychological Review, 69,* 379–399.

Shanab, M., & Yahya, K. (1977). A behavioral study of obedience in children. *Journal of Personality and Social Psychology, 35,* 530–536.

Sieber, J. E. (1992). *Planning ethically responsible research: A guide for students and internal review boards.* Newbury Park, CA: Sage.

Warwick, D. P. (1980). *The teaching of ethics in the social sciences.* Hastings on Hudson, NY: Hastings Center.

Watson, J. B., & Rayner, R. (1920). Conditioned emotional reactions. *Journal of Experimental Psychology, 3,* 1–4.

Whitbeck, C. (1987). *The engineer's responsibility for safety: Integrating ethics teaching into courses in engineering design.* Proceedings of the annual meeting of the American Society of Mechanical Engineers, Boston.

Whitbeck, C. (1992). The trouble with dilemmas: Rethinking applied ethics. *Professional Ethics, 1,* 119–142.

Notes

1. This research was supported by Grant SBR–9310458 from the National Science Foundation to Celia B. Fisher and Fordham University.
2. We are grateful to Michelle Caban, Michael Collins, Roseanne Diubaldo, Yvette Martens, and Colleen O'Sullivan for their assistance in scoring the pretests and posttests.

Incorporating Evolutionary Theory Into the Teaching of Psychology

Peter Gray

Teaching is, or should be, a scholarly activity. To teach psychology well, we must think about and attempt to make sense of psychology's fundamental ideas. As teachers, we might view ourselves not merely as conveyers of information and other people's ideas but as philosophers trying to figure out what is worth conveying. It is up to us to decide what—out of all that has been said and done in the history of psychology—is worth passing on to the next generation of psychologists and consumers of psychology. Our choices of what ideas to teach and our effectiveness in conveying the evidence and logic behind them will inspire some students to continue in psychology and will dissuade others. The ideas we plant today will germinate in a few bright minds and help define the discipline in 10 or 20 years. We might engage ourselves more than we now do in debate about what ideas to teach. What classic theories should be dropped, or taught simply as history, because they have been superseded by more useful theories? What theories or principles should be added or given more weight due to their growing contribution? What organizing themes are most useful?

Toward helping to provoke more of that kind of debate, I present herein a particular view concerning what to teach. My thesis is that we should devote far more attention than we do to evolutionary theory in our psychology courses. Evolutionary theory is the only truly integrative theory that psychology can ever have; it provides a foundation for critical thought about every idea in psychology that is, explicitly or implicitly, a statement of human nature. Instead of the peripheral position that it now occupies, evolutionary theory should be a central component of the introductory course and an integral part of almost every other course. In this article, I describe some of the advantages of incorporating evolutionary theory into our courses and, more briefly, examine some misconceptions that seem to have inhibited many teachers of psychology from doing so.

What Do We Gain by Incorporating Evolutionary Theory Into Our Courses?

The basic premise of evolutionary theory is accepted by nearly all psychologists as well as biologists. It can be stated simply as follows: All living species, including humans, achieved their present forms through a process of natural selection in which those randomly occurring genetic changes that helped individuals to survive and reproduce were passed along from generation to generation, and those that hindered survival and reproduction were lost. This premise has a clear, far-reaching implication for psychology. It implies that all of the complex biological mechanisms under-lying human behavior and experience—including the mechanisms of perception, learning, memory, thought, motivation, and emotion—came about because they promoted the survival and reproduction of our ancestors. The incorporation of evolutionary theory into our courses can provide us and our students with (a) a basis for thinking critically about classic psychological theories; (b) a basis for understanding psychology's recent shift away from grand, general theories to narrower, domain-specific theories; (c) an antidote to the tendency to overemphasize pathologies and underemphasize adaptive functions in psychology; and (d) a basis for understanding the rationales for cross-species comparisons in psychology.

A Basis for Thinking Critically About Classic Psychological Theories

Theories in psychology are theories about human nature and, as such, are theories about products of evolution by natural selection. This is true even of those theories that place the greatest weight on the influence of the present environment or culture. The theory that all complex human behavior is shaped by operant conditioning is a theory about human nature, as is the theory that all complex human behavior can be understood as the playing out of culturally acquired roles. For any theory about human nature, we can ask: How plausible is it that natural selection would have produced the psychological mechanisms posited or implied by this theory? What aspects of the theory are easily reconciled with evolution and what aspects are not? Attempts to answer such questions can lead us and our students to identify the fundamental tenets of the theory and to think about them critically. Here I illustrate how an evolutionary perspective can raise critical questions about classic theories in developmental, personality, and social psychology. Space is lacking here to develop any of the critiques fully, so please read them only as hints for further thought.

Application to Piaget's theory of cognitive development. According to Piaget, the mind as a whole undergoes a series of metamorphoses, each of which can be characterized by the existence of a particular kind of mental scheme that underlies all of the person's thought at that stage (Inhelder & Piaget, 1958). The final stage, reached at about age 13, is that of formal operational schemes, defined as schemes that manipulate mental symbols in mathematically logical ways regardless of the symbols' referents.

Because Piaget proposed this theory as universal, it is reasonable to raise questions about it from an evolutionary perspective, such as the following: Is the type of scheme postulated for each stage well designed to solve the range of survival-related problems that children encounter (or would have encountered in our evolutionary past) at that stage? Does Piaget's image of the developing child as a dispassionate scientist figuring out the lawful nature of the world fit reasonably with cross-cultural findings about children's behavior? Does formal operational reasoning characterize adult thinking worldwide; in particular, does it characterize adult thinking in hunter–gatherer people, who live in ways most comparable to those in which humans evolved? How is such reasoning linked to finding food, warding off enemies, engaging in reciprocal exchanges, obtaining and retaining mates, and raising children? When adults reason about survival-related problems, do they really manipulate contentless symbols, or do they think in concrete symbols manipulated according to the different means–end schemes that apply to the different categories of problems?

These are the kinds of questions that an evolutionary perspective begs us to ask about Piaget's theory, but they are not the questions that Piaget himself asked. Although Piaget came to psychology with a biological background and used biological terms to describe the process of mental growth, he did not bring a Darwinian perspective to bear. If he had, his theory may have taken a different shape from the one we teach to our students.

An evolutionary perspective forces us to transcend our parochial niche of the world when we develop or critique theories of human nature. From an evolutionary perspective, Piaget's theory seems ethnocentric. Formal operational reasoning is indeed a developmental goal of schools and colleges in Europe and North America (a goal that may or may not ever be achieved), and the preoperational and concrete operational stages of Piaget's theory seem to match reasonably well the curriculum demands of the early school grades. Piaget appears to reject the influence of schooling in his emphasis on the role of self-motivated discovery and his minimization of the value of teaching, but he seems to posit that the Euro-American school curriculum, in an abstract form, is a universal developmental sequence endemic to the human mind.

Application to Freud's theory of personality. Freud's emphasis on sex, aggression, and unconscious reasoning may seem superficially to be consistent with an evolutionary view, but his manner of explaining and elaborating on them do not. Freud's conception of evolution was overtly Lamarckian, not Darwinian; unlike modern evolutionists, he believed that individual development in humans mirrors human history (MacDonald, 1986; Nesse & Lloyd, 1992). If Freud had come to psychology with a Darwinian orientation, he would have attempted to reconcile his theories with natural selection. How plausible is it that natural selection would have led to incestuous wishes as the most primitive form of the human sex drive or to a death instinct as the foundation for aggression or to primary process thought (which fails to distinguish reality from fantasy) as the most fundamental form of human reasoning? (For a summary of these aspects of Freud's theory, see Hall, 1979.) To the degree that such characteristics exist in humans, they would seem to be most plausibly described as secondary, emergent, maladaptive consequences of characteristics that evolved to serve other, adaptive functions. Freud's general approach

was almost the inverse of a modern evolutionary approach. He took maladaptive characteristics (characteristics that are detrimental to the person's survival and reproduction, and would probably have been so in the past as well) as the primary psychological characteristics, and he showed how they could, through secondary means, be channeled toward adaptive ends. An evolutionary view, in contrast, requires that the primary functions of all biological mechanisms be adaptive (if not now, then at least in our evolutionary past) and that maladaptive effects be explained as secondary functions.

Freud's theory of defense mechanisms might, with some modification, be reconciled with evolutionary theory. One possibility is that defenses serve for anxiety a function analogous to that served by endorphins for pain (Goleman, 1985; Nesse & Lloyd, 1992). As is true of pain, anxiety generally promotes survival but is sometimes more harmful than helpful. Sometimes there is no adaptive way to reduce anxiety through acting on its source in the external world, and defense mechanisms may have evolved as imperfect but generally adaptive means to reduce anxiety at those times. Another possibility is that the ultimate function of defense mechanisms is not relief from anxiety, as Freud thought, but impression management (Alexander, 1979; Nesse & Lloyd, 1992; Trivers, 1985). People who appear calm, capable, and prosocial are typically more successful at securing the admiration and cooperation of others than are people who appear anxious, incompetent, or antisocial; people who believe (right or wrong) that they are calm, capable, and prosocial may find it easier to project themselves as such than people who do not harbor those beliefs. Thus, defense mechanisms may have evolved as means for hiding one's insecurities and antisocial motives from oneself for the ultimate purpose of hiding them from others.

Application to Maslow's and Rogers's humanistic theories of personality. An evolutionary perspective applied to humanistic personality theories could help overturn the common criticism that such theories are unscientific or products of sentimental wishful thinking. Maslow's (1970) needs hierarchy—with physiological needs at the base, social needs in the middle, and actualizing needs at the top—would make evolutionary sense if it were modified somewhat. Survival requires that the physiological needs be met immediately. The social needs, although not quite as immediately demanding, are also of constant concern; as social beings, our survival and reproduction depend on our being accepted and approved of by other people. From an evolutionary perspective, the actualizing needs, which include the needs to play, explore, and create, may be relabeled and reconceptualized as *educative needs.* In the course of evolution, those individuals who spent their free time (the time they did not have to devote to lower level needs) at playful, exploratory, and creative activities may thereby have acquired skills and knowledge that made them more flexible in adapting to future crises, more attractive to potential mates, and more valued by their community than people who spent their free time simply waiting for the next immediate survival demand.

The emphasis of humanistic theory on the "real self" as a phenomenological entity distinct from "conditions of worth" imposed by others (Rogers, 1959) may also be reconciled with an evolutionary perspective. For sound evolutionary reasons, people need the approval of others; for equally sound evolutionary reasons, people exploit that need by reserving approval for actions that meet their own (the approvers') self-interests. Evolutionary theorists have described extensively, for example, the ways in which the self-interests of children conflict with even the long-term genetic self-interests of their parents (Dawkins, 1976). Given the constant, often unconscious attempts at manipulation that occur in human interactions, a sense of one's real self may well be an evolved, imperfect but generally adaptive means of keeping one's own needs distinct from those of others.

Although the basic premises of humanistic theories can be reconciled with evolutionary theory, further elaboration of those premises from an evolutionary perspective would lead to substantial modification of them. No modern evolutionist would paint as benign a picture of self-interested, self-directed activity as that painted by humanistic theorists. To be complete, humanistic theory must give more weight than it now does to self-motivated, self-interested aggression and exploitation. The antisocial motives are as much a product of evolution as the prosocial motives, and social structures must operate to keep the former in check.

Application to theories in social psychology. In the area of social psychology, evolutionary thinking is too often regarded as an alternative to the traditional approach rather than as a complement. When evolutionary thinking is applied to social psychological issues (e.g., see Kenrick, 1994), it is usually applied only to those topics—notably aggression, cooperation, and mating strategies—that seem to define the field of sociobiology and in a manner that ignores the findings and theory that define traditional social psychology.

Social psychologists have identified many reliable effects of the immediate social environment on the individual's thought and behavior (see Smith & Mackie, 1995, or any other recent textbook of social psychology). These include the passive bystander effect (failure to help when other bystanders are present), the foot-in-door effect (increased likelihood of complying to a large request after complying to a small one), social facilitation and interference (improved performance on some tasks and worsened performance on others, when observers are present), and group polarization (development of a more extreme view on an issue as a result of discussing it with like-minded others). All such effects can be described superficially, in behavioral terms, without reference to the psychological mechanisms that underlie them. But social psychologists, like nearly all psychologists, are curious about mechanisms and do probe below the surface. As a result, they have developed deeper theories to explain the superficial phenomena, such as impression management theory, social comparison theory, and equity theory. These theories are implicitly statements about human nature: People care about the impressions they make on others and attempt to control those impressions; people understand themselves by comparing themselves to others; people are concerned that they get a fair deal in their relationships with others. In teaching social psychology, we might ask students to think about all such theories from an evolutionary perspective. How would the tendencies to think and behave in ways predicted by the theories tend to promote survival and reproduction? How might the theories be modified to be even more reconcilable with an evolutionary perspective? What new research might be generated to test the modified theories?

A Basis for Understanding Psychology's Shift Toward Specific-Process Theories

For the past 3 decades, psychology has been shifting from a *general-process* perspective toward a *specific-process* perspective. Whereas the former encouraged the development of grand theories that could account for a broad range of behavioral phenomena with a few general psychological mechanisms or processes, the latter encourages the search for many different mechanisms or processes, each of which accounts for a relatively restricted set of phenomena.

The general-process bias in psychology originated partly from the field's historic link to philosophy and from early psychologists' admiration of physics. Philosophers and physicists specialize in the search for general processes. The shift toward specific-process theories has come as part of an increasingly explicit recognition that psychology is a branch of biology, not of physics. All psychological mechanisms are biological mechanisms. Biological mechanisms are products of history, built gradually by chance mutations coupled with natural selection. The mechanisms persist to the degree that they help the genes that create them to survive from one generation to the next. Teaching psychology explicitly from an evolutionary perspective provides students with a means of understanding the value of the specific-process approach, which on the surface seems less exciting than the grand theories of the past. (For more on the evolutionary rationale for specific processes, see Buss, 1995; Cosmides & Tooby, 1994.)

The specific-process perspective in animal learning. The role of evolutionary thinking in the shift toward a specific-process perspective is perhaps clearest in the study of animal learning. Before the mid-1960s, research in animal learning was dominated by behaviorism, the epitome of a general-process perspective. Behaviorists assumed that essentially all examples of learning can be understood in terms of a few general processes, particularly those of classical and operant conditioning. From that perspective, researchers could study learning in salivating dogs or bar-pressing rats and believe they were identifying fundamental laws of learning in general. The laws that explained a rat's learning to press a bar for food were deemed to be so general that they could account for a child's learning language or a sparrow's learning to find food.

The assumption that all learning involves the same processes and principles began to crumble in the late 1960s and early 1970s. Laboratory researchers in North America, who had been working in the tradition of behaviorism, became increasingly concerned with the "misbehavior" of animals in learning situations. To explain patterns of behavioral change that did not fit with standard accounts of operant and classical conditioning, researchers began to think about instincts and adaptive functions in the natural environment (e.g., Bolles, 1970). At the same time, the work of European ethologists was becoming well known to psychologists. Ethology was conceived initially to be the study of instincts, but ethologists found they could not study instincts without studying learning (Tinbergen, 1951, 1963). Instinctive behaviors do not develop in a vacuum; their development depends on experiences in ways that fit anyone's broad definition of learning.

How do young goslings learn which adult goose to follow? How do sparrows learn to sing their local dialect? How do chickadees remember the many locations where they have hidden food? How do buntings learn the cues that direct their migratory flight? How do rats in nature learn to find food? How do rats learn what is food and what is not? The answer to each of these questions is a separate story, and each one involves specific learning mechanisms that are integral components of survival-related instincts. None of these examples is well explained by the grand theories of classical or operant conditioning. Today psychologists who study learning commonly view it not as a single process or small set of processes but as a term referring to a large number of different adaptive processes that all happen to involve neurally mediated changes in an individual's behavioral responses to particular environmental situations (see Johnston & Pietrewicz, 1985; Marler & Terrace, 1984).

In retrospect, it is not surprising that different examples of learning, which serve different ends, should involve different mechanisms. By analogy, consider two adaptive processes of the skin: When skin is exposed to continuous friction, it produces a callus, which helps protect it from damage due to subsequent friction; when skin is exposed to intense sunlight, it becomes darkened by melanin, which helps protect it from damage due to subsequent sunlight. Similar terms can be used to describe these two adaptive processes superficially, but no researcher would assume that they are the same process or are governed by the same underlying mechanism or follow the same laws with respect to the timing between stimulus application and adaptive change. No researcher who learned how one mechanism works would assume that he or she had thereby learned also how the other one works. The same mechanism that makes calluses cannot make suntans.

When the kind of sensory input is different, the kind of response is different, and when the adaptive function is different, the mechanism must also be different (although some portions of the mechanism may be shared). That seems obvious when we think of adaptive processes of the skin. Why is it not equally obvious when we think of those adaptive processes that are labeled *learning*? Perhaps the common label, *learning*, is itself part of the problem; we tend automatically to think that labels apply to concrete entities not abstract categories. Recognition that learning refers to a category of evolved biological processes, which serve various functions linked to survival and reproduction, helps us remove our blinders.

Specific-process theories in cognitive development. The evolution-based, specific-process perspective that emerged in the field of animal learning is beginning to influence human developmental psychology. For any behavioral capacity that is common to humans, we can ask four questions concerning its development: (a) What is the developed form of the capacity and what function does it serve? (b) What innate knowledge, drives, and behavioral tendencies provide the biological basis for the capacity and its development? (c) What environmental supports are required for the capacity to develop? (d) What variations in the capacity occur as a result of variations in the environment? From the specific-process perspective, answers to these questions will vary from one domain of development to another.

The domain in which the specific-process perspective has been most conspicuously applied is language acquisition. Since Chomsky's early writings in the 1950s (e.g., Chomsky, 1959), psychologists have been confronted with the argument that language could not possibly be learned from scratch, based solely on all-purpose, general learning mechanisms. Rather, some fundamental knowledge of language must be built into the human organism, and some special learning mechanisms must guide the child's acquisition of the specific version of human language to which he or she is exposed. Pinker's (1994) *The Language Instinct* provides a lucid account of the answers for language development to each of the four questions just mentioned.

Books comparable to Pinker's (1994) could be written for other domains of development. *The Physics Instinct* might describe the development of the child's understanding of the physical environment. Infants apparently come into the world prewired to perceive three-dimensional space (e.g., Bower, Broughton, & Moore, 1970), to know certain universal principles of solid objects and their movement (e.g., Baillargeon, 1994; Spelke, 1994), and to behave in ways that provide them with information about the unique qualities of objects around them. Beginning in the first few days after birth, infants look longer at novel objects than at familiar ones. Beginning at 5 or 6 months, infants engage in a form of combined manual and visual exploration of novel objects referred to as *examining* (Oakes & Tellinghuisen, 1994; Ruff, 1986). They hold the object in front of their eyes, turn it this way and that, view it from various angles, squeeze it, mouth it, and pass it from one hand to the other. Nobody has to teach them to examine objects, just as nobody has to teach them to attend to language or to babble.

Likewise, *The Psychology Instinct* could describe the child's innate knowledge about some of the universal characteristics of human minds and relationships, and it could describe inborn drives and tendencies that lead the child to understand the unique minds and relationships in his or her portion of the world. Another book, *The Culture Instinct*, could describe the innate drives and tendencies that lead a developing person to attend to, acquire, and expand on the skills, ideas, values, and social roles and rules that characterize and promote acceptance and survival in the particular culture of which he or she is a part. That book would no doubt devote many pages to social play, which occurs cross-culturally in certain universal forms (Johnson, Christie, & Yawkey, 1987) and seems designed by evolution to promote practice of culture-specific skills (Groos, 1901) and understanding of culture-specific roles and rules (Vygotsky, 1933).

An Antidote to the Tendency to Pathologize in Psychology

An evolutionary perspective can help us counter students' and many psychologists' bias to overemphasize pathology and ignore adaptive functions in accounts of behavior and psychological states. An analogous situation exists in the field of medicine. Due to the influence of what is called *Darwinian medicine*, symptoms that were once viewed only as harmful consequences of disease or other physiological conditions are now often considered to be adaptive responses to those conditions (Williams & Nesse, 1991). Fever is now known to help fight disease by killing temperature-sensitive infectious organisms (Kluger, 1991); coughing, sneezing, vomiting, and diarrhea may all help expel pathogens from the body (Williams & Nesse, 1991); and the so-called morning sickness that is common in the first trimester of pregnancy may help protect the developing fetus from teratogens during the phase of development when its tissues are most sensitive to them (Profet, 1992).

Clinical psychology likewise is beginning to profit from the evolutionary perspective. The fact that nearly all people have the capacity to become depressed in response to particular conditions or anxious in response to other conditions suggests that such states, at least when they occur at moderate levels, may be adaptive responses to the conditions that produce them. Perhaps moderate depression promotes realistic self-appraisal and life change following repeated failure (Nesse, 1990); perhaps the various anxiety disorders are linked to normal anxiety states that evolved because they promoted survival by enhancing vigilance in dangerous situations (Marks & Nesse, 1994). Today, when Prozac is prescribed for mild depression and Valium for mild anxiety, the question of whether such states are useful is of considerable practical importance.

Psychology has long tended to treat emotions in general as pathologies rather than adaptations. The most explicit example of this tendency is seen in the writings of early behaviorists, who saw no need for a concept of emotions as internal states and considered "emotional behavior" to be a breakdown in normal behavioral functioning (e.g., Duffy, 1941). As one illustration of how an evolutionary analysis can help us understand the adaptive value of emotional behavior, consider the tendency of infants and young children in our culture to protest against going to bed. They cry; they claim to be afraid of the dark, afraid of monsters. Why? Years ago, Watson (1928) argued essentially that such behavior is pathological and derives from parents' overindulgence and spoiling of their children. Remnants of that view persist in books on baby care (e.g., Spock & Rothenberg, 1985). But something is clearly missing from that explanation. Why should indulgence lead to this particular protest and not some other? Why does it not lead children to protest against candy, toys, or sunlight? A more complete and plausible answer to the original question can be derived from cross-cultural research combined with evolutionary thought.

In essentially all non-Western cultures, infants and young children sleep in the same room and usually in the same bed with one or more adult caregivers (Barry & Paxson, 1971), and bedtime protest is absent (Morelli, Rogoff, Oppenheim, & Goldsmith, 1992). What infants protest, apparently, is not going to bed per se, but going to bed alone, in the dark, at night. An obvious function of this protest becomes apparent when one considers existing hunter–gatherer cultures, in which any infant left alone at night would be in serious danger from nighttime predators (Konner, 1982). In the history of our species, infants who grew frightened and cried out to elicit adult attention when left alone at night would have been more likely to survive to pass their genes on to another generation than those who placidly accepted their fate.

A Basis for Thinking Critically About Cross-Species Comparisons

Many psychologists study other animal species to learn about humans, and all undergraduate psychology students read and hear about such research. However, if students lack a foundation in evolutionary theory, they are poorly equipped to appreciate such research or to think critically about it. Without a foundation in evolution, students cannot recognize that two fundamentally different kinds of comparisons can be made across species and that the two serve fundamentally different purposes. One kind of comparison focuses on *homologies*, which are similarities between species that are due to their common ancestry; the other focuses on *analogies*, which are similarities due to convergent evolution.

Homologies are useful for research on the mechanisms of behavior. Because convergent evolution can produce similar behaviors that operate through different mechanisms, researchers who seek to understand the physiological mechanism of some behavior in humans through experiments on other species should study species in which the relevant behavior is homologous, not analogous, to that in humans. Homologies are also useful for tracing the evolutionary origins of particular human behaviors. Darwin (1872/1965) pioneered the use of homologies for this purpose in his comparisons of the facial expressions of emotions in humans with those in various species of monkeys and apes. Modern extension of this work has led, for example, to the hypothesis that the human happy smile and human greeting smile have separate evolutionary origins (Hooff, 1972; Redican, 1982). Analogies are useful for identifying the ultimate functions of specific behavioral characteristics (Lorenz, 1974). For example, researchers interested in the question of the functions of different mating patterns—monogamy, polygyny, or polyandry—have used comparison by analogy as their primary tool (Dewsbury, 1988; Trivers, 1972). What is common in the ecology of such otherwise differing species as geese, foxes, and gibbons that might have led them independently to evolve monogamous mating systems?

Given the advantages of using an evolutionary perspective in the teaching of psychology, why do so many psychology instructors avoid it? One answer is simply tradition. People teach what they have learned, and because relatively few psychologists have learned much about evolution, relatively few teach it. In addition, many psychologists hold misbeliefs about evolutionary theory or its role in psychology, which they cite as justification for avoiding evolutionary theory in their thought and teaching. I discuss briefly three of the most common of these misbeliefs.

Three Beliefs About Evolutionary Theory That May Lead Psychologists to Avoid It

The Belief That Evolution Is Relevant Only to Certain "Biological" Realms of Psychology

Some psychologists apparently avoid evolutionary theory because they think it is relevant only to certain realms of psychology, not to the field as a whole. Some associate it specifically with the study of aggression, cooperation, and mating strategies—the topics that have been most emphasized so far by people who call themselves sociobiologists or evolutionary psychologists. But all of psychology is biological. All behavioral mechanisms are the products of evolution by natural selection. In this article, I tried to indicate how an evolutionary perspective can help promote critical thinking and suggest research questions in widely diverse areas of psychology (see also Buss, 1995).

The Belief That Evolutionary Analyses Are Not Useful in Promoting Social Change

Many people go into psychology because they are interested in social change. Theories that emphasize only the role of the immediate environment or culture in shaping behavior may seem, superficially, to be more useful to them than do theories that emphasize evolution. We can do something about our immediate environment, not about our past evolution, and most reformers certainly are not advocating eugenics as a means of human betterment.

Such superficial reasoning, however, is based on a false dichotomy between nature and nurture, and it deprives reformers of useful ideas and information. Any theory about how environment or culture influences human beings is, implicitly, a theory of human nature, and any theory about human nature is, implicitly, a theory about the environmental conditions likely to elicit aspects of that nature. All human behavior emerges from an interplay between evolved human tendencies and the social–environmental conditions in which individual humans develop and interact. Evolution did not endow us with instincts that play themselves out, dumbly and blindly, regardless of environmental conditions. Rather, evolution endowed us with tendencies to behave in particular ways in response to particular conditions.

The real dichotomy is not between nature and nurture but between general-process and specific-process views of human nature. According to the general-process view, human nature consists only of certain very general learning processes, and we can use our understanding of them to shape any kind of behavior we wish to shape. According to the specific-process view, evolution has endowed us with a wide variety of different mechanisms and tendencies for dealing with different problems linked to our survival and reproduction. According to this view, different social problems and their solutions may rest in different aspects of human nature, each of which must be thought about anew from an evolutionary perspective.

As one example, consider again the problem of children's bedtime protest. From the general-process perspective, there is no practical value in bringing an evolutionary analysis to bear on this problem; we can simply apply principles of learning. Through firmness, conditioning, or good examples, we can teach our children to go peaceably to bed. Contrarily, according to the specific-process perspective, an evolutionary analysis is useful. If that analysis indicates that children's bedtime protest is linked to an evolved fear of being alone in the dark, then an effective solution to the problem may not rest on firmness, conditioning, or good examples but on our changing children's sleeping arrangements so they feel less alone and abandoned.

As another example, consider the social problem of men's violence toward women. In the United States, an estimated 2 million women are beaten by their husbands each year, and one eighth of all murders involve men killing their wives (Smuts, 1992). Based on studies of the contexts in which such violence occurs, and using cross-cultural and cross-species comparisons, Smuts (1992, 1995) and Wilson and Daly (1992) developed a compelling case for understanding such violence as part of an evolved tendency in men to take a proprietary interest in the sexual lives of their wives. The major immediate cause of husbands' violence toward their wives, in the United States and elsewhere, is sexual jealousy (Counts, Brown, & Campbell, 1991; Daly & Wilson, 1988). According to this analysis, a tendency in men to respond violently when they perceive (rightly or wrongly) that their wives have been sexually unfaithful evolved because such behavior, over the course of evolutionary history, more often increased than decreased the rate of men's own paternity of their wives' children. Such an analysis neither implies that men's violence toward women is justifiable, inevitable, or resistant to social influence nor is it necessarily incompatible with social pathology theories. As Smuts pointed out, cultures differ in the degree of such violence; within any given culture, great variation exists among individual men. In fact, based on cross-cultural evidence combined with evolutionary logic, Smuts (1992) developed hypotheses concerning the social conditions that increase or decrease the probability that such violence will occur. Those hypotheses would be useful to anyone working toward social change aimed at improving the lives of women.

The Belief That Evolutionary Explanations Cannot Be Tested

The most frequently stated objection, in my experience, to the use of evolutionary theory in psychology is that evolutionary accounts amount to mere speculation and cannot be tested empirically. Although this objection is an understandable reaction to some of the more careless uses of evolutionary reasoning, it does not fairly characterize the enterprise in general.

All theorizing involves speculation. If a statement were not speculative, we would not call it a theory. Speculating (creating theories) is a valued activity in every science and in every realm of psychology. An advantage of an evolutionary perspective in psychology is that it provides guidance and boundaries to speculation. Far from promoting wildness, it promotes constraint. The evolutionary perspective insists that our theories about underlying psychological mechanisms must be compatible with the empirical data we are trying to explain and with the principle of natural selection. Each theory must be consistent with the idea that, over the course of evolutionary history, the mechanism has tended to promote individuals' survival and reproduction.

Theories in psychology developed from an evolutionary perspective are, like any other theories, testable to the degree that they make predictions about observable phenomena. Each of the specific evolution-based theories mentioned in this article can be elaborated into a set of reasonable predictions about the contexts and specific forms in which the behaviors are most likely to occur. Alternative theories of the evolutionary function of a human tendency can be pitted against one another if the theories make different predictions about the manner or contexts in which the tendency is manifested in people or if they make different predictions as to which other animal species will manifest analogous tendencies. Such tests are standard practice in evolutionary psychology.

Conclusion

Most scholars would place Darwin's theory of evolution by natural selection at or near the top of a list of most profound ideas ever developed concerning the study of human beings. The theory has clear implications for psychology, which have long been recognized but, even today, are remarkably unexploited. When we familiarize students with evolutionary theory and show them how it can help guide thought and research in each realm of psychology, we help students get a better education and help make psychology a more exciting and effective science. I hope that the "hints" provided in this article will encourage teachers of psychology to think creatively about many ways to use evolutionary theory in their courses, to promote deeper understanding, critical thinking, and advancement of the discipline.

References

Alexander, R. D. (1979). *Darwinism and human affairs*. Seattle: University of Washington Press.

Baillargeon, R. (1994). How do infants learn about the physical world? *Current Directions in Psychological Science, 3*, 133–140.

Barry, H., III, & Paxson, L. (1971). Infancy and early childhood: Cross-cultural codes, 2. *Ethnology, 10*, 466–508.

Bolles, R. C. (1970). Species-specific defense reactions and avoidance learning. *Psychological Review, 77*, 32–48.

Bower, T. G. R., Broughton, J. M., & Moore, M. K. (1970). Infant response to approaching objects: An indicator of response to distal variables. *Perception and Psychophysics, 9*, 193–196.

Buss, D. M. (1995). Evolutionary psychology: A new paradigm for psychological science. *Psychological Inquiry, 6*, 1–30.

Chomsky, N. (1959). A review of B. F. Skinner's "Verbal behavior." *Language, 35*, 26–58.

Cosmides, L., & Tooby, J. (1994). Beyond intuition and instinct blindness: Toward an evolutionarily rigorous cognitive science. *Cognition, 50*, 41–77.

Counts, D., Brown, J. K., & Campbell, J. C. (Eds.). (1991). *Sanctions and sanctuary: Cultural perspectives on the beating of wives*. Boulder, CO: Westview.

Daly, M., & Wilson, M. (1988). *Homicide*. Hawthorne, NY: Aldine de Gruyter.

Darwin, C. (1965). *The expression of the emotions in man and animals*. Chicago: University of Chicago Press. (Original work published 1872)

Dawkins, R. (1976). *The selfish gene*. Oxford, England: Oxford University Press.

Dewsbury, D. A. (1988). The comparative psychology of monogamy. In D. W. Leger (Ed.), *Comparative perspectives in modern psychology: Nebraska Symposium on Motivation, 1987* (pp. 1–50). Lincoln: University of Nebraska Press.

Duffy, E. (1941). An explanation of "emotional" phenomena without the use of the concept "emotion." *Journal of General Psychiatry, 25*, 283–293.

Goleman, D. (1985). *Vital lies, simple truths*. New York: Simon & Schuster.

Groos, K. (1901). *The play of man*. New York: Appleton.

Hall, C. S. (1979). *A primer of Freudian psychology: 25th anniversary edition*. New York: Mentor.

Hooff, J. A. van (1972). A comparative approach to the phylogeny of laughter and smiling. In R. A. Hinde (Ed.), *Non-verbal communication* (pp. 209–241). Cambridge, England: Cambridge University Press.

Inhelder, B., & Piaget, J. (1958). *The growth of logical thinking from childhood to adolescence*. New York: Basic Books.

Johnson, J. E., Christie, J. F., & Yawkey, T. D. (1987). *Play and early childhood development*. Glenview, IL: Scott, Foresman.

Johnston, T. D., & Pietrewicz, A. T. (Eds.). (1985). *Issues in the ecological study of learning*. Hillsdale, NJ: Lawrence Erlbaum Associates, Inc.

Kenrick, D. T. (1994). Evolutionary social psychology: From sexual selection to social cognition. *Advances in Experimental Social Psychology, 26*, 75–121.

Kluger, M. J. (1991). The adaptive value of fever. In P. A. Mackowiak (Ed.), *Fever: Basic mechanisms and management* (pp. 105–124). New York: Raven.

Konner, M. J. (1982). *The tangled wing: Biological constraints on the human spirit*. New York: Harper & Row.

Lorenz, K. Z. (1974). Analogy as the source of knowledge. *Science, 185*, 229–234.

MacDonald, K. (1986). Civilization and its discontents revisited: Freud as an evolutionary biologist. *Journal of Social and Biological Structures, 9*, 307–318.

Marks, I. M., & Nesse, R. M. (1994). Fear and fitness: An evolutionary analysis of anxiety disorders. *Ethology and Sociobiology, 15*, 247–261.

Marler, P., & Terrace, H. (Eds.). (1984). *The biology of learning*. Berlin: Springer-Verlag.

Maslow, A. H. (1970). *Motivation and personality* (2nd ed.). New York: Harper & Row.

Morelli, G. A., Rogoff, B., Oppenheim, D., & Goldsmith, D. (1992). Cultural variation in infants' sleeping arrangements: Questions of independence. *Developmental Psychology, 28*, 604–613.

Nesse, R. M. (1990). Evolutionary explanations of emotions. *Human Nature, 1*, 261–289.

Nesse, R. M., & Lloyd, A. T. (1992). The evolution of psychodynamic mechanisms. In J. H. Barkow, L. Cosmides, & J. Tooby (Eds.), *The adapted mind: Evolutionary psychology and the generation of culture* (pp. 601–624). Oxford, England: Oxford University Press.

Oakes, L. M., & Tellinghuisen, D. J. (1994). Examining in infancy: Does it reflect active processing? *Developmental Psychology, 30*, 748–756.

Pinker, S. (1994). *The language instinct*. New York: Morrow.

Profet, M. (1992). Pregnancy sickness as adaptation: A deterrent to maternal ingestion of teratogens. In J. H. Barkow, L. Cosmides, & J. Tooby (Eds.), *The adapted mind: Evolutionary psychology and the generation of culture* (pp. 327–365). Oxford, England: Oxford University Press.

Redican, W. K. (1982). An evolutionary perspective on human facial displays. In P. Ekman (Ed.), *Emotion in the human face* (pp. 212–280). Cambridge, England: Cambridge University Press.

Rogers, C. R. (1959). A theory of therapy, personality, and interpersonal relationships, as developed in the client-centered framework. In S. Koch (Ed.), *Psychology: A study of a science* (Vol. 3, pp. 184–256). New York: McGraw-Hill.

Ruff, H. A. (1986). Components of attention during infants' manipulative explorations. *Child Development, 57*, 105–114.

Smith, E. R., & Mackie, D. M. (1995). *Social psychology*. New York: Worth.

Smuts, B. (1992). Male aggression against women: An evolutionary perspective. *Human Nature, 3*, 1–44.

Smuts, B. (1995). The evolutionary origins of patriarchy. *Human Nature, 6*, 1–32.

Spelke, E. (1994). Initial knowledge: Six suggestions. *Cognition, 50*, 431–445.

Spock, B., & Rothenberg, M. B. (1985). *Dr. Spock's baby and child care* (rev. ed.). New York: Pocket Books.

Tinbergen, N. (1951). *The study of instinct*. Oxford, England: Oxford University Press.

Tinbergen, N. (1963). On aims and methods of ethology. *Zeitschrift für Tierpsychologie, 20*, 410–433.

Trivers, R. L. (1972). Parental investment and sexual selection. In B. Campbell (Ed.), *Sexual selection and the descent of man: 1871–1971* (pp. 136–179). Chicago: Aldine.

Trivers, R. L. (1985). *Social evolution*. Menlo Park, CA: Benjamin/Cummings.

Vygotsky, L. S. (1978). The role of play in development. In L. S. Vygotsky (Author) & M. Cole, V. John-Steiner, S. Scribner, & E. Souberman (Eds.), *Mind in society: The development of higher psychological processes* (pp. 92–104). Cambridge, MA: Harvard University Press.

Watson, J. B. (1928). *Psychological care of infant and child*. New York: Norton.

Williams, G. C., & Nesse, R. M. (1991). The dawn of Darwinian medicine. *The Quarterly Review of Biology, 66*, 1–22.

Wilson, M., & Daly, M. (1992). In J. H. Barkow, L. Cosmides, & J. Tooby (Eds.), *The adapted mind: Evolutionary psychology and the generation of culture* (pp. 289–322). Oxford, England: Oxford University Press.

Note

This article is based partly on a paper presented at the Seventeenth Annual National Institute on the Teaching of Psychology, St. Petersburg Beach, FL, January 1995.

Practice Versus Review Exams and Final Exam Performance

William R. Balch

Research on self-assessment in college students shows that learners generally overestimate their mastery (Balch, 1992; Sjostrom & Marks, 1994) or potential mastery (Prohaska, 1994) of material before testing as well as their performance after testing (Balch, 1992; Boud & Falchikov, 1989; Doleys & Renzaglia, 1963). Several researchers have obtained similar findings when students rated their confidence in their comprehension of recently read material and then took a test on the material (Glenberg & Epstein, 1985, 1987; Glenberg, Sanocki, Epstein, & Morris, 1987; Morris, 1990). In these studies, calibration (i.e., the correlation between confidence ratings and subsequent test performance) was generally low.

However, increased assessment accuracy might result in better academic performance because it would allow students to modify (e.g., increase or improve) their studying for an upcoming test. Previous research has suggested the validity of this hypothesis that I call the *assessment-accuracy* hypothesis and that I test in this study. Several studies have shown that above-average students can predict their test performance more accurately than below-average students (e.g., Balch, 1992; Boud & Falchikov, 1989; Jacobson, 1990; Maki & Berry, 1984; Prohaska, 1994; Sjostrom & Marks, 1994). Such findings demonstrate a link between self-assessment and academic performance. However, they do not establish that more accurate assessment actually causes better performance.

To establish a causal relation between assessment accuracy and performance, one must experimentally manipulate the former and measure the latter. One likely type of manipulation involves a practice test that students take, receiving scores to assess their preparation for a subsequent test. Previous research has established that practice tests improve calibration in laboratory comprehension tasks (Glenberg et al., 1987) and can contribute to improved performance on national, standardized tests (e.g., Frierson, 1987; Ligon, 1983).

In this study, I manipulated assessment accuracy in an introductory psychology course and then compared the final-exam performance of two groups, both of which saw the same sample final exam. A *practice* group took the sample exam as a test and immediately afterward received an objective assessment of their performance by scoring the test according to a key showing both the questions and answers. However, a *review* group saw only the key to the exam (without taking the exam as a test or being assessed) and simultaneously performed a control task. The assessment-accuracy hypothesis tested here holds that accurate assessment of preparation improves academic performance.

Therefore, according to this hypothesis, the practice-exam group should score higher than the review-exam group on the final.

Method

Participants

Of 168 students, 134 volunteered for this study. All were undergraduates enrolled in two sections of an introductory psychology course that I taught at Pennsylvania State University, Altoona, during the fall semester of 1996. To compensate participants and offset possible detrimental effects of the sample-exam treatments on final-exam scores, students received 3 points of extra credit (6% of the maximum final-exam score) for participating.

Procedure

To assign students to one of two sample-exam treatments, I first ranked them with respect to their all-but-final percentages. These percentages were based on 175 points that could be earned on previous multiple-choice quizzes and tests. Then, to ensure that the average all-but-final percentages of each sample-exam group were as similar as possible, I paired students of adjacent ranks (Rank 1 and Rank 2, Rank 3 and Rank 4, etc.) and carried out random assignment to sample exam on each pair.

Both the practice and review groups received the same sample exam, consisting of 25 multiple-choice questions selected (with editing of some of the items) from the test bank for Benjamin, Hopkins, and Nation (1994). The sample-exam sessions occurred during the last class of the semester. I conducted a 25-min session with only volunteers preassigned to one of the sample-exam treatments, followed by a second 25-min session with only volunteers preassigned to the other treatment. Across the two introductory psychology sections, I counterbalanced the order of these treatments.

Practice-exam group. Volunteers in the two practice-exam sessions totaled 68. I told them that they were going to take a practice final exam consisting of multiple-choice questions that were similar in style and general content—but not identical—to those that would appear on the final exam. In addition, I assured the volunteers that although they would receive extra credit for taking the practice exam, their scores on this exam would not count toward their grades.

I showed the sample-exam questions to the practice-exam students by using an overhead projector and a set of four transparencies presented for 3 min apiece, while students recorded their answers by circling one of four letters on answer sheets. Afterward, students exchanged sheets and scored the practice exams according to the key (i.e., the questions with correct answers indicated). Students took 4 min to score the practice exam, with 1 min allowed for each keyed transparency. Then they received their own tests back, along with a self-grading sheet on which a percentage and grade (A, A–, B, C+, C, D, or F) were indicated for each of the possible numerical scores. After students graded themselves by writing the appropriate letter in the space provided on the sheet, I explained that this grade indicated both their current level of preparation for the final and my prediction of how well they would do on the final exam with no further preparation.

Review-exam group. Volunteers in the two review-exam sessions totaled 66. The review procedure varied from the practice-exam procedure only with respect to the way in which I presented the sample exam to the volunteers. I showed them only the keyed transparencies, which had correct answers indicated for each question. Instead of taking the sample exam as a test and being assessed, they spent 3 min (per transparency) performing an expectancy-rating task that served as a control for (a) the familiarization with the questions that the practice-exam volunteers received, and (b) the approximate effort or attention required of those volunteers. In this task, they rated each sample-exam question in terms of how much they would expect a similar question when taking the final exam, by circling one of four numbers on a rating sheet: 1 (*definitely unexpected*), 2 (*moderately unexpected*), 3 (*moderately expected*), or 4 (*definitely expected*). Then, to control for the time required to score the practice exam, I had the review-exam students put aside their rating sheets and view the keyed transparencies once more, allowing 1 min per transparency.

Class-standing categories. I divided volunteers for each of the two sample-exam treatments into three class-standing categories based on their previously determined all-but-final point totals. The lowest ranking third of the students in each sample-exam group was designated as "low"; the middle ranking third as "medium"; and the highest ranking third as "high."

Final exam and helpfulness ratings. One week after participating in the sample-exam sessions, students in both sections of the course took the final exam. This exam consisted of 50 multiple-choice questions covering the entire course. Although it included no items from the practice exam, the final exam came from the same test bank and covered the same general topics. I used two different random orders for the exam, with each being divided approximately evenly within each of the six Sample-Exam Treatment × Class Standing groups.

The last page of each final-exam booklet was a rating sheet on which students rated the helpfulness of the sample exam in their preparation for the final exam. Each participant gave a rating by circling a number on a 11-point scale ranging from 0 (*not helpful at all*) to 10 (*extremely helpful*). As instructed, students took the final exam first and then completed the helpfulness-rating sheet.

Results

To equate the numbers of students in the practice-exam and review-exam groups, I dropped the highest ranking and lowest ranking student (based on their all-but-final percentages) from the practice-exam group. Thus, there were 66 students (22 in each of three class-standing categories) in each of two sample-exam groups. Except when noted, my statistical conclusions are based on two 2 × 3 (Sample-Exam Treatment × Class Standing) ANOVAs: one on the final-exam percentage scores and the other on the helpfulness ratings. To determine statistical significance for all analyses, I used an alpha level of .05.

Final-Exam Percentage Scores

The top half of Table 1 shows the percentage scores of the practice and review groups on the final exam. Note that across class-standing categories, the practice group scored significantly higher ($M = 63.27$, $SD = 11.66$) than the review group ($M = 59.30$, $SD = 9.92$) and that the effect of sample-exam treatment was significant, $F(1, 126) = 4.43$, $p < .05$. The class-standing effect was also significant, $F(1, 126) = 63.68$, $p < .001$. Moreover, post hoc Scheffé tests on the means of the class-standing categories revealed that all three pairwise differences were significant, $ps < .001$. Students having high class standing scored higher ($M = 75.05$, $SD = 11.68$) than those having either low ($M = 49.14$, $SD = 11.89$) or medium ($M = 59.69$, $SD = 8.60$) class standing, and the latter students scored higher than those having low standing. Finally, the Sample-Exam Treatment × Class Standing interaction was not significant ($F < 1$), indicating that the advantage of the practice over the review treat-

Table 1. Final-Exam Percentage Scores and Helpfulness Ratings After Practice Versus Review Exams

| | Exam | | | |
| | Practice | | Review | |
Class Standing	M	SD	M	SD
Final-exam % scores				
Low	51.36	12.88	46.91	10.81
Medium	61.64	9.59	57.73	7.47
High	76.82	12.26	73.27	11.08
Helpfulness ratings				
Low	5.59	1.47	4.14	1.81
Medium	4.36	2.22	3.96	2.24
High	5.82	1.71	3.96	1.84

Note. n = 22. Helpfulness ratings are based on a scale ranging from 0 (*not helpful at all*) to 10 (*extremely helpful*).

ment did not differ significantly for different class-standing categories.

Helpfulness Ratings

The bottom half of Table 1 shows the helpfulness ratings that the practice and review groups gave to their respective sample-exam tasks after having completed the final exam. For all class-standing categories, students rated the practice task significantly higher ($M = 5.26$, $SD = 1.83$) than the review task ($M = 4.02$, $SD = 1.97$) in terms of how much they believed it helped them in their preparation for the final, $F(1, 126) = 14.13$, $p < .001$. However, class standing had no significant effect on the ratings, $F(2, 126) = 2.09$, $p > .10$, or the Sample-Exam Treatment × Class Standing interaction, $F(2, 126) = 1.72$, $p > .10$.

Post Hoc Analyses of Sample-Exam Tasks

To test the possibility that the practice-exam and review-exam tasks required significantly different degrees of cognitive effort, I compared the interitem reliabilities (i.e., consistencies in responding to different items) of these two tasks. To determine the interitem reliability of the practice-exam answers, I calculated the correlation between the item-difficulty indexes (percentage of students who answered a given question correctly) obtained in each of the two practice-exam sessions, $r(24) = .70$, $p < .001$. Then, to determine the reliability of the expectancy ratings, I calculated the analogous correlation between the mean ratings obtained in the review-exam sessions, $r(24) = .87$, $p < .001$. Finally, to test the difference between the two reliability coefficients, I performed a two-tailed test comparing the correlations (Comrey, Bott, & Lee, 1989, p. 228). This test revealed no significant difference, $z = 1.55$, $p > .10$. In that participants in one task were no more consistent in their responses than participants in the other task, both tasks appeared to require similar degrees of attention and cognitive effort.

Furthermore, if the expectancy-rating task required relatively little cognitive effort, then the review volunteers might perform no better on the final than nonvolunteers. The average final-exam scores of the 31 nonvolunteers present for the exam—consisting of 15 low, 8 medium, and 8 high class-standing students—was 51.77%. However, the average of the mean scores for the three class-standing categories of the review group (weighted by 15/31, 8/31, and 8/31, respectively) was 56.51%. The significantly lower performance of the nonvolunteers, $t(30) = 2.10$, $p < .05$, does not support the notion that the review treatment was trivial with respect to cognition.

Discussion

The findings obtained here support the assessment-accuracy hypothesis and extend previous research on the effects of practice tests. For instance, Glenberg et al. (1987) found in a laboratory study that being assessed on a practice test improved students' accuracy of predicting their performance on a similar test given afterward. Because that research suggests that practice tests increase self-assessment accuracy, students may also use such assessment—as they apparently did in this study—to modify their studying and improve their subsequent test performance. In addition, these results are consistent with educational research showing that practice tests contribute to improved performance on standardized tests (e.g., Frierson, 1987; Ligon, 1983). In particular, by controlling for factors such as familiarization with sample-exam questions, this study helps isolate assessment accuracy as a cause of improved final-exam scores in introductory psychology. Furthermore, there was no interaction between sample-exam treatment and class standing. Thus, students at all levels of academic ability benefit from an objective assessment of their preparation for an upcoming final.

The helpfulness-rating data suggest further that the practice-exam students were aware of the potential benefit of this assessment. Compared to the review group, the practice students rated the sample exam more helpful in preparing them for the final. Therefore, accurate assessment of their degree of preparation for the final exam could have motivated them to adjust their subsequent studying. In particular, students whose practice-exam scores were lower than they expected may have knowingly increased the amount or quality of their study for the final. However, this conclusion would be strengthened if future research shows the same result for helpfulness ratings made at the time of the sample-exam treatments. In this study, students made their ratings only in retrospect.

To interpret the results unambiguously as supporting the assessment-accuracy hypothesis proposed here, the nature of the review-exam treatment needs further elaboration. More clearly a control for familiarization, the review treatment may have been less effective in its other function of controlling for cognitive effort. If effort were indeed greater for the practice group than for the review group, the better performance of the former might be explained by the levels-of-processing theory (e.g., Craik, 1979; Matlin, 1994, pp. 75–86). This view would hold that the practice group performed better than the review group because the former applied deeper or more effortful cognitive processing to the sample-exam questions. Yet this position is arguably circular (Matlin, 1994, pp. 85–86; Nelson, 1977), unless depth of processing is measured independently of the performance variable in question (final-exam scores in this case). Even with such independent measures, the levels-of-processing theory is inherently difficult to rule out. To do so, one would have to establish that two tasks are similar with respect to these measures, but such evidence would be weak because it merely supports the null hypothesis.

Despite these problems, I attempted to address to the levels-of-processing argument by performing the post hoc analyses of sample-exam tasks reported in the Results section. One of these analyses compared the interitem reliabilities of the practice and review tasks. Suppose, for instance, that the expectancy-rating task was more shallow than the sample-exam-taking task. Then the review group might pay less attention or exert less effort than the practice group. If so, the expectancy ratings of the former group should show more variance due to random error than the sample-exam answers of the latter; therefore, the interitem reliability should be lower. Because there was no significant difference in the two interitem reliabilities, participants in each group appeared to perform their tasks with reasonable consistency and attention to the individual questions of the sample exam.

The levels-of-processing view also suggests that the presumably more shallow review task should do little to improve final-exam performance beyond that of non-volunteering students, who received no sample-exam treatment at all. However, the review-exam students performed significantly better than nonvolunteers on the final. Of course, this result may possibly reflect a sample bias stemming from lower motivation on the part of the non-volunteers.

Based on these admittedly rough analyses, there is no evidence of a difference between the sample-exam treatments with respect to the depth of processing applied to the sample exam. Still, such a difference might be detectable by other measures. In future research, for instance, participants could perform sample-exam treatments individually to allow for measuring response times to each question and comparing the mean response times of the two treatments.

Even if such processing-related differences were found, however, they would not necessarily influence final-exam performance. Note that the final-exam questions differed from those on the sample exam, in that they covered different subtopics within the same general topics. Therefore, deeper processing of the specific sample-exam questions by the practice-exam group—during a period of only 25 min—would not guarantee higher scores than the review-exam group on the final. The assessment-accuracy hypothesis appears to be a more convincing explanation of the practice group's higher performance. This view suggests that the practice group received information motivating them toward more or better study of a larger body of course material during the week between the sample exam and the final exam. Certainly, the practice-exam volunteers may have used deeper cognitive processing in such studying than the review-exam volunteers. However, their superior final-exam performance apparently stemmed from the assessment of their preparation for the final and the effect on subsequent studying that the practice exam provided, rather than from specific facts learned as a result of processing during the practice exam per se.

Note that the practice-exam procedure used here involved both practice and assessment of performance. Therefore, each element of this procedure may have contributed to the higher final-exam scores of the practice group. However, the effects of accurate assessment alone—apart from practice—might be more precisely isolated by a design that included both a practice-and-assessment group and a practice-without-assessment group. I did not include the latter manipulation in this study for two reasons. First, practice without assessment would be complicated by the fact that self-assessment skill varies with academic ability (e.g., Balch, 1992; Sjostrom & Marks, 1994). Therefore, better students would receive reasonably good self-assessment of performance even if none were provided explicitly. In addition, if the practice test were for an exam that counted in the course, students would justifiably expect to receive their scores on the practice version before taking the real exam. However, such problems might be overcome by a study in which researchers used a laboratory task and selected volunteers whose self-assessment ability was initially low.

Finally, the results suggest a practical implication regarding what students commonly call "old tests." Teachers sometimes provide copies of exams given in previous years, so that students will have an idea of what to expect on current exams. This technique is similar to the review-exam procedure used in this study. However, because practice appears to benefit students more than review, teachers might consider using questions from their old tests on a practice exam. If kept short, practice exams are not particularly time consuming. For instance, the procedure used in this study—including presenting the questions, scoring the exam, and self-grading—took a little less than 25 min. The potential benefits of a practice exam may well be worth the time it takes.

References

Balch, W. R. (1992). Effect of class standing on students' predictions of their final exam scores. *Teaching of Psychology, 19,* 136–141.

Benjamin, L. T., Jr., Hopkins, J. R., & Nation, J. R. (1994). *Psychology* (3rd ed.). New York: Macmillan.

Boud, D., & Falchikov, N. (1989). Quantitative studies of student self-assessment in higher education: A critical analysis of findings. *Higher Education, 18,* 529–549.

Comrey, A. L., Bott, P. A., & Lee, H. B. (1989). *Elementary statistics: A problem-solving approach* (2nd ed.). Dubuque, IA: Brown.

Craik, F. I. M. (1979). Levels of processing: Overview and closing comments. In L. S. Cermak & F. I. M. Craik (Eds.), *Levels of processing in human memory* (pp. 447–461). Hillsdale, NJ: Lawrence Erlbaum Associates, Inc.

Doleys, E. J., & Renzaglia, G. G. (1963). Accuracy of student prediction of college grades. *Personnel and Guidance Journal, 41,* 528–530.

Frierson, H. T. (1987). Combining test-taking intervention with course remediation. *Journal of the National Medical Association, 79,* 161–165.

Glenberg, A. M., & Epstein, W. (1985). Calibration of comprehension. *Journal of Experimental Psychology: Learning, Memory, & Cognition, 11,* 702–718.

Glenberg, A. M., & Epstein, W. (1987). Inexpert calibration of comprehension. *Memory & Cognition, 15,* 84–93.

Glenberg, A. M., Sanocki, T., Epstein, W., & Morris, C. (1987). Enhancing calibration of comprehension. *Journal of Experimental Psychology: General, 116,* 119–136.

Jacobson, J. M. (1990). Congruence of pretest predictions and post-test estimations with grades in short answer and essay tests. *Education Research Quarterly, 14,* 41–47.

Ligon, G. D. (1983). Preparing students for standardized testing. In W. F. Hathaway (Ed.), *Testing in the schools* (pp. 19–27). San Francisco: Jossey-Bass.

Maki, R. H., & Berry, S. L. (1984). Metacomprehension of text material. *Journal of Experimental Psychology: Learning, Memory, & Cognition, 10,* 663–679.

Matlin, M. W. (1994). *Cognition* (3rd ed.). New York: Harcourt Brace.

Morris, C. C. (1990). Retrieval processes underlying confidence in comprehension judgments. *Journal of Experimental Psychology: Learning, Memory, & Cognition, 16,* 223–232.

Nelson, T. O. (1977). Repetition and depth of processing. *Journal of Verbal Learning and Verbal Behavior, 16,* 151–171.

Prohaska, V. (1994). "I know I'll get an A": Confident overestimation of final course grades. *Teaching of Psychology, 21,* 141–143.

Sjostrom, K. P., & Marks, A. (1994). Pretest and posttest confidence ratings in test performance by low-, medium-, and high-scoring students. *Teaching of Psychology, 21,* 12–16.

Notes

1. This study was supported by a faculty-development grant from Pennsylvania State University.
2. I thank Brenda K. Balch for her assistance in conducting the four sample-exam sessions and William G. Engelbret for helpful theoretical retical discussions.

Holistic Grading of Written Work in Introductory Psychology: Reliability, Validity, and Efficiency

Robert J. Madigan
James J. Brosamer

Many college faculty agree that writing assignments are valuable additions to college classes. For Boyer (1987), the ability to communicate well in writing and speaking is one of the hallmarks of an educated person. He listed the development of writing skills among the major objectives of a college education. The growth and influence of the writing- across-the-curriculum movement is well attested (Griffin, 1982; Maimon, 1982; McLeod, 1988). Its relevance to psychology courses was explored in a special issue of this journal (Nodine, 1990). In addition to developing writing skills, there are other reasons to include written work in courses. Writing is a special mode of learning (Emig, 1977); it can improve critical thinking (Fulwiler, 1982) by encouraging writers to scrutinize the language expressing their thoughts. Written examinations may produce better mastery of course material than do multiple-choice tests (Frederiksen, 1984).

The cost of written work is that it must be read and graded. The prospect of the grading task, coupled with the availability of multiple-choice questions from textbook publishers, prompts many teachers to eliminate written work from large classes. Apart from the difficulties of grading, there are legitimate questions about the quality of grading by faculty members whose formal training in writing may not exceed that of their students. White (1989) reported that many faculty members overemphasize mechanical aspects of writing at the expense of the more important conceptual and organizational components.

Holistic grading may offer a way to address issues of workload and quality in evaluating written work. In holistic scoring, the grader places a writing sample in one of a small number of descriptive categories (typically five or six) based on the grader's overall impression of the work (White, 1985). Each category is described by three or four sentences that identify its salient characteristics.

This article describes our adaptation of holistic scoring to written work in a medium-sized introductory psychology class in which all grading was done by teaching assistants (TAs). This situation required an efficient system that could easily be taught to new TAs. But a useful scoring system must also provide students with reliable and valid judgments of their written work. Intergrader reliability was a concern in our study because the graders had no prior training in the assessment of writing. It is natural to question whether psychology TAs can make valid judgments about the writing skills of freshmen.

In the following sections, we describe a holistic scoring system developed for this course and present data on its efficiency, reliability, and validity. The grading system was created for a General Psychology course taught in a lecture format to about 100 students. During the semester, a typical student wrote 4,000 words on essay exams and paper assignments. The primary grading was done by a TA and supervised by the course instructor.

The Scoring Approach

The holistic scoring methods developed for the course evolved from examples presented by White (1985) but differ from his in order to meet the pedagogical objectives of General Psychology. The course instructor intended the writing component of the course to foster content mastery and to support the development of students' writing skills, whereas White was concerned only with the assessment of writing skill. New holistic scoring categories were developed to allow each writing sample to be given two scores, one for content and another for quality of expression. This distinction between content and writing skill tells the students that the ability to write well is important, and it provides them with direct feedback about the quality of their written work. The relative magnitude of the content and writing-skill scores was determined by the instructor's sense of their relative pedagogical importance for the course. Content was weighted 80%, and writing skill was weighted 20%.

Another difference between our approach and White's (1985) was to represent each holistic category by a range of numeric values for grading purposes. The specific numerical values associated with each category were determined by the instructor based on experience with the course and grading preferences. The TA assigned a score from the range to indicate the quality of the student's work within the category.

The course generated two different types of written work: (a) responses to short-answer essay-test questions and (b) short papers. Scoring criteria were developed for each.

Essay Test Scoring

Weekly tests consisted of eight multiple-choice and two essay questions. Ten essay questions were distributed in advance on a weekly study guide; two of the questions were selected for the weekly test. Students also received handouts describing the grading system and suggesting ways of doing well on the tests. Students were encouraged to prepare for the test by writing and revising trial answers to the 10 questions. A typical answer was 80 words. Madigan and Brosamer (1990) described the testing system in more detail. Table 1 presents the scoring system for these essay-test answers. The essays were graded by giving up to 20 points for the content of the answer and up to 5 points for writing skill. The grader read the student's work and assigned points for content and writing skill according to the categories given in Table 1.

Short-Paper Scoring

Students could also earn course points by writing optional homework assignments. Only the most commonly selected option is discussed here: two 500- to 1,000-word papers describing the application of psychological principles to the student's life. These two papers were structured around Holland's (1985) manual, which suggests self-improvement exercises based on psychological principles in such areas as study skills, progressive relaxation, and relating to children. The two short papers described the students' experiences with these projects. Table 2 shows the scoring system for the papers. Each paper was given up to 60 points for its content and 15 points for writing skill.

The TA was discouraged from writing comments on the papers. Evidence supporting the efficacy of instructor comments to improve student writing comes from studies in which students revised earlier drafts based on instructor feedback (Willingham, 1990; Ziv, 1984). This was not the

Table 1. Grading Criteria for Essay Test Questions

Content Score[a]	Criteria
0–5	The answer is largely irrelevant to the question or shows major conceptual confusions.
6–13	The answer does not address significant portions of the question or contains significant factual errors.
14–19	The answer responds appropriately to all parts of the question but does not include sufficient depth, or it includes irrelevant material, or it contains minor factual errors.
20	The answer addresses the question completely. It is concise and may contain original observations or examples. There is no irrelevant material.

Writing-Skill Score[b]	Criteria
0	The answer is clearly inappropriate to the question.
1	The answer is so lacking in coherence and unity that it is very difficult to follow, or the answer is so brief that it says almost nothing.
2	The answer does not develop in a manner appropriate to the question; in addition, the material is not presented in a unified, coherent paragraph.
3	Either the answer does not develop in a manner appropriate to the question or the answer is a poorly constructed paragraph.
4	The answer is a unified, coherent paragraph that addresses the question appropriately. It adequately develops and expresses the writer's thoughts.
5	The answer is a well developed, unified, and coherent paragraph that skillfully addresses the question. The writing is more than adequate; it is good.

[a]Ideas, supporting facts, and reasoning. [b]Organizing and expressing idea.

Table 2. Grading Criteria for Short-Paper Assignments

Content Score	Criteria[a]
0–44	The paper does not come to terms with the assignment. Content areas are ignored or misconstrued, or there are major errors in the interpretation of psychological principles central to the assignment.
45–49	The paper ignores several content areas or shows a misunderstanding of the principles involved.
50–54	The paper ignores more than one content area of the assignment but shows the writer's ability to appreciate key ideas and principles.
55–59	The paper slights or ignores one of the content areas of the assignment. The writer demonstrates a clear understanding of the assignment and the psychological principles involved.
60	The paper deals fully with all content areas specified for the assignment and shows a clear understanding of the underlying psychological principles.

Writing-Skill Score	Criteria
1–8	There is little development of ideas or no clear progression from one part of the assignment to another. There may be serious, frequent errors in sentence structure, usage, and mechanics.
9–11	The paper is organized enough to allow the reader to move through it, but there may be disjointedness or lack of focus in some sections. The paper may contain errors in mechanics, usage, and sentence structure.
12–14	The paper is not as carefully organized or reasoned as the full credit paper, but it is organized into unified, coherent sections and is largely free from serious errors in mechanics, usage, and sentence structure.
15	The paper shows careful organization and orderly thinking. The transitions between content areas are smooth; the paper may organize the content areas creatively to improve the readability of the paper; and the author may make thoughtful comments. It is virtually free from errors in mechanics, usage, and sentence structure.

[a]Content requirements included an appropriate introduction, descriptions of the chosen exercise and the psychological principles

case here. Furthermore, handwritten comments are exceedingly time-consuming. Students did receive a model answer when their tests were handed back, and they were encouraged to discuss tests and papers with the TA.

Scoring Reliability

Method

Reliability was assessed by comparing the grades assigned by a first-year graduate student and an undergraduate psychology senior, inexperienced as a TA. The graduate student had served as the TA for the course during two semesters. The TA spent about 4 hr training the psychology senior in the scoring methods. Two essay-test answers written in a previous class were available for 30 students. The answers were typed on separate sheets of paper and scored by the two assistants using the criteria in Table 1.

To assess the reliability of Table 2's scoring criteria for short papers, a set of 23 papers graded during the semester by the TA were also graded by the psychology senior. All papers were typed.

Results

The reliabilities for content scores given to essay-test answers were .91 and .95 for the two questions analyzed. The writing-skill scores for these questions had reliabilities of .61 and .75. The short-paper scores yielded a content reliability of .68 and a writing-skill reliability of .71.

Scoring Validity

Method

The validity analysis focused on whether the writing-skill scores given by the TAs were consistent with judgments of writing skill made by better trained evaluators of written work. Two experienced instructors of freshman composition read the same essay-test answers and short papers that had been previously scored by the TAs. The English instructors worked independently of each other and judged the essays separately from the papers. They were told to assign each writing sample to one of five categories based on its quality. *Writing quality* was defined as a "subjective term" that "generally refers to a writer's ability to express thoughts in a clear, organized, and interesting manner." No other constraint was placed on their judgments except that they assign at least one essay to each of the five quality categories. They were unfamiliar with the grading systems presented in Tables 1 and 2. Data from the English instructors were analyzed to determine interscorer reliability, and then their judgments were pooled to arrive at a mean writing-quality judgment for each writing sample. These values were correlated with the pooled writing-quality scores assigned by the TAs. This analysis assessed the agreement between the writing-quality judgments of the TAs and those of experienced composition instructors.

Results

When the English instructors sorted the same writing samples into five writing-quality levels, their interscorer reliability was .68 for the test essays and .65 for the short papers. The average of the TAs' writing-skill scores were correlated with the corresponding judgments of the English instructors and yielded .73 for the essay answers and .48 for the short papers.

Scoring Efficiency

Method and Results

The third area of interest was the efficiency of the scoring system. Time required to score each essay-test answer was recorded over a semester. Scoring times were also obtained for a sample of 26 of the short papers.

The typical answer was 79.9 words. The average time required to score it was 58 s. The median short-paper length was 741 words; short papers required an average of 4 min, 5 s to grade. These grading times do not include activities such as totaling points and recording scores.

General Discussion

The scoring systems presented here have acceptable interscorer reliabilities. As a point of reference, the reliability of the system developed for writing samples collected in the California State University English Equivalency Examination is estimated to be about .78 (White, 1985). That system has been carefully refined and is administered by experienced, trained judges.

The writing-skill judgments of the essay-test answers made by psychology TAs had impressive validity. We conclude that the psychology TAs are able to use holistic scoring criteria to make writing-skill judgments about paragraph-length test answers that are comparable to the judgments of professional raters who are better trained and more experienced.

However, the agreement between the TAs and the teachers of freshman composition was not as high for the short papers. We attribute this to the more complex nature of the short-paper assignments. The criteria used by the TAs to judge writing skill were made deliberately simple, and it may be that the English instructors took more factors into account when they judged writing quality. They had been instructed to judge writing quality based on the extent to which the writers' thoughts were expressed in clear, organized, and interesting ways. They may have understood this to imply aspects of diction and style not captured by the writing-skill categories in Table 2.

The use of somewhat different criteria to judge the short papers may explain why there was high reliability between the two psychologists and between the two English instructors, yet only moderate agreement across the two disciplines. The holistic scoring system of Table 2 focuses primarily on the organization of the short papers. We do not know if the criteria could be successfully expanded to include other important features of writing without compromising reliability. We suspect it would be difficult. Although the validity coefficient was not as high as we had hoped, judgments of the TAs were in substantial agreement with those of sophisticated professionals in English. Students received reliable and useful information about at least one major dimension of their writing.

The data show that grading efficiency, the third major concern of the project, is satisfactory. The total amount of time spent grading about 4,000 words written by a typical student in our introductory course is about 38 min (30 min to score 30 essay-test answers and 8 min for two 750-word short papers).

Our holistic grading approach appears to have reasonable reliability, validity, and cost efficiency. It has functioned well for 3 years, serving almost 600 students under three different TAs. Student feedback about the course has been solicited each semester, and not one complaint has been directed at the philosophy or mechanics of the grading system. Perhaps the strongest testimony supporting the practicality of the grading system is the fact that it continues to be in place and that each student in the course continues to write about 4,000 words during the term. Because the grading burden is shifted to a TA, the instructor serves as a supervisor, consultant, and quality-control monitor. The possibility that the demands of grading will lead the instructor to eliminate written work from the course is, therefore, reduced. Competent, committed TAs are essential, but they have not been difficult to find.

References

Boyer, E. L. (1987). *College: The undergraduate experience in America*. New York: Harper & Row.

Emig, J. (1977). Writing as a mode of learning. *College Composition and Communication, 28*, 122–128.

Frederiksen, N. (1984). The real test bias. *American Psychologist, 39*, 193–202.

Fulwiler, T. (1982). Writing: An act of cognition. In C. W. Griffin (Ed.), *Teaching writing in all disciplines* (pp. 15–26). San Francisco: Jossey-Bass.

Griffin, C. W. (Ed.). (1982). *Teaching writing in all disciplines*. San Francisco: Jossey-Bass.

Holland, M. K. (1985). *Using psychology* (3rd ed.). Boston: Little, Brown.

Madigan, R., & Brosamer, J. (1990). Improving the writing skills of students in introductory psychology. *Teaching of Psychology, 17*, 27–30.

Maimon, E. P. (1982). Writing across the curriculum: Past, present, and future. In C. W. Griffin (Ed.), *Teaching writing in all disciplines* (pp. 67–74). San Francisco: Jossey-Bass.

McLeod, S. H. (Ed.). (1988). *Strengthening programs for writing across the curriculum*. San Francisco: Jossey-Bass.

Nodine, B. F. (Ed.). (1990). Psychologists teach writing [Special issue]. *Teaching of Psychology, 17*(4).

White, E. M. (1985). *Teaching and assessing writing*. San Francisco: Jossey-Bass.

White, E. M. (1989). *Developing successful writing programs*. San Francisco: Jossey-Bass.

Willingham, D. B. (1990). Effective feedback on written assignments. *Teaching of Psychology, 17*, 10–13.

Ziv, N. D. (1984). The effect of teacher comments on the writing of four college freshmen. In R. Beach & L. S. Birdwell (Eds.), *New directions in composition research* (pp. 362–380). New York: Guilford.

Notes

1. A portion of this article was presented at the annual meeting of the American Psychological Association, Atlanta, GA, August 1988.
2. We thank Gloria Collins, Lynette Derrickson, Donna Kleppin, and Tamra Matlock for their help with the study and Jodi Madigan and Susan Johnson for helpful comments on an earlier draft of this article.

Rating Class Participation: The Prof/Peer Method

Kenneth B. Melvin

As faculty, we typically grade a variety of student performances. Some evaluations are easily made: Even a computer can grade a multiple-choice test. But essay exams, student presentations, and term papers are less objective. Among the most subjective criteria is class participation. Indeed, some faculty members recommend that it be avoided (e.g., Carter, 1977). Yet, in seminar classes, class participation plays a crucial role and warrants evaluation.

For the past few years, I have used a method of rating class participation that combines professor ratings with peer (student) ratings. Peer evaluations offer certain advantages. For example, high interobserver reliability coefficients have been found in a number of peer-evaluation studies (e.g., Kaess, Witryol, & Nolan, 1961; Kane & Lawler, 1978). Furthermore, peer evaluations have shown considerable validity (Hollander, 1965; Kane & Lawler, 1978).

Despite these valuable attributes, peer evaluations are not widely used (Landy, 1985). Possible reasons for this neglect include: (a) lack of exposure to rated behaviors, (b) leniency effects, and (c) lack of acceptance by ratees. The prof/peer method addresses these problems.

First, as Kane and Lawler (1978) noted, peers must have exposure to each other's relevant behaviors. For example, one of the problems with faculty peer evaluations is the typical brief exposure to the ratee's teaching (Cederblom & Lounsbury, 1980). For those using the prof/peer method, the classroom experience provides the necessary exposure.

Another valuable facet of this method is the use of the forced-distribution approach, which eliminates leniency errors. Like Kane and Lawler (1978), Love (1981) noted the superiority of peer ranking over peer rating (due to leniency errors in ratings). The forced distribution is more similar to ranking than rating. Also, the forced distribution is easier to do than ranking, especially in large classes. One can also adjust the categories within the forced distribution—those used here reflect my perception and value of class participation in these specific courses.

Finally, peer evaluations often are not well accepted by the ratees (Landy, 1985; Love, 1981). With the prof/peer procedure, the peer ratings serve as a backup to the professor's ratings, thus alleviating the acceptance problem. A description of the prof/peer method and an analysis of its effectiveness are presented here.

Method

Students in seven classes (N = 144) were rated on class participation. There were four sections of Psychology of Motivation; these sections were scheduled during a 3-week interim term, met for 3.5 hr per day, and were taught in seminar fashion. The other courses were: a seminar on Motivation in Industry, a seminar on Theories of Motivation, and Industrial Psychology. Class participation counted as 10% to 50% of the total course grade.

At the beginning of the course, students were told that the quality and quantity of class participation would be rated, but they were not informed of the peer rating system. Some students covertly participate in that they engage in all class activities except discussion. Thus, I stated that the lowest participant's grade would be a C– unless the student was excessively absent.

I kept an informal record of students' class contributions throughout the term. On the next to last day, the students were asked to rate their peers as a supplement to my ratings. I drew the seminar table on the blackboard and wrote in each student's name in the appropriate place. Any absent students were identified by their usual location and physical description.

To reduce the effects of leniency errors, a forced distribution was used. All students placed all other students (but not themselves) in three categories of class participation—high, medium, or low. Students were instructed to place an approximately equal number of students within each category, but not to rank ratees within a category. A median peer rating was computed for each student on a 3-point scale ranging from *low* (1) to *high* (3). To determine the class participation grade, each student received my grade and the median peer rating of class participation (these peer rating scores also were translated into letter grades, e.g., 2.8 would be an A). If the peer rating was at least one letter grade higher than mine, the two grades were averaged. If the peer rating was lower than mine, only my grade counted. In a typical class, only two or three final participation grades are adjusted upward by the peer ratings.

To check for consistency between faculty and student ratings, my letter grades were changed to ranks and correlations were computed with the ranks of median peer ratings. Other standard evaluation forms were given to rate the teacher, course, and grading procedures.

Results

Given the platykurtic nature of the distributions, Spearman's rho was used for correlational analyses. The results indicate a high degree of consistency between class participation grades given by the professor and median peer ratings (see Table 1).

Standardized brief teacher/course evaluation forms are routinely given each semester. On a 5-point scale, teacher/course mean student evaluations ranged from 4.0 to 4.9 (see Table 1). Two Psychology of Motivation sections received a different form with the statement, "The procedure for grading was fair." The mean ratings by students were 4.1 and 4.4. Obviously, these evaluations reflect more than how class participation was graded, but any marked dissatisfaction should have been reflected in lower ratings than these. With the three most recent classes, a more specific evaluation of the class participation rating was conducted. The statement, "This method of grading was fair to the student,"

Table 1. Student Evaluations and Correlations Between Professor and Peer Ratings of Class Participation

Year	Course	N	% Weight	Student Evaluations			Rho
				Teacher	Course	Grading	
1983	Psychology of Motivation	15	50	—	—	—	.83*
1985	Psychology of Motivation	27	50	4.7	4.6	4.1	.85*
1986	Psychology of Motivation	27	33	4.8	4.6	4.4	.90*
1986	Motivation in Industry	17	10	4.1	4.0	—	.90*
1987	Industrial Psychology	17	10	4.7	4.4	4.5	.84*
1987	Psychology of Motivation	23	33	4.9	4.7	4.4	.89*
1987	Theories of Motivation	18	20	—	—	—	.90*

*p < .01.

was rated on a 5-point scale ranging from *strongly disagree* (1) to *strongly agree* (5). The mean rating for class participation was 4.03. Only 4 of 56 students (7.6%) rated the prof/peer method of grading class participation a 2 (unfair) and no student selected alternative 1.

Sometimes the most meaningful result is the simplest—I believe this to be true in this case. Of 144 students enrolled in the seven courses, not one has complained or argued about the assigned grade for class participation.

Discussion

The peer ratings correlated highly with the professor's class participation grades. If one considers the professor an observer (or participant observer), these correlations would be evidence of high interobserver reliability. If one considers the professor's rating as analogous to a supervisor's rating, these correlations can be considered evidence of concurrent validity. A possible limitation on the generality of these findings might be that only one professor was involved. However, the consistency of the correlations across seven classes, some of which varied widely on a number of dimensions, argues for the generality of these results.

Another variable to be considered is class size. These classes ranged from 15 to 27 students. With more than 27 to 30 students, class participation is difficult to rate. Whether or not the technique will be valuable with very small classes (e.g., 10 students or fewer) is an open question.

Introducing a class participation grade, in my opinion, structures the reinforcement contingencies and thus inspires participation. The prof/peer method appears to make the evaluation of participation acceptable to students. In this case, course and teacher evaluations by students were all respectable and the prof/peer method was deemed as fair.

As Love (1981), Cederblom and Lounsbury (1980), and others pointed out, one problem with peer evaluations is a lack of ratee acceptance. My use of the peer ratings as a backup rating seems to increase acceptance. I note that the

professor should carefully explain the procedure. In an early class, I skimmed over the technique: Several students complained, "I don't want to be rated by other students," until the method was explained in more detail.

In summary, I believe the prof/peer method is an acceptable and fair way of evaluating class participation. It is efficient and takes about 20 min of class time and 1 hr or so of simple statistics. Finally, if a student complains about the participation grade, we have a new option. Instead of pontificating about our professorial expertise, we can simply support our grade with the peer evaluation.

References

Carter, K. R. (1977). Student criterion grading: An attempt to reduce some common grading problems. *Teaching of Psychology, 4,* 59–62.

Cederblom, D., & Lounsbury, J. W. (1980). An investigation of user acceptance of peer evaluations. *Personnel Psychology, 33,* 564–580.

Hollander, E. P. (1965). Validity of peer nominations in predicting a distant performance criterion. *Journal of Applied Psychology, 49,* 434–438.

Kaess, W. A., Witryol, S. L., & Nolan, R. E. (1961). Reliability, sex differences, and validity in the leaderless group discussion technique. *Journal of Applied Psychology, 45,* 345–350.

Kane, J. S., & Lawler, E. E. (1978). Methods of peer assessment. *Psychological Bulletin, 85,* 555–586.

Landy, F. J. (1985). *Psychology of work behavior* (3rd ed.). Homewood, IL: Dorsey.

Love, K. B. (1981). Comparison of peer assessment methods: Reliability, validity, friendship bias and user reaction. *Journal of Applied Psychology, 66,* 451–457.

Note

I thank Brenda D. Hinkle for her able technical assistance.

Study Strategy Portfolio: A Project to Enhance Study Skills and Time Management

Gabriele B. Sweidel

Students often visit during office hours complaining that they studied for hours but failed the test. Many factors may account for students' unsatisfactory test scores: poorly constructed tests, insufficient motivation, low aptitude, personal reasons, problems with time management, or poor study skills. I suspect that poor study skills and time management are leading factors. I teach a unit on the application of

the cognitive approach to learning in the classroom that deals with metacognition, memory strategies, reading comprehension, and study techniques. Students have great difficulty with this information and often tell me that they use the same study strategy for all tests regardless of the nature of the course; they never heard of mnemonics, they do not preview, review, or make questions for readings; they do not use the headings in a book; and they read textbooks in the same way that they read books for pleasure. This information indicates that many students need help learning how to study. Angelo and Cross (1993) stressed that students "need to learn how to assess their own learning. If they are to become self-directed, lifelong learners, they also need instruction and practice in self-assessment" (p. 9).

To address this problem, I devised a project called a *study strategy portfolio* (SSP). The SSP is intended to help students (a) outline and commit to a study plan—although not as formal as a contract, a written commitment may encourage students to follow the plan (Griffin & Watson, 1978); (b) begin to examine their study strategies and techniques; (c) relate their study plan to their test outcome; (d) make changes as necessary to facilitate their performance; and (e) use self-reflection to assess their performance during the semester.

The project was introduced in two Educational Psychology classes. The 87 student participants were primarily education majors or postbaccalaureate students. The portfolio consists of students' replies to surveys administered throughout the term, assessing their study plans, journal entries for each test, and an end-of-semester reflective essay. My goal is to expose students to information that can help them study; through critical analysis and self-reflection they decide which method works best for them.

Procedure

To facilitate their understanding of study strategies, at the beginning of the semester, students receive a copy of an article by Derry (1990) outlining tactics for learning verbal information and procedural knowledge and for developing "mental support tactics" (p. 117). Information from the article is reviewed at the beginning of the semester, and the cognitive approach to learning is presented approximately halfway through the semester.

Before beginning the project, I encourage students to be honest in their replies to the survey and in writing in their journals. Students complete two short-answer surveys and two journal entries for each test. The surveys and journal entries are structured to encourage self-monitoring and self-reflection concerning studying. The first survey is designed to help students commit to a study plan; it is completed 1 week before the first test. Students write out their study plans (e.g., where, when, and how they plan to study and specific strategies they plan to use). In addition, they respond to the following questions: (a) How do you know when you have studied enough?, (b) How do you monitor your studying?, (c) What will you do to maintain your motivation?, (d) Explain how you go about reading the chapter(s), and (e) How many hours or days do you plan to study? The night before the test, students complete a journal entry reflecting on their study plan. Specifically, they address (a) if they followed the original plan or made modifications, (b) emotional preparedness, (c) actual hours studied, (d) if they expect to make changes for the next test, and (e) their expected grade. After finishing the test, students complete another survey concerning their perceptions about the test, their anxiety level, their anticipated grade,

and their study plan. The two surveys and the journal entry are handed in with the test. The SSP is reviewed and graded and individual feedback is supplied for each student. My comments might suggest switching strategies or place of study, or I might ask a student to think about what he or she does to check reading comprehension.

The last journal entry is completed after students review their graded test. Students comment on their satisfaction with the grade, study plan, successful tactics, and possible modifications for future tests. This journal entry is collected with the surveys for the next test. Students receive a single letter grade for the two surveys and two journal entries for each test. The same procedure is used for all four tests; thus there are two surveys and two journal entries (one grade) for each test. The survey questions and journal entries all deal with cognitive strategies, affect, and self-reflection, but they do so at different times to help students examine the process of studying.

After reviewing students' responses for the first test, I realized that some students did not use a plan and had difficulty answering some questions, particularly those requiring metacognition. For example, the question, "How do you know when you have studied enough?" was answered as "I just know." I expected the journal entry to include self-reflection, critical analysis of study strategies as related to the test score, and comments indicating that students are thinking about the process. Between Test 1 and Test 2, I ask students with good SSPs if I could use their portfolios as examples, and I distribute copies to everyone at the next class session to illustrate what was expected.

At the end of the semester, students type a three- to five-page reflective essay. Students discuss their study plans and strategies, modifications made, satisfaction with their performance, and any benefits derived from scrutinizing their study habits. The folder with all the journal entries and survey questions is handed in with the reflective essay to provide the instructor with a comprehensive review of each student. The students' final grade is the average of the grade for the reflective essay and the four grades for the SSP for each test. I look for correct identification of the strategies used, a discussion of the pros and cons, and indications of why and how these strategies work for them. Students are expected to address the relation between their grades and their study techniques in their critical essay. The SSP accounts for 20% of the final grade.

Student Evaluations

After the portfolios and reflective essays are collected and graded, students are asked to voluntarily complete an anonymous questionnaire. The questionnaire is intended to provide me with feedback for future use of this project.

Combining the two classes, 76 (87% response rate) students completed the questionnaire. As displayed in Table 1, student response was overwhelmingly favorable. Not only did students enjoy the project, but most believed they had a greater self-awareness concerning their studying, and many changed their study habits and developed new techniques. One student wrote, "My grades improved, which was the supporting factor that helped me to realize that my revised

Table 1. End-of-Semester Study Portfolio Survey

Question	Yes	No	Somewhat
1. Did you enjoy the project?	44[a]	6	50
2. Was the project helpful?	80	5	15
3. Did you make any changes in your studying?	86	11	—
4. Have you applied anything that you have learned while keeping the study portfolio in your other classes?	67	33	—
5. Was it difficult to complete the project?	83	17	—
6. Do you think you are now a better "study-er" because of this project?	82	18	—
7. Would you recommend that I use the project again?	82	18	—

Note. n = 76.
[a]Responses reported in percentages.

study techniques were working. I was more structured and organized in budgeting time and material to be covered."

In response to the question, "Did you make any changes in your studying?," students answering "yes" were asked to check which of the following changes they made: (a) changed strategies based on review of my study plan (52% indicated they made this change), (b) developed new strategies never used before (38%), (c) budgeted time better (58%), (d) followed a plan for the first time (32%), (e) set goals (40%), and (f) increased studying efficiency (54%). One student wrote, "All of these choices sound like what has occurred. I also noticed that I liked to study and learn, which never happened before."

Key to the application of new strategies is generalization to other classes. One student responded, "In some of my other classes, since I've implemented my new study techniques, I've noticed some gains in scores on my tests plus I retain much more of what I've studied."

Discussion

This project has many benefits. It forces students to examine their study skills as a process and to look for relations between the process and the outcome. It can help students (a) develop time management skills, (b) learn new strategies, (c) examine the difference between strategies intended for long-term and short-term storage, and (d) evaluate their plans. For many students, responding to the survey questions, "How do you know when you have studied enough or comprehended the material?," it stimulates metacognitive awareness.

There are also benefits for teachers using this project. The SSP facilitates the teaching of material on the cognitive approach to learning. Because students are examining their cognitive strategies, the instructor can use a discussion format rather than a lecture format. Using student-generated examples of their study plans, a critical analysis of strategies and the structure of memory is easily accomplished with students as active participants and not just note takers. The feedback that the SSP provides to teachers about students' study strategies is also valuable. This information may point to areas needing class discussion. Furthermore, it is an opportunity to provide feedback specific to a student's individual needs, sometimes fostering a bond not readily created in larger class sections.

Many students were critical of the time necessary to fill out the surveys and journal entries. Each survey or journal entry can take up to 30 min to complete. Students perceive this as time they could be studying. I view this as an opportunity to discuss time management. Students should be advised at the beginning of the semester that this project deals with time management and that completing the forms is one of the learning aspects of this project. Sharing this information in the beginning of the semester and discussing the pros and cons of the project throughout the semester may also help students cope with the time factor.

A drawback to this project is the large block of time necessary to read and respond to student portfolios for each test. Some portfolios are read in 5 min; others can take up to 15 min if you suggest changes in their study plan. It is not enough just to grade the portfolios. Students need feedback about their study plans, particularly for the first two tests. However, helping students become more efficient and effective learners is a powerful reward for the teacher. For students in Educational Psychology, the SSP may serve a dual purpose; someday they can share their knowledge of study techniques, goals, and plans with their students.

References

Angelo, T. A., & Cross, K. P. (1993). *Classroom assessment techniques: A handbook for college teachers* (2nd ed.). San Francisco: Jossey-Bass.

Derry, S. J. (1990). Putting learning strategies to work. In D. Hamachek (Ed.), *Educational psychology reader: Toward the improvement of schooling* (pp. 113–120). New York: Macmillan.

Griffin, D. E., & Watson, D. L. (1978). A written, personal commitment from the student encourages better course work. *Teaching of Psychology, 5*, 155.

Note

Portions of this article were presented at the American Psychological Society's Institute on the Teaching of Psychology, June 1995, New York.

Student Expectations of Course and Instructor

Angela H. Becker
Stephen F. Davis
Loretta Neal
Cathy A. Grover

On the first day of each semester, students and faculty meet in the classroom with one common goal—the acquisition of knowledge—at least this is the perception that most faculty members appear to take with them to the first class meeting. Unfortunately, we do not know if students share this view. A reasonable amount is known about the plethora of student misconceptions of psychology (see Brown, 1983; Gutman, 1979; Lamal, 1979; McKeachie, 1960; Vaughan, 1977), but very little is known about student expectations.

Although the exact nature of these expectations remains elusive, there appear to be two general types: One type concerns students' expectations of their performance in, and benefits from, the course (i.e., personal expectations); the second concerns expectations associated with the instructor. Our study was designed to provide some data about these expectations. We developed two questionnaires: The first assessed precourse expectations; the second evaluated how those expectations had been met at the end of the course.

Method

Questionnaires

Precourse expectations. The Precourse Questionnaire consisted of nine questions. The first seven dealt with such topics as age, gender, number of semesters in college, major, and so on. Question 8 asked the students to "Describe (in as much detail as you care to) six expectations/goals you have for yourself as a student in this course"; Question 9 asked them to "Describe (in as much detail as you care to) six expectations you have of your instructor."

Postcourse expectations. The Postcourse Questionnaire was designed to determine how well the course met students' expectations. It consisted of a series of questions each having "yes" (this goal was accomplished), "no" (this goal was not accomplished), or "not one of my expectations" as response alternatives. The items were chosen to reflect the most frequent responses to the Precourse Questionnaire. One set of 16 items covered the goals students had listed for themselves, and the second set of 20 items covered the goals they had listed for the instructor.

Subjects and Procedure

Both questionnaires were administered to 393 first-semester freshmen (283 women, 110 men) enrolled in 10 sections of Introduction to Psychology at Emporia State University.[1] The same investigator administered the questionnaires to all classes. The Precourse Questionnaire was completed during the second class meeting; the Postcourse Questionnaire was completed during the last class meeting before the final exam.

Results

Precourse Expectations

Demographic data from the Precourse Questionnaire indicated that ages ranged from 17 to 53 years (M = 19.36) for the women and from 18 to 30 (M = 18.88) for the men. However, most of the students (83% of the women, 87% of the men) were 18 or 19 years old. The two most frequently cited reasons for taking the course were "required for the major" or "to satisfy a general education requirement."

Responses to Questions 8 and 9 dealing with the personal and instructor expectations, respectively, were subjected to descriptive and inferential analyses. A 2 × 2 unweighted means, split-plot analysis of variance (ANOVA) was performed to evaluate the influence of Gender (female vs. male) and Type of Expectation (personal vs. instructor) on the number of expectations listed on the Precourse Questionnaire. Results yielded significance only for the Type of Expectation, $F(1, 391) = 30.42$, $p < .001$. Although the students generated more personal (M = 4.25) than instructor (M = 3.60) expectations, in both cases they fell far short of the 6 that were requested.

Visual inspection of the precourse data indicated natural clusters or categories of responses for personal (16 categories) and instructor (20 categories) expectations. Subsequently, the individual responses were independently assigned, by gender and type of expectation, to one of these categories by two of the investigators. A high level of agreement (r = .93) was recorded for these judgments. For women

---

[1]In a second study, the questionnaires were administered to 168 sophomore and junior students enrolled in Developmental Psychology or Applied Psychology. Because the results of this investigation did not differ substantially from those of this study, these data have not been incorporated herein. The replicability of these data, however, is noteworthy.

and men, the five most frequently listed personal and instructor expectations appear in Table 1 and Table 2.

Postcourse Expectations

One hundred seventy-nine women and 75 men completed the Postcourse Expectations Questionnaire. The decrease in number of respondents from precourse ($n = 393$) to postcourse ($n = 254$) reflects the operation of two factors—students who dropped the course and students who did not attend the final class period. Due to inconclusive data, neither factor appears most important.

The number of responses in each category was calculated for each subject. These data were subjected to a split-plot ANOVA incorporating Gender (female vs. male) as a between-subjects factor, and Type of Expectation (personal vs. instructor) and Type of Response (yes—expectation was met, no—expectation was not met, or not an expectation) as within-subjects factors. This analysis yielded significance for Gender, $F(1, 252) = 4.52$, $p < .05$; Type of Expectation, $F(1, 252) = 8.98$, $p < .01$; Type of Response, $F(2, 504) = 762.51$, $p < .001$; and Type of Expectation × Type of Response, $F(2, 504) = 119.68$, $p < .001$. Newman–Keuls tests evaluated the significant response type main effect and indicated that there were significantly more ($p <$

Table 1. Five Most Frequently Listed Precourse Personal Expectations for Women and Men

	Expectation (%)
Women[a]	
Get a good grade/pass the class	12.3[b]
Learn and understand	9.2
Learn more about psychology	9.1
Learn more about human behavior/emotions	9.0
Develop good study habits, stay awake	8.8
Men[c]	
Get a good grade/pass the class	12.8
Learn more about psychology	9.9
Learn and understand	9.2
Develop good study habits, stay awake	8.8
Earn an A/B	7.6

[a]$n = 1,884$ responses. [b]Number of responses in category divided by the total number of responses made by the appropriate sample. [c]$n = 964$ responses.

Table 2. Five Most Frequently Listed Precourse Expectations of the Instructor for Women and Men

	Expectation (%)
Women[a]	
Make the material understandable	17.0[b]
Be patient, openminded, fair	14.0
Make class interesting, fun, exciting	11.0
Give extra help	9.6
Be able to talk at students' level	5.1
Men[c]	
Make the material understandable	12.9
Be patient, openminded, fair	12.6
Make class interesting, fun, exciting	9.2
Give extra help	8.8
Be able to talk at students' level	6.5

[a]$n = 1,660$ responses. [b]Number of responses in category divided by total number of responses made by the appropriate sample. [c]$n = 859$ responses.

Table 3. Five Most Frequently Met Postcourse Personal Expectations for Women and Men

	Expectation (%)
Women[a]	
Come to class on time/regularly	91.0[b]
Learn more about human behavior/emotions	85.0
Learn how to deal with certain people	81.5
Enjoy class/have fun	80.0
Get to know myself better	79.0
Men[c]	
Learn more about human behavior/emotions	82.0
Enjoy class/have fun	81.0
Develop good study habits/stay awake	73.5
Come to class on time/regularly	72.0
Learn how to deal with certain people	71.0

[a]$n = 179$. [b]Percentage of subjects in the respective group who felt the particular expectation had been met. [c]$n = 75$.

Table 4. Five Most Frequently Met Postcourse Instructor Expectations for Women and Men

	Expectation (%)
Women[a]	
Be pleasant, cheerful, friendly	87.5[b]
Know the material well	86.0
Get along well with students	85.0
Care about students	84.0
Allow students to express their opinions	80.0
Men[c]	
Be patient, openminded, fair	81.5
Be pleasant, cheerful, friendly	76.0
Relate class to everyday, current events	75.0
Get along well with students	74.0
Know the material well	72.5

[a]$n = 179$. [b]Percentage of subjects in the respective group who felt the particular expectation had been met. [c]$n = 75$.

.01) yes (M personal = 9.48, M instructor = 13.58) than no (M personal = 1.70, M instructor = 1.54) or not (M personal = 4.47, M instructor = 1.22) responses.

Relevant to this project was the significant Type of Expectation × Type of Response interaction. Simple main effects analyses comparing the number of personal responses versus the number of instructor responses within each type of response category probed this effect. These analyses indicated that there were significantly more yes responses, $F(1, 504) = 7.32$, $p < .01$, for the instructor than for the personal questions. Conversely, significantly more not responses, $F(1, 504) = 4.08$, $p < .05$, were made for the personal questions than for the instructor. The distribution of no responses did not differ reliably between the instructor and personal questions, $F(1, 504) = 1.17$, $p < .25$.

For women and men, the five most frequently met personal and instructor expectation categories are included in Table 3 and Table 4.

Discussion

The questionnaires clearly tapped the goals that students have for themselves and the instructor in this course. Students found it easier, however, to list precourse personal expectations, as opposed to expectations for the instructor.

A comparison of precourse expectations with postcourse expectations is informative. Although students typically did not list 6 expectations at the beginning of the semester, they agreed to having had nearly 10 such expectations met by the end of the course. Clearly, the students' expectations were not formulated sufficiently enough at the beginning of the semester to allow their written expression. Possibly the impact of the just-completed course or simply having to indicate agreement or disagreement with items listed on the Postcourse Questionnaire resulted in the dramatic increase in the number of satisfied personal expectations. The same trend was observed in students' expectations of the instructor.

Concerning the content of the personal expectations at the beginning of the semester, both women and men expressed concern about: (a) the grade they hoped to achieve, (b) learning in general and learning about psychology in particular, and (c) study habits and staying awake in class. All these areas reflect realistic, if not commendable, expectations. By the end of the semester, achievement of a certain grade had slipped from the top 5 expectations that were met. In its place, we find satisfaction for the more interpersonal aspects of the course. The increase in such concerns could represent a recency effect, because the sections on social, abnormal, and therapy were presented toward the end of the course. Of those items that were ranked among the top 5 on the Precourse Questionnaire but not on the Postcourse Questionnaire, most were ranked in the top 10 on the Postcourse Questionnaire. The priority placed on interpersonal aspects in the postcourse surveys is consistent with data reported by Zanich and Grover (1989), who found that psychology majors and nonmajors reported more interest in topics of an interpersonal nature than in hard science aspects of the introductory course.

Students' expectations of the instructor at the beginning of the semester primarily concerned an enjoyable class and sensitivity to student needs. By the end of the course, however, students had added another dimension. They expected the instructor to know the material being taught. Also, they seemed to place less emphasis on the need to make the class fun and exciting.

Concerning these student expectations, the question becomes: "What does this information mean to us as teachers?" Several suggestions are worth considering. First, students' initial concern with grades might be partially alleviated by receiving clear, direct information concerning grading policies and the specific calculation of grades for the class in question. Similarly, students' persistent expectation of developing good study habits might be enhanced in the introductory course by devoting a lecture period to this topic during the first week of class. Many students will insist that they already know how to study, but many more will probably thank you for your efforts after they take the first test.

In discussing the project with colleagues, someone inevitably points out that among the students' precourse expectations are several suggestions for specific topics they deem important. The same colleagues greet these suggestions with such statements as "I do not intend to change the content of my course to please the students' whims." This, of course, is up to the individual instructor. It is perhaps more important than meeting every personal and course expectation to use the type of survey presented here to provoke students' reflection of their own loosely defined expectations. This information can then be used to introduce a discussion about the goals and content of your course. In other words, use information from a survey, such as the one described here, to improve your own performance and that of your students.

References

Brown, L. T. (1983). Some more misconceptions about psychology among introductory psychology students. *Teaching of Psychology*, *10*, 207–210.

Gutman, A. (1979). Misconceptions of psychology and performance in the introductory course. *Teaching of Psychology*, *6*, 159–161.

Lamal, P. A. (1979). College students' common beliefs about psychology. *Teaching of Psychology*, *6*, 155–158.

McKeachie, W. J. (1960). Changes in scores on the Northwestern Misconceptions Test in six elementary psychology courses. *Journal of Educational Psychology*, *51*, 240–244.

Vaughan, E. D. (1977). Misconceptions about psychology among introductory psychology students. *Teaching of Psychology*, *4*, 138–141.

Zanich, M. L., & Grover, D. E. (1989). Introductory psychology from the standpoint of the consumer. *Teaching of Psychology*, *16*, 72–74.

Note

Portions of this article were presented at the 1988 meeting of the American Psychological Association, Atlanta, GA.

The Semantic Profile Technique for Measuring Students' Impressions of Psychology Courses

William B. Davidson
William J. House
O. Joseph Harm

Many universities use standardized student ratings to gauge and improve their faculty's teaching performance. Such ratings typically focus heavily on characteristics of the instructor rather than on specific course content. In making course refinements, however, students' reactions to specific aspects of a course can be helpful. The method described herein is an adaptation of the semantic differential technique (Osgood, Suci, & Tannenbaum, 1957) that measures the meanings that people attach to certain target words. A semantic profile has several bipolar dimensions (e.g., simple–complex) that describe people's impressions of a particular entity; for a course evaluation, the entity is a psychological term. The semantic differential technique has been widely applied to a variety of measurement situations (e.g., Snider & Osgood, 1969), but it has rarely been used in course evaluations, and then only to compare different courses (Hoste, 1981).

We use the semantic differential technique to measure students' reactions to psychological terms in their course. The semantic profiles generated for each term provide a basis for comparing students' impressions of different parts of the course and for gauging the reactions of particular groups of students. The technique can be easily adapted to fit other courses and instructors.

We describe how to use the technique and analyze the results. Also, we report relations between the semantic ratings and several individual difference variables that reflect students' achievement or level of interest. These relations tested the criterion-related validity of the ratings and show how we used the feedback to change our course.

We expected four individual difference variables to affect semantic ratings: (a) mastery of course material; (b) psychological mindedness, which is the capacity to be empathic; (c) achievement via independence, which is the drive to do well in settings that encourage initiative and independence of thought; and (d) learning-oriented academic style, which is the tendency to place greater value on the acquisition of knowledge for personal enrichment than on the acquisition of grades in school (Eison & Pollio, 1986). We predicted that students with high scores on each of these variables would rate the psychological terms toward the positive pole of the semantic dimensions.

Method

Materials

Using a 5-point scale, students rated six or seven key terms in their introductory psychology course on 12 semantic dimensions (see Table 1 for a list). Semantic dimensions appeared in the same order for each psychological term, and the positive poles were counterbalanced for dimensions with a clear positive or negative connotation. All students rated six terms that varied in inclusiveness: *psychology* (broad); *emotion, memory,* and *personality* (chapter level); and *reinforcement* and *unconscious* (within-chapter level). Some students rated a seventh, broad term: *science.* We chose the more inclusive terms to gauge reactions to the course as a whole or to compare ratings of different chapter topics. We chose the two specific (within-chapter) terms because they are often misunderstood by students, and we wanted feedback about them. We used just enough terms to sample the different levels of inclusiveness but not exhaust them. Therefore, we could test the utility of a relatively longer list of semantic dimensions without risking erosion in students' concentration.

The individual difference variables were measured with the 28-item Psychological-Mindedness scale and the

36-item Achievement-via-Independence scale of the California Psychological Inventory (CPI; Gough, 1987) and with the 32-item *LOGO* II Scale of learning-oriented versus grade-oriented academic style (Eison & Pollio, 1989). Two sections took the CPI scales on the first day of class; two other sections took the *LOGO* II.

Procedure

Two instructors collected semantic ratings on the last day of class in six sections of introductory psychology (average *n* = 35) over 3 years. The exercise took about 15 min.

Results and Discussion

To ascertain whether the course produced a desired impact on students, we constructed a semantic profile of each term's 12 mean ratings. Table 1 illustrates the mean dimension scores for two terms. To gauge the students' impression of a term, we typically compare the dimension mean scores with those of another term (presented with *t* values) or with the means for all terms (presented with *z* values). Note that the ratings for *emotion* and *reinforcement* differed on several dimensions. We typically find differences, indicating that the terms elicit different impressions and that the ratings are not unduly influenced by a response set. Interpretations of the profile for each term will vary depending on an instruc-

Table 1. Mean Semantic Scores for Two Psychological Terms

| | Psychological Term | | | | |
| | Emotion | | Reinforcement | | |
Semantic Dimension	M (SD)	z^a	M (SD)	z^a	t^b
Unfamiliar–familiar	4.38 (0.77)	1.05	3.78 (0.99)	−0.02	5.42*
Cold–warm	3.70 (0.88)	0.81	3.15 (1.02)	−0.33	4.64*
Simple–complex	4.02 (1.14)	0.37	3.18 (1.15)	−0.92	5.89*
Sad–happy	3.37 (0.74)	0.08	3.28 (0.98)	−0.10	<1
Easy–hard	3.28 (1.12)	0.08	3.04 (1.19)	−0.29	1.67
Dull–interesting	4.08 (0.80)	0.19	3.53 (1.04)	−0.69	4.71*
Useless–useful	4.20 (0.93)	0.13	4.15 (0.95)	−0.04	<1
Unpleasant–pleasant	3.43 (0.84)	−0.02	3.23 (1.10)	−0.38	1.64
Concrete–abstract	3.32 (1.06)	0.32	2.43 (1.07)	−0.97	6.68*
Dislike–like	3.77 (0.83)	0.15	3.45 (1.05)	−0.46	2.70*
Irrelevant–relevant	3.98 (0.92)	−0.02	3.91 (1.00)	−0.11	<1
Inhumane–humane	4.05 (0.83)	0.38	3.44 (1.04)	−0.62	5.17*

Note. N = 128.
[a]Compares term mean with grand mean for semantic dimension.
[b]Compares means for two terms.
*p < .01.

Table 2. Regression Relations Between Semantic Ratings and the Individual Difference Variables

Semantic Dimension	Standardized Regression Coefficient for Individual Differences[a]				
	Grade	PY	AI	LO	GO
Unfamiliar–familiar	.12**	−.14	−.02	.13**	−.07
Cold–warm	.02	.20**	−.27**	.06	.10*
Simple–complex	.05	−.15*	.20**	.17**	.01
Sad–happy	−.04	.04	−.16*	.09	.14**
Easy–hard	−.05	.05	−.04	.04	−.13**
Dull–interesting	.27**	.31**	−.44**	.44**	.06
Useless–useful	.25**	.14*	−.10	.17**	.08
Unpleasant–pleasant	.01	.27**	−.35**	.08	.01
Concrete–abstract	.19**	−.30**	.23**	−.02	.06
Dislike–like	.17**	.10	−.32**	.23**	.02
Irrelevant–relevant	.25**	−.10	.32**	.19**	.02
Inhumane–humane	.07	−.04	−.10	.13**	.04

Note. PY = psychological mindedness; AI = achievement-via-independence; LO = learning orientation; GO = grade orientation.
[a]Positive coefficient indicates that a high score on the individual difference varialbe is associated with positive pole of semantic dimension.
*p < .05. **p < .01.

tor's goals. Our students often confuse negative reinforcement with punishment, so their rating *reinforcement* as less complex than other terms suggested that we had been successful in communicating about it. One semester we found a disturbing tendency for students to rate *psychology* in the direction of *inhumane*. They made these ratings immediately after a discussion of the highly manipulative, social-influence experiments of Milgram and Asch. We suspected that the reaction to this topic had generalized. In later semesters, we emphasized the debriefing procedure and cost-benefit analysis of scientific inquiry, and the semantic ratings shifted toward *humane*.

To test the responsiveness of the ratings to four individual differences, we performed multiple regression analyses. In separate equations for each semantic dimension, we regressed the ratings, collapsed across all psychological terms, against the individual difference scores. We operationalized "mastery of course material" as the students' course grade and entered it first into each regression, partly to control for any overlapping variance with the other individual differences. We analyzed the two personality variables in regressions separate from those for academic style because they had different samples of students.

Table 2 presents standardized regression coefficients associated with the individual differences. Positive coefficients indicate that students who scored high on the individual difference variable tended to rate concepts toward the positive end of the semantic dimensions. As predicted, the semantic ratings were quite responsive to all four individual difference variables. Usually the direction of the relations was expected and confirmed our course goals. For example, students with high grades or an achievement orientation rated the course terms as more relevant, and students who were psychological minded or learning oriented rated the terms as more interesting. However, the direction of certain relations was surprising. Achievement-oriented students, who as a group performed well in the course, apparently did not like the process. They rated the terms as more cold, dull, unpleasant, and disliked, which prompted us to make some refinements in the course. We suspected that the course was too structured for their taste, so we added some assignments that rewarded initiative and self-directed search. Overall,

the responsiveness of ratings to individual differences validates the semantic technique.

To adapt the technique to fit different courses or instructors, select psychological terms and semantic dimensions for which feedback is desired. To assure that students remain attentive, we recommend using fewer semantic dimensions—perhaps four to six—if many psychological terms are rated. Although the selection of dimensions and terms is individualistic, we find feedback especially helpful from the semantic perspectives of mastery (e.g., unfamiliar–familiar), difficulty (e.g., easy–hard), attitude (e.g., dull–interesting), and applicability (e.g., useless–useful). Also, we recommend using broad terms to draw global inferences about a course and using specific terms that are hard to grasp, difficult to present, or have several meanings (e.g., unconscious). The semantic technique can be administered at the end of a course or intermittently during a course to measure students' reactions to many psychological terms in a particular section or chapter. The semantic information can be helpful in making decisions about how to improve a course and also in verifying that a desired impact has been achieved.

References

Eison, J., & Pollio, H. (1986). A multidimensional approach to the definition of college students' learning styles. *Journal of College Student Personnel, 27*, 434–443.

Eison, J., & Pollio, H. (1989). *LOGO II bibliographic and statistical update*. Cape Girardeau: Southeast Missouri State University, Center for Teaching and Learning.

Gough, H. (1987). *California Psychological Inventory administrator's guide*. Palo Alto, CA: Consulting Psychologists Press.

Hoste, R. (1981). Course appraisal using semantic differential scales. *Educational Studies, 7*, 151–163.

Osgood, C., Suci, G., & Tannenbaum, P. (1957). *The measurement of meaning*. Urbana: University of Illinois Press.

Snider, J., & Osgood, C. (1969). *Semantic differential technique: A sourcebook*. Chicago: Aldine.

Note

Part of this research was presented at the annual meeting of the American Psychological Society, San Diego, June 1992.

Motivation in the College Classroom: What Students Tell Us

Edmund J. Sass

The topic of motivation is a broad and complex one that deals with the arousal, selection, direction, and persistence of all types of behavior (Biehler & Snowman, 1982). Although motivation is an abstract concept, psychologists assume that it is at least partially responsible for individual differences in the initiation and persistence of goal-directed behavior.

Because of the complex nature of motivation, I use an activity with my Educational Psychology students that encourages them to think critically about what makes their classes more or less "motivating." The original purpose of this activity was to make the concept of classroom motivation as concrete and relevant as possible, but it also provides insights into those aspects of a class that students associate with high or low motivation.

The activity is straightforward. Students are asked to analyze two recent class periods, one in which they were highly motivated and one in which their motivation was very low. They identify specific aspects of each class that influenced their level of motivation and also determine which types of classes typically result in very high and very low motivation for them.

Individual perspectives are then shared with other students in small groups, and each group is asked to reach consensus on a list of characteristics that contribute to high and low motivation. A group reporter shares these characteristics with the class. I write their views on the board and develop a composite list, combining similar characteristics into more general categories.

Since 1981, I have used this activity in 22 class sections enrolling more than 700 students and have kept the composite list produced in each section. Although there is some variation from class to class, each list of characteristics associated with high motivation almost always includes the same eight characteristics or categories. These categories, as well as explanations and examples drawn from my notes of student comments, are provided here. They are listed in order of importance as determined by the rankings of 61 students from my fall 1988 class. In these rankings, enthusiasm and relevance were virtually tied for first. Organization was a relatively close third, with the others scoring considerably lower.

1. *Enthusiasm.* Teachers in these classes have high energy levels, and their interest in and enjoyment of the subject matter are obvious. As the students often put it, "How can teachers expect us to be interested in a topic if they don't seem interested in it."

2. *Relevance* (relatedness). Course material is seen as relevant, applicable, and important by the students. They can relate it to their experiences and career goals. Teachers often make this relevance explicit to students through explanation and examples.

3. *Organization* (well-planned, prepared). Teachers of these classes do not "wing it." Their classes are organized, and their preparation is obvious. To put it in the students' words, "We can see that they've done their homework, which makes us feel more of a responsibility to do ours."

4. *Appropriate Difficulty Level.* Most students see the class as challenging but "doable." The instructor's expectations are not so simple as to "insult their intelligence," yet most students perceive the material to be understandable and the tests to be fair and "passable."

5. *Active Involvement.* Students are actively engaged in classroom learning, which may involve group discussion or other hands-on activities. In a lecture class, students may be actively involved through frequent questioning by the instructor.

6. *Variety.* The same instructional techniques are not used in every class. Monotony is avoided by using a variety of strategies such as lecture, discussion, media, or discovery learning.

7. *Rapport.* The teachers are perceived as approachable and friendly. They appear interested in the students and their learning. They talk to students before and after class, know at least some of their names, and create a comfortable classroom climate.

8. *Use of Appropriate Examples.* Course material is made real, concrete, and understandable through the use of appropriate examples and related anecdotes. This quality is particularly crucial in a lecture class.

Not surprisingly, the characteristics of classes viewed as nonmotivating are essentially the opposite of those just described. Characteristics on this list typically include: lack of variety (generally all lecture), disorganization, little or no active involvement, and a perceived lack of enthusiasm and interpersonal warmth on the part of the instructor.

Although there has not been much empirical research on motivation in the college classroom, my findings are essentially consistent with previously published work. For example, Clegg (cited in Cashin, 1979) reported that areas of course evaluations that correlate most highly with college student motivation are typically related to teacher enthusiasm, expressiveness, and organization. Cashin (1979) offered a number of suggestions for improving motivation, including the use of a variety of teaching techniques, establishing relevance, using learning tasks at the appropriate level of difficulty, and improving student–teacher relationships. Lowman (1984) stated that student motivation toward work outside the classroom is increased when the teacher is enthusiastic and the course material is seen as relevant. Others emphasized the importance of classroom climate (Gleason, 1986; Hanna & McGill, 1985) and getting students actively involved as ways of increasing their intrinsic motivation (Watson & Stockert, 1987).

Though my list of student perceptions of the types of classes likely to result in high motivation is no panacea, I believe that incorporating at least some of these characteristics into one's classes will help to increase student motivation. As my findings demonstrate, motivation is not determined exclusively by achievement motivation (i.e., the desire to make a "good grade"), course content, class hour, or other variables over which faculty have little control. Rather, what we do as teachers has a major impact on students' willingness to make initial and persistent efforts in our classes.

References

Biehler, R. F., & Snowman, J. (1982). *Psychology applied to teaching* (4th ed.). Boston: Houghton Mifflin.

Cashin, W. E. (1979, August). *IDEA paper no. 1: Motivating students*. (Available from the Center for Faculty Evaluation and Development, Kansas State University, Manhattan, KS 66502)

Gleason, M. (1986). Better communication in large courses. *College Teaching, 34*, 20–24.

Hanna, S. J., & McGill, L. T. (1985). A nurturing environment and effective teaching. *College Teaching, 33*, 177–180.

Lowman, J. (1984). *Mastering the art of teaching*. San Francisco: Jossey-Bass.

Watson, D. L., & Stockert, N. A. (1987). Ensuring teaching and learning effectiveness. *Thought and Action, 3*(2), 91–104.

Introductory Psychology From the Standpoint of the Consumer

Mary Lou Zanich
David E. Grover

More than 50 years ago, Ruch (1937) stated that college teachers and textbook writers of elementary psychology "are obliged to analyze the 'market' and to create a product which meets a human need" (p. vi). Ruch surveyed students who had completed their first course in psychology to determine their interest in various topics traditional to psychology at the time. Ruch found that students were primarily interested in understanding themselves (e.g., personality and character) and in the application of psychology to practical problems (e.g., how to study and the training of children). In a more recent attempt to use student reactions in determining course content, Brown (1980) found student interest high in the areas of learning and memory, emotion, drugs and their effects, and mental health.

We surveyed entry-level psychology majors and nonmajors before and after they took the introductory course. Our specific purposes were to: (a) determine if students' interests have changed since Ruch's (1937) survey, (b) determine if taking the introductory course has short-term effects on students' interests, (c) determine if the interests of entry-level psychology majors are different from those of nonmajors, and (d) examine the implications of students' interests for course structure and emphasis.

Method

Subjects

Subjects were students enrolled in four sections of General Psychology at Indiana University of Pennsylvania. Three of the sections were designed for nonpsychology ma-

jors (pretest $n = 132$, posttest $n = 129$), and one was designed for psychology majors (pretest $n = 44$, posttest $n = 36$). Posttest sample size was reduced by student course withdrawals; in addition, the data from six psychology majors were excluded from the posttest because they failed to complete the second page of the survey. Student participation was in partial satisfaction of a course requirement for research involvement.

Survey Instrument and Procedure

An 80-item interest survey was generated by selecting topics from each of the "Chapter Objectives" listed in the instructor's resource manual (Bolt, 1986) accompanying the text used in the course (Myers, 1986). Four to 6 items were selected to represent the general coverage of each chapter; 10 items duplicated the 10 most interesting topics from the Ruch (1937) survey. Students were told that each item was a topic that might be included in a general psychology course and were asked to indicate their personal interest in each topic using a 5-point scale ranging from *not very interesting* (1) to *very interesting* (5). The survey was administered the first and last day of class in the fall semester of 1987.

Results

Students indicated a reasonably high interest in all topics (M = 3.60), which did not change from pre- to posttest. The highest level of interest was in topics dealing with states of consciousness, memory, personality (especially psychopathology), and gender/interpersonal issues (M = 4.10). The topics of least interest were physiological processes, sensory processes, language processes, and the history and structure of modern psychology (M = 2.90). Patterns of interest were consistent from pre- to posttest with an increase of interest in psychopathology being the only noticeable change, r (78) = .95, p < .01. (Accordingly, all data presented are posttest data; see Table 1.) When topics from within a textbook chapter are combined, the same pattern emerges (see Table 2); again, students show less interest in the hard science areas of psychology (e.g., sensation) than in areas more closely related to individual student needs (e.g., gender and memory).

Table 1. Mean Ratings for Specific Topics of Most and Least Interest

Rank[a]	Topic	Mean Rating
1	Possible function of dreams	4.36
2	Why people are attracted to each other	4.25
3	Hypnosis	4.23
4	How to improve your memory	4.20
5	Sexual motivation/variations in sexual behavior	4.10
6	How to study effectively	4.08
7	Types of psychological disorders	4.08
8	Why do people develop mental disorders	4.05
9	What causes forgetting	4.00
10	Improving your personality	3.99
71	Subfields of modern psychology	3.12[b]
	Concepts and their formation	3.12[b]
72	Relationship between thought and language	3.10
73	Structure of language	3.01
74	How the visual system works	2.97
75	Theories of language development	2.88
76	How the auditory system works	2.84
77	Learning of nonsense syllables	2.84
78	Historical roots of modern psychology	2.80
79	Theories of color vision	2.78
80	Endocrine system	2.74

[a]Rank of topic on the 80-item survey. [b]Topics receiving the same mean rating were assigned the same rank.

Table 2. Mean Interest Ratings of Textbook Chapter Content

Rank[a]	Chapter Content	Psychology Majors	Other Majors
1	States of consciousness	4.29	4.04
2	Memory	4.02	3.97
3	Abnormal/therapy	4.15	3.88
4	Gender	3.72	3.74
5	Motivation	3.88	3.69
6	Personality	3.91	3.67
7	Development	3.87	3.65
8	Social behavior	3.79	3.61
9	Emotion	3.62	3.49
10	Perception	3.49	3.36
11	Learning	3.52	3.25
12	Physiology	3.27	3.26
13	Study of psychology	3.48	3.14
14	Thought/language	3.45	3.09
15	Sensation	2.98	3.06

[a]Rank based on combined weighted ratings of psychology and other majors.

Table 3. 1987 Rank of Most Interesting Topics on Ruch's 1937 Survey

1937 Rank	Topic	1987 Rank Psychology Majors	1987 Rank Other Majors
1	Understanding your personality problems	22	10
2	Improving your personality	7	12
3	Human motives	31	32
4	Psychology applied to the training of children	63	58
5	Techniques for solving everyday problems	11	41
6	The problem of heredity versus environment	54	54
7	Development of character	20	13
8	Psychological factors in crime and delinquency	10	27
9	Why do people develop mental disorders	5	8
10	How to study effectively	16	5

Patterns of responding were not significantly different for psychology majors and nonmajors either before or after the course: Both rs (78) > .87; both ps < .01. Psychology majors showed consistently higher levels of interest overall (M = 3.75) than did nonmajors (M = 3.50), except for the topic of sensory systems.

Finally, the results of this survey were compared to those from Ruch's (1937) survey. Four of Ruch's 10 most interesting topics were perceived by majors, nonmajors, or both as being among the 10 most interesting topics on our survey (see Table 3). These common topics dealt with personality, psychological disorders, and the practical applications of psychology. With two exceptions, the remainder of Ruch's 10 topics ranked in the top half of our survey.

Discussion

Our data indicate that students' interests center around their most immediate needs: to do well as students (memory), to relate to other people (gender and interpersonal relationships), to understand themselves (personality), and, in a more abstract way, to understand the variety of their own experiences (states of consciousness). In addition, interest is high in the area of psychopathology, representing the common public perception of psychology as being clinically oriented. It is not surprising that students show the least interest in the more traditional, "hard-core" scientific areas of psychology; this is not, after all, what psychology is perceived to be. Also, the discussion of these topic areas (thought, language, sensation, perception, and physiology) involves the description of processes that are often automatic. Therefore, explanations of these processes may be deemed unnecessary (i.e., the processes "just happen" and can thus be "taken for granted").

These preferences are consistent with the general findings of Ruch's (1937) and Brown's (1980) surveys, although the specific content that is of high and low interest is expressed by different topics. These differences reflect more of a change in the nature of psychology than a change in the nature of students (e.g., we know and talk more today about states of consciousness and sexual behavior). In essence, our consumers—both past and present—want to know what people do and why they do it.

Our results also indicate that entering psychology majors do not choose psychology as their field of study because of prior substantial interest in specific topics within the field (i.e., psychology majors' response patterns match those of nonmajors). However, psychology majors do show a slightly higher overall interest in the full range of topics that constitute psychology. For both groups, patterns of interest are highly resistant to change. Being exposed to an introductory course does not significantly alter incoming predilections. What was or was not interesting before taking the course remains so afterward.

Finally, Lenthall and Andrews (1983) suggested that the organization of an effective introductory course take into account entry-level students' cognitive skills, motivation, and interests. A course organized around the interests measured here and with some consideration for logical sequencing would present course material in approximately the reverse order of the traditional sequencing of topics in most introductory textbooks.

References

Bolt, M. (1986). *Instructor's resource manual to accompany Psychology David G. Myers*. New York: Worth.

Brown, L. T. (1980). What the consumer thinks is important in the introductory psychology course. *Teaching of Psychology, 7,* 215–218.

Lenthall, G., & Andrews, D. (1983). Psychological seduction: Effective organization of the introductory course. *Teaching of Psychology, 10,* 137–139.

Myers, D. G. (1986). *Psychology*. New York: Worth.

Ruch, F. (1937). *Psychology and life*. New York: Scott, Foresman.

The Create-A-Game Exam: A Method to Facilitate Student Interest and Learning

Joy L. Berrenberg
Ann Prosser

Multiple-choice exams, short-answer exams, essay exams, oral exams, term papers, and class projects are traditional methods for assessing a student's mastery of course material. Although all such evaluations should engage the student in the process of reviewing and synthesizing the course material, many students, even the brightest, apply the "least effort principle" in their preparations. Often their review is cursory and involves rote memorization rather than organized analysis.

It is generally assumed that students learn and retain more when they are actively and personally involved with the course material. Although a number of class projects facilitate this type of involvement (e.g., Brožek & Schneider, 1973; Coffield, 1973; Gurman, Holliman, & Camperell, 1988; McAdam, 1987), relatively few examination procedures incorporate this active approach. One example of such an approach allows students to comment on or justify their answers on multiple-choice exams (Dodd & Leal, 1988; Nield & Wintre, 1986). This procedure encourages more thinking and less rote memorization. Another procedure involves innovative and integrative essay questions in a History of Psychology course (Berrenberg, 1990). Presumably, such questions force students to organize and synthesize the material. Benjamin (1979) described an exam "game" in which teams of students compete to identify portraits of famous figures in psychology. He suggested that the element of fun in this kind of exam helps to motivate students to learn more. Ackil (1986) and Carlson (1989) described two teacher-designed games that motivate students to learn factual material and prepare for exams. Note, however, that these last examples are not used to evaluate student performance.

To expand the options for active, personally involving evaluation procedures, we developed an examination technique in which students create a game for a particular subject area. The procedure is designed to engage students' creative talents and to encourage detailed review and synthesis of course material. Unlike assignments that require students to write their own exam questions, the create-a-game exam requires students to develop a structure (e.g., game categories) to present factual material. In many instances, it also requires students to make fine distinctions regarding the difficulty of the material (e.g., how many points to offer for a correct answer). Furthermore, the number of questions students prepare for a game usually exceeds the number requested for a write-your-own exam exercise (most students write 100 or more questions), thus requiring a more thorough review of course material. Finally, the create-a-game exam encourages students to think about and present material in creative and innovative ways that may improve understanding as well as retention.

Our approach can be readily adapted to any course in psychology and used to supplement or replace other evaluation methods. The resulting games may be played with fellow class members, thus providing additional review of course content. What follows is a description of the create-a-game technique developed in a History of Psychology course.

Procedures and Grading

We have used the create-a-game exam as part of a take-home exam in a senior level History of Psychology course. Students answer one or more integrative essay questions and develop a History of Psychology game. Working individually, students have 2 weeks to complete the exam and game. Instructions for the game portion of the exam are:

Create a "History of Psychology Game." It may be a board game, word game, trivia game, or whatever. It must cover a broad range of information pertinent to the history of psychology. Include rules, game board, game pieces, or whatever is needed to play the game. Have fun and be creative!

Your game will graded on the basis of (a) the accuracy of information, (b) the breadth of coverage (e.g., game covers a variety of historical time periods, events, theories, ideas, figures in the history of psychology), (c) your understanding of course material as evidenced in meaningful organization of game material (e.g., information is grouped into appropriate categories, such as Greek Philosophers, French Positivism, Neo-Behaviorists), (d) neatness of game materials (e.g., readable instructions, game cards), and (e) originality.

We do not provide examples of games because we do not want to limit creativity. Although we have used the procedure as an individual project, it should also work well as a group assignment.

Most students satisfy the criteria so the resulting distribution of exam scores is negatively skewed. The proportion of students who do a substandard job on the game is lower than it is for other assignments. We generally make the game portion of the exam worth 25% of the course grade, which seems appropriate for the amount of time and effort involved.

The completed games, or some sample thereof, can be effective teaching techniques. We have used one full class period before an objective exam to allow students to play the games of their choice as a way of providing painless review of material.

Examples of Games

The most common games include take-offs on Jeopardy, Trivial Pursuit, and Life. Four examples of games developed by students are described next.

1. *Psychological Trivia.* In this game, the players compete for points by correctly answering questions from one of several categories (e.g., functionalism, psychoanalysis, the mind–body problem). The easiest questions in a category are worth 100 points (e.g., Who was the founder of psychoanalysis?); the most difficult questions are worth 500 points (e.g., What is the title and publication date of Dewey's famous "founding" paper on functionalism?).

2. *Freud's Inner Circle.* The object of this game is to move Freudian tokens (e.g., small cigars, toilet seats) around a game board, answer questions correctly, and accumulate enough points to move to Freud's inner circle in the middle of the game board. Once in the circle, players must demonstrate their knowledge of Freud's position or risk getting "kicked out." Variations of this basic "board and dice" game have been called The Rat Maze, The Therapeutic Couch, The Funny Farm, and Psychomania.

3. *Psych-Out.* This game consists of a board with photographs of famous figures in the history of psychology. Upon landing on a square associated with a particular face, players must name the figure and as many of his or her contributions to psychology as possible. The more they know, the more points they earn.

4. *Psychogories.* This game is similar to Gin Rummy or Go Fish; the object is to be the first to accumulate complete sets of cards. Players are dealt 10 cards, each of which states a theory, belief, or assumption (e.g., reinforcement plays an important role in learning, higher mental processes cannot be studied experimentally). Cards are drawn and discarded until a player's hand is full of completed sets. A set consists of three or more theoretically compatible cards (e.g., all ideas held in common by behaviorists, gestaltists). Psychogories is a conceptually challenging game because the categories are not indicated on the cards and players must determine for themselves which ideas constitute sets.

Student Response

Students are generally enthusiastic about the create-a-game exam. This enthusiasm is demonstrated by the amount of time and effort they put into their creations: one student sculpted and fired ceramic game pieces, another hand-printed 200 question cards in beautiful calligraphy, another found and copied onto the game board old photographs of Wundt's lab and other psychological memorabilia. In a recent term, 63% of the students in a class of 65 found designing the game to be an "extremely useful" method for learning course material, and 77% said using the games for review was an "extremely useful" way to spend class time. Many students spontaneously mentioned the create-a-game procedure in the comment section of the course evaluation. One student said the procedure was a "refreshing change" from traditional exams. Another said designing the game helped him to "learn history inside-out." Others described the exam as "personally involving," "lots of fun," "a really worthwhile exercise," and "a painless way to learn."

In conclusion, the create-a-game technique is a method for evaluation that actively engages students in the review and organization of course material. It could easily be incorporated into a variety of courses.

References

Ackil, J. E. (1986). PhysioPursuit: A trivia-type game for the classroom. *Teaching of Psychology, 13,* 91.

Benjamin, L. T., Jr. (1979). Instructional strategies in the history of psychology. *Teaching of Psychology, 6,* 15–17.

Berrenberg, J. L. (1990). Integrative and goal-relevant essay questions for history and systems courses. *Teaching of Psychology, 17,* 113–115.

Brožek, J., & Schneider, L. S. (1973). Second summer institute on the history of psychology. *Journal of the History of the Behavioral Sciences, 9,* 91–101.

Carlson, J. F. (1989). Psychosexual pursuit: Enhancing learning of theoretical psychoanalytic constructs. *Teaching of Psychology, 16,* 82–84.

Coffield, K. E. (1973). Additional stimulation for students in history and systems. *American Psychologist, 28,* 624–625.

Dodd, D. K., & Leal, L. (1988). Answer justification: Removing the "trick" from multiple-choice questions. *Teaching of Psychology, 15,* 37–38.

Gurman, E. B., Holliman, W. B., & Camperell, K. (1988). Oral application questions as a teaching strategy. *Teaching of Psychology, 15,* 149–151.

McAdam, D. (1987). Bringing psychology to life. *Teaching of Psychology, 14,* 29–31.

Nield, A. F., & Wintre, M. G. (1986). Multiple-choice questions with an option to comment: Student attitudes and use. *Teaching of Psychology, 13,* 196–199.

Note

Portions of this article were presented at the annual meeting of the American Psychological Association, Boston, MA, August 1990.

A Method for Enhancing Student Interest in Large Introductory Classes

William Buskist
Devin Wylie

Although students generally prefer small classes over large classes (Gleason, 1986; McKeachie, 1994), many introductory college courses enroll large numbers of students. The problem is a familiar one: Smaller classes offer a more personalized atmosphere, whereas larger classes are more economical and offer an opportunity for a few extraordinary teachers to influence large numbers of students. Because college enrollment remains high and colleges and universities generally do not have enough faculty to teach small classes, large classes, especially at the introductory level, seem to be here to stay.

What faculty need in this situation is an effective way of recreating the small classroom atmosphere in large classrooms (Benjamin, 1991). According to Herr (1989), involved students usually learn material better than uninvolved students. Involving students in course activities in small classes is easier in part because of the instructor's familiarity with the students and relative logistical ease.

Student–teacher rapport also is essential to the learning environment (Herr, 1989). Classroom discussion allows students and the instructor to build two-way relationships and open channels for further communication. This relationship helps personalize the class for the students. Herr suggested that instructors may increase rapport in their classes by (a) holding personal conferences with students to increase communication and produce a more relaxed atmosphere in and out of the classroom, (b) showing interest in students by being alert to changes in their classroom behavior, (c) using relationships established from previous classes to show interest in students' background and progress, and (d) showing enthusiasm for the topic being taught.

If instructors know students' names, they can call on specific students to answer questions. According to Chism (1989) and Herr (1989), coming to class early and staying after class to answer specific questions or to chat with students are also good ways for instructors to get to know their students and to make them feel individually recognized.

According to Benjamin (1991), the most important variables involved in teaching large classes are the students' attitudes toward the topic, the students' attitudes toward the instructor, and the teaching method used. To improve teaching technique, an instructor may seek new interactive exercises to engage students in the learning process. One suggestion given by Benjamin is the use of an autobiographical questionnaire, which students complete early in the term. In Benjamin's words,

> I ask them to list their hometown, year in college, and major. I ask them why they are taking the course and what they hope to get out of it. . . . I ask them about their job (if they work) and about what they like to do when they are not being students. I also ask them if there is anything they would like to ask me or anything else they would like for me to know about them. (p. 69)

Incorporating the information gathered from this type of exercise into the class allows students to see how their responses compare to those of others in the class. These data are unique in that they apply specifically to the students in the class and may reveal interesting information about the students themselves.

Perhaps a more efficient means of involving students in the class is to ask more focused questions that address specific, relevant topics of high interest to students. The instructor may then incorporate students' answers throughout the term in contexts applicable to the presentation of corresponding psychological principles or theory. The remainder of this article describes such a method.

At the beginning of a recent term, 605 Auburn University students in three sections of an introductory psychology course responded in writing to the following question: "What one thing in your life, if you could change it today, would have the most immediate and profound positive impact in your life?" This question developed out of one-to-one conversations with students in previous sections of the course who were interested in the relevance of psychology to their lives. The intent of using the question in class is to motivate students to think about how the topics in the course might apply to them and how they might use course content for self-improvement.

Just prior to posing this question, we project a copy of the following instructions on a large screen and read them aloud to the class:

> In a few minutes, you will have the chance to participate in a class project worth one extra credit point toward your final grade in this course. Your participation is entirely voluntary. Right now we are passing out an "informed consent form," which explains what the project involves, how the information we collect about you may be used, and what your rights are as a participant in this project. In brief, this project involves your anonymous answer to a single question: "What one thing in your life, if you could change it today, would have the most immediate and profound positive impact in your life?" We are interested in your responses to this question because they help us to develop ways to make the class more interesting and relevant to what you may be experiencing in your lives. If, after reading this form, you decide you would like to participate, please sign on the appropriate line. If you do not wish to participate, please do not sign it. If you have any questions about this exercise or your participation in it, do not hesitate to ask them now.

Once all the forms are collected, we project a copy of the question on the screen along with instructions not to place any identifying information on their responses and to limit their responses to three to five words. We also read the question and the instructions aloud. Next, we give students 3 or 4 min to respond. We then collect the answers and later that same day categorize them according to problem or issue type, such as low self-esteem, financial concerns, emotional adjustment, and so on. (The categories often change from term to term and depend wholly on student responses; we do not use preestablished categories into which we attempt to force student responses.) During the next class period, we list students' responses in decreasing order of frequency and according to gender. This presentation has two effects. First, it allows students to become aware of the types of issues that their peers are confronting, many of which are similar to issues that they themselves are facing. Second, it demonstrates similarities and differences in how men and women respond to this question. For example, women generally stress religion and spiritual concerns more, and men usually stress issues related to grades more. Throughout the remainder of the term, we refer to students' responses to the question when discussing relevant concepts and issues (i.e., self-esteem, stress, attitude-behavior correspondence, and self-control).

An analysis of student responses this term to this question revealed, in decreasing order, that the most prevalent concerns among female students were exercising more and losing weight (19%), increasing self-esteem and outgoingness (19%), studying more and procrastinating less (14%), becoming more spiritual or religious (11%), and developing a more positive attitude about others and life (7%). Among men, the chief concerns were (in decreasing order) studying more and procrastinating less (23%), increasing self-esteem and outgoingness (21%), exercising more and losing weight (9%), developing a more positive attitude about others and life (5%), and becoming more spiritual or religious (5%). Many students are surprised that so many men reported they have self-esteem problems. We point out that this reaction is typical of the stereotypes many people hold about differences between men and women.

Personal issues and concerns, such as those expressed by students responding to the question that we posed to them, fit easily into classroom lectures and provide fertile ground for discussion. In addition to those topics alluded to earlier, we make explicit attempts to address many of these concerns. Following are several general examples:

1. Motivation (What psychological variables may prevent students from making important changes in their lives?)
2. Learning (What environmental variables may prevent students from accomplishing such changes and how might students control these variables to produce such changes?)
3. Development (To what extent does the ability to make such life changes reflect social and emotional maturity?)
4. Personality and intelligence (How is success in later life related to the changes students currently wish to make in their lives and how are these changes related to personality variables and intelligence?)
5. Stress and coping (How is failure to make such changes a source of stress and what are the best coping strategies to deal with such failure?)

In short, there is no shortage of ways in which we integrate students' responses to our question into class discussions about basic psychological principles and theory. In fact, we developed several of our course lectures (e.g., those covering self-control, stress and coping, and mental health and physical well-being) specifically from student responses to the question.

Fortunately, students rarely mention serious psychological problems in their responses. However, this exercise does seem to make some students feel comfortable in discussing their responses with us during office hours, which sometimes leads to discussion of more serious problems, such as extremely high anxiety, depression, or abuse. In such cases, we do two things. First, when a student begins to disclose information about a personal problem, such as alcohol or drug abuse, we immediately, but gently, tell him or her that it is beyond our roles as teachers to serve as counselors in such matters. Second, we refer the student to the appropriate counseling services on campus.

Because student responses to this question may change from term to term, the value of this exercise rests in the technique itself and not the particular data set it generates. Once we pose the question and present student responses to the class, students begin to feel more comfortable talking about everyday issues related to course content. For example, they often raise questions regarding strategies for intervention for certain problems and ask for written sources that they may consult. We, too, follow up our original question by asking related questions over the course of the term. Of course, our questions depend on specific issues that students identified in their responses to the original question. For example, we ask students to describe how the theories and methods of self-control described in the text might apply to those students who said that they would like to exert more control over their diet, exercise, or time-management regimens. The class then offers suggestions for developing a specific plan, based on course content, that these students might consider as an intervention. When necessary, we offer modifications and elaborations of students' suggestions to make them conform to empirically tested psychological principles and strategies.

Many teachers of introductory psychology believe that their course should show their students how psychology can be applied to important issues in their students' everyday lives. We have described a technique—involving one simple question—by which teachers may make direct contact with issues of concern to students, become sensitive to what is happening in their students' lives, demonstrate psychology's relevance in addressing these issues, and increase student interest in their course. Our students respond enthusiastically to this approach with other questions and comments and appreciate its insightful contributions to their personal development.

References

Benjamin, L. T., Jr. (1991). Personalization and active learning in the large introductory psychology class. *Teaching of Psychology, 18,* 68–74.

Chism, N. V. (1989). *Large enrollment classes: Necessary evil or not necessary evil?* (Rep. No. 20444–361). Columbus: Ohio State

University, Center for Teaching Excellence. (ERIC Document Reproduction Service No. ED 334 875)

Herr, K. U. (1989). *Improving teaching and learning in large classes: A practical manual* (revised). Fort Collins: Colorado State University, Office of the Instructional Services. (ERIC Document Reproduction Service No. ED 312 215)

Gleason, M. (1986). Better communication in large courses. *College Teaching, 34,* 20–24.

McKeachie, W. J. (1994). *Teaching tips: A guidebook for the beginning college teacher* (9th ed.). Lexington, MA: Heath

Notes

1. Portions of this article were presented by the first author at the 19th Annual National Institute on the Teaching of Psychology, St. Petersburg Beach, FL, January 1997.
2. The authors wish to thank Charles L. Brewer, Randolph A. Smith, and several anonymous reviewers for their helpful comments in revising earlier versions of this manuscript.

Motivating Students to Read Journal Articles

David M. Carkenord

Exposing students to the topics and content of current journal articles is a goal of many undergraduate psychology courses. As Suter and Frank (1986) noted, by reading journal articles, students can see the application of methodological concepts in actual research settings. in addition, reading published research can help develop critical reading and thinking skills (Anisfeld, 1987; Chamberlain & Burrough, 1985). Yet, motivating students to read the articles can be difficult. Chamberlain and Burrough (1985) speculated that students skim assigned articles rather than attend carefully. Thus, it is necessary to investigate strategies aimed at increasing the frequency with which students read journal articles.

Various authors attempted to increase the motivation of students to read published literature. Buche and Glover (1980) described an experimental study in which students who were given a minicourse (instructions and guidelines on reading journal articles) read articles at a significantly higher frequency than control subjects who received no instruction. Although these results are encouraging, the authors admitted that generalizations of their findings are limited. Chamberlain and Burroughs (1985) discussed a question-based technique in which students were instructed to answer specific questions pertaining to an assigned article. The authors did not, however, report any data concerning the frequency with which the articles were read. Suter and Frank (1986) described a similar question-based approach with classic journal articles but presented no data addressing the issue of frequency of reading.

It is important to ensure that students actually read assigned articles. This article describes a technique that motivates students to read and summarize articles.

The Present Technique

Selecting the Articles

The technique was used in an industrial psychology (I/O) course and a consumer psychology course (both 200-level courses). Article selection was based on four criteria suggested in part by Poe (1990), Price (1990), and Suter and Frank (1986): (a) high correspondence between the article topic, course content, and textbook material; (b) high correspondence between the technical level of the article and students' competence (e.g., lack of excessive or advanced statistical analyses); (c) high expected student interest; and (d) generally short length ($M = 5.4$ pages, $SD = 2.0$, range = 3 to 10 pages). A complete list of the readings for both classes is available from the author.

The Assignment

One article was assigned to be read each week, except for the weeks in which a test was scheduled. Students were informed that the class would discuss the article for 10 to 15 min on the due date and that material from the article would appear on the test. In general, students were given at least 1 week to locate and read the article. Students were requested to write a summary and critique of each article on an 8 × 5 in. index card, highlighting the major points and conclusions of the article and providing their critique and opinion of the reading. The front and back of one card was usually ample space for the summaries; only one student consistently used two notecards. At the conclusion of the class discussion of the article, students who submitted their card received 1 point extra credit (cumulatively worth approximately 4% of total course points). Although the extra credit was not contingent on the quality of the summary, most students wrote thorough and accurate summaries.

In addition to earning extra credit, students were allowed to use their notecards during the subsequent test. In general, two or three articles were covered per test. The notecards were returned just before test distribution to ensure that no lecture or textbook notes were written on the cards. Both multiple-choice and short-answer/essay test items were specifically taken from the articles and referred explicitly to them (e.g., "Based on the article by. . . ."). Inclusion of these test items encouraged students to read the articles carefully and provide accurate summaries. Because the articles had been previously discussed in class, I tried to write test questions based on information that had not come up during the discussion. My usual strategy was to touch on the articles' major points during the discussion and to write test items on more specific details from the article. In the most recent courses, test items based on the readings comprised an average of 18.2% of the test material.

Those students who did not submit a notecard on the due date were encouraged to read the articles before the test. However, these students were not allowed to complete a card for extra credit or to use the card during the test. No specific penalty was enacted if students chose not to do the readings (i.e., they would not directly lose course credit).

Assessment

Objective Assessment

To evaluate students' motivation to read the articles, the total percentage of notecards submitted (which estimates the readings completed) was calculated. On average, the 34 students in both classes (n = 21 in I/O and n = 13 in consumer) submitted a summary notecard for 73.7% of the readings throughout the semester. Twelve of the 34 students (35%) submitted a notecard for every reading; only 1 student submitted no notecards.

The extra credit improved final course grades for 11 of the 34 students (32.4%) by one letter grade. Three students (8.8%) could have improved their final grade if they had submitted cards on all the readings.

Table 1 displays the mean percentage of correct responses on the article-based test items for students who did and did not submit notecards. For 17 of the 22 articles assigned (across both classes), students using their notecards during the tests got a higher percentage of the test items correct than students without notecards.

Student Assessment

Student attitudes concerning the technique were surveyed anonymously at the end of the term. Four items were each rated on a 5-point scale ranging from *strongly disagree* (1) to *strongly agree* (5). Responses on these items indicated very favorable attitudes: "Receiving extra credit motivated me to read the articles" (M = 4.2, SD = 1.4); "The fact that I could use the notecards during the tests motivated me to read the articles" (M = 4.4, SD = 1.3); "Doing the additional readings increased my knowledge of the subject matter" (M = 4.0, SD = 1.0); and "Overall, reading the articles provides a good learning experience" (M = 4.2, SD = 0.9). Clearly, students recognized and responded favorably to the connection between reading the articles and the positive implications for their course grade—both on tests and for extra credit. Students also believed that reading the articles enhanced their learning.

The survey also asked students to report the percentage of articles they had read during the term. Thirty-one of the 34 students in the classes reported reading 50% or more of the

Table 1. Mean Percentage of Correct Responses on Article-Based Test Items as a Function of Card Submission

Article	Consumer		I/O	
	Card	No Card	Card	No Card
1	84	41	71	88
2	80	33	87	43
3	84	78	94	100
4	89	75	87	80
5	100	20	86	43
6	78	50	97	90
7	99	54	90	50
8	88	80	78	33
9	97	100	98	71
10	30	67	93	100
11	—	—	100	40
12	—	—	94	60
M	83	60	90	67

Note. An 11th article was assigned in the consumer course, but no test items were developed from it.

articles, although only 28 students submitted notecards on 50% or more of the articles. Eighteen of the 34 students reported reading 100% of the articles, whereas 12 students submitted notecards on all articles. These discrepancies are likely the result of students reading articles after the due date in preparation for the test. This would explain why the percentage of correct responses to article-based test items is relatively high even for some students who did not submit cards (see Table 1).

Finally, the survey contained an open-ended item soliciting additional opinions about the technique. Ten students wrote additional comments, which were generally positive, about the readings in general (e.g., "I think it does help me understand research" and "I've learned a lot from [the readings] and have actually enjoyed most of them!") and the extra credit opportunity in particular (e.g., "If any teacher gives me a chance for extra credit, I take it" and "Extra credit also gives a chance to reward people who go the extra mile").

Three students did, however, express concerns. One commuter student had difficulty scheduling adequate library time. Two students expressed the opinion that the articles should be mandatory because test items covered the readings. These two responses were intriguing, but I do not know what motivated them.

Discussion

The technique outlined herein was effective in motivating most students to read assigned journal articles, and students' attitudes toward the technique were very favorable. Beyond the primary benefit of getting students to read the articles, the technique has other benefits. First, with most students having read an article, class discussion of the material can be lively and productive. Students are willing to add to the discussion not only as a result of having read the article but also because they have a summary of the article (notecard) in their possession for easy reference in answering questions or adding comments. Furthermore, at the end of the course, students have a permanent file of information that may be of future use. I strongly encourage students to maintain their notecards for later reference, and many students tell me that they have made an effort to keep the cards.

Some instructors may take slight offense at the decidedly operant "carrot-and-stick" approach of the technique—motivating students to read articles with extra course credit rather than a primary emphasis on the importance of knowledge acquisition. Admittedly, research suggests that many instructors are uncomfortable with the entire concept of extra credit (Norcross, Horrocks, & Stevenson, 1989). Practical experience, however, indicates that most students do not read textbooks or journal articles as a result of their intrinsic interest and desire to learn. The present technique attempts to integrate the importance of learning with students' desires and expectations for tangible rewards. Awarding extra credit for reading a journal article may be more constructive than awarding extra credit for non-academic factors (i.e., attendance), and it is a form of extra credit that is equally available to all students. If an instructor holds negative views of extra credit, the approach may be modified so that students receive no extra credit but are allowed to use their notecards on tests. Such a modification may also prompt students to read the assigned articles.

This approach to motivating students has applications in any course that incorporates the reading of journal articles. Instructors are encouraged to use the technique and report their impressions of its value.

References

Anisfeld, M. (1987). A course to develop competence in critical reading of empirical research in psychology. *Teaching of Psychology, 14,* 224–227.

Buche, D. D., & Glover, J. A. (1980). Teaching students to review research as an aid for problem solving. *Teaching of Psychology, 7,* 206–209.

Chamberlain, K., & Burrough, S. (1985). Techniques for teaching critical reading. *Teaching of Psychology, 12,* 213–215.

Norcross, J. C., Horrocks, L. J., & Stevenson, J. F. (1989). Of barfights and gadflies: Attitudes and practices concerning extra credit in college courses. *Teaching of Psychology, 16,* 199–203.

Poe, R. E. (1990). A strategy for improving literature reviews in psychology courses. *Teaching of Psychology, 17,* 54–55.

Price, D. W. W. (1990). A model for reading and writing about primary sources: The case of introductory psychology. *Teaching of Psychology, 17,* 48–53.

Suter, W. N., & Frank, P. (1986). Using scholarly journals in undergraduate experimental methodology courses. *Teaching of Psychology, 13,* 219–221.

Note

I thank Ruth L. Ault and three anonymous reviewers for their helpful comments and suggestions on an earlier version of this article.

7. DISCUSSION EXERCISES AND GROUP ACTIVITIES

Consider the Opposite: Opening Minds Through In-Class Debates on Course-Related Controversies

Thomas Lee Budesheim
Arlene R. Lundquist

Students encounter complex and often controversial issues in psychology. As educators, we strive to give students a full appreciation of these complex issues so they may see the strengths and weaknesses of all sides. Moreover, we try to help students acquire the skills necessary to critically and objectively evaluate other complex and controversial issues on their own. The in-class debate is one potentially valuable tool that educators use to instruct students on controversial topics in psychology as well as to facilitate their development of analytic skills. Several articles have attested to numerous benefits that come from using in-class debates in teaching psychology (Bauer & Wachowiak, 1977; Berg, 1979; Elliot, 1993; Gorman, Law, & Lindegren, 1981; Moeller, 1985; Smith, 1990). In-class debates involve active and cooperative learning, stimulate critical thinking and student interest, facilitate discussion, and can improve oral communication skills. Nevertheless, it may be premature to conclude that all the educational effects of in-class debates are uniformly positive. There is reason to worry that, unless carefully structured, such debates may inadvertently serve to strengthen existing beliefs rather than promote objective analysis of an issue. In short, students who participate in and observe such debates may not be critically evaluating all sides of an issue.

We begin with three assumptions. The first assumption is that one of the many purposes of higher education is to expose students to ideas, information, and perspectives that would otherwise be absent from their experiences. Second, students should be objective when evaluating the relative merits of both sides of an issue. Hence, they must learn to critically evaluate their own existing beliefs. Finally, we assume that critical and objective analysis is a habit of thought not commonly formed in most students and therefore must be actively created and reinforced through structured intervention.

If left to their own devices, students may selectively process information in a manner that reinforces existing biases. Evidence suggesting this possibility comes from Lord, Ross, and Lepper (1979), who demonstrated that when partisans (i.e., individuals with definite preexisting attitudes) read mixed evidence regarding capital punishment (some evidence indicated it was an effective deterrent and some evidence indicated it was ineffective), the partisans emerged with more extreme rather than less extreme attitudes on the controversy. Lord et al. argued that these individuals engaged in a "biased assimilation" of the evidence. That is,

participants accepted quickly and easily any information that supported their existing beliefs but were skeptical and critical of any information contradicting their existing beliefs on the issue. As a result, those who favored a particular position became even more in favor of that position and those opposed to that position became even more opposed to that position. The danger implied by this research is that through the process of biased assimilation, students become experts on those things they wish to be true, amassing a mountain of "facts" consistent with their personal beliefs while discarding information inconsistent with their views. Their mental scales of judgment tilt overwhelmingly in favor of their own positions and they become convinced that they know something that may not be so (cf. Gilovich, 1991).

If in-class debates reinforce and polarize preexisting opinions, one need not abandon the debate tool and the many benefits it can offer. Rather, one can conduct the debate in such a way that it corrects the tendency toward biased assimilation. Lord, Lepper, and Preston (1984) demonstrated that a *consider-the-opposite strategy* was effective in correcting the biased assimilation process. Although exhortations to be fair and unbiased had little effect on how participants processed information, requiring participants to explain and defend an opposing position did reduce or eliminate the effects of biased assimilation. The educational implications of this research are simple: Instructors should require students to defend positions that are inconsistent with the students' existing opinions if instructors hope to broaden students' perspectives and achieve greater objective analysis of the issues.

Instructors who conduct in-class debates, however, commonly allow students to choose which side of an issue they would like to defend (e.g., Elliot, 1993; Gorman et al., 1981). Instructors who allow students to choose their positions may do so to promote students' sense of involvement and voice in the process and in hopes of encouraging interest and general satisfaction with the debate experience. An instructor also may worry that a student debater's performance is hindered when asked to defend a position contrary to his or her privately held opinion.

We examined the effects of in-class debates on students' attitudes toward the issues debated, their debate performances, and their subjective evaluations of the debate experience. We systematically assigned people to argue in favor of a position that was either consistent or inconsistent with their attitude on the issue. Based on the research by Lord et al. (1979) and Lord et al. (1984), we hypothesized that (a) students who argued a position consistent with their views would strengthen their existing attitude (a biased assimilation effect), (b) students who simply listened to the mixed evidence presented during the debate would also exhibit a biased assimilation effect and strengthen their existing attitudes, and (c) students who argued a position inconsistent with their views would show movement away from their preexisting attitudes toward a more neutral position, thus demonstrating a nonbiased assimilation of the information.

Method

Participants

Participants were students in three upper-level psychology courses: Cognitive Psychology ($n = 27$), Marriage and Family Issues ($n = 24$), and Multicultural Issues in Psychology ($n = 21$).

Materials

We conducted three debates each in the Multicultural Issues course and the Marriage and Family Issues course and four debates in the Cognitive Psychology course on various course-related controversies. The debates covered a variety of topics ranging from "Can subliminal messages influence our attitudes and behavior?" (a cognitive topic) to "Are intelligence tests that reveal differences between racial and ethnic groups valid or are these tests culturally biased?" (a multicultural issues topic). Students were responsible for researching their topic and presenting arguments and evidence (preferably empirical) in support of their assigned position.

Procedure

At the beginning of the semester, we gave students a brief description of the controversies and polled them concerning their opinions. Students indicated for each issue which side they favored (pro or con) and their confidence that their opinion was correct using a 7-point scale ranging from 1 (*not at all confident*) to 7 (*very confident*). Thus, each student's attitude on an issue could be represented by a number ranging from −7 (*very confidently opposed*) to +7 (*very confidently in favor*). We calculated the magnitude of students' attitude shifts by comparing their scale judgments before the debates to those immediately after each debate. Positive scores indicated that individuals became more confident in their prior attitude (e.g., attitude shifts from +3 to +6 and from −4 to −7 would both receive scores of +3) whereas negative scores indicated that individuals shifted away from their prior attitude, either becoming less confident or expressing some degree of confidence in the opposing view. Due to restricted range, the largest positive score possible was +6 (a shift from +1 to +7 or −1 to −7), but negative scores could be as high as −14 (i.e., a shift from −7 to +7).

Approximately 1 to 2 weeks after polling students' opinions on the issues, we assigned students to a particular debate and to argue a position either consistent or inconsistent with their existing opinion. A team of three or four students represented each side of an issue. Whenever possible, we attempted to construct each team such that some members were arguing a position consistent with their private opinion and some were arguing a position inconsistent with their private opinion. Following the arguments in each debate, the debaters and the remainder of the class again indicated which side of the issue they now favored and their degree of confidence that their opinion was correct (on scales identical to those used at the beginning of the semester). We gave nondebating students evaluation forms on which they evaluated each individual debater along two scales concerning (a) the quality of information presented and (b) the persuasiveness of the presentation. Students made each judgment on an 11-point scale ranging from 0 (*worthless*) to 10 (*outstanding*). After making these judgments, the student audience and the instructor made comments and questioned the panels for the remainder of the period.

Some characteristics of the debates varied across instructors. In two of the three classes, each debater had 4 min to present his or her arguments and evidence. Turns alternated between the opposing sides until each person had presented. Informal cross-examinations and rebuttals from the opposing sides took place during general class discussion. In the third class, one member of each group gave an opening statement to introduce their perspective on the issue. These opening statements had a limit of 3 min for each side. Each side prepared two questions to pose to the opposing side during the debate. The two teams debated these four questions for 5 min each with free-flowing discourse between the two teams. After the teams debated all four questions, one member from each team provided a closing statement to summarize their position and the main points of the debate. The instructor limited each closing statement to 3 min.

Results

Measure of Biased Assimilation and Attitude Change

We compared students' attitude judgments made well before the debate and immediately after each debate and classified students into one of four categories: (a) became more confident in their initial attitude, (b) did not change their attitude or confidence, (c) became less confident in their initial attitude, and (d) switched their attitude to the opposing side. Results indicated that students' roles during the debate altered how the debate affected their attitudes (see Table 1). As suggested by the biased assimilation hypothesis, the majority of those who argued for a position consistent with their initial attitude grew more confident that their attitude on the issue was correct. If we combine those classified as becoming more confident in their initial attitude with those classified as having no change in their existing attitude confidence, it is evident that the vast majority of those who argued a position consistent with their attitude maintained that attitude ($M = 88\%$). In contrast, the majority of those who argued for a position inconsistent with their existing attitude either became less confident in their initial attitude or switched their attitude to the opposing

Table 1. Distribution of Change in Attitudes As a Function of Position Argued

| | Position Argued | | |
| | Consistent With Attitude[a] | Inconsistent With Attitude[b] | Audience Member[c] |
Predebate to Postdebate Change in Attitude			
Cognitive Psychology			
Became more confident	83	0	24
No change in confidence	17	0	17
Became less confident	0	7	17
Switched sides	0	93	42
Marriage and family issues			
Became more confident	64	36	32
No change in confidence	18	18	23
Became less confident	9	27	25
Switched sides	9	18	20
Multicultural issues in psychology			
Became more confident	50	27	34
No change in confidence	30	9	34
Became less confident	10	18	6
Switched sides	10	46	26
Overall			
Became more confident	67	19	29
No change in confidence	21	8	23
Became less confident	6	16	16
Switched sides	6	57	32

Note. Given in percentages.
[a]$n = 33$. [b]$n = 37$. [c]$n = 160$.

side of the issue. Thus, the vast majority of those who argued a position inconsistent with their own private opinion weakened their attitude position ($M = 73\%$). A chi-square analysis, comparing those who argued consistent or inconsistent with their initial attitude, revealed a significant difference in the number whose attitude positions were maintained and the number whose attitude positions were weakened, $\chi^2(1, N = 70) = 28.23, p < .001$.

A similar pattern emerged when analyzing the magnitude of shifts in students' attitude positions after the debates. Those who argued consistent with their own private opinion generally became slightly more confident in their position ($M = +.64, SD = 3.31$) whereas those who argued inconsistent with their initial position generally shifted away from their prior position ($M = -5.84, SD = 5.62$), $t(69) = 5.80, p < .01$.

We had predicted that the student audience would tend to engage in biased assimilation as well. However, audience members (pooled across the three classes) were as likely to maintain their initial attitude ($M = 52\%$) as they were to weaken their initial attitude ($M = 48\%$). This pattern of student audience members' reactions differed significantly from that exhibited by the debaters arguing consistent with their private position, $\chi^2(1, N = 193) = 15.02, p < .001$, and those arguing inconsistent with their private position, $\chi^2(1, N = 197) = 7.08, p < .01$. We obtained similar results when analyzing the magnitude of students' attitude shifts. Student audience members exhibited a slight tendency to shift away from their original position ($M = -2.86, SD = 4.80$) rather than to strengthen their confidence in their initial position. Thus, student audience members did not exhibit the same biased assimilation pattern as those who argued consistent with their prior attitude position, $t(191) = 3.99, p < .01$, and the student audience members did not appear to dramati-

cally reduce their confidence in their original position as did students who argued inconsistent with their prior position, $t(196) = -3.33, p < .01$.

Despite the commonalties across the three classes, there were some systematic differences among them. We compared attitude changes in the three classes for each of the positions argued (consistent with attitude, inconsistent with attitude, or audience member). Students who argued a position consistent with their attitude were likely to maintain their attitude position, and this tendency did not vary across the three classes, $\chi^2(2, N = 33) = 2.62, p > .20$. Likewise, the magnitude of their attitude shifts did not vary significantly across the three classes, $F(2, 30) = 1.45, p > .25$. In contrast, students who argued a position inconsistent with their attitude were more likely to weaken their attitude position in the Cognitive Psychology course ($M = 100\%$), than in either the Marriage and Family Issues course ($M = 45\%$) or the Multicultural Issues course ($M = 64\%$), $\chi^2(2, N = 37) = 10.27, p < .01$. Additionally, students who argued a position inconsistent with their prior opinion shifted away from their prior opinion more dramatically in the Cognitive Psychology course ($M = -9.67$) than in the Multicultural Issues course ($M = -5.41$) or the Marriage and Family course ($M = -1.09$), $F(2, 35) = 11.80, p < .01$.

Similarly, student audience members were more likely to weaken their attitude position in the Cognitive Psychology course ($M = 59\%$) than in the Marriage and Family Issues course ($M = 45\%$) or the Multicultural Issues course ($M = 32\%$), $\chi^2(2, N = 160) = 7.94, p < .02$. The magnitude of these shifts was also greater for student audience members in the Cognitive Psychology course ($M = -3.85$) than for those in the Multicultural Issues course ($M = -2.21$) or in the Marriage and Family Issues course ($M = -1.65$), $F(2, 157) = 3.48, p < .04$. Subsequent analyses found no significant difference between the distributions of attitude change for the Multicultural Issues course and the Marriage and Family Issues course (all $\chi^2 < 2$, $p > .15$).

We conducted a 3 (debate position: consistent, inconsistent, neutral) × 3 (class: Cognitive Psychology, Multicultural Issues, Marriage and Family Issues) ANCOVA on the magnitude of attitude shifts, using participants' initial attitude positions as a covariate. The covariate did not account for a significant portion of the variance ($B = .037$, $t < .60$, $p > .50$). Consistent with results described previously, the analysis confirmed that the positions participants defended significantly affected the magnitude of attitude change, $F(2, 220) = 17.29$, $p < .001$. The type of course also had a significant influence, $F(2, 220) = 4.34$, $p < .02$, and interacted with debate position in determining the magnitude of attitude change, $F(4, 220) = 3.25$, $p < .02$.

Evaluations of Debate Performance

One potential drawback to assigning people to argue a position inconsistent with their existing attitude is that their performance may be handicapped. Perhaps their enthusiasm for the research required is diminished and their oral presentation of the material will lack the conviction it otherwise would have had if they had argued for their private position. The results do not support this contention. The student audience judged the quality of information[1] presented by those who argued consistent with their private opinion ($M = 8.22$, $SD = .77$) to be as strong as for those who argued a position inconsistent with their private opinion ($M = 8.10$, $SD = .99$), $t(38) < 1$, $p > .3$. Similarly, the student audience judged those who argued consistent with their initial attitude to be no more persuasive ($M = 8.10$, $SD = .91$) than those who argued inconsistent with their initial attitude ($M = 7.91$, $SD = 1.16$), $t(38) < 1$, $p > .3$. Hence, arguing for or against one's initial private opinion had no effect on debaters' performance.

Ratings of the Debate Experience

An end of the semester evaluation (along the 11-point scale) indicated that students generally enjoyed being a participant in one of the debates ($M = 7.32$, $SD = 2.12$) and reported learning a great deal from the preparation for and participation in a debate ($M = 8.72$, $SD = 1.19$). Their overall ratings of the debates (as both spectator and participant) were that they were enjoyable ($M = 8.34$, $SD = 1.38$) and that they learned a great deal from the debates ($M = 8.40$, $SD = 1.33$). Due to the fact that ratings of the debate experience were anonymous, we were unable to determine if those who argued for or against their initial opinion differed in their ratings of the debate experience. However, these ratings were typically quite high, suggesting that the position one had to defend did not adversely affect their enjoyment of the experience or how much they learned from their debate.

---

[1]Research by Smith (1990) suggested that peer ratings of student debates correlate highly with instructor ratings. We therefore used the student ratings as a measure of the debaters' performance.

Discussion

The ability to see different sides of an issue and to evaluate each objectively is a hallmark of science. Students must learn to question their assumptions, ask new questions, consider novel solutions, and evaluate their possibilities evenhandedly. These mental habits will promote meaningful contributions to the science of psychology. As educators, one tool we can use to promote these mental habits is the in-class debate in which we require students to defend a position with which they disagree.

When students receive evidence and arguments on both sides of a controversial psychological issue, do they soften their positions as they learn more about the merits of the two opposing sides? The answer to this question depends on two factors: the position the students argued during the debate and the nature of the material debated. The results support two main conclusions. First, students who argued a position consistent with their initial attitude almost always maintained or strengthened that attitude. Second, students who argued a position inconsistent with their initial attitude were likely to weaken their confidence in that attitude or change their attitude to the opposing position. Despite the commonalties across the three courses, some differences among the three courses did emerge. One possible explanation for these differences is that students were more likely to maintain or strengthen their initial attitudes when the debates concerned familiar topics connected to deep-seated values. Such debates dominated the Multicultural Issues course and the Marriage and Family Issues course, but not the Cognitive Psychology course.

This research demonstrates that biased assimilation occurs when students argue for their existing position on an issue and may be likely to occur when simply listening to a debate on a controversial issue that involves personal values. Biased assimilation was much less likely to occur when students considered the opposite by defending a position with which they disagreed. In fact, these students often became proponents of the opposing position (this switch to an opposing position was particularly likely to occur in the cognitive psychology course). Thus, it could be that student debaters are more likely to believe whatever position they must defend. This tendency may be due in large part to the fact that students are relatively uninformed on the issues, and as they research the topic, they look primarily for evidence to support the side we required them to defend (cf. Einhorn & Hogarth, 1978). As they acquire information supporting their side, they become convinced of the position. When later exposed to arguments and evidence supporting the other side, then they are motivated to dismiss them as invalid or insufficient to maintain their newly formed attitude. One could also offer a cognitive dissonance explanation for this pattern of results. That is, students we assign to defend a position contrary to their initial attitude may change their attitude so as to be consistent with their behavior.

Some alterations to the debate procedures we used could retain the beneficial reduction of biased assimilation we found while eliminating the tendency for students to adopt any position instructors assign them to defend. Instructors could tell students to research both sides of an issue and to prepare arguments on both sides of an issue, but instructors would not tell students until shortly before the debate which side they would defend. Alternatively, instructors could assign students to defend one position during the in-class oral arguments but to defend the opposing position in a written assignment. The requirement to defend both positions would eliminate the tendency to adopt a single position only because one had to defend it. At the same time, a reduction in biased assimilation may still occur because students must give careful consideration to evidence on both sides of an issue rather than simply confirming their preferred position. Whatever procedures instructors adopt, it is important that they carefully construct the format of the exercise to encourage students to consider the opposite. Only then are students likely to be more open to new perspectives and spend less time reinforcing old beliefs.

References

Bauer, G., & Wachowiak, D. (1977). The home-court advantage: A debate format for the teaching of personality. *Teaching of Psychology, 4,* 190–192.

Berg, B. (1979). Panel discussions in the classroom. *Teaching of Psychology, 6,* 242–243.

Einhorn, H. J., & Hogarth, R. M. (1978). Confidence in judgment: Persistence of the illusion of validity. *Psychological Review, 85,* 395–416.

Elliot, L. B. (1993). Using debates to teach the psychology of women. *Teaching of Psychology, 20,* 35–38.

Gilovich, T. (1991). *How we know what isn't so: The fallibility of human reason in everyday life.* New York: Free Press.

Gorman, M. E., Law, A., & Lindegren, T. (1981). Making students take a stand: Active learning in introductory psychology. *Teaching of Psychology, 8,* 164–166.

Lord, C. G., Lepper, M. R., & Preston, E. (1984). Considering the opposite: A corrective strategy for social judgment. *Journal of Personality and Social Psychology, 47,* 1231–1243.

Lord, C. G., Ross, L., & Lepper, M. R. (1979). Biased assimilation and attitude polarization: The effects of prior theories on subsequently considered evidence. *Journal of Personality and Social Psychology, 37,* 2098–2109.

Moeller, T. G. (1985). Using classroom debates in teaching developmental psychology. *Teaching of Psychology, 12,* 207–209.

Smith, R. A. (1990). Are peer ratings of student debates valid? *Teaching of Psychology, 17,* 188–189.

Note

A partial report of this research was presented at the meeting of the Midwestern Psychological Association, Chicago, May 8–10, 1997.

Cooperative Learning and Critical Thinking

James L. Cooper

In many ways, college teaching has remained largely unchanged since the days of the medieval university. This article recommends cooperative learning as one alternative to the lecture method, which has dominated college pedagogy during the last few hundred years, and suggests possible reasons why cooperative learning may foster the critical-thinking skills that appear to be lacking in many of our students. These suggestions are tentative for several reasons. First, there is no generally agreed-on definition of *critical thinking* (Kurfiss, 1988). Second, the main effect of cooperative learning on numerous student outcome measures has been replicated in hundreds of studies (D. W. Johnson & R. T. Johnson, 1989), but problems exist in addressing how cooperative learning may be causally linked to increases in critical thinking among college students. At least five properties define cooperative learning, and systematic research on the efficacy of each in promoting positive student outcomes is still quite scarce, particularly on college populations. Third, cooperative learning is not a unitary technique; there are at least 50 different forms of cooperative learning, ranging from student-directed to teacher-structured methods (Kagan, 1992).

Cognitive Disequilibrium

In most cooperative-learning structures, heterogeneous teams of students work on a common problem. This approach often leads to cognitive disequilibrium, which may produce what D. W. Johnson, R. T. Johnson, and Smith (1991a) called *epistemic curiosity,* as students seek out information to help them resolve the conflict. The confluence of differing approaches to an issue may lead students to move from what Perry (1970) called *egocentric, dualistic thinking* to more mature, relativistic thinking. If cooperative learning is properly structured, it can foster divergent thinking much more than the lecture technique. In lectures, students often hear a highly skilled problem solver resolve complicated issues without hearing the diversity of ideas that went into the lecturer's ultimate resolution. Too often, students then copy down the end product of an interesting and complicated problem for regurgitation on a test containing items calling for rote responses.

Model–Practice–Feedback Loop

In many cooperative-learning structures, students seek out information from readings, lecture, or other sources and then practice or apply the information within their groups, receiving feedback from other group members and the teacher concerning the adequacy of their verbal and written responses. This structure appears to be consistent with McKeachie's (1988) three elements that make a difference in college students' thinking skills: (a) discussion among students, (b) explicit emphasis on problem-solving procedures and methods using varied examples, and (c) verbalization of methods and strategies. Astin (1992) completed an extensive statistical analysis of the data gathered in his longitudinal study of what works in undergraduate education. He concluded that curricular issues had little impact on a variety of cognitive and affective student outcomes. The two variables that had, by far, the most impact on these outcomes were student–student and student–faculty interactions. Astin called for greatly increased use of cooperative learning in the undergraduate curriculum as a vehicle for fostering the development of liberal education. D. W. Johnson, R. T. Johnson, and Smith (1991b) reported that cooperative learning allows students to process information more efficiently and effectively than more traditional forms of instruction. In addition, they reported that the oral rehearsal associated with cooperative learning increases the likelihood that information will be placed in long-term storage for future retrieval.

Developmental Stages

Vygotsky (1978) and others indicated that students may learn best when taught by persons at more proximal stages of development than their professors. However, the novice receiving information from a somewhat more expert student–colleague is not the only one who gains from cooperative learning. Webb (1982), Dansereau (1988), and others found that the person giving an explanation actually gains more from a cooperative-learning discussion than the person receiving the explanation. Such teaching to other students may require elaboration and other metacognitive strategies that foster critical thinking concerning the content under review.

Giving a Voice to Students

Belenky, Clinchy, Goldberger, and Tarule (1986) and their colleagues in the women's ways of knowing movement spoke forcefully for the idea of knowledge as a social construction. They argued against overly competitive systems of instruction and against the idea of an authoritarian, lecture format of instruction in which knowledge is delivered to passive students. Members of this movement called for the establishment of communities of learners who help one another form connections between what is currently known and newly constructed knowledge. They preferred that a teacher be a midwife or coach to new knowledge, rather than an oracle dispensing pat resolutions to complicated issues. Although Belenky et al.'s original concern was with women, they and others have extended their argument to include ethnic minorities and those whose voices have not been heard due to the White, middle-class, European view that has dominated curricular and pedagogical decisions in many colleges. One can argue that many minority, nontraditional, and at-risk students may perform better using cooperative learning relative to lecture and lecture–discussion pedagogies. Treisman (1985) indicated that minority students' performance in calculus is significantly related to using small groups, and Frierson (1986) found similar results for African-American students taking a statewide nursing exam. Millis (1990) pointed out how cooperative learning is consistent with principles proven to be effective with the adult learner.

In examining the appropriateness of cooperative learning relative to traditional lecture and lecture–discussion methods of instruction, we should ask "Who does most of the complicated, difficult thinking in the classroom?" In properly structured cooperative learning, students perform most of the active, critical thinking with continuous support and feedback from other students and the teacher.

When should we use cooperative learning? According to D. W. Johnson et al. (1991b), who summarized a D. W. Johnson and R. T. Johnson (1989) meta-analysis,

> cooperative learning is indicated whenever the learning goals are highly important, mastery and retention are important, the task is complex or conceptual, problem solving is desired, divergent thinking or creativity is desired, quality of performance is expected, and higher level reasoning strategies and critical thinking are needed. (p. 40)

References

Astin, A. W. (1992). *What matters in college? Four critical years.* San Francisco: Jossey-Bass.

Belenky, M. F., Clinchy, B. M., Goldberger, N. R., & Tarule, J. M. (1986). *Women's ways of knowing: The development of self, voice, and mind.* New York: Basic Books.

Dansereau, D. F. (1988). Cooperative learning strategies. In C. E. Weinstein, E. T. Goetz, & P. A. Alexander (Eds.), *Learning and study strategies: Issues in assessment, instruction, and evaluation* (pp. 103–120). New York: Academic.

Frierson, H. T. (1986). Two intervention methods: Effects on groups of predominantly black nursing students' board scores. *Journal of Educational Psychology, 69,* 101–108.

Johnson, D. W., & Johnson, R. T. (1989). *Cooperation and competition: Theory and research.* Edina, MN: Interaction Book.

Johnson, D. W., Johnson, R. T., & Smith, K. A. (1991a). *Active learning: Cooperation in the college classroom.* Edina, MN: Interaction Book.

Johnson, D. W., Johnson, R. T., & Smith, K. A. (1991b). *Cooperative learning: Increasing college faculty instructional productivity* (ASHE–ERIC Higher Education Report No. 4). Washington, DC: The George Washington University, School of Education and Human Development.

Kagan, S. (1992). *Cooperative learning*. San Juan Capistrano, CA: Resources for Teachers.

Kurfiss, J. G. (1988). *Critical thinking: Theory, research, practice, and possibilities* (ASHE–ERIC Higher Education Report No. 2). Washington, DC: Association for the Study of Higher Education.

McKeachie, W. (1988). Teaching thinking. *Update, 2*, 1.

Millis, B. J. (1990). Cooperative learning strategies for continuing education faculty. In M. C. Natelli & T. F. Kowalik (Eds.), *Continuing education: A critical reflection. Proceedings of the 1990 Annual Conference of Region II, National University Continuing Education Association* (pp. 41–49). Binghamton, NY: National University Continuing Education Association. (ERIC Document Reproduction Service No. ED 324 455)

Perry, W. G. (1970). *Forms of intellectual and ethical development in the college years: A scheme*. New York: Holt, Rinehart.

Treisman, P. (1985). A study of the mathematics performance of black students at the University of California, Berkeley (Doctoral dissertation, University of California, Berkeley, 1986). *Dissertation Abstracts International, 47*, 1641–A.

Vygotsky, L. S. (1978). *Mind in society: The development of higher psychological processes*. Edited by M. Cole, V. John-Steiner, S. Scribner, & E. Souberman. Cambridge, MA: Harvard University Press.

Webb, N. M. (1982). Student interaction and learning in small groups. *Review of Educational Research, 52*, 421–445.

Note

Preparation of this article was supported in part by a grant from the Fund for the Improvement of Postsecondary Education.

In-Class Collaborative Learning: Practical Suggestions From the Teaching Trenches

Peter J. Giordano
Elizabeth Yost Hammer

Meyers's (1997) article on the use of collaborative learning groups is an excellent overview of pedagogical issues pertinent to the use of collaborative groups in the classroom. The aim of this article is to supplement Meyers's discussion with additional practical suggestions on starting in-class groups, maintaining their effectiveness, and anticipating common problems. As many teachers have discovered, poorly planned group work can be disastrous, resulting in a waste of class time and a variety of student complaints. The suggestions in this article have come from a variety of sources, including conversations with colleagues on our campus and at teaching conferences, the literature on collaborative learning, workshops presented by our Teaching Center, and mostly from trial and error in the teaching trenches.

Getting Started

One effective way to form the first group of the semester is to capitalize on proximity and friendship by having students form groups of four or five from those sitting closest to them. We tell students that this group will be their in-class learning group for the next few weeks.

Once we have formed groups, we hold a discussion on how groups fail and how they succeed. For example, in the first few class meetings, we distinguish between group tasks (the goals) and group processes (how the goals are reached). We underscore that creating meaningful tasks is our responsibility, but that effective group processes depend on the students' cooperative work together. We acknowledge that some students may not like groups or may feel socially awkward participating in them. We also stress that although students may feel shy at first, they will become more confident by getting to know others and speaking in front of them.

In classes in which we use collaborative group work, we intentionally establish productive group norms on the first day of class. Instead of reading over the syllabus, we put students in groups, ask them to read the syllabus, and then generate at least one question about its content. We have found this procedure a reliable means of generating discussion about important aspects of the course.

Another way to get groups off to a good start, particularly in introductory classes, is to allow students to develop guidelines for effective group work. In this task, we ask groups to spend a few minutes brainstorming about guidelines that should help groups function effectively. Next, each group shares its guidelines with the class, and we develop a composite list to distribute later to all class members. A list compiled by a recent introductory class included the following guidelines: be open-minded; communicate, cooperate, and distribute work evenly; be responsible (e.g., read materials); and be willing to compromise.

Maintaining and Using Groups Effectively

In our experience, in-class groups need some continuity to help them run smoothly. Conversely, when a particular group is not working well because of interpersonal dynamics, there needs to be a vehicle for change. We have found it useful to change groups after every unit exam. Thus, by the end of the semester, students have been in a variety of groups and have worked with almost everyone in the class. We change the groups by simply having students count off by the number of groups needed.

Students benefit more from group activity when structure is provided. We encourage groups to appoint a time keeper and a note taker, although the instructor can appoint students to these roles. When we have organized groups and given them a task, we leave for a few minutes to allow groups to get started. By leaving, we resist the temptation to give groups guidance before they have worked out problems themselves. After a few minutes, we check to be sure there are no major problems and that they understand the task. Although we are available to answer questions, we do not interact with the groups too much because when we do students rely on our input rather than the group's ideas.

When designing tasks for in-class group work, one way to start is to look through lecture notes for the day. What are the main topics to cover? Is there a way to divide the major topics and have groups present them? For example, when discussing biopsychology in the introductory course, each group can cover a different structure (or set of structures) of the brain. Each group should identify the structure on a model of the brain or on an overhead and describe its major functions. Students can then use the model or the overhead as they present to the class.

Once groups have completed the task, group reports allow the whole class to benefit from each group's work. One good way to get groups to report is to use a die. Number off each group member, roll the die, and the die selects who reports. This technique prevents the group from selecting the most outspoken person each time. The social pressure of possibly reporting also guards against a group member being totally uninvolved. However, we are always careful to give students an "out" if they absolutely do not want to report. We simply tell them that if we roll their number and they do not feel like reporting, they may decline to speak. Few students decline, but the option seems to enhance the level of trust in the classroom.

Regarding the style of reporting, we have found it helpful to tell groups they may not read from their textbooks while reporting. This suggestion ensures that students must understand the information enough to restate it in their own words. When groups engage in discussion or critiques of material, an effective way to have them report is to have them write the major points on a blank overhead. Then when they report they can show the overhead to the class and discuss the main points (Lutsky, 1997). Note that it is important for the professor not to restate all the information after the groups report. Restating conveys to the rest of the class that you will say what is important as soon as the group gets done and discourages students from learning from each other. This temptation is hard to resist.

Anticipating Problems

There will always be students who say they do not work well in groups. These students will say group work is a waste of time and they came to learn from the professor—the expert. We respect this opinion but try to convey that group work models the way many real-world situations operate. We encourage them to try to find value in what may seem like an alien process by allowing them to talk through their frustrations with us. Other students might not like their particular group. In actuality, students rarely complain about this issue. They seem to find relief in knowing that group composition periodically changes.

Some students might complain because they do not have pages of organized notes from lectures. Group work seems inherently "messier." Because of this possible problem, we encourage the note taker in each group to take good notes. We also tell students that we will photocopy the group's notes (one-page maximum) for each group member.

Just as in class discussion, an opinionated student can become a group dominator. Switching roles (e.g., reporter, note taker) often and changing groups at each unit minimizes this problem. Also, making all students feel accountable for the group work can help. In extreme situations, at the end of class we might discreetly talk with the dominating student.

From the student's perspective and for pedagogical reasons, it is important to make exams or other evaluative procedures relevant to group work. One possibility is deriving essay questions directly from group tasks. For example, if a group task is to compare and contrast the activation-synthesis and psychoanalytic theories of dreams, then an essay question on an exam might tap this same issue.

Conclusions

Collaborative learning groups are not a panacea for the teaching profession, but we have found them a rewarding addition to lectures. They have helped us kick the lecture habit (Zachry, 1985) and given us strength to overcome the Atlas complex (Finkel & Monk, 1983), the feeling that professors are primarily responsible for student learning. When used effectively, collaborative learning groups help students take greater responsibility for their own learning.

References

Finkel, D. L., & Monk, G. S. (1983). Teachers and learning groups: Dissolution of the Atlas complex. In C. Bouton & R. Y. Garth (Eds.), *Learning in groups: Directions for teaching and learning* (pp. 83–97). San Francisco: Jossey-Bass.

Lutsky, N. (1997, February). *Over my head: How overheads can aid lecture and discussion.* Paper presented at the Southeastern Conference on the Teaching of Psychology, Kennesaw, GA.

Meyers, S. A. (1997). Increasing student participation and productivity in small-group activities for psychology classes. *Teaching of Psychology, 24,* 105–115.

Zachry, W. H. (1985). How I kicked the lecture habit: Inquiry teaching in psychology. *Teaching of Psychology, 12,* 129–131.

Note

We thank Randolph A. Smith, three anonymous reviewers, and Elliott Hammer for helpful comments on a draft of this article. We also thank Jerry Cederblom and Diane Gillespie at the University of Nebraska, Omaha who gave us many helpful ideas during a Collaborative Learning Workshop on our campus.

Case Study Pedagogy to Advance Critical Thinking

Sharon A. McDade

For many instructors, case studies and discussion method pedagogy are newly discovered teaching strategies recently introduced into many disciplines for which lecture and small-group discussion used to be the norm. Although interest in case studies as a teaching mechanism is new, the pedagogy itself is very old—as old as the ancient storytellers who told a narrative (case) to promote children's individual discovery of wisdom, knowledge of the surrounding world, and development of the thought processes of survival. The goals of storytelling in those ancient cultures were similar to our goals in using case studies today: to foster critical thinking and reflection so that students learn how to learn on their own.

The terminology of this pedagogy is a good place to begin. The terms *case study* and *discussion method* are often used interchangeably, although the terms come at the topic from different directions. Case study refers to the vehicle of the pedagogy; that is, the use of a case—a written description of a problem or situation—to present a problem for analysis. Discussion method refers to the process of the pedagogy; that is, the method of an instructor facilitating a structured, preplanned discussion to lead students through the process of analyzing a piece of material. Although a case study is most often analyzed through facilitated in-class discussion, a case can also be the foundation for simulations, role-plays, written exercises, and a wide variety of other pedagogical methods. Conversely, discussion method teaching can center around any number of devices that trigger analysis. The discussion-triggering vehicle is often discipline specific; for example, a floor plan in architecture, a patient's chart in medicine, a poem in literature, a newspaper article in political science, and a statistical table in economics.

A case is a particular type of document created for specific purposes. Although case studies have long been used in research, particularly qualitative research, the cases used for teaching are usually specifically crafted to support intensive discussion and detailed analysis. A case is a story about a situation that is carefully designed to include only facts arranged in a chronological sequence. A teaching case ends before the conclusion of the story; students provide the analysis and speculate, based on their analysis, on possible solutions and conclusions. The purpose of a teaching case study is to create in the classroom realistic laboratories for applying research techniques, decision-making skills, and critical-thinking analysis.

A case study/discussion method provides a unique learning experience. Students prepare by analyzing the case (identifying key characters, determining central issues, and assessing internal and external climate and forces). They must identify objectives and goals for key characters by putting themselves in the shoes of those characters. This first-person analysis includes ascertaining resources, constituencies, and constraints; determining sources and nature of conflicts, and the dynamics of behavior; isolating decisions to be made; identifying alternatives; and anticipating and assessing consequences of decisions and actions. As a foundation for this analysis, students must apply theoretical paradigms and constructs, thus deriving theory from practice and practice from theory.

A teacher also prepares differently for a case study/discussion method class. Instead of preparing an outline of statements as for a lecture, the teacher prepares an outline of questions to facilitate the discussion and lead students through the thought process of analysis and application. The resulting classroom experience is far different from the typical question-and-answer format that many teachers accept as discussion. Question-and-answer formats are usually one-shot discussions—a question is answered, a topic is cleared, then on to the next question and topic. Discussion method teaching builds on ideas, a progression of thinking from one point to the next logical point, a guiding of students through a sequence of critical thinking in which the students think out loud to share their thinking processes with the teacher and their student colleagues.

The learning outcomes of this teaching process are different from those of a typical lecture or small-group discussion. The learning outcomes are typically not facts but the critical-thinking process itself, which has been modeled for students by the instructor and their student colleagues and in which they themselves have participated. Although a lecture may force students to generate pages of notes about facts or theory, in a case study/discussion method classroom, students take notes on the process, particularly the conclusions, lessons, or applications clarified at the end of the class. Learning outcomes may not be easily evaluated by conventional testing but should be evaluated by testing the process of thinking—the process of critical analysis. This suggests that case study/discussion method teaching is not the solution for all teaching goals. Some lessons, even courses, particularly those in which foundation factual or theoretical knowledge must be conveyed, may be better taught through lecture and other related pedagogies. Contrarily, case study/discussion method teaching is a better pedagogy for teaching and modeling thinking processes. All pedagogies have appropriate places in a curriculum, and a complete curriculum should include a wide variety of pedagogies to appeal to the learning styles of all students.

Case study/discussion method teaching provides a particularly useful tool for advancing critical thinking because it actively involves students in their own learning process. Arguments for the use of case study/discussion method pedagogy as a primary vehicle to achieve these goals are powerful:

1. It models critical thinking and provides a laboratory in which students can practice and advance their critical thinking skills.
2. It emphasizes the process of analyzing information.

3. It is contextually based; that is, students must understand contextual nuances and make references and analyses accordingly.
4. It challenges students to identify and challenge assumptions about situations and about their own beliefs.
5. It encourages students to imagine alternatives and explore these for strengths and weaknesses.
6. It helps students to integrate learning by incorporating theory into practice and practice into theory.
7. It enables students to develop critical-listening skills because listening to and understanding the nuances and diversity of the thinking processes of others is as important as developing one's own thinking.
8. It provides opportunities for students to develop and test theories about how people and organizations function.
9. It helps students to develop teamwork and collaborative learning as students work together in small groups and in the classroom to solve the problems presented by the case with the best means possible to serve the most goals.

10. It helps students to experience, explore, and test alternative ways of thinking.
11. It facilitates the consideration of different perspectives as other students present ideas, analyses, and solutions that no one student may have thought of.

Although there is value in a case study as a teaching document and much of the learning comes from the individual analysis that students do in preparing for class, the real potency of this pedagogy is in the facilitated classroom discussion. A well planned facilitator/teacher can take a class to levels of sophisticated analysis and insights impossible for the students to achieve on their own. Students are stretched to new levels of thinking. The lessons of the case studies go beyond the specific story; they are generalizable to similar situations and experiences. The benefit in life after the classroom occurs when students recognize a real-life situation as similar to one from a case study and that the same steps of analysis and problem solving can be applied. Case studies, as teaching vehicles, and discussion method, as a teaching process, model research and professional practice so that teachers and students are winners.

Writing to Discuss: Use of a Clustering Technique

Deborah G. Ventis

Writing is receiving increasing attention as an important tool in teaching. A clustering technique developed by Rico (1983) to improve writing skills was adapted by Henry (1985, 1986) to facilitate thinking in classroom settings. *Clustering* involves writing down a word or phrase and engaging in free association. Each association is written down and connected to the original stimulus by an arrow or line. If associations generate further associations, chains of associated words are produced. It is assumed that the writer will be motivated to write further about the connections made during the clustering exercise and that the connections will provide direction for the writing that follows. Henry concluded that clustering improves understanding and retention of concepts by providing students with an approach to learning that facilitates thinking. Teaching thinking skills is also an important component of class discussion (Lowman, 1984). This article describes the use of clustering as an impetus for class discussion.

Discussion, although a common teaching technique, has received relatively little research attention. Dunkin (1986) noted that much of the research on discussion has focused on the merits of lecture versus discussion. He concluded that research results suggest the choice of discussion for which the objectives are higher cognitive learning and attitude change. In addition to teaching thinking skills, Lowman (1984) summarized the educational objectives of discussion as clarifying course content, revealing students' attitudes, fostering student involvement, and building interpersonal skills (e.g., student motivation, rapport, and independence).

Discussion may occur in a number of different contexts within the classroom. Aamodt and Keller (1981) observed that the success or failure of small discussion groups used in teaching psychology depends on unsolicited student participation. They established that students experiencing high levels of social anxiety had low levels of participation in discussion.

Social anxiety may be exacerbated when discussion section instructors have relatively little contact with the students. I used the clustering technique to facilitate participation in discussion and to provide additional information for evaluating student performance.

Participants were 14 men and 24 women enrolled in two sections of an Introductory Psychology laboratory–discussion class. A list of assignments and topics is provided in the syllabus for the course, which is available from the author.

The clustering technique used was essentially the same as that described by Henry (1985, 1986). At the beginning of each class section, the instructor presented a word relevant to the topic of the readings for that day (e.g., for a discussion on homosexuality in one of the sections the students were given the word *preference*; in the other section, they were

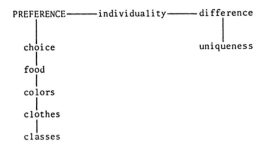

```
PREFERENCE————individuality————difference
    |                              |
  choice                       uniqueness
    |
  food
    |
  colors
    |
  clothes
    |
  classes
```

Preference connotes choice, and this "personal freedom" results in individuality. People have preferences and, thus, differences about almost every aspect of life.

(At the end of the discussion):
    In our discussion today, we touched on the pathological/social stigma of homosexuality. We questioned what was "normal" in terms of sexual preference, and we discussed society's reaction toward homosexuals. It was interesting to note that many of us described preference as a person's personal choice, but when we directed the word preference to have a sexual connotation, heterosexuality was believed to be right.

Figure 1. Example of a cluster and written comments produced during a discussion of homosexuality.

given the word *normality*). Students were asked to write associations they had to the word. After about 1½ or 2 min, they were also asked to write a brief explanation of an association or pattern of associations. Approximately 3 min was allowed for this part of the writing process. Figure 1 is an example of a cluster and written comments.

Use of the clustering technique to facilitate discussion involved using the students' written material as a framework for the discussion. After listening to the instructor's introductory remarks on the topic to be discussed, each student reported on his or her written responses; some students relied on reading what they had written, others read what they had written and commented on it, still others commented on what they had written without directly reading their work. At the end of the discussion that followed, students were asked to write for another 3 to 5 min. They were told that they could use this time for making summary comments, recording things they did not get to say or did not want to say in front of the class, or their general reactions to the class.

Evaluation

Students were encouraged to write down their thoughts about their readings for the discussions and comments about their laboratory sessions in the same notebooks in which they kept their clustering exercises and discussion comments. Midway through the semester, the students turned in these logs for feedback. They were provided with a plus, a check, or a minus to indicate that they were doing an excellent job in keeping their log, fulfilling the requirement for keeping the log, or had omissions or deficiencies they needed to correct to meet the requirement, respectively. At the end of the semester, they received a letter grade on their logs based on the same general criteria. Their final grade for the course included grades for their discussion class participation and lab class participation.

Effectiveness of the clustering technique was evaluated anonymously by the students at the end of the semester through the use of a questionnaire devised by the instructor. Students rated questions on the usefulness of the writing portion of the class on a scale ranging from *useless* (1) to *very helpful* (10). Students rated their writing most helpful in allowing them to express their opinions ($M = 7.8$), moderately helpful in organizing thoughts about the reading material ($M = 6.7$) and facilitating discussion ($M = 6.5$), and neutral with respect to helping with writing skills ($M = 4.8$).

Students were also asked if they had taken a discussion section connected with the department's other semester of Introductory Psychology. Of the 10 students who answered affirmatively and responded to a question concerning whether they found the writing portion of the present course a useful addition, 7 responded yes, and 3 responded no.

Finally, in a section reserved for comments and suggestions, of the 23 students who made remarks, 8 students commented directly on the usefulness of the writing assignment for the discussion portion of the class, and 2 commented on the writing assignment they did for the laboratory portion of the class. Of the remaining comments, 8 were general comments on the class, 4 focused on the criteria used for grading, and 1 was a general comment about psychology. The positive comments about the writing portion of the course included statements about help with formulating ideas (e.g., "helped me realize my own opinions," "writing about an issue really makes you think about it"), getting the discussion going (e.g., "the word association and brainstorming at the beginning of discussion was good because it started things off," "the brainstorming part at the beginning is helpful in getting things started," "usually getting started in a discussion is hard, and by opening class with everyone saying something about what they had written makes it easier for everyone to keep adding comments"), and participation (e.g., "this was a good way for everyone to be able to participate," "oftentimes I had trouble contributing to class discussions. This way . . . showed the prof that I did the work and had some comprehension of it"). The only negative comments about the writing portion of the course were made by one student who endorsed doing the associations, but thought that "the writing after that and especially at the end is pretty useless," and another who said that "It was very hard to write about experiments . . . because so little was said after the experiment I wasn't always sure of the purpose" (the laboratory meetings of the course were all coordinated by another faculty member and taught by student assistants so the discussion leader had no control over their content).

The clustering technique had a number of advantages for the instructor. Areas of agreement and disagreement, relevant concepts, and misconceptions or omissions were readily apparent from the comments made during the initial round of responses at the beginning of each class. Similarly, reading the comments written at the end of class confirmed that students' thinking was stimulated by the discussion, and sometimes opinions were changed or the relevance of the topic to other areas was recognized. In short, the technique was useful in realizing several of the objectives Lowman (1984) cited for class discussion: teaching thinking skills, revealing students' attitudes, and fostering student involvement.

Although Henry (1985) emphasized that "writing to learn is an entirely different form of writing from that used for evaluative purposes. . . . Grading is unnecessary" (p. 90), use of the clustering technique also provided valuable information beyond verbal participation on which to base grades for the discussion section. As noted by one student, the written work showed the instructor what the students had learned, even when they did not discuss it with the entire class. An unexpected bonus was the usefulness of the written work in verifying the identities of students who had made particularly interesting comments during the discussions; many of the views expressed in class appeared in the written work.

Clustering can be a useful addition to any course in which discussion is desired. I have used it on the first day of class to ascertain students' attitudes and beliefs about the topic of the course (undergraduate and graduate research and developmental psychology courses). It is also helpful in stimulating discussion about specific topics when a lecture is eliciting yawns and blank stares. As an impetus for discussion, the clustering technique is most useful in provoking comments from every class member. Using the technique in large classes forces each student to think about a response and may be effective in increasing involvement and improving the quality of discussion, even if only some students participate.

References

Aamodt, M. G., & Keller, R. J. (1981). Using the Self-Consciousness Scale to predict student discussion group participation. *Teaching of Psychology, 8,* 176–177.

Dunkin, M. J. (1986). Research on teaching in higher education. In M. C. Wittrock (Ed.), *Handbook of research on teaching* (3rd ed., pp. 754–777). New York: Macmillan.

Henry, L. H. (1985). Clustering: Writing (and learning) about economics. *College Teaching, 34,* 89–93.

Henry, L. H. (1986, November). Clustering. In C. L. Mett (Moderator), *Writing to learn: Activities in a variety of disciplines.* Panel discussion conducted at the State Council of Higher Education for Virginia conference on The Academic Profession in Virginia and the Nation, Norfolk, VA.

Lowman, J. (1984). *Mastering the techniques of teaching.* San Francisco: Jossey-Bass.

Rico, G. (1983). *Writing the natural way.* Los Angeles: Tarcher.

Note

An earlier version of this article was presented at the Tenth National Institute on The Teaching of Psychology, St. Petersburg, FL, January 1988.

8. DIVERSITY IN THE INTRODUCTORY CLASSROOM

Suggestions on Teaching International Students: Advice for Psychology Instructors

Dave S. Collingridge

According to Cushner (1987), an increasingly global society makes it necessary for many individuals to live, work, and think cross-culturally. One domain where cross-cultural awareness is important is in colleges and universities. The number of foreign students attending American colleges and universities has increased steadily over the last four decades (Davis, 1996). A large number of international students register in psychology courses to satisfy a general education requirement, out of interest, or because psychology is their major. Psychology professors should be aware of a number of issues when teaching these students.

In most cases, international students try to adjust and fit into the culture of the schools they attend. However, some cultural differences can create unfortunate situations for students, professors, and schools. In this article, I present a limited discussion of these issues. I raise a few of the common concerns expressed to me by international students. By presenting these pertinent topics, I hope to increase awareness of matters associated with teaching this segment of the student population. In the first section, I consider helping international students feel like equal participants in the classroom setting, an issue that applies to all students. The second concerns U.S. immigration and legal policies that professors should know with regard to international students. Although violations of these legal policies may occur accidentally, they can create unfortunate circumstances for international students and the schools they attend.

Communication Issues

There are a few issues of which psychology professors should be cognizant when instructing and interacting with non-native English speaking students. Giving attention to these special considerations will make learning psychology more interesting and beneficial for many international students. First, teachers should be aware of language barriers. Although most schools require a test of proficiency in the English language for English as a second language (ESL) students, many of these students experience difficulties with sophisticated terminology. These students would benefit if teachers also provided simpler terms or definitions whenever they use more difficult words. Such an approach ensures that international students understand the material and helps them advance their English vocabularies. Similarly, teachers should also be aware that international students may find slang, colloquial expressions, and references to culturally specific events confusing. In addition, some students may shy away from classroom discussions because they believe that their English skills are inadequate or in their home culture it is inappropriate to publicly question people in positions of authority. This predicament can place such students at a disadvantage if instructors assess classroom participation when assigning grades.

Second, different cultures often embrace varying methods for addressing instructors. Although the commonly accepted method of address in American universities is "Dr. Jones" or "Professor Jones," some international students may be accustomed to more colloquial expressions such as "Mr. Jones" or "Allan" (Mr. Jones's first name). Instructors can avoid uncomfortable situations regarding appropriate titles and forms of address by informing all students of the preferred mode of address at the beginning of the semester. This approach will help international students feel more comfortable when approaching and communicating with professors.

Finally, international students occasionally lack adequate English writing skills. They may experience difficulties with grammar and expression of ideas. These problems can create difficulties in a profession such as psychology, which relies heavily on clear and effective written communication. If an international student submits a paper containing poor grammar and expression, a professor can do one of three things: (a) he or she can give an honest, lower grade that reflects the quality of work in the paper and bypass the opportunity to counsel with the student on ways to improve; (b) give a higher than deserved grade if the correct ideas are present; or (c) give the honest, deserved grade and counsel with the student on ways to ameliorate the writing. I endorse the last approach. The first approach provides no help to the student and ignores an instructor's responsibility to educate students. The second approach is unfair and reinforces poor habits. The third, preferred approach is equitable and demonstrates a willingness to help students overcome a unique barrier.

There are a couple of approaches to assist international students who experience language difficulties. First, instructors can grade essays on a point system that provides separate evaluations on key components such as writing, content, American Psychological Association style, and creativity. This approach will provide international students with specific feedback on the strengths and weaknesses of their papers. Second, often all that is needed is a native English speaker to proofread the student's work to point out grammatical errors; therefore, professors should encourage and, if necessary, help international students find someone who can proofread their papers. Some institutions have an ESL program or writing labs from which international students can get help on essay writing. The proofreader could be a friend or a fellow student. It may even be possible and propitious for professors to urge students to submit drafts of essays. In any case, counseling students with grammatical difficulties to seek assistance in the form of proofreading can engender peer interaction and help international students improve their writing skills, thus enabling them to get more out of their psychology education. Furthermore, according to Waller (1994), when students evaluate each other's written work, additional benefits occur, such as an increased sense of community and shared responsibility for learning. Developing a sense of community among one's peers is a positive step toward helping international students integrate into the culture of the schools they attend ("International Student Guide to the United States of America," 1996).

Legal Issues

There are two legal issues of which professors should be aware with regard to international students. First, U.S. immigration law requires that these students maintain a full course of study (Fragomen, Del Rey, & Bell, 1997). With few exceptions, full-time enrollment at most schools is 12 credit hours for undergraduates and 9 credit hours for graduate students. These requirements suggest that professors should be careful when counseling students about dropping a course. Students who fail to maintain a full course of study may be considered "out of status" and as such must qualify for reinstatement. Being out of status disqualifies students for F–1 visa benefits such as campus employment and re-entry into the United States (Fragomen et al., 1997).

Second, when employing international students as research or teaching assistants, professors should be aware that, if these students work before the required employment documentation is complete, the school may be fined up to $10,000 (Aliens and Nationality Act, 1997), in the event that an audit of the school's financial records reveals the mistake. This statute should not deter psychology professors from hiring international students, who often rely heavily on departmental employment. The onus is on the student and the department staff in charge of student employment to ensure that appropriate hiring procedures are followed. Nevertheless, it is in everyone's best interest if psychology professors are aware of the requirement to have documenta-

tion in place before assigning paid duties to international students. Finally, professors should also note that international students are limited to 20 hr of work per week, except during holidays or recess breaks (Fragomen et al., 1997).

Conclusions

In this article, I addressed a few of the pertinent issues regarding teaching psychology to international students. However, not all international students are alike. These students can be as different as the countries from which they originate. Thus, instructors should give careful consideration to the varied needs of the diverse international student population. Having some knowledge of the various cultures and educational practices around the world could help teachers meet this group's educational needs. Instructors can gain this knowledge by reading, attending multicultural seminars, meeting with multicultural community organizations, and by discussing cultural issues with international students. Finally, the communication issues discussed in this article do not apply only to international students. For example, many undergraduates suffer from poor writing skills, become confused with sophisticated language use, and are uncertain about how to address teachers. Hence, this article will help instructors be sensitive to the educational needs of all students, regardless of cultural status.

References

Aliens and Nationality Act, 8 C. F. R. § 274a.10(c) (1997).

Cushner, K. H. (1987). Teaching cross-cultural psychology: Providing the missing link. *Teaching of Psychology, 14,* 220–224.

Davis, T. M. (Ed.). (1996). *Open doors: Report on international educational exchange.* New York: Institute of International Education.

Fragomen, A. T., Del Rey, A. J., & Bell, S. C. (1997). *Immigration procedures handbook.* New York: Thomson Information Services.

International student guide to the United States of America. (1996). Pittsburgh, PA: Spindle.

Waller, J. E. (1994). Philosophies of psychology: A discovery process for undergraduates. *Teaching of Psychology, 21,* 33–35.

Note

I thank Darhl Pedersen, Brent Slife, and Ted Okawa for critiquing this article. Always consult appropriate legal resources for information regarding immigration rules and procedures.

On Teaching About the Cultural Relativism of Psychological Constructs

Carolyn Zerbe Enns

Questions about the universality of a self-contained identity have emerged from the results of multicultural personality research studies, which have found that concepts of the self often vary across cultures (Hoare, 1991; Shweder & LeVine, 1984). Hoare (1991) stated that "identity is inseparable from the specific culture that shapes it" (p. 51), and Markus and Kitayama's (1991) extensive review concluded that culture influences one's inner thoughts, feelings, and actions and, consequently, the manner in which the self is organized. The multicultural approach reflected by recent studies moves beyond past efforts merely to compare cultures and demonstrates an appreciation for the diversity and complexity of human experience. This perspective recognizes that human behavior must be understood in its sociocultural context and explores both similarities and differences between and within various cultural, ethnic, and racial groups (Pedersen, 1991).

Material related to multicultural psychology has appeared in introductory psychology texts (e.g., Allen & Santrock, 1993), texts on multicultural psychology (Matsumoto, 1993; Triandis, 1994), handbooks and articles on the teaching of psychology (e.g., Bronstein & Quina, 1988; Whitten, 1993), and teaching tools for the psychology of women (e.g., DeFour & Paludi, 1991; Mays, 1988; Paludi, 1990). However, past discussions on teaching a more inclusive psychology of personality have focused primarily on gender (e.g., Enns, 1989; Torrey, 1987). Multicultural issues have received only limited attention in teaching materials for personality courses, with the exception of Bronstein's (1988) proposal for a sociocultural approach and Engler's (1991) chapter on Zen Buddhism.

Many personality texts and courses survey the major historical personality theories and research that are embedded within a Western, middle-class perspective on psychological health and then evaluate theories according to this world view (Enns, 1989). As a consequence, students may develop narrow and ethnocentric views of healthy human functioning and be unprepared to deal with an increasingly pluralistic society. If current immigration and birth patterns continue, the majority of residents in the United States will be People of Color within our students' lifetimes (Comas-Diaz, 1992). Thus, the teaching of multicultural approaches to psychology is central to helping our students survive and succeed in a changing society.

The first section of this article summarizes recent research and theory on multicultural personality issues. It pays special attention to the concepts of individualism and collectivism because they are widely studied by social scientists, represent important dimensions for understanding diverse construals of the self within and across cultures, and serve as useful tools for teaching about the ways in which culture influences behavior and personality (Triandis, 1994). The second portion of the article discusses teaching methods that can be used to convey this content.

Psychology, Personality Theory, and Individualism

American psychology has historically emphasized the centrality of the individual, independent self in identity formation (Hoare, 1991). Healthy individuals in our culture are defined as self-actualizing and self-directed. They exhibit self-acceptance, self-confidence, self-esteem, high self-efficacy, internal locus of control, self-respect, and a positive self-concept. Personality researchers are interested in the degree to which people engage in self-monitoring, self-handicapping, self-talk, self-disclosure, and self-control. Qualities such as personal competence, autonomy, mastery, and uniqueness are highly valued.

Healthy psychological functioning is typically associated with the construction of distinctive boundaries between the self and others (Sampson, 1988), and the absence of these boundaries is referred to by terms such as *fusion, enmeshment,* and *codependency.* Sampson (1977, 1988) described American culture as characterized by self-contained individualism and stated: "The self-contained person is one who does not require or desire others for his or her completion or life; self-contained persons either are or hope to be entire unto themselves" (Sampson, 1977, p. 770). This person "contains unto him or herself all the esteemed and valued qualities of the culture" (p. 772).

Waterman (1984) identified four theoretical perspectives that contain the core components of individualism in personality theory. They include (a) Erikson's (1968) view of healthy identity, which entails knowledge and consistency of one's personal goals, values, and characteristics; (b) Rotter's (1966) concept of internal locus of control, which involves the perception of control over one's reinforcements; (c) Kohlberg's (1981) notion that the highest level of moral development is associated with personal, principled ethical thinking; and (d) Maslow's (1956) description of self-actualization, which defines *healthy persons* as those who are "dependent for their own development and continued growth upon their own potentialities" (p. 176), whose "determinants of satisfaction and of the good life are for them now inner-individual and not social" (p. 176), and who have "become strong enough to be independent of the good opinion of other people, or even of their affection" (p. 176). Each of these theories has contributed significantly to our understanding of healthy personality in the Western world.

They exemplify the high value placed on autonomy, independence, and personal uniqueness in American culture. However, these notions of healthy behavior may be seen as isolating and unhealthy in more collective cultures (Hui, 1988).

The centrality of the individual self in current research and theory is at least partially demonstrated by the increased use of *self* as a prefix to describe psychological constructs. Whereas the 1969 version of *Psychological Abstracts* used 8 categories including *self* as a prefix for organizing and searching for existing research, the 1979 version contained 19 categories with *self* prefixes, and the 1989 version included 33 such categories (Hoare, 1991). Given the large volume of research available on these topics, our students will see the individual self as a universal and central component of personality.

Individualism and Collectivism and Core Personality Variables

Although traditional approaches to personality continue to dominate the field, a growing body of theory and research is providing insight about the cultural relativity of personality (e.g., Cousins, 1989; Markus & Kitayama, 1991; Trafimow, Triandis, & Goto, 1991; Triandis, 1989; Triandis, Bontempo, Villareal, Asai, & Lucca, 1988; Triandis, McCusker, & Hui, 1990; Weisz, Rothbaum, & Blackburn, 1984; Wheeler, Reis, & Bond, 1989). Authors have used the terms *individualism* and *collectivism* to contrast two different types of cultures (e.g., Triandis et al., 1988). Persons from individualistic cultures tend to value *idiocentric* personal characteristics that are associated with a person's unique qualities. In contrast, persons from collective cultures tend to value *allocentric* characteristics associated with the subordination of personal goals to group goals (Triandis, 1989). Markus and Kitayama (1991) also coined definitions of the *independent self* and the *interdependent self* to denote the most typical self-definitions associated with these contrasting cultures. Cultures that tend to value individualism and the independent self include a sizable portion of Americans (especially Whites) and many Western Europeans. Cultures that tend to value a more collective view of the world and interdependent self-definitions include many minority cultures within the United States; many Asian, African, and Latin-American cultures; and some Southern European cultures (Markus & Kitayama, 1991).

Differential levels of endorsement of collective and individualistic values are likely to have an impact on views of the self, views of maturity, the experience of emotion, methods of coping, one's relationship to groups, and one's views of achievement and work. For the purpose of definition and illustration, I contrast individualistic/independent concepts with collectivist/interdependent concepts as though they are two discrete, bipolar categories. However, these dimensions should be seen as a continuum of behaviors or constructs rather than as opposites.

Views of the self. The Western, individualistic self is typically described in abstract terms. Individuals tend to see themselves as stable across situations and emphasize the importance of internal qualities and attributes. Personal goals and uniqueness pave the way for mature action that is marked by autonomy and the affirmation of inner characteristics through self-assertion (Markus & Kitayama, 1991). In contrast, the person from a collectivist culture is likely to define himself or herself in an interdependent fashion; the self may vary across situations or contexts. Rather than emphasizing personal distinctiveness, this person is likely to stress his or her similarity to a group, view roles and obligations to a group as central aspects of self-definition, and value restraint and harmony. *Maturity* is defined as the ability to eliminate artificial boundaries between the self and the environment, as well as the capacity to adjust to the environment and demonstrate concern for the community's well-being and future (Engler, 1991; Markus & Kitayama, 1991). For individualists, the adage "The squeaky wheel gets the grease" is an extension of the value placed on self-expression and interpersonal directness; for contextualists, the proverb "The nail that stands out gets pounded in" is an extension of the ability to detect and respond appropriately to subtle nonverbal cues and the willingness to restrain oneself from self-promotion.

Support for these hypotheses about the self-structure come from several studies in which students from collectivist (e.g., Chinese) and individualist (e.g., White North American) cultures were asked to complete sentences beginning with the words "I am." North American students were more likely to respond to this task with idiocentric statements such as "I am intelligent" and were less likely than persons from more collectivist cultures to complete sentences with statements that indicated membership in a group, such as a religion, family, or ethnic group (Trafimow et al., 1991; Triandis et al., 1990).

When Cousins (1989) asked Japanese and American students to make 20 statements about themselves, he found that Japanese students provided more context-specific and concrete descriptions (e.g., playing tennis during the weekend) than did American students, who described themselves with more abstract psychological traits (e.g., optimism). However, when respondents were asked to make statements about themselves in a specific context, Japanese students were more likely to describe themselves with a specific trait label (e.g., optimism or friendliness) and Americans were more likely to provide qualified statements (e.g., sometimes lazy at home). Cousins concluded that the noncontextualized task represented an artificial and less relevant format for Japanese students; the opposite was true for American students.

Finally, in a comparison of students' endorsements of various values, individualists were more likely to choose items such as independent, daring, adopting one's own goals, and equality. In contrast, those with a more collectivist orientation scored higher on values such as loyalty, humility, honoring parents and elders, family security, true friendship, accepting one's position in life, and discovering a sense of belonging (Triandis et al., 1990).

Emotion and motivation. Culture influences one's self-perceptions as well as one's emotions and cognitions. Due to the centrality of self-expression, the individualistic self is more likely to experience ego-oriented emotions, such as pride and anger; the interdependent self is more likely to experience other-oriented emotions, such as sympathy, shame, or feelings of interpersonal connectedness. The ego-focused emotions of anger or pride are an extension of the individualistic person's unique self-defined internal attributes, whereas the other-focused emotions of the collective self maintain and support harmonious relationships. Individuals from interdependent cultures are also more likely to report other-oriented motivations, such as affiliation, the need to emulate others, or deference (Markus & Kitayama, 1991).

When collectivists experience ego-focused emotions, such as anger, they are more likely to feel these emotions with members outside of their primary circle of relationships, whereas individualists often feel these emotions with significant others. For example, Chinese respondents were more likely than Americans to describe anger in response to situations involving individuals outside their circle of acquaintance (Stipek, Weiner, & Li, 1989). Leung (1988) also found that Chinese respondents were less likely than Americans to engage in conflict with a friend and more likely than Americans to pursue conflict with a stranger, suggesting that the value of self-restraint applies primarily to the collectivist's in-group, which represents one's primary source of self-definition.

Markus and Kitayama (1991) proposed that ego- or self-focused emotions foster and promote an independent and active self. Matsumoto, Kudoh, Scherer, and Wallbott (1988) found that American students reported more physiological symptoms and experienced feelings longer and more intensely than Japanese students. In contrast to the Western stereotype that Asians are "repressed" (Leong, 1986), the lower intensity of emotion described by these Japanese students may reflect a successful outcome of learning to live harmoniously rather than needing to demonstrate one's distinctiveness within a group.

Relationships and groups. Relationships and group membership are important to individuals from both individualistic and collectivist cultures, but they tend to differ in their nature and roles. Markus and Kitayama (1991) indicated that persons with an independent construal of the self see others as reference points for self-evaluation and social comparison; persons with an interdependent self-construal see others as providing self-definition that may vary in different groups. Consistent with the important of self-expression, individualists are more likely to participate in a variety of groups and place importance on meeting people, joining groups, and exiting groups. The length of group membership depends on the degree to which a group meets one's private needs. In contrast, interdependent individuals tend to be members of fewer groups that are more enduring in nature and defined according to important roles. Cooperation within groups is emphasized, and members build skills in maintaining relationships with important others. Although individualists tend to hold specific, well-defined, and segmented expectations for groups, collectivists are more likely to have more significant, wide-ranging, and diffuse expectations of groups.

Within individualistic cultures, horizontal relationships with spouses, friends, and colleagues tend to be of primary importance; within collectivist cultures, vertical/hierarchical relationships between a boss and employee or between a parent and child tend to take on greater significance. Horizontal relationships allow the self-contained person to express individuality, and vertical relationships preserve the collectivist's sense of interdependence and harmony across generations or social boundaries (Triandis et al., 1988). Hierarchical relationships allow the collectivist to fulfill important obligations and develop personal attachment to a parent or a work supervisor with whom lifelong identification may occur (Weisz et al., 1984).

Comparing the relationships between Chinese and American students, Wheeler et al. (1989) found that Chinese students participated in fewer long-lasting interactions and that they disclosed more than their American counterparts. Compared to American students, Chinese students communicated with fewer partners. Chinese students also experienced more group interactions and engaged in more task activities rather than recreational activities. These findings about Chinese students seem consistent with behavior that one would expect in a collective culture in which individuals often define themselves within a narrow in-group that is relatively permanent.

Achievement and coping. Consistent with individualistic cultural values, the separate self values personal initiative, self-reliance, and achievement as coping mechanisms and tends to take internal responsibility for both success and failure. In contrast, the collectivist is more likely to value making a contribution to a group effort, more likely to express modesty or self-effacement in the face of success, and less likely than the individualist to make internal attributions for either success or failure (Markus & Kitayama, 1991). In support of this principle, Chandler, Shama, and Wolf (1983) demonstrated that men in collective cultures are less likely to make internal attributions for failure than men in individualist cultures, and they concluded that this pattern may reduce the stress of daily living.

Within Western culture, the association between perceived control or internal locus of control (LOC) and positive mental health has been revealed through many studies (for reviews, see Burger, 1993; Phares, 1991; Potkay & Allen, 1986). However, this orientation toward success or coping is not highly valued in many collectivist cultures. Weisz et al. (1984) suggested that, rather than thinking of LOC as internal or external, researchers should differentiate between primary and secondary control. The goal of primary control, which is most evident in individualistic cultures, is to shape current realities by acting directly on the environment. The goal of secondary control, which is more evident within collectivist cultures, is to become aligned with nature, fate, and current realities. The person gains a sense of well-being and control by interpreting events in ways that provide a sense of meaning or experiences vicarious satisfaction through connections with important others.

Members of collectivist cultures are no more conforming and no less achievement oriented than Westerners; self-reliance, competition, and achievement merely take on different meanings. In individualist cultures, self-reliance implies that one has freedom to act according to personal wishes; in collectivist contexts, self-reliance means that one will avoid being a burden on the group (Triandis et al., 1988; Triandis et al., 1990).

On the dangers of overgeneralization. Although Triandis (1989) suggested that the collective–individual continuum will help researchers test how personality varies across cultures, he also cautioned against viewing these contrasting values as two discrete categories. There is much variation between and within cultures regarding how and to what degree independence and interdependence are emphasized, and some individuals may value both independence and interdependence. Members of primarily individualistic cultures, such as Americans, may define themselves in ways that are most consistent with a collective world view, and members or collectivist cultures may adopt self-definitions that resemble those of most Westerners. The multicultural literature parallels some theories that women's identity is based primarily on affiliation (e.g., Gilligan, 1982). However, the primary foundation for the relationship models of women's identity is a Western perspective. In contrast to the inseparability of self and other found in many collectivist cultures, the self-in-relation models focus on the importance of valuing connection and independence in a society that is primarily self-oriented (Lykes, 1985).

The collective–individual dimension may be modified by gender, a person's economic class background, minority or majority status within a culture, and level of acculturation to a dominant culture. Intragroup differences should not be overshadowed by discussions of intergroup differences. When intergroup differences are overemphasized, the personality student may develop rigid categories that limit understanding of individual differences.

Teaching Strategies

One of the most straightforward strategies for teaching about multicultural psychology involves asking students to read one of the research reviews on cultural variations of personality (e.g., Markus & Kitayama, 1991; Triandis, 1989) and lecturing about the material summarized in the previous sections. However, given the nonconscious ways in which Western concepts permeate our thinking about healthy and normal behavior, it is difficult to convey a full appreciation for alternative world views through traditional teaching methods alone. By using experiential strategies, instructors and students can examine and critique popular personality research constructs from a multicultural perspective. The following section describes a critical thinking approach to evaluating the concept of LOC and suggests ways of using self-awareness activities and autobiographical materials.

Demonstrating the Cultural Relativity of Personality Constructs: The Example of LOC

Discussion of the strengths and limitations of external–internal LOC (Rotter, 1966, 1990) represents a useful method for examining the narrowness of Western personality theory for several reasons. First, LOC is one of the most extensively studied variables in the history of personality psychology (Phares, 1991; Rotter, 1990). As early as 1975, Rotter counted over 600 studies that used an internal–external LOC measure (cited in Potkay & Allen, 1986), and studies in the 1990s continue to explore concepts such as perceived LOC. Rotter (1990) reported that his 1966 monograph on external–internal LOC had received at least 4,700 citations. Second, LOC has been identified as one of the central components of individualism (Waterman, 1984). Third, psychologists have suggested specific ways in which LOC should be modified to encompass the life experiences of individuals from other cultures (D. W. Sue, 1978; Weisz et al., 1984).

When introducing this lecture–discussion session in a personality class, I ask students to respond to selected items of a LOC scale (see, e.g., Burger, 1993; Engler, 1991; Potkay & Allen, 1986; Rotter, 1966). After students score their questionnaires, class time is used to review the concept of internal–external LOC and some of the major research findings about this concept. Students then examine the items of the LOC scale and identify ways in which items associated with primary or Western view of control are connected with internal LOC (e.g., I deserve credit for most of my accomplishments), whereas items associated with secondary control or collectivist values are related to external LOC (e.g., We are likely to be swept up in the ebb and flow of events).

Important content for the class session includes discussion of relations between internal–external control and a host of variables, such as achievement, adjustment, and mastery. Internal LOC has been associated with persistence in the face of failure, high achievement, enjoyment of challenge, ability to cope with stress, and viewing oneself as independent; external LOC is associated with more negative outcomes (for reviews, see Potkay & Allen, 1986; Phares, 1976, 1991). The instructor should then note that People of Color and individuals from non-Western cultures tend to score in a more external direction and that this result has often been interpreted negatively (D. W. Sue, 1978). However, an external orientation is connected to health or secondary control in many Asian cultures (Weisz et al., 1984; see also the previous section on achievement and coping). Secondary control provides a sense of meaning and purpose as individuals adapt to existing realities. Fate, good or bad luck, or serendipitous events may be seen as realities that one accepts in order to achieve harmony with others and the world. Thus, some of the items associated with internal LOC or primary control (e.g., I deserve credit for most of my accomplishments) may be related to low levels of adjustment in non-Western cultures because it implies a lack of knowledge of the centrality of healthy interdependence. The terms *secondary control* and *primary control* more accurately depict the way in which individuals orient themselves to the world than the phrases *external LOC* and *internal LOC*. Furthermore, secondary control is not associated with negative connotations as is external LOC. Weisz et al. (1984) provided numerous examples of secondary control that can be used for illustration and lecture.

The instructor may also lead a discussion concerning the practical implications of primary–secondary control for subgroups within American culture, especially People of Color and vulnerable populations (Thompson & Spacapan,

1991). Although internal or primary coping patterns are generally more adaptive within the majority culture (Parkes, 1984), secondary control represents a more adaptive method of coping within some populations (see Reich & Zautra, 1991; Schulz, Heckhausen, & Locher, 1991; Taylor, Helgeson, Reed, & Skokan, 1991). Burger (1989) also observed that primary control is related to a strong sense of personal responsibility, which may contribute to personal stress, interfere with effective coping, and increase self-blame for failure. Furthermore, when external circumstances, such as prejudice and poverty, impinge on one's opportunities and success, internal LOC may lead to discouragement and failure (D. W. Sue, 1978).

Discussion of the external–internal LOC construct provides an opening for the instructor to introduce basic frameworks that support Western personality theory. The class can be asked to generate a list of qualities associated with healthy personality in typical Western cultures (for a comprehensive list, see Katz, 1985). The instructor and students then contrast this list with some of the values of many collectivist cultures, such as subtlety of communication, mature dependence, preservation of harmony, or the belief that fate plays a major role in shaping outcomes (see Markus & Kitayama, 1991; Weisz et al., 1984). As a final step, class interaction can be used to generate a list of important components of multicultural personality theory.

The activities outlined herein provide one method to help students test personality theories for their inclusiveness and generalizability to other cultures. A similar set of activities can be organized around other significant concepts, such as self-monitoring, self-esteem, or self-efficacy.

Self-Awareness Activities

In order for students to understand the role of culture in personality formation, it is important for them to become aware of aspects of their own culture that are often implicit and only dimly understood at a conscious level (Pedersen, 1988). Some of the most useful activities for developing self-awareness include experiential exercises, such as role-plays, role reversals, and simulation games. Case studies, discussion of critical incidents in cultural communication, and exposure to other cultures are also useful (D. W. Sue & D. Sue, 1990). I briefly describe two activities that are particularly useful for increasing self-awareness in personality theories courses.

Within small groups, students respond to the following questions: What is your own cultural/ethnic/racial background? How did your family describe this identity to you as you were growing up? How did this ethnic identity influence the way you and your family related to your community and friends? What is the impact of your racial/ethnic identity on your self-definition, personality style, and/or relationships with others (for a variation of this exercise, see Tsai & Uemura, 1988)? Even in relatively homogenous groups, students discover diversity. After students discuss these questions for approximately 15 min, full class discussion can be used to identify themes, commonalities, and differences that were identified in smaller groups. Increased awareness of unique and diverse life experiences facilitates understanding

of the complex intersections of culture, ethnicity, and race and decreases the likelihood that students will develop stereotypes.

Because much of culture is internalized and implicit, class members often have difficulty describing their culture in words. In another exercise, I ask students to draw pictures of their personal cultures by using crayons, markers, and symbols. After they depict their cultures in symbolic ways, class members label specific aspects of the culture and describe their culture to other members of a small group (for a variation of this exercise, see Pedersen, 1988). Ideally, small-group discovery-oriented discussion is followed by full class discussion of themes and variations. A valuable outcome of this exercise is students' increased knowledge of how their world views influence their symbols and pictures. The typical picture by a White American student includes many separate symbols or small pictures that depict specific parts of his or her culture such as home, religion, personal preferences, and family values. However, international students from more collectivist cultures tend to create more unified, holistic images in which a central theme of interdependence emerges. For example, a Chinese student's picture included symbols of the sky, a bird, and the green earth, which represented the interconnectedness of all aspects of life. Alternatively, a South African student drew specific parts of her culture within one large circle that represented the interdependence between individuals, the soil, and deceased individuals. When students compare the similarities and differences among their pictures, they often gain a clear visual perspective of how individualistic and collectivist cultures may influence personality and world view.

Using Autobiography to Teach About Diversity

Because it is difficult for students to understand alternative world views by talking abstractly about culture, I assign the reading of a brief autobiography by a woman whose Asian-American family lived in a relocation camp during World War II (Wakatsuki-Houston & Houston, 1973). The value of this and other autobiographical accounts is that they concretely and graphically depict ways in which collective and individualistic values influence personality. The autobiography also illustrates how numerous factors, such as biculturalism, acculturation, economic class, gender, individual differences, historical events, immigration patterns, and racism, intersect in complex ways to influence personality (Tsai & Uemura, 1988). Biographical, fictional, or literary accounts of people's lives can also be used as tools to help students apply personality constructs in the real world (Boyatzis, 1992; Carlson, 1992; Mueller, 1985).

Autobiographies provide students with additional information for evaluating personality theory. As part of a final take-home test or paper for the personality course, I ask students to choose two characters from the book they have read and illustrate how two major personality theorists would assess the personalities of book characters. In addition, students evaluate the strengths and limitations of these theories for understanding the characters' personalities and discuss whether the theories account for cultural variations and external forces, such as racism, historical events, and immigration, that influence these individuals. Students often demonstrate a more mature understanding of culture and personality when considering how these issues relate to specific people.

Concluding Comments

Comas-Diaz (1992) predicted that, as the demographics of the United States continue to change dramatically, "many of the so-called universal principles of human behavior will be perceived as examples of cultural myopia at best, or cultural imperialism at worst" (p. 90). In light of our growing knowledge about the cultural relativism of personality, we must teach a more pluralistic and multicultural orientation in a wide variety of psychology courses. Although I discussed constructs and examples that can be most easily integrated into the personality theories course, the concepts and activities can also be adapted to other courses, such as introductory psychology, abnormal psychology, developmental psychology, and social psychology.

References

Allen, L., & Santrock, J. W. (1993). *Psychology: The contexts of behavior.* Madison, WI: Brown & Benchmark.

Boyatzis, C. J. (1992). Let the caged bird sing: Using literature to teach developmental psychology. *Teaching of Psychology, 19,* 221–222.

Bronstein, P. (1988). Personality from a sociocultural perspective. In P. Bronstein & K. Quina (Eds.), *Teaching a psychology of people: Resources for gender and sociocultural awareness* (pp. 60–67). Washington, DC: American Psychological Association.

Bronstein, P., & Quina, K. (Eds.). (1988). *Teaching a psychology of people: Resources for gender and sociocultural awareness.* Washington, DC: American Psychological Association.

Burger, J. M. (1989). Negative reactions to increases in perceived control. *Journal of Personality and Social Psychology, 56,* 246–256.

Burger, J. M. (1993). *Personality* (3rd ed.). Pacific Grove, CA: Brooks/Cole.

Carlson, J. F. (1992). From metropolis to never-neverland: Analyzing fictional characters in a personality theory course. *Teaching of Psychology, 19,* 153–155.

Chandler, T. A., Shama, D. D., & Wolf, F. (1983). Gender differences in achievement and affiliation attributions. *Journal of Cross-Cultural Psychology, 14,* 241–256.

Comas-Diaz, L. (1992). The future of psychotherapy with ethnic minorities. *Psychotherapy, 29,* 88–94.

Cousins, S. (1989). Culture and selfhood in Japan and the U.S. *Journal of Personality and Social Psychology, 56,* 124–131.

DeFour, D. C., & Paludi, M. A. (1991). Integrating scholarship on ethnicity into the psychology of women course. *Teaching of Psychology, 18,* 85–90.

Engler, B. (1991). *Personality theories.* Boston: Houghton Mifflin.

Enns, C. Z. (1989). Toward teaching inclusive personality theories. *Teaching of Psychology, 16,* 111–117.

Erikson, E. H. (1968). *Identity: Youth and crisis.* New York: Norton.

Gilligan, C. (1982). *In a different voice.* Cambridge, MA: Harvard University Press.

Hoare, C. H. (1991). Psychosocial identity development and cultural others. *Journal of Counseling and Development, 70,* 45–53.

Hui, C. H. (1988). Measurement of individualism–collectivism. *Journal of Research in Personality, 22,* 17–36.

Katz, J. H. (1985). The sociopolitical nature of counseling. *The Counseling Psychologist, 13,* 615–624.

Kohlberg, L. (1981). *The philosophy of moral development.* San Francisco: Harper & Row.

Leong, F. T. L (1986). Counseling and psychotherapy with Asian-Americans: Review of the literature. *Journal of Counseling Psychology, 33,* 196–206.

Leung, K. (1988). Some determinants of conflict avoidance. *Journal of Cross-Cultural Psychology, 19,* 125–136.

Lykes, M. B. (1985). Gender and individualistic vs. collectivist bases for notions about the self. In A. J. Stewart & M. B. Lykes (Eds.), *Gender and personality: Current perspectives on theory and research* (pp. 268–295). Durham, NC: Duke University Press.

Markus, H. R., & Kitayama, S. (1991). Culture and the self: Implications for cognition, emotion, and motivation. *Psychological Review, 98,* 224–253.

Maslow, A. H. (1956). Self-actualizing people: A study of psychological health. In C. E. Moustakas (Ed.), *The self* (pp. 160–194). New York: Harper Colophon.

Matsumoto, D. (1993). *People: Psychology from a multicultural perspective.* Pacific Grove, CA: Brooks/Cole.

Matsumoto, D., Kudoh, T., Scherer, K., & Wallbott, H. (1988). Antecedents and reactions to emotions in the United States and Japan. *Journal of Cross-Cultural Psychology, 19,* 267–286.

Mays, V. M. (1988). Even the rat was white and male: Teaching the psychology of Black women. In P. Bronstein & K. Quina (Eds.), *Teaching a psychology of people: Resources for gender and sociocultural awareness* (pp. 142–146). Washington, DC: American Psychological Association.

Mueller, S. C. (1985). Persons in the personality theory course: Student papers based on biographies. *Teaching of Psychology, 12,* 74–78.

Paludi, M. A. (1990). *Exploring–teaching the psychology of women: A manual of resources.* Albany: State University of New York.

Parkes, K. R. (1984). Locus of control, cognitive appraisal, and coping in stressful episodes. *Journal of Personality and Social Psychology, 46,* 655–668.

Pedersen, P. (1988). *A handbook for developing multicultural awareness.* Alexandria, VA: American Association for Counseling and Development.

Pedersen, P. (1991). Multiculturalism as a generic approach to counseling. *Journal of Counseling and Development, 70,* 6–12.

Phares, E. J. (1976). *Locus of control in personality.* Morristown, NJ: General Learning Press.

Phares, E. J. (1991). *Introduction to personality* (3rd ed.). Glenview, IL: Scott, Foresman.

Potkay, C. R., & Allen, B. P. (1986). *Personality: Theory, research, and applications.* Monterey, CA: Brooks/Cole.

Reich, J. W., & Zautra, A. J. (1991). Experimental and measurement approaches to internal control in at-risk older adults. *Journal of Social Issues, 47,* 143–158.

Rotter, J. B. (1966). Generalized expectancies for internal versus external control of reinforcement. *Psychological Monographs, 80*(Whole No. 609).

Rotter, J. B. (1990). Internal versus external control of reinforcement: A case history of a variable. *American Psychologist, 45,* 489–493.

Sampson, E. E. (1977). Psychology and the American ideal. *Journal of Personality and Social Psychology, 35,* 767–782.

Sampson, E. E. (1988). The debate on individualism: Indigenous psychologies of the individual and their role in personal and societal functioning. *American Psychologist, 43,* 15–22.

Schulz, R., Heckhausen, J., & Locher, J. L. (1991). Adult development, control, and adaptive functioning. *Journal of Social Issues, 47,* 177–196.

Shweder, R. A., & LeVine, R. A. (Eds.). (1984). *Culture theory: Essays on mind, self, and emotion.* Cambridge, England: Cambridge University Press.

Stipek, D., Weiner, B., & Li, K. (1989). Testing some attribution–emotional relations in the People's Republic of China. *Journal of Personality and Social Psychology, 56,* 109–116.

Sue, D. W. (1978). World views and counseling. *Personnel and Guidance Journal, 56,* 458–462.

Sue, D. W., & Sue, D. (1990). *Counseling the culturally different* (2nd ed.). New York: Wiley.

Taylor, S. E., Helgeson, V. S., Reed, G. M., & Skokan, L. A. (1991). Self-generated feelings of control and adjustment to physical illness. *Journal of Social Issues, 47,* 91–110.

Thompson, S. C., & Spacapan, S. (1991). Perceptions of control in vulnerable populations. *Journal of Social Issues, 47,* 1–22.

Torrey, J. W. (1987). Phases of feminist re-vision in the psychology of personality. *Teaching of Psychology, 14,* 155–160.

Trafimow, D., Triandis, H. C., & Goto, S. G. (1991). Some tests of the distinction between the private self and the collective self. *Journal of Personality and Social Psychology, 60,* 649–655.

Triandis, H. C. (1989). The self and social behavior in differing cultural contexts. *Psychological Review, 96,* 506–520.

Triandis, H. C. (1994). *Culture and social behavior.* New York: McGraw-Hill.

Triandis, H. C., Bontempo, R., Villareal, M. J., Asai, M., & Lucca, N. (1988). Individualism and collectivism: Cross-cultural perspectives on self-ingroup relationships. *Journal of Personality and Social Psychology, 54,* 323–338.

Triandis, H. C., McCusker, C., & Hui, C. H. (1990). Multimethod probes of individualism and collectivism. *Journal of Personality and Social Psychology, 59,* 1006–1020.

Tsai, M., & Uemura, A. (1988). Asian Americans: The struggles, the conflicts, and the successes. In P. Bronstein & K. Quina (Eds.), *Teaching a psychology of people: Resources for gender and sociocultural awareness* (pp. 125–133). Washington, DC: American Psychological Association.

Wakatsuki-Houston, J., & Houston, J. D. (1973). *Farewell to Manzanar.* New York: Bantam.

Waterman, A. S. (1984). *The psychology of individualism.* New York: Praeger.

Weisz, J. R., Rothbaum, F. M., & Blackburn, T. C. (1984). Standing out and standing in: The psychology of control in America and Japan. *American Psychologist, 39,* 955–968.

Wheeler, L., Reis, H. T., & Bond, M. H. (1989). Collectivism–individualism in everyday social life: The middle kingdom and the melting pot. *Journal of Personality and Social Psychology, 57,* 79–86.

Whitten, L. A. (1993). Infusing Black psychology into the introductory psychology course. *Teaching of Psychology, 20,* 13–21.

Note

This article is based on a paper presented at the annual meeting of the Midwestern Psychological Association, Chicago, IL, May 1992.

Confronting Heterosexism in the Teaching of Psychology

Jane M. Simoni

The science and pedagogy of psychology are not practiced in a cultural vacuum. As Denmark (1994) suggested, "we must realize that psychology is not value free but rather is a creation of the culture and context in which it has developed" (p. 334). One prevailing aspect of the dominant culture of the United States is heterosexism, defined here as the belief that heterosexuality is the only natural and acceptable sexual orientation and the irrational hatred and discrimination directed at those deemed nonheterosexual (Simoni, 1996). In this country, religious institutions have demonized lesbians and gay men (Boswell, 1980), the general populace has largely harbored antigay attitudes (Herek, 1991), and the courts have historically failed to protect the rights of lesbian and gay male individuals (Rivera, 1991).

This prevailing bias has created a psychology of heterosexuality so entrenched in our notions about human behavior that it is "as the water is to fish, wholly nonconscious and relatively unchallenged" (Brooks, 1992, p. 203). Brooks described the heterosexist bias in psychology as based on the following four assumptions: (a) Lesbianism and homosexuality have to be explained, (b) adult sexual orientation is determined by early childhood experience, (c) lesbianism and homosexuality are negative outcomes of childhood socialization, and (d) lesbians are masculine and masculine women are pathological or gay men are effeminate and effeminate men are pathological (p. 204). Despite the dearth of evidence to support these assumptions and the research since Hooker (1957) that contradicts them (see Garnets & Kimmel, 1993; Gonsiorek & Weinrich, 1991), many psychologists persist in holding these beliefs.

The heterosexist bias in clinical psychology can be traced to the field's psychoanalytic roots. Although many quote Freud (1935/1960) as writing to the mother of a homosexual son that "homosexuality is assuredly no advantage, but it is nothing to be ashamed of, no vice, no degradation, it cannot be classified as an illness . . . ," they often omit the rest of his sentence, ". . . we consider it to be a variation of the sexual function, produced by a certain *arrest of sexual development*" [italics added] (p. 423). Later psychoanalytic theorists asserted the pathology of homosexuality, continuing to view it as a fixated and immature state (Bieber & Bieber, 1979; Socarides, 1968, 1978). Until 1973, homosexuality was classified as a mental disorder in the American Psychiatric Association's *Diagnostic and Statistical Manual of Mental Disorders* (DSM; Kirk & Kutchins, 1992; Morgan & Nerison, 1993).

Identifying, confronting, and defying heterosexism in the field of psychology should be part of the task of an effective instructor. Success in this endeavor requires breaking the customary silence on the topic and challenging its omission from the traditional psychology curriculum. An indication of this omission is that only one article since this journal's inception in 1974 (i.e., McCord & Herzog, 1991) directly addresses the issue of teaching about homosexuality.

In place of a model of homosexuality based on pathology and rooted in heterosexist bias, instructors should present an affirmative perspective based on an appreciation of diversity (L. D. Garnets, personal communication, March 29, 1995; King, 1988) and rooted in empirical research (see Garnets & Kimmel, 1993; Gonsiorek & Weinrich, 1991; Hooker, 1957). Such a model is supported by the American Psychological Association (APA), which in 1975 adopted the following resolution:

> Homosexuality per se implies no impairment in judgment, stability, reliability, or general social and vocational capabilities: Further, the APA urges all mental health professionals to take the lead in removing the stigma of mental illness that has long been associated with homosexual orientations. (Conger, 1975, p. 633)

An affirmative model stresses the equivalent status of heterosexuality and homosexuality, with homosexuality seen as a natural variant in human sexuality. Lesbians and gay men are acknowledged to be equal to heterosexuals in their psychological adjustment and in their capacity to love, relate, and contribute to society. Social psychological and developmental models are used to understand lesbian and gay male experiences and the process of coping with a marginal status. The increasing acceptance of this model is demonstrated by the growth of the literature incorporating an affirmative approach (see Appendix) and the courage, creativity, and commitment shown by many psychologists in their teaching and advocacy within the field.

In this article, I present a rationale for adopting an affirmative model of homosexuality in the psychology curriculum, a critique of the treatment of homosexuality in psychology textbooks, and some suggestions for avoiding heterosexist bias and incorporating an affirmative model in the pedagogy of psychology.

Rationale for a More Inclusive Curriculum

Beyond adherence to APA's directive, there are other compelling reasons for psychologists to challenge heterosexism in their classrooms. The fear, ignorance, and prejudice concerning lesbians and gay men on college campuses and the resulting harassment and violence have been well documented (Comstock, 1991; Herek, 1991). Such negative attitudes and harmful behaviors jeopardize the well-being of all in the university community. Instructors contribute to this devaluation of lesbian and gay male stu-

dents when they ignore or omit them in their teaching. An incomplete curriculum suggests to lesbian and gay male students that they are "deviant, psychologically abnormal, invisible, or, at best, barely tolerated" (Crumpacker & Vander Haegen, 1993, p. 95). Because the issue of homosexuality is rarely considered in high school courses, the college curriculum may be students' first exposure to accurate and unbiased information and their first opportunity to discuss the topic in a structured academic setting (Watter, 1987). Covering this topic is especially important in introductory psychology and survey courses because classes devoted exclusively to homosexuality are rare and often not attended by those who might have the most to learn.

Learning to teach what we have been taught to omit about lesbians and gay men is important to heterosexual students as well. Accurate information compels them to confront their prejudice and move beyond their limited world views. They are given the opportunity to recognize the dangerous consequences of complicity in even mild statements or acts of heterosexism (Crumpacker & Vander Haegen, 1993).

Several points raised by Denmark (1994) in her discussion of the need to "engender" psychology in terms of women's issues are relevant to teaching about homosexuality. She indicated that we are compelled to challenge biased perspectives with our students so that they may obtain an accurate view of the world. She reminded us of our duty to make students careful consumers of information so that they can challenge fallacious stereotypes and harmful generalizations. Finally, she advised that challenging the discipline's unfounded assumptions makes psychology a stronger science and profession.

Critique of Psychology Textbooks

Relevant to the discussion of teaching about homosexuality is an examination of how the subject is treated in textbooks often required for psychology courses. Researchers have evaluated the treatment of lesbianism in women's studies textbooks (Zimmerman, 1982) and women's literature anthologies (Hickok, 1982). Others have examined the treatment of homosexuality in introductory psychology textbooks from 1975 to 1979 (McDonald, 1981), college-level health science textbooks (Newton, 1979), and human sexuality textbooks (Whitlock & DiLapi, 1983). A perusal of psychology textbooks before 1988 indicated that the psychology of lesbians and gay men, when considered at all, was often restricted to a reference to the declassification in the third edition of the DSM usually followed by a discussion on etiological theories and reparative therapies (King, 1988). Such discussions were often relegated to chapters on abnormal psychology and psychopathology. Restricting the mention of homosexuality to one section or chapter, usually one related to sexual dysfunction, has been termed *ghettoization* (Whitlock & DiLapi, 1983).

Methodology

Textbook sample. I reviewed a convenience sample of 24 textbooks published between 1991 and 1995—six textbooks each in the areas of introductory, social, developmental, and abnormal psychology. Although there is no statistical basis for claiming this sample is representative, the striking similarity among recently published textbooks in each area argues for the generalizability of the findings.

Definitions. How authors define terms relating to sexual orientation often reveals their perspective; therefore, the glossary of each textbook was examined for definitions of the terms *lesbian, gay,* and *homosexual.* In addition, because an affirmative approach involves comparable treatment of homosexuality and heterosexuality, I also looked for the terms *heterosexual* and *sexual orientation.*

Quantity of coverage. To gather data on the quantity of coverage of lesbian and gay male issues, the number of index headings or subheadings for the five terms mentioned earlier (and derivatives thereof, e.g., *gay male* or *homosexual orientation*) were tallied. Moreover, the detailed tables of content were scanned for sections likely to include relevant passages. All major passages were probably identified because most indexes were highly comprehensive. Length of each passage in number of pages, or fraction thereof rounded up to one-half page, was determined.

Context and content of coverage. To assess the context of the coverage, I noted whether relevant passages were limited to sections on sex or sexuality, in other sections only, or in both types of sections. The general thematic content of

the coverage was identified. Because the range of topics was somewhat circumscribed, simply listing the topics covered was possible.

Quality of coverage. As an indicator of the quality of coverage, I devised a measure that combined quantity, context, and content of the coverage. Terms for the categories were based on those used in a review of the treatment of African American women in psychology of women textbooks (Brown, Goodwin, Hall, & Jackson-Lowman, 1985). *Poor* textbooks did not mention homosexuality (exclusion) or restricted its coverage to a focus on sexuality or etiology (segregation). *Fair* textbooks defined at least one term in the glossary or cited one in the index. In addition, a *fair* textbook included one passage on homosexuality that did not focus mainly on its etiology and was not included in a section on sexuality (tokenism). *Good* textbooks met the criteria for *fair* textbooks and also mentioned lesbians and gay men in contexts such as parenting or relationships. *Good* textbooks often included photos of identifiable lesbians and gay men or used them as examples in contexts that were entirely unrelated to homosexuality (integration).

Results

Definitions. As shown in Table 1, the lack of lesbian and gay male coverage began in the glossary, with the vast majority of textbooks excluding definitions for the terms

Table 1. Coverage of Homosexuality in 24 College Psychology Textbooks

Evaluation Criteria	Textbook Subject Area			
	Introductory	Social	Developmental	Abnormal
Quantity of coverage				
Index citations (range/*M*)	0–10/4.8	0–8/2.3	1–10/4.2	1–10/2.9
Pages (range/*M*)	0–5.5/2.8	0–7.5/1.9	1.5–2.5/2.5	1–8/4.0
	n	*n*	*n*	*n*
Glossary definitions				
Gay	1	0	1	1
Heterosexual	0	0	1	1
Homosexual	1	0	1	1
Lesbian	1	0	1	4
Sexual orientation	1	0	3	0
Content of coverage				
Homophobia/prejudice	3	3	4	5
AIDS & gay men	4	3	3	3
DSM declassification	4	0	2	6
Origins of homosexuality	6	1	3	2
Other	2	2	1	6
Relationships	1	3	3	2
Gay families/parenting	2	0	2	2
Prevalence	2	0	2	1
Identity formation/coming out	2	1	2	0
Ethnic minority issues	2	0	0	0
Context of coverage				
Not in any section	0	2	0	0
In sexuality section(s) only	4	0	1	1
In other section(s) only	0	1	1	0
In both types of sections	2	3	4	5
Quality of coverage				
Good (integration)	2	3	0	3
Fair (tokenism)	0	0	4	1
Poor (exclusion/segregation)	4	3	2	2

gay, lesbian, or *homosexual.* Not a single social psychology textbook glossary defined any of the five terms examined. *Homosexual* and *sexual orientation* were the most frequently defined terms; only one textbook included a definition for *heterosexual.*

The definitions for *homosexuality* and *sexual orientation* varied widely. The most heterosexist versions focused on sexual behavior, referring to a lifestyle, choice, or condition, and failed to comparably define heterosexuality. For example, Bootzin, Acocell, and Alloy (1993) defined homosexuality as "a condition characterized by sexual activity directed toward one's own sex" (p. G–10) and included none of the other terms in their glossary. One of the best definitions of *sexual orientation,* "an enduring sexual attraction toward members of either one's own sex (homosexual orientation) or the other sex (heterosexual orientation)" (p. G–14), appeared in Myers (1992).

Quantity of coverage. Three textbooks (two social and one introductory) included no index citations for any of the five terms. As shown in Table 1, the mean numbers of index citations for each subject area were fairly comparable. This limited indexing was reflected in the low quantity of material in the textbooks; most referred to lesbians and gay men or their concerns on fewer than three pages. Two textbooks did not mention the topic.

Context of coverage. Review of sections of the textbooks in which the material related to homosexuality was found revealed mixed results according to subject area. Authors of introductory textbooks were most likely to include this material only in sections related to sexuality. Social and developmental textbook authors distributed the information more evenly throughout the textbook, and authors of abnormal psychology textbooks were least likely to restrict content on homosexuality to a chapter on sexual disorders and dysfunction. When they did, they often changed the chapter titles to something more appropriate (e.g., Abnormality and Variation in Sexual Behavior, Bootzin et al., 1993) or relegated the discussion to a box (as in Sue, Sue, & Sue, 1994).

Content of coverage. The most recurring topics were homophobia and prejudice, AIDS and gay men, the declassification of homosexuality as a mental illness in the *DSM,* and the origins of homosexuality. Focus on the origins of homosexuality seems excessive, especially when no allusion to the possible origins of heterosexuality were explored. Especially disturbing was the scant coverage of ethnic minority issues and homosexuality; only 2 of the 24 textbooks mentioned these topics.

Quality of coverage. Over half the textbooks reviewed were rated *poor.* Either they completely excluded any content addressing homosexuality or lesbians and gay men or they completely segregated such content in sections on sexuality. The omission was particularly glaring in sections such as Attraction: Liking and Loving Others (Myers, 1993). These textbooks are representative of those described in King's (1988) review and suggest that calls for

more inclusive coverage and increasing visibility in the intervening years have gone largely unheeded.

Four textbooks were rated *fair;* they offered only token coverage of homosexuality. Developmental psychology textbooks were most likely to receive this rating. In one such textbook (Cole & Cole, 1993), there was no mention of the specified terms in the glossary, although under the term *homosexuality,* the index included page references for homosexual identity, orientation, behavior, stigma, and stages of development. However, all references were to one 2-page box that concerned mainly a four-stage model of coming out. A close scanning of the rest of the text revealed no other references to lesbians and gay men or the issue of homosexuality.

Seven *good* textbooks succeeded in presenting several issues related to homosexuality and integrating this content across diverse sections. For instance, Wade and Tavris (1993) discussed kissing as a learned behavior and an acquired taste. Accompanying photos displayed three kissing couples, one of two Latina women. In considering the diversity of the U.S. population, Rubin, Peplau, and Salovey (1993) do not limit their discussion to ethnic diversity; they also mentioned gay men, lesbians, and bisexual women and men. Beside a description of how various couples are seen in marital therapy, Comer's (1992) textbook displays a gay male couple.

Discussion of Textbook Review

This evaluation of 24 college-level textbooks in introductory, social, developmental, and abnormal psychology revealed scant attention to psychological issues related to lesbians and gay men. Although some textbooks are beginning to do a fair job of covering homosexuality, most disturbing was the lack of systematic incorporation of references to lesbians and gay men in contexts unrelated to their sexual orientation.

For example, a textbook may mention homosexuality in relation to sex but then neglect to refer to it at all in sections on commitment, intimacy, parenting, and other aspects of relationships, as if these were exclusively heterosexual domains. Under such generic headings as "Attraction," textbook authors almost always referred exclusively to heterosexual attraction. Such misleading and assumptive restriction conveys the notion that, compared to heterosexuality, homosexuality is deviant, less important, and less natural. Even more disturbing is the complete absence of homosexual content in a textbook. This type of omission has been interpreted as an implied antihomosexual statement to the student (Newton, 1979).

Teaching About Homosexuality

The findings indicate that most textbooks offer insufficient coverage of homosexuality for college psychology courses. To complement textbooks, instructors must rely on supplementary materials and activities. In his review of the literature on teaching about homosexuality in sex education courses, Watter (1987) pointed out that many modalities have been suggested (i.e., lectures, role-playing, audiovisual materials, and guest speakers) but that a scientific evaluation is needed to determine the most efficacious of strategies for teaching about homosexuality. Although such a task is beyond the scope of this article, some suggestions are offered.

Before teaching about homosexuality and the heterosexist biases in psychology, the instructor must deal with his or her own homophobia. The willing instructor should read materials by or about lesbians and gay men, consult with them or those who specialize in this area, and talk with peers who are also attempting to eradicate bias from their classrooms. This exercise is important for the lesbian or gay male instructor as well as the heterosexual one.

Because usually only a small portion of any psychology class can be devoted specifically to homosexuality, appropriate information and messages must be conveyed. Ideas for course content can be selected from the resources and references lists at the end of this article. Topics might include coming out as part of the developmental process; the origins of sexual orientation (not homosexuality only!); the intersections of heterosexism, sexism, and racism; the social and historical context of institutionalized heterosexism; lesbians and gay men as a minority group; or the formation and alteration of heterosexist attitudes. These discussions should reflect the demographic diversity of lesbians and gay men and, therefore, should incorporate issues of ethnicity (see Greene, 1994), gender, and aging. Most important, discussion of same-sex relationships and sexuality should not be covered in lectures on psychopathology or deviant sexuality anymore than discussion of heterosexual relationships would be.

Apart from a specific discussion of homosexuality, instructors should use examples of lesbians and gay men in neutral contexts. I have done this successfully with test items such as the following one: "Jose is besieged with grief and insomnia after the sudden death of Mario, his partner of 10 years. Jose's symptoms are indicative of a diagnosis of . . . ?" In considering interpersonal attraction, which textbooks almost always describe only in terms of male–female attraction, Fontaine (1982) described to her class the situation of Marita and Joan who are attracted to each other and would like to live together after high school but have conflicts because of different class backgrounds. Fontaine then asked the class how the two teenagers might try to resolve these issues within their relationship.

Didactic presentation of information may not be adequate. Experiential as well as cognitive components may be needed to challenge students' assumptions and prejudices. Pedagogies that validate personal experiences affirm the feminist injunction that the personal is political, raise students' political consciousness, and decrease their alienation from intellectual material (Crumpacker & Vander Haegen, 1993). One experiential strategy is the presentation of panels of lesbians and gay men who speak openly about themselves and their experiences and field questions from the class. In such panels, women and people of diverse ethnic backgrounds are necessary to prevent dismissal of the issue due to the belief that it is pertinent only to Anglo-American men. A demographically diverse panel will demonstrate the heterogeneity within the lesbian and gay male community and facilitate the discussion of negotiating a double or triple minority status. McCord and Herzog (1991) summarized topics in which undergraduates were most interested (e.g., AIDS, same-sex marriages, and child rearing); their list of 13 topics could help prepare less experienced panelists. In the absence of panelists, other sources such as films, videos, and slides may be more readily available (Russo, 1981). An instructor might also try clever exercises that involve more active participation. One such exercise begins by asking students to identify their "petual orientation" as either cat lovers or dog lovers (Weber, 1990; Weinrich, 1987). Other exercises involve having students wear a pin advocating gay pride all day or read a book in public in which the words *gay* or *lesbian* are prominent on the cover.

Finally, lesbian or gay male educators may consider coming out. Lesbians and gay men of Color who can afford to come out in their work are particularly needed as role models. Although coming out publicly is not always feasible (Browning, 1987; Harbeck, 1991; Khayatt, 1992) and may depend on one's gender, ethnicity, class, rank, and the climate of the department, visibility can counter negative stereotypes that are only perpetuated by the absence of upstanding lesbians and gay men in influential positions (Lance, 1987).

Consequences of Inclusion

Finally, here is a word to instructors on what to expect. Students tend to overestimate the attention paid to ordinarily neglected topics. For example, one student complained that a Women's Studies course reader included too many lesbian writers when, in fact, less than 10% of the readings were by lesbian authors. In addition, content related to homosexuality is generally an emotionally laden issue. Heterosexual students may fear being blamed for societal homophobia or pressured to adopt a progay position; lesbian and gay male students may have great hopes of affirmation coupled with fears that suspected homophobia in others may become apparent (Browning, 1987). They also may take umbrage at having to educate others. Anticipated consequences, however, are often more negative than actual results. In a recent abnormal psychology section comprising almost 400 students, many of my students commented that they liked the "socio-cultural approach," appreciated the attempts to address "more delicate issues," and found that the "homosexual angles enhanced the presentation of the material and the class as a whole."

Only one student complained about a lesbian and gay male panel presentation by saying it was a "moral issue." Religious protestations against inclusion of content related to lesbians and gay men should be addressed by emphasizing the scientific and psychological nature of the material. The focus should be on recognizing and respecting differences, not pathologizing or demonizing them. The class can be informed that religious tenets have been used historically to justify oppression of other minority groups (e.g., Native Americans and African slaves) and must, therefore, be critically examined from a scientific perspective. Referrals to the growing number of lesbian and gay male religious organizations or assignment of supplementary readings on the issue of religion and homosexuality (e.g., Boswell, 1980; Davidson, 1986; Griffin, Wirth, & Wirth, 1986) may be helpful.

Conclusion

A survey of recent textbooks in the areas of introductory, social, developmental, and abnormal psychology revealed some progress but still generally scant attention to any aspect of the psychological issues related to lesbians and gay men beyond discussion of the *DSM* declassification and etiology. Instructors need to actively seek textbooks that present affirmative views of lesbians and gay men and reinforce publishers of these textbooks. Even the most inclusive textbooks, however, must be supplemented with lecture material or additional readings. Instructors not confident in their ability should consult with others more knowledgeable as well as begin to educate themselves and challenge their own belief systems. Instructors who learn to teach about the lives of lesbians and gay men will provide a more inclusive pedagogy of psychology for their students and, perhaps, prompt an intellectual awakening for themselves.

References

*Textbooks included in the survey.
**Textbooks included in the survey but not cited in text.

**Aronson, E., Wilson, T. D., & Akert, R. M. (1994). *Social psychology: The heart and the mind*. New York: HarperCollins.

**Berk, L. E. (1993). *Infants, children, and adolescents*. Needham Heights, MA: Allyn & Bacon.

Bieber, I., & Bieber, T. B. (1979). Male homosexuality. *Canadian Journal of Psychiatry, 24*, 409–421.

**Bigner, J. J. (1994). *Individual and family development*. Englewood Cliffs, NJ: Prentice Hall.

*Bootzin, R. R., Acocell, J. R., & Alloy, L. B. (1993). *Abnormal psychology: Current perspectives* (6th ed.). New York: McGraw-Hill.

Boswell, J. E. (1980). *Christianity, social tolerance, and homosexuality*. Chicago: University of Chicago Press.

**Brehm, S. S., & Kassin, S. M. (1993). *Social psychology* (2nd ed.). Boston: Houghton Mifflin.

Brooks, W. K. (1992). Research and the gay minority: Problems and possibilities. In N. J. Woodman (Ed.), *Lesbian and gay lifestyles: A guide for counseling and education* (pp. 201–215). New York: Irvington.

Brown, A., Goodwin, B. J., Hall, B. A., & Jackson-Lowman, H. (1985). A review of psychology of women textbooks: Focus on the Afro-American woman. *Psychology of Women Quarterly, 9*, 29–38.

Browning, C. (1987, August). *The process of teaching lesbian/gay psychology: Student and educator issues*. Paper presented at the annual meeting of the American Psychological Association, New York.

**Carlson, N. R., & Carlson, M. (1993). *Psychology: The science of behavior* (4th ed.). Needham Heights, MA: Allyn & Bacon.

*Cole, M., & Cole, S. R. (1993). *The development of children* (2nd ed.). New York: Freeman.

*Comer, R. J. (1992). *Abnormal psychology*. New York: Freeman.

Comstock, G. D. (1991). *Violence against lesbians and gay men*. New York: Columbia University Press.

Conger, J. J. (1975). Minutes of the Annual Meeting of the Council of Representatives. *American Psychologist, 30*, 620–651.

**Craig, G. J. (1992). *Human development* (6th ed.). Englewood Cliffs, NJ: Prentice Hall.

Crumpacker, L., & Vander Haegen, E. M. (1993). Pedagogy and prejudice: Strategies for confronting homophobia in the classroom. *Women's Studies Quarterly, 21*(3 & 4), 94–105.

Davidson, D. (1986). The spiritual dimension of the gay experience. *Christopher Street, 9*, 29–33.

**Deaux, K., Dane, F. C., & Wrightsman, L. S. (1993). *Social psychology in the 1990s* (6th ed.). Belmont, CA: Brooks/Cole.

Denmark, F. L. (1994). Engendering psychology. *American Psychologist, 49*, 329–334.

Fontaine, C. (1982). Teaching the psychology of women: A lesbian–feminist perspective. In M. Cruikshank (Ed.), *Lesbian studies: Present and future* (pp. 70–80). Old Westbury, NY: Feminist Press.

Freud, S. (1960). Letter to the mother of a homosexual son. In E. L. Freud (Ed.) and T. Steven & J. Stern (Trans.), *Letters of Sigmund Freud* (pp. 423–424). New York: Basic Books. (Original letter written in English in 1935)

Garnets, L. D., & Kimmel, D. C. (Eds.). (1993). *Psychological perspectives on lesbian & gay male experiences*. New York: Columbia University Press.

Gonsiorek, J. C., & Weinrich, J. D. (Eds.). (1991). *Homosexuality: Research implications for public policy*. Newbury Park, CA: Sage.

Greene, B. (1994). Ethnic-minority lesbians and gay men: Mental health and treatment issues. *Journal of Consulting and Clinical Psychology, 62*, 243–251.

Griffin, C. W., Wirth, M. J., & Wirth, A. G. (1986). *Beyond acceptance: Parents of lesbians and gays talk about their experiences*. Englewood Cliffs, NJ: Prentice Hall.

Harbeck, K. M. (Ed.). (1991). Coming out of the classroom closet: Gay and lesbian students, teachers, and curricula [Special issue]. *Journal of Homosexuality, 22*(3 & 4).

Herek, G. M. (1991). Stigma, prejudice, and violence against lesbians and gay men. In J. C. Gonsiorek & J. D. Weinrich (Eds.), *Homosexuality: Research implications for public policy* (pp. 60–80). Newbury Park, CA: Sage.

Hickok, K. (1982). Lesbian images in women's literature anthologies. In M. Cruikshank (Ed.), *Lesbian studies: Present and future* (pp. 132–147). Old Westbury, NY: Feminist Press.

**Holmes, D. S. (1994). *Abnormal psychology* (2nd ed.). New York: HarperCollins.

Hooker, E. (1957). The adjustment of the male overt homosexual. *Journal of Projective Techniques, 21*, 18–31.

Khayatt, M. D. (1992). *Lesbian teachers: An invisible presence*. Albany: State University of New York Press.

King, N. (1988). Teaching about lesbians and gays in the psychology curriculum. In P. A. Bronstein & K. Quina (Eds.), *Teaching a psychology of people: Resources for gender and sociocultural awareness* (pp. 168–175). Washington, DC: American Psychological Association.

Kirk, S. A., & Kutchins, H. (1992). *The selling of DSM: The rhetoric of science in psychiatry*. New York: Aldine de Gruyter.

Lance, L. M. (1987). The effects of interaction with gay persons on attitudes toward homosexuality. *Human Relations, 6*, 329–336.

**Lippa, R. A. (1994). *Introduction to social psychology* (2nd ed.). Pacific Grove, CA: Brooks/Cole.

McCord, D. M., & Herzog, H. A. (1991). What undergraduates want to know about homosexuality. *Teaching of Psychology, 18*, 243–244.

McDonald, G. (1981). Misrepresentation, liberalism, and heterosexual bias in introductory psychology textbooks. *Journal of Homosexuality, 6*, 45–59.

Morgan, K. S., & Nerison, R. M. (1993). Homosexuality and psychopolitics: An historical overview. *Psychotherapy, 30*, 133–140.

*Myers, D. G. (1992). *Psychdogy* (3rd ed.). New York: Worth.

*Myers, D. G. (1993). *Social psychology* (4th ed.). New York: McGraw-Hill.

Newton, D. E. (1979). Representations of homosexuality in health science textbooks. *Journal of Homosexuality, 4,* 247–253.

**Papalia, D. E., & Wendkosolds, S. (1993). *A child's world: Infancy—adolescence* (6th ed.). New York: McGraw-Hill.

**Rathus, S. A. (1993). *Psychology* (5th ed.). New York: Harcourt Brace.

Rivera, R. R. (1991). Sexual orientation and the law. In J. C. Gonsiorek & J. D. Weinrich (Eds.), *Homosexuality: Research implications for public policy* (pp. 81–100). Newbury Park, CA: Sage.

*Rubin, Z., Peplau, L. A., & Salovey, P. (1993). *Psychology.* Boston: Houghton Mifflin.

Russo, V. (1981). *Celluloid closet: Homosexuality in the movies.* New York: Harper & Row.

**Sarason, I. G., & Sarason, B. R. (1993). *Abnormal psychology: The problem of maladaptive behavior* (7th ed.). Englewood Cliffs, NJ: Prentice Hall.

**Sigelman, C. K., & Shaffer, D. R. (1995). *Life-span human development.* Pacific Grove, CA: Brooks/Cole.

Simoni, J. M. (1996). Pathways to prejudice: Predicting heterosexist attitudes with demographics, self-esteem, and contact with lesbians and gay men. *Journal of College Student Development, 37,* 68–78.

**Smith, E. R., & Mackie, D. M. (1995). *Social psychology.* New York: Worth.

Socarides, C. W. (1968). *The overt homosexual.* New York: Grune & Stratton.

Socarides, C. W. (1978). *Homosexuality.* New York: Aronson.

*Sue, D., Sue, D., & Sue, S. (1994). *Understanding abnormal behavior* (4th ed.). Boston: Houghton Mifflin.

*Wade, C., & Tavris, C. (1993). *Psychology* (3rd ed.). New York: HarperCollins.

Watter, D. N. (1987). Teaching about homosexuality: A review of the literature. *Journal of Sex Education and Therapy, 13,* 63–66.

Weber, A. L. (1990). Teaching tips for social psychology. *Contemporary Social Psychology, 14,* 226–228.

Weinrich, J. D. (1987). *Sexual landscapes.* New York: Charles Scribner's Sons.

Whitlock, K., & DiLapi, E. M. (1983). Friendly fire: Homophobia in sex education literature. *Interracial Books for Children Bulletin, 14,* 20–23.

**Wilson G. T., O'Leary, K. D., & Nathan, P. (1992). *Abnormal psychology* (2nd ed.). Englewood Cliffs, NJ: Prentice Hall.

**Zimbardo P. G., & Weber, A. L. (1994). *Psychology.* New York: HarperCollins.

Zimmerman, B. (1982). One out of thirty: Lesbianism in women's studies textbooks. In M. Cruikshank (Ed.), *Lesbian studies: Present and future* (pp. 128–131). Old Westbury, NY: Feminist Press.

Appendix: Additional Resources

Boston Lesbian Psychologies Collective. (Ed.). (1987). *Lesbian psychologies: Explorations and challenges.* Urbana: University of Illinois Press.

Committee on Lesbian and Gay Concerns. (1990). *A selected bibliography of lesbian and gay concerns in psychology: An affirmative perspective.* Washington, DC: American Psychological Association.

D'Augelli, A. R. (1991). Teaching lesbian and gay development: A pedagogy of the oppressed. In W. G. Tierney (Ed.), *Culture and ideology in higher education* (pp. 214–233). New York: Praeger.

Forrister, D. K. (1992). The integration of lesbian and gay content in direct practice courses. In N. J. Woodman (Ed.), *Lesbian and gay lifestyles: A guide for counseling and education* (pp. 51–65). New York: Irvington.

Garnets, L. D., & Kimmel, D. C. (1991). Lesbian and gay male dimensions in the psychological study of human diversity. In J. D. Goodchilds (Ed.), *Psychological perspectives on human diversity in America* (pp. 137–192). Washington, DC: American Psychological Association.

Green, B., & Herek, G. M. (Eds.). (1994). *Psychological perspectives on lesbian and gay issues: Vol. 1. Lesbian and gay psychology: Theory, research, and clinical applications.* Thousand Oaks, CA: Sage.

Herek, G. M., Kimmel, D. C., Amaro, H., & Melton, G. B. (1991). Avoiding heterosexist bias in psychological research. *American Psychologist, 46,* 957–963.

Lee, J. A. B. (1992). Teaching content related to lesbian and gay identity formation. In N. J. Woodman (Ed.), *Lesbian and gay lifestyles: A guide for counseling and education* (pp. 1–22). New York: Irvington.

Schieder, E. (1993). Integrating lesbian content. *Women's Studies Quarterly, 21*(3 & 4), 46–56.

Refer also to APA Division 44, the National Gay and Lesbian Task Force, and lesbian and gay male community and professional organizations.

Note

This research was supported in part by National Cancer Institute Training Grant 5 T32 CA09492 and the Aaron Diamond Foundation. I thank Linda Garnets and Karina Walters for their comments on earlier drafts of this article.

Infusing Black Psychology Into the Introductory Psychology Course

Lisa A. Whitten

One of the most exciting challenges of teaching the introductory psychology course is exploring a wide range of topics. Many teachers of introductory courses would welcome the opportunity to include material on Black psychol-ogy and would benefit from exposure to ideas and information for developing lectures on these subjects. In this article, I provide a review of the literature, a brief introduction to Black psychology, curriculum resources, a lecture outline, and small-group activities. I also provide student reactions to lectures on these topics. In the first course, the influence of social, political, and economic factors on psychological functioning must be clearly understood. The topic of Black psychology should be infused into the introductory course to communicate to students that these forces influence the full spectrum of psychological concerns. Students' knowledge about how and why humans function should include an understanding of variations in psychological functioning among racial and ethnic groups.

Rationale for Infusing Black Psychology

Introductory psychology textbooks give scant coverage to race, class, and the range of larger social forces that affect one's psychological functioning. By infusing Black psychology into the course, one can emphasize, when appropriate, the impact of social, political, and economic factors on human development. These issues must be addressed in order to provide students with a thorough introduction to psychology. Race and culture can serve as unifying threads throughout the course. The experience of African-Americans, in particular, may facilitate the understanding of other groups, such as women, the physically disabled, and homosexuals, that have experienced discrimination.

My student evaluations reveal that some students believe that racial and cultural factors are irrelevant to psychology, perhaps because their textbooks do not address these subjects. Covering these topics in class validates their importance. If this information is not presented, students may believe that psychologists have not investigated the important variables of race and culture and that African-American psychologists have not contributed scholarly work to the field. Given the importance of role modeling, this latter belief could discourage some African-American students from pursuing careers in psychology. Finally, given the recent upsurge of racial conflict on college campuses, the introductory psychology course could also educate students about racial and cultural differences and the development and reduction of prejudice. Students should be exposed to the research and theories of African-American and other scholars on these issues.

Review of Introductory Psychology Textbooks

I surveyed the indexes of 25 textbooks to determine the extent of their treatment of several topics related to Black psychology: race, racism, culture, Black, and prejudice. All of these texts included material on at least one of these topics, but in some cases this information was limited to only one page. Gleitman (1987) had many references to culture, as did Price, Glickstein, Horton, Sherman, and Fazio (1987) and Wade and Tavris (1987). Roediger, Rushton, Capaldi, and Paris (1987) included 12 references to Black people and a total of 24 additional references to the key terms. In general, intelligence testing was a popular issue, as was prejudice, which was mentioned in 19 textbooks. Only 6 of the 25 texts use the word *racism*, and only 8 refer to the word

race. These data suggest that textbook authors, for the most part, do not consider race and culture important variables in psychological development, and/or they do not deem them crucial for introductory courses. A new textbook by Allen and Santrock (in press) integrates material on culture and ethnicity in each chapter of the text and the instructor's manual. It will be very useful to instructors who are interested in placing more emphasis on these topics.

Another shortcoming is that these textbooks (including Allen & Santrock, in press) do not refer to Black psychology as an alternative approach, despite a considerable amount of published literature on the topic, including the *Journal of Black Psychology*, which had its inception in 1974, and publications by Akbar (1981); Baldwin (1986); Baldwin and Bell (1985); Boykin, Franklin, and Yates (1979); Harrison (1982), R. Jones (1972, 1978, 1980, 1989, 1991); Myers (1985); Nobles (1972, 1976, 1978, 1986, 1987); and White and Parham (1990).

Review of the Literature on Teaching Black Psychology

A literature review revealed two articles on teaching Black psychology (Fairchild, 1984, 1988) and one on Black studies in psychology (Hicks & Ridley, 1979). Fairchild (1984) advocated incorporating Black psychology into the general psychology course starting with the first lecture on the history of psychology. Later, Fairchild (1988) outlined curriculum resources for teaching courses in Black psychology. Hicks and Ridley (1979) reviewed undergraduate catalogs for their inclusion of courses related to Black studies in psychology. An article on teaching a Black family course by Hill-Collins (1986) presented a "Myths of Black Families" questionnaire for use on the first day of class. Since its inception in 1974, the journal *Teaching of Psychology* has published only two articles that focus on race or culture. DeFour and Paludi (1991) provided a useful course outline for integrating scholarship on women of Color into the psychology of women course. Cushner (1987) described a culture assimilator, an exercise that facilitates teaching cross-cultural concepts to people with limited intercultural or international experience. Given the plethora of curriculum materials on other topics for the introductory psychology course, scholars should develop more materials related to teaching about race and culture.

Definition of Black Psychology

Black psychology, also called African psychology by Akbar (1981), Baldwin (1986), Nobles (1972), and others, seeks to develop a theoretical framework for understanding African-Americans (and other people of African descent), challenging the assumption that Blacks are psychologically inferior. It considers the full range of African-American experience; Nobles (1972) stated that Black psychology "is more than the darker dimension of general psychology" (p. 18). Rather, it is a distinct and well developed area of investigation within the field of psychology.

Although there are several opinions on when Black psychology began (Fairchild, 1984; Jackson, 1982; White &

Parham, 1990), Jackson dated Black psychology to the 1920s when African-American researchers began to address some of the biased notions promoted by White researchers about African-American people. White and Parham (1990) suggested that Black psychology began with the establishment of the Association of Black Psychologists in 1968. Guthrie (1976) and White and Parham (1990) highlighted some of the early contributions of Black psychologists. Students should be aware that early in this century, well before the Civil Rights movement, African-American scholars were investigating topics related to the psychology of African-American people.

R. Jones (1972) identified four themes in Black psychology:

> The first theme is a deemphasis on deficiency based hypotheses about black behavior, and second, a concurrent emphasis upon the positive aspects of black behavior which have permitted survival—though not without scars—in a racist society. . . . A third theme is a rejection of white normative standards when understanding and assessing black behavior. . . . A fourth theme is a quest for explanations of black behavior rooted not only in psychological phenomena but also in social and economic factors as well which serves to maintain the system which serves to subjugate blacks psychologically. Thus, certain psychological states of blacks are described within the context of environmental forces which create and maintain them. (p. xii)

Table 1. Outline for Black Psychology Lecture

Introduction
  Brief History of African-Americans
    The Origin of African-Americans
    The Triangle Slave Trade
    The Civil Rights Movement
  The Black Psychology Model
    Definition of Black Psychology
    The Importance of Using African-Americans as a Standard
      When Studying African-Americans
    Trends in the Study of African-Americans
      G. Stanley Hall
      Cultural Deficit/Cultural Deprivation/Cultural Difference
      Blaming the Victim
  How Race/Culture Affect Development
    Poverty
    Social Policy
    Prejudice
    Institutional Racism
    Stress/Illness
Application
  Scholarship on African-American Families
  Relation Between Family Style and History
  Attempts to Correct Misperceptions
  Impact on Policy Decisions
Discussion
  Large Group
    Student Reactions
  Small-group Activities
    Structured Activities
Conclusion
  Critique of Black Psychology Model
  Racial Attitudes
    What You Can Do to Make a Difference
  Future Trends in Black Psychology
  Importance for All People of Understanding the Relations
    Among Culture, Race, Politics, Economics, and Psychological
    Functioning

R. Jones (1972) further noted that, although the authors of the 1972 edition of *Black Psychology* recognize both individual differences among African-Americans and overlap between the behaviors of African-Americans and Whites, there are "forces operative in American society which shape and influence black Americans" (p. xii). Scholars using the Black psychology perspective seek to understand how these influences affect the psychological development and functioning of African-Americans and to illuminate the etiology and impact of racism.

Some authors (e.g., Baldwin, 1981, 1986; Nobles, 1972; Williams, 1981) asserted that a different theoretical framework, using African philosophical assumptions as a basis, is necessary for an accurate understanding of African-American psychological functioning. For example, Black psychology asserts that psychologists should focus on spirituality and one's relationship to nature as important elements of personality and should note that, from an African perspective, the survival of the group supersedes the survival of individuals (Mbiti, 1970; Nobles, 1972).

The Black Psychology Lecture

Infusing race and culture throughout the semester can decrease their emotional volatility. In addition, one or two lectures (depending on the length of each class) focusing specifically on Black psychology can serve to explicate major themes. Table 1 provides a sample lecture outline, and Table 2 presents guidelines for infusing topics into the introductory psychology course. Table 3 includes some curriculum resources available to instructors.

Table 2. Suggestions for Infusing Material on Black Psychology Into the Introductory Psychology Curriculum

Developmental psychology
  Cultural/racial variations in childrearing
  Educational/intelligence testing
  Child abuse
  Differences in infant mortality and general morbidity and
    mortality
Biological bases of behavior
  Early misconceptions about Africans's cranial capacity
  Health issues
  AIDS
Family
  Variations in family constellations and dynamics
  Impact of the welfare system and migration on families
Learning
  Cultural and racial variations in learning style
  Special education
  African-American male academies
Intelligence
  Bias in intelligence testing
  Strength of African-American children
Abnormal psychology
  Bias in diagnosis and treatment
  Impact of environmental factors/social class
  Cross-cultural/cross-racial counseling
Social psychology
  Racism
  Prejudice
  Attitude change
  Black on Black crime
  Gang behavior

Table 3. Curriculum Resources

Journals

Black Scholar
Published bimonthly. Individual, $30.00; institutional, $50.00. P.O. Box 2869, Oakland, CA 94609.

College Teaching
Published six times a year. Individual, $26.00; institutional, $46.00. 1–800–365–9753.

Feminist Teacher
Published three times a year. Individual, $12.00; institutional, $20.00. Ballentine 442, Indiana University, Bloomington, IN 46405.

Journal of Black Psychology
Published twice a year. Individual, $30.00; institutional, $50.00. Association of Black Psychologists, Inc., P.O. Box 55999, Washington, DC 20040–5999, (202) 722–0808.

Journal of Black Studies
Published four times a year. Individual, $42.00; institutional, $112.00. Sage Publications, Inc., 2455 Teller Road, Newbury Park, CA 91320, (805) 499–0721; fax (805) 499–0871.

Journal of Multicultural Community Health
Published quarterly. Free subscriptions available to municipal, state, and federal agencies, as well as public schools and universities and nonprofit community based organizations. Individual, $25.00; institutional, $35.00; student, $15.00. 125 Worth Street, Room 502, New York, NY 10013.

Journal of Negro Education
Published quarterly. Individual, $16.00; institutional, $28.00. Circulation Department, Journal of Negro Education, P.O. Box 311, Howard University, Washington, DC 20059, (202) 806–8120.

Radical Teacher
Published three times a year. Individual, $10.00. Box 102, Kendall Square Post Office, Cambridge, MA 02142.

Sage: A Scholarly Journal on Black Women
Published twice a year. Individual, $15.00; institutional, $25.00. Sage Women's Education Press, Inc., Box 42741, Atlanta, GA 30311, (404) 681–3643.

Transformations
Published twice a year. Price not listed. Sylvia Baer, Editor, Gloucester County College, Tanyard Road, Sewell, NJ 08080, (609) 468–5000, x207; fax (609) 468–9462.

Western Journal of Black Studies
Published quarterly. Individual, $20.00; institutional, $25.00. Washington State University Press, Pullman, WA 99164–5190, (509) 335–3518.

Other Periodicals

American Visions
Published bimonthly. $30.00. Visions Foundation, Inc., Carter G. Woodson House, 1538 Ninth Street NW, Washington, DC 20002, (202) 462–1779.

The Black Collegian
Published four times a year. Students, $5.00. Black Collegian Services, 1240 South Brand, New Orleans, LA 70125, (504) 824–5694.

Black Issues in Higher Education
Published twice monthly. $40.00. Cox, Matthews & Associates, Inc., 10520 Warwick Avenue, Suite B–8, Fairfax, VA 22030, (703) 385–2981; fax (703) 385–1839.

Teaching Professor
Published monthly except July and August. $39.00. Magna Publications, Inc., 2718 Dryden Drive, Madison, WI 53704–3006, (608) 249–2455.

(continued)

Table 3. Curriculum Resources *(Continued)*

Black Excellence
Published five times during the academic year. $11.00. NAFEO Excellence, Inc., Lovejoy Building, 400 12th Street NE, Washington, DC 20002, (202) 543–9112.

Emerge
Published monthly with combined issues in December/January and July/August. $14.97. Emerge Communications, Inc., 599 Broadway, New York, NY 10012.

Audiotapes and Videotapes

The Association of Black Psychologists, Inc., P.O. Box 55999, Washington, DC 10040–5999, (202) 722–0808 (audiotapes and videotapes).

Mind Productions, Inc., P.O. Box 11221, Tallahassee, FL 32302 (audiotapes of Na'im Akbar).

Proud to be . . . a Black Video Collection, One Kendall Square, Building 600, Suite 125, Cambridge, MA 02139, (617) 868–8965.

Films for the Humanities and Sciences, Multicultural Studies on Video, P.O. Box 2053, Princeton, NJ 08543–2053, (800) 257–5126.

Books

African Psychology Institute (1982)
Chicago Center for Afro-American Studies and Research, Inc. (1981)
R. Jones (1978)
McKeachie (1986)

Articles

Rothenberg (1984, 1988)
Shaw and Wicker (1981)
Smith and Stewart (1983)
Whitten (in press)

Background

A brief history of African-Americans in the U.S. is necessary because most students have not taken this course in high school or college. Students should be exposed to the notions that African-American history began in Africa, not in slavery (Franklin & Moss, 1988), and that the impact of a group's history on their psychological functioning is important. The fact that African-Americans have retained many elements of African culture should be noted (Foster, 1983; Herskovitz, 1941; Holloway, 1990; Sudarkasa, 1975, 1980; Turner, 1949).

In this section, the instructor can present examples of early misconceptions about the psychology of African-American people. For example, enslaved people who attempted to escape were sometimes diagnosed with drapetomania, which means "running away madness" (Thomas & Sillen, 1972, p. 2). From a Black psychology perspective, running away is an indication of a healthy desire to be free and to take initiative to acquire freedom, not a pathological behavior that requires diagnosis. Another example is found in an article by Hall (1905), who suggested that African-Americans and Whites are so different that they require completely distinct medical treatments.

Beliefs (both erroneous and accurate) related to African-American family dynamics (Billingsley, 1968; Hill, 1972; Pipes-McAdoo, 1988; Sudarkasa, 1975, 1980) and child development (Torrence, 1982) can also be presented briefly. Students should know that some psychological constructs (e.g., intelligence, self-esteem, and family health) and some physical characteristics (e.g., cranial size and lip size) have been used in an attempt to document the presumed inferiority of African-American people. Research by Dillard (1972), Thomas and Sillen (1972), and Ryan (1976) can be useful in defining cultural deprivation and cultural difference theories and emphasizing how one's perspective determines one's conclusions. According to Thomas and Sillen (1972),

> The concept of "cultural deprivation" places the emphasis on the psychological characteristics of the poor individual himself—his language use, perceptual level, cognitive style, emotional attributes. As one sociologist has observed, poverty nowadays is often discussed as if it were a personal trait rather than a social condition. This shift has important consequences. It means a redirection of concern, from overcoming the objective circumstances of poverty to altering the attributes of people who are poor. (pp. 67–68)

Cultural difference theories, on the other hand, recognize variations in human behavior without placing a value judgment on the behavior or the people. Intergroup variations are seen as acceptable and adaptive rather than as pathological deviations from the standards of the group in power. The continuing role of African-American psychologists and others in dispelling these beliefs can be illuminated.

Definition

Black psychology focuses on the unique experience of African-American people and the relation between this experience and the environment. It is important for students to know that scholars are attempting to understand the behavior of African-American people without overlooking or minimizing strengths, adaptability, achievements, and health. Some African-American psychologists believe that African-Americans were stripped of much of their culture and forced to take on a new incompatible culture that has led to psychological difficulties. Black psychological perspectives (also known as Afrocentric or Africentric perspectives) are designed to reconnect African-Americans with these African cultural features.

It is also useful to define the terms *ethnicity*, *race*, and *culture*. The definitions of ethnicity and race are especially complicated. A brief review of the definitions (*Webster's New Collegiate Dictionary*, 1973) revealed little agreement among the three definitions, fostering confusion. Yetman (1985) pointed out that ethnicity and race are socially defined phenomena. He also noted that *ethnic* is derived from the Greek word *ethnos*, meaning people. According to Yetman (1985),

> An ethnic group is defined on the basis of its cultural characteristics. Ethnicity, or the sense of belonging to a particular ethnic group, thus implies the existence of a distinct culture or subculture in which group members feel themselves bound together by a common history, values, attitudes, and behaviors—in its broadest sense, a sense of peoplehood—and are so regarded by other members of the society. (p. 6)

On the other hand, Yetman (1985) defined *race* as follows:

> A society therefore defines a social category as a race when it isolates certain *physical characteristics* [emphasis added], perceives them to be innate and inherited, and magnifies their importance as differentiating factors. These physical characteristics are usually believed to be related to other immutable mental, emotional or moral characteristics such as intelligence. (p. 8)

The physical traits used to define a race can vary from society to society, such that a person identified as Black in one country may not be defined as Black in another.

Berreman (1986) noted that some authors distinguish between race and ethnicity, but asserted that " 'ethnic' has increasingly been used to refer to all social distinctions based on birth or ancestry, be they associated with race, language, or anything else" (p. 24), and he adopted this usage. I recommend not using the terms *race* and *ethnicity* interchangeably. The instructor must clarify at the outset which definitions are being used.

Application

At this point in the lecture, one can describe a particular area of investigation in detail. The African-American family is an excellent topic because it has received considerable attention in the media and scholarly journals. Billingsley (1968), Blassingame (1979), Boyd-Franklin (1989), Foster (1983), Hill (1972), and Nobles (1978) provided relevant information. The study of Black English, adolescence, and learning are other useful areas. Instructors can ask students to provide examples of stereotypes about African-American families, their language, and their values. One can reemphasize the distinction between the cultural difference and cultural deprivation models, as well as the importance of social class variations among African-Americans.

Instructors often mention the value of joining professional associations at some point in the term. In this lecture, students can be told about the Association of Black Psychologists (ABPsi) and provided with the address of the national office and the local chapter. To mitigate against a sense of exclusion (D. Papademas, personal communication, February 24, 1989) often experienced by White students when instructors address cultural and racial issues, ABPsi should be included on a list of organizations relevant to many ethnic and racial groups (Table 4). Students should also know about *A Resource Manual for African-American Psychology Students* (DeFour, Whitten, & Johnson, 1992) that offers guidelines for preparing for, applying to, and thriving in graduate school, as well as other resources, most of which could be useful to any psychology major. The role of African-American psychologists as social activists should be stressed, particularly in relation to the psychological testing of African-American children in California (Bay Area Association of Black Psychologists, 1972).

Lecture Summary and Conclusions

A critique of the Black psychology model must be included and compared and contrasted with other models, such as feminist psychology and the psychology of disability.

Table 4. Organizational Resources

American Orthopsychiatric Association
19 West 44th Street, Suite 1616, New York, NY 10036,
  (212) 345–5770.

American Psychological Association
750 First Street NE, Washington, DC 20002–4242,
  (202) 336–5500.

American Psychological Society
1511 K Street NW, Suite 345, Washington, DC 20005–1401,
  (202) 783–2077.

Asian American Psychological Association
Nolan Zane, Graduate School of Education, University of
  California, Santa Barbara, Santa Barbara, CA 93106,
  (805) 893–8564; fax (805) 893–3324.

Association of Black Psychologists, Inc.
P.O. Box 55999, Washington, DC 20040–5999, (202) 722–0808.

Association of Black Social Workers
1969 Madison Avenue, New York, NY 10035, (212) 348–0035.

Association of Black Women in Higher Education
Jacqueline A. Kane, Cultural Education Center, Room 5A55,
  Empire State Plaza, Albany, NY 12230, (518) 474–5313.

National Black Child Development Institute
1463 Rhode Island Avenue, Washington, DC 20005,
  (202) 387–1281.

National Conference on Undergraduate Research, Conferences &
  Institutes
2174 Annex Building, University of Utah, Salt Lake City, UT
  84112, (801) 581–5809; fax (801) 581–5809. (Some travel
  funds available.)

National Council for Black Studies
Jacqueline Wade, Ohio State University, 1030 Lincoln Tower,
  1800 Cannon Drive, Columbus, OH 43210, (614) 292–1035;
  fax (614) 292–2713.

National Hispanic Psychologists Association
Mary DeFerreire, Texas Department of Mental Health and Mental
  Retardation, Austin State Hospital, 4110 Guadalupe, Austin, TX
  78751–4296, (512) 452–0381, x4802; fax (512) 478–2044.

Society of Indian Psychologists
Candice Fleming, National Center for American Indian and
  Alaska Native Mental Health Research, University of Colorado
  Health Science Center, 4200 East 9th Avenue, Campus Box
  C24–917, Denver, CO 80262, (303) 270–4600.

Society Organized Against Racism in Higher Education, Inc.
237 Cushing Hall, Northeastern University, Boston, MA 02115,
  (617) 437–2612.

Students and Youth Against Racism
P.O. Box 1819, Madison Square Station, New York, NY 10159,
  (212) 741–0633.

World Federation for Mental Health
Richard Hunter, Deputy Secretary General, 1021 Prince Street,
  Alexandria, VA 22314–2971, (703) 684–7722.

This approach will place Black psychology in the larger context of the study of disenfranchised people. Students should realize that some scholars have promoted similar distorted ideas about women, the physically disabled, immigrants, and other people of Color. One can encourage students to take courses, write term papers on these topics, and/or get involved with professional and student groups that seek to eradicate bias and discrimination and to correct racist and biased scholarship.

Student Reactions

Student reactions during and after lectures of this type have been diverse. Both African-American and White students have had strong reactions. Each semester, at least one African-American student comments on the value of the lecture. Numerous students assert that they have never taken other courses that addressed race and racism. They are curious about other courses I teach, and many have taken them. Other students have noted in evaluations that the inclusion of material on African-Americans is a strength of the course. These reactions indicate that African-American students who take a course in which the instructor infuses Black psychology may be more motivated to continue in the field.

The intensity of my students' responses suggests that the Black psychology lecture should be presented after rapport has been established with the class, especially when students' backgrounds are quite varied. Students sometimes make negative comments about the instructor on their course evaluations (i.e., the instructor is racist, hates White people, or only talks about racism, which has nothing to do with psychology). These comments reveal the difficulty many students experience when they encounter ideas about race that are different from their own or when they believe that race and culture are not the purview of psychology. I discuss strategies for managing emotional reactions in an article that will appear in the journal *Transformations* (Whitten, in press).

Small-Group Activities

Research on racial stereotypes in elementary school students suggests that the most effective method of attitude change is small-group interaction in multicultural contexts (Aronson, 1987). Fairchild (1984) suggested that teachers of Black psychology should strive to place students in "cooperative and equal status relationships that require that they collectively share in the responsibility for the course of instruction" (p. 57). In addition to attending the lecture on Black psychology, students can discuss and apply some of the relevant concepts in small, less formal groups using a variety of activities. Ideally, instructors will assign students to groups that facilitate multicultural contact, except when focusing on their own cultural or racial group. My experience suggests that many White students do not devote time to considering the impact of race and ethnicity on their development. Even in racially homogenous settings, students can be divided according to geographic origin, ethnicity, religion, gender, or history of immigration. Alternatively, each group can do an exercise focusing on different racial or ethnic groups and then compare notes. A list of possible group activities is presented in Table 5. After about 30 min, each

Table 5. Small-Group Activities

1. Write intelligence test questions that tap knowledge about a specific cultural group and that people outside the group would fail.
2. Design a parent training program that takes into account the unique features of a particular cultural group.
3. Develop a program to improve racial self-concept of African-American (or immigrant or refugee) preschoolers.
4. Develop a drug/AIDS prevention program that takes into account students' racial/cultural diversity and their varying notions about and experience with drugs/sexuality.
5. Present debates in which two opposing positions of a controversial topic regarding race (e.g., the impact of single parent homes, interracial marriage, and transracial adoption). Each person must present an aspect of the argument.
6. Administer the African Self-Consciousness Scale (Baldwin & Bell, 1985) and have students discuss in small groups how it compares and contrasts with their own experience.

group can present its ideas to the larger group. The instructor can distribute specific written outlines for each project to provide structure. Students can submit written summaries based on their group's discussion and/or research.

Aronson (1987) and Lucher, Rosenfield, Sihes, and Aronson (1976) conducted innovative research on teaching in multicultural elementary school classrooms using a technique called the *jigsaw method*. Students read parts of a larger written assignment on which they will be tested. Individuals explained the material in their paragraphs to the rest of the group after consulting with other students who read the same segment of the project. This technique increased academic performance, self-esteem, and fondness for school and diminished negative racial stereotypes; it could prove fruitful in the introductory psychology classroom as well. Students may also generate test questions from a segment of a chapter or other material. Carroll (1986) used the jigsaw method in a psychology laboratory course and found that it improved student evaluations of the course, allowed more students to complete the course in one term, and resulted in more complex research projects. He concluded that the jigsaw method is "an excellent motivational device and has the pedagogical value of calling on the distinctive backgrounds, experiences, and abilities of different students" (p. 210).

Faculty Issues

Broadening the college curriculum is difficult for some faculty. For example, an advertisement by the National Association of Scholars (1989) stated that "the idea that the traditional curriculum 'excludes' the contributions of all but males of European descent is patently false" (p. 23). To make the suggested changes, some faculty will need training and encouragement from administrators, students, and colleagues. Faculty could arrange for special training sessions on presenting material about race and culture and on using small-group exercises. Ongoing informal discussions among faculty can also provide a forum for sharing ideas and strategies. In addition, African-American guest speakers could be invited to teach a class about Black psychology, especially on campuses with few African-American faculty.

Conclusion

Exposure to perspectives on race and culture could enhance the quality of students' college experiences, even at colleges with a racially diverse student body where interaction among groups is often limited. Providing a new context for understanding cultural/racial differences may influence some students to challenge their prejudices and reach out to other students. The lectures, readings, and exercises should help students understand cultural and racial differences, celebrate rather than denigrate them, and dispel fears and myths about groups.

Teaching Black psychology affords an excellent opportunity to relate psychology to other disciplines, such as sociology, anthropology, literature, history, art, and music. Students can be encouraged to pursue these areas in future coursework, and they will be more likely to do so when they are clear about the relations among the disciplines.

Faculty can also apply this curriculum model to work on other people of Color, immigrants, refugees, women, the disabled, homosexuals, and the elderly. Depending on the composition of the student body, one may develop similar curricula for other groups. For some students, recognizing that psychological research and theories have led to a skewed understanding of many oppressed groups can make the ideas put forth by Black psychology more acceptable. The infusion of Black psychology should not leave students with the impression that African-Americans are the only group that western psychology has misinterpreted due to the use of theories based on the notion of cultural deprivation. In addition to drawing these comparisons, the unique experience of each ethnic, racial, or gender group should also be outlined and documented.

Another goal of this curriculum and the teaching strategies associated with it is to increase the number of African-Americans pursuing psychology as a career. The number of African-Americans pursuing doctoral degrees in psychology has always been low and has dropped over the last 10 to 12 years (J. Jones, 1987). Students should recognize that psychology is relevant to African-American people, that African-American scholars have contributed to the literature in meaningful ways, and that mentors are available.

Future research on curriculum development in Black psychology should investigate how these lectures alter students' perceptions of African-American people, poverty, and racism. Evaluative procedures could measure gains in knowledge as well as changes in attitudes and self-esteem in African-American and other students. Additional work on curriculum development in Black psychology should be published to enhance both the exposure of faculty to this area and their skill in teaching this material.

It is unrealistic to expect that infusing material on Black psychology into a single course can radically change the misconceptions and prejudices some students harbor about African-American people. This material can stimulate students' inquisitiveness about the impact of social, political, economic, and cultural forces on psychological functioning and development, and it can challenge students to consider these issues when analyzing their own lives and the lives of people they encounter.

References

African Psychology Institute. (1982). *The African Psychology Institute training module handbook*. Tallahassee, FL: Author.

Akbar, N. (1981). Cultural expression of the African-American child. *Black Child Journal, 2*(2), 6–15.

Allen, L., & Santrock, J. W. (in press). *Psychology: The contexts of behavior*. Madison, WI: Brown.

Aronson, E. (1987). Teaching students what they think they already know about prejudice and desegregation. In V. P. Makosky (Ed.), *The G. Stanley Hall lecture series* (Vol. 7, pp. 69–84). Washington, DC: American Psychological Association.

Baldwin, J. (1981). Notes on an Africentric theory of Black personality. *Western Journal of Black Studies, 5*, 172–179.

Baldwin, J. (1986). African (Black) psychology: Issues and synthesis. *Journal of Black Studies, 16*, 235–249.

Baldwin, J., & Bell, Y. R. (1985). The African self-consciousness scale: An Africentric personality questionnaire. *Western Journal of Black Studies, 9*, 61–68.

Bay Area Association of Black Psychologists. (1972). Position statement on use of IQ and ability tests. In R. Jones (Ed.), *Black psychology* (pp. 92–94). New York: Harper & Row.

Berreman, G. D. (1986). Race, caste and other invidious distinctions in social stratification. In N. R. Yetman (Ed.), *Majority and minority: The dynamics of race and ethnicity in American life* (4th ed., pp. 21–39). Boston: Allyn & Bacon.

Billingsley, A. (1968). *Black families in White America*. Englewood Cliffs, NJ: Prentice-Hall.

Blassingame, J. (1979). *The slave community: Plantation life in the antebellum south*. New York: Oxford University Press.

Boyd-Franklin, N. (1989). *Black families in family therapy*. New York: Guilford.

Boykin, A. W., Franklin, A. J., & Yates, J. F. (1979). *Research directions of Black psychologists*. New York: Russell Sage.

Carroll, D. W. (1986). Use of the jigsaw technique in laboratory and discussion classes. *Teaching of Psychology, 13*, 208–210.

Chicago Center for Afro-American Studies and Research, Inc. (1981). *Guide to scholarly journals in Black studies*. Chicago: Peoples College Press.

Cushner, K. H. (1987). Teaching cross-cultural psychology: Providing the missing link. *Teaching of Psychology, 14*, 220–224.

DeFour, D., & Paludi, M. (1991). Integrating scholarship on ethnicity into the psychology of women course. *Teaching of Psychology, 18*, 85–90.

DeFour, D., Whitten, L., & Johnson, S. (1992). *A resource manual for African-American psychology students* (4th ed.). New York: New York Association of Black Psychologists/Association of Black Psychologists.

Dillard, J. L. (1972). *Black English*. New York: Vintage.

Fairchild, H. (1984). Teaching Black psychology. *Western Journal of Black Studies, 8*, 55–60.

Fairchild, H. (1988). Curriculum design for Black (African-American) psychology. In P. A. Bronstein & K. Quina (Eds.), *Teaching a psychology of people: Resources for gender and sociocultural awareness* (pp. 134–141). Washington, DC: American Psychological Association.

Foster, H. J. (1983). African patterns in the Afro-American family. *Journal of Black Studies, 14*, 201–232.

Franklin, J. H., & Moss, A. A., Jr. (1988). *From slavery to freedom* (6th ed.). New York: McGraw-Hill.

Gleitman, H. (1987). *Basic psychology* (2nd ed.). New York: Norton.

Guthrie, R. V. (1976). *Even the rat was White: A historical view of psychology*. New York: Harper & Row.

Hall, G. S. (1905). The Negro in Africa and America. *Journal of Genetic Psychology 12*, 350–368.

Harrison, A. (1982). *Conference on empirical research in Black psychology final report*. Washington, DC: Ford Foundation.

Herskovitz, M. (1941). *The myth of the Negro past*. Boston: Beacon.

Hicks, L., & Ridley, S. (1979). Black studies in psychology. *American Psychologist, 34*, 597–602.

Hill, R. (1972). *The strengths of Black families*. New York: Emerson Hall.

Hill-Collins, P. (1986). Getting off to a good start: The first class in Black family studies. *Teaching Sociology, 19*, 193–195.

Holloway, J. E. (1990). *Africanisms in American culture*. Bloomington: Indiana University Press.

Jackson, G. (1982). Black psychology: An avenue to the study of Afro-Americans. *Journal of Black Studies, 12*, 241–260.

Jones, J. (1987, June). *Student recruitment and retention: A marketing and program development job for psychology*. Invited address at the National Conference on Graduate Education in Psychology, University of Utah, Salt Lake City.

Jones, R. (Ed.). (1972). *Black psychology*. New York: Harper & Row.

Jones, R. (Ed.). (1978). *Sourcebook on the teaching of Black psychology* (Vols. 1–2). Washington, DC: Association of Black Psychologists.

Jones, R. (Ed.). (1980). *Black psychology* (2nd ed.). New York: Harper & Row.

Jones, R. (Ed.). (1989). *Black adult development and aging*. Berkeley, CA: Cobb & Henry.

Jones, R. (Ed.). (1991). *Black psychology* (3rd ed.). Berkeley, CA: Cobb & Henry.

Lucher, G. W., Rosenfield, D., Sihes, J., & Aronson, E. (1976). Performance in the interdependent classroom: A field study. *American Educational Research Journal, 13*, 115–123.

Mbiti, J. (1970). *African religions and philosophy*. New York: Doubleday.

McKeachie, W. J. (1986). *Teaching tips, a guidebook for the beginning college teacher* (8th ed.). Lexington, MA: Heath.

Myers, L. J. (1985). Transpersonal psychology: The role of the Afrocentric paradigm. *Journal of Black Psychology, 12*, 31–42.

National Association of Scholars. (1989, November 8). Is the curriculum biased? A statement by the National Association of Scholars. *Chronicle of Higher Education*, p. A23.

Nobles, W. W. (1972). African philosophy: Foundations for Black psychology. In R. Jones (Ed.), *Black psychology* (pp. 18–32). New York: Harper & Row.

Nobles, W. W. (1976). Extended self: Rethinking the so-called Negro self-concept. In R. L. Jones (Ed.), *Black psychology* (2nd ed., pp. 99–105). New York: Harper & Row.

Nobles, W. W. (1978). Toward an empirical and theoretical framework for defining Black families. *Journal of Marriage and Family, 13*, 679–688.

Nobles, W. W. (1986). *African psychology: Toward its reclamation, reascension and revitalization*. Oakland, CA: Black Family Institute.

Nobles, W. W. (1987). Psychometrics and African-American reality: A question of cultural antimony. *The Negro Educational Review, 38*(2–3), 45–55.

Pipes-McAdoo, H. (1988). *Black families* (2nd ed.). Beverly Hills: Sage.

Price, R. H., Glickstein, M., Horton, D. L., Sherman, S. J., & Fazio, R. (1987). *Principles of psychology* (2nd ed.). Glenview, IL: Scott, Foresman.

Roediger, H. L., Rushton, J. P., Capaldi, E. D., & Paris, S. G. (1987). *Psychology* (2nd ed.). Boston: Little, Brown.

Rothenberg, P. (1984). Teaching "racism and sexism in a changing America." *Radical Teacher, 24*, 2–5.

Rothenberg, P. (1988). Integrating the study of race, gender, and class: Some preliminary observations. *Feminist Teacher, 3*(3), 37–42.

Ryan, W. (1976). *Blaming the victim* (rev. ed.). New York: Vintage.

Shaw, L. L., & Wicker, D. G. (1981). Teaching about racism in the classroom and in the community. *Radical Teacher, 21,* 9–14.

Smith, A., & Stewart, A. J. (1983). Approaches to studying racism and sexism in Black women's lives. *Journal of Social Issues, 39*(3), 1–15.

Sudarkasa, N. (1975). An exposition on the value premises underlying Black family studies. *Journal of the National Medical Association, 67,* 234–239.

Sudarkasa, N. (1980). African and Afro-American family structure: A comparison. *Black Scholar, 11,* 37–60.

Thomas, A., & Sillen, S. (1972). *Racism and psychiatry.* New York: Bruner/Mazel.

Torrence, E. P. (1982). Identifying and capitalizing on the strengths of Black children. In C. R. Reynolds & B. Gutkin (Eds.), *The handbook of school psychology* (pp. 481–500). New York: Wiley.

Turner, L. D. (1949). *Africanisms in the Gullah dialect.* Chicago: University of Chicago Press.

Wade, C., & Tavris, C. (1987). *Psychology.* New York: Harper & Row.

Webster's new collegiate dictionary. (1973). Springfield, MA: G. & C. Merriam.

White, J., & Parham, T. (1990). *The psychology of Blacks: An African-American perspective.* Englewood Cliffs, NJ: Prentice-Hall.

Whitten, L. (in press). Managing emotional reactions to controversial topics in the multicultural classroom. *Transformations.*

Williams, R. (1981). *Collective Black mind: An Afrocentric theory of Black personality.* St. Louis, MO: Williams & Associates.

Yetman, N. R. (Ed.). (1985). *Majority and minority: The dynamics of race and ethnicity in American life* (4th ed.). Boston: Allyn & Bacon.

Notes

1. This article is based on a paper presented at "Undergraduate Teaching of Psychology: Ideas and Innovations," State University of New York, Farmingdale, NY, March 1987.
2. I thank Wade Nobles, George Stricker, Eloise C. Whitten, Frederica Brown, and Paul Dunn for their assistance on earlier drafts of this article.

9. TEACHING CRITICAL THINKING

Using Riddles and Interactive Computer Games to Teach Problem-Solving Skills

John H. Doolittle

Ruggiero (1984) took the approach, popular among psychologists, of characterizing the problem-solving process as having two complementary phases: production and judgment. In the production phase, which he associated with creative thinking, potential solutions to the problem are generated. In the judgment phase, which he associated with critical thinking, the ideas generated are evaluated. This approach seems to elevate the importance of teaching students how to generate ideas to a level approaching the importance of being able to evaluate ideas. However, a closer examination of the evaluation process shows that it, too, frequently calls on the problem solver to think creatively (J. H. Doolittle, 1992b). For example, if one is evaluating the assertion, "He must be the killer; he's holding the murder weapon!," part of what one needs to do is to generate ways in which someone could be holding a murder weapon and not be the killer. This process includes generating various scenarios or models (Johnson-Laird, 1983), which may or may not involve images, and then judging their plausibility (Kaufmann, 1980).

The purpose of this article is to suggest exercises and activities to help students become better idea generators using riddles and computer games as the context in which problem solving occurs.

Flexibility and Metacognition

Flexibility, which is the process of generating a variety of types of potential solutions, may be more important to good problem solving than *fluency*, which is the process of generating more potential solutions regardless of type. For students to become more flexible as solutions generators, they need to be made aware of the types of solutions that they are generating. This process, one aspect of self-monitoring or metacognition, is at the heart of successful problem solving and can be improved in the important area of verbal associations by having students construct word tables.

In constructing word tables, students brainstorm as many associations as they can think of to a word such as *fish*. The generation of associations should take approximately 2 min. Next, have them categorize the associations they generated. Each will produce a word table with categories, such as kinds of fish (guppy, trout, etc.), parts of a fish (fin, gills, etc.), things you take fishing, and so on. An interesting phenomenon then occurs: Students not only begin to add new

associations, such as salmon and scales, to the table but also begin to add new categories, such as places where fish live. J. H. Doolittle and Bourg (1991) showed that brief training with generating associations to one word was followed by increased production on an unrelated, follow-up word. More recently, I assigned 10 word tables as a supplemental homework exercise for those of my students who scored in the lowest 20% of the class on a verbal-association measure. On a later and more difficult verbal-association quiz, 80% (12 of 15) of these remedial students passed a test of verbal associations as compared with 53% (32 of 60) of the other students, who were not required to produce word tables. It may be that any activity that causes problem solvers to pause, retrieve relevant information from memory, and examine their production is beneficial.

Flexibility and Mental Models

The notion of thinking as the construction and manipulation of mental models (Johnson-Laird, 1983) suggests another realm for flexibility training. Riddles, puns, jokes, and other word-association games help students shift mental models. The primary skill learned in these exercises is a willingness to let go of an unsuccessful solution or model. It provides a way to circumvent the common problem of functional fixedness in which problem solvers are not able to go beyond the usual functions of an object. Jokes and riddles work because the listener develops a likely model or interpretation, which then proves to be incorrect. For example, in the joke, "Question: How do porcupines make love? Answer: Very carefully!," the question leads to a distant and clinical mental model of the mechanics of mating, which the answer switches to a porcupine's perspective of the dangers of being close. The popularity of jokes, puns, and riddles suggests that people enjoy the surprise of shifting mental models in certain situations. This built-in source of motivation can be tapped by the instructor to make the learning of thinking skills fun.

The enjoyment of riddles, as opposed to jokes and puns, calls on the listener to at least attempt to shift the model. In the riddle, "What's black and white and read all over?" (answer: newspaper), which works better as a spoken riddle, the solver is fooled by words *black* and *white* to misinterpret *read* as *red*. Psycholinguists call these *garden path* sentences because the reader is misled "down the garden path" by key words in the sentence that suggest another meaning than the one that is intended. To use riddles as a teaching tool, I decided to generate riddles in a sequence from easy to difficult so that solvers would have a reasonable chance of solving each riddle while building their skill level (J. H. Doolittle, 1991). An example of a college-level riddle is as follows: "What you did to the letter, / Before it then was sent; / You memorized the poem, / Not knowing what it meant." (write/rote) Riddles like this from the *Dr. DooRiddles* series or other riddles can be selected for appropriate difficulty level and read aloud to the class or presented on an overhead transparency. In these exercises, students must be cautioned against blurting out answers so that others will have a period of quiet in which to generate models and possible word tables. Popular parlor games, such as 20 Questions and Charades foster model flexibility as well. Because these group activities can inhibit the production of some students, computer riddle exercises have been developed (J. H. Doolittle & T. A. Doolittle, 1992a, 1992b) to allow individuals to solve riddles without social judgment and without getting completely stuck.

Visualization and Imagination

A process similar to the use of jokes and riddles to encourage cognitive flexibility occurs when we read or listen to a story. Symbols and sounds are converted into visual images, models, and scenarios that we continuously transform and examine in order to comprehend the text. Because readers and listeners have to construct their own mental models, these experiences have been shown to be beneficial to the development of students' imaginations when compared to comprehension based on film presentations (Greenfield & Beagles-Roos, 1988). Presumably, television and other visual media provide images and models so that the production of mental models and creative imagination on the part of the recipient are less necessary. In interactive–fiction experiences, such as those available as computer software, one is a participant in rather than a recipient of the story. Although participants make maps and other notations as they move about an imaginary world, it is their mental representation of that world that allows them to speculate about the possibilities of a given scene. For example, in the all-text computer program, "Cursed Castle" (J. H. Doolittle, 1992a), the student must see the dirt floor of the dungeon as a potential hiding place in addition to its more usual use.

Students solving interactive–fiction problems on a computer generate a variety of solutions, but they may become frustrated on finding that not one of their solutions leads to progress toward the goal. This frustration can quickly build into discouragement and a sense of failure and must be countered by either the sequencing of task difficulty or the judicious application of hints. For example, in "Hangtown" (J. H. Doolittle, 1989b), students must frighten off a vicious dog barring the entrance to a miner's shack by threatening the dog with the carcass of a huge rattlesnake. Because most students do not think of this right away, the software monitors each student's progress and introduces a hint after a judicious amount of floundering has occurred. In this case, the next time the student is in the vicinity of the dead rattle-

snake, the student is informed that a coyote has strolled by, seen the dead snake, and run off in terror. If this hint does not work, the student is later given a more direct hint. To determine when and where hints are necessary, the software can record which obstacles are the hardest to overcome and where students seem to get stuck. The student can then retrieve this information and improve the flow of the program.

Empirical Evidence for the Effectiveness of Using Riddles and Computer Games for Training Students to Be Problem Solvers

During the past 8 years, I have gathered preliminary data using a quasi-experimental design. The comparison group was several sections of my introductory psychology classes at California State University, Sacramento. Two experimental groups received practice with the riddles and computer games described earlier—students in my freshman-level critical-thinking course and students enrolled in the Summer Academic Study Program (SASP) at the University of California School of Medicine, Davis. Several dependent measures were used: Cornell Critical Thinking Text (Level X; Ennis & Millman, 1985), the Ennis–Weir Critical Thinking Essay Test (Ennis & Weir, 1985), the Remote Associates Test of creativity (Mednick & Mednick, 1967), the Creative Reasoning Test (J. H. Doolittle, 1989a), the Unusual Uses Test of creativity (Guilford, Merrifield, & Wilson, 1958), the Purdue Non-Language Test of intelligence (Tiftin, Gruber, & Inaba, 1957), and the Coopersmith Inventory of self-esteem (Coopersmith, 1981). Although the introductory psychology students did not show gains on these measures beyond chance expectation, students in the critical-thinking courses and the SASP students showed statistically significant gains on all of these measures (most at $p < .01$). Many of these differential gains have been replicated in five or more different semesters.

Independent analyses conducted by the Dean's Office at the University of California Medical School, Davis, have indicated an improvement for SASP students in grade point average, undergraduate dropout rates, and medical school admission and retention rates.

Although these results are highly encouraging, they must be viewed as preliminary because of the quasi-experimental design used, the fact that there were some year-to-year changes in the type of test used to assess critical thinking, and the fact that these analyses do not indicate the relative benefits of the various educational experiences of these students.

Conclusions

The principal barriers to a society of better problem solvers may simply be that too few teachers are attempting to teach students the skills of creativity. As teachers plunge into these waters, it may be useful if they follow these few precepts: (a) make cognitive flexibility the top priority; (b) if flexibility is not forthcoming, focus on metacognition; (c) provide tasks that are rich in imagery; and (d) closely monitor the frustration level of students so that the tasks will be fun.

References

Coopersmith, S. (1981). *Coopersmith Inventory*. Palo Alto, CA: Consulting Psychologists Press.

Doolittle, J. H. (1989a). *The Creative Reasoning Test*. Pacific Grove, CA: Critical Thinking Press & Software.

Doolittle, J. H. (1989b). *The hangtown trilogy*. Pacific Grove, CA: Critical Thinking Press & Software.

Doolittle, J. H. (1991). *Dr. DooRiddles*. Pacific Grove, CA: Critical Thinking Press & Software.

Doolittle, J. H. (1992a). *Adventures in danger*. Pacific Grove, CA: Critical Thinking Press & Software.

Doolittle, J. H. (1992b, August). *Imagining possibilities: A neglected aspect of critical thinking training*. Paper presented at the International Conference on Critical Thinking and Educational Reform, Rohnert Park, CA.

Doolittle, J. H., & Bourg, T. M. (1991, April). *The effects of metacognitive training on a word-association task*. Paper presented at the meeting of the Western Psychological Association, San Francisco.

Doolittle, J. H., & Doolittle, T. A. (1992a). *Escape from the pyramid of riddles*. Pacific Grove, CA: Critical Thinking Press & Software.

Doolittle, J. H., & Doolittle, T. A. (1992b). *The riddle mysteries*. Pacific Grove, CA: Critical Thinking Press & Software.

Ennis, R. H., & Millman, J. (1985). *Cornell Critical Thinking Test (Level X)*. Pacific Grove, CA: Critical Thinking Press & Software.

Ennis, R. H., & Weir, E. (1985). *Ennis–Weir Critical Thinking Essay Test*. Pacific Grove, CA: Critical Thinking Press & Software.

Greenfield, P., & Beagles-Roos, J. (1988). Radio vs. television: Their cognitive impact on children of different socioeconomic and ethnic groups. *Journal of Communication, 38*, 71–91.

Guilford, J. P., Merrifield, P. R., & Wilson, R. C. (1958). *Unusual Uses Test*. Orange, CA: Sheridan Psychological Services.

Johnson-Laird, P. N. (1983). *Mental models: Toward a cognitive science of language, influence, and consciousness*. Cambridge, MA: Harvard University Press.

Kaufmann, G. (1980). *Imagery, language, and cognition*. New York: Columbia University Press.

Mednick, S. A., & Mednick, M. T. (1967). *Remote Associates Test*. Boston: Houghton Mifflin.

Ruggiero, V. R. (1984). *The art of thinking*. New York: Harper & Row.

Tiftin, J., Gruber, A., & Inaba, K. (1957). *Purdue Non-Language Test*. Chicago: Science Research Associates.

Engaging Students' Intellects: The Immersion Approach to Critical Thinking in Psychology Instruction

Peter Gray

All college teachers have seen the evidence: Students write down absurdities without apparently noticing that they are absurd; feed back, undigested, the precise and sometimes peculiar words that a lecture or the textbook used in an example or definition; and recite facts but miss the ideas to which the facts pertain. Clearly, students often fail to bring their intellectual abilities to bear on their academic endeavors. For at least the past 30 years, educators have debated the causes and possible solutions to this problem. Their writings can be classified roughly into two camps.

According to one camp, students fail to think critically because they are deficient in the general ability to do so. The remedy, according to this camp, is to teach critical thinking explicitly, either in separate courses or in segments of existing courses. Advocates of this explicit-instruction approach typically define *critical thinking* as a set of skills or cognitive steps for reaching correct decisions or assessing the truth or falsity of statements (e.g., Ennis, 1962). The underlying assumption is that these skills are (a) specifiable; (b) teachable through explicit description of each skill and

exercises for practicing it; and (c) sufficiently general that, once learned, they can be used for thinking critically about a wide variety of issues (Ennis, 1989). Consistent with this view, textbooks have been written for courses in critical thinking (e.g., Browne & Keeley, 1990); some textbooks in traditional subject areas now include separate critical thinking sections within chapters, in which a formula for critical thinking is applied to some issue relevant to the chapter.

People in the other camp favor an immersion approach. They argue that students fail to think critically in our courses not so much from lack of ability as from lack of will. From this view, critical thinking is best thought of as a disposition or attitude, which can be turned on or off, rather than as a skill, which one either has or does not have. For example, McPeck (1981) defined critical thinking as "a disposition of reflective skepticism" (p. 6), and Siegel and Carey (1989) described it as "less a set of sure-fire procedures than an attitude of inquiry" (p. 26). Immersionists do not deny that critical thinking involves cognitive steps, but they argue that the steps vary in innumerable, unspecifiable ways that depend on such factors as the kind of problem, the kind of information available, the thinker's specific goals, and the thinker's unique style of reasoning. Moreover, the steps are implicit, not explicit; critical thinkers focus attention on the issue and information about which they are thinking, not on a set of learned steps for thinking. Thus, immersionists argue, attempts to outline, teach, or use a general formula for critical thinking are futile. Any such formula simply becomes one more thing to memorize, one more thing to learn uncritically. People become better critical thinkers through engaging in critical thinking.

Immersionists argue that students will think critically and become better at it if they are immersed in a social environment that offers interesting ideas to think about, models of critical thinking to emulate, and rewards for (or at least toleration of) their own critical thoughts (McPeck, 1981; Prawat, 1991; Smith, 1990). As a rule, they contend, classrooms have not been that kind of environment, so students have learned to turn off the critical-thinking attitude in their academic work.

Whether or not immersionists are right about the futility of explicit instruction in critical thinking, they are surely right in their view that critical thinking can bloom among students only if students actually engage in it as they study subjects other than critical thinking. For many years, I have tried to teach my undergraduate psychology courses in a manner that is consistent with the immersion approach. My overriding goal is to teach in such a way that students will define their task as thinking about ideas in psychology, not simply learning (which to students often means memorizing) psychology. The remainder of this article describes some methods that I have found to be most helpful toward achieving that goal.

Providing Something to Think About: Ideas as the Units of the Course

If we want students to think about what we teach, then our teaching must focus on ideas. An idea, almost by definition, is something to think about. Ideas are the basic units of an academic discipline. Psychology is a set of ideas about the mind and behavior that have accumulated and evolved over time. Some of these are accepted today as part of the discipline's foundation, and others are actively investigated as hypotheses. If we want students to approach psychology as scholars, we must put ideas on center stage in our teaching and relegate the specific findings, techniques, facts, terms, and famous people to the role of supporting cast.

If chosen properly, ideas are more general than facts and more specific than themes. Facts (e.g., the fact that electrical stimulation in the lateral hypothalamus can elicit feeding behavior) should be brought in when appropriate to substantiate ideas but should not be the basic units of a course. Facts are too narrow, perceived as unchallengeable, and uninteresting except as related to ideas. Themes (e.g., the theme that we are influenced by our social environment) should emerge in a course and help tie ideas together but, again, should not be the basic units. They are too general

eral to be possibly wrong or to provide the basis for specific predictions. Ideas, by contrast, are sufficiently general to be interesting and sufficiently narrow to be testable. To test them we must discuss evidence, and that is how interest in a course develops; that is how students can experience the excitement of scholarship and research.

Every area of psychology, even those that seem to be most factual, can be viewed as a set of ideas. For example, an important idea in physiological psychology is that the nervous system is divisible into functionally discrete components, and the components operate in a hierarchical manner to control behavior. This idea is interesting and debatable, and it can serve as a vehicle for introducing neuroanatomy and factual material in physiological psychology. Here is a sample of other ideas, each from a different realm of psychology. Perception involves an unconscious, unselective first stage followed by a conscious, selective second stage. Human beings come into the world with special biological mechanisms for learning language. The human mind actively defends itself from certain kinds of knowledge as a way of reducing anxiety (the theory of defense mechanisms). The self-concept is a social product; its general nature depends on the person's culture, and the specifics depend on the reactions of others to the person.

When preparing a list of ideas to teach, certain guidelines are useful. First, each idea should be important to the subject of the course, as that subject is generally understood by psychologists. We have at least some obligation to teach conventional psychology. Second, each idea should be such that it can be stated clearly and can, in principle, be tested empirically. Psychology is a science, and a basic rule of science is that ideas are worthwhile to the degree that they are testable. Finally, each idea should be exciting to the instructor. If I am excited, I have a chance to excite my students; if I am not, I have no chance. If I have difficulty feeling excited about some central idea of the field—an idea that I feel obliged to teach—then I must think about that idea some more or do some additional reading to find the excitement. I must ask such questions as: Where did this idea originate?, Why was it exciting to its originators?, and What important controversies center on this idea? The pursuit for answers to such questions makes the idea exciting.

After preparing a list of ideas, the next step in planning an idea-centered course is to choose readings that convey and discuss those ideas. No textbook will fit any given instructor's set of ideas exactly, but some will fit better than others. In choosing a textbook you may ask: Do most of the ideas that I want to teach stand out in this book? Are they clear? Are they presented in a thoughtful, interesting way? In some courses, the ideas may be conveyed better with primary readings than with a textbook.

Regardless of how clearly ideas are presented in the readings, lectures can bring them forth even more clearly. Some lectures may highlight several of the main ideas in the readings, so students can read or reread in a way that focuses on the ideas. Other lectures may be devoted to a single idea. My single-idea lectures typically follow a certain pattern. I begin: "Good morning; the idea that I want to talk about today is. . . ." Then I state the idea (already written on the chalkboard or projected from a transparency); elaborate on it to make it clear; present examples to illustrate it and show its importance; ask students if they can think of additional examples; say something about the idea's history (including the people who developed it and the context in which they did so); ask students if they can think of ways to test the idea; and, finally, describe one or more actual research studies that support, refute, or delimit the idea. In the process, I may introduce some technical terms, talk about a famous person or two, and discuss some methodological aspects of the research; but the focus throughout is on the idea. The main goal is to have students understand, appreciate, and think about the idea.

Providing Models of Thought

It is useful to distinguish between the explicit and implicit content of a course. Explicit content includes information in readings and lectures, stated goals of the course, and assignments and suggestions for achieving those goals. In an idea-centered course, explicit content consists of a set of ideas, the elaboration of those ideas in readings and lectures, and various assignments and suggestions designed to help students think about the ideas. Implicit content is more subtle and more important. It is the set of messages conveyed by the manner in which the explicit content is presented. It includes attitudes about the subject under discussion, attitudes about the students, and expectations about what the students will do vis-à-vis the subject. The explicit and implicit messages can conflict, and when they do the implicit message wins. The explicit message may say, "Here is this interesting idea and some evidence pertaining to it for you to think about and evaluate." But that will have little effect if the implicit message is, "Here is so-and-so's idea and some facts pertaining to it, which you should memorize to do well on the test."

If we want students to think critically about an idea, then the implicit as well as explicit message must be that the idea is something to think critically about. I know of no other way to convey that message than to present the idea in the context of critical thought. If an idea in a lecture or a chapter comes across clearly as something that the lecturer or author is thinking about, then students will grasp it as something to think about. If students experience the genuine thinking of the lecturer or author in a way that invites them to participate, then at least some of them will accept the invitation.

The Instructor as Thinker

Most instructors cannot fake an implicit message, at least not for long. Students can see through our feigned interest or pretended thought and judge implicit messages to be part of a long string of pedagogical tricks played on them over the years. If we want to convey the message that a particular idea is something to think about, then we must really think about the idea. This is the most important meaning of the common statement that scholarship and teaching go hand in hand, and it is as true of the introductory course as it is of advanced seminars. To be good instructors of introductory psychology, we must be philosophers; we must be interested

in and prepared to think critically about the ideas that make up the foundation of psychology.

The best way to prepare an idea-based lecture is to think through the idea critically yourself, working through the logic and evidence just as you would when preparing to discuss it with colleagues. There is no need to condescend. I believe that any important idea or argument in psychology can be understood by an average first-year undergraduate, if the idea or argument is clearly stated and the student is trying to understand it. Condescension—which may take the form of watering down ideas or presenting facts instead of ideas—contributes to the implicit message, "You are a mere student, you have a lot to learn before you can really understand and think about these ideas." This is the message students have received throughout their formal education; it is the main reason they enter our courses with the assumption that they will learn or be taught, rather than think.

If you attempt in each lecture to convey your own best thinking about the idea under discussion, then you will grow mentally as you teach, you will be enthusiastic toward your teaching, and your students will experience your thinking and enthusiasm. At least some of your students will begin to think along with you and experience the same joy in playing with ideas that led you to choose an academic career in the first place. Using this process, you will also gain respect for your students and increasingly invite them in as genuine collaborators, unpretentiously using phrases such as, "Am I making sense?" or "I can't think of any other explanation, can you?"

Class Demonstrations as Opportunities for Mutual Thought

A lecture need not be just talk. Demonstrations and class experiments provide an enjoyable change of pace and can contribute to the implicit message that you and your students are doing psychology, not just teaching it and learning it. With a little imagination, many classic experiments in psychology can be replicated in class (as the pages of *Teaching of Psychology* have so frequently shown). Each demonstration or experiment becomes an opportunity for students and instructor to think together, as students pose possible explanations of the results and speculate on what may have happened had certain conditions been a little different. I have a battery of experiments and demonstrations for my introductory psychology classes, and each year I make up a new one or two to try out.

As one example, I routinely demonstrate group polarization before students have read the social influence chapter in their textbook. I first have each student declare on a Likert scale how strongly he or she agrees or disagrees with some proposition (e.g., the proposition that the next test should be essay rather than multiple-choice), then I divide them into like-minded groups for discussion. After the discussion, I have them again declare the strength of their agreement or disagreement. The results are always consistent with group polarization: Those who initially agreed with the proposition agree even more strongly after discussing it, and those who initially disagreed disagree even more strongly. When I then ask the class to speculate on why the results came out as they did, they often generate all the explanations of group polarization that social psychologists have proposed and tested over the years. When I then ask them to suggest a procedure for testing one explanation or another, they usually produce the outlines of a reasonable study.

What do students learn in that exercise? They learn in a memorable way the meaning of group polarization; but, far more important, they learn that they can think like psychologists; they can come up with plausible explanations of an observed phenomenon and can think of ways of testing those explanations. Students in one class were so enthusiastic about one of their explanations of a demonstration that they convinced me to repeat it in another class, varying the conditions in a certain way, to see if I would get the different result that they predicted would occur. To their delight, their prediction was confirmed.

Providing Study Techniques That Foster Thought

For some students, providing substance for thought and models of it is not enough. Some need extra help in overturning long-standing habits of intellectual passivity, especially in their approach to textbooks and other readings. Too often students focus so narrowly on term definitions and facts that they miss the overriding ideas to which the definitions and facts pertain. "How could I possibly have received a D on that test?" complained one student some years ago, "I memorized every definition in the chapters and the names of all the researchers." To prevent that kind of experience, I now teach my students some techniques, including those described later, designed to help them keep the main ideas in mind and to think about the more specific information in the context of those ideas.

Asking Students to Make the Course's Implicit Questions Explicit

One technique, which I have found to be especially useful, was developed by Marcia Heiman (1987) as part of a program to help students get more out of their college education. Heiman's program grew out of research at the University of Michigan, directed by Dale Brethower, that systematically compared the study methods of successful and unsuccessful college students. The most striking finding was that successful students engage in a mental dialogue with authors and lecturers. They continuously form hypotheses, and they read or listen to confirm or disconfirm those hypotheses (Heiman, 1987). The aim of Heiman's program is to teach students who have been unsuccessful to become engaged with their readings and lectures in the way that successful students do.

As a first step, Heiman (1987) taught students to infer and write out the questions that the course's readings and lectures are trying to answer. She told them that every statement in a chapter or a lecture is part of an attempt to answer some question and that the statement will make sense only if they know what the question is. Some authors and lecturers simplify the student's task by stating each question explicitly before trying to answer it, but more often the

questions are implicit. To a student who has not inferred the questions, the statements aimed at answering them are bits of nonsense. Heiman taught students to read their textbook a section (or subsection) at a time using the following procedure; (a) Skim the section, using such cues as the section's heading, the first sentence of every paragraph, and figure captions to infer the section's main question or questions; (b) write the question or questions in the margin; (c) read the section carefully with an aim of answering the question or questions; and (d) if necessary, rephrase the question or questions in the margin to fit the actual contents of the section. She also instructed students to leave wide margins in their lecture notebooks and use that space to write the questions that their notes are designed to answer.

Controlled studies at Boston College and elsewhere have shown that Heiman's (1987) program significantly increases students' grade point averages and decreases their likelihood of withdrawal from courses. Reports from my own students suggest that the question-inferring technique works through the following means:

1. It keeps the mind alert and focused on the content while reading or listening.
2. It promotes curiosity, because the explicit phrasing of a question by the student tends to induce a desire to know the answer.
3. It serves as a guide for review and further study. To review, students can read the questions they have written in the margin and try to answer them.
4. Perhaps most important, the process of thinking about the author's or lecturer's questions helps engender a questioning attitude in students. The student may begin to think of important questions that the author or lecturer missed or may begin to see the flaws in the author's or lecturer's answers. When that happens, the student is thinking like a scholar.

Teaching Students to Make Question Maps and Hierarchical Review Charts

Students can also be shown how to summarize information in their readings in ways that promote active thought. One technique that Heiman (1987) recommended is the construction of question maps. This technique is a derivative of the question-inferring method just discussed. When students write out questions regarding the information in a chapter, they may find that some questions keep recurring, applied each time to a different item. A question map is simply a two-dimensional grid that lists recurring questions along one axis and the items to which they are applied along the other. An example of such a chart that may be used to summarize part of a chapter on personality theories is shown in Figure 1. As another example, in a chart summarizing a chapter on social influence, the columns may represent different influence phenomena (e.g., social inhibition, social facilitation, social loafing, Asch conformity effect, group polarization, etc.), and the rows may represent questions about the definition of the effect, real-life examples of it, how it is demonstrated in the laboratory, conditions under which it occurs or does not occur, and theories offered to explain it. To complete the chart, students may fill the boxes

Personality Theories

Questions	Freud's psycho-dynamic theory	Adler's psycho-dynamic theory	Rogers's human-istic theory	Rotter's social learning theory	Eysenck's trait theory
What human motives are emphasized?					
What mental structures are posited?					
What sorts of differences among individuals are emphasized?					
What does it posit as the developmental causes of indivi-dual differences?					
What kinds of evidence were important in developing the theory?					

Figure 1. Sample question map, which a student might prepare to summarize part of a textbook's chapter on personality theories.

with key words or abbreviations that hint at each question's answer.

Question maps are especially useful for identifying the similarities and differences among related theories or phenomena; they help students prepare for test questions of the "compare and contrast" type. Also, in producing such charts, students begin to understand that certain kinds of questions are common to psychology or specific branches of it, which helps them see how psychologists think.

Another kind of review chart, which I find to be even more effective than question maps, is the hierarchical summary chart that depicts relations among broad ideas or phenomena and the more specific ideas, phenomena, and lines of evidence pertaining to them. An example of such a chart, based on the discussion of classical conditioning in an introductory psychology textbook, is presented in Figure 2. The second level in this hierarchy contains, in abbreviated form,

the basic ideas that the text offers concerning classical conditioning. Thus, the box on the left may be expanded to read, "The idea that Pavlov's work on conditioning was very important to the historical development of psychology as a science." As another example, the box on the right may be expanded to, "The idea that some aspects of classical conditioning are better understood from a cognitive rather than behavioral perspective." The third level in the hierarchy shows how each idea is fleshed out or supported by the text.

Producing such charts is not as difficult as it may at first seem, yet it does require some intellectual effort. The information in most textbooks is organized hierarchically, with different levels marked by different kinds of headings—a fact that many students do not notice until it is explicitly pointed out to them. To produce the chart, students must focus on the logic of the author's organization and sometimes supplement that with some organization of their own. This requires that they think about the information more deeply than would be necessary to produce more conventional crib sheets or lists of key terms, people, and research studies. For example, to know where to place a certain experiment by Rescorla on the chart in Figure 2, they must understand why Rescorla did the experiment and what it has to do with the cognitive perspective on classical conditioning.

Once the chart is prepared, it is a marvelous tool for review. A dozen pages of text can be summarized on 1 page, visually organized in a way that preserves the lines of argument and interrelations of ideas. Computer scientists and cognitive psychologists have long known that hierarchical structures are the most efficient means to represent complex, logically related bodies of information. The hierarchical review chart helps students take advantage of that fact.

Requiring Students to Write Out Their Own Questions

The study procedures described so far are recommended in my courses, but the procedure to which we now turn is required. Because I believe that questioning is the essence of critical thinking and scholarship, I require students to write out and hand in questions on each reading assignment. In this assignment, I am not asking for the author's questions, which were answered by the reading, but for the students'

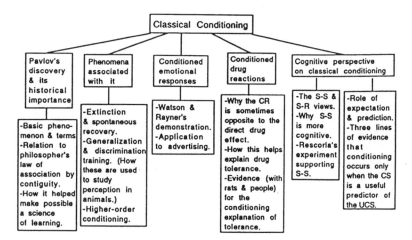

Figure 2. Sample hierarchical review chart, which a student might prepare to summarize the discussion of classical conditioning in a textbook.

own questions, which were stimulated by the reading but not answered by it.

The first time I made this assignment in my introductory psychology course I was amazed at how hard it was for some students to understand. They were so used to thinking of questions as things that teachers ask and students answer that the idea that they should have questions seemed upsetting to them, One student, complaining about the assignment, put it this way: "I understand everything in the chapter; I don't have any questions. Do you want me to pretend I don't understand something?" My gut-reaction answer to him, "If you understand it, and have thought about it, you must have questions," was not very helpful.

I now avoid that kind of misunderstanding by explaining the assignment carefully from the beginning, with the aid of a handout. The handout begins with the words, "To think is to question." It then describes the kinds of questions that may come to mind while reading a passage of text—such as questions about the evidence or logic behind some claim, the exact meaning of a somewhat murky concept, or possible implications or extensions of an idea or research finding. The handout then advises students to jot down such questions as they read and, after finishing the chapter, to select five of them from different parts of the chapter and elaborate on each in a paragraph that explains the question clearly, shows its linkage to something in the chapter, and shows some of the student's own thought behind or about the questions.

Most students like this assignment after doing it a few times. They gradually get the knack of reading in a questioning manner and discover that this makes their task more fun. The questions that students generate through this assignment also become the fodder for small-group discussions, to which we turn now.

Holding Discussion Meetings at Which Students Really Discuss

Critical thinking is fundamentally a social phenomenon; it derives from dialogue. In dialogue, one person makes a statement and another, in the attempt to understand or elaborate, asks a question or makes a related statement. In this back-and-forth exchange, the original statement is corrected, clarified, or used as the foundation to build a larger argument. When we think things through alone we engage in an internal dialogue. It is as if we imagine how others would respond to our initial statement and in that way we correct, clarify, or build on our own germinal thought. A sad fact of university life—at least on the campuses that I have observed—is that many undergraduates rarely discuss with each other or with anyone else the academic ideas that they are studying. Their lack of dialogue about the ideas is part and parcel of the passive, absorptive mental stance that they take toward their studies.

To ensure that students engage in at least some dialogue about the ideas in my introductory psychology course, I divide them into groups of about 6 to 10 students each for weekly discussion meetings. Each group is led by an undergraduate teaching assistant (TA), whom I select based on previous excellent course performance and demonstrated enthusiasm about ideas in psychology. These TAs receive credit through a teaching experience seminar. In addition to leading the weekly meetings, TAs attend all lectures, study the textbook, and attend a weekly seminar meeting with me to discuss the course content, which I lead in much the same manner that I expect them to adopt in the meetings that they lead.

Each discussion meeting is devoted to a different chapter or pair of chapters in the textbook. Students must bring to the meeting their set of written questions for the chapter or chapters. At a typical meeting, the TA may begin by asking each member to read his or her most important question. Usually, one or more of these questions provokes controversy, and discussion follows. The TA does not take the role of an expert but rather acts primarily as a presider, moderating the discussion, keeping it on track, and elevating it by asking for logic or asking people to describe the evidence they would need to be convinced of a particular idea. Sometimes a group will decide that it wants my opinion on something or that an idea in the text needs elaboration. The TA brings that report to me, and, if I think it warranted, I will present the requested opinion or elaboration as part of a subsequent lecture.

Because the groups are small and are led by a nonthreatening but enthusiastic and capable TA who is essentially a peer, most students participate actively at every meeting. I evaluate the discussion groups through a number of means, including direct observation and questions on an anonymous course evaluation form. The results convince me that real discussions occur, most students become engaged in them, and sometimes the discussions continue long after the official period is over.

The discussion-group system has benefits beyond the discussions themselves. The TAs tutor students who need extra help (they teach the study methods described earlier), are sought out for advice about a wide range of issues pertaining to their college experiences, and provide a bridge between me and the large number of students whom I do not get to know personally. The discussion groups also promote friendships. Some students, especially commuters, report that without the discussion group they would not have become acquainted with anyone in the course. Some have told me 1 year or more later that they are still close friends with one or more former members of their group.

Testing and Grading To Reward Thought

Like everyone else, students are pragmatic. They gear their efforts toward solving the problems of life. The problem of life that college poses to most students is getting good grades, not thinking deeply about academic ideas. It does not help to blame students for this. Their view is quite rational. We have invented the grade and made it the wage for scholastic effort; people will work for the wage and will interpret as frivolous any activity that does not bring it.

If students believe they can do well on tests by memorizing, they will memorize. If they believe they can do better by thinking, they will think. But many students are not likely to believe the latter unless it is proven to them. As McPeck

(1990) pointed out, they are used to tests that ask questions such as, "What is the definition of W?" or "Who discovered X and when?" or "What did Y believe about Z?" Such tests require that students store temporarily a lot of miscellaneous information, but they do not require that students organize the information in a coherent manner, attend to the evidence behind it, or even understand it in a way that allows them to do anything with it other than recite it. From experience, students know that the surest route to a good grade with such questions is to feed back the exact words used in the textbook or the lecture; any deviation may be interpreted as wrong. They also know that the correct answer on multiple-choice items often comes verbatim from the textbook or lecture.

Thinking is tapped by questions that ask students to do something with the information that was not already done for them by the author they read or the lecturer they heard. "How does X compare with Y?" is a good thought question if X and Y were both discussed in the textbook but were not directly compared there. Thinking is also tapped by questions that focus on logic and evidence, which cannot be efficiently encoded and fed back without intervening thought. I tell students that I will not ask them a question such as, "What is the S–S theory of classical conditioning?" or "Which theory of classical conditioning has the most support—the S–S or the S–R?" but will ask them questions such as, "Describe one line of evidence supporting the S–S theory of classical conditioning over the S–R theory."

Such questions are easier to ask (but harder to grade) with essay tests than with multiple-choice tests, but they are not impossible with the latter. For example, concerning the experiment by Rescorla supporting the S–S theory (included in Figure 2), a multiple-choice item may describe an experiment like his but with an opposite result, and then it may ask which of several theories about classical conditioning (including the S–S and S–R theories) is supported by that result. A student who had simply memorized which theory was supported in the textbook without understanding the logic would choose the wrong answer.

Occasionally students accuse me of being tricky with questions like that. I used to try to defend myself from that charge, but I do not any more. I now say, with a degree of genuine empathy,

> Yes, I suppose that's true; but I don't know any other way, in such a large class, to test how well you've thought about the ideas and evidence in the course. Perhaps you can just accept me as tricky and assume that your task is to outsmart me by thinking deeply about the ideas in the course and by thinking carefully about each question on the test.

By the time the first test is graded and discussed in class, most students are convinced that I am to some degree measuring the depth of their thought about ideas and evidence.

So those who performed well feel rewarded for their efforts in that direction, and at least some of the others feel motivated to approach me or their TA for help in learning the study techniques designed to promote thought and discourage rote memory.

Conclusion

Over the years, I have observed that the procedures described in this article help stimulate critical thought and discussion in my courses. Sometimes I forget to use them, and sometimes I am too busy to use those that are time consuming; but when I do use them, my teaching is more effective than when I do not. I value thoughts from readers about other ways to encourage critical thinking in the context of psychology instruction. I hope that research on the teaching of psychology will begin to focus more on procedures for encouraging reflective skepticism and a spirit of inquiry.

References

Browne, M. N., & Keeley, S. M. (1990). *Asking the right questions: A guide to critical thinking* (3rd ed.). Englewood Cliffs, NJ: Prentice-Hall.

Ennis, R. H. (1962). A concept of critical thinking. *Harvard Educational Review, 32*, 81–111.

Ennis, R. H. (1989). Critical thinking and subject specificity: Clarification and needed research. *Educational Researcher, 18*(3), 4–10.

Heiman, M. (1987). Learning to learn: A behavioral approach to improving thinking. In D. N. Perkins, J. Lochhead, & J. Bishop (Eds.), *Thinking: The second international conference* (pp. 431–452). Hillsdale, NJ: Lawrence Erlbaum Associates, Inc.

McPeck, J. E. (1981). *Critical thinking and education.* Oxford, England: Martin Robertson.

McPeck, J. E. (1990). *Teaching critical thinking: Dialogue and dialectic.* New York: Routledge.

Prawat, R. S. (1991). The value of ideas: The immersion approach to the development of thinking. *Educational Researcher, 20*(2), 3–10.

Siegel, M., & Carey, R. F. (1989). *Critical thinking: A semiotic perspective.* Bloomington, IN: ERIC Clearinghouse on Reading and Communication Skills.

Smith, F. (1990). *To think.* New York: Teachers College, Columbia University.

Note

This article is based partly on a paper presented at the Fourteenth Annual National Institute on the Teaching of Psychology, St. Petersburg Beach, FL, January 1992.

Inquiring Minds Really Do Want to Know: Using Questioning to Teach Critical Thinking

Alison King

I believe that the hallmark of a critical thinker is an inquiring mind.[1] Simply put, good thinkers are good questioners. Whatever they see, hear, read, or experience, they are constantly analyzing it, puzzling over its significance, searching for explanations, and speculating about relations between that experience and what they already know. Good thinkers are always asking What does this mean?, What is the nature of this?, Is there another way to look at it?, Why is this happening?, What is the evidence for this?, and How can I be sure? Asking questions such as these and using them to understand the world around us is what characterizes critical thinking. Isidor Rabi, the 1944 Nobel Prize winner in physics, told the story of how he learned to be a questioner as a very young boy. When he returned home from school each day, his mother, instead of asking him what he had learned in school that day (as most other mothers did), asked him what good questions he had asked that day. According to Rabi, this daily greeting from his mother had a profound influence on the development of his inquiring mind.

If good thinkers are good questioners, then is the reverse true? Are good questioners good thinkers? Do inquiring minds really want to know? If we could teach our students to ask good questions, would that improve their critical thinking? Results of my own program of research on inquiry-based learning (King, 1989, 1990, 1991, 1992, 1994a) suggest that the answer is yes.

A Model of Inquiry

The overall emphasis of the model of inquiry presented herein is on helping students develop a habit of inquiry so that they can learn to ask thoughtful questions—of themselves and of each other—about the material they read, hear in lectures, and encounter during class discussions. Such a habit of inquiry learned and practiced in class can be applied also to their everyday lives: to what they see on television, read in the newspaper, observe in the popular culture, and hear during interaction with friends and colleagues, as well as to decisions they make about personal relationships, consumer purchases, political choices, and business transactions.

Thus, the model's focus is on autonomous learning that is inquiry based. This model turns around the notion of inquiry-based instruction and places the responsibility (as well as the skill) for learning on the student. In inquiry-based instruction, the instructor asks the students leading questions to elicit from them information and inferences, predictions, and so on about that information. By contrast, in this inquiry-based learning model, students learn a skill for asking

such questions on their own—autonomously—whether they are studying alone at home, working independently in class, or participating in a discussion group within the class. An important feature of inquiry-based learning is that the students are not merely searching for correct answers to the instructor's questions (which may or may not be relevant to individual students' own learning needs); rather, they are posing and answering questions that address their own lack of understanding, specific gaps in knowledge, and particular misconceptions. Because such questioning and answering activity is personally meaningful to them, students are more likely to be making the kinds of mental connections between concepts that are more memorable for them.

What Are Thought-Provoking Questions?

In any classroom, the level of thinking that occurs is influenced by the level of questions asked. We can use particular questions to induce in students whatever specific thinking processes we wish. For example, when questions are factual (e.g., What is a schema?), the tendency is for only facts to be recalled (in this case, a memorized definition); however, when questions are thought provoking (e.g., How do schemas differ from scripts?, and Explain how a schema would facilitate problem solving in the following scenario.), then critical thinking is more likely to occur. Thought-provoking or critical-thinking questions require students to go beyond the facts to think about them in ways that are different from what is presented explicitly in class or the text. Critical-thinking questions activate critical thinking in both the questioner and the responder. More specifically, critical-thinking questions induce high-level cognitive processes, such as analysis of ideas, comparison and contrast, inference, prediction, evaluation, and the like.

Unfortunately, researchers have shown that, when students are asked to generate questions on their own, they usually pose factual rather than thought-provoking ones (Dillon, 1988; Flammer, 1981; Kerry, 1987; King, 1990). Therefore, if we want students to generate thoughtful questions spontaneously, we need to teach them how to do so. By teaching our students to ask critical-thinking questions, we can promote the development of their inquiring minds.

Guiding Students To Create Their Own Critical-Thinking Questions

We can train students to generate their own effective and relevant critical-thinking questions by providing them with the structure and guidance of exemplar questions. Table 1

---

[1]This position has been developed more fully in King (1994b).

Table 1. Guiding Critical Thinking

Generic Questions	Specific Thinking Skills Induced
What are the strengths and weaknesses of . . . ?	Analysis/inferencing
What is the difference between . . . and . . . ?	Comparison–contrast
Explain why . . . . (Explain how . . . .)	Analysis
What would happen if . . . ?	Prediction/hypothesizing
What is the nature of . . . ?	Analysis
Why is . . . happening?	Analysis/inferencing
What is a new example of . . . ?	Application
How could . . . be used to . . . ?	Application
What are the implications of . . . ?	Analysis/inferencing
What is . . . analogous to?	Identification of and creation of analogies and metaphors
What do we already know about . . . ?	Activation of prior knowledge
How does . . . affect . . . ?	Analysis of relationship (cause–effect)
How does . . . tie in with what we learned before?	Activation of prior knowledge
What does . . . mean?	Analysis
Why is . . . important?	Analysis of significance
How are . . . and . . . similar?	Comparison–contrast
How does . . . apply to everyday life?	Application to the real world
What is a counterargument for . . . ?	Rebuttal to argument
What is the best . . . , and why?	Evaluation and provision of evidence
What is a solution to the problem of . . . ?	Synthesis of ideas
Compare . . . and . . . with regard to	Comparison–contrast
What do you think causes . . . ? Why?	Analysis of relationship (cause–effect)
Do you agree or disagree with this statement: . . . ? What evidence is there to support your answer?	Evaluation and provision of evidence
What is another way to look at . . . ?	Taking other perspectives

Note. From "Comparison of Self-Questioning, Summarizing and Notetaking Review as Strategies for Learning From Lectures" by A. King, 1992, *American Educational Research Journal, 29.* Copyright 1992 by the American Educational Research Association. Reprinted by permission of the publisher. Also from *Changing College Classrooms: New Teaching and Learning Strategies for an Increasingly Complex World* (p. 24) edited by D. Halpern, 1994, San Francisco: Jossey-Bass. Copyright 1994 by Jossey-Bass. Adapted by permission.

contains some examples of general thought-provoking question stems and the thinking processes each is expected to induce. Students use these generic questions as prompts to guide them in formulating their own specific questions pertaining to the material to be learned. They simply adapt the generic thought-provoking question stems for use by filling in the blanks with specific content relative to the topic being covered. They are encouraged to generate questions to which they do not already know answers. In my program of research, my co-workers and I found that, when students are provided with that set of exemplar question stems (or a subset of it) and coached while they practice generating their own questions, they learn the skill very quickly and their learning is markedly enhanced (King, 1990, 1992, 1994a).

These question stems can be used in many ways by psychology students to enhance their own thinking and learning. Some applications are cooperative-learning strategies (e.g., reciprocal peer questioning), others are based on individual student use, and others combine individual learning and group learning (e.g., readers' questions—such as David Letterman's "viewer mail" questions).

Reciprocal Peer Questioning

After listening to a class lecture, my students use the generic question stems and work independently to generate two or three questions based on the lecture material. Next, in pairs or small groups, they engage in peer questioning, taking turns posing their questions to their partner or group and answering each other's questions in a reciprocal manner. Then, as a whole class, we share some of the questions and ideas that have arisen in the small groups and discuss them further.

For example, in my educational psychology class, during our study of human intelligence, one of the topics we cover is theories of multiple intelligences. In one class session, I present material on the two theories. Then, I display the list of generic question stems on the overhead projector and ask students to select stems appropriate to their learning needs and generate two or three thoughtful questions on the topic of multiple intelligences using those question stems as a guide. After about 3 min, I signal them to turn to their neighbors, form their discussion groups, and begin the reciprocal peer questioning and responding discussion process with which they have become familiar. Some of the actual questions written by one such group are as follows:

Why is the concept of multiple intelligence important?

Explain why it is necessary—or beneficial? Who benefits? Why is it better than the old one-dimensional theory?

How does Sternberg's theory of multiple intelligences differ from Gardner's?

What are the implications of the idea of multiple intelligences for a second grade teacher in a multicultural classroom?

Compare Sternberg's theory and Gardner's with regard to their probable influence on the public schools.

How do the theories of multiple intelligences apply to everyday life?

Students continue discussing the topic of multiple intelligences by asking and answering each others' questions until I signal them to stop. Then, in the whole-class context, students share some of the ideas generated in their group discussion, and together we clarify any misunderstandings about multiple intelligences that have arisen.

In reciprocal peer questioning, it is important that students not ask and answer their questions in a rote manner without concern for fully discussing an issue before going on to another question. I have found that often within one 8- to 10-min discussion session some of the student groups have time to pose only one question because the discussion that ensues from that one question is so extensive. Asking probing follow-up questions is an effective way to extend the discussion on a particular point. For example, the second question mentioned earlier (Explain why it is necessary—or beneficial? Who benefits? Why is it better than the old one-dimensional theory?) is a follow-up question asked by the same student who posed the initial question, and this probes students to explore further into the first question asked.

Colleagues of mine (e.g., N. M. Webb, personal communication, May 1992) who have used this inquiry model report that the process can be time-consuming; however, the quality of the discussion in their classes is greatly improved. They have also noted that this questioning strategy allows students to phrase their confusions (e.g., What is the more appropriate analysis to use in this case, repeated measures or analysis of covariance, and why?) and lack of understandings (e.g., Why is that situation an example of the Piagetian construct of ego-centrism?) and receive information to address their needs. When students work in collaborative inquiry with a partner or a small group using this model, they are more willing to risk asking stupid questions or questions to which they do not already know an answer. One of the benefits of this approach is that circulating about the room listening to the small groups as they answer and discuss their questions is very helpful. It is a way for me to determine how well the class understands the material and which individual students do not. This is good feedback about my instructional process because it tells me which concepts need to be clarified and what material we need to consider longer.

Readers' Questions

Getting students to complete reading assignments before class is a perennial problem for most of us. To stimulate my students to complete their readings before class, I have them use the generic question stems shown in Table 1 to generate three or four thoughtful questions on the material as they are reading it before the class meets. At the beginning of each class session, they turn in their questions to me as an assignment (and keep a copy for themselves). I use these questions in two ways. First, I use them to stimulate discussion during that class session—rather like the questions in the "viewer mail" segment on David Letterman's television show. I shuffle through the students' questions, select ones to read aloud, and initiate either small-group or whole-class discussion. Second, when I review the questions after class, the questions that a particular student generated tell me a

great deal about that student's level of understanding of the material covered—or even whether the student has actually read the material. At the end of the semester, I review each student's contribution of questions from the entire semester for quality and comprehensiveness. Furthermore, I sometimes use the questions generated by students as items on course exams (see discussion that follows).

Alternative Applications for Individual Student Use

In the individual or self-questioning version of this strategy, students use the question stems to guide them to generate their own thought-provoking questions after listening to a lecture or reading assigned material. Then, they answer those questions fully on their own. This form of questioning and answering is very useful as a way to study the material in preparation for class and exams.

Why Is This Model Effective?

These generic question stems are effective in promoting students' critical thinking because they act as cognitive prompts to induce analysis, inference, evaluation, comparison and contrast, and other high-level cognitive processes with regard to specific aspects of the material being studied (King, 1992; Pressley et al., 1992). Simply formulating the thought-provoking questions, despite whether they are answered, requires students to think critically about the material. In the process of generating such questions, students are forced to identify the main ideas presented and think about how those ideas relate to each other and to the students' own prior knowledge and experience. When they respond to other students' critical-thinking questions (or their own), they are compelled to engage in further critical thinking because they must explain concepts, defend their ideas, give examples, and show that they really understand (Bargh & Schul, 1980; Cobb, 1988; Mugny & Doise, 1978; Webb, 1989). According to current theories of information processing, when students think about material in these ways, they process the ideas more thoroughly than if they were simply memorizing it. During this extensive processing, they are building complex cognitive networks, connecting the new ideas together and linking them to what they already know. When students develop such extensive cognitive representations of the new material, they are more likely to remember it.

The effectiveness of reciprocal peer questioning and other cooperative-learning applications of the inquiry model can also be attributed partially to theories of the social construction of knowledge. According to social constructivism (e.g., Bearison, 1982; Damon, 1983; Mugney & Doise, 1978; Perret-Clermont, 1980; Vygotsky, 1978), when we are engaged in peer interaction, we discover that our own perceptions, facts, assumptions, values, and general understandings of the material differ to a greater or lesser extent from those of others. When confronted with these conceptual discrepancies, we want to reconcile the conflicts. To do so, we must negotiate understanding and meaning. And this negotiation, this co-construction of meaning, occurs through explaining concepts and defending our own views to each other. Reciprocal peer questioning promotes this process of exposing and reconciling cognitive discrepancies by controlling the direction of the discussion. For example, when students ask and answer thought-provoking questions, such as What do you think would happen if . . . ?, they tap in to each others' different views on the matter. Once these differing views or conflicting information are exposed, individuals are requested to elaborate, explain, justify, and engage in other sociocognitive behaviors that may lead to reconciling those differences and reaching negotiated meaning. According to Cobb (1988), when we are engaged in such meaning negotiation, we are continually restructuring our own thinking.

The inquiry model also serves a metacognitive role. *Metacognition* is the awareness, monitoring, and control of one's cognitive processes. Awareness of the purpose of a task, monitoring one's attention to a lecture, selecting specific learning strategies to use, monitoring one's progress toward a goal, identifying mistakes, monitoring one's understanding all are examples of metacognition in action. Asking and answering thoughtful questions functions as a metacognitive self-testing experience, giving students the chance to monitor their understanding of the topic before moving too far into the material.

Fostering Questioning Through Modeling

We can further promote student use of these critical-thinking questions by modeling the use of such questions ourselves. Those general critical-thinking questions can be used by any instructor in any subject area to guide that instructor to ask subject-specific questions relevant to any content. Asking students to back up their assertions and examine their thinking through such questions as Why do you think so? and What is your line of reasoning here? provides further opportunity to model critical-thinking questioning. I use the question stems during class to pose questions to stimulate thinking and discussion as well as to construct examination questions and other forms of course evaluation.

Evaluation

In any course, assessment must be congruent with the kinds of learning emphasized in class. When critical thinking is emphasized and promoted during the semester, all tests, assignments, and final exams should reflect this emphasis. Specifically, such evaluation should be designed to assess students' understanding of course material, rather than their ability to recall memorized information. Therefore, exam questions should require the kinds of thinking emphasized in class sessions: explanation; analysis; and integration of concepts, theories, processes, and so on. I use the generic critical-thinking questions in constructing appropriate examination questions and other assignments for my students. I have even built an entire examination from questions students themselves have written and contrib-

uted. Why not? By the time of the final exam, they have become just as proficient as I at constructing thoughtful questions. For their course term paper, I have my students generate and answer a question of their own. Essentially, the term paper consists of their answer to a question they themselves have posed about an educational psychology topic, issue, or construct that interests them (the paper cannot be a reiteration of some part of the text, and students must use several primary sources).

Conclusion

In my educational psychology classes, I use this model of inquiry in its various applications: reciprocal peer questioning, readers' questions, and modeling. The model enhances student learning, promotes self-regulated learning, and provides students the structure and motivation to prepare well for class. The consistent feedback that I get on student evaluations of my teaching is that students really learn how to think in my class.

References

Bargh, J. A., & Schul, Y. (1980). On the cognitive benefits of teaching. *Journal of Educational Psychology, 72*, 593–604.

Bearison, D. J. (1982). New directions in studies of social interactions and cognitive growth. In F. C. Serafica (Ed.), *Social–cognitive development in context* (pp. 199–221). New York: Guilford.

Cobb, P. (1988). The tensions between theories of learning and instruction in mathematics education. *Educational Psychologist, 23*, 78–103.

Damon, W. (1983). The nature of social–cognitive change in the developing child. In W. F. Overton (Ed.), *The relationship between social and cognitive development* (pp. 103–142). Hillsdale, NJ: Lawrence Erlbaum Associates, Inc.

Dillon, J. T. (1988). *Questioning and teaching: A manual of practice.* New York: Teachers College Press.

Flammer, A. (1981). Towards a theory of question asking. *Psychological Research, 43*, 407–420.

Halpern, D. (Ed.). (1994). *Changing college classrooms: New teaching and learning strategies for an increasingly complex world.* San Francisco: Jossey-Bass.

Kerry, T. (1987). Classroom questions in England. *Questioning Exchange, 1*(1), 32–33.

King, A. (1989). Effects of self-questioning training on college students' comprehension of lectures. *Contemporary Educational Psychology, 14*, 1–16.

King, A. (1990). Enhancing peer interaction and learning in the classroom through reciprocal questioning. *American Educational Research Journal, 27*, 664–687.

King, A. (1991). Improving lecture comprehension: Effects of a metacognitive strategy. *Applied Cognitive Psychology, 5*, 331–346.

King, A. (1992). Comparison of self-questioning, summarizing and notetaking-review as strategies for learning from lectures. *American Educational Research Journal, 29*, 303–323.

King, A. (1994a). Autonomy and question asking: The role of personal control in guided student-generated questioning. *Learning and Individual Differences, 6*, 163–185.

King, A. (1994b). Roads to empowerment: Teaching and learning critical thinking through questioning. In D. Halpern (Ed.), *Changing college classrooms: New teaching and learning strategies for* an *increasingly complex world* (pp. 13–38). San Francisco: Jossey-Bass.

Mugny, G., & Doise, W. (1978). Sociocognitive conflict and the structure of individual and collective performances. *European Journal of Social Psychology, 8,* 181–192.

Perret-Clermont, A. (1980). *Social interaction and cognitive development in children.* New York: Academic.

Pressley, M., Wood, E., Woloshyn, V. E., Martin, V., King, A., & Menke, D. (1992). Encouraging mindful use of prior knowledge:

Attempting to construct explanatory answers facilitates learning. *Educational Psychologist, 27,* 91–109.

Vygotsky, L. S. (1978). Internalization of higher psychological functions. In M. Cole, V. John-Steiner, S. Scribner, & E. Souberman (Eds.), *Mind in society: The development of higher psychological processes* (pp. 52–57). Cambridge, MA: Harvard University Press.

Webb, N. M. (1989). Peer interaction and learning in small groups. *International Journal of Educational Research, 13,* 21–39.

Using Writing to Develop and Assess Critical Thinking

Carole Wade

Perhaps the second most frequently asked question about critical thinking (after "What is it?") is "How, exactly, do you get students to do it?" Although there is no magical formula that will answer this question, I concluded, after many years of experimenting with different approaches, that writing is an essential ingredient in critical-thinking instruction. Writing tends to promote greater self-reflection and the taking of broader perspectives than does oral expression (Pennebaker, Czajka, Cropanzana, & Richards, 1990). Written assignments ensure the participation of every student—a basic requirement for active learning (Mathie, 1993). In class discussions, students usually articulate or defend only what they already believe; with written assignments, an instructor can encourage the development of dialectic reasoning by requiring students to argue both (or three, four, or five) sides of an issue. In class discussions, words cannot easily be taken back, qualified, or reconsidered. In contrast, written assignments can be structured to allow students to try again if their first attempt to address an issue was unsuccessful; this is a great advantage because the revision and refinement of ideas is integral to critical thinking. Finally, in class discussions, rewards, in the form of attention, may go to students who are glib rather than thoughtful. Writing allows time for reflection and a careful consideration of reasons for taking a position or making an assertion.

Before one can design critical-thinking assignments, of course, one must have a clear idea of the goal. Some years ago, my colleague Carol Tavris and I (Wade & Tavris, 1987) settled on a definition of critical thinking as "the ability and willingness to assess claims and make objective judgments on the basis of well-supported reasons" (pp. 308–309). This definition, we thought, had the advantage of including dispositions (the "willingness") as well as skills ("the ability"). It left room for both logic and empirical evidence as the basis for judgments and did not imply the existence of a single correct answer. It also emphasized the positive aspects of critical thought. In late adolescence and young adulthood, people tend to be skeptical that anything

can be rationally known, thus regarding knowledge as entirely subjective or idiosyncratic. Usually they have not yet developed the capacity to weigh and evaluate competing arguments or knowledge claims according to rules of evidence or general principles of inquiry (King & Kitchener, 1994; King, Kitchener, Davison, Parker, & Wood, 1983; Kitchener & King, 1981; Welfel & Davison, 1986). Focusing solely on logical fallacies in arguments or defects in empirical data could reinforce students' extreme relativism and even lead to intellectual nihilism. Therefore, we concluded, critical-thinking instruction must also encompass the creative construction of ideas.

Although dozens of specific skills and dispositions are involved in critical thinking (Ennis, 1986; Halonen, 1986; Halpern, 1989), we decided to focus on eight general activities that critical thinkers, in line with our basic definition, should be able to perform. These activities ask students to (a) ask questions and be willing to wonder, (b) define problems clearly, (c) examine evidence, (d) analyze assumptions and biases, (e) avoid emotional reasoning, (f) avoid oversimplification, (g) consider alternative interpretations, and (h) tolerate uncertainty. There are other valid and useful ways to divide up the critical-thinking "pie." However, our guidelines are general enough to subsume several other commonly mentioned components of critical thought, and eight has proven to be a good number—within the limits of working memory and realistic in terms of what can be achieved in a semester course that must also cover basic content. Since creating our original formulation, we have incorporated these guidelines into our lectures and our writings (e.g., Tavris & Wade, 1994; Wade & Tavris, 1993). We have also developed a set of short written assignments for our introductory psychology classes and, with Sarah Cirese, I (Wade & Cirese, 1991) have developed a similar set for the human sexuality course. Collectively, the assignments for each course cover all eight guidelines.

For each major topic in the course, there is an assignment consisting of two or three questions. I usually allow students to select any six assignments to complete during the term. Because I wish to make critical thinking an intrinsically rewarding activity that develops into a lifelong habit, I do not grade the responses. However, I do write comments on the papers, and all six assignments must be done in order to receive a grade in the course. Unsatisfactory responses are returned without credit and with constructive suggestions for improvement. Students may then redo the assignment or complete a different one in its place. At the end of each unit, I usually read some of the best answers so that students can learn from the ideas of others. The number of assignments required and the length of responses encouraged can be adjusted for very large classes. In the rest of this article, I describe a few of the items in these assignments. Others could easily be formulated to accomplish the same goals.

Ask Questions, and Be Willing to Wonder

All intellectual inquiry starts with a good question. At the beginning of the term, I ask students, after they have read the first chapter of the text and scanned the table of contents, to generate three questions they would like to see answered in the course. Questions that are vague or unclear or that are not psychological in nature are returned for revision. I also ask the students to explain why they consider the three questions they selected to be especially important. Then, I type up the questions and distribute them so that students can see what interests others in the class. During the semester, I make sure to address each question in some manner. When there is little or no evidence on an issue, I ask students how they would go about gathering some. This simple exercise not only involves students immediately in the course but also gives me information about what students think psychology is and what topics most concern them.

Another exercise asks students to use what they have learned about the scientific method to generate questions about a specific psychological issue. In the human sexuality course, for example, I ask students what questions they should ask about a drug reputed to have aphrodisiac properties before assuming that it will improve people's love lives. Good responses may include such questions as, "Have there been actual studies of such properties, or is the 'evidence' merely anecdotal?," "If there has been research, was a control group used?," and "Were there any adverse side effects?" A similar item for introductory psychology asks students to think of three questions they should ask about a self-help book before taking its advice seriously, based on what they know about scientific and critical thinking. Good responses may include such questions as, "Does the writer cite empirical evidence to support his/her claims?," and "Does the writer try to reduce all problems to a single cause?"

Define the Problem

To think critically, students need to understand that the way one formulates a question or problem affects its susceptibility to empirical investigation as well as the answer or solution that one ultimately reaches. I use several types of assignments to get these ideas across. In one approach, which I use during a unit on methodology, I ask students to judge whether various questions are phrased in such a way that they can be addressed by research:

Psychology seeks knowledge through observation, experimentation, and measurement. However, some questions cannot be answered empirically. Decide whether or not scientific research could possibly provide an answer to each of these questions, and explain your decision briefly: (a) Is abortion on demand bad for society?; (b) Do people talk more after they have eaten than when they are hungry?; (c) Does jogging lead to a positive mental attitude?; (d) Are the incomes of doctors related to the grades they made in medical school?; (e) Which emotion is stronger, love or anger?; (f) Are breast-fed babies more alert than bottle-fed babies?; (g) Will people be more moral in the year 2020 than they are now?

It is interesting to note that a few students over the years have misunderstood this item. Instead of evaluating the susceptibility of the questions to scientific study, they try to answer them ("Yes, I think jogging probably does enhance mental health. A guy I know. . . ."). These students apparently have learned that they should try to answer any question they read, and they seem to do so almost reflexively!

A second approach asks students to generate several possible definitions of a term (e.g., *success* in the evaluation of psychotherapy) and speculate on how these definitions may lead to different conclusions. And a third approach has students think about their own definition of a term:

Professor A tells a female student that she looks very attractive in an outfit she's wearing. Professor B makes a joke in class about a female student's "sexiness." Professor C tells a student he would like to date her after the semester is over. Professor D flirts with a student and asks her out to dinner and a movie. Professor E invites a student to sit on his lap. Which, if any, of these professors are guilty of sexual harassment? Give reasons for your answer.

Answers to this item can be used to initiate a discussion of how concepts are socially constructed and how they can influence legal and ethical judgments.

Examine the Evidence

Kuhn (1989) showed that adults as well as children often cannot distinguish between a causal explanation on the one hand and supporting evidence on the other, and they fail to recognize that explanations are useful only if their possible falsehood can be tested against evidence. For students who have not previously been challenged to think critically, "evidence" may amount to personal anecdote or simply a restatement of the explanation. An important goal of all psychology instruction is to get students to appreciate that not all opinions regarding psychological issues are created equal—that some are supported by strong evidence or reasons, whereas others are mere speculation or are based on weak evidence.

One approach is simply to ask students to cite evidence from the textbook or lecture to support a position. For example, they may be asked to give three specific reasons for supporting or opposing the implementation of a token economy in a first-grade classroom, citing findings they have read about in a unit on operant conditioning. Another tack is to ask what sorts of evidence would be useful for studying a question:

> No one really understands why father–daughter incest is so common in this country. One hypothesis is that men are socialized to express closeness primarily in sexual or physical ways. How could this hypothesis be studied to find out if it is correct or not? What kind of evidence might be relevant?

Another type of item requires an understanding of selective perception and the confirmation bias:

> Susan opposes a proposed law that would forbid discrimination against gay men and lesbians in housing and employment. "Every gay person I've met is unhappy and disturbed," she says, "and so I wouldn't want to have to work with one." What is wrong with Susan's evidence?

Finally, one can ask students to reflect on the personal and social reasons that people often have for resisting empirical evidence:

> Despite the fact that controlled research has failed to support the existence of PMS in most women, many people continue to believe that in most women (but not most men), monthly hormone fluctuations cause mood swings and other emotional symptoms. Give three possible reasons why this belief persists, despite the lack of strong supporting evidence.

Analyze Assumptions and Biases

This guideline calls on students to identify not only other people's assumptions but also their own, a task that is difficult when an issue is controversial. One method is to ask students to identify the assumptions that underlie a particular conclusion. For example, in a unit on heritability, I use this item:

> Jean wants to become a widget maker. After reading in a magazine that widget-making ability, which involves manual dexterity, is partly heritable, and noting that her parents have terrible manual skills, Jean concludes that she should choose a different occupation. What mistaken assumptions is Jean making?

A good answer may point out that (a) Jean assumes heritability estimates are applicable to individuals, (b) parents low in some skill cannot have a child who is high in that skill, and (c) heritable abilities are untrainable. (Students need a thorough understanding of heritability before attempting this particular item.)

I also sometimes use an item that asks students to think of factors that are ignored in both genetic and personality ex-

planations of drug addiction. My purpose is to direct students' attention to sociocultural factors and make them aware of a widespread assumption in our culture that intrapsychic explanations are the only ones possible. A good response on this item (which most students find extremely difficult) may mention poverty, discrimination, and cultural messages that encourage the pursuit of easy, immediate gratification and biochemical solutions to problems. To do well on an item of this sort, students need to recognize the possibility of interactions and the problems inherent in reductionistic, single-cause explanations of complicated problems.

Avoid Emotional Reasoning

In teaching this guideline, I must take care not to imply that critical thinking is bloodless, solemn, and dispassionate. Research suggests that certain moods and emotions can actually have a salutary effect on cognition (Isen, 1984; Mayer, 1986). In various kinds of tasks, positive emotions can facilitate creative problem solving, the integration of cognitive material, the perception of interconnections, and flexibility in categorization (Isen & Daubman, 1984; Isen, Daubman, & Nowicki, 1987; Murray, Sujan, Hirt, & Sujan, 1990). Moreover, moods and emotions direct our attention, often in adaptive ways, and motivate performance. The lesson of this guideline, however, is that people who hold conflicting views may feel equally passionate or emotional about the rightness of their position and that the intensity of a person's commitment to a belief has no bearing on its truth or validity.

One strategy for increasing students' awareness of emotional reasoning is to have them identify appeals to emotion in political campaigns and commercial advertising. Another approach is to ask students to consider some issue and propose arguments or evidence that someone with a position opposed to their own may offer. Many people find this activity confusing or emotionally threatening (Kuhn, 1989). They may resist stating an argument that they disagree with or have difficulty even imagining the possibility of counterarguments or counterevidence. For example, although most students can give three arguments for legalizing hard drugs and three arguments against (citing evidence from a unit on drug use), some will protest that there are legitimate arguments on only one side of the issue (usually the "against" side).

Avoid Oversimplification

Oversimplification includes either-or thinking and overgeneralizing from limited samples or data. Many students start their psychology education with a long list of pop psychology oversimplifications (e.g., that everyone is either right brained or left brained), so there is plenty of raw material to draw on in teaching this particular guideline.

One simple strategy is to ask students to make distinctions that draw attention to the complexity of behavior. For example:

> In what situations might a 10-year-old child be a better eyewitness than a 40-year-old, and vice versa?

Many students recognize that the nature of the event to be recalled (e.g., a Little League game vs. a money-laundering conspiracy) and the different cognitive schemas of children and adults could influence the accuracy of recall at different ages. Similarly, one may teach the dangers of oversimplification by asking students to speculate on the possible pros and cons of some practice (e.g., the possible negative and positive effects of television watching on a child's intellectual development).

Consider Other Interpretations

This guideline encourages students to look beyond the first, obvious explanation for a phenomenon, event, or finding and to recognize that "the facts" do not automatically end debate on an issue. One type of item that I use asks students to generate alternative hypotheses on their own:

Some people are said to be "emotional" because of the intensity of their emotional responses. Instead of being happy, sad, or afraid, they are euphoric, devastated, or terrified. Suggest three hypotheses that might help explain why some people are more emotionally intense than others.

Another type of item focuses on the interpretation of correlational findings:

For each of these hypothetical findings, suggest at least two alternative explanations, taking into account different possible relations between cause and effect: (a) A study finds that men who have frequent sex tend to have higher testosterone levels than those who have sex less often. (b) A study finds that after surgical removal of their ovaries women tend to be less interested in sex than they were before.

Items can also be written to draw attention to the consequences of differing interpretations in daily life. For example, students can be asked to consider how altering their interpretations of everyday hassles may reduce the stressfulness of these events.

Tolerate Uncertainty

The first seven guidelines all work to promote greater tolerance of ambiguity. Teachers can also focus on such tolerance explicitly by having students identify questions not answered by the text or in lecture (see Halonen, 1986) or by asking students to consider whether there is sufficient evidence to draw conclusions about certain claims. One item I use in a unit on memory raises the issue of how a therapist can know whether a suddenly recalled repressed memory is accurate. So far, research cannot help us distinguish false memories from reliable ones in the absence of objective corroboration. Thus, in the current debate about false memories, in which many are willing to take extreme positions (e.g., there is no such thing as a repressed memory, or nearly all patients are remembering accurately), the wisest response may be to reserve judgment.

During the years that I have been using these and similar exercises, I have learned that, although not all students will do well on them, most do make progress during the semester. By using such exercises or other strategies for encouraging critical thinking, we will learn much more about the way our students' minds work and become more critical thinkers ourselves.

References

Ennis, R. H. (1986). A taxonomy of critical thinking dispositions and abilities. In J. B. Baron & R. J. Sternberg (Eds.), *Teaching thinking skills*. New York: Freeman.

Halonen, J. (Ed.). (1986). *Teaching critical thinking in psychology*. Milwaukee: Alverno Productions.

Halpern, D. F. (1989). *Thought and knowledge: An introduction to critical thinking* (2nd ed.). Hillsdale, NJ: Lawrence Erlbaum Associates, Inc.

Isen, A. M. (1984). Toward understanding the role of affect in cognition. In R. S. Wyer, Jr. & T. K. Srull (Eds.), *Handbook of social cognition* (Vol. 3, pp. 179–236). Hillsdale, NJ: Lawrence Erlbaum Associates, Inc.

Isen, A. M., & Daubman, K. A. (1984). The influence of affect on categorization. *Journal of Personality and Social Psychology, 47,* 1206–1217.

Isen, A. M., Daubman, K. A., & Nowicki, G. P. (1987). Positive affect facilitates creative problem solving. *Journal of Personality and Social Psychology, 52,* 1122–1131.

King, P. M., & Kitchener, K. S. (1994). *The development of reflective judgment in adolescence and adulthood: From unsubstantiated beliefs to reasoned conclusions*. San Francisco: Jossey-Bass.

King, P. M., Kitchener, K. S., Davison, M. L., Parker, C. A., & Wood, P. M. (1983). The justification of beliefs in young adults: A longitudinal study. *Human Development, 26,* 106–116.

Kitchener, K. S., & King, P. M. (1981). Reflective judgment: Concepts of justification and their relationship to age and education. *Journal of Applied Developmental Psychology, 1,* 89–111.

Kuhn, D. (1989). Children and adults as intuitive scientists. *Psychological Review, 96,* 674–689.

Mathie, V. A. (1993). Promoting active learning in psychology courses. In T. V. McGovern (Ed.), *Handbook for enhancing undergraduate education in psychology* (pp. 183–214). Washington, DC: American Psychological Association.

Mayer, J. D. (1986). How mood facilitates cognition. In N. E. Sharkey (Ed.), *Advances in cognitive science* (pp. 290–314). Chichester, UK: Ellis Horwood.

Murray, N., Sujan, H., Hirt, E. R., & Sujan, M. (1990). The influence of mood on categorization: A cognitive flexibility interpretation. *Journal of Personality and Social Psychology, 59,* 411–425.

Pennebaker, J. W., Czajka, J. A., Cropanzana, R., & Richards, B. C. (1990). Levels of thinking. *Personality and Social Psychology Bulletin, 16,* 743–757.

Tavris, C., & Wade, C. (1994). *Psychology in perspective*. New York: HarperCollins.

Wade, C., & Cirese, S. (1991). *Thinking critically about human sexuality: A workbook to accompany* Human Sexuality (2nd ed.). San Diego: Harcourt Brace.

Wade, C., & Tavris, C. (1987). *Psychology* (1st ed.). New York: Harper & Row.

Wade, C., & Tavris, C. (1993). *Critical and creative thinking: The case of love and war*. New York: HarperCollins.

Welfel, E. R., & Davison, M. L. (1986). The development of reflective judgment during the college years: A 4-year longitudinal study. *Journal of College Student Personnel, 27,* 209–216.

10. WRITING TO LEARN, LEARNING TO WRITE

Novels as Case-Study Materials for Psychology Students

Joan C. Chrisler

Goals often expressed by professors include improving their students' ability to write clearly, to think critically, and to apply these skills to their lives outside the classroom. Because "thinkers and writers become better thinkers and writers by thinking and writing" (Eble, 1976, p. 92), it is clear that frequent short writing assignments requiring students to present their own opinions and analyses will do more to develop students' skills than will the traditional end of term paper. The most effective assignments will be those without answers readily obtainable from published sources.

A good way to encourage the application of thinking and writing skills to daily life is to base assignments on the types of activities students are likely to engage in outside the classroom (e.g., reading novels). Several writers (Bennett, 1985; Williams & Kolupke, 1986; Zeren & Schultz, 1988) have suggested team teaching psychology and literature as a way of improving writing, critical thinking, and perceived relevance of psychological theory and research. These courses generally apply the major theories of personality and motivation to the interpretation of literary works and can be taught as one course with the two instructors alternately presenting material (Williams & Kolupke, 1986) or as the coordinated teaching of introductory psychology and basic composition courses (Bennett, 1985; Zeren & Schultz, 1988). This article describes an assignment for psychology students based on a literary work.

Writing Assignment

Students are given a list of novels, biographies, and autobiographies (see Table 1) describing cases of schizophrenia, depression, multiple personality, personality disorders, and organic brain syndromes. Many of these books have been made into films which the students have seen. I prefer that they choose a book with which they are not familiar so that they approach the character with an open mind, rather than through the film director's point of view. Students are to read their book and prepare a 5- to 10-page paper about the main character.

The students are cautioned that this paper is not to be a typical book report and that they are not to summarize the plot. Rather, they should adopt the perspective of a psychotherapist and prepare a case study of the book's main character. The students' task is to describe and discuss the character's behavior; specifically, they must address the following questions: (a) What are the character's symptoms? (b) Into which *DSM–III* category does the character fit and why? (c) What type of therapeutic treatment did the character receive? (d) What treatment would you recommend if you were the therapist? (e) Which theory of mental illness best explains the development of the character's symptoms?

Discussion

The answers to the questions are not as obvious as they may seem. For example, although most of the books give the main character's diagnosis, some of the older books use categories that are no longer in the *DSM–III* or that have been renamed. This situation forces the students to compare their

Table 1. Suggested Readings for a Case-Study Assignment

Axline, V. (1976). *Dibs in search of self.* New York: Ballantine.

Barnes, M., & Berke, J. (1972). *Mary Barnes: Two accounts of a journey through madness.* New York: Harcourt.

Gordon, B. (1980). *I'm dancing as fast as I can.* New York: Bantam.

Greene, H. (1964). *I never promised you a rose garden.* New York: New American Library.

Guest, J. (1982). *Ordinary people.* New York: Ballantine.

Hodgkins, E. (1964). *Episode: A report on an accident inside my skull.* New York: Atheneum.

Kesey, K. (1975). *One flew over the cuckoo's nest.* New York: New American Library.

Keyes, D. (1982). *The minds of Billy Milligan.* New York: Bantam.

Levonkron, S. (1978). *The best little girl in the world.* Chicago: Contemporary Books.

Mee, C. (1978). *Seizure.* New York: Evans.

Naylor, P. (1977). *Crazy love.* New York: Morrow.

Neufeld, J. (1970). *Lisa bright and dark.* New York: New American Library.

Plath, S. (1975). *The bell jar.* New York: Bantam.

Rebeta-Burditt, J. (1986). *The cracker factory.* New York: Bantam.

Reed, D. (1976). *Anna.* New York: Basic Books.

Rubin, T. (1986). *Jordi.* Mattituck, NY: Amereon.

Rubin, T. (1986). *Lisa and David.* Mattituck, NY: Amereon.

Schatzman, M. (1973). *Soul murder: Persecution in the family.* New York: Random House.

Schreiber, F. (1974). *Sybil.* New York: Warner.

Sechehaye, M. (1985). *Autobiography of a schizophrenic girl.* New York: New American Library.

Sheehan, S. (1983). *Is there no place on earth for me?* New York: Random House.

Thigpen, T., & Cleckley, H. M. (1985). *The three faces of Eve.* Augusta, GA: Cleckley-Thigpen.

Vonnegut, M. (1975). *The Eden express.* New York: Bantam.

Wexler, S. (1970). *The story of Sandy.* New York: American Library.

Wolf, E. (1969). *Aftershock.* New York: Putnam.

list of symptoms to the textbook or directly to the *DSM–III* to find the category that best fits the character. Sometimes students disagree with the diagnosis given to the character by the book's author. Points are awarded for a good argument in favor of the student's choice of diagnosis, and I try to avoid suggesting that there is one right answer in every case.

The therapeutic treatments the characters receive are so varied that this is perhaps the most interesting section for the students to write about. The older books describe treatment techniques that are no longer in use (e.g., hydrotherapy or wrapping patients in cold, wet sheets and tying them to their beds) or that have been recognized as inappropriate or ineffective for particular types of illness (e.g., psychoanalysis for acute schizophrenics). This gives students the opportunity to object to the treatments and to argue in favor of other approaches. Students will gain a better understanding of therapy in action as they read about the character's experiences. Characters in these books take medications of various kinds and receive electroconvulsive and insulin shock treatments. They participate in individual, group, and family therapy with therapists who use psychodynamic, cognitive, behavioral, and humanistic techniques. Students are usually good at identifying which therapy the character receives.

The last question—which theory of mental illness best explains the development of the character's symptoms?—is the most difficult to answer and instructors may decide not to assign it to lower level classes. Less sophisticated and less able students regularly assume that the perspective given by the book's author is the best one and adopt it without question. It is disheartening to read paper after paper stating that psychoanalytic theory best explains the development of schizophrenia as students disregard biochemical and genetic evidence in their up-to-date textbooks and adopt the opinion of an author of a novel or biography written 20 or 30 years ago. Return of the papers is always followed by a discussion of the fact that the books' authors have constructed cases that fit their points of view and the fact that the student authors must do the same.

All books on the list are interesting and well written; most have been best sellers, and students enjoy reading them. Paperback editions of most of the books are widely available in bookstores; the older, out-of-print books can be found in most public libraries. The books give students a better idea of what it is like to experience mental illness than do textbook descriptions of symptoms. Reading about the characters seems to promote empathy for the mentally ill as much as writing about them promotes critical thinking.

This is a versatile assignment; I have used it in both Introductory Psychology and Abnormal Psychology classes with students from the community college level to the university level. Upper division students usually write more sophisticated papers than lower division students do, but all complete the assignment and benefit from it. Because of the number of possible characters and the variety of approaches one can take to describe them, I never tire of reading these papers and am surprised at how often I, too, learn something from this assignment.

References

Bennett, S. M. (1985). Coordinated teaching of psychology and composition: A valuable strategy for students and instructors. *Teaching of Psychology, 12,* 26–27.

Eble, K. E. (1976). *The craft of teaching: A guide to mastering the professor's art.* San Francisco: Jossey-Bass.

Williams, K. G., & Kolupke, J. (1986). Psychology and literature: An interdisciplinary approach to the liberal curriculum. *Teaching of Psychology, 13,* 59–61.

Zeren, A. S., & Schultz, N. L. (1988, March). *Classifying the character of Esther Greenwood.* Paper presented at the conference on the Teaching of Undergraduate Psychology, Farmingdale, NY.

Critiquing Articles Cited in the Introductory Textbook: A Writing Assignment

Karen C. Gareis

Although upper level psychology courses frequently require that students read journal articles, descriptions of techniques to help students comprehend and interpret what they read are rare (Chamberlain & Burrough, 1985) and are generally too sophisticated for the introductory course (e.g., Chamberlain & Burrough, 1985; Klugh, 1983; Osberg, 1991; Suter & Frank, 1986). Only Keller (1982) described a technique for introductory psychology students, who wrote critiques of journal articles in the form of letters to their parents. However, the critiques focused on article interest, usefulness, and relation to experience and class material rather than on methodology.

The introductory course is many students' only exposure to psychology, so it is essential to provide them with the knowledge and skills to be critical consumers of the research reports they will encounter in the popular media. For students who take additional psychology courses, the benefits of methodological proficiency are self-evident. The following assignment has at least four benefits: (a) It allows students to practice using research terms and concepts that may be emphasized throughout the introductory course; (b) it exposes students to primary research in the field, which does not normally occur until upper level classes; (c) it gives instructors a chance to read articles outside their own field, which helps meet the challenging breadth of the introductory course; and (d) it promotes critical thinking about textbook presentations of research. Students should come to appreciate the monumental task involved in writing a textbook and gain a healthy skepticism about relying on secondary sources for information, even sources as legitimate as highly regarded introductory psychology textbooks (e.g., Atkinson, Atkinson, Smith, & Bem, 1993).

Todd and Morris (1992) discussed the self-perpetuating nature of erroneous academic folklore, arguing that psychology textbooks are both a repository of such folklore and a primary means of its dissemination. Vicente and de Groot (1990) used a virus metaphor in their historical tracing of distortions of de Groot's work on recall with chess masters, finding that the number and severity of such errors actually increased over time. Loftus (1974) reported that secondary sources tend to exaggerate the strength of the "cocktail party phenomenon," in which one's own name penetrates consciousness despite inattention; in fact, this occurred only 33% of the time in the original study (Moray, 1959). Rosenthal, Soper, Coon, and Fullerton (1993) pointed out that developmental psychology texts routinely overstate how much is known about the number of human genes, which can mislead students about scientific uncertainty. Given the ramifications of these inaccuracies, psychology instructors should do what they can to avoid spreading them.

Critiquing Articles

Students choose a study presented in their textbook and find the original article. The focus of the assignment is research methods, so students should look for empirical articles and avoid books, case studies, or reviews. To help students choose appropriately, I tell them to avoid *American Psychologist* and *Psychological Bulletin* in favor of empirically oriented journals, such as *Journal of Personality and Social Psychology*, and to look for Method, Results, and Discussion headings. Because students have complete citations, I just need to tell them how to find specific journals; they are also encouraged to consult library reference staff. The assignment is fully described in the syllabus, so I only spend about 15 min of class time discussing it.

In preparation for the assignment, students read Peplau (1988), which describes parts of a journal article, defines common statistical terms, and indicates that even technical articles restate key findings in plain English, requiring little statistical sophistication to understand. In addition, students have had three class hours on research methods, including practice identifying the method, variables, operational definitions, and flaws in short descriptions of studies. I reinforce these concepts by questioning students about studies that come up in later units.

Students read the article and write a 5-page paper consisting of (a) a one-page summary describing the hypothesis, variables, operational definitions, method, and results using terms from the research methods unit; (b) a critical evaluation, including any compliments on or criticisms of method, operational definitions, sample, and so forth; (c) a discussion of how the study illustrates course concepts; and (d) a comparison of the primary source with its description in the text. They also turn in a copy of the article.

Students can consult with me and with teaching assistants if they need help. Typically, about one third come in to ensure that their articles are appropriate and that they have identified variables and interpreted results accurately. When students seem intimidated by Results sections, I remind them to look for plain-English statements.

Grading takes only as much time as for traditional assignments of similar length. Students tend to choose short, straightforward articles that I can read quickly. Grading criteria include correct use of research terms and accurate description of the study, thoughtful and well-reasoned evaluation, thorough demonstration of knowledge of pertinent course concepts, and accurate and thoughtful comparison of primary and secondary sources. Introductory students may not be capable of sophisticated methodological critiques, but they can apply their knowledge of the trade-offs between experimental and correlational designs, examine operational definitions critically, and contemplate external validity and ethics.

Evaluation

When I offered the assignment as extra credit, 58 of 135 students completed it. When I required it in a summer course, 27 of 28 students did the assignment. The quality of the papers was quite high, with an average grade of B+ in both classes. Students responded to six evaluation items on a 5-point scale ranging from *strongly disagree* (1) to *strongly agree* (5). They were also asked to provide general comments and suggestions for improving the assignment. Because the extra-credit version of the assignment was due at the end of the semester, evaluation forms were distributed when papers were returned; students were asked to bring them to the final class or to leave them in my mailbox. Only 22 students complied, so their ratings may not be representative. When the assignment was required, students were asked to turn in evaluations with their papers; 24 of 27 did so.

Students who turned in evaluations gave the assignment fairly high marks, particularly when it was offered for extra credit (see Table 1). Looking for a specific article offered a rather painless introduction to library research, a new skill for many first-year students. An unexpected benefit was that students who consulted reference staff were advised to use PsycLIT to preview articles for appropriateness and interest; they reported saving time and enjoying using the database. As many authors have stressed the need for bibliographic instruction in psychology courses (e.g., Baxter, 1986; Cameron & Hart, 1992; Merriam, LaBaugh, & Butterfield, 1992), this assignment could usefully be combined with more formal training in library research.

The first time I assigned this paper I did not adequately emphasize article selection guidelines; a few students inadvertently chose review articles, which made it virtually

Table 1. Student Evaluations of Assignment

Questionnaire Item	Extra Credit[a]		Required[b]	
	M	SD	M	SD
1. Clearer understanding of research.	4.41	0.80	3.83	1.17
2. Think critically about research.	4.36	0.23	3.87	1.10
3. Learn more about course topics.	4.23	0.81	3.79	1.10
4. Think critically about textbook presentation.	4.41	0.73	3.63	1.10
5. Was interesting.	4.36	0.85	3.50	1.10
6. Should be required.	3.68	1.32	3.71	1.27

Note. Items were scored on a scale that ranged from *strongly disagree* (1) to *strongly agree* (5).
[a]*n* = 22. [b]*n* = 24.

impossible for them to complete the assignment. Requiring that articles be approved in advance would both prevent this problem and encourage students to start the assignment early.

Students reported that they learned more about psychological research and appreciated the opportunity to see original sources, as indicated by comments such as "This assignment gave me the chance to look at an actual journal, which I most likely never would have on my own!" and "I am glad that I did this assignment because it helped me understand the complexities of psychological research studies." Students found the articles challenging to read but not insurmountable. Many students had difficulty limiting their summaries to one page, but they benefit from extracting an article's essential points and describing it concisely.

Students also believed that the assignment encouraged them to think critically about psychological research and expanded on course topics: "The assignment was a challenge to me to read more deeply and critically on the topic I was researching." Several students were disappointed at being constrained to articles cited in the textbook. However, focusing on text articles allows them to compare primary and secondary sources and simplifies the library search. Students agreed that the assignment encouraged them to think more critically about the textbook's presentation of research.

Some students did find errors and distortions in the textbook, ranging from mild to more serious. For instance, in describing Darley and Latané's (1968) diffusion of responsibility experiment, the text authors wrote that group sizes were two, three, and six (Atkinson et al., 1993, p. 757); actually, the middle group had four members. More seriously, the text inaccurately described Godden and Baddeley's (1975) study of context and memory with scuba divers. The authors converted the within-subject study to a between-subject design and incorrectly claimed that divers in one condition "recalled 40% less" than divers in another (Atkinson et al., 1993, p. 308); this figure should only be 32%. Information about such errors can be incorporated into lectures, and the publisher can also be notified of discrepancies between the textbook and primary sources.

Students reported that the assignment was interesting and enjoyable and that it would prepare them for future classes: "I think doing something like this in an introductory course is *awesome* because it prepares you for later, more advanced courses in psychology, where we'll actually have to do things like this." A further advantage of the assignment for me was the chance to read original research articles on topics outside my own specialization. Many students chose to track down classic articles, which were of particular interest and worth photocopying as sources of supplemental lecture material.

References

Atkinson, R. L., Atkinson, R. C., Smith, E. E., & Bem, D. J. (1993). *Introduction to psychology* (11th ed.). Fort Worth, TX: Harcourt Brace.

Baxter, P. M. (1986). The benefits of in-class bibliographic instruction. *Teaching of Psychology, 13*, 40–41.

Cameron, L., & Hart, J. (1992). Assessment of PsycLIT competence, attitudes, and instructional methods. *Teaching of Psychology, 19*, 239–242.

Chamberlain, K., & Burrough, S. (1985). Techniques for teaching critical reading. *Teaching of Psychology, 12*, 213–215.

Darley, J. M., & Latané, B. (1968). Bystander intervention in emergencies: Diffusion of responsibility. *Journal of Personality and Social Psychology, 8*, 377–383.

Godden, D., & Baddeley, A. D. (1975). Context-dependent memory in two natural environments: On land and under water. *British Journal of Psychology, 66*, 325–331.

Keller, R. A. (1982). Teaching from the journals. *Teaching Sociology, 9*, 407–409.

Klugh, H. E. (1983). Writing and speaking skills can be taught in psychology classes. *Teaching of Psychology, 10*, 170–171.

Loftus, E. F. (1974). On reading the fine print. *Quarterly Journal of Experimental Psychology, 26*, 324.

Merriam, J., LaBaugh, R. T., & Butterfield, N. E. (1992). Library instruction for psychology majors: Minimum training guidelines. *Teaching of Psychology, 19*, 34–36.

Moray, N. (1959). Attention in dichotic listening: Affective cues and the influence of instructions. *Quarterly Journal of Experimental Psychology, 11*, 56–60.

Osberg, T. M. (1991). Teaching current advances in psychology: Student and instructor advantages. *Teaching of Psychology, 18*, 41–42.

Peplau, L. A. (1988). Introduction: Reading research reports in social psychology. In L. A. Peplau, D. O. Sears, S. E. Taylor, & J. L. Freedman (Eds.), *Readings in social psychology: Classic and contemporary contributions* (2nd ed., pp. 1–5). Englewood Cliffs, NJ: Prentice Hall.

Rosenthal, G. T., Soper, B., Coon, R. C., & Fullerton, R. (1993). The misrepresentation of scientific uncertainty: The number of genes in the human cell. *Journal of Instructional Psychology, 20*, 333–339.

Suter, W. N., & Frank, P. (1986). Using scholarly journals in undergraduate experimental methodology courses. *Teaching of Psychology, 13*, 219–221.

Todd, J. T., & Morris, E. K. (1992). Case histories in the great power of steady misinterpretation. *American Psychologist, 47*, 1441–1453.

Vicente, K. J., & de Groot, A. D. (1990). The memory recall paradigm: Straightening out the historical record. *American Psychologist, 45*, 285–287.

Note

I thank Ruth L. Ault and three anonymous reviewers for helpful comments and suggestions on an earlier draft of this article.

Improving the Writing Skills of Students in Introductory Psychology

Robert Madigan
James Brosamer

Can an introductory psychology course help students develop writing proficiency while they master course material? Our effort to design such a course was motivated by a conviction shared by many (e.g., White, 1985) that the college curriculum in general should develop students' writing skills. The writing-across-the-curriculum movement (Griffin, 1982) reflects this educational objective with its emphasis on the importance of teaching writing in all disciplines. The advocates of writing across the curriculum have had some success in persuading faculty not to hold their colleagues in English solely responsible for the teaching of writing, but, as yet, there is no consensus about how to integrate writing assignments into courses in ways that are pedagogically sound and logistically practical. In this article, we discuss our experiences in developing effective and manageable writing assignments in a freshman psychology class of about 100 students.

At our institution, the introductory psychology course attracts a broad cross section of freshmen who have selected it to meet their general degree requirements. One of us (RM) had worked for several years to incorporate written assignments into the introductory psychology course; the result was a course design that used frequent essay exams and several short papers. This article discusses our experiences with student writing in the context of the essay exams.

There were pedagogical reasons for the essay exams, apart from any consideration of improving composition skills. Essay exams encourage students to take more extensive notes and to study in a more organized way than they do when given multiple-choice exams (Richards & Friedman, 1978), and essay tests produce better mastery of the course material (Frederiksen, 1984). These considerations led to a course format that presented students with essay questions on 13 weekly quizzes. Examples of these questions are given in Table 1. There was a great deal of variation in the length of the answers, but the average was about 80 words. A study guide listing 10 questions was distributed during the class period preceding each quiz. The students were told that they would be writing answers to two of the questions appearing on two of the most recent study guides. They were encouraged to practice writing their answers before the quiz and were told that part of their grade (5 points out of 30) would depend on their *writing*, a term further described for them as "complete sentences and reasonable grammar." (Of the remaining points, 20 were awarded for content and 5 for legibility.) It was suggested that part of the preparation for the test should include prewriting activities, such as outlining and organizing the material as well as editing and revising trial answers. When the quizzes were returned each week, the students also received two sample answers ("among the best in the class") to one of the essay questions. The two were selected to show different writing styles and approaches. For the typical student, weekly quizzes and the final exam involved writing about 2,500 words.

Study 1

In Study 1, we looked for evidence of improvement during the semester. We compared essays students wrote early in the semester with those they wrote for the final exam. Because the final exam consisted of 6 essay questions selected from the 26 questions that had appeared on the previous 13 tests, the students responded to some of the same questions early and late in the semester.

Method

A total of 94 students registered for the course, and 84 were assigned grades. A teaching assistant scored the weekly quizzes, spending an average of about 1 min per essay question assigning scores for legibility (5 points), content (20 points), and writing quality (i.e., "complete sentences and reasonable grammar"; 5 points).

The essays we selected for comparison were written in response to the same question appearing on the second quiz and the final: "Give an example of the use of the experimental method." No sample answer had been given for this question. Usable data were available for 55 students. The at-

Table 1. Examples of Essay Questions Used in Study 1

1. Why is it said that the experimental method can demonstrate causality but the correlational method cannot?
2. Describe in general the functioning of the autonomic nervous system. Why is this of interest to psychologists?
3. A child's language skill develops in an orderly way. Describe three important milestones in this process and say roughly the age at which each might be expected.
4. Give an example of the use of biofeedback to teach the control of a function regulated by the autonomic nervous system, and point out how this is an example of operant conditioning.
5. Using results from animal studies, discuss the effects of deficient early environments on later development.
6. Discuss the social learning view of child behavior problems by describing how children acquire deviant behavior and the approach that social learning therapists take in helping parents of difficult children.
7. Say why reliability and validity are critically important characteristics of psychological tests.
8. Describe some of the cognitive characteristics of moderately depressed persons and relate these to Beck's cognitive therapy for depression.

trition resulted from some students missing either the first test or the final exam or not responding to the critical question (students could omit one question on the final). Four students were excused from the final on the basis of their high scores during the semester.

The essays from the second quiz and the final for the 55 students were typed onto a single sheet in random order. Four judges read the pairs of essays and selected one as the better of the two according to a 6-point scale anchored as follows: *top essay significantly better* (1), *top essay slightly better* (2), *top essay, but essays are very close* (3), *bottom essay, but essays are very close* (4), *bottom essay slightly better* (5), and *bottom essay significantly better* (6). Judges were the authors and two teaching assistants from the English department who had previously taught freshman composition but were unfamiliar with this study.

Results

We examined agreement among the ratings of the four judges. Intercorrelations ranged from .57 to .65 with a median interrater agreement of .62, reflecting the difficulty of the task. The four ratings of each writing sample were averaged to create the measure of writing improvement used in the study. The average rating was more stable than individual ratings; its theoretical reliability was .87 (Winer, 1971).

In order to average the ratings across all subjects, the numbers were converted so that a score of 1 corresponded to a rating that the early essay was significantly better and a score of 6 corresponded to a judgment that the essay on the final was significantly better. A score of 3.5 was at the midpoint of this scale. The average of the writing samples from all subjects was 3.72 (SD = 1.5), which is slightly in favor of the essay written on the final. A t test showed that this was not significantly different from 3.5, $t(54) = 1.07$. There was no statistically significant improvement in the students' writing over the semester.

Discussion

The outcome of Study 1 was surprising. We had expected that students who wrote often during the semester and who were given encouragement to attend to their writing would show improvement by the final exam. This was not the case. Essays composed at the beginning of the term were indistinguishable in quality from those written in the last week. The writing may have produced unmeasured benefits for the students in terms of the way they took notes and studied for tests, but it did not result in a measurable improvement in the quality of their written expression.

At this point, we reconsidered the writing tasks and processes involved and made two changes in the writing component of the course. First, in order to concentrate the students' writing efforts more precisely, we restricted the kinds of essays they composed. Second, we refined the scoring system to give students more direct feedback on writing quality. The purpose of Study 2 was to determine whether this more focused approach would produce demonstrable improvements in writing quality over the semester.

Study 2

The required freshman composition course at our institution approaches expository writing through practice with specific rhetorical patterns or modes. Students write themes that require classical rhetorical skills, such as comparison and contrast or causal analysis. We looked to these rhetorical patterns for models of writing appropriate to our limited setting and found four rhetorical patterns that were particularly well suited to writing short, expository compositions on concepts treated in introductory psychology. The four patterns were exemplification, definition, comparison and contrast, and process analysis.

Although some of the material from freshman composition was incorporated into the psychology course, there was no explicit linkage between the two courses. The fact that introductory psychology may be taken before, after, or concurrently with freshman English made a close coordination of material infeasible.

An important consequence of selecting the rhetorical patterns as models for the student essays was that we found it necessary to revise or replace virtually all the essay questions on the study guides. Table 2 gives examples of these questions grouped by rhetorical mode. The difference between these questions and those in Table 1 is that the earlier ones are concerned solely with the content of the expected answer and offer no guidance on what might be an appropriate form or method of rhetorical development for the answer. The new questions give clear directions for development.

Method

The four rhetorical forms (definition, exemplification, comparison and contrast, and process analysis) were introduced gradually during the term. For the first 5 weeks, all study guide essay questions required either definition or exemplification. Students received a handout during the first week of the course with suggestions for answering questions requiring these two rhetorical types. In the sixth week, comparison and contrast questions were introduced with an appropriate handout. Process analysis was added in the ninth

Table 2. Examples of Essay Questions Used in Study 2

Definition
1. Define the concept of hemispheric specialization as it applies to the cerebral cortex.
2. Define reliability in the context of a psychological test.

Exemplification
1. Use an example involving Weber's law to explain the concept of a difference threshold.
2. Use an example to show why a lie detector may not always detect lies.

Comparison and Contrast
1. Compare and contrast negative reinforcement and punishment.
2. Use comparison and contrast to present the important characteristics of the id and the ego.

Process Analysis
1. Explain the process by which the Minnesota Multiphasic Personality Inventory was constructed.
2. Describe the process of parent–child bonding.

week. Sample essays showing examples of full-credit answers to one of the exam questions were distributed each week.

The writing component of the essay scoring system was modified to place less emphasis on writing mechanics and more on the students' ability to develop a topic effectively. The 5-point scoring category "complete sentences and reasonable grammar" was changed to *development*, a term defined as the organization of content. Handouts provided development strategies appropriate to the rhetorical form called for by the type of question.

The methodology of Study 1 was used to examine whether this approach was effective in helping the students improve their writing skills. Students wrote answers to the same question on their second exam in the third week of the course and on the final exam: "Use an example drawn from a behavioral study to illustrate the relation between the early environment and neural development." Each of the 36 essay pairs available for this study was typed on a single sheet of paper in random order. Three judges rated each pair of essays on the same scale used in Study 1. The raters were one of the authors (JB) and the same two English teaching assistants used previously.

Results

The interrater agreements for the three judges were similar to those reported in Study 1, ranging from .51 to .74 with a median of .59. Ratings were averaged across raters and corrected for the random order of the essay pairs so that a score of 1 indicated that the early essay was significantly superior and a score of 6 showed the later essay to be significantly better. The midpoint on this scale was also 3.5, which indicates the two essays are of equal quality. The overall average rating for the essays in Study 2 was 4.2 (*SD* = 1.3), which is significantly above 3.5, $t(35) = 3.16$, $p < .01$.

Discussion

We found it more difficult to make a measurable improvement in writing than we had expected. Our first study showed that it is simply not enough to require writing and to encourage quality in compositions by grading on sentence structure and grammar. This approach had little effect on what the judges recognized as writing quality.

Study 2 dealt with only one of four rhetorical modes introduced in the course (exemplification). Our impression is that writing in the other rhetorical forms also showed marked improvement over the semester; it would be surprising if this were not the case. Definition, comparison and contrast, and process analysis are more demanding rhetorical forms than exemplification, so they provide even more opportunities for repeated practice and feedback to help students.

Success of the writing component in Study 2 was probably attributable, in the main, to restricting essays to particular rhetorical formats. This narrower focus required us to be more specific in two ways. First, the exam questions were revamped so that each one called for the development of a single topic according to an identified format. Second, each

of the sample answers illustrated a general rhetorical principle that students could apply to future essay questions.

The change in the grading system probably helped too. In Study 1, students were told that the 5 points for writing were awarded for complete sentences and reasonable grammar. By changing the grading basis to development in Study 2, we shifted emphasis from the editing component to the conceptual component of the writing task. This change should have encouraged students to focus their efforts on what we believed to be more important writing skills. The change also brought our approach into better agreement with the advocates of writing across the curriculum who see the writing process as primarily an attempt to create or share meaning (Emig, 1977) rather than a technical exercise in the production of correct sentences.

One unusual feature of our approach is that writing improvement occurs in the context of examinations. This came about somewhat accidentally because the pedagogical reasons for frequent essay examinations were more to support mastery of the material than to develop writing skill. However, the testing format worked out well for both objectives. We believe a number of factors contributed to its success. The format was helpful to students attempting to master the overwhelming amount of material covered in the introductory course. Distributing potential essay questions before the tests helped students structure and focus the material. The specific rhetorical modes also provided students with useful models of thought (Fulwiler, 1982) that aided in the assimilation of important course ideas. Access to the set of possible essay questions before the test allowed students to engage in prewriting activities, such as organizing, planning, and practicing trial answers, before the exam; they improved their writing as they mastered the course content. This approach is reasonable and helpful in the introductory course, but it is probably not pedagogically appropriate for more advanced, specialized courses that lend themselves to other strategies for testing and assigning written work.

We have continued to develop the writing component of this course. Students' essays are now scored for writing skill rather than development, and points are awarded for the extent to which essays are unified, coherent paragraphs appropriate to the various question formats. Writing skill appears to be a more meaningful concept to the students than development. We have also begun distributing a poorly written sample answer to each week's quiz along with one full-credit sample answer. We have data suggesting that many of our students are deficient in discriminating good from bad writing; the sample answers we distribute are meant to strengthen that discrimination.

The set of rhetorical formats used in the course has also been refined. Because one major objective is to emphasize the empirical nature of psychology, we have adapted the rhetorical mode of process analysis specifically to the process of the experiment. Process analysis questions now have one of two specific formats: "Describe an actual experiment that showed . . ." and "Design a plausible experiment to investigate. . . ." In the first of the new formats, the student writes a coherent, unified paragraph approximating a brief abstract of a study previously described in the course. In the second, the student uses the rhetorical format to think empirically about a psychological topic. These additions bring the number of rhetorically based patterns to five. The course begins with exemplification and definition. Comparison and contrast is introduced in Week 3, "Describe an experiment" in Week 5, and "Design an experiment" at midsemester.

The improvement in writing skills shown by the second study was modest, which is, perhaps, a reasonable achievement for a course whose primary purpose is an introduction to psychology. It is difficult to know the extent to which the writing skills students developed in the course will be useful to them in other situations requiring writing. We would expect good generalization to settings that require the creation of short, focused essays. The specific rhetorical patterns themselves may be sources of additional benefit because each of the rhetorical modes, such as comparison and contrast, is an analytical tool of general applicability.

References

Emig, J. (1977). Writing as a mode of learning. *College Composition and Communication, 28,* 122–128.

Frederiksen, N. (1984). The real test bias. *American Psychologist, 39,* 193–202.

Fulwiler, T. (1982). Writing: An act of cognition. In C. W. Griffin (Ed.), *Teaching writing in all disciplines* (pp. 15–26). San Francisco: Jossey-Bass.

Griffin, C. W. (1982). *Teaching writing in all disciplines.* San Francisco: Jossey-Bass.

Richards, J. P., & Friedman, F. (1978). The encoding versus the external storage hypothesis in note taking. *Contemporary Educational Psychology, 3,* 136–143.

White, E. M. (1985). *Teaching and assessing writing.* San Francisco: Jossey-Bass.

Winer, B. J. (1971). *Statistical principles in experimental design* (3rd ed.). New York: McGraw-Hill.

Note

We thank Ken Baker, Joan Kleppe, and Sonya Plourde for their help with the data analysis.

The Psychology Portfolio: Promoting Writing and Critical Thinking About Psychology

Cheryl A. Rickabaugh

The writing across the curriculum movement has greatly changed the teaching of undergraduate writing. Proponents of writing across the curriculum assert that the writing class is no longer the exclusive domain of the English Department and that all academic departments should teach undergraduate writing skills. Many teachers of psychology have taken up this challenge and developed techniques to strengthen student writing in psychology courses (e.g., Beers, 1985; Blevins-Knabe, 1987; McGovern & Hogshead, 1990; Snodgrass, 1985; Spiegel, Cameron, Evans, & Nodine, 1980).

Many psychology teachers, however, have hesitated to emphasize writing in their courses. Boice (1990) described a number of common concerns of faculty involved in writing across the curriculum programs. For example, faculty frequently are concerned about the impact that additional writing assignments may have on their workload. Writing assignments also may produce negative reactions from students who complain about the extra work involved or their weak writing skills. Thus, when revising a course to include additional writing assignments, it is important to consider the effect of these assignments on faculty and student workloads.

My primary goal was to develop a series of written assignments that would require students to write on a regular basis. As Boice (1982) pointed out, students frequently suffer from writing-related anxiety, which leads to procrastination and, subsequently, poor-quality "binge writing." He suggested that students' written output is of better quality when they are required to submit regular, shorter assignments rather than one large course assignment (i.e., a traditional term paper due at the end of the semester).

My second goal was to incorporate more critical thinking exercises into my courses by requiring students to apply theoretical principles or empirical findings from psychology to their everyday lives. Thus, I developed a series of self-directed laboratory projects that students could conduct independently outside of class. These projects required students to evaluate the course content critically by application to real-world phenomena. Because students conducted these projects outside of class, I had more time available during class time for lectures, discussion, and other activities. The assignment of individual projects also ensured that each student became actively involved with the course material. Hence, the projects provided me with more freedom to plan in-class activities and provided students with topics for critical essay assignments that were collected in a course portfolio.

Psychology Portfolio Assignments

Portfolio assignments were handed out on a weekly basis. For example, during a module on attribution theory, students were asked to survey a small number of their friends to ascertain the nature of the last excuse they had made to someone. Then, students were asked to identify the nature of the attributions underlying each excuse (e.g., situational vs. dispositional) and determine whether the attributional patterns they observed were consistent with excuse theory (Snyder & Higgins, 1988).

The assignments generally conformed to Weber's (1984) three-part essay assignment format. Students were asked to describe the observation that served as the basis for the assignment. Then, they summarized the psychological theory or research that would be applied in an analysis of this observation. Finally, they evaluated the fit of the theory or research to their experience. Students' weekly handouts provided detailed guidelines for each assignment. The assignments typically required students to write two to three typed pages.

Coordination of portfolio assignments with weekly course topics was important because it encouraged students to complete assigned readings and to attend class regularly. Thus, each assignment was handed out in class when the weekly course topic was introduced. Completed assignments were due the following week in class when the next assignment was handed out. In order to do well, students had to synthesize and integrate material from the course in their essays; students could not simply summarize the textbook or lecture material. The application portion of the assignments required students to evaluate the course material critically in light of the observations discussed in their essays. Thus, assignments were designed to require students to analyze and interpret their observations within the context of course material that they were currently mastering.

I also thought it was critical to provide prompt feedback to students. Toward that end, I attempted to return each essay by the next class meeting. I used Weber's (1984) 5-point grading scale, which makes global assessments of writing quality and application of theoretical concepts. Although written comments were provided when appropriate, the standardized format of the assignments made it very easy to assess students' comprehension of psychological theory and research, facilitated grading, and may have reduced subjectivity in assigning scores. Teachers with large classes might implement this assignment without significantly increasing their workload by using the 5-point grading scale and omitting written comments.

The portfolios constituted a significant portion of the students' grades in each course. The complete portfolio for each course consisted of 10 assignments. Assignments were due weekly unless a test was scheduled that week. Students were allowed 1 week to complete each assignment. Although each assignment was worth a maximum of 5 points, the total portfolio constituted 25% of the students' grades (equivalent to one examination). This grading structure was intended to minimize students' anxiety about the relation of each individual assignment to the final course grade while emphasizing that the portfolio was important and could be used to offset a poor exam performance.

Student Evaluations

Four classes (two sections of Introduction to Psychology, one section of Personality Theories, and one section of Social Psychology) assessed the effectiveness of the psychology portfolio method at the end of the semester by completing a 10-item questionnaire. Students responded to 9 evaluative items using a 5-point scale ranging from *strongly disagree* (1) to *strongly agree* (5). The 10th item asked students to estimate the amount of time they spent completing the average portfolio assignment. Finally, students provided their own comments about the portfolio method. Questionnaires were administered in class; however, students were assured that their responses would be anonymous. With the exception of a few absentees, all students participated in the survey ($N = 96$). The questionnaire items and the sample means and standard deviations are presented in Table 1.

Students responded favorably to the portfolio method, saying that it was more interesting than writing a term paper. In addition, the portfolio assignments appeared to increase student involvement in the course; respondents indicated that they could relate the assignments to their own lives and that the assignments had helped them to develop individual interests in the subject matter.

Perhaps more important, students wrote on a regular basis. Furthermore, students appeared not to resent the increased workload or to think that the assignments required too much work. Students produced 20 to 30 typed pages during the 13-week semester. Thus, students wrote substantially more than if a traditional term paper had been assigned. Although students reported a highly variable number of hours preparing their assignments, the weekly deadlines appeared to be useful in increasing the amount of time students consistently spent writing about psychology.

Students also reported that the assignments facilitated their understanding of the text and lecture material. These assignments were designed to require students to apply the course content outside of the classroom. To do well, students were forced to go beyond mere regurgitation of the facts and to think critically. The nature of these assignments encouraged students to become actively engaged in the course content and to apply psychological research and theory in a real-world setting. Furthermore, the provision of

Table 1. Student Evaluations of Assignment

Questionnaire Item	M	SD
1. The portfolio assignments were more interesting than writing a term paper.	4.39	1.03
2. The assignments were appropriate for the level of this class.	4.11	.92
3. I could relate the portfolio assignments to my life.	4.05	.97
4. The assignments made me interested in psychology.	3.82	1.06
5. I enjoyed the assignments.	3.66	1.03
6. The assignments involved too much work.	2.16	1.02
7. These assignments helped me understand the textbook and lecture material better.	4.19	.99
8. The assignments were integrated well into the course.	4.32	.80
9. The assignments should be due on a regular basis (perhaps three times/semester) rather than weekly.	2.72	1.56
10. On the average, how much time (in hours) did you spend working on each assignment?	2.19	1.13

Note. Items 1 through 9 were scored on a scale that ranged from *strongly disagree* (1) to *strongly agree* (5).

prompt, weekly feedback was important for students to assess their mastery of the course content.

Conclusion

For the most part, I believe that the portfolio method met the goals established when I began revising my courses. Since my initial experimentation with the method, I have incorporated portfolio assignments into three additional courses. Without significantly increasing my own workload, I was able to incorporate critical thinking assignments into my courses. Furthermore, student reactions to the additional out-of-class projects were favorable. The overall positive attitudes reported by these students is encouraging when one considers that the average written output for each student was 20 to 30 typed pages per semester. Hence, the portfolio method also appeared to be successful in promoting students' writing skills while minimizing procrastination and anxiety, as indicated in students' comments on the evaluation.

References

Beers, S. E. (1985). Use of a portfolio writing assignment in a course on developmental psychology. *Teaching of Psychology, 12,* 94–96.

Blevins-Knabe, B. (1987). Writing to learn while learning to write. *Teaching of Psychology, 14,* 239–241.

Boice, R. (1982). Teaching of writing in psychology: A review of sources. *Teaching of Psychology, 9,* 143–147.

Boice, R. (1990). Faculty resistance to writing-intensive courses. *Teaching of Psychology, 17,* 13–17.

McGovern, T. V., & Hogshead, D. L. (1990). Learning about writing, thinking about teaching. *Teaching of Psychology, 17,* 5–10.

Snodgrass, S. E. (1985). Writing as a tool for teaching social psychology. *Teaching of Psychology, 12,* 91–94.

Snyder, C. R., & Higgins, R. L. (1988). Excuses: Their effective role in the negotiation of reality. *Psychological Bulletin, 104,* 23–35.

Spiegel, T. A., Cameron, S. M., Evans, R., & Nodine, B. F. (1980). Integrating writing into the teaching of psychology: An alternative to Calhoun and Selby. *Teaching of Psychology, 7,* 242–243.

Weber, A. (1984). Teaching tips for social psychology. *Contemporary Social Psychology, 10,* 9–10.

Notes

1. Earlier versions of this article were presented at the annual meeting of the Western Psychological Association, Los Angeles, April 1990, and the National Institute on the Teaching of Psychology, St. Petersburg, FL, January 1992.
2. I thank Anna Marie Napoli and three anonymous reviewers for their helpful comments on a draft of this article.

Effective Feedback on Written Assignments

Daniel B. Willingham

When a writer seeks an editor, the writer is asking "Am I communicating my ideas?" or, more precisely, "How can I better communicate my ideas on my next draft?" Instructors try to fulfill that editorial function by providing feedback on student papers, but other concerns come into play. Instructors provide feedback to justify a grade. They serve as authorities who tell the students whether they understand the material they have learned; in their strictest role, teachers tell students whether they have fulfilled the assignment. All of these functions are valid, and may be emphasized in varying degrees for different students. The focus here is on the first function, the one all writers seek—criticism that motivates an improved paper and motivates improved writing skills.

How can instructors provide comments to students that emphasize improved future drafts rather than the evaluation of the current draft? Instructors comment on the content of papers and on the mechanics. Usually, comments on content are rather general: "This part of the paper doesn't make sense" or "this argument needs shoring up." Comments on mechanics are usually quite specific: Misspellings are pointed out, errors in grammar are corrected, and so on. I contend that the goal of commenting should be kept in mind when selecting the degree of specificity of comments on content and mechanics. If the goal of commenting is to improve future drafts and to improve the student's writing, then comments should encourage the student to think about how the draft could be improved; the specificity of comments is the key variable in promoting that mind-set.

Comments on Content

The most important principle in providing feedback is to encourage the student to be his or her own editor. The student must consider whether the paper will make sense to the reader. Is the argument clear? Is the logic of the paper explicit? Does the author anticipate and refute counterarguments? If writers can read their papers the way a naive reader would, they will reduce their errors by 50%.

One way to encourage such reading is simply to tell the student what you heard in the paper, without making any judgments. The goal is to get the student to follow the thoughts of a naive reader. For example, the instructor might write: "First you said X, so I thought you would write about Y, but then you brought Z in, so I figured the paper would connect X and Z. But then you brought in Q and I was confused. . . ." This sort of commenting works well not only for the style and organization of a paper but for its argument as well: "Because you brought up A, I, as the reader, immediately think of B as a counterargument. You'd better say something about B."

Another way to encourage students to edit their work is to ask questions. Instead of telling students what to do, ask leading questions. This technique is designed to keep students in the process and to initiate dialogues between students and instructors, instead of setting up instructors as oracles, with students guessing what sort of prose to lay at their feet until they grow impatient and tell them so. Do not let comments be the last words between teacher and student. Remember, when anyone writes a paper he or she thinks is good, it is not easy to understand a mistake, even when it is pointed out. Comments should be part of an ongoing conversation between teacher and student.

Some writing instructors suggest asking the entire class to turn in with their paper their own evaluation of its strengths and weaknesses, which is an interesting way of initiating the dialogue. This guarantees that the instructor will be able to respond not only to the paper but also to the student's thoughts on the paper, which is what the dialogue is about. Such an exercise may make students think about their draft in broad terms as they write it, which is all for the best. Certainly it will force them to do so when they turn in their rough draft, and that gives them a good start on their second draft. Another benefit is that it probably makes the instructor's job of commenting a bit easier.

Finally, the instructor should be sure to say something positive about the paper. It is easy to leave well enough alone and point out only the flaws. Even if the paper seems terrible, it is important to point out those things the student did well for two reasons. First, negative comments from start to finish may wound the student's ego so deeply that he or she will simply give up on the paper or even on the class. Second, students learn as much from being told what they have done well as they do from being told what they have done poorly.

Comments are not helpful when they are either too specific or not specific enough. At one end of the spectrum, the instructor may effectively take over the paper by suggesting precisely what should be changed. Brannon and Knoblauch (1982) referred to this process as appropriating the student's text. The instructor's comments draw attention to the purposes in commenting rather than to the paper itself. In so doing, the instructor encourages the student to satisfy the teacher rather than to perceive and repair what the paper lacks. The student's goal for the paper changes from "Here are some things I think are important" to "Here's what I guess you want me to do." By asking questions in comments appropriation of the text can be prevented. The student is required to generate improvements in the paper, rather than to execute improvements as directed by the instructor.

The instructor may be even more specific in his or her comments by actually rewriting portions of the paper, which never helps the student. It does not encourage students to be their own editors; instead they learn to retype what the instructor has written, and, worse yet, they will never take out anything the instructor writes. Even if the paper goes through many more drafts and what was added becomes irrelevant, come hell or high water, the instructor's prose will appear.

When comments are very specific about what the student should do to change the paper, the instructor's purpose in commenting is no longer to improve the next draft. Yes, the instructor will like the draft more because it is studded with his or her prose, but the comments did not help the student learn to write. Hyperspecific comments evaluate the prose, but they do not help students improve their writing ability, because the opportunity to improve the text is taken away from them. The message from such comments is: "You did this wrong. I had better show you how to do it right. You sit back and watch me."

At the other end of the spectrum, a lack of specificity can be a problem in instructor's comments. Somers (1982), in a study of college teachers' comments on student writing, found they were frequently unspecific about what part of the text their comments applied to. Teachers gave instructions that could be put on any essay, like "Think more about what you're thinking about" or "Think about your audience." The irony is that if the commentors had thought about their audience, they would never make such comments.

You can tell a student what is wrong with a text. If a sentence or paragraph is vague, point out the multiple interpretations. If a student consistently writes awkward sentences, then show why a few are awkward: "This phrase makes me think you're going to talk about X, but then you talk about Y" and "This phrase connotes P and you're talking about Q."

Occasionally an instructor, consciously or unconsciously, will write comments that are personally insulting. Unfortunately, such comments are frequently the most memorable. My most memorable comment came from an English professor in regard to an in-class essay. The only comment was "No. C+." Think back on the most memorable comment you ever received on a paper. It is a good bet that the comment is equally negative and personal and, therefore, unhelpful. If the professor does not tell the student what was wrong with an essay, then the implicit message is "This essay is not worth commenting on. You are so far gone I can't be bothered to try to correct your mistakes."

Insulting comments are frequently a symptom that the instructor does not know what is wrong with a paper. The instructor knows the paper is bad but cannot offer specific criticisms or advice so the teacher blasts the student. Comments like "You haven't thought about this enough" or "Your writing is so bad no one could be expected to understand what you're saying" are typical.

There are some tricks to try if one cannot identify a paper's problem. Set the paper aside for 1–2 days, then reread it. Ask a colleague to look at it. If still left speechless, have the student come in during office hours and ask him or her about the paper. The student may have fairly good insight. If not, tell the student what seems to need work and be satisfied. No one wins every time. But do work hard to figure out what exactly the paper lacks. Do not be vague. The most insulting and unhelpful comment one can write (without getting personal) is "vague." Students will look at the comment, shrug their shoulders and say "Looks okay to me."

Vague comments, like hyperspecific comments, change the function of the feedback on papers. Vague comments do not help the student write a better draft because they do not provide enough direction. They tell the student that something is wrong, but do not help the student learn how to fix it. The only message is that something is wrong. Again, the function of feedback changes from improvement of the draft to evaluation of the student.

Comments on Mechanics

What about the mechanics of a paper? How should one handle grammar, syntax, and so on, as opposed to content? Again, the motivation must be to improve future drafts and future papers.

An overemphasis on the mechanics of writing is the way instructors most frequently appropriate a student's text. Mallonee and Breihan's (1985) informal study of college instructors found that comments on the mechanics of writing constituted the "chief object of [faculty] attention" (p. 214). Marius (1987) contended that mechanics are emphasized to the exclusion of all else in high school, and, therefore, students frequently carry over the idea to college that mechanics count for all. Grammar is important; spelling is important—but students already know this! Rather than confirm this fact for them with red ink, instructors should emphasize the issues that they tend to underemphasize.

If students know the mechanics of writing are important, why do they make so many mechanical mistakes? An obvious answer is that writing correct prose is difficult and requires practice; it would be expecting too much of college students to write error-free papers. This answer is, on a second look, not so obvious. What is difficult about proofreading carefully and using a dictionary? The correction of typographical and spelling errors requires patience more than anything else. Consider that papers students submit for English classes consistently contain fewer mechanical errors than papers they submit for content courses (Mallonee & Breihan, 1985). Sometimes it is casualness with language rather than ignorance that results in substandard mechanics. Using grammar correctly may be more difficult than avoiding typographical and spelling errors, but not prohibitively so. College students take courses like organic chemistry and computer programming; learning English grammar is a good bit easier than learning the principles in either of these courses. Most school systems begin teaching grammar between the seventh and ninth grade. Surely mastery of grammar is not too difficult for college students.

But how will students master grammar? How can students be encouraged to work on the mechanics of writing? Again, the question of the specificity of the instructor's comments comes to the fore. Students will not benefit from reading the hyperspecific corrections written by their instructors. Most college students have been reading such corrections for years; if they were helpful, then they would have helped by now. The way to learn grammar is to work out grammatical problems yourself.

This reasoning indicates that the instructor should highlight mechanical errors on the paper but have the student correct them. This strategy will not work because the student will not take the time to find the correct answers. Any student motivated enough to do that learned correct grammar long ago. Instead, instructors must take a hard line. They should make it clear that technical competence is expected. If a student turns in a draft with many errors on it, write "You have many mechanical errors here. Please correct them. See me if you don't understand the mechanics of writing."

Am I advocating an abandonment of students with problems? No. My motivation is to improve student writing, and I contend that students will be more likely to learn the mechanics of writing by instructors requiring technical competence than by instructors correcting of technical incompetence. This argument is predicated on the assumption that college students can achieve technical competence largely on their own. This argument should not be construed as a stone wall for those students for whom grammar poses a real stumbling block that they have difficulty surmounting. There will be some college students for whom the mechanics of writing are genuinely difficult to master. Ideally, a psychology instructor will have the time and expertise to work with such students to help them learn the basic and the fine points of grammar and usage. If the instructor does not have the time and expertise, these students should be directed to places where they can get help: to the appropriate English courses or to writing centers on campus, if they are available.

This is a hard line. But a hard line is appropriate because (a) most students can minimize or eliminate mechanical errors, (b) students benefit more from working out problems and solutions to grammar problems than from reading the instructor's corrections, (c) it takes a great deal of the instructor's time to flag all these errors, and (d) an overemphasis on mechanics may distract students from problems of content.

Content and Mechanics — A Hierarchy of Comments

Much of the foregoing discussion focused on getting students to think about their audience as they write papers. This advice also applies to instructors as they write comments. They must think about the student's perspective in reading these comments in order to make them useful. It may not be clear to the student which comments are more or less important. The errors that are easy to correct are frequently the most obvious—errors at the sentence level. Sometimes the instructor even provides the correction; the student may correct the misspellings and errors of usage and unclear phrases and figure that the draft is perfect, while failing to notice the marginal comment "This part of your argument needs more support."

A hierarchy must be easily discernible in the instructor's comments. The student should know immediately which aspects of the paper need the most work, which need less work, and which aspects have been handled well. Writers may or may not be able to make those judgments themselves. Even if students were able to make such judgments when asked, they may not do it spontaneously.

The easiest way to make the hierarchical structure of comments apparent is to write a long comment at the end of the paper and to make explicit what the student needs to work on. The relative importance of each of the problems should be raised and suggestions should be made. Too often, the most important comment will be a phrase like "develop the argument for separable memory systems further," which may get buried among other comments or, even worse, may go unnoticed in a margin.

The instructor should not only list the most important comment first and label it as important, but should also describe in appropriate detail why it needs work. Why is the argument for separable memory systems insufficient? Is it unclear? In what way? Are there counterarguments that the author should have anticipated? The comments should tell the writer the ways in which you, the reader, found the paper lacking or confusing. The student thought the argument for separable memory systems was strong when the draft was turned in and will not see that it is weak on reading it a second time, even when knowing the instructor thinks it is.

Finally, a hierarchical structure to comments allows the instructor to emphasize the improvement of the paper and future papers, rather than to emphasize the grade. Rather than writing an evaluation of the paper, the instructor's message can be "here's the most important thing you can do to make this paper even better." The emphasis is on teamwork between the instructor and student on improving the draft, rather than on the evaluation of the student's work.

References

Brannon, L., & Knoblauch, C. H. (1982). On students' rights to their own texts: A model of teacher response. *College Composition and Communication, 33*, 157–166.

Mallonee, B. C., & Breihan, J. R. (1985). Responding to students' drafts: Interdisciplinary consensus. *College Composition and Communication, 36*, 213–231.

Marius, R. (1987). *Impressions of student writing at Harvard*. (Available from Expository Writing Center, Freshman Union, 12 Quincy Street, Cambridge, MA 02138)

Somers, N. (1982). Responding to student writing. *College Composition and Communication, 33*, 148–156.

Notes

1. Much of the content of this article comes from a series of workshops and meetings held through the Graduate Writing Fellow Program at Harvard University. I thank Sue Lonoff and Lenny Cassuto for their able leadership of the Program and Harvard University for supporting it.
2. Roger Brown, Sue Lonoff, Barbara F. Nodine, and Elizabeth Willingham provided many helpful comments on earlier drafts.

Psychology on a Disk: Then What?

Thomas Brothen

Two questions seem appropriate for instructors to ask about commercially produced software. They may wonder: "How could I use that in my course?" and "Why would I want to bother with that?" In this review, I proceed under the assumption that readers of this section of *Teaching of Psychology* are considering the first and not the second question. I assume further that readers of this review are seeking practical information that could help them improve their courses with computer-assisted instruction.

Psychology On A Disk (POAD) is a set of 13 computer-assisted exercises contained on one disk designed to be used by students as an out-of-class exercise (a network version is available by special arrangement). The primarily text-based (little multimedia—animation, video, etc.) program is available in MS–DOS® and Macintosh® versions and sells for $13.50. Instructors adopting the software package through their campus bookstores receive a demonstration disk that explains each exercise, a master disk (for replacing damaged student disks), and an Instructor's Manual containing information about how to use the programs. The publisher also promises telephone technical support.

Each of the 10 regular and 3 advanced options exercises first presents a conceptual background and its relation to the exercise, then gives operating instructions and ends with a rationale. The demonstration disk adds tips on how instructors may use the exercises. Some exercises provide students with a data printout. POAD records exercise completions on a progress report that students can print and turn in. Users access individual exercises through a Main menu. Some exercises "trap" students by requiring completion before returning to the menu (pressing control-break bypasses this requirement) because they are experiments that do not make sense unless finished. Students need to budget at least 15 to 20 min for each exercise. More time is required, however, if a student does not take some tasks seriously.

Exercise Summaries

Horizontal–Vertical Illusion: The task in this exercise is to adjust a vertical line emanating upward from the middle of a horizontal line until both are the same length. This is done under three conditions of 10 trials each: without feedback, with feedback (indication of where the correct length is after the adjustment is made), and without feedback again. After the last condition, students see a graph that represents their performance under each condition. The computer generates a table of deviations from the correct length for each condition. Presumably, the first condition will be least accurate, the feedback condition will show rapid improvement, and the last condition will show learning. The exercise is essentially a within-subjects experiment showing the effects of feedback on length perception.

Guilt Detection: Students role-play a crime scenario in which they are a thief being questioned by police with a guilt detection technique. Told to "try not to think of the crime," students complete a word association task. After the task, they learn that some of the words were critical (i.e., related to the crime: *cash, purse*) and some neutral (e.g., *red, heavy*). Their typed responses are not important but their response latencies are. Both neutral and critical words then appear on screen with their associated latencies and averages. Students should see that the critical words have longer latencies. In addition to being a simulation of a lie detection procedure, the exercise is a within-subjects experiment on the effects of word relevance on response latency.

Shaping: Students are to shape the behavior of a rat that has already been trained to press a bar. Reinforcing successive approximations, students train the rat to press harder until it reaches a criterion. A number representing the force of each press appears on screen and students choose whether to reinforce the response. Students can select from four levels of difficulty. For example, in the "easy" level the rat tolerated 56 straight reinforcements from me before it was satiated and quit, saying "Whew! I'm full!" In the "very hard" level students have to maintain a fine balance between reinforcing and not reinforcing or the rat will either satiate or its behavior will extinguish. The progress report indicates which level the student achieved. This simulation of the shaping process is realistic and engaging.

Short-Term Memory: This exercise is an experiment requiring students to recall trigrams. In the first of four conditions they type each trigram after it appears. In three delay conditions (5, 10, and 15 s) they have to complete subtraction problems that appear on screen before typing the trigram. If students do not complete enough problems the trial is not recorded. This exercise holds the student captive so the integrity of the experiment is upheld. I took a shortcut by writing down the trigrams to see what the data looked like, but I still had to do the subtractions. I wondered whether students would do the same. On completing the experiment, students see bar graphs representing their performance. To make sure students understand the graphs, they must correctly answer a question about them before going further. As with other instances in which students must answer before continuing, the computer pauses and responds only to a correct answer. Students then see a table of their correct trigrams by condition. In addition to demonstrating the effect of delay on short-term memory, this is also a within-subjects experiment that provides data students can analyze.

Cognition in Recall: The authors of the program say this one-participant experiment with relatively few trials makes it different from most experiments on cognition. After a practice trial that illustrates the procedure, students see 48 words presented one at a time. They then type as many as they can (free recall). If they do not type enough words they must repeat the task. Again, I cheated by writing down most of the words to get enough data to evaluate the program—and wondered if students may also take this shortcut. The data display illustrates intrusions, primacy/recency, and category clustering (e.g., how many words they typed correctly fit into the body part category). Students perform several operations in this long and comprehensive exercise. They memorize words, type words, rate their certainty about whether words appeared, and view the data in several interesting ways. The explanation during and after the data collection and presentation is very complete and the program emphasizes the importance of taking notes to aid memory. This exercise is a demonstration of the memory process and provides a wealth of data that students could use in research projects. However, it is in a format that would prove difficult for most students without supplemental instructions from their instructor on its objectives and how to use it.

Insight: Students doing this exercise encounter an unusual task. They play a word matrix game against the computer. If they cannot win they can try another game that involves adding numbers in a matrix to get 15 before the computer does. They should soon realize (with or without hints from the computer) that they are playing variants of tic-tac-toe. This insight makes it easy to win. In fact, the same sequence of moves results in a win every time. This exercise is different from those summarized previously in that it does not provide data and serves only to illustrate the concept of insight.

Evaluating Your Personality: In this simulation, students experience firsthand the P. T. Barnum effect. After answering a set of bogus questions the computer supposedly analyzes the answers and student data from other exercises (they must complete the first six before this one) to produce a personality profile. Shortly after students see their profiles a message blinks that "It was a hoax!" followed by a complete explanation.

Making Interpersonal Judgments: Students see brief personality descriptions (two trait words in a short sentence) attributed to six men and six women. They then see all six trait words and must indicate whether they were used to describe men more, women more, or both equally. Four of the words are listed as neutral, one (analytical) is listed as traditionally "male" and one (compassionate) traditionally "female." Students then see a display of their guesses and the actual usage (equal for men and women for all words). If students say the male adjective was used to describe men more and the female adjective was used to describe women more, the computer discusses this as an example of illusory correlation. This simulation of person perception processes could also serve as a within-subjects experiment on the effects of sex stereotypes.

Cooperation and Competition: Students engage in a simulation of the prisoner's dilemma game against four opponents in sequence for 12 trials each. They can choose to give themselves 1 point or the opponent 3 points. A scoreboard tells what score is necessary for each game to be complete with each opponent and tallies the points after each trial. Each of the opponents uses a different strategy with the fourth one being truly contingent—selfishness and generosity are returned in kind. In this simulation, mutual reinforcement equals cooperation and a win is reaching the criterion point total no matter what total the opponent reaches. An informative explanation and discussion follow.

Segregation in a Snack Bar: Students see an 8 × 8 matrix of boxes occupied by 60 Xs and Os signifying two types of people. The program highlights those people "unhappy" because they do not have a high enough percentage of similar others near them. The student's task is to move people until everyone is "happy" with the seating pattern. (In the MS–DOS® version this involves typing "A2 to B3," etc., whereas the Macintosh® version moves people with a mouse click.) What results is a segregated seating pattern with Xs and Os clumped together. Once everyone is happy the student sees a distribution of people before and after. Students answer a question designed to show understanding of the distribution, and then may change the parameters (proportions of Xs and Os; percentage of similar others that results in satisfaction) and do the exercise again. However, returning to the main menu requires starting from the beginning. This clever simulation demonstrates how the appearance, if not the fact, of segregation results from personal preferences.

Neural Basis of a Visual Illusion: This advanced exercise shows the Hermann Grid and explains it by having students run a simulation of neural excitation–inhibition. This exercise is too advanced for most introductory psychology students and any user would have to pay close attention to the opening explanation. The simulation presents a grid with 10 cells across the top. Students enter values of light excitation for each and the resulting level of activity of each cell is represented by a white square that moves up or down depending on the number (0–9) entered. Adjacent squares also move up (excitation) or down (inhibition) depending on the value entered. Students must enter the proper values to match patterns that explain the Hermann Grid. This complex teaching simulation illustrates how vision operates by explaining an illusion through actively involving students.

Developing a Psychological Test: This advanced exercise has students develop a test to identify sufferers of a new disorder (narapoia). After six screens of introduction about test development and how the simulation works, students can review 60 items that have already been tested with narapoids and controls. They select 12 items after seeing data on how the questions were supposedly answered by the two groups and decide how the question should be scored. Then, they field test the instrument, and the percentages of hits and misses determines whether they must revise it. Basically, they need to pick items that discriminate, no matter what the item asks. This simulation of the empirical test development process is very realistic and is likely to be very engaging for students.

Scatterplots and Correlations: This advanced exercise has students construct scatterplots of data supplied by the computer. They move points along the *x* and *y* axes of a graph to their proper bivariate locations. After plotting several points (the computer allows only correct plotting), the best fit line and the correlation coefficient appear. Next, students see how low, medium, and high correlations appear as scatterplots. Then, students estimate correlations from different scatterplots until they get five correct (with a margin of error ± .10). Finally, students can enter up to 40 pairs of whole numbers (0–999) and watch the scatterplot build, the regression line drawn, and the correlation coefficient appear. The exercise teaches students about scatterplots and correlation and also provides them with a tool to compute correlations with their own sets of bivariate data.

Evaluation

In all the exercises, the software looks good, works well, and actually does what it claims to do. It is user friendly and instructors can feel confident that even their computer illiterate students will be able to master it. The Macintosh® version looks newer and allows use of the mouse and pull down menus. The MS–DOS® version looks older because it lacks these features and uses graphics text mode in some places. One important question that should always be asked about software is whether what it does could be done as well without a computer. The answer for this program is most emphatically no—unless time and labor were limitless. An instructor could certainly sit in front of a student while he or she plotted each bivariate pair in a set of data and provide immediate feedback on correct placement but that obviously makes little sense. The software is definitely not of the page-turning variety.

To get an impression of how students would react to the software, I gave it to a senior undergraduate teaching assistant and asked her to evaluate the exercises as a beginning student might. She had some minor complaints such as the two memory tasks being "too challenging" and wondered whether introductory psychology students would benefit as much as more advanced students. Overall, she was positive—liking very much the "research focus" of many of the "really fun" exercises and the "cool graphs." She praised the software for delivering "theory and then practical application," and the "experiential nature" of activities, such as the shaping exercise, saying she knew the theory but having to actually do it made it real for her.

The developers of POAD have created a set of exercises that teach by actively involving students. The program is intrusive—unlike some software, POAD requires students to follow directions and quizzes them at crucial points. It does not punish mistakes in these instances but rather, waits for a correct response. If students get lazy and do not want to do subtraction problems in the short-term memory exercise, it simply makes them do the task over. I think this is an effective pedagogical technique the developers could have used even more. It is amazing to watch students scroll quickly through carefully prepared computer assisted instruction directions and then turn to their neighbors or raise their hands to ask what they are supposed to do. The exercises also have a great deal of depth to them. Students could simply complete them and learn something. They could also go much deeper and use them to generate data for research projects.

The title of this review asks "then what?" because instructors are faced with the question of how to use resources like POAD. They also have to evaluate student behavior on assignments, decide how assignments fit into the course, what students are supposed to learn from them, and how they should be graded. The authors of POAD have provided part of the answer. Students can turn in a printed copy of the progress report, which lists the exercises and the date completed. To prevent students from simply typing a false report, the printout has the student's name and identification number (which students enter the first time they use the disk) and a number series that can be decoded using the Instructor's Manual. This is certainly a legitimate solution to the issue—simply completing the exercises would give students experience "doing" psychology. However, most instructors are probably looking for more course integration, if not more and better ways to evaluate students' learning.

It seems that the first problem for instructors is timing. Each exercise may be self-contained and need no explanation from the instructor but when to have students do them is important. For example, one may want students to read the learning chapter before doing the shaping exercise. Instructors need to examine each exercise to determine where it fits into their course. Some exercises are very topic specific and others could serve several purposes. For example, the horizontal–vertical illusion exercise is related to sensation-perception, but really is about two other things: the effects of feedback on performance and research design. It could also be a research project if students were to pool their data to compare the performance of men and women or other easily constituted groups. Some topics have more than one exercise and instructors probably should consider how to spread them throughout the term.

I applaud the effort of the POAD developers to make it self-contained. Over the years I have examined software that has left me wondering what to do with it and wondering even more what students would make of it. POAD is turn-key software that students could buy, use, and learn from without any instructor intervention. However, that is unlikely to happen: Students would ask how it affects their grade and instructors need an answer.

As with any instructional materials, the more motivated the students, the less instructors will have to be concerned with the issue of context. Some students will be able to use POAD independently to expand their knowledge of psychology. With most students in most introductory psychology classes, instructors will have to make the context more prescriptive. Students should know when to do each exercise, what they are to gain from doing it, and how they will be evaluated (write a research report, have a test on the concepts covered, etc.).

POAD is definitely worth a closer look. Instructors can contact CMS Software for a demo disk, review it, and make decisions about how they could use it. As a tool in the hands of a creative instructor, the exercises could be interesting and educational for students.

Developing Visual Displays for Lecture-Based Courses

Michael A. Seaman

According to the information-processing model (Atkinson & Shiffrin, 1968), a relatively small portion of what a person sees actually makes it to working memory, and an even smaller portion is processed for storage in long-term memory. Although many articles describe the positive effects of visual presentations (Kulik, Kulik, & Cohen, 1980), instructors must examine both the content and form of their presentations to ensure that students understand and remember presented material. One presentation tool commonly used is the visual display (e.g., chalkboard writing, overheads, slides, pictures).

With the advent of presentation software for the personal computer, an instructor can prepare professional-looking displays that combine text, illustrations, symbols, or other images. In the past, visual displays contained text, pictures or previously constructed illustrations, or photographs. There is no longer a need to depend on preexisting materials. Instructors can now create visual displays that specifically address the goals of the course.

In this article, I draw on cognitive theory and personal experience to discuss visual displays. First, I review the benefits of visual displays. I then categorize displays and relate these types to the goals of the presentation. Finally, I propose principles for developing visual displays.

Benefits of Visual Displays

There are several cognitive and logistical benefits to using visual displays in lectures. The cognitive resources that students typically allocate to the clerical chore of note taking can be redirected toward the presentation itself when the lecturer uses visual displays and provides copies of these displays to students. This alternative gives students the opportunity to think about newly presented information so that the process benefits of note taking (DiVesta & Gray, 1972) can be realized. I find that students ask more questions when I use visual displays, possibly indicating that they are thinking about the information as it is presented, rather than afterward.

Visual displays can redirect note taking so that students focus their attention on main points. The student's task becomes one of organizing supporting material around the main points offered in the visual display. This procedure promotes organizational processing that is at an optimal depth-of-processing level, somewhere between no processing (i.e., clerical note taking) and simple elaboration (Kiewra, 1985a). Students still take responsibility for adding information to visual displays, but these notes are personalized explanations added to a supporting framework (Kiewra, 1985b) rather than mere transcripts.

Instructors can present nonlinear information in a nonlinear fashion with a visual display. This presentation highlights major concepts and relations between concepts at the outset of the presentation. For example, consider presenting a concept map to a class of students (Novak & Gowin, 1984). In concept maps, the instructor represents concepts as circles around terms and the hierarchical relations between concepts as lines and prepositional links. Drawing a concept map on the chalkboard does not accurately or completely represent the hierarchy until the map is complete. Showing the entire concept map at once provides the correct representation immediately.

Colors used in visual displays capture attention and help organize material. The color of text or a graphic cues students to the category or purpose of a particular presentation element. Mayer (1984) identified such cues as a major aid to text comprehension.

Instructors can distribute visual displays in a variety of formats. Displays prepared with presentation software are stored in computer files. Students can view these files as a slide show with viewing software. Many presentation software manufacturers provide viewing software free of charge. Printouts of visual displays are useful as a starting point for student notes. Without this framework to build on, student notes are often sketchy and are less effective at aiding in comprehension and recall (Kiewra, 1985b). Transferring visual displays to a course World Wide Web page makes the displays accessible to any student connected to the Internet.

My informal observations suggest positive learning outcomes from using visual displays. These outcomes replicate the informal observations of Beins (1984) who used slides that were primarily photographs and figures in his lectures.

The most obvious change is that I can now cover more material in a course at a pace that feels more relaxed, and there is more time for questions and student–teacher interaction. The increased interaction with students does not appear to be solely the result of a relaxed pace. As suggested earlier, students spend far less time on clerical tasks and more time thinking about the content of the presentation. Before, the questions focused on making certain the student took accurate notes (e.g., "Could you repeat that definition?", whereas now the questions are for clarifying understanding (e.g., "Could you give another example?"). The free access to visual displays eliminates the verbatim dictation that I used to frequently observe. Students also use these displays to catch up quickly after an absence.

The students' open-ended evaluations of my courses contain many references to the visual displays and the "workbook" (a bound set of printouts of these displays) that I provide. In the evaluation of a recent course, 47 of the 51 students commented on the visual displays. One of these students suggested that I put a table of contents in the workbook, whereas the other 46 made emphatic and positive remarks. Typical comments about my "slides" (as my visual displays were referred to by students) included: "Slide photocopies were instrumental and vital to learning." "Slides were very effective and the book to go with them is great!" "The book of slides made note taking much easier since we could concentrate on learning the concept rather than writing everything down." "The instructor's supplementing text of slides presented was instrumental in clarifying abstract and confusing concepts presented." "The slide presentation was much more beneficial than lecture alone would have been."

Visual Display Categories

Individual visual displays can serve many purposes. Consider a visual display as a means to help reach a single lecture goal. For example, I prepared one lecture to teach measurement concepts and established several goals for this lecture: Outline the main elements of measurement, define terms, describe the uses of these terms, give examples, and check to see if communication has been effective and a correct understanding has been achieved. I use one or more visual displays to help me reach each goal. These goals lead to a typology of visual displays, briefly described in the following section.

Introductory Display

An introductory display presents a new topic in general terms and outlines the elements of the topic. Such a display acts as an advance organizer. Mayer (1979) demonstrated that advance organizers are especially useful when material is unfamiliar. The primary purpose of the introductory display is to show how the topics relate to a general theme. Figure 1 is a sample introductory display.

Text Display

Text displays present words, and thus are an alternative to writing on the chalkboard. Text displays give definitions and present basic facts or more complex information. These

Addressing Threats to Internal Validity

- Standardize conditions so that groups or individuals are equated on as many variables as possible except the independent variable.
- Obtain information on participants in order to ascertain that characteristics across groups or individuals are similar.
- Obtain information on components of the study so as to identify potential threats.
- Choose an appropriate design using an experimental method that will control for or minimize the most serious threats.

Figure 2. A sample text display.

displays save time, presenting complete information in a fraction of the time it would take to write the material on a chalkboard. One disadvantage to them is the temptation to rush through such displays without giving students adequate time to process the information. Therefore, pacing is essential. An effective way to use the time savings is to verbally elaborate on the visual presentation. Mayer and Sims (1994) demonstrated that the simultaneous presentation of verbal and visual instruction can lead to greater learning than successive verbal and visual presentations. Figure 2 shows a sample text display.

Graphic Representation

Graphic representations show relations among objects or concepts. One may use geometric figures to illustrate relations. Various thicknesses of lines represent various degrees of relations, whereas lines of differing colors or types can show different types of relations. Placement of objects on a display can use proximity of objects to one another to illustrate similarities and differences. Promoting such internal connections facilitates learning (Mayer, 1984).

Pictures incorporated in visual displays can enhance meaning. The clip art in presentation software is useful for this purpose. Figure 3 is a sample graphical representation. The figure is black and white, but on the actual display the circles are shaded with different colors to differentiate sets from subsets.

Example Display

Example displays put new concepts in a familiar context. Examples aid comprehension by building external connections for the new knowledge (Mayer, 1984). When a relation is made between new information and existing information, it establishes a metaphorical link from the unknown to the known. Example displays may have brief text accompanying corresponding pictures or graphs, as shown in Figure 4.

Sampling

- **Types of Populations**
  - Target Population
  - Accessible Population
- **Purpose of Sampling**
- **Types of Samples**
  - Simple Random Sample
  - Stratified Random Sample
    - Equal Strata Selections
    - Proportional Strata Selections
  - Cluster Sample
  - Systematic Sample
  - Convenience Sample
- **Sample Size**

Figure 1. A sample introductory display.

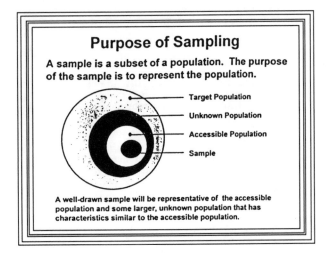

Figure 3. A sample graphical representation.

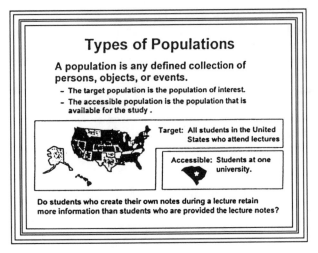

Figure 4. A sample example display.

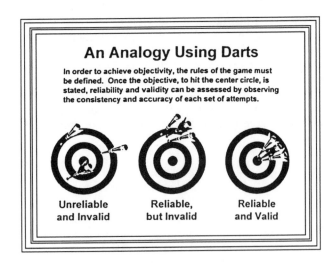

Figure 5. A sample review display.

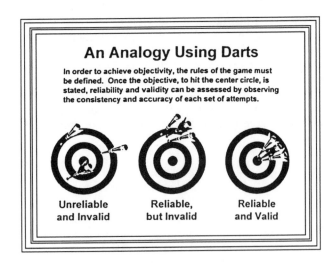

Figure 6. A sample questions display.

Review or Summary Display

Review displays summarize the presented information, highlight main points, and review the organization of presented concepts. Such summaries may take the form of an outline, similar to the introductory display, but they are not restricted to this approach. Other possibilities include a flow chart, a concept map, an inclusive example that illustrates all major components of the presentation, or a brief textual summary such as may be found at the end of a textbook chapter. The purpose is to facilitate the construction of a schema of the material (Rumelhart & Ortony, 1977). Figure 5 is a popular analogy that I chose as a summary for a lecture on the characteristics of measurement.

Questions Display

Figure 6 shows an illustrative questions display. I use such displays as a means of starting a discussion at the beginning of each class. Because students have out-of-class access to all the displays I show, they use the questions displays as a means of reviewing the material from the previous lecture.

By the next class period, they are ready to discuss the questions when I project them onto the screen, prior to beginning new material.

Principles of Construction for Visual Displays

I have based the principles of constructing visual displays listed here on ideas from cognitive psychology and personal experience (both positive and negative). A more comprehensive discussion can be found in books on graphics design (e.g., Tufte, 1983, 1990, 1997).

Consider Goal of Display

The type of display that will be most effective is apparent when there is a known goal. For instance, when the goal is to present a fact, a text display, or text accompanied by clip art, is sufficient. If the goal is to show the application of a concept, an example display is appropriate.

Keep Textual Information Short

Because of the power of visual learning, text on slides should be subservient to the visual focus. Ritchey (1982) demonstrated that recall from visual learning is superior to recall from text learning. Short phrases or headings are more likely to blend in as part of the graphic, whereas long explanations detract from the visual material. The exception to this rule is when the material is not visual, as in the case of a formal definition. Text displays have their place in a presentation, but too much text on a display meant to promote visual learning can limit effectiveness.

Restrict Delivery to One Main Concept Per Display

Isolating concepts is a way to keep information in manageable units consisting of few propositions (Anderson, 1990). The ability of a student to understand the material and create a knowledge representation for the concept is dependent on having the working resources with which to store and process those components of the idea that are fundamental and form the core of the idea. Using more than one main concept per slide requires the student to take additional time to survey the slide and isolate concepts before committing them to long-term memory.

Exemplify Concepts After Presenting Them

Concepts placed in context facilitate learning (Solso, 1988; Wittrock, 1974). Examples put new information in a familiar context and relate new knowledge to existing knowledge. The context provided by the example must be familiar, so instructors should consider the backgrounds and interests of the students when formulating examples.

Use Colors to Categorize

Colors can help organize information (Berry & Dwyer, 1982; Dwyer & Moore, 1992). Concepts and topics are distinguished from one another when visually categorized with colors. When defining a term, for instance, the term can be in one color and the explanation in another, so as to clarify the object of the explanation. I use a different background color every time I switch main headings (e.g., from "Characteristics of Measurement" to "Internal Validity"). In addition, I use the same text colors for a particular element of the display (e.g., white text for examples). Thus, students can use both context and color to recognize the purpose of the text.

Use Visual Elements When Possible

Many studies demonstrate that visual learning can positively affect cognitive processes such as recall and problem solving (e.g., Anglin, 1986; Ritchey, 1982; Yang & Wedman, 1993). Frequent use of pictures, diagrams, and graphs promotes learning. In some cases, the supporting visual may be germane to the topic or illustration. For instance, displaying a scatterplot when presenting the topic of reliability is almost a necessity. Often, though, the visual may simply be a supporting device. Even a picture that does not directly explain a concept can provide a visual representation in

memory to which the student can link supporting ideas. (For a discussion of imagery as a facilitative learning process, see McDaniel & Pressley, 1987.)

Summarize Information at the End of a Topic

One disadvantage of putting a single concept at a time on a visual display is that the connections between concepts may not be apparent to the learner. The interaction of two concepts often results in a separate concept that is just as important as the individual parts. For instance, teaching the research concepts of internal and external validity separately, with a different set of examples illustrating each, is a reasonable organizational strategy. Once students have mastered these concepts, however, it is also important to compare and contrast these two types of validity, illustrating how external validity depends on internal validity.

Insert Questions

Frequent testing can improve student performance (Fulkerson & Martin, 1981; Kika, McLaughlin, & Dixon, 1992; Peckham & Roe, 1977). To implement an informal form of testing, insert an occasional question display. This procedure has a number of benefits, including providing impetus for class discussion, offering students a self-check of their understanding, alerting the instructor to any conceptual misunderstandings, and allowing students to familiarize themselves with questions before a formal examination.

Concluding Comments

The most apparent disadvantages of producing and using visual displays in lectures are logistical, although modern presentation software is easy to use and relatively inexpensive. I used Powerpoint (1995), but there are many similar presentation software packages, including ASAP Word-Power (1996), Freelance Graphics (1997), Persuasion (1996), and Hyperstudio (1997). Software reviewers (e.g., Garelik, 1996; Gottesman, 1996; Grunin, 1996a, 1996b, 1996c; Patz, 1996a, 1996b; Seymour, 1996) have described and critiqued these programs and others. Bsales (1996) reviewed the computer hardware options available for making these presentations.

Academe has a long way to go to take full advantage of existing technology, in no small part because of tight budgets. Nonetheless, there are inexpensive ways to incorporate visual displays into a lecture. Presentation software provides one method. This software has become increasingly user friendly, and removes much of the work formerly associated with preparing visual displays. The results can be impressive.

Cognitive principles and personal experience suggest that the inclusion of visual displays in the lecture facilitates learning. Studies are needed that formally focus on the outcomes associated with such use. Based on my informal observations, I predict that these experiments will show favorable results with regard to content coverage, student attitudes, and student achievement.

References

Anderson, J. R. (1990). *Cognitive psychology and its implications* (3rd ed.). New York: Freeman.

Anglin, G. J. (1986). Prose relevant pictures and older learners' recall of written prose. *Educational Communication and Technology, 34,* 131–136.

ASAP WordPower [Computer software]. (1996). San Jose, CA: Software Publishing Corporation.

Atkinson, R. C., & Shiffrin, R. M. (1968). In K. W. Spence (Ed.), *The psychology of learning and motivation: Advances in research and theory* (Vol. 2, pp. 89–195). New York: Academic.

Beins, B. (1984). The use of slides in psychology classes: Do they help or are they an invitation to sleep? *Teaching of Psychology, 11,* 229–230.

Berry, L. H., & Dwyer, F. M. (1982). Interactive effects of color realism and learners' IQ on effectiveness of visual instruction. *Perceptual and Motor Skills, 54,* 1087–1091.

Bsales, J. M. (1996, March 12). Presentation hardware: Tools for the big show. *PC Magazine, 15,* 222–223.

DiVesta, F. J., & Gray, S. G. (1972). Listening and notetaking. *Journal of Educational Psychology, 63,* 8–14.

Dwyer, F. M., & Moore, D. M. (1992). Effect of color coding on visually and verbally oriented tests with students of different field dependence levels. *Journal of Educational Technology Systems, 20,* 311–320.

Freelance Graphics [Computer software]. (1997). Cambridge, MA: Lotus.

Fulkerson, F. E., & Martin, G. (1981). Effects of exam frequency on student performance, evaluations of instructor, and test anxiety. *Teaching of Psychology, 8,* 90–93.

Garelik, D. (1996, March 12). Corel presents. *PC Magazine, 15,* 215, 217–218.

Gottesman, B. Z. (1996, March 12). Novell presentations 3.0. *PC Magazine, 15,* 226, 229.

Grunin, L. (1996a, March 12). Adobe Persuasion. *PC Magazine, 15,* 201–202.

Grunin, L. (1996b, March 12). Harvard Graphics for Windows 95. *PC Magazine, 15,* 218, 220.

Grunin, L. (1996c, March 12). Lotus Freelance Graphics 96 for Windows 95. *PC Magazine, 15,* 220, 224.

Hyperstudio [Computer software]. (1997). El Cajon, CA: Roger Wagner.

Kiewra, K. A. (1985a). Investigating notetaking and review: A depth of processing alternative. *Educational Psychologist, 20,* 23–32.

Kiewra, K. A. (1985b). Providing the instructor's notes: An effective addition to student notetaking. *Educational Psychologist, 20,* 33–39.

Kika, F. M., McLaughlin, T. F., & Dixon, J. (1992). Effects of frequent testing of secondary algebra students. *Journal of Educational Research, 85,* 159–162.

Kulik, C. C., Kulik, J. A., & Cohen, P. A. (1980). Instructional technology and college teaching. *Teaching of Psychology, 7,* 199–205.

Mayer, R. E. (1979). Twenty years of research on advance organizers: Assimilation theory is still the best predictor of results. *Instructional Science, 8,* 133–167.

Mayer, R. E. (1984). Aids to text comprehension. *Educational Psychologist, 19,* 30–42.

Mayer, R. E., & Sims, V. K. (1994). For whom is a picture worth a thousand words? Extensions of a dual-coding theory of multimedia learning. *Journal of Educational Psychology, 86,* 389–401.

McDaniel, M. A., & Pressley, M. (Eds.). (1987). *Imagery and related mnemonic processes.* New York: Springer-Verlag.

Novak, J. D., & Gowin, D. B. (1984). *Learning how to learn.* Cambridge, England: Cambridge University Press.

Patz, J. T. (1996a, March 12). ASAP. *PC Magazine, 15,* 202, 204.

Patz, J. T. (1996b, March 12). Microsoft Powerpoint for Windows 95. *PC Magazine, 15,* 224, 226.

Peckham, P. D., & Roe, M. D. (1977). The effects of frequent testing. *Journal of Research and Development in Education, 10,* 40–50.

Persuasion [Computer software]. (1996). Mountain View, CA: Adobe.

Powerpoint [Computer software]. (1995). Redmond, WA: Microsoft.

Ritchey, G. H. (1982). Pictorial detail and recall in adults and children. *Journal of Experimental Psychology: Learning, Memory, and Cognition, 8,* 139–141.

Rumelhart, D. E., & Ortony, A. (1977). The representation of knowledge in memory. In R. C. Anderson, R. J. Spiro, & W. E. Montague (Eds.), *Schooling and the acquisition of knowledge* (pp. 99–136). Hillsdale, NJ: Lawrence Erlbaum Associates, Inc.

Seymour, J. (1996, March 12). Presentation graphics: Show business. *PC Magazine, 15,* 193, 195–196.

Solso, R. L. (1988). *Cognitive psychology* (2nd ed.). New York: Allyn & Bacon.

Tufte, E. R. (1983). *The visual display of quantitative information.* Cheshire, CT: Graphics Press.

Tufte, E. R. (1990). *Envisioning information.* Cheshire, CT: Graphics Press.

Tufte, E. R. (1997). *Visual explanations: Images and quantities, evidence and narrative.* Cheshire, CT: Graphics Press.

Wittrock, M. C. (1974). Learning as a generative process. *Educational Psychologist, 11,* 87–95.

Yang, C. L., & Wedman, J. F. (1993). A study of the conditions influencing analogical problem solving. *Journal of Research and Development in Education, 26,* 213–221.

Developing a Web-Assisted Class: An Interview With Mark Mitchell

Jeanne M. Slattery

JMS: You have become active in developing Web-assisted classes. How did this come about?

MM: After wandering into some conference presentations that dealt with the Web, I realized that the

Web could help me solve several problems that I think most professors face.

JMS: Such as?

MM: I want students to become more involved in and outside of the classroom. I want students to talk more to each other and to me. I want them to be engaged in the material and to have ready access to resources that they find interesting or helpful. A class Web page can increase communication, interest, and learning.

JMS: How is a class Web page different from other kinds of Web pages?

MM: The goals are different. Rather than making a pretty page with fancy graphics, you are meeting some educational objective. Your objective may be to present course information in a completely different way, to stimulate the student's curiosity, to get them to communicate more with you, to get them to talk more to each other, or to get them to master certain basic concepts.

JMS: That means we need to identify our goals before producing a page.

MM: Right. Otherwise, you're not going to accomplish your educational objectives and your students will wonder, "Why is the teacher making us do this?"

JMS: What's the simplest way to begin using the Web to support a class?

MM: A very simple way would be to have a Web page that has your name, your e-mail address, and links to your favorite sites. That way your students can reach you at the touch of a button by clicking on your e-mail address. They can learn more about you by following the links you like to visit. That would be a modest beginning point. Such a page would be easy to construct and would help students get to know you and talk to you.

It's amazing how much such a simple page can increase interactions with students and their perceived connectedness with their professor. For example, Santoro (1997) reported that students taking an e-mail class rated it as being the class in which they had the most personal contact with the professor—despite seeing the professor only twice, both times on videotape.

JMS: What's the next step?

MM: Add material to make the page more dynamic. For example, you could post a "hot site of the week," announcements, and answers to frequently asked questions.

JMS: I'm curious about the "hot site of the week." What kinds of things could you do there?

MM: Suppose you're teaching General Psychology and you're in the research methods section. In that case, you might have a link to the Skeptical Inquirer page. Or, if you're talking about the brain and there's some late-breaking news, like there's a conference on the brain at the White House, you could link to that.

JMS: Sounds fun. What about more advanced uses? What else can the Web do for you?

MM: To further improve the communication between you and your class, you can put your syllabus on the Web. That way, students can't lose it and they can preview it even before they register for the class. During the term, you can modify it quite easily. Similarly, you can also make assignments, handouts, old exams, and old papers readily available to students. If these assignments are already on computer, converting them to Hypertext Markup Language (HTML) is very easy. Converter programs will, at the touch of a button, convert your word-processed document into HTML.

With a little more work, you can increase student-to-student communication by making a class discussion list. Many professors report that Web-based discussions are much better than in-class discussions (Brooks, 1997). You can also increase student-to-student communication by making a class yearbook. You can easily capture images by either using a digital camera or by using a regular camera, and then asking your developer to put the pictures on a disk. Regardless of how you do it, everyone's photo, interests, and e-mail address can be readily incorporated into the yearbook file. Such a yearbook could help students collaborate on class projects outside of class as well as form study groups.

Finally, and most ambitiously, you can put your class notes on the Web.

JMS: What are the advantages of putting your class notes on the Web? Why not just photocopy them and hand them out?

MM: There are at least four advantages to putting your notes on the Web. First, you can link easily to other people's resources so you don't have to invent your own. You can take the best of what other people have to offer. Second, you can use links to make connections between course concepts more salient. Students can click on a link and instantly see how new material links back to what they learned earlier in the term. For example, when talking about the dopamine hypothesis of schizophrenia, you could link to your previous discussion on neurons. Third, you can reproduce color photographs, overheads, animations, and video clips. These resources especially help the student who learns visually, but I think they help all your students. Until the Web, some professors argued quite convincingly against using visual aids because students could not incorporate those aids into their notes. With the Web, the argument that students cannot review visual aids is less convincing. Fourth, you can incorporate interactive activities, such as quizzes and tutorials.

JMS: You are describing some Web-based strategies that are very different than traditional styles of teaching. You are increasing your students' ability to get to other resources and your ability to make connections with other resources.

MM: Right. When I took General Psychology, the only guide I had for getting resources that went beyond the text was the list of further readings at the end of the chapter. I don't think anyone in the class went to the library to check out those resources. Similarly, I don't think my teachers, as good as they were, took advantage of what other teachers had done. As scientists, we are proud that we have built on what others have done, but as teachers, we have not done a great job of building on others' accomplishments.

JMS: And the Web provides an easy way to stand on the shoulders of others.

MM: Yes.

JMS: What do you see as the advantages of this style of teaching? Has it panned out the way you thought it would?

MM: For the better students, it has. They do better on exams, ask more interesting questions, and do much more optional reading than they had before. More students earn As than before.

JMS: What about the rest of your students?

MM: Most students like the Web. However, there have been problems. Some students have trouble learning the technology, and others initially object to what they perceive as extra work. A few students think they don't have to come to class, but they may be the same ones who don't think they have to read the textbook. Also, a couple of students initially felt it was unfair that classmates who don't attend could still get the notes from the Web site.

JMS: How do you address those problems? How do you get students to feel good about using this technology?

MM: Some problems solve themselves. For example, after the first exam, students see that the students who didn't attend class don't do well, so that's the end of the attendance issue. Getting students comfortable with the technology, on the other hand, does not happen automatically. I spend much more class time than I ever thought I would dealing with Web issues. For example, we go to the computer lab at least twice a semester, whereas I thought once would be quite sufficient.

JMS: Do you build in some incentives for using your page?

MM: Yes, I've found that I've had to. Not all students are self-regulated learners. Therefore, I employ Web-based quizzes and assignments. Some professors post grades on the Web. Of course, if you post grades on the Web, you should use code names. Other professors post old exams. Some even offer hints about quiz questions and extra credit.

JMS: This makes it almost difficult not to use the Web page.

MM: Right. I warn students on the first day of class that I will expect them to spend time outside of class using the Web.

JMS: Speaking of time, how much professor time would be involved in creating a Web page?

MM: I would advise spending about a week deciding what you want your Website to look like. Then, I would recommend spending a weekend learning HTML. Admittedly, you can avoid learning HTML and, most of the time you will be having an HTML editor program, such as Netscape Gold, do the coding for you. However, there will be times when you want to "clean up" what the HTML editor has done; knowing HTML is useful for that.

The next step would be to get the text for your pages into HTML. This will probably take less than a week because there are computer programs that automatically converts word-processed documents into HTML documents. Once you have a set of pages, you need to get them on a server so they will be "on the net." If your own personal computer will be the server, your page can be up and running in anywhere between 5 min and 1 hr. If you have to put it on the campus server, then the time spent depends on how cooperative and how comprehensible your campus's computer people are. After your "bare bones" page is up and running, you might spend from 5 min to 5 hr a week for a month, getting the links and graphics you want as well as testing the site. Once it's working fairly well, you might still want to spend up to 1 hr a week improving the site and keeping it current.

JMS: HTML editors to do HTML coding for you, programs to convert text into HTML, servers, this sounds expensive. What does setting up a Web page cost?

MM: In the best-case scenario, nothing. Your word processor may already have the ability to save and convert text files. Even if it doesn't, if you understand the basics of HTML, you can produce HTML from your word processor. Similarly, you may be able to create simple graphics using your word processor. Once you have the pages, you just need a server. The server might be your existing office computer, the university's computer, or the computer of an organization that offers free Web sites for nonprofit organizations.

JMS: What would be a more expensive scenario?

MM: You can spend between $40 and $200 dollars for an HTML editor and HTML converter. You might spend $50 to $200 for an image editor. If you decide to put a database on the Web, you could spend $1,000 for a Web-friendly database program. If you want to have the prettiest Web site of all your friends, you could spend $1,000 on a graphics program, a color scanner, a digital camera, and collections of clip art. If you then decide you are going to produce and download actual movies, you could spend another $500 to $50,000 getting software for that. In other words, if you want to spend a lot of money, you can.

JMS: What about the cost to the student?

MM: That's a tricky question. Technically, it's free as long as they use an on-campus computer. However, there is some understandable concern that students with computers will have an edge over those who don't. To deal with this problem, some professors allow students to access their Web site only from campus computer labs (Santoro, 1997).

JMS: I don't think that "solution" would be very popular with some of my returning adult students.

MM: No. Furthermore, it clearly negates one of the advantages of the Web—being able to access information any time from anywhere.

JMS: Would you give any advice to someone starting to develop a Web-assisted class?

MM: Once you've decided on your goals and tried to limit your Web page to achieving those goals, I think there are four things you can do to make the site "student useful." First, use links as much as possible. Academics are not used to hyperlinks. We're used to linear thought, writing out long dissertations where one thought follows another very sequentially. You have to exercise your imagination and ask yourself, "What could I link this to?"

Second, use graphics. Students love visuals, and cognitive psychologists tell us that most of us are visual learners.

Third, include many navigational aids. It's very easy to get lost in hyperspace. Link every page back to your main page. If you have a long page, have at least one link back to the top of the page. At the top of each page, include a title so students know where they are.

Fourth, involve students in the process. Ideally, involve the whole class. Involving students will reduce your workload, and students can do much of this work as well as, or better than, you can. They have more time to surf the Web than you do and they know what interests them better than you do. At the very least, involve a student assistant.

JMS: Can you expand on that? How would you involve students?

MM: Students can find relevant links and give a short summary of the site they linked to. Students can contribute a personal example of a principle discussed in class. Students can design a cartoon, image, or animated graphic that illustrates a concept. I know that my students have more artistic ability than I do.

JMS: How do you get the students' graphics onto a Web page?

MM: If the students used a computer to create the graphic, you can easily convert the graphic into a format that is Web compatible by using any of a number of commonly available shareware programs, all of which are under $50. If the student did not use a computer, you can make the pictures Web compatible by using a color scanner. There are many scanners for under $300 that will do the job.

JMS: What resources are out there to help us with this process? What makes designing a Web-assisted class easier to do?

MM: Imitate sites that you like. You can follow links from the site referenced at the end of this article to find pages that you like. The mechanics of copying on the Web are frighteningly easy. In Netscape, for example, you just click on "View Source." If you think that is too much work, you can buy programs like "Web Whacker" that will automatically copy a site for you. However, just because it's easy to copy, doesn't mean it's legal. Copyright law still applies. Nevertheless, you can borrow the basic ideas from a site you like. Furthermore, you can often get permission to link to another person's resources or borrow elements of their page.

JMS: You're describing examples out there. Are there sites that we can go to, to figure out how to develop a stronger Web-assisted class?

MM: Yes. Just access the site referred to at the end of this article (Mitchell, 1997). That site links you to a tutorial that provides a very gentle introduction to using HTML, as well as to a guide for making Web pages from Netscape Gold. I've also posted a page that outlines the basic decisions and processes that should be addressed in developing a Web-assisted classroom.

JMS: I see what you mean about it being convenient to access the information you want by just clicking on a link or two. I also see the value of using Web technologies for those of us whose schools are hooked up to the Internet. But what if your school is not hooked up?

MM: Even then, you could distribute Web-based course materials to your students by putting Web files on a computer in a computer lab or by giving each student a disk. Your students could have the syllabus, class notes, sample papers, tutorials, and animations. However, you would lose the ability to interact with students over the Internet. Furthermore, you would lose the ability to link to external sites—unless you get permission to copy those sites.

JMS: Wouldn't the students need to use a browser to open the Web files?

MM: Yes, but the most popular browsers—Internet Explorer, Netscape, and Mosaic—are free for students.

JMS: What do you project for the future? How do you think things will change?

MM: I think that the gap between the "techies" and the average instructor is going to shrink tremendously. Most things that you would want to do on the Web, you'll be able to do—regardless of your level of computer expertise. Already, there are programs that allow you to construct Web pages without knowing any HTML. Within 2 years, anyone who wants to have their class syllabus, grade book, discussion group, or yearbook on the Web will have it—as long as their school is hooked up to the Web. Likewise, any teacher who wants to do testing on the Web will be able to do so easily. Finally, programs that automatically collect and analyze test and survey responses will be more commonly available. Consequently, professors will be able to go into every class knowing what concepts the class has mastered, what topics students want to discuss, and what the class thinks about key issues. To go beyond that, we'll need people to come up with more imaginative uses of the Web. The technology is there—it's just waiting for us noncomputer scientists to discover how to use it.

Resources

Brooks, D. W. (1997). *Web-teaching: A guide to designing interactive teaching for the World Wide Web.* New York: Plenum.

Mitchell, M. (1997). *Resources for developing a Web-assisted class* [Online]. Retrieved March 1, 1998 from the World Wide Web: http://psy1.clarion.edu/mm/Webclass.html

Santoro, G. M. (1997, April). *Design principles for online learning environments.* Paper presented at the meeting of the Pennsylvania Academy for Computer and Information Science Education, Clarion, PA.

Computer-Assisted Instruction as a Supplement to Lectures in an Introductory Psychology Class

Everett L. Worthington, Jr.
Josephine A. Welsh
C. Ray Archer
Erica J. Mindes
Donelson R. Forsyth

Introduction to Psychology serves as a general introduction to psychological research and theory. By tradition, much of the learning in the course comes from reading the textbook and attending lectures. Recent technological developments, however, offer instructors an additional method for teaching psychology's content and process. Computer-assisted instruction (CAI) continues to evolve, ultimately offering several advantages. Interactive CAI can engage students. Rather than passively receiving information, students help generate information. Material is also paced to fit individuals' needs. Computerized study guides can improve students' overall level of mastery. Also, testing may be improved if students complete tests on computer screens and receive immediate feedback about their performance.

What educational benefits are gained by using CAI in psychology as a discipline and, more specifically, in introductory psychology? Only a few studies have investigated CAI in introductory psychology (e.g., Conn, Stafiniak, DiPasquale, & Harper, 1988; Welsh & Null, 1991), but several researchers have studied CAI as part of a course in experimental psychology (Chute, 1986; Goolkasian, 1989; Monahan, 1993; Perone, 1991; Petty & Rosen, 1990). Evaluation research in psychology outlines specific goals that CAI should produce. Outcome measures should include both learning and enjoyment components. In particular, we need to ask whether CAI experiences produce increased general learning in the course, learning of the concepts in which students completed exercises, enjoyment of the course, and enjoyment of the CAI experiences (Chute, 1986; Conn et al., 1988; Duncan, 1993; Isaacs, Costenbader, Reading-Brown, & Goodman, 1992; C. L. C. Kulik & J. A. Kulik, 1991; J. A. Kulik & C. L. C. Kulik, 1987; Lambert & Lenthall, 1989; McNeil & Nelson, 1991; Monahan, 1993; Niemiec & Walberg, 1987; Perone, 1991; Petty & Rosen, 1990; Ransdell, 1990).

Many design issues arise when evaluating the efficacy of CAI. One of the most pernicious is possible selection bias when comparing two classes that receive different treatments. After a thorough review of the literature, Duncan (1993) suggested participant variables that should be controlled: interest in the subject, prior knowledge of an area (Tobias, 1987), computer anxiety (Lambert & Lenthall, 1989), and generalized anxiety (Tobias, 1987). Trowbridge (1987), for example, took into account age, gender, grade point average (GPA), and family income. Liefeld and Herrmann (1990) controlled academic major, number of previous courses in the major, score on an English aptitude test, and semester CPA. Some researchers have matched groups for equality on critical variables. Underwood and Underwood (1987) matched groups on reading ability, IQ scores, and a pretest of ability to classify objects.

Duncan (1993) also articulated the controversy over the proper choice of dependent variable. Some argue for domain-specific measures, such as objective indices that focus on the concepts examined in CAI experiences (Duncan, 1991; Petty & Rosen, 1990; Welsh & Null, 1991). Others argue for more generalized measures of learning (Hannafin & Carney, 1991). Still others argue that student attitudes toward CAI or toward the specific software used in the class are proper dependent variables (Cordell, 1991; Duncan, 1991; Goolkasian, 1989; Lambert & Lenthall, 1989).

Our research responds to Duncan's (1993) methodological suggestions by examining the impact of CAI through the use of a quasi-experimental design (Cook & Campbell, 1979). To determine if students who complete CAI exercises in addition to attending traditional lectures outperform students who only attend lectures, two large sections of introductory psychology were matched on critical variables recommended by Duncan (1993), and CAI was incorporated into one of these sections.

The impact of CAI participation was assessed in several ways. First, students in both sections completed an identical final examination. All items on the final examination were covered in the lecture or the text; questions on material examined only in the CAI sections would have been unfair. However, some items on the final examination were also addressed by one CAI experience. The final examination, therefore, yielded two indices of student outcomes: overall examination score and examination score for CAI-supplemented items. The independent variable was the presence or absence of a weekly CAI session as a supplement to lecture. We predicted that students in the CAI section would outperform students in the no-CAI section.

Method

Participants

Participants attended Virginia Commonwealth University. They registered for introductory psychology without computer-assisted learning (no CAI; $n = 246$) or with computer-assisted learning (CAI; $n = 196$).

The instructor was a man who had taught introductory psychology for 18 years. CAI sections were conducted by two male graduate teaching assistants with one semester of experience conducting the sections before the semester in which the study was performed.

Procedure

We used a quasi-experimental design. Two sections of the course were offered in spring 1993. Students self-selected into sections through university registration procedures using a registration booklet that explained that one section was scheduled to meet an additional 50 min per week with a focus on CAI. Students in the no-CAI section did not complete the CAI exercises. At the beginning of the semester, research assistants collected demographic data from the university registrar to ensure that no systematic differences in demography between the CAI and no-CAI sections existed. Sections were matched on instructor, lecture, and textbook. The instructor gave the same lectures on the same days in each class, keeping a diary to note any differences that might affect student response to the lecture. In addition, each day of class, the instructor rated the relative response of students to lecture. The same textbook (Myers, 1992) was used in both sections.

In the second week of the semester, after the period for adding and dropping courses but before the first CAI 50-min session, students completed a demographic questionnaire with additional questions concerning students' attitudes toward and experience with computers and factors affecting their decision to enroll in the class with CAI or no CAI. Students in the CAI section rated the degree to which they expected to enjoy the CAI. All students completed a questionnaire in which they rated their preference for small, medium, and large classes.

A pre–postexperimental design was used to assess increases in learning over the course of the semester. An 18-question (fill-in-the-blank and short-answer) quiz was administered as a preliminary index of student knowledge of psychology. Students were told that this was part of an evaluation of learning in the class and were urged to do their best. Two forms of the quiz were used—one for each section—and the order was counterbalanced in the administration of the quiz at the end of the semester.

Students in the CAI section attended a 50-min class each week and completed one or more of the following types of computerized exercises: simulations of psychological processes, demonstrations of classic experiments, and tutorials. Simulations taught concepts such as hemispheric specializations, visual illusions, Piagetian conservation tasks, and statistical correlations. Several exercises demonstrated such classic experiments as Sperling's (1960) iconic memory study and Deutsch and Krauss's (1960) trucking game. Tutorials helped students understand processes such as neuron construction and functioning. Software used to provide these exercises was mostly PsychSim (Ludwig, 1986), which was available to the course instructor with Myers's (1992) text. Students in the CAI group performed two or three exercises per week. Students in the no-CAI group attended lectures only.

In the 3rd and 14th weeks of the course, the instructor audiotaped the same lecture in both classes. Those audiotapes were later rated for equivalence by listeners who were blind to section. At seven lectures throughout the semester, unannounced roll calls were taken to assess any differences between the two groups in student attendance at lectures.

In the 14th week of the course, the instructor administered (a) a quiz on course content (the counterbalanced version of the initial quiz), (b) institutionally mandated anonymous student evaluations of instruction to measure the perceived quality of the instructor and the course (Cordell, 1991; Duncan, 1991; Goolkasian, 1989; Lambert & Lenthall, 1989), and (c) a self-reported (nonanonymous) evaluation of the course on which students rated their enjoyment and the helpfulness of the course. All students who took the CAI class were asked, "Knowing what you do now that the semester is over, if you had it to do over again, and if you had a completely free choice without scheduling constraints, would you prefer this course with or without labs?" (Responses were coded as prefer with labs, mixed opinions or doesn't make any difference, or prefer without labs.)

During the same week, interviews with students from the CAI section were conducted. Seven students were selected at random from the students attending lectures in the CAI class and participated in a 20-min structured interview with the instructor. Items covered were as follows: (a) Tell me what you thought of the exercises. (b) Sometimes people race through the exercises without thinking; did you actually do the exercises or did you sometimes move quickly through them? (c) Did you use the study guide during the [CAI 50-min sessions]? (d) Which exercises (if any) did you particularly like? (e) Which (if any) did you dislike? (f) How did the exercises help (if the student had expressed that they had helped)? (g) Can you suggest anything that could be done differently with the [CAI 50-min sessions] that would help future students?

After the 15th week of the course, the same comprehensive final examination was administered to each section as a measure of generalized learning (Hannafin & Carney, 1991). (No other hourly examinations throughout the semester were the same.) Students had seen half the questions on the final examination; this half was drawn from a bank of 308 questions that students could study ahead of time. Of the 80 questions on the final exam, 15 critical items tested information covered in the CAI sessions (also covered in the book or lecture). Ten of the 15 critical items had not been seen previously, whereas 5 were in the question bank.

After the semester was completed and final grades had been submitted, students' presemester GPAs were obtained from university student records to use as a covariate in data analyses.

Results

Testing for Matched Sections

We tried to control some variables that may influence why people select one course over another. Demographic variables used to identify any systematic differences between sections included age, gender, and race (Trowbridge, 1987). The mean age for both classes was 22, and the standard deviation for both sections was 4. Specific data for gender and race are presented in Table 1. There was no difference in gender between the two groups, $\chi^2(1, N = 442) = .28$, $p > .05$. Similarly, race did not differ between the no-CAI and CAI classes; $\chi^2(4, N = 442) = 6.18$, $p > .05$.

Academic factors examined to test for matched groups included GPA (Duncan, 1993), class status (Tobias, 1987), reason for scheduling the course (Sawyer, 1988), and attrition rates (Duncan, 1993). Presemester GPA was used as a covariate in analyses. The 246 no-CAI students consisted of 112 freshmen, 60 sophomores, 33 juniors, 16 seniors, and 25 special students. Of the 196 CAI students, 108 were freshmen, 47 sophomores, 17 juniors, 3 seniors, and 21 special students. There was some difference in distribution of students by class status, $\chi^2(4, N = 442) = 10.49$, $p < .05$. The no-CAI section contained 45% freshmen, and the CAI class contained 55% freshmen.

We used a chi-square test to determine whether CAI or no-CAI students selectively took PSY 101 as a requirement or an elective. Of the 246 students in the no-CAI class, 123 reported taking the course because it was required, 80 took it as an elective, and 43 did not answer the question. Of the 196 students in the CAI class, 101 took the course because it was required, 63 took it as an elective, and 32 did not answer. There was no significant difference, $\chi^2(1, N = 442) = .04$, $p > .05$. The fraction of enrolled students who dropped the course was assessed by dividing the number of students who received grades at semester's end by the number of students enrolled in the class at the end of the first week (after add–drop week was complete). Of the 246 students in the no-CAI class at the end of the first week, 16 (6.5%) withdrew from the course before the official withdrawal date (halfway through the semester). Of the 196 students in the CAI class, 10 (5.3%) officially withdrew. There was no significant difference between classes in rates of withdrawal, $\chi^2(1, N = 442) = .39$, $p > .05$.

We also examined personal reasons that led students to choose one section over another, including the presence or absence of an additional CAI 50-min session of class, scheduling convenience, and preferred size of classes. An analysis of variance (ANOVA) revealed that scheduling convenience and preferred class size influenced students' choices in selecting either CAI or no-CAI sections. The no-CAI

students were more likely to have chosen that section because it fit their schedule ($M = 4.0$, $SD = 1.1$) than were the CAI students ($M = 3.7$, $SD = 1.2$), $F(1, 387) = 6.15$, $p < .05$. Students who took the no-CAI class preferred larger class sizes than students who took the CAI classes, $\chi^2(3, N = 442) = 13.3$, $p < .01$. For the no-CAI class, 73 (30%) of the 246 students preferred small classes, 62 (25%) preferred moderate-size classes, 52 (21%) preferred large classes, 27 (11%) preferred very large classes, and 32 (13%) had missing data. For the CAI class, 83 (42%) of the 196 students preferred small classes, 53 (27%) preferred moderate-size classes, 23 (12%) preferred large classes, 12 (6%) preferred very large classes, and 25 (13%) had missing data.

Students' ratings of ability, comfort, and familiarity with computers did not differ between the two groups, all $ps > .05$. Overall, our tests for matching subjects between groups revealed that, although students self-selected into either the CAI groups or no-CAI, only class status and preference for class size differed between the two groups. The CAI group had significantly more freshmen than the no-CAI group; the CAI group preferred smaller classes, whereas the no-CAI group preferred larger classes. Demographic variables, academic factors, and attitudes toward computers did not differ between the two groups.

Validity Checks for Controlled Variables of Instructor and Lecture

Ideally, for good experimental control, by the end of the course students should have rated the instructor equally in both sections (Duncan, 1993; C. L. C. Kulik & J. A. Kulik, 1991). On the anonymous institutional evaluations of the instructor, students rated the instructor on a scale ranging from 1 (*poor*) to 5 (*outstanding*). In the no-CAI class, the mean rating was 4.2 ($SD = .8$); in the CAI class, the mean rating was 4.1 ($SD = .9$), $t(280) = 1.71$, $p > .05$.

Each day, the instructor rated the relative response of students to lecture. Class response was rated as equal for 14 lectures, CAI was better for 7 lectures, and no CAI was better for 8 lectures. Instructor-rated student response to lectures did not differ, $\chi^2(2, N = 442) = 2.99$, $p > .05$.

The same two lectures (from early and late parts of the semester) in each class were audiotaped and rated by listeners who were blind to the class. Relative ratings (When A and B were randomized, was Lecture A better, equal to, or worse than Lecture B?) were made by three undergraduate students not in the course to determine whether systematic differences (in content, lecture style, and audience participation) were apparent. No rater judged there to be any difference between the two lectures on any of the three dimensions.

Anonymous ratings of the course taken from the institutional student evaluations of instruction administered in the last 2 weeks of the course showed no difference between the no-CAI class ($M = 3.8$, $SD = .8$) and the CAI class ($M = 3.7$, $SD = 1.0$), $t(276) = .65$, $p > .05$.

Learning

Learning was assessed through difference scores on an 18-item pre–postquiz, comprehensive final examination

Table 1. Demographic Comparisons Between No-CAI and CAI Groups

Variable	No-CAI		CAI	
	n	%	*n*	%
Gender				
Men	107	43	80	41
Women	139	57	116	59
Race				
African American	55	22	50	25
Native American				
Aborigines	3	1	2	1
Asian	20	8	7	4
Latino/Latina	7	3	2	1
Caucasian	161	65	135	69

scores, critical item scores (those final exam questions reflecting material covered not only in the lecture and text but also in the CAI sessions), and anonymous self-reports of learning. On the short-answer and fill-in-the-blank quiz, students answered a mean of .5 (no CAI) and .4 (CAI) of 18 questions correctly at pretest. At posttest, students answered a mean of 4.8 (no CAI) and 4.3 (CAI) questions correctly. There was no difference between no-CAI and CAI classes on mean recall learning, $F(1, 310) = .22$, $p > .05$.

The comprehensive final examination consisted of 80 multiple-choice questions. One technical problem was considered. Some students, usually those who were doing poorly in the class, did not take the final exam. Conceivably, differential attrition at the final exam by no-CAI and CAI students could influence the mean performance of the groups. Attrition before the final for no-CAI students (8.5% of those who had taken the other exams) did not differ from attrition before the final for CAI students (7.7%); thus, final exam scores for only the students taking the final exam were analyzed (no CAI, $n = 204$; CAI, $n = 168$). Of the 80 questions, the no-CAI students answered a mean of 54.6 questions correctly ($SD = 11.0$). The CAI students answered a mean of 57.8 questions correctly ($SD = 10.9$). A hierarchical multiple regression (on GPA, attendance, and class) was used to determine whether class affected score on the final exam. First, initial GPA was entered. Second, we entered the number of student absences obtained from unannounced roll calls taken at seven randomly selected lectures. Finally, class (no CAI or CAI) was entered. Means and standard deviations for each variable are given in Table 2. Initial GPA significantly predicted score on the final exam, $R^2 = .48$, $F(1, 370) = 338.7$, $p < .001$. Frequency of attendance at lecture did not significantly affect final exam score, R^2 change = .00, $F(2, 369) = 3.6$, $p > .05$. Even after controlling for initial GPA and attendance, class type predicted final exam score, R^2 change = .01, $F(3, 368) = 7.3$, $p < .01$.

Final exams contained 15 critical questions that were covered in the CAI exercises as well as in the book or lecture. Those questions were analyzed separately from questions covered only in the readings or the lectures (Duncan, 1991; Petty & Rosen, 1990; Welsh & Null, 1991). A hierarchical multiple regression was used to determine whether class type affected score on the 15 critical items. Students in the no-CAI class answered a mean of 8.3 correctly ($SD = 2.7$), and students in the CAI classes answered a mean of 10.2 correctly ($SD = 2.3$). The predictor variables were entered in the same order as in the previous analysis. Initial GPA significantly predicted score on the critical items, $R^2 = .32$, $F(1, 370) = 171.5$, $p < .001$. Once again, attendance at Lecture did not significantly affect critical item score, R^2 change = .00, $F(2, 369) = 1.1$, $p > .05$. Even after controlling for initial GPA and attendance, class type predicted critical item score, R^2 change = .09, $F(3, 368) = 56.3$, $p < .001$.

Taken together, analyses of the final examination scores and the 15 critical items suggest that the critical item score made a difference in final exam scores between the no-CAI and CAI groups. As a post hoc analysis, we tested the predictive value of CAI after removing the critical items from final examination scores. Predictor variables of including GPA, attendance, and class were entered into a hierarchical multiple regression analysis. Using a modified final exami-

Table 2. Means and Standard Deviations for Important Variables

Variable	No-CAI		CAI	
	M	SD	M	SD
Final exam[a]*	54.6	11.0	57.8	10.9
Critical items (final exam)[b]*	8.3	2.7	10.2	2.3
Initial GPA[c]	2.4	.9	2.5	.8
Attendance at lecture[d]	6.1	1.7	6.0	2.3
Familiarity with computers[e]	2.9	.9	2.9	1.0
Comfortable with computers[e]	3.1	1.0	3.2	1.2
Experience with computers[e]	2.5	.9	2.5	1.1
Fit schedule[e]	4.0	1.1	3.7	1.2

[a]Mean number of multiple-choice items correct of 80 items. [b]Mean number of items correct of 15 items. [c]GPA based on courses taken at Virginia Commonwealth University on a 4.00 system. [d]Number of times present in lecture during 7 unannounced roll calls. [e]Rated on a scale ranging from 1 (*not at all*) to 5 (*extremely*).
*$p < .01$.

nation score, after removing the variance from GPA and attendance at lecture (as in previous analyses), class type did not predict modified final examination scores, R^2 change = .006, $F(3, 359) = 1.279$, $p > .05$. In sum, the predictive value of CAI disappeared when the critical item score was removed from the final examination score. The critical item score from items covered in the text, lecture, and CAI sessions made the difference in final examination scores.

Students in no-CAI and CAI classes did not differ in their anonymous ratings of self-reported learning. Both rated learning 3.6, $t(278) = .01$, $p > .05$.

Post Hoc Analysis

Because preference for size of class differed for students who took the CAI versus the no-CAI class, we conducted an attribute-by-treatment analysis. Students were divided into those who preferred small, moderate-size, large, and very large classes. Preference for class size was crossed with class type (no CAI and CAI). We hypothesized that students preferring smaller classes would perform better in the CAI class and students preferring larger classes would perform better in the no-CAI class. A 4 × 2 (Preferred Class Size × Class) ANOVA with final exam score as the dependent variable revealed that the main effect for class was significant, $F(1, 332) = 7.10$, $p < .01$, but neither the main effect for preference for class size, $F(3, 332) = .81$, $p > .05$, nor the interaction, $F(3, 332) = .09$, $p > .05$, was significant. A 4 × 2 (Preferred Class Size × Class) ANOVA with number of critical items answered correctly on the final exam as the dependent variable showed that the main effect for class was significant, $F(1, 332) = 40.74$, $p < .001$, but neither the main effect for preference for class size, $F(3, 332) = 1.81$, $p > .05$, nor the interaction, $F(3, 332) = .23$, $p > .05$, was significant.

Supplemental Analyses: Responses of Students Who Took the CAI Class

For students in the CAI class, correlations were calculated for the precourse expectations about liking computerized exercises, end-of-course ratings of the degree to which students found the CAI enjoyable and helpful, score on the final exam, and score on the 15 critical items (see Table 3).

Precourse expectations that students would like computerized exercises were unrelated to later ratings of enjoyment or helpfulness and to measures of learning. End-of-course ratings of enjoyment and helpfulness were related to each other but were unrelated to learning. Measures of learning were related to each other but not to subjective ratings of expectation, enjoyment, or helpfulness of the CAI exercises.

Students who took the CAI class responded to the stimulus: Knowing what you do now that the semester is over, if you had it to do over again, and if you had a completely free choice without scheduling constraints, would you prefer this course with or without (CAI) labs? Of the 163 who responded, 106 (65%) said they preferred the class with CAI; 25(15%) had mixed opinions or said it did not make any difference; 32 (20%) preferred the class without CAI.

Structured Interviews

Seven students were selected at random from the CAI class and participated in a 20-min structured interview with the instructor. The interview covered the following points.

(a) Tell me what you thought of the exercises. All seven expressed positive reactions to the exercises; two confessed to initial negative reactions to having to spend an extra 50 min each week, but both said that after the course, they were glad to have had the exercises.

(b) Sometimes people race through the exercises without thinking; did you actually do the exercises or did you sometimes move quickly through them? All seven professed taking the exercises seriously.

(c) Did you use the study guide during the [CAI sessions]? Four of the seven students said they used the study guide regularly; two said they used it once or twice; one never used it.

(d) Which exercises did you particularly like? Most liked exercises on perception and memory. Three liked the exercise on the neuron. One liked the exercise on Piaget.

(e) Which did you dislike? One disliked the Piaget exercise. Two disliked all exercises that made the students read a lot and did not involve them in activities.

Table 3. Correlation Matrix for Expectations About CAI, Ratings of Enjoyment and Helpfulness of CAI, and Performance on Measures of Learning

	Expect (1)	Enjoy (2)	Help (3)	Final Exam (4)	Critical (5)
1	1.00				
2	.02	1.00			
3	−.05	.92*	1.00		
4	.07	.02	.05	1.00	
5	.05	−.02	.04	.75*	1.00

Note. Expect = precourse expectations that students would enjoy the CAI exercises, 1 (*not at all*) to 5 (*extremely*); Enjoy = end-of-course ratings of whether students enjoyed the CAI exercises, 1 (*extremely unenjoyable*) to 7 (*extremely enjoyable*); Help = end-of-course ratings of whether students found the CAI exercises helpful, 1 (*extremely unhelpful*) to 7 (*extremely helpful*); Final Exam = score (number correct of 80 questions) on the final exam; Critical = number of items answered correctly of the 15 critical items.
*$p < .01$.

(f) How did the exercises help [if the student had expressed that they had helped]? Students expressed various reasons for the helpfulness of the exercises, including creating interest, helping review, and reinforcing lecture by looking at the material in a different way.

(g) Can you suggest anything that could be done differently with the [CAI sessions] that would help future students? Some suggested increasing the length of the CAI sessions so students would have more time to use study guides and having more quizzes. One suggested emphasizing the same topics in lecture that were emphasized in the CAI session.

Discussion

CAI exercises, as a supplement to traditional lecture, produced additional learning in an introductory psychology class. Students neither differentially withdrew from the class after beginning the CAI sections nor did they differentially fail to take the final exam (due to grades that were so low that the course could not be passed even with good performance on the examination).

In testing the effectiveness of CAI, several variables were controlled—more variables than previous research has considered. We examined student characteristics (age, gender, and race), class status, whether the course was required or taken as an elective, experience with computers, and variables concerning reasons for taking the course (see Duncan, 1993). Of those, only the variables concerning reasons for taking the class differed between the two classes. For example, students did not elect the CAI or no-CAI class because of the presence or absence of CAI per se, but they chose one class over the other because of the fit with their schedule or their preferred size of class. Results of an Attribute × Treatment (Preferred Class Size × Class) analysis revealed that presemester preferences for class size did not affect performance on the final exam as a whole or on the critical items covered in the CAI exercises. This finding supports the results of C. L. C. Kulik and J. A. Kulik's (1991) meta-analysis of 254 controlled studies that examined student attribute-by-treatment comparisons. Similar conclusions were reached after qualitative reviews of the literature by Duncan (1993) and Ransdell (1993).

Initial GPA predicted performance on the final examination, but higher attendance at lectures did not. This effect can be explained by the fact that, after the critical items were removed from the final examination, no differences in performance between the groups were detected. The groups differed according to those areas that not only were discussed in lecture but also were reinforced during the computer sessions. Even after controlling for GPA and attendance, exposure to CAI resulted in higher performance on the final examination, although only 1% of the variance was accounted for by the CAI exercises. Similar findings were obtained when performance on critical items was used as the dependent variable, but only 9% of the variance was accounted for by participation in the CAI exercises. In the CAI class, students spent 3.5 hr per week of classroom activity (performing exercises and demonstrations, reviewing the study guide, and taking six short multiple-choice quizzes on the material covered in the course) rather than 2.67 hr per week with the no-CAI class. Gains from participating in CAI exercises were modest.

Extra time spent on the study guide and quizzes may have accounted for better performance of students in the CAI class on the final examination, but this is unlikely. Most students in the no-CAI class purchased written study guides, which included the same material that was available in CAI. By identifying test items as either general material or critical items representing CAI domain-specific information, we were able to determine whether additional class time spent doing CAI increased overall learning or domain-specific learning. Essentially all of the increased performance was attributable to domain-specific performance on the items covered in the CAI exercises. Students in the CAI class, on average, answered three more questions correctly than did students in the no-CAI class; however, students in the CAI class correctly answered two more of the critical items covered in the CAI exercises. This result suggests that it was not additional time spent reviewing the study guide, taking quizzes, or mere additional time dealing with the content of the course that affected performance. Rather, the time spent completing the specific exercises translated into gains in learning that material; this is congruent with Castellan's (1993) study.

Most students who completed the class were positive toward the experience, as revealed by the supplemental analyses and the structured interviews. Positive reactions to the CAI exercises, better performance on the final examination, and better performance on critical items could not be accounted for by expectations before the course. Furthermore, positive reactions to the exercises were unrelated to performance on the examination or the critical items. These findings suggest that CAI allows people to learn, assuming they participate in the exercises, regardless of whether the students enjoy the exercises.

Our results offer modest support for including CAI exercises as a supplement to traditional lectures in introductory psychology (Conn et al., 1988; Welsh & Null, 1991). However, the gains in knowledge were limited to the content covered in the particular exercises used in the CAI sessions. We did not test whether a similar review or discussion session offered to the no-CAI group would have increased learning for those students with no access to computerized assistance. Although such alternatives to CAI have been shown to increase knowledge, computerized exercises have been shown to increase learning in significantly less time with fewer staff resources (Welsh & Null, 1991). Learning is domain specific, and software must be chosen with this in mind. CAI can increase learning in introductory psychology, but it cannot improve knowledge it did not cover.

References

Castellan, N. J., Jr. (1993). Evaluating information technology in teaching and learning. *Behavior Research Methods, Instruments, & Computers, 25,* 233–237.

Chute, D. L. (1986). MacLaboratory for psychology: General experimental psychology with Apple's Macintosh. *Behavior Research Methods, Instruments, & Computers, 18,* 205–209.

Conn, G., Stafiniak, P., DiPasquale, M. C., & Harper, L. (1988). Effects of teaching an introductory psychology laboratory using a computerized research tool. *Behavior Research Methods, Instruments, & Computers, 20,* 184–187.

Cook, T. D., & Campbell, D. T. (1979). *Quasi-experimentation, design, and analysis issues for field settings.* Chicago: Rand McNally.

Cordell, B. J. (1991). A study of learning styles and computer-assisted instruction. *Computers & Education, 16,* 175–183.

Deutsch, M., & Krauss, R. M. (1960). The effect of threat upon interpersonal bargaining. *Journal of Abnormal and Social Psychology, 61,* 181–189.

Duncan, N. C. (1991). CAI-enhanced exam performance in a research design course. *Behavior Research Methods, Instruments, & Computers, 23,* 324–327.

Duncan, N. C. (1993). Evaluation of instructional software: Design considerations and recommendations. *Behavior Research Methods, Instruments, & Computers, 25,* 223–227.

Goolkasian, P. (1989). Computerized laboratories for psychology instruction: How successful are they? *Behavior Research Methods, Instruments, & Computers, 21,* 148–150.

Hannafin, M. J., & Carney, B. W. (1991). Effects of elaboration strategies on learning and depth of processing during computer-based instruction. *Journal of Computer-Based Instruction, 18,* 77–82.

Isaacs, M., Costenbader, V., Reading-Brown, M., & Goodman, G. (1992). Using a computer simulation in research, training, and evaluation of school psychologists. *Behavior Research Methods, Instruments, & Computers, 24,* 165–168.

Kulik, C. L. C., & Kulik, J. A. (1991). Effectiveness of computer-based instruction: An updated analysis. *Computers in Human Behavior, 7,* 75–94.

Kulik, J. A., & Kulik, C. L. C. (1987). Review of recent research literature on computer-based instruction. *Contemporary Educational Psychology, 12,* 222–230.

Lambert, M. E., & Lenthall, G. (1989). Effects of psychology courseware use on computer anxiety in students. *Computers in Human Behavior, 5,* 207–214.

Liefeld, J. P., & Herrmann, T. F. (1990). Learning consequences for university students using computerized mastery testing. *Educational Technology, Research & Development, 38,* 19–25.

Ludwig, T. (1986). *Program diskette for PsychSim: Interactive graphic simulation for psychology.* New York: Worth.

McNeil, B. J., & Nelson, K. R. (1991). Meta-analysis of interactive video instruction: A 10-year review of achievement effects. *Journal of Computer-Based Instruction, 18,* 1–6.

Monahan, J. S. (1993). A computer lab for undergraduate psychological research. *Behavior Research Methods, Instruments, & Computers, 25,* 295–297.

Myers, D. G. (1992). *Psychology* (3rd ed.). New York: Worth.

Niemiec, R., & Walberg, H. J. (1987). Comparative effects of computer-assisted instruction: A synthesis of reviews. *Journal of Educational Computing Research, 3,* 19–37.

Perone, M. (1991). Computer-based methodology laboratories: An undergraduate course in experimental psychology. *Behavior Research Methods, Instruments, & Computers, 23,* 121–126.

Petty, L. C., & Rosen, E. F. (1990). Increase in mastery level using a computer-based tutorial/simulation in experimental psychology. *Behavior Research Methods, Instruments, & Computers, 22,* 216–218.

Ransdell, S. E. (1990). Using a real-time replay of students' word processing to understand and promote better writing. *Behavior Research Methods, Instruments, & Computers, 22,* 142–144.

Ransdell, S. (1993). Educational software evaluation research: Balancing internal, external, and ecological validity. *Behavior Research Methods, Instruments, & Computers, 25,* 228–232.

Sawyer, T. A. (1988). The effects of computerized and conventional study guides on achievement in college students. *Journal of Computer-Based Instruction, 15,* 80–82.

Sperling, G. (1960). The information available in brief visual presentations. *Psychological Monographs, 74*(Whole No. 498).

Tobias, S. (1987). Learner characteristics. In R. Gagne (Ed.), *Instructional technology: Foundations* (pp. 207–231). Hillsdale, NJ: Lawrence Erlbaum Associates, Inc.

Trowbridge, D. (1987). An investigation of groups working at the computer. In D. E. Berger, K. Pezdek, & W. Banks (Eds.), *Applications of cognitive psychology: Problem solving, education and computing* (pp. 47–57). Hillsdale, NJ: Lawrence Erlbaum Associates, Inc.

Underwood, G., & Underwood, J. D. M. (1987). The computer in education: A force for change? In F. Blacker & D. Osborne (Eds.), *Information technology and people: Designing for the future* (pp. 167–190). Letchworth, England: British Psychological Society.

Welsh, J. A., & Null, C. H. (1991). The effects of computer-based instruction on college students' comprehension of classic research. *Behavior Research Methods, Instruments, & Computers, 23,* 301–305.

Section II
Demonstrations and Activities
in Introductory Psychology

Invertebrates in the Classroom

Charles I. Abramson

Laboratory courses in animal behavior offer university and high school students a unique educational experience. While attempting to maintain or increase the quality of such experiences, instructors can choose among several low cost programs using gerbils (Hunt & Shields, 1978; Plant, 1980), chickens (Ackil & Ward, 1982; Rowland, Jordan, & Orson, 1984), or fishes (Weiss, 1980).

This article describes an inexpensive program using invertebrates as subjects in conditioning demonstrations and experiments. Although invertebrates are standard subjects in many biology courses, their potential value for psychology courses is not well known. To familiarize psychology instructors with the many uses of invertebrates in conditioning experiments, the invertebrate program is presented in tabular form. The reader will need to consult the relevant references to obtain details for any demonstration. The invertebrates chosen for this program are ants, earthworms, honeybees, and planarians. They were selected on the basis of laboratory adaptability, availability of apparatus, and unequivocal demonstrations of learning ability.

Invertebrates offer several advantages over more traditional laboratory animals. First, they are inexpensive to procure and maintain. Cockroaches, for example, can survive without food and water for 30 days (Longo, 1970). They can be ordered from commercial suppliers or brought from home. Second, students can train their own subject in a variety of mazes, runways, shuttleboxes, and operant chambers costing a few dollars rather than hundreds of dollars. Apparatus can often be manufactured from plastic tubes and connectors. Third, invertebrates can easily be used under the proper conditions (McConnell, 1967a; Ratner, 1967) to demonstrate principles of the comparative analysis of learning, biochemistry of learning, behavioral pharmacology, physiological psychology, and economics. Fourth, students can take part in some of the classic controversies in animal behavior such as the relative importance of stimulus–stimulus (SS) versus stimulus–response (SR) associations, learning of planarians, taste-aversion learning, RNA transfer experiments, and the role of genetic versus environmental factors in learning.

To assist the instructor in preparing demonstrations, this paper is divided into four sections: (a) review articles, (b) procuring and maintaining subjects, (c) apparatus, and (d) demonstrations. For convenience, tables accompany each of these sections.

Review Papers

The most comprehensive series of reviews about invertebrate learning appear in Corning, Dyal, and Willows (1973, 1975). Volume 1 of this 3-volume set includes chapters on protozoans, planarians, and earthworms. Learning of crabs, snails, bees, ants, and roaches is covered in volume 2. The final volume contains discussions of octopus and plant learning. Other reviews include the chemical changes associated with invertebrate learning (Corning & Ratner, 1967; Thorpe & Davenport, 1964), foraging behavior (Hassell & Southwood, 1978), and statements regarding the importance of invertebrate learning in behavior theory (Farley & Alkon, 1985; Quinn, 1984; Sahley, 1984). Instructors interested in neuroanatomy and physiology can find much material in Bullock and Horridge (1965) and to a lesser extent in Corning et al. (1973, 1975). Instructors are encouraged to consult Table 1 to obtain reviews on specific invertebrates. All of the reviews contain information on learning; many also include suggestions on how to ensure stable performance.

Procuring and Maintaining Subjects

In purchasing invertebrates from commercial suppliers, instructions on feeding and maintenance typically accompany each order. If additional information is required (e.g., materials for nest construction) it can be found in Lutz, Welch, Galtsoff, and Needham (1937/1959) and Best (1978). Commercially constructed nests for ants, bees, earthworms, and fruitflies are available from Connecticut Valley Biological Supply Co. Table 2 presents a list of suppliers, their addresses, and some of the invertebrates that can be purchased.

Apparatus

There is a rich variety of apparatus available for the study of invertebrate behavior. Descriptions of this equipment can be found in published reports. Most apparatus can be constructed from inexpensive materials; however, some of it

Table 1. Review Papers

Animal	Source
Ant	Alloway (1973)
Bee	Wells (1973); Menzel & Bitterman (1983)
Earthworm	Ratner (1967); Dyal (1973)
Fruitfly	McGuire (1984); Tully (1984)
Housefly	McGuire (1984)
Planarian	McConnell (1967b); Corning & Riccio (1970); Corning & Kelly (1973)
Roach	Alloway (1973)

**Table 2. Commercial Suppliers
of Invertebrate Material**

Source	Animal
Carolina Biological Supply Co. Burlington, NC 27215	Bee Fruitfly Housefly
Connecticut Valley Biological Supply Co. Southampton, MA 01073	Ant Earthworm Planarian
Uncle Milton Industries 10459 West Jefferson Blvd. Culver City, CA 90230	Ant

can be purchased commercially. For example, a planarian maze/classical conditioning arena, which eliminates handling, is available from Connecticut Valley Biological Supply Co., as is a fruitfly conditioning chamber suitable for genetic analysis. The type of apparatus reported in the literature ranges from simple runways and mazes to automated shuttleboxes and operant chambers (see Table 3). A major advantage of automated apparatus is that it minimizes handling and, depending on the type of invertebrate used, minimizes emotional reactions associated with using "bugs" in the classroom. Nevertheless, automated apparatus is more difficult to construct. When using an apparatus, it is often desirable to program contingencies automatically. In keeping with the basic philosophy of the invertebrate program that is low in cost and flexible, several references to inexpensive programmers are included in Table 3.

Demonstrations

Table 4 cites references that will enable an instructor to produce demonstrations of classical, instrumental, and avoidance conditioning. There is also a section of that table

labeled "Special Topics," which cites experiments concerned with physiological and genetic manipulations. An attempt was made to select experiments that could be performed in a 2-hour laboratory period, although this was not always possible. Where possible, experiments that use controls were selected; however, some uncontrolled experiments were intentionally included. It has been my experience that students obtain a stronger foundation in experimental design when asked to interpret a poorly controlled experiment than if they are simply told to follow the instructions of one that is well controlled. Of course, nothing prevents the instructor from improving a deficient design. For convenience, the experiments are listed under general headings. If more detailed information is required, such as class of reinforcer (i.e., appetitive or aversive), simply consult the reference list.

Conclusions

Over the past several years, I have used invertebrates as a supplement to rodent programs, a source for independent student projects, and lecture/guest lecture demonstrations. Invertebrates are well suited for lecture demonstrations because they are easily transported and can be placed upon an overhead projector for mass viewing. The choice behavior of an ant, for instance, can be demonstrated to a large audience by placing a T maze on the projector.

In a laboratory course, the ability to supplement rodent experiments with invertebrates adds flexibility. Students can explore a problem, such as reversal learning, across the evolutionary scale or study a series of problems with one class of organism. Especially appealing is the ability to conduct classical conditioning experiments without being limited to conditioned suppression or general activity conditioning of rats confined in student-operant conditioning chambers. Invertebrate experiments are also a wonderful

Table 3. Instrumentation Used in the Study of Invertebrate Behavior

	Type	Animal	Reference
Unautomated:	Runway	Ant Earthworm Roach	Abramson, Miler, & Mann (1982) Reynierse & Ratner (1964) Longo (1970)
	Maze	Ant Bee Earthworm Fruitfly Roach Planarian	Schneirla (1933); Vowles (1964) Menzel & Erber (1972) Datta (1962) Dudai (1977); Drudge & Platt (1979) Longo (1964) Best & Rubinstein (1962); Corning (1964)
	Free-Flying Situation	Bee	Couvillon & Bitterman (1980); Abramson (1985)
Automated:	Operant Chamber	Ant Bee Planarian Roach	Abramson, Collier, & Marcucella (1977) Sigurdson (1981a, 1981b) Crawford & Skeen (1967) Rubadeau & Conrad (1963)
	Shuttlebox	Ant Bee Housefly	Abramson et al. (1977, 1982) Abramson (1985) Leeming & Little (1977)
	Running Wheel	Earthworm Fruitfly Housefly Roach	Marian & Abramson (1982) DeJianne, McGuire, & Pruzan-Hotchkiss (1985) Miller, Bruner, & Fukuto (1971) Ball (1972)
Programming Equipment:	Calculator Computer Integrated Circuit	— — —	Robinson (1979) Nicholls & Potter (1982) Wolach (1979)

Table 4. **Demonstrations of Invertebrate Learning Suitable for the Classroom**

Procedure	Animal	Initial Demonstration	Manipulation
Classical Conditioning	Bee	Sigurdson (1981a) Bitterman, Menzel, Fietz, & Shäfer (1983) Abramson (1985)	CS preexposure Bitterman et al. (1983) Abramson & Bitterman (1985) Compound Conditioning Couvillon & Bitterman (1982) Couvillon, Klosterhalfen, & Bitterman (1983) Second Order Conditioning Bitterman et al. (1983)
	Earthworm	Ratner & Miller (1959a) Peeke, Herz, & Wyers (1967)	CS-US Interval Ratner & Miller (1959b) Wyers, Peeke, & Herz (1964) Herz, Peeke, & Wyers (1967) Intertrial Interval Ratner & Miller (1959b) Ratner & Stein (1965) Reinforcement Probability Wyers et al. (1964)
	Planarian	Thompson & McConnell (1955) Griffard (1963) Fantl & Nevin (1965) Block & McConnell (1967) Corning & Freed (1968)	None
Instrumental Conditioning	Ant	Schneirla (1943) Vowles (1964) Martinsen & Kimeldorf (1972) Stratton & Coleman (1972) Abramson (1981) Morgan (1981) Abramson (1983)	Partial Reinforcement Fleer & Wyers (1963) Ramos (1966) Reinforcement Probability Simmel & Ramos (1965) Fleer (1972) Reversal Learning Fleer (1972) Time Allocation DeCarlo & Abramson (1985)
	Bee	Couvillon & Bitterman (1980) Sigurdson (1981a)	Contrast Couvillon & Bitterman (1984) Sigurdson (1981a) Delay of Reinforcement Couvillon & Bitterman (1980) Partial Reinforcement Robacker & Ambrose (1978) Sigurdson (1981a, 1981b) Probability Learning Sigurdson (1981a) Reversal Learning Sigurdson (1981a)
	Earthworm	Datta (1962) Zellner (1966)	Intertrial Interval Datta (1962) Probability Learning Sigurdson (1981a) Reversal Learning Datta (1962)
	Fruitfly	Quinn, Harris, & Benzer (1974) Dudai (1977) Booker & Quinn (1981) Hewitt, Fulker, & Hewitt (1983) DeJianne et al. (1985)	US Intensity Dudai (1977)
	Roach	Szymanski (1912) Ebeling, Wagner, & Reierson (1966) Ebeling, Reierson, & Wagner (1968) Freckleton & Wahlsten (1968) Longo (1970) Pritchatt (1970)	None
Signalled Avoidance	Ant	Abramson & Russ (1985)	None
	Bee	Abramson (1985)	None
	Earthworm	Ray (1968)	None
	Roach	Chen, Aranda, & Luco (1970)	None

(Continued)

Table 4. *(Continued)*

Procedure	Animal	Initial Deminstration	Manipulation
Unsignalled Avoidance	Bee Roach	Abramson (1985) Longo (1964)	None None
Special Topics			
Drugs	Ant Earthworm	Kostowski, Beck, & Meszaros (1965) Kostowski & Tarchalska (1972) Arbit (1964)	— —
Genetic Analysis	Fruitfly	Quinn et al. (1974) Dudai (1977) Booker & Quinn (1981) Hewitt et al. (1983)	—
Lesions	Ant Earthworm	Vowles (1964, 1967) Ratner & Miller (1959b) Ratner & Stein (1965) Zellner (1966)	— —

source for independent student projects and provide a data base to test the generality of results and interpretations of vertebrate experiments.

Although I have only informal data supporting the benefits of using invertebrates, there is no reason to believe that the intellectual rewards of an experimental animal course or animal demonstration depend upon vertebrates. In fact, some of the most difficult experiments in psychology, such as those involving lesions, cannibalistic transfer, and genetic variations, can be performed inexpensively only with invertebrates.

The material cited enables an instructor or student to acquire background information, maintain various invertebrates, and create automated or manual demonstrations on a wide range of topics with minimal expense. A laboratory course based entirely on invertebrates may be a bit too radical although, with a severely limited budget, there is no reasonable alternative that permits as much flexibility.

References

Abramson, C. I. (1981). Passive avoidance in the California harvester ant *Pogonmyremex californicus*. *Journal of General Psychology, 104,* 29–40.

Abramson, C. I. (1983, April). *Resistance to extinction as a function of reinforcement magnitude and punishment in the harvester ant.* Paper presented at the meeting of the Eastern Psychological Association, New York.

Abramson, C. I. (1985). *Aversive conditioning in honeybees (Apis mellifera).* Manuscript submitted for publication.

Abramson, C. I., & Bitterman, M. E. (1985). *Latent inhibition in honeybees (Apis mellifera).* Manuscript submitted for publication.

Abramson, C. I., Collier, D. M., & Marcucella, H. (1977). An aversive conditioning unit for ants. *Behavior Research Methods and Instrumentation, 9,* 505–507.

Abramson, C. I., Miler, J., & Mann, D. W. (1982). An olfactory shuttlebox and runway for insects. *Journal of Mind and Behavior, 3,* 151–159.

Abramson, C. I., & Russ, R. C. (1985). *Demonstration of discrete-trial signalled avoidance learning in the carpenter ant (Componotus herculeanus).* Manuscript submitted for publication.

Ackil, J. E., & Ward, E. F. (1982). Chickens in the classroom: Introductory laboratory courses in experimental psychology. *Teaching of Psychology, 9,* 107–108.

Alloway, T. M. (1973). Learning in insects except *apoidea.* In W. C. Corning, J. A. Dyal, & A. O. D. Willows (Eds.), *Invertebrate learning: Vol. 2. Arthropods and gastropod mollusks* (pp. 131–171). New York: Plenum.

Arbit, J. (1964). Learning in annelids and attempts at the chemical modification of this behavior. *Animal Behaviour, 13*(Suppl. 1), 83–87.

Ball, H. J. (1972). A system for recording activity of small insects. *Journal of Economic Entomology, 65,* 129–132.

Best, J. B., & Rubinstein, I. (1962). Maze learning and associated behavior in planaria. *Journal of Comparative and Physiological Psychology, 55,* 560–566.

Best, R. L. (1978). *Living arthropods in the classroom.* Burlington, NC: Carolina Biological Supply Company.

Bitterman, M. E., Menzel, R., Fietz, A., & Schäfer, S. (1983). Classical conditioning of proboscis extension in honeybees (*Apis mellifera*). *Journal of Comparative Psychology, 97,* 107–119.

Block, R. A., & McConnell, J. V. (1967). Classically conditioned discrimination in the planarian, *Dugesia dorotocephala. Nature, 215,* 1465–1466.

Booker, R., & Quinn, W. G. (1981). Conditioning of leg position in normal and mutant *Drosophila. Proceedings of the National Academy of Sciences of the United States of America, 78,* 3940–3944.

Bullock, T. H., & Horridge, G. A. (1965). *Structure and function of the nervous systems of invertebrates* (Vols. 1–2). San Francisco: W. H. Freeman.

Chen, W. Y., Aranda, L. C., & Luco, J. V. (1970). Learning and long- and short-term memory in cockroaches. *Animal Behavior, 18,* 725–732.

Corning, W. C. (1964). Evidence of right-left discrimination in planarians. *Journal of Psychology, 58,* 131–139.

Corning, W. C., Dyal, J. A., & Willows, A. O. D. (1973). *Invertebrate learning* (Vols. 1–2). New York: Plenum.

Corning, W. C., Dyal, J. A., & Willows, A. O. D. (1975). *Invertebrate learning* (Vol. 3). New York: Plenum.

Corning, W. C., & Freed, S. (1968). Planarian behavior and biochemistry. *Nature, 219,* 1227–1229.

Corning, W. C., & Kelly, S. (1973). Platyhelminthes: The turbellarians. In W. C. Corning, J. A. Dyal, & A. O. D. Willows (Eds.), *Invertebrate learning: Vol. 1. Protozoans through annelids* (pp. 171–224). New York: Plenum.

Corning, W. C., & Ratner, S. C. (Eds.). (1967). *Chemistry of learning*. New York: Plenum.

Corning, W. C., & Riccio, D. (1970). The planarian controversy. In W. Byrne (Ed.), *Molecular approaches to learning and memory* (pp. 107–150). New York: Academic.

Couvillon, P. A., & Bitterman, M. E. (1980). Some phenomena of associate learning in honeybees. *Journal of Comparative and Physiological Psychology, 94*, 878–885.

Couvillon, P. A., & Bitterman, M. E. (1982). Compound conditioning in honeybees. *Journal of Comparative and Physiological Psychology, 96*, 192–199.

Couvillon, P. A., & Bitterman, M. E. (1984). The overlearning-extinction effect and successive negative contrast in honeybees (*Apis mellifera*). *Journal of Comparative Psychology, 98*, 100–109.

Couvillon, P. A., Klosterhalfen, S., & Bitterman, M. E. (1983). Analysis of overshadowing in honeybees. *Journal of Comparative Psychology, 97*, 154–166.

Crawford, F. T., & Skeen, L. C. (1967). Operant responding in the planarian: A replication study. *Psychological Reports, 20*, 1023–1027.

Datta, L. G. (1962). Learning in the earthworm *Lumbricus terrestris*. *American Journal of Psychology, 75*, 531–553.

DeCarlo, L. T., & Abramson, C. I. (1985). *Time allocation as a measure of behavior in the ant*. Manuscript submitted for publication.

DeJianne, D., McGuire, T. R., & Pruzan-Hotchkiss, A. (1985). Conditioned suppression of proboscis extension in *Drosophila melanogaster*. *Journal of Comparative Psychology, 99*, 74–80.

Drudge, O. W., & Platt, S. A. (1979). A versatile maze for learning and geotaxic selection in *Drosophila melanogaster*. *Behavior Research Methods and Instrumentation, 11*, 503–506.

Dudai, Y. (1977). Properties of learning and memory in *Drosophila melanogaster*. *Journal of Comparative Physiology, 114*, 69–89.

Dyal, J. A. (1973). Behavior modification in annelids. In W. C. Corning, J. A. Dyal, & A. O. D. Willows (Eds.), *Invertebrate learning (Vol. 1). Protozoans through annelids* (pp. 225–290). New York: Plenum.

Ebeling, W., Reierson, D. A., & Wagner, R. E. (1968). Influence of repellency on the efficacy of blatticides. IV. Comparison of four cockroach species. *Journal of Economic Entomology, 61*, 1213–1219.

Ebeling, W., Wagner, R. E., & Reierson, D. A. (1966). Influence of repellency on the efficacy of blatticides. I. Learned modification of behavior of the German cockroach. *Journal of Economic Entomology, 59*, 1374–1388.

Fantl, S., & Nevin, J. A. (1965). Classical discriminations in planarians. *Worm Runner's Digest, 7*, 32–34.

Farley, J., & Alkon, D. L. (1985). Cellular mechanisms of learning, memory, and information storage. *Annual Review of Psychology, 36*, 419–494.

Fleer, R. (1972). Some behavioral observations on the ant *P. californicus*, with special reference to habit-reversal learning. *Dissertation Abstracts International, 33*, 2370. (University Microfilms No. 72–30, 477)

Fleer, R. E., & Wyers, E. J. (1963). Partial reinforcement in the ant *Pogonomyrex californicus*. *American Psychologist, 18*, 444.

Freckleton, W. C., Jr., & Wahlsten, D. (1968). Carbon dioxide induced amnesia in the cockroach *Periplaneta americana*. *Psychonomic Science, 12*, 179–180.

Griffard, C. D. (1963). Classical conditioning of the planarian *Phagocata gracilis* to water flow. *Journal of Comparative and Physiological Psychology, 56*, 597–600.

Hassell, M. P., & Southwood, T. R. E. (1978). Foraging strategies of insects. *Annual Review of Ecology and Systematics, 9*, 75–98.

Herz, M. J., Peeke, H. V. S., & Wyers, E. J. (1967). Classical conditioning of the extension response in the earthworm. *Physiology and Behavior, 2*, 409–411.

Hewitt, J. K., Fulker, D. W., & Hewitt, C. A. (1983). Genetic architecture of olfactory discriminative avoidance conditioning in *Drosophila melanogaster*. *Journal of Comparative Psychology, 97*, 52–58.

Hunt, K., & Shields, R. (1978). Using gerbils in the undergraduate operant laboratory. *Teaching of Psychology, 5*, 210–211.

Kostowski, W., Beck, J., & Meszaros, J. (1965). Drugs affecting the behaviour and spontaneous bioelectric activity of the central nervous system in the ant, *Formica rufa. Journal of Pharmacy and Pharmacology, 17*, 253–255.

Kostowski, W., & Tarchalska, B. (1972). The effects of some drugs affecting brain 5-HT on the aggressive behaviour and spontaneous electrical activity of the central nervous system of the ant, *Formica rufa. Brain Research, 38*, 143–149.

Leeming, F. C., & Little, G. L. (1977). Escape learning in houseflies (*Musca domestica*). *Journal of Comparative and Physiological Psychology, 91*, 260–269.

Longo, N. (1964). Probability learning and habit reversal in the cockroach. *American Journal of Psychology, 77*, 29–41.

Longo, N. (1970). A runway for the cockroach. *Behavior Research Methods and Instrumentation, 2*, 118–119.

Lutz, F. E., Welch, P. S., Galtsoff, P. S., & Needham, J. G. (Eds.). (1959). *Culture methods for invertebrate animals*. New York: Dover. (Original work published 1937)

Marian, R. W., & Abramson, C. I. (1982). Earthworm behavior in a modified running wheel. *Journal of Mind and Behavior, 3*, 67–74.

Martinsen, D. L., & Kimeldorf, D. J. (1972). Conditioned special avoidance behavior of ants induced by X-rays. *Psychological Record, 22*, 225–232.

McConnell, J. V. (Ed.). (1967a). *A manual of psychological experiments on planarians*. Ann Arbor, MI: Journal of Biological Psychology.

McConnell, J. V. (1967b). Specific factors influencing planarian behavior. In W. C. Corning & S. C. Ratner (Eds.), *Chemistry of learning* (pp. 217–233). New York: Plenum.

McGuire, T. R. (1984). Learning in three species of Diptera: The blow fly *Phormia regina*, the fruit fly *Drosophila melanogaster*, and the house fly *Musca domestica*. *Behavior Genetics, 14*, 479–526.

Menzel, R., & Bitterman, M. H. (1983). Learning by honeybees in an unnatural situation. In F. Huber & L. Markl (Eds.), *Behavioral physiology and neuroethology* (pp. 206–215). Heidelberg: Springer-Verlag.

Menzel, R., & Erber, J. (1972). The influence of the quantity of reward on the learning performance in honeybees. *Behaviour, 41*, 27–42.

Miller, T., Bruner, L. J., & Fukuto, T. R. (1971). The effects of light, temperature, and DDT poisoning on housefly locomotion and flight muscle activity. *Pesticide Biochemistry and Physiology, 1*, 483–491.

Morgan, R. F. (1981). Learning in submerged *Formica rufa*. *Psychological Reports, 49*, 63–69.

Nicholls, R. J., & Potter, R. M. (1982). An inexpensive computer and interface for research in the behavioral sciences. *Behavior Research Methods and Instrumentation, 14*, 532–533.

Peeke, H. V. S., Herz, M. J., & Wyers, E. G. (1967). Forward conditioning, backward conditioning and pseudoconditioning sensitization in the earthworm (*Lumbricus terrestris*). *Journal of Comparative and Physiological Psychology, 64*, 534–536.

Plant, L. (1980). The gerbil jar: A basic home experience in operant conditioning. *Teaching of Psychology, 7*, 109.

Pritchatt, D. (1970). Further studies on the avoidance behavior of *Periplaneta americana* to electric shock. *Animal Behaviour, 18*, 485–492.

Quinn, W. G. (1984). Work in invertebrates on the mechanisms underlying learning. In P. Marler & H. S. Terrace (Eds.), *The biology of learning* (pp. 197–246). Berlin: Springer-Verlag.

Quinn, W. G., Harris, W. A., & Benzer, S. (1974). Conditioned behavior in *Drosophila melanogaster*. *Proceedings of the National Academy of Sciences of the United States of America, 71*, 708–712.

Ramos, F. (1966). *Rate of extinction as a function of varying schedule of reinforcement in the harvester ant P. californicus*. Unpublished master's thesis, California College, Los Angeles, CA.

Ratner, S. C. (1967). Annelids and learning: A critical review. In W. C. Corning & S. C. Ratner (Eds.), *Chemistry of learning* (391–406). New York: Plenum.

Ratner, S. C., & Miller, K. R. (1959a). Classical conditioning in earthworms, *Lumbricus terrestris*. *Journal of Comparative and Physiological Psychology, 52*, 102–105.

Ratner, S. C., & Miller, K. R. (1959b). Effects of spacing of training and ganglia removal on conditioning in earthworms. *Journal of Comparative and Physiological Psychology, 52*, 667–672.

Ratner, S. C., & Stein, D. G. (1965). Responses of worms to light as a function of intertrial interval and ganglion removal. *Journal of Comparative and Physiological Psychology, 59*, 301–305.

Ray, A. J. (1968). Instrumental light avoidance by the earthworm. *Communications in Behavioral Biology, 1*, 205–208.

Reynierse, J. H., & Ratner, S. C. (1964). Acquisition and extinction in the earthworm, *Lumbricus terrestris*. *Psychological Record, 14*, 383–387.

Robacker, D. C., & Ambrose, J. T. (1978). Random partial reinforcement in the honeybee: Effect on asymptotic performance and resistance to extinction. *Journal of Apiculture Research, 17*, 182–187.

Robinson, G. H. (1979). Programming experiments with pocket programmable calculators. *Behavior Research Methods and Instrumentation, 11*, 61–63.

Rowland, D. L., Jordan, E. K., & Orson, M. (1984). On the use of chicks as experimental laboratory subjects. *Teaching of Psychology, 11*, 45–46.

Rubadeau, D. O., & Conrad, K. A. (1963). An apparatus to demonstrate and measure operant behavior of arthropoda. *Journal of the Experimental Analysis of Behavior, 6*, 429–430.

Sahley, C. L. (1984). Behavior theory and invertebrate learning. In P. Marler & H. S. Terrace (Eds.), *The biology of learning* (pp. 181–196). Berlin: Springer-Verlag.

Schneirla, T. C. (1933). Motivation and efficiency in ant learning. *Journal of Comparative Psychology, 15*, 243–266.

Schneirla, T. C. (1943). The nature of ant learning: II. The intermediate stage of segmental maze adjustment. *Journal of Comparative Psychology, 35*, 149–176.

Sigurdson, J. E. (1981a). Automated discrete-trials techniques of appetitive conditioning in honeybees. *Behavior Research Methods and Instrumentation, 13*, 1–10.

Sigurdson, J. E. (1981b). Measurement of consummatory behavior in honeybees. *Behavior Research Methods and Instrumentation, 13*, 308–310.

Simmel, E. C., & Ramos, F. (1965). Spatial-probability learning in ants. *American Zoologist, 153*, 228.

Stratton, L. O., & Coleman, W. P. (1972). Maze learning and orientation in the fire ant (*Solenopsis saevissima*). *Journal of Comparative and Physiological Psychology, 83*, 7–12.

Szymanski, J. S. (1912). Modification of the innate behavior of cockroaches. *Journal of Animal Behavior, 2*, 81–90.

Thompson, R., & McConnell, J. V. (1955). Classical conditioning in the planarian, *Dugesia dorotocephala*. *Journal of Comparative and Physiological Psychology, 48*, 65–68.

Thorpe, W. H., & Davenport, D. (Eds.). (1964). *Learning and associated phenomena in invertebrates*. Animal Behavior Supplement 1, London: Bailliere, Tindall & Cassell.

Tully, T. (1984). Drosophila learning: Behavior and biochemistry. *Behavior Genetics, 14*, 527–557.

Vowles, D. M. (1964). Olfactory learning and brain lesions in the wood ant (*Formica rufa*). *Journal of Comparative and Physiological Psychology, 58*, 105–111.

Vowles, D. M. (1967). Interocular transfer, brain lesions, and maze learning in the wood ant *Formica rufa*. In W. C. Corning & S. C. Ratner (Eds.), *Chemistry of learning* (pp. 425–447). New York: Plenum.

Weiss, C. S. (1980). An inexpensive animal laboratory course. *Teaching of Psychology, 7*, 193–195.

Wells, P. H. (1973). Honey bees. In W. C. Corning, J. A. Dyal, & A. O. D. Willows (Eds.), *Invertebrate learning (Vol. 2). Anthropods and gastropod mollusks* (pp. 173–185). New York: Plenum.

Wolach, A. H. (1979). *Programming schedules of reinforcement with integrated circuits*. Chicago: K.D.V.H.E.

Wyers, E. J., Peeke, H. V. S., & Herz, M. J. (1964). Partial reinforcement and resistance to extinction in the earthworm. *Journal of Comparative and Physiological Psychology, 57*, 113–116.

Zellner, D. K. (1966). Effects of removal and regeneration of the suprapharyngeal ganglion on learning, retention, extinction and negative movements in the earthworm *Lumbricus terrestris L*. *Physiology and Behavior, 1*, 151–159.

In-Class Poster Sessions

Brian N. Baird

An unfortunate fact of teaching is that the opportunities for creative, individualized student activity tend to decrease in direct proportion to the number of students in a class. Instructors seeking a way around this dilemma may find in-class poster sessions a practical and rewarding solution.

Poster sessions have been described by Chute and Bank (1983) and in a slightly different form as "fairs" for high school students by Benjamin, Fawl, and Klein (1977). This article presents a more detailed description of how poster sessions can be conducted in classes ranging from small seminars to large introductory sections.

Poster Session Project Description and Requirements

My in-class poster sessions resemble the poster sessions held at professional and scientific conferences. Instead of each student submitting a paper that only the instructor reads, students present projects to their classmates in poster session format. Depending on the class size, we hold poster sessions on sequential days, with a portion of the class simultaneously presenting their posters at various locations in the room while the remaining students circulate to discuss, evaluate, and give feedback. The students then evaluate the projects, with the instructor reserving the right to assign final grades.

During the second week of class, students receive a handout describing the rationale, requirements, and procedures for the poster sessions. In an effort to promote creativity and diversity, poster sessions are not limited to written papers. Instead, I offer the more general requirement that the students present projects. These projects, which I must approve, may be anything from traditional papers or research studies to auditory, video, or other artistic presentations. All projects require some combination of written and visual presentation during the poster sessions. To assist students in understanding the requirements, I place examples of papers, videos, and audio productions from previous students on library reserve. Although most students grasp the nature of the assignment on their own, instructors using this activity for the first time may wish to provide class time to discuss ideas and options for poster sessions. Instructors may also wish to present examples of their own work in poster session format. If students still have difficulty understanding the assignment, the two-stage approach (discussed later) provides opportunities to observe the work of other students and to receive additional feedback and direction.

All projects must meet three criteria that also serve as the bases for grading: (a) extended research beyond the information available from text or lecture materials, (b) critical thinking and analysis of the subject matter, and (c) clear communication of the information and ideas. For the purpose of this assignment, *critical thinking* is defined rather broadly as doing more than just reporting what others have written on a topic. Students are expected to evaluate, synthesize, interpret, and critique information, not just paraphrase. I discuss each of the criteria in the handout and in class.

Three Steps to Developing Posters

A three-step approach to developing posters is helpful. First, early in the semester, students are given a written description of poster project requirements. I then suggest that students explore their textbooks, personal experiences, or other sources to identify topics they would like to pursue. Students are also encouraged to find one or two other students with whom they would like to work on a project. Students must then submit a one-page proposal describing the topic they will address, the methods they will use, any ethical considerations, and the responsibilities of each student in the group.

The one-page descriptions give me a chance to ensure that the proposed projects are within the students' abilities and do not pose significant risks or other ethical concerns. The descriptions also let me brainstorm with students, suggest possible resources or approaches, and help anticipate or iron out problems.

After approving the project proposals, I schedule a date for initial presentation of the projects. During the semester, students present their projects on two occasions. The first presentation is given midway through the semester. This presentation allows students an opportunity to present what they have completed and receive feedback from their peers.

Setting a midsemester presentation date helps reduce the last minute "cramming" guaranteed to accompany assignments that are due at the end of the semester. Of greater importance is the opportunity for students to give and receive feedback. During the first poster session presentation, students' work will be reviewed by half of the other students in the class. Before this session, I instruct students in the value of such feedback and how best to give and receive it. This approach encourages students to learn from one another and to appreciate the value of the process of revision (Baird & Anderson, 1990). A recent student demonstrated this value by placing a sign beside his paper that read, "Tear it up please. I want your suggestions." Encouraging students to share their work and constructive criticism with others establishes a precedent that will serve them well throughout their educational experience.

A third benefit of the initial session is that the opportunity to observe the work of other students encourages project improvement among all participants. In the traditional model of assigned papers, only the instructor sees and evaluates student work. In such situations, students know only what they have produced and have no way to compare or contrast their work with that of their peers. The poster session, on the other hand, provides an opportunity for students to learn from comparison. The midsemester presentation leaves time for improvements.

A final benefit of the poster session and the two-stage presentation is that complaints concerning grades diminish. When students have no opportunity to observe the quality of their peers' work, they do not know why they received a particular grade. Poster sessions do not entirely solve this problem, but many students seem more ready to accept the grade their projects earn. As one student admitted, "When you gave me a C on my project I was mad at first, but then I saw what some of the other students had done and I understood. Now I want to make my final version a lot better."

Following the initial presentation of posters, I schedule the final step in the process for the next to last week of the semester. At this time, students present their revised projects. Presentation during this week allows time to grade and give feedback before the semester ends.

Session Logistics

Because students often choose similar topics, I review the first proposals and schedule presentations on different days to avoid redundancy. After topics are selected and assigned, a printed program describes what will be presented and by whom during the poster sessions. Copies of this program are distributed in advance to build a sense of the importance of the event. I also post the programs so other students or faculty may attend the sessions.

Along with balancing the content of the poster sessions, the instructor must consider the number of posters to be presented and how much time will be available for students to visit each poster. In large introductory classes, I allow the nonpresenters approximately 5 min to visit each poster that day. I also follow this time limit as I circulate among the posters to evaluate and discuss them with the students. If two or three students collaborate on each project, we can review posters for a lecture class of 50 to 60 students in 2 or 3 days. For larger classes, I schedule more presenters on a given day, with the trade-off being less time for interaction or the inability of all the students to visit all of the posters for that day. For smaller, upper division classes, I allow 10 to 15 min for each poster presentation. The added time permits greater discussion of presumably more advanced topics and projects.

Another suggestion is to take a signed, written roll on each day of the poster sessions. Although most students look forward to presenting their own work and attending the other days to view the posters of others, some attend only on the days of their presentations. Such absences are unfair to students who attended the first presentations. Absent students also defeat the goal of having students learn from each others' posters. Making attendance mandatory at all sessions is regrettable but necessary to ensure equal participation.

We hold poster sessions in a classroom where students spread out around the perimeter and display their material either on tables or the wall. Poster sessions require a room that is large enough for students to have at least 5 to 8 ft in which to present their posters, with several feet between adjacent posters.

At the students' request, we recently held poster sessions in the informal, club-like, student union cafeteria. This allowed others outside the class to join the session and circulate among the posters. The response was positive, and other instructors say that they will follow suit with their classes.

Grading

As noted earlier, students participate in grading posters. This approach reduces the grading burden on the instructor and encourages students to evaluate the quality of their own work and that of others. Unfortunately, my experience suggests that when students are asked to grade others they tend to give everyone As. Such generosity is understandable, but it does not require students to consider what "quality work" means, and it is unfair to those students who have clearly produced superior work. To address this problem, give students the grading criteria before they grade any projects. The session program lists these criteria, and students assign each project a grade for each of the three criteria. Students record the grades on the programs and then return the programs anonymously at the end of each session. Even with these measures, the instructor should reserve the right to assign final grades. The instructor may wish to recognize exceptional effort that students might overlook or reduce the grade of mediocre projects that students graded too highly.

One final grading issue concerns the evaluation of collaborative projects. Most students find collaboration instructive and enjoyable. In some instances, however, students complain that they carried all the load while their partners

did little or none of the work. With grades assigned on a per project basis, all students connected with the project receive the same grade, although some may not have earned it. I know of no solution that is entirely satisfactory. Asking students to identify their role during the proposal phase, then giving them an opportunity to individually grade their own project, as well as their contribution and that of their partners, may be useful. This approach at least provides a way for students to tell the instructor who in their group they felt earned what grade.

Student Evaluation of Poster Sessions

To assess student reactions to the poster sessions, I prepared a brief evaluation form and distributed it to two introductory psychology sections that participated in the poster sessions. I asked students to complete these forms anonymously and return them as part of the end of semester course evaluation. Abbreviated items from the questionnaire and response frequencies for each item are presented in Table 1.

Table 1. Poster Session Evaluation Results

1. Did the poster sessions increase interaction among students and provide exposure to other students' learning styles?

A	B	C	D	E
58%	37%	5%		

2. By viewing other students work, do you feel you were able to gain more information about other topics that Interested you?

A	B	C	D	E
73%	25%	2%		

3. The poster sessions involved three steps—the original proposal, the first session, and the final session. Do you feel this was a valuable approach?

A	B	C	D	E
74%	22%	4%		

4. How valuable was it for you to have the opportunity to do something other than a written paper?

A	B	C	D	E
75%	21%	4%		

5. What is your reaction to the process of you grading other posters?

A	B	C	D	E
34%	36%	25%	5%	

6. What is your reaction to having other students grade your work?

A	B	C	D	E
37%	38%	15%	8%	1%

7. Overall, how would you rate the effectiveness of the poster session format?

A	B	C	D	E
63%	33%	4%		

8.[a] What percentage of your course grade do you think the poster session should comprise?

% of Grade	0%	10%	15%	20%	25%	30%	Selected
	3%	43%	28%	17%	4%	1%	4%

9. As a student, would you prefer to follow this format or go back to the term paper approach?

Poster	Term Paper	No Answer
93%	0%	7%

Note. A represents a *very positive* response to an item, C is *neutral,* and E is *very negative.* N = 73.
[a]The top row for this item indicates the percentage of the final grade the students think the posters should comprise. *Selected,* in the top row, means the grade value of the poster sessions would vary and students would choose for themselves how much their poster contributes to their final grade. The bottom row indicates the percentage of students preferring a given grade percentage for the poster sessions.

The overall response to the poster sessions was positive as revealed in Table 1. Students indicated that the poster sessions were a valuable activity and that the main goals of the sessions were achieved. Some students expressed ambivalence about grading other students' papers and having their own work graded by peers. Even in these areas, however, the responses were almost all positive.

The clearest indication of support for poster sessions was seen in response to the last item of the survey. When asked if they would prefer to follow the poster session format or the standard term paper approach, 100% of those who responded to the question favored the poster sessions.

References

Baird, B. N., & Anderson, D. D. (1990). Writing in psychology. *The Teaching Professor, 4*(3), 5.
Benjamin, L. T., Jr., Fawl, C. T., & Klein, M. (1977). The fair—Experimental psychology for high school students. *American Psychologist, 32*, 1097–1098.
Chute, D. L., & Bank, B. (1983). Undergraduate seminars: The poster session solution. *Teaching of Psychology, 10*, 99–100.

Note

I thank Gayle Robbins for her assistance in developing the activities described in this article.

The Science Fair: A Supplement to the Lecture Technique

Thomas A. Fish
Ian H. Fraser

Poster sessions and science fairs have been used as substitutes for undergraduate seminar courses (Chute & Bank, 1983) and as devices to educate the public (Benjamin, Fawl, & Klein, 1977). Chute and Bank (1983) found that students responded favorably to poster sessions, indicating that they had learned a great deal from the experience. Benjamin et al. (1977) advocated that the science fair be used as a mechanism to deal with public misconceptions of psychology as a scientific discipline. They pointed out, however, that fairs do not compensate for the lack of appropriate instruction.

Science fairs and poster sessions have two major benefits. First, these organized events, if open to the public, can be an educational experience. Second, they can be an effective learning medium for advanced undergraduate students.

We were interested in studying the possible benefits of the fair for undergraduates in an introductory psychology course. Such benefits might include allowing the student to explore in depth a topic of interest; promoting cooperation and discourse among students, as well as between students and instructors; motivating students to exert more effort in their course work; and allowing for the practical and theoretical exploration of a topic (Fish, 1988). We compared the retrospective impressions of introductory psychology courses for students who did and students who did not experience a fair component.

Description of Science Fair Component

During the first week of classes, students were informed that they would he required to do a major project suitable for presentation at a science fair to be held near the end of the second semester. Their science fair contributions would be worth 30% of their final grade and be based on the quality of individual projects and on contributions to various science fair student committees. The remainder of their course grade would be based on test and final exam performance. From one to three classes (each with approximately 60 students) have participated in the event in any given year.

Individual Projects

To encourage creative expression, we gave students little direction regarding their projects. All topics and formats were welcomed as long as the topic was relevant to psychology and the format involved the active participation of science fair visitors.

After all topics had been approved (by the 6th week of the first semester), classes participating in the science fair attended an information meeting that included a narrated slide presentation focusing on previous science fairs. The meeting was designed to stimulate enthusiasm for the event, give students a clear understanding of the type of space that would be available for individual projects, and provide specific examples of projects that have received both high and low grades.

Committees

Students volunteered to serve on one or more committees. Committee activities included designing a program for visitors, promoting the event, fund-raising, and coordinating procedures for setting up and taking down projects.

171

Class Presentations

Approximately 2 weeks before the science fair, students presented their projects to classmates. This format allowed students to practice their oral presentations and receive suggestions for improving them. They also had a chance to learn about the work of their peers.

The Science Fair

More than 1,000 people have attended the science fair each year. Visitors have included university and high school students, community groups, and the general public. Each student describes his or her project to approximately 100 visitors.

Grading Procedures

A few days after the science fair, students met with instructors to discuss the strengths and weaknesses of their individual efforts and to negotiate a grade.

Examples of Projects

Projects have covered many facets of psychology. One student with a spinal cord injury gave fair visitors an opportunity to negotiate access to campus buildings in a wheelchair. Another student demonstrated a biofeedback machine. Others have built their own tachistoscopes, mazes, and perceptual illusions. Still others chose to share the experience of staying at a shelter for the homeless.

Evaluation Study

Participants

Participants were 3rd- and 4th-year students in upper level psychology classes. Thirty had conducted a science fair project in the previous 3 years, and 80 had experienced other introductory formats.

Materials

Students anonymously reported their retrospective impressions of their introductory psychology course by responding to 14 questionnaire items using a 5-point Likert scale ranging from *not at all* (1) to *to a great degree* (5). They also answered four questions about their pursuit of a major.

Results

Table 1 indicates the mean student ratings for each questionnaire item and the *t* values comparing the science fair students to the students with other course formats. In addition to these findings, 65% of the science fair participants (vs. 41% of other format students) were also more likely to have taken other courses from their introductory psychology instructor, $\chi^2(1, N = 30) = 5.56$, $p < .05$. However, science fair and other format students did not differ in their (a)

Table 1. Mean Student Evaluation Ratings for Science Fair and Other Formats

Item	Science Fair	Other Formats	t
Opportunity to explore interests	36.2	3.14	2.20*[a]
Prepared for other courses	4.03	3.49	2.23*[b]
Understood basic principles	4.00	3.57	1.80*[b]
Principles applied to everyday life	3.97	3.59	1.87*[b]
Course effort	4.20	3.27	2.12*[b]
Learned from text	4.40	3.94	1.83*[a]
Learned from instructor	3.97	3.30	2.05*[a]
Improved oral skills	2.77	2.64	n.s.[b]
Improved written skills	2.57	2.43	n.s.[b]
Discussed with those not enrolled	3.14	2.99	n.s.[a]
Understood research	3.41	3.46	n.s.[a]
Enjoyed class	4.13	3.87	n.s.[b]
Learned from classmates	2.35	2.48	n.s.[a]
Learned from research	3.17	2.74	n.s.[b]

[a]107 *df.* [b]108 *df.*
*$p < .05$.

grade point average (GPA) in psychology, (b) desire to major or to achieve honors in psychology, and (c) desire to pursue a graduate degree or career in psychology.

Discussion

Results indicated that ratings of introductory courses with a science fair component compared favorably with ratings for courses with other formats. Although students missed some regular classes to plan for a science fair, this lost time did not appear to detract from ratings of their learning experience. Science fair participants actually reported a better understanding of psychological principles and their application, as well as better preparation for subsequent psychology courses.

Results also indicated that students gave comparable ratings for improving oral and written skills and providing discussion opportunities. Furthermore, no differences were detected in student ratings of how much they learned from their classmates or from personal research. It is important to note that science fair ratings were compared with combined ratings of collaborative research (Reither & Vipond, 1989) and self-paced (Bourque & Hughes, 1991) courses specifically designed to encourage small-group research and discussion and to provide opportunities for improvement of oral and written skills. Thus, the science fair appears to be a valuable alternative for instructors.

Science fair participants reported exerting more effort and learning more from their textbook and instructor than did students experiencing other formats. They were also more likely to take additional courses from their introductory psychology instructors. Because up to three different instructors have coordinated the science fair in any given year, these results are not likely due to particular instructor characteristics. It appears, therefore, that positive regard for the unique qualities of the science fair generalizes to the instructors involved.

It is important to remember that the results represent differences in student beliefs about the quality of their learning experience and do not necessarily translate into demonstrable learning benefits. Moreover, the sample included no introductory students who did not take more psychology courses. Although science fair courses received higher ratings on a number of indices, science fair participants did not differ from other format students in GPA for subsequent psychology courses or in their desire to pursue further studies. Despite these caveats, results indicate that the science fair is a useful pedagogical tool that can be successfully adapted for introductory courses with a lecture format. It provides a unique and valuable learning experience for students and instructors.

References

Benjamin, L. T., Jr., Fawl, C. L., & Klien, J. (1977). The fair: Experimental psychology for high school students. *American Psychologist, 32,* 1097–1098.

Bourque, W. L., & Hughes, G. R. (1991, June). *The Keller plan still works.* Paper presented at the Annual Conference of the Society for Teaching and Learning in Higher Education, Halifax, Nova Scotia.

Chute, D. L., & Bank, B. (1983). Undergraduate seminars: The poster session solution. *Teaching of Psychology, 10,* 99–100.

Fish, T. A. (1988, June). *Begged, borrowed, and stolen: Nontraditional approaches to teaching.* Paper presented at the Enhancement of University Teaching Conference, Sackville, New Brunswick.

Reither, J. A., & Vipond, D. (1989). Writing as collaboration. *College English, 51,* 855–867.

Note

We gratefully acknowledge the editorial assistance of Daizal Samad and Ruth L. Ault.

Rap Singing as an Icebreaker for Large Classes

E. Rae Harcum

In order to provide small classes for our advanced courses and seminars, our psychology department enrolls up to about 310 students in sections of our introductory courses. Because most students in these large classes are first-year students, an additional burden is placed on the instructor, particularly during the fall term, to create extra exercises and demonstrations that will put new college students at ease and establish rapport.

Wulff, Nyquist, and Abbott (1987) reported that only 18% of the students in their survey preferred classes of more than 200 students. The primary reasons for disliking large classes were limited learning interactions with the instructor and feelings that the instructor could not show an interest and concern for students as individuals.

The purpose of my article is to suggest a way for dealing with similar concerns of students in a large introductory class. The exercise has worked well for me. It requires little time and skill to perform. The instructor sings a brief, self-composed rap song during the first class of the semester. Because this style of singing is popular, it enjoys the familiarity and other advantages of a fad. To the best of my knowledge, no reports of similar approaches have been reported in the literature.

Preparation and Performance

It took me about 15 min to compose the 16-line piece presented later. There is no virtue in agonizing over the writing because the rap loses some of its appeal if it is too tightly written. The purpose of the exercise is not to demonstrate either the compositional or performance skills of the instructor. Great care must be taken to ensure that the exercise does not appear to make the class a captive audience for showcasing the instructor's talents—real or imagined. A mediocre level of performance is probably best for an effective result; a performance that is too inept or too slick may not achieve its purpose. The song itself should convey an educational message to the students in order to maintain its legitimacy as a classroom exercise. It can provide some useful redundancy for an important point in the orientation lecture.

I ask for about six volunteers from the class to provide backup rhythm by hand clapping, along with perhaps a recorded background rhythm. I do not have the confidence to perform without a written script, but suspect that the impact would be greater if the rap were memorized or even composed spontaneously in front of the class. The class is very tolerant when I muff the lines or falter in the rhythm.

A rap that works well for me is the following:

Seeking Help

I'm Professor Harcum and I come here to say,
Psychology class is not the place to play.
For freshman people and the seniors, too,
There's much to learn before you're through.
So keep on working on the syllabus,
To dis that old semester-end fuss,
'Cause life is not all just fun and games,
Before you know it you'll go down in flames.

So if you see you're gonna fall,
Give Professor H a mighty quick call,
Be very sure he will try to please,
But in this place we've no guarantees.
The professors here may be very weird,
But not as bad as you might have feared.
We know the hassles here can get your goat,
Just be sure we know we're in the same darn boat.

Evaluation

Formal evaluation of this demonstration would be superfluous. The most important feedback is immediate, protracted, and thunderous applause as well as rows of revealing smiles.

In addition, students have volunteered comments about the effectiveness of the exercise in reducing first-day tension and anxiety and in creating a positive image of the instructor as a warm, approachable person. One student reported the following strong endorsement: "When you did that rap, you really had us in the palm of your hand." Perhaps even more convincing are the secondhand reports from other persons who have been told about the rap performance. According to such reports, it conveys a sense of enthusiasm by the instructor for the goals of the course and a feeling that the instructor is trying to establish a good relationship with the class. It establishes a tenor for the remainder of the semester.

Discussion

Critics may argue that this exercise is too much like a circus to be appreciated by college students. Although I admit it is a touch theatrical, this exercise is entirely consistent with good principles of teaching and professional behavior. For example, Dewey (1946) and James (1958) emphasized the importance of tying our lessons to the existing motivations of our students. James (1958) expressed this principle in the following way:

Any object not interesting in itself may become interesting through becoming associated with an object in which an interest already exists. The two associated objects grow, as it were, together: the interesting portion sheds its quality over the whole; and thus things not interesting in their own right borrow an interest which becomes as real and as strong as that of any natively interesting thing. (p. 74)

Therefore, James's (1958) advice for teaching a person is clear: "Begin with the line of his native interests, and offer him objects that have some immediate connection with these" (p. 75).

This advice is consistent with my own experience and philosophy of teaching, as a cooperative effort between teacher and student. As many have said, anyone can lay out the facts and principles for the student to learn, but a good teacher induces and enables the student to become receptive to this information. Without such receptivity, the learning is poor indeed.

However, two notes of caution should be emphasized. First, given the effectiveness of rap singing, the instructor will be tempted to use it again when student enthusiasm seems to be flagging. As with all good interest-provoking techniques, it can lose its appeal with overexposure. A second note of caution concerns the instructor's personal style. As Aronson (1987) pointed out, it is unwise to use a teaching style that is inconsistent with one's own personal style. If the instructor is not reasonably comfortable with rapping another icebreaker should be considered. Nevertheless, the students will appreciate the effort if you try.

References

Aronson, J. R. (1987). Six keys to effective instruction in large classes: Advice from a practitioner. In M. G. Weimer (Ed.), *Teaching large classes well* (pp. 31–37). San Francisco: Jossey-Bass.

Dewey, J. (1946). *Problems of men.* New York: Philosophical Library.

James, W. (1958). *Talks to teachers.* New York: Norton. (Original work published 1899)

Wulff, D. H., Nyquist, J. D., & Abbott, R. D. (1987). Student perceptions of large classes. In M. G. Weimer (Ed.), *Teaching large classes well* (pp. 17–30). San Francisco: Jossey-Bass.

Integrating Disability Awareness Into Psychology Courses: Applications in Abnormal Psychology and Perception

Stephen A. Wurst
Karen Wolford

The mandate for higher education to provide education to students "otherwise qualified" who have learning disabilities, emotional problems, and other handicaps was outlined in Section 504 of the Rehabilitation Act of 1973 (Scott, 1990). Accordingly, instructors and nondisabled students should understand the concepts of learning disability and emotional disorder and know the unique needs of people affected by these conditions. This need for understanding is especially important because the number of disabled students attending college has steadily risen. Hippolitus (1987) estimated that 18,300 students with learning disabilities were admitted to colleges in 1985, and another 7% to 20% will experience some type of emotional disorder during their college career.

Increasing disability awareness of nondisabled students and faculty is also vital due to the prevalent stigma of disability. The stigma of mental illness is more prominent and documented (O'Grady, 1988), but the stigma of being physically disabled is also widespread (e.g., Fichten & Amsel, 1988). Burgo (1992) stated that the attitudinal barriers that society holds toward the disabled are far more insidious than structural barriers.

On our campus, the Committee of Services for Students with Disabilities and the Dean of Students Office attempt to heighten awareness through a 2-day Disability Awareness Program. Three major components of the program are as follows: (a) Nondisabled faculty and students can "adopt" a disability for the day, (b) faculty are encouraged to provide classroom activities that increase awareness, and (c) speakers are scheduled to address these issues. Such disability simulations have been used successfully not only in colleges and graduate schools (Glazzard, 1979) but also in high schools (Hallenback & McMaster, 1991) and elementary schools (T. W. Jones, Sowell, J. K. Jones, & Butler, 1981).

Three Program Components

We describe in this article how we incorporated the three components in abnormal psychology and perception courses. We also specify possible discussion topics to be used after each event.

Disability Simulation

Nondisabled individuals could select a visual impairment that simulated macular degeneration (using light-filtered glasses from the Eye Research Institute of Boston that block the central area of the visual field), a hearing deficit (using Flents Model No. 241 sound-reducing earplugs), a motor disability (using a wheelchair, using crutches, or wearing splints on the fingers of their dominant hand), or a psychological disability (not talking for the day). Participants received any equipment they needed for the simulation in the morning and then conducted their daily activities while simulating the disability. At the end of the day, participants returned the equipment and were asked to complete a questionnaire about their experiences. At a reception afterward, the nondisabled students could interact socially with students with disabilities.

In the abnormal psychology course, participants discussed the stigmatizing process (E. Jones et al., 1984), using their experiences as examples. The discussion in the perception course focused on two rationales for studying perception. The first is that senses tend to be taken for granted. Participants related the general difficulties they encountered and

acknowledged the importance of preserving their senses by avoiding high-risk behavior that may result in injuries to the sensory organs. The second rationale is that perception is fundamental to psychology (e.g., Goldstein, 1990). To show the role perception plays in learning and memory, students itemized their difficulties during classes in which they simulated the disability, and they noted the relation between perception and emotion (e.g., Zimbardo, Andersen, & Kabat, 1981).

Classroom Activities

Three activities were used in two abnormal psychology sections (ns = 40 and 90) to introduce the topic of childhood disorders and learning disabilities, such as dyslexia and dysgraphia. One activity included projecting overhead transparencies backward while students attempted to take notes. The second activity instructed students not to say any word containing the letter e (to simulate expressive language disorders). The third activity was a mirror-tracing demonstration (using a Lafayette Instruments Mirror Tracer Model No. 31010) to approximate a learning disorder. Two volunteers attempted to draw a line within the boundaries of a maze while looking at their hand and the maze in a mirror, which reverses the image. Volunteers described the frustration of performing the task.

These activities were intended to give students insight into the emotional aspect of the disorder, rather than the exact experience. The instructor explained how students with learning disabilities face this kind of struggle continuously and how individual differences in learning styles occur in students with and without disabilities. The controversies in dyslexia research (e.g., Solan, Sutija, Ficarra, & Wurst, 1990; Vellutino, 1987) can then be fully described.

Speakers

A third important, although not novel, technique to increase students' awareness is to use speakers who can help students empathize with people with disabilities and understand different disorders. In abnormal psychology, effective speakers have been a person with bipolar disorder and another whose relative committed suicide despite professional treatment. Students can write a reaction paper after hearing the speakers.

Evaluation of the Simulation Activity

From the perception class of 24 students, 18 (11 women, 7 men) students volunteered to participate in exchange for class credit. Twelve students simulated an auditory disability, and 6 simulated a visual disability. The 6 students who did not participate cited scheduling conflicts as the reason.

Students who adopted a disability completed a two-section questionnaire about their experiences. One part was a semantic differential probing the participants' emotional experience during the simulation. Results are presented in Figure 1. For presentation purposes, the positive emotions are listed on the left side of the graph, and the negative

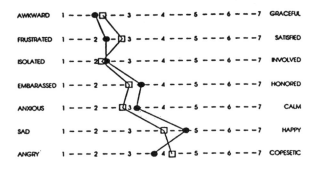

Figure 1. Mean ratings on the semantic differential scales as a function of type of disability simulated (filled circles indicate visual; open squares indicate auditory).

emotions are listed on the right (Sommer & Sommer, 1991).

Visual and auditory participants responded similarly and mostly in the negative direction. The strongest negative reactions were for *awkward* and *isolated*, followed by *frustrated* and *anxious*. Somewhat surprising, the *happy–sad* and the *copesetic–angry* scales were not as intense as the other reactions.

The second part of the questionnaire asked 10 open-ended questions concerning the participants' experiences and their attitudes. Four of these questions are relevant to this article. Did participants see people with disabilities differently after simulating their disability? Participants mentioned the challenges of routine tasks that nondisabled people take for granted ($n = 11$), emotional empathy with people with disabilities ($n = 7$), and the mental and physical strength of people with disabilities ($n = 2$).

Did participants view nondisabled people differently? Participants noted how nondisabled people act toward people with disabilities ($n = 9$), such as being "distant," "judgmental," "not as friendly," and "ignoring." Participants also wrote how "lucky" nondisabled people are ($n = 3$). Such responses support our major goals to have students (a) empathize with people with disabilities, (b) understand the stigma associated with disability, and (c) not to take their senses for granted.

How would the participants change their interactions with people with disabilities? Students said they would be "more sensitive" or "more patient" with people with disabilities ($n = 7$), they would speak louder to hearing-impaired people ($n = 3$), they would offer assistance more ($n = 3$), and they would be more respectful ($n = 2$). One student said the exercise would not change her interactions much because she already respected and interacted with people with disabilities.

How did the simulated disability affect participants' ability to function in class? Not surprising, all auditory disability participants mentioned that they had to listen more closely to the instructor, whereas visual disability participants cited their difficulties in seeing the overheads and chalkboard and in writing notes. Two auditory disability participants mentioned that they became less attentive and had more daydreams; two others reported being distracted by ambient sounds, especially when the class divided into small discussion groups. These results should prompt teachers to be more sensitive to the needs of students with disabilities.

Conclusions

These activities have been used successfully in teaching abnormal psychology and perception. They can also be used in other psychology courses, such as introductory and developmental psychology. Faculty interested in these activities may contact their office that serves students with disabilities to develop demonstrations for the entire college community. We recommend that college curricula address issues concerning the rights and needs of the differently abled in a variety of classroom and extracurricular settings to ensure all members of our society the rights and acceptance they deserve. After structural and attitudinal barriers are eliminated, people with disabilities can flourish and contribute more fully to society and to everyone's self-awareness.

References

Burgo, I. (1992, Spring). Opening doors to dignity. *Villanova Magazine*, pp. 2–7.

Fichten, C., & Amsel, R. (1988). Thoughts concerning interaction between college students who have a disability and their nondisabled peers. *Rehabilitation Counseling Bulletin, 32*, 22–40.

Glazzard, P. (1979). Simulation of handicaps as a teaching strategy for preservice and inservice training. *TEACHING Exceptional Children, 11*, 101–104.

Goldstein, E. B. (1990). *Sensation and perception*. Belmont, CA: Wadsworth.

Hallenback, M. J., & McMaster, D. (1991). Disability simulation for regular education students. *TEACHING Exceptional Children, 23*, 12–15.

Hippolitus, P. (1987). *College freshmen with disabilities preparing for employment*. Washington, DC: President's Committee on Employment of the Handicapped.

Jones, E., Farina, A., Hastorf, A., Markus, H., Miller, D., & Scott, R. (1984). *Social stigma: The psychology of marked relationships*. New York: Freeman.

Jones, T. W., Sowell, V. M., Jones, J. K., & Butler, L. G. (1981). Changing children's perceptions of handicapped people. *Exceptional Children, 47*, 365–368.

O'Grady, T. (1988). Community psychiatry: A changing locus of rejection? *Perspectives in Biology and Medicine, 31*, 324–340.

Scott, S. S. (1990). Coming to terms with the "otherwise qualified" student with a learning disability. *Journal of Learning Disabilities, 23*, 398–405.

Solan, H., Sutija, V., Ficarra, A., & Wurst, S. A. (1990). Binocular advantage and visual processing in dyslexic and control children as measured by visual evoked potentials. *Optometry and Vision Science, 67*, 105–110.

Sommer, B., & Sommer, R. (1991). *A practical guide to behavioral research: Tools and techniques*. New York: Oxford University Press.

Vellutino, F. R. (1987). Dyslexia. *Scientific American, 256*(3), 34–41.

Zimbardo, P. G., Andersen, S. M., & Kabat, L. G. (1981). Induced hearing deficit generates experimental paranoia. *Science, 212*, 1529–1531.

Note

We thank the SUNY–Oswego Learning Enhancement Office, Committee for Services to Students with Disabilities, and the Dean of Students Office, especially Inez Alfors and Kathy Evans. We also thank Monica Everett for her assistance with the literature review, and Barbara Watters, Kevin Wallace, Ruth Ault, and three anonymous reviewers for their helpful comments.

Combining the Use of Progressive Writing Techniques and Popular Movies in Introductory Psychology

Scott H. Hemenover
Jeffrey B. Caster
Ayumi Mizumoto

Although writing assignments are a common feature of introductory psychology, most students in such courses are freshmen and are unfamiliar with how to write college papers. The ambiguity of the writing process may produce anxiety that can attenuate performance. In addition, instructors seldom give students complete control over selection of their paper topics. For example, students may have to read a novel and write a paper discussing psychological concepts found in that novel. Because the instructor typically selects the books before the semester begins, those chosen may not meet the interests of the students and consequently fail to spark their motivation for writing a paper.

We believe the ambiguity of the writing process and the lack of control inherent in traditional paper assignments produces low motivation. Low motivation may result in many students completing a paper the night before it is due. As a result, students may not adequately process and reflect on what they learned, resulting in a less beneficial educational experience.

One way to address these issues is through the use of progressive writing techniques focused on popular movies. Past research has demonstrated that progressive writing (i.e., writing one section of a paper at a time, providing feedback on each section, and allowing students to rewrite each section) improves writing quality and motivation (e.g., Dorazio, 1984; Kalia, 1984; Schierhorn, 1991). In addition, movies promote classroom discussion, enthusiasm, and enjoyment (Bolt, 1976; Conner, 1996; Desforges, 1994); self-reported learning (Conner, 1996; Dorris & Ducey, 1978); and critical thinking (Anderson, 1992). Because combining the use of progressive writing with the benefits of movies should help students improve their writing and increase motivation, we designed a paper assignment utilizing both these elements.

Method

Participants

The sample consisted of 173 students (69 men and 104 women) taking an introductory psychology course at a large Midwestern University. Most students were freshman (65%) or sophomores (23%), with few juniors (10%) or seniors (2%) and few psychology majors (5%).

Materials

Paper assignment. To facilitate writing quality we gave students a three-page tutorial that described a six-step writing process, including descriptions and illustrative examples of all the sections to be covered in the paper. First, students chose a topic in psychology that interested them and turned in a brief description of that topic. Because numerous students chose topics that were too broad for this assignment (e.g., schizophrenia), we provided suggestions as to how they might narrow these topics (e.g., focusing just on the treatment of schizophrenia). We left which aspect of their topic students focused on up to them.

Because summary writing improves text comprehension (e.g., Radmacher & Latosi-Sawin, 1995), students next read about their topic in the textbook and wrote a one-page summary of their reading. Although students could use other resources (e.g., journal articles), we did not require them to do so (and most did not). We checked for conceptual understanding of the relevant topic(s), made corrections when necessary, and returned these summaries to the students.

Third, students chose and viewed a movie relevant to their topic. We list the most frequently chosen topics and movies in Table 1. We instructed students to view the movie several times and to take notes relevant to their topic. We told students to view the movie's depiction of their topic critically and to note discrepancies between the movie and course content. Although most students chose appropriate movies, some did not (e.g., watching *Sybil* [Babbin & Petrie, 1976] for a paper on schizophrenia). We suggested alternative movies to these students or instructed them to continue looking for a more appropriate movie. This situation served as an excellent learning opportunity because many students discussed with us whether a given movie was appropriate for their topic.

Table 1. Student Paper Topics and Related Movies

Topic	Movie
Stress	*Falling Down* (1993)
Dissociative identity disorder	*Sybil* (1976)
	Raising Cain (1992)
Alcoholism	*When A Man Loves A Woman* (1994)
Dreams	*Nightmare On Elm Street* (1985)
Autism	*Rain Man* (1988)
Aggression	*Speed* (1994)
Amnesia	*Regarding Henry* (1991)
Group behavior	*Clueless* (1995)
Schizophrenia	*One Flew Over the Cuckoo's Nest* (1975)
Rape	*The Accused* (1988)
Child development	*Boyz 'n' the Hood* (1991)
Taste aversion	*Dying Young* (1991)
Prejudice	*Man Without A Face* (1993)
Intelligence	*Dumb and Dumber* (1994)
Memory	*Dad* (1989)
Mental retardation	*What's Eating Gilbert Grape* (1993)
Mental illness	*Fisher King* (1991)

Fourth, students wrote a summary of their movie, and we provided editorial feedback. Fifth, students wrote an outline for their paper, including five sections. In the introduction students summarized the major points of their paper, in the topic summary students summarized their reading on their topic, and in the movie summary students summarized their chosen movie. In the integration students discussed appropriate illustrations of their topic as well as any inconsistencies between the movie and course content. Finally, in the conclusion students discussed their personal reactions to what they learned.

We provided editorial feedback on the outlines and returned them to the students. For the sixth step students wrote the final paper. We instructed students that the topic summary, movie summary, and outline should be rewritten versions of the originals, taking into consideration instructor feedback.

Assignment evaluation. We assessed student perceptions of the assignment with several items on an end-of-semester course evaluation. We included three items using a 7-point scale ranging from 1 (*strongly disagree*) to 7 (*strongly agree*) and one item in a multiple choice format that asked whether students had learned more, the same, or less in writing this paper in comparison to past papers.

Paper quality. The percentage of possible paper points earned by each student served as a measure of paper quality.

Results

Most students agreed that completing one section at a time helped them write a high quality paper, and a majority liked choosing their own paper topic (see Table 2). The overall paper performance was good ($Mdn = 85\%$), and the distribution was substantially skewed (i.e., skewness = -1.79) with almost half (44%) the students earning more than 90% of the points. Approximately half the students (48%) believed they learned more writing this paper than they had completing past papers, with a somewhat smaller proportion (44%) responding that they had learned the same as for previous papers. Finally, a third of the students

agreed that they were more motivated for this paper than for previous papers.

Conclusions

These results indicate that our assignment was successful in helping students write quality papers. Students believed the progressive approach improved their writing, they liked having control over their paper topics, and roughly half earned over 90% of the paper points.

Somewhat inconsistent with our expectations, only half of our students believed that their learning was superior compared to past assignments. Considering the favorable grade distribution, this finding is puzzling. It may be that some of our students completed past assignments using progressive writing, as almost half found their learning equivalent to past assignments.

Motivation level was lower than expected. This finding is consistent with self-reported learning and may be due to our students' past experiences with progressive writing. In addition, our measure of motivation may not have been valid. We assessed overall motivation and did not ask about the specific aspects of the assignment expected to increase motivation (e.g., watching a movie). Students may have been unaware that watching a movie had an impact on their overall motivation. Lastly, because only 5% of our students were psychology majors, they may have been reluctant to admit high motivation for any psychology assignment.

To help instructors successfully implement this assignment we have several recommendations. First, the writing steps should be widely spread out across the semester. Students will appreciate the breaks, and the time between writing steps will allow the grader(s) sufficient time to compose conscientious feedback. Second, instructors should allow students to do the assignment in pairs, an arrangement that will reduce the grading burden and may offer further advantages through cooperative learning (Johnson, Johnson, & Holubec, 1990). Finally, some students may choose movies unfamiliar to the instructor(s), making fair grading difficult. To prevent this problem, instructors should encourage the use of popular (feature-length) movies. If students choose an unfamiliar movie, instructors should view it prior to grading the relevant paper(s).

Overall this assignment appears to foster high quality writing and therefore is a useful alternative to the typical paper assignments in introductory psychology courses. Students in such courses may favor watching movies over reading a book, and our data suggest that they appreciate the progressive writing approach. In addition, because identifying incorrect representations of psychological phenomenon in movies may engage critical thinking, more advanced courses may also benefit from this and similar assignments.

References

Anderson, D. D. (1992). Using feature films as tools for analysis in a psychology and law course. *Teaching of Psychology, 19,* 155–158.

Table 2. Student Responses to End of Semester Course Evaluation

Item	Agree (%)	Strongly Agree (%)	Total (%)
Doing the paper a section at a time helped me write a high quality paper.	31.3	28.9	60.2
I was more motivated to do the paper assignment than in previous classes with a paper assignment.	24.4	13.4	37.8
I liked being able to choose my own paper topic.	39.0	46.3	85.3

Note. The data in this table represent the two most positive options on our 7-point scale.

Babbin, J. (Executive Producer), & Petrie, D. (Director). (1976). *Sybil* [Videotape]. (Available from CBS/Fox Video)

Bolt, M. (1976). Using movies based on literature in teaching psychology. *Teaching of Psychology, 3,* 189–190.

Conner, D. B. (1996). From Monty Python to *Total Recall*: A feature movie activity for the cognitive psychology course. *Teaching of Psychology, 23,* 33–35.

Desforges, D. M. (1994). Applying theories of development: An exercise for teaching adolescent psychology. *Teaching of Psychology, 21,* 245–246.

Dorazio, P. A. (1984). Teaching composition: A way to improve it. *Community College Review, 12,* 29–31.

Dorris, W., & Ducey, R. (1978). Social psychology and sex roles in films. *Teaching of Psychology, 5,* 168–169.

Johnson, D. W., Johnson, R. T., & Holubec, E. J. (1990). *Cooperation in the classroom.* Edina, MN: Interaction Book.

Kalia, N. N. (1984). The sociological book review. *Teaching Sociology, 11,* 213–217.

Radmacher, S. A., & Latosi-Sawin, E. (1995). Summary writing: A tool to improve student comprehension and writing in psychology. *Teaching of Psychology, 22,* 113–115.

Schierhorn, A. B. (1991). The role of the writing coach in the magazine curriculum. *Journalism Educator, 46,* 46–53.

Note

Portions of this article were presented at the 69th annual meeting of the Midwestern Psychological Association in Chicago on May 8–10, 1997.

From the Laboratory to the Headlines: Teaching Critical Evaluation of Press Reports of Research

Patricia A. Connor-Greene

Undergraduate education in psychology should help students understand scientific methodology and improve their critical thinking. These are important skills, given the frequency with which research findings are reported in the mass media. People tend to perceive the press as an objective source of information, despite the fact that subjective decisions determine what is reported (Howitt, 1982). Constrained by space limitations, newspaper and magazine depictions of research findings often omit essential information that would permit the reader to evaluate adequately the strength of the research conclusions. News summaries often distort research findings by sensationalizing the results, minimizing discussion of the research limitations, and confusing correlation with causation (Jacobs & Eccles, 1985).

The distinction between correlation and causation is essential to understanding research methods and statistics (Boneau, 1990). Although a recent analysis indicated that correlational designs are discussed in 87% of introductory psychology textbooks (Hendricks, Marvel, & Barrington, 1990), I often hear upper level students make causal statements when describing correlational studies. The frequency of this error highlights the need to develop teaching strategies that emphasize this important distinction.

The exercise described in this article involves a collaborative, active-learning task in which students use information about the scientific method to analyze a newspaper account of a research study. The technique is designed to increase students' awareness of the distinction between correlation and causation and to encourage them to become critical consumers of research reported in the popular press. I use this exercise in abnormal psychology classes, but it is also appropriate for introductory psychology and other courses that address research methods.

The Class Exercise

Students are given a homework assignment to study the research methods chapter in their textbook and be prepared to discuss these concepts in class. During the next class period, each student is assigned to a small group of 4 or 5 people. One member of each group serves as recorder, and each group member is expected to participate in the small-group discussion. Every student is given a copy of an article from *USA TODAY* titled, "Gay Men Show Cell Distinction" (Snider, 1991; see Appendix) and the following list of questions to be addressed by the group.

1. What conclusion does this article imply? What statements in the article suggest this conclusion?
2. Is this conclusion warranted by the study described? Why or why not?
3. Is the title an accurate summary of the study described? Why or why not?
4. Can this study "prove . . . being gay or lesbian is not a matter of choice," as the task force spokesman suggests? Why or why not?
5. What questions do you have after reading this article?
6. If you had the power to create guidelines for the press's reporting of a research study, what would you recommend?

Class Discussion

After each group addresses these questions (which takes approximately 40 min), the entire class reconvenes to discuss the group responses. At this point, I provide excerpts, via overhead projector, from the original research article published in *Science* (LeVay, 1991) that is the subject of the *USA TODAY* article. Students identify omissions and distortions in the newspaper's account of the original research study. By examining both the newspaper article and the original research report, they can now identify flaws or unanswered questions in the original study and recognize any misrepresentation of the research in the newspaper article.

Usually the small-group responses to the questions are very similar. All groups interpret the newspaper article (Snider, 1991) as implying that male homosexuality is caused by smaller brain cell nuclei. They cite the statements "The debate over the *roots* of homosexuality has been going on a long time, but this finding 'suggests a *biological phenomenon*'" (p. 1D) and "It might explain '*why* male homosexuality is present in most human populations'" (p. 1D) [all italics added] as suggesting causality.

In deciding whether this implication of causality is warranted by the research study as described, students discuss the requirements for a true experimental design. They recognize LeVay's (1991) study as a correlational design because it simply identifies a relation between size of brain cell nuclei and sexual orientation. Discussing alternative interpretations of this association (e.g., sexual orientation could affect size of brain cell nuclei, rather than the reverse; the differences may be caused by a third variable) helps to clarify the seriousness of the error of confusing correlation and causation.

Students note two problems with the title of the newspaper article. First, they think the title suggests that all cells are different in gay men, but the news article refers only to brain cell nuclei. (The difference is actually much more specific than implied in the news article; it is only one area of the anterior hypothalamus.) Second, the title suggests that gay men are the "different" ones, but the article reports gay men's brain cell nuclei to be similar in size to those of women. Consequently, the "different" ones are actually the heterosexual men. Then we discuss the political and social context in which *normal* and *deviant* are defined and how subjectivity and bias can occur in the formulation of research questions and in the interpretation and reporting of findings.

The quote from the news article (Snider, 1991) that the study can "prove . . . being a gay or lesbian is not a matter of choice" (p. 1D) provides an excellent opportunity to discuss the nature of scientific experimentation and the inappropriateness of the term *prove* in science.

Students generate questions after reading the news article (Snider, 1991), setting the stage for discussion of the specifics of LeVay's (1991) study. After obtaining information from LeVay's article, students are able to identify limitations in the study itself. (For example, the heterosexual men were "presumed" to be heterosexual; for all but two of them, there was no available information on sexual orientation; there was no comparison of heterosexual and homosexual women; the actual cause of death can vary greatly among AIDS patients; and the brain cell nuclei differences could be a result of the disease process itself.)

Students always ask "How did this study get published? How could a respectable scientist confuse correlation and causation?" At this point, I show them several quotes from LeVay's (1991) article in which he pointed out the speculative and preliminary nature of his research, identified limitations of his study, and emphasized that it is correlational and does not permit causal inferences. Then students see that the *USA TODAY* article (Snider, 1991) sensationalizes LeVay's results and that Snider, not LeVay, confused correlation with causation.

In addition, I show the students the following excerpt from "Is Homosexuality Biological?" (1991), which appeared in the same issue of *Science* as LeVay's (1991) article.

> Lest eager believers jump to too many conclusions, LeVay points out that his finding *contains no direct evidence that the difference he has observed actually causes homosexuality*. He and others in the field acknowledge that the paper *needs replication*, since such studies are difficult and somewhat subjective. "Simon is very good; he's extremely well-equipped to make those observations," said one neuroscientist who is familiar with LeVay's work. *"But we ought to put off big speculation until it is confirmed."* (p. 956) [all italics added]

Clearly, speculation was not put off until LeVay's (1991) findings were replicated; the study was widely reported in the print media and on the network news. Nearly all the students in my class had heard or read about this study and were surprised to learn that the research did not address causality. The extensive media coverage, contrasted with the preliminary nature of the research itself, helps students recognize that factors other than scientific merit may determine degree of media attention and that science and the reporting of science are not value-free.

Students generated recommendations for changing the press's approach to reporting scientific research. These recommendations included discussing limitations of studies, improving accuracy of headlines, distinguishing between correlational and experimental studies, providing a full reference citation to enable the reader to locate the original research article, and making the degree of media attention proportional to the scientific strength of the study.

Individual Assignment

After completing the class exercise, students were individually assigned to find a newspaper or magazine summary of research and compare it to the original journal article. Their written critiques assessed the accuracy of the popular press article and discussed important omissions or distortions in the popular press article (e.g., limitations of the study and accuracy of the title).

Because some popular press articles contain serious distortions and others are accurate summaries, this assignment helps students become critical evaluators rather than simply dismissing all popular press articles as flawed. Several weeks are needed for this assignment. Most students reported that although press summaries of research were easy to find, many of these articles failed to include a citation sufficient to locate the original article.

Evaluation and Conclusions

The day after participating in the class exercise, students ($N = 33$) anonymously completed a four-item questionnaire using a scale ranging from *very much so* (1) to *not at all* (5). The items and mean ratings are as follows: (a) This exercise gave me a clearer understanding of correlational research ($M = 1.70$), (b) this exercise will help me evaluate media reports of research more critically in the future ($M = 1.55$), (c) this exercise was interesting ($M = 1.61$), and (d) it was helpful to work in groups for the class exercise ($M = 1.61$). Students' written comments, such as "It gives me a good idea of how to look at articles critically," "newspaper articles need to be examined much more closely than I've done previously," and "this will help me remember the difference between correlational and experimental studies," suggested positive aspects of the exercise. Students were also asked for written comments after completing their individual assignment. Overall, students perceived the assignment as valuable.

The class exercise and individual assignment encourage students to apply information learned in class to their outside experiences (i.e., reading the newspaper), which makes their learning more personally relevant. The exercises help students understand why the popular press is not an appropriate source of information to be used in writing term papers. The fact that the press typically emphasizes results and not methods convinces students that they can properly evaluate the strengths and weaknesses of a study only after examining the original source. Greater awareness of the importance of precision in reporting research methods and findings should encourage students to be more critical of information they read in newspapers, journal articles, and textbooks.

References

Boneau, C. A. (1990). Psychological literacy: A first approximation. *American Psychologist, 45*, 891–900.

Hendricks, B., Marvel, M. K., & Barrington, B. L. (1990). The dimensions of psychological research. *Teaching of Psychology, 17*, 76–82.

Howitt, D. (1982). *Mass media and social problems.* New York: Pergamon.

Is homosexuality biological? (1991). *Science, 253*, 956–957.

Jacobs, J., & Eccles, J. (1985). Gender differences in math ability: The impact of media reports on parents. *Educational Researcher, 14*(3), 20–25.

LeVay, S. (1991). A difference in hypothalamic structure between heterosexual and homosexual men. *Science, 253*, 1034–1037.

Snider, M. (1991, August 30). Gay men show cell distinction. *USA TODAY*, p. 1D.

Notes

1. I thank Charles L. Brewer, Ruth L. Ault, and the anonymous reviewers for their helpful comments.
2. Requests for reprints should be sent to Patricia A. Connor-Greene, Department of Psychology, Clemson University, Clemson, SC 29634–1511.

Appendix

Gay Men Show Cell Distinction
By Mike Snider
USA TODAY

A new study of the brain suggests a biological difference between homosexual and heterosexual men.

The debate over the roots of homosexuality has been going on a long time, but this finding "suggests a biological phenomenon," says neurologist Dennis Landis, Case Western Reserve University, Cleveland, in comments accompanying the study in today's *Science*.

It might explain "why male homosexuality is present in most human populations, despite cultural constraints."

In a study of the brain cells from 41 people, 25 of whom had died from AIDS, certain brain cells of heterosexual men had nuclei that were more than twice as large as those in homosexual men, says researcher Simon LeVay, Salk Institute for Biological Studies.

The difference was apparently not caused by AIDS, because it was constant in a comparison of cells from heterosexual and homosexual male AIDS victims. LeVay also found homosexual men's cells similar in size to women's.

Robert Bray, spokesman for National Gay and Lesbian Task Force, called the study "fascinating."

"If used ethically, (it) can shed light on human sexuality and prove what we've always believed—being a gay or lesbian is not a matter of choice.

"Used unethically, the data could reinforce the political agenda of anti-gay groups that advocate 'curing' or 'repairing' homosexuals—the notion that gay people could be made straight by tweaking a chromosome here or readjusting a cell there."

Note

A Sweet Way to Teach Students About the Sampling Distribution of the Mean

Jennifer L. Dyck
Nancy R. Gee

Although statistical textbooks usually provide an example of constructing a sampling distribution of the mean, these examples are often abstract and require the student to conceptualize the process of selecting a number of samples of a certain size from a theoretical population. Zerbolio (1989) suggested one technique for presenting examples of sampling distributions, in which the instructor uses imaginary bags of marbles and chips to demonstrate the concepts. Although this technique may allow students to more easily visualize the process of creating sampling distributions, some may still have difficulty understanding the process and

may respond more readily to a concrete, hands-on example. Concrete examples increase understanding of abstract, scientific concepts (Brown & Kane, 1988; Chen, Yanowitz, & Daehler, 1995) because students are more likely to pay attention to and use relevant information from examples, as compared to attending to and using relevant information from abstract instructions (LeFevre & Dixon, 1986), Therefore, we developed a hands-on, in-class demonstration, during which students create an actual sampling distribution of the mean using M&M's®. To test the effectiveness of our concrete example, we compared performance and attitudes of two statistics classes, with one class receiving the M&M demonstration and the other class receiving equivalent instruction using a textbook example.

Method

Participants

A total of 63 undergraduate students (14 men, 49 women) enrolled in a sophomore-level introductory statistics course in the Psychology Department at the State University of New York, College at Fredonia participated for partial course credit. We treated all participants ethically (American Psychological Association, 1992). The control group as well as the experimental group received the M&M's, the content of the information presented was equivalent in the two groups, and they had the same textbook as a reference. Therefore the control group was not deprived of information that could have affected their final grade in the course.

Materials

We used forty-eight 1.69-oz packages of plain M&M's in this experiment. The students had their own calculators, and an overhead projector displayed a table of random numbers.

We constructed a class survey for assessing student attitudes toward the demonstration. The survey included four questions on assessment of learning, three questions on enjoyment of class, and two questions on negative feelings. We included questions on negative feelings primarily to avoid a positive response bias. The instructor referred to the textbook example as a demonstration in lecture so that the same survey questions were appropriate for both the textbook example and the M&M demonstration. Students answered all questions using a 7-point Likert scale ranging from 1 (*completely disagree* or *not at all*) to 7 (*completely agree* or *very well*).

We constructed a quiz consisting of 10 questions about the sampling distribution of the mean. Nine of the questions were multiple choice, and one question was a fill-in-the-blank question. The following is an example question:

When constructing a distribution of the means, the larger the sample size, the ____ the distribution of the means will be ____.
a.) more likely, rectangular
b.) less likely, rectangular
c.) more likely, normal
d.) less likely, normal
e.) the question is irrelevant because the distribution of the means is always the same shape regardless of sample size.

One additional question at the end of the quiz asked whether the student was repeating the class.

Design and Procedure

The participants in this study were enrolled in one of two sections of a statistics course taught by the same instructor. One section was randomly assigned to the experimental condition; the other section to the control condition. In the experimental class, 7 were repeating the course. In the control class, 4 were repeating the course. The two classes were not statistically different from each other, as measured by scores on their first exam prior to the experiment (control: $M = 74.49$, $SD = 8.84$; experimental: $M = 77.66$, $SD = 12.44$), $t(66) = 1.21$, $p > .05$. This analysis included all students in both classes, including repeating students. Both classes had progressed to the same place in the course syllabus. On the day of the experiment, 34 students attended the experimental class, and 29 students attended the control class.

Both classes received the same lecture on the sampling distribution of the mean. Midway through the lecture, the experimental group received the M&M demonstration (described subsequently), and the control group received a textbook example (described subsequently). Following the lecture, both groups completed the quiz and then the class survey. Students did not know how they had performed on the quiz when they completed the class survey. Students in the control condition each received a package of M&M's after handing in their quiz and survey.

M&M demonstration. All students received one package of M&M's. They opened their packages, separated their M&M's according to color, counted the number of M&M's of each color, and recorded these numbers. After recording the numbers, students could eat the M&M's.

The students determined the color of the M&M's used in the demonstration (blue) by class vote. The instructor arbitrarily chose a sample size of 5 because of time constraints. At this point, the instructor raised the issue of sample size, pointing out that larger sample sizes are better, but time constraints made this small sample size necessary. Students then numbered off, beginning with 1 for the first student and ending with the last student. The instructor displayed a table of random numbers with the overhead projector. Beginning at a random line in the random number table, the instructor read five numbers one at a time, and the appropriate students reported the number of blue M&M's in their package. The instructor wrote these five numbers on the chalkboard, and each student calculated the mean of those five numbers. The instructor drew the axes of a histogram on the chalkboard, plotting the mean of the first sample on the histogram as one data point. We used sampling with replacement for this demonstration, therefore the instructor generated the next sample of five numbers in the same manner. The instructor again wrote the numbers from this second sample on the chalkboard, and the students in the class calculated the mean for that sample. The instructor then plotted this second mean on the histogram. The instructor followed this procedure for approximately 20 samples of size five. Because this demonstration uses sampling with replacement, this demonstration is also successful with small class sizes. At this point, the overall shape of the distribution began to emerge. Students then calculated the mean of the 20 sample means. This number represented the estimate of the mean of the sampling distribution of the mean (expected value).

The students individually reported the number of blue M&M's they had. They then calculated the mean of the population of blue M&M's for the class. As expected, the mean of the population of blue M&M's was almost the same as the estimate of the mean of the sampling distribution. The mean of the sampling distribution is not always exactly equivalent to the population mean with this demonstration, but typically, there are only small differences. If the two means are not exactly equivalent, the instructor can take the opportunity to discuss the impact of sample size and the number of samples drawn.

After the class calculated the mean of the population, the instructor continued with the lecture emphasizing the following main points:

1. The mean of the sampling distribution of the mean is the same as the population mean.
2. The variance of the sampling distribution of the mean is always smaller than that of the population.
3. The shape of the sampling distribution of mean is normal (unimodal and symmetrical).

The M&M demonstration took approximately 30 min.

Textbook example. To create an informationally equivalent example, we used an example from chapter 7, "Hypothesis Tests with Means of Samples" in the statistics textbook required for the course (see Figure 7–3, Aron & Aron, 1994, p. 183). This example described the process of constructing a sampling distribution of means using the same procedure involved in the M&M demonstration except that the content of the example involved numbering hypothetical ping pong balls instead of physically counting M&M's. In both the M&M demonstration and the textbook example, the instructor drew a histogram on the chalkboard and detailed the process of sampling and calculating means. As in the M&M demonstration, the instructor emphasized the three main points of the lecture following the example.

Results and Discussion

Quiz Results

We scored the quizzes, calculated the total number of correct answers for each student, and analyzed these data using an independent samples t test. We excluded data from students who were repeating the course. The results revealed that the experimental group ($M = 7.96$, $SD = 1.43$) performed significantly better than the control group ($M = 6.72$, $SD = 2.01$) on the quiz, $t(50) = 2.59$, $p < .05$.

Survey Results

We analyzed the attitude survey data with a two-way mixed model ANOVA. The between subjects variable was learning condition (control or experimental), and the within subjects variable consisted of the nine survey questions. We eliminated one student from this analysis who did not complete all of the questions on the survey, leaving a total of 62 participants. The main effect of learning condition, $F(1, 60) = 36.73$, $p < .01$, the main effect of questions, $F(8, 480) = 133.76$, $p < .01$, and the interaction, $F(8, 480) = 18.70$, $p < .01$, were all significant. We conducted simple main effects analyses on the interaction because it was significant and because it contains the effect of interest here. The simple main effects analyses presented in Table 1 show that the experimental group rated each of the Assessment of Learning questions significantly higher than did the control group. It appears from the students' assessments that those who participated in the M&M demonstration believed they learned more about the distribution of the mean than those who received the textbook example. For the enjoyment of class questions, the experimental group had higher ratings

Table 1. Summary of the Simple Main Effects Analysis of the Significant Instruction by Questions Interaction

| | | Instruction Group | | | |
| | | Experimental | | Control | |
	F	M	SD	M	SD
Assessment of learning					
I learned more today than usual in this class.	6.15*	4.82	1.19	4.07	1.18
I think that today's demonstration made the concepts we covered much more clear than is typically true of this class.	32.64*	5.79	1.00	3.96	1.50
How well do you think you understand the distribution of the means?	15.65*	5.62	0.74	4.70	0.92
How helpful was today's demonstration in understanding the distribution of the means?	25.48*	6.35	0.85	5.04	1.20
Enjoyment of class					
Today's class was more fun than the typical day in Dr. Gee's statistics class.	29.91*	5.79	1.15	4.07	1.33
Today's class stands out as a particularly good class in comparison to the average class in statistics.	27.94*	5.50	1.14	3.89	1.26
How much did you enjoy today's demonstration of the distribution of the means?	40.50*	6.24	0.89	4.57	1.17
Negative feelings					
I felt like I was wasting my time today.	16.31*	1.11	0.33	2.07	1.33
I was more bored than usual today in class.	11.61*	1.38	0.74	2.42	1.60

Note. All F scores have df = (1, 60). Students rated questions on a 7-point Likert scale ranging from 1 (*disagree completely* or *not at all*) to 7 (*agree completely* or *extremely helpful*).
*p < .05.

for each of these questions than did the control group. This finding suggests that the students enjoyed the M&M demonstration more than the textbook example. Additionally, the experimental group rated the negative feelings questions significantly lower than the control group. This result suggests that the experimental group felt significantly more positive about the demonstration than did the control group and also that there was not a positive response bias in the data. This pattern of the experimental group rating the assessment of learning questions and the enjoyment of class questions high, as compared to the low ratings of the control group, followed by the two groups reversing their ratings for the negative feelings questions, explains the significant interaction. Overall, the survey data suggest that, according to the students' own opinions, they learned more, enjoyed class more, and felt more positive when they participated in the M&M demonstration as compared to the textbook example demonstration.

These results indicate that the students viewed the M&M demonstration as a fun and effective way to learn about the sampling distribution of the mean. Additionally, the results from the quiz provide an objective measure that indicates that the students did learn more from the M&M demonstration than from the textbook example.

Conclusions

It appears that the M&M demonstration is an effective way to convey the theoretical concept of the sampling distribution of the mean to statistics students. The instructor can also expand this demonstration to include a concrete example of variability. When the students calculate the population mean (i.e., the entire class), they can also calculate the population standard deviation and compare it to

the standard error of the mean, which the students can calculate from the sample means generated in class. This part of the demonstration also works well for us, but we sometimes delete it due to time constraints, as in the experiment presented here. In addition to using M&M's for teaching students about sampling distributions, M&M's are also effective for teaching students about basic sampling concepts (Smith, in press). Besides the educational benefits of using M&M's for demonstrating sampling concepts and distributions, another positive aspect is that students have consistently mentioned to us that they enjoy receiving candy in class from their instructor!

References

American Psychological Association. (1992). Ethical principles of psychologists and code of conduct. *American Psychologist, 47,* 1597–1611.

Aron, A., & Aron, E. N. (1994). *Statistics for psychology.* Englewood Cliffs, NJ: Prentice Hall.

Brown, A. L., & Kane, M. J. (1988). Preschool children can learn to transfer: Learning to learn and learning from example. *Cognitive Psychology, 20,* 493–523.

Chen, A., Yanowitz, K. L., & Daehler, M. W. (1995). Constraints on accessing abstract source information: Instantiation of principles facilitates children's analogical transfer. *Journal of Educational Psychology, 87,* 445–454.

LeFevre, J., & Dixon, P. (1986). Do written instructions need examples? *Cognition & Instruction, 3,* 1–30.

Smith, R. A. (in press). A tasty sample(r): Teaching about sampling using M&M's. In L. T. Benjamin, Jr., B. F. Nodine, R. M. Ernst, & C. Blair-Broeker (Eds.), *Activities handbook for the teaching of psychology* (Vol. 4). Washington, DC: American Psychological Association.

Zerbolio, D. J., Jr. (1989). A "bag of tricks" for teaching about sampling distributions. *Teaching of Psychology, 16,* 207–209.

"The Eye of the Beholder": A Classroom Demonstration of Observer Bias

Miriam D. Goldstein
J. Roy Hopkins
Michael J. Strube

Human beings are neither objective nor accurate processors of information: We often see what we want or expect to see and tend to remember information that is consistent with our schemas or expectations (Mischel, Ebbesen, & Zeiss, 1976; Snyder & Swann, 1978; Snyder & Uranowitz, 1978). In other words, prior theories or hypotheses have a strong impact on the processing of new information.

Biases in human perception have important implications for scientific research. The researcher, being human, is not immune to such bias. Indeed, extensive research has demonstrated that hypotheses held by researchers can have a strong influence on the obtained data (Anderson, 1983; Rosenthal, 1963; Rosenthal & Rosnow, 1969). Thus, it is not surprising that issues of experimenter bias and observer fallacies are often highlighted in psychology courses of all levels (see Aronson, Ellsworth, Carlsmith, & Gonzales, 1990; Neale & Liebert, 1986).

We created a demonstration in which students experienced directly the powerful effects of observer bias. We led students to believe that they would be monitoring the self-report accuracy of a subject (actually a trained confederate) who was expected to display a decrease in performance across trials due to alcohol consumption. Students reported a trend that was consistent with the expectancy yet was not present in the behavior observed; the confederate actually drank apple juice and displayed consistent behavior across trials.

Format of the Demonstration

Participants and Procedure

Students in an experimental psychology class were led to believe that they would observe a demonstration of subject response bias. We explained that researchers such as Nisbett and Wilson (1977) suggested that self-report is often inaccurate, thus rendering the validity of measures based on self-report questionable. We told students that a subject would be unable to report accurately an obvious decrement in performance due to alcohol consumption. In other words, we suggested that students would be more objective than the subject, or less likely to display a bias, in reporting the subject's level of performance.

After being told that she was about to participate in a study of motor coordination, the subject (a trained confederate) engaged in three trials of a mirror-tracing task (see Mednick, 1964). In this task, subjects must trace within the outline of a double-lined star with only a mirror's reflection to guide them. The subject was instructed to trace the pattern with a pencil while looking only at the mirror, not directly at her hand or the pattern. The subject used her right hand and traced clockwise. At the beginning of each trial, the subject placed the point of her pencil between the boundaries of the figure at an indicated starting point. When signalled by the experimenter, she began tracing the figure as rapidly as possible, trying not to go out of the boundary lines. At first, this task is very difficult. With practice, however, one becomes able to fill in the star quite easily (Mednick, 1964). To assure consistent performance across trials, the confederate was trained before the demonstration to maintain a constant rate and constant number of errors (i.e., number of times she crossed the outline of the star). Despite such training, slight performance changes could occur in the actual demonstration. Moreover, one runs the risk that the tracings will vary in a consistent manner (e.g., become worse across trials). Thus, it is advisable to obtain quality ratings of the tracings from objective judges after the demonstration. Another limitation of this variation is that our confederates had a difficult time keeping their performance consistent while following a verbal and nonverbal script.

To avoid these difficulties, we have also run the demonstration with pretraced stars so that the confederate needs only to concentrate on time to complete the task. All three stars are identical. To assure that the tracings are not obviously identical, each tracing is rotated clockwise (i.e., the master tracing is copied onto the other forms at a different angle). Students do not suspect that the tracings are not actually completed during the demonstration (their view of pencil–paper contact is obstructed). However, to reduce potential suspicion, we invite students to attempt the tracing task, using blank forms pulled from a drawer (this procedure also serves to illustrate the difficulty of the task). The pretraced forms are located at the bottom of the pile of forms and, with a little sleight of hand, can be easily placed on the apparatus during the demonstration.

We provided our confederate with a detailed script for her behavior. Once she began to trace, she counted silently for 20 s, remarked "okay," counted another 20 s, smiled, counted another 20 s, and remarked "This isn't easy" (during Trial 1), "This is hard" (during Trial 2), and "This is difficult" (during Trial 3). She then counted another 20 s, laughed, counted another 20 s, and announced that she was finished. The confederate's performance on each trial was inconspicuously timed to assure equivalent performance time across trials.

Before each trial, the confederate consumed what students believed was a mixture of rum and cola. To reduce possible suspicion and increase realism, the drinks were prepared in class, using a can of cola, a shot glass, and a rum bottle actually containing apple juice. After each trial, the traced star was passed around for students to see. Students were then given a questionnaire that asked them to "rate the effect of the alcohol on the subject's speech and behavior" and to "rate the effect of alcohol on the subject's performance." Students were provided with a 10-point scale ranging from *no effect* (1) to *strong effect* (10) and were instructed to circle the number that corresponded to their answers. Students were instructed not to put their names on the questionnaires. The answer sheets were collected after each trial. The confederate completed what students believed to be similar ratings; presumably, her answers were to be used to assess the accuracy of her self-reports. Actually, the confederate circled random responses.

In order to give the "alcohol" time to take effect, the confederate was given a 15-min break after each trial. During this time, we proceeded with class activities.

After the final trial and collection of all answer sheets, we revealed that in this demonstration we expected the students, not the subject, to exhibit bias. We explained that the subject was in fact a trained confederate and that she had not consumed alcohol. We also told the students that we planned to analyze their answers to see whether they had indeed displayed an observer bias. We described what pattern of results would offer support for a bias and what pattern would offer support for objective rating. During the next class period, which focused on experimenter and subject biases, we presented the results described in the following section.

Results

Overview

In this section, we present empirical evaluation of two variations of the demonstration that we have used in past years. In the first variation (hereafter Demonstration 1), the confederate is actually performing the tracing task. We recommend using Demonstration 1 if the students will have a clear view of the tracing apparatus. In the second variation of the demonstration (hereafter Demonstration 2), the tracings are objectively identical.

Demonstration 1

The confederate's performance times for the three trials were highly consistent (Trial 1 = 1.46 min, Trial 2 = 1.39 min, and Trial 3 = 1.41 min). Students' ratings of the effects of alcohol on the confederate's speech, behavior, and performance were analyzed using a repeated measures analysis of variance (ANOVA). Significant linear trends were found for speech and behavior ($M_1 = 1.29$, $M_2 = 1.60$, and $M_3 = 3.00$), $F(1, 13) = 10.95$, $p < .006$; and for performance ($M_1 = 1.43$, $M_2 = 2.14$, and $M_3 = 4.07$), $F(1, 13) = 18.91$, $p < .001$. Thus, students rated the effect of alcohol as increasing across the trials for speech, behavior, and performance.

Demonstration 2

We ran this variation in two sections of an experimental psychology class. Because the results did not differ across sections, the following results refer to both sections combined.

The confederate's performance times for the three trials were highly consistent (Trial 1 = 2.18 min, Trial 2 = 2.20 min, and Trial 3 = 2.17 min). Students' ratings of the effects of alcohol on the confederate's speech, behavior, and performance were analyzed using a repeated measures ANOVA. Significant linear trends were found for speech and behavior ($M_1 = 1.50$, $M_2 = 2.69$, and $M_3 = 2.85$), $F(1, 26) = 19.90$, $p < .001$; and for performance ($M_1 = 2.30$, $M_2 = 3.30$, and $M_3 = 4.70$), $F(1, 26) = 19.89$, $p < .001$. As in Demonstration 1, students rated the effect of alcohol as increasing across the trials for speech, behavior, and performance.

Evaluation

Following the discussion, students completed an anonymous questionnaire reporting whether they personally succumbed to observer bias and whether they thought the deception involved in the demonstration was justified. The purpose of this questionnaire was twofold. First, it allowed us to assure that students were not upset or anxious about being deceived. Second, it allowed us to examine whether students were convinced that they individually succumbed to the observer bias. We think that the responses to these questions revealed that the demonstration was effective. In a recent class, 25 of 27 students agreed that their expectations influenced their observations, and all students thought that the deception was justified. One student wrote: "Although we can learn through lecture that we are all biased, you just *proved* it to us. You couldn't have done that without deception." Another student commented: "I'm glad I was fooled. I'll scrutinize and think more when I plan an experiment. I want to avoid these flaws."

Discussion

Both variations of our demonstration allow students to experience personally the powerful effects of prior expectations on perception. Results verify that our demonstrations are effective in producing an observer bias.

This demonstration is an excellent tool to use in both experimental and introductory psychology classes. Although bias in information processing is a well-established finding, we believe that students were more appreciative of this effect after they experienced it personally. The demonstration has led easily into a discussion of both experimenter and subject biases and other experimentation issues, such as reliability and validity of measures. For example, we pointed out that students served as the measurement instrument in this demonstration. They were to observe and record a subject's behavior and performance. Were their measurements valid? Probably not: The students' measurement of the confederate's behavior and performance was biased by their expectations and thus did not reflect the actual behavior and performance. It follows that their recordings were not a valid measure of the confederate's behavior, because they did not measure what they set out to measure. Similarly, to the extent that the students' bias reflects random and, thus, nonreplicable variance, the students' measurements were not reliable. The effects of expectations on perception outside of the lab (e.g., stereotypes) can also be discussed.

Students have eagerly shared their thoughts about why they fell prey to the bias, often providing specific examples of neutral behaviors that they had processed in an expectation-consistent manner. For example, one student commented that, during the final trial, he had thought that a smile indicated "tipsiness." Similarly, a student noted that she now realized that a comment made by the confederate during the last trial ("this is difficult") was not different from a comment made in an earlier trial ("this is hard"). At the time of the demonstration, however, she had thought that the comment in the last trial indicated greater difficulty in performance, which she had attributed to the alcohol consumption.

Students also remarked on how they actively distorted their reports. One student commented that, even when she thought there was no difference in performance, she rationalized that there must be a difference. She ignored certain things that the subject did at times but noticed and exaggerated their meaning at other times. Such comments can be used to illustrate the difference between demand characteristics (i.e., subjects report what they think the experimenter wants to hear) and observer bias (subjects see what they expect to see), both of which contribute to explaining the results of our demonstration. Another student noted that he watched for signs, such as blinking, that he thought were characteristic of someone under the influence. One student had an interesting insight into one possible source of observer biases. She said "Don't you think it would be dangerous for us all not to think that her behavior was influenced at least a little bit by the alcohol?" Her intriguing question led to a discussion of whether biases and heuristics (or cognitive shortcuts) are indeed errors (see Funder, 1987).

Although we have demonstrated that students succumbed to observer bias and that they can articulate the reasons why they thought they did so, another important issue is whether our students actually learned from the demonstration. We addressed this question in two ways. First, at the beginning of the semester, we provided students with a manuscript containing numerous methodological problems and APA-style violations. Embedded in the manuscript was an example of a potential observer bias. Students handed in a list of detected methodological problems and APA-style violations several times throughout the semester to demonstrate their progressive mastery of course material and to hone their ability to evaluate research critically. Students handed in their lists for the first time before the demonstration and for the second time 2 weeks after the demonstration. None of the students detected the observer bias before the class demonstration, but seven (22%) did after the class demonstration.

Because the manuscript described earlier was fairly long and complex, we sought other ways to demonstrate that students had learned the concept of observer bias. In an exam that followed the class demonstration by 3 weeks, we presented students with a brief description of a hypothetical study and instructed them to identify its major problems. One of the major problems involved a potential observer bias. Eleven students (35%) detected the bias. The seven students who detected bias in the manuscript also detected bias in the exam.

In summary, our demonstration provides students with a lively and memorable introduction to observer biases. Students' personal involvement in the demonstration should improve learning.

References

Anderson, C. A. (1983). Abstract and concrete data in the perseverance of social theories: When weak data lead to unshakable beliefs. *Journal of Experimental Social Psychology, 19*, 93–108.

Aronson, E., Ellsworth, P. C., Carlsmith, J. M., & Gonzales, M. H. (1990). *Methods of research in social psychology.* New York: McGraw-Hill.

Funder, D. (1987). Errors and mistakes: Evaluating the accuracy of social judgment. *Psychological Bulletin, 101,* 75–90.

Mednick, S. A. (1964). *Learning.* Englewood Cliffs, NJ: Prentice-Hall.

Mischel, W., Ebbesen, E. B., & Zeiss, A. M. (1976). Determinants of selective memory about the self. *Journal of Consulting and Clinical Psychology, 44,* 92–103.

Neale, J. M., & Liebert, R. M. (1986). *Science and behavior: An introduction to methods of research.* Englewood Cliffs, NJ: Prentice-Hall.

Nisbett, R. E., & Wilson, T. (1977). Telling more than we can know: Verbal reports on mental processes. *Psychological Review, 84,* 231–259.

Rosenthal, R. (1963). On the social psychology of the psychological experiment: The experimenter's hypothesis as unintended determinant of experimental results. *American Scientist, 51,* 268–283.

Rosenthal, R., & Rosnow, R. L. (Eds.). (1969). *Artifact in behavioral research.* New York: Academic.

Snyder, M., & Swann, W. B. (1978). Hypothesis-testing processes in social interaction. *Journal of Personality and Social Psychology, 36,* 1202–1212.

Snyder, M., & Uranowitz, S. W. (1978). Reconstructing the past: Some cognitive consequences of person perception. *Journal of Personality and Social Psychology, 36,* 941–950.

Note

We thank Tammy Hershey and David Stotz for their contributions to this project and Saera Khan for her superb performance as the confederate in Demonstration 2. We also thank Ruth L. Ault and several anonymous reviewers for their helpful comments on a draft of this article.

A "Handy" Way to Introduce Research Methods

David E. Johnson

Several studies have found that left-handers are underrepresented in older age ranges (Coren & Halpern, 1991; Fleminger, Dalton, & Standage, 1977; Halpern & Coren, 1988). Many of these studies reveal relations similar to the one graphically presented in Figure 1, which is adapted from Coren and Halpern (1991).

Coren and Halpern (1991) suggested two possible explanations for this relation. First, left-handers learn to become right-handed due to implicit or explicit environmental pressures. This *modification hypothesis* implies that left-handers convert to being right-handed over time due to the physical and social difficulties encountered living in a right-handed world. For example, most tools, equipment, and common articles (e.g., scissors) require right-handed operation for optimal performance: Conversely, the data might suggest that left-handers have increased mortality rates across the life span that selectively eliminate them from the population (the *elimination hypothesis*).

Coren and Halpern (1991) attempted to determine the viability of these hypotheses by examining data on various topics (e.g., birth stress, environmental risk factors, maturational variables, and immune system variables) and concluded that the elimination hypothesis is more tenable than the modification hypothesis. Left-handers, on average, experienced birth stress more often, experienced higher accident rates, suffered higher rates of immune and autoim-

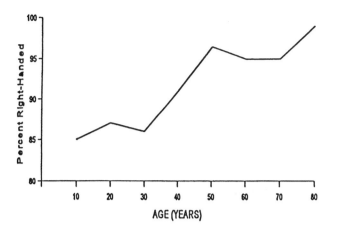

Figure 1. Percentage of right-handers in the population as a function of age. *Note.* From "Left-Handedness: A Marker for Decreased Survival Fitness," by S. Coren and D. F. Halpern, 1991, *Psychological Bulletin, 109,* p. 91. Copyright 1991 by the American Psychological Association, Inc. Adapted with permission.

mune dysfunction, and died younger as compared with right-handers.

Students find the relation between handedness and mortality intriguing. Because of their interest, I developed a simple classroom activity based on this research that requires students to think about the processes scientists consider when doing research.

Method

The activity requires minimal preparation. Familiarity with the basic core of studies in this area is required. I recommend reading Coren and Halpern (1991) and Porac and Coren (1981) at a minimum. Prepare an overhead transparency (or another method of visual presentation) that contains Figure 1.

Typically, I begin the class period by placing Figure 1 on the overhead projector and asking the class the following questions: "What does this graph mean?" "How do you explain it?" "Based on your explanation, how would you decide if your explanation is tenable?" Students organize themselves into groups of five or six to discuss their responses to these questions. Often students' initial response is to express disbelief in the veracity of the data. Spirited discussion results, and students often vigorously disagree about the potential causes of the handedness–mortality relation. Most believe that the data are a result of changes from left- to right-handedness.

After 15 to 20 min of discussion, the groups report the results of their discussion to the entire class. During the group reports, I note responses that address factors requiring further treatment in the discussion with the whole class. Afterward, I summarize and discuss the importance of the issues raised during the class discussion.

I usually implement this activity during the first week of classes because textbooks often present introductory material on research methods in the first chapters. I use the activity in various courses, such as Honors General Psychol-

ogy, Research Methods, and Behavioral Neuroscience. In research methods or physiological psychology courses, reading some core articles to facilitate discussion of more advanced topics in future class periods can be instructive for students.

Results and Discussion

Many benefits result from this exercise. First, students practice reading and interpreting a line graph (Figure 1), an important skill for understanding research reports.

Second, at least some students recognize the fact that Figure 1 can be interpreted in at least two ways (i.e., modification vs. elimination). I emphasize that these two explanations form a dichotomy that is similar to the nature versus nurture debate that runs through much of psychology. The modification hypothesis focuses more on environmental variables; the elimination hypothesis centers more on biological variables, some of which have genetic origins.

Third, some students realize that acceptance of the modification or elimination explanation depends on how the data in Figure 1 were collected. Essentially, they realize that a cross-sectional methodology may yield a different result from a longitudinal design. Usually, this realization is based on the possibility that subjects born 50 to 80 years ago made the sinistral to dextral change due to more intense social pressures as compared with younger subjects. In upper division courses, I present Coren and Halpern's (1991) data and rationale for discounting this explanation.

Fourth, students always ask, "Who is left-handed?" They point out that some people do some things left-handed and other things right-handed. This observation highlights the need for operational definitions of variables. We discuss ways to operationalize the handedness variable, and I present some definitions used in the literature. For example, Peters and Perry (1991) defined left-handers as those who used the left hand to write, whereas Halpern and Coren (1988) assigned left-handedness to baseball players in their study if the players batted and pitched with the left hand.

Fifth, students mention some of the same variables that Coren and Halpern (1991) tested. For example, almost every class suggests the possibility of increased accident rates for left-handers, genetic variables, and prenatal variables.

Finally, some authors disagree with Coren and Halpern's (1991) conclusion that elimination is the better explanation for this relation (e.g., Dellatolas et al., 1991; Fudin, Renninger, Lembessis, & Hirshon, 1993; Harris, 1993a, 1993b; Hugdahl, Satz, Mitrushina, & Miller, 1993; Peters & Perry, 1991). In research methods classes, we discuss disagreements among researchers that are based on different methodologies or statistical analyses. Introduction to scholarly debate can be accomplished by having students read some of the published replies to these criticisms (e.g., Coren & Halpern, 1993; Halpern & Coren, 1993).

In my most recent Honors General Psychology course, I asked students (*N* = 25) if they believed the activity should be used in future classes. Twenty-four of the 25 students answered in the affirmative.

In summary, this activity can be used in various courses. Students find the topic interesting, and it provides an engaging way to present diverse research issues.

References

Coren, S., & Halpern, D. F. (1991). Left-handedness: A marker for decreased survival fitness. *Psychological Bulletin, 109*, 90–106.

Coren, S., & Halpern, D. F. (1993). A replay of the baseball data. *Perceptual & Motor Skills, 76*, 403–406.

Dellatolas, G., Tubert, P., Castresana, A., Mesbah, M., Giallonardo, T., Lazaratou, H., & Lellouch, J. (1991). Age and cohort effects in adult handedness. *Neuropsychologia, 29*, 255–261.

Fleminger, J. J., Dalton, R., & Standage, K. F. (1977). Age as a factor in the handedness of adults. *Neuropsychologia, 15*, 471–473.

Fudin, R., Renninger, L., Lembessis, E., & Hirshon, J. (1993). Sinistrality and reduced longevity: Reichler's 1979 data on baseball players do not indicate a relationship. *Perceptual & Motor Skills, 76*, 171–182.

Halpern, D. F., & Coren, S. (1988). Do right-handers live longer? *Nature, 333*, 213.

Halpern, D. F., & Coren, S. (1993). Left-handedness and life span: A reply to Harris. *Psychological Bulletin, 114*, 235–241.

Harris, L. J. (1993a). Do left-handers die sooner than right-handers? Commentary on Coren and Halpern's (1991)

"Left-handedness: A marker for decreased survival fitness." *Psychological Bulletin, 114*, 203–234.

Harris, L. J. (1993b). Left-handedness and life span: Reply to Halpern and Coren. *Psychological Bulletin, 114*, 242–247.

Hugdahl, K., Satz, P., Mitrushina, M., & Miller, E. N. (1993). Left-handedness and old age: Do left-handers die earlier? *Neuropsychologia, 31*, 325–333.

Peters, M., & Perry, R. (1991). No link between left-handedness and maternal age and no elevated accident rate in left-handers. *Neuropsychologia, 29*, 1257–1259.

Porac, C., & Coren, S. (1981). *Lateral preferences and human behavior.* New York: Springer-Verlag.

Notes

1. A version of this article was presented at the annual meeting of the American Psychological Association, Los Angeles, August 1994.
2. Correspondence concerning this article should be addressed to David E. Johnson, Department of Psychology, John Brown University, Siloam Springs, AR 72761; e-mail: djohnson@acc.jbu.edu.

Publication Bias: A Computer-Assisted Demonstration of Excluding Nonsignificant Results From Research Interpretation

Todd C. Riniolo

Publication bias is an impairment to accurate interpretation of published literature. Publication bias, the increased likelihood of publication of a manuscript describing significant rather than nonsignificant findings, can arise either from researchers' failure to submit nonsignificant results for publication or journal reviewers' rejection of articles based on nonsignificant findings. Recent evidence suggests that publication bias can pose a serious impediment to accurate interpretation of research results (Berlin, Begg, & Louis, 1989; Easterbrook, Berlin, Gopalan, & Matthews, 1991; Simes, 1986) and can alter meta-analytic results designed to estimate effect sizes from published studies (Dear & Begg, 1992). Although formal studies have shown that the majority of articles published in journals are filled with positive results (Bozarth & Roberts, 1972; Sterling, 1959), introductory research methods textbooks (e.g., Graziano & Raulin, 1989; Ray, 1993) often fail to alert students that published research findings may be a biased representation of true population differences.

The cumulation of individual studies to derive an accurate interpretation of the literature is tied intimately to the Central Limit Theorem (CLT). First, the CLT states that drawing repeated samples from a given population (or differences between populations) will yield a nearly normal sampling distribution of means when the sample sizes are approximately 25 or larger for both normal and nonnormal parent populations (Hopkins & Glass, 1978). From this sampling distribution of means, the mean of the sampling distribution is an accurate estimate of the true population mean. If the full range of results from repeated sampling is not available, such as when nonsignificant findings are not published, the CLT does not accurately reflect the true population mean. Similarly, if the researcher does not have access to the full range of results because of publication bias, interpretation of the literature occurs from a biased sample. Second, the CLT states that as sample size increases, the variability (i.e., the standard error) of the sampling distribution of means decreases according to the function: $\sigma/\sqrt{N}$. A decrease in the standard error as sample size increases results in greater statistical precision to detect differences (i.e., greater statistical power) because the individual distributions being compared constrict, resulting in a smaller distributional overlap between groups.

The purpose of this article is to provide a computer-based simulation, based on tenets of the CLT, of the effects of excluding nonsignificant findings from research interpretation. The concept of publication bias may seem abstract to the student at the introductory level, and a classroom demonstration can provide a concrete and visual example to supplement class lecture and discussion.

Method

Procedure

I obtained results in this article from 10,000 trials; however, you can use 1,000 or 100 trials for the class exercise when quick processing time is essential. Processing time requires less than 5 min for 1,000 trials and less than 1 min for 100 trials on a 486-based personal computer (16MB RAM) running at 66MHz.

I performed a power analysis (desired power level as a function of effect size, significance level, and sample size) using the power function in Sigmastat 1.0 (Jandel Scientific, 1994) to approximate a 25%, 50%, and 80% chance of reaching statistical significance for two-tailed t tests (α = .05) between Group 1 ($M = 106.36$, $SD = 10$) and Group 2 ($M = 100$, $SD = 10$). The population difference between groups corresponds to $d = .636$ (Cohen, 1988). Results used for this demonstration are as follows: (a) $1 - \beta = .245$ ($n = 9$ for each group), (b) $1 - \beta = .5$ ($n = 20$ for each group), and (c) $1 - \beta = .802$ ($n = 40$ for each group). The numbers used in this demonstration can change, but are conceptually easy to interpret and understand (e.g., differences between populations on IQ scores).

The demonstration consists of the following series of steps:

1. Provide the class with a refresher of the CLT.
2. Run the simulation with the various sample sizes starting with $1 - \beta = .50$, $1 - \beta = .245$, and $1 - \beta = .802$. Record the mean results comparing the full range of results with significant results only. Print the graph after each simulation or use the figures from this article for illustration.
3. Lead a discussion of the results.
4. Instruct the class to browse through recent journals comparing significant versus nonsignificant findings to provide students with firsthand experience of the proportion of positive versus negative findings in the journals.

You may change the effect size difference between populations or sample sizes associated with this demonstration. For example, you may wish to compare the effects of publication bias on small, medium, and large effect size differences (Cohen, 1988) in the population while maintaining a constant sample size.

Programming

I created the program for this demonstration in Matlab 4.0 (Math Works, 1995) with Statistics Toolbox (Math Works, 1996). The logic of the program was to use a "for" loop to draw random samples from a given population (i.e., a normal distribution) for 2 groups and to perform t tests. The random number generator is a scalar whose value changes each time it is referenced and transforms values of a uniform generator according to the algorithm described by Forsythe, Malcolm, and Moler (1977). I then labeled results as being significant or nonsignificant, allowing for easy access to compare the full distribution versus significant results only. The program appears in Table 1.

Results

Figure 1 (solid line) illustrates the full range of mean difference scores from Group 1 and Group 2 with power set at .5, giving an equal chance of obtaining significant or nonsignificant results. Findings are consistent with the CLT ($M = 6.34$, $SD = 3.16$), which predicts an accurate estimation of the true difference between groups (6.36 as defined by the random number generator) from the mean of the sampling distribution. Figure 1 (dashed line) illustrates the distribution of significant results only. Of the 10,000 trials, 4,996 were significant ($M = 8.78$; $SD = 1.99$). As shown by Figure 1, exclusion of negative findings produces a positively biased distribution, which results in the biased estimation of the between groups difference.

Figure 2 (solid line) shows that despite low power (.245), the full range of results still provides an accurate estimate of group differences ($M = 6.42$; $SD = 4.66$). However, when significant results only ($n = 2,532$) are examined ($M = 11.95$; $SD = 2.71$), a large overestimation of the true difference occurs from the limited distribution (Figure 2, dashed line). With power raised (.802), the full range of results (Figure 3, solid line) also provides an accurate estimate of true group differences ($M = 6.39$; $SD = 2.25$). Although overestimating the true difference ($M = 7.14$; $SD = 1.75$; $n = 8042$), this power level provided the least biased estimate of the true difference using only significant results (Figure 3, dashed line).

Discussion

Results from this demonstration are consistent with the CLT. First, inclusion of the full range of results accurately estimates the true difference between groups (i.e., an accurate interpretation of the literature derived from an unbiased sample). As shown in Figures 1, 2, and 3, exclusion of nonsignificant results biases the available distribution, impairing the interpretation by the researcher. For example, exclusion of nonsignificant results may result in a treatment (e.g., a new drug therapy for hypertension) or a group difference (e.g., gender) being represented by the literature as a greater difference than exists in the population. Second, results based on smaller samples are prone to a greater bias when nonsignificant results are excluded because of the reduction of statistical precision resulting in an increase in distributional overlap.

This demonstration provides an important lesson for psychology students that is often absent in introductory research textbooks and provides a vehicle for discussion of the more philosophical issues associated with the evolution of publication bias. Perhaps publication bias has arisen from the dichotomous nature of hypothesis testing that allows re-

Table 1. Publication Bias Program

```
SAM=input('Input number of samples to be drawn from a population:    ');
SUB=input('Input number of subjects in each group:    ');
MEAN_=input('Input the Mean for group 1:    ');
ES=input('Input the Population Mean difference between groups:    ');
STD_=input('Input the Standard Deviation for both groups:    ');
for n=1:SAM                    %for loop to generate # of trials
GRP1=(randn(SUB,1)*STD_)+MEAN_;
GRP2=(randn(SUB,1)STD_)+MEAN_+ES;
[h(n,1)]=ttest2(GRP1,GRP2);    %independent t-tests
Mean_dif(n,1)=mean(GRP2) - mean(GRP1);
  if h(n,1) == 1;              %flagging significant results
  reject_(n,1)=Mean_dif(n,1);
  else;
  reject_(n,1)= (abs(MEAN_*STD_+10000))*(-1);
  end;
end;
MIN_1=min(Mean_dif);MAX_1=max(Mean_dif);MM1=MIN_1:MAX_1;
%setting graph axis
R=sort(reject_);K=find(R(abs(MEAN_*STD_+10000))*(-1));
P=K(1,1);E=max(K);reject_2=R(P:E,1);
subplot(2,1,1); hist(Mean_dif,MM1);title('Full Distribution');ylabel('Frequency');
subplot(2,1,2); hist(reject_2,MM1);
title('Significant Results Only');ylabel('Frequency');
total_rej=sum(h);mean_diff=mean(Mean_dif);
std_diff=std(Mean_dif);reject_a=mean(reject_2);
reject_std=std(reject_2);
fprintf('Number of "Significant" Trials          =    %6.3f\n',total_rej);
fprintf('Mean Difference using the Full Distribution =   %6.3f\n',mean_diff);
fprintf('Standard Deviation of the Full Distribution =    %6.3f\n',std_diff);
fprintf('Mean Difference of "Significant" Trials    =    %6.3f\n',reject_a);
fprintf('Standard Deviation of "Significant" Trials =    %6.3f\n',reject_std);
clear;
```

searchers to interpret only significant findings. As Hedges (1984) pointed out, when a study fails to reach statistical significance, interpretation is difficult, often resulting in unpublished manuscripts or published manuscripts with incomplete reporting of nonsignificant findings. Additionally, the ability to interpret only significant results may have contributed to the widespread overconfidence of social scientists about the probability that statistically significant findings will replicate (Cohen, 1994; Oakes, 1986; Tversky & Kahneman, 1971). Shaver (1993) recommends philo-

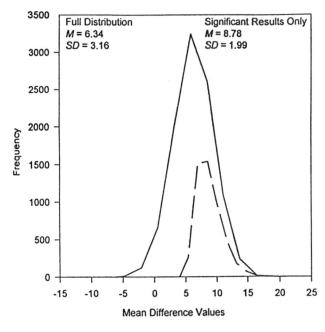

Figure 1. Frequency distributions of mean difference scores for the full distribution (solid line) and significant results only (dashed line) with $1 - \beta = .500$.

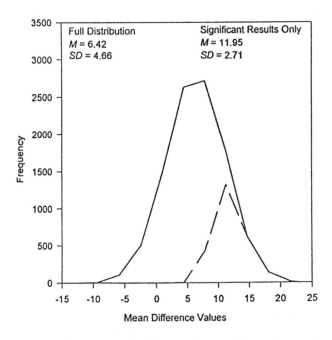

Figure 2. Frequency distributions of mean difference scores for the full distribution (solid line) and significant results only (dashed line) with $1 - \beta = .245$.

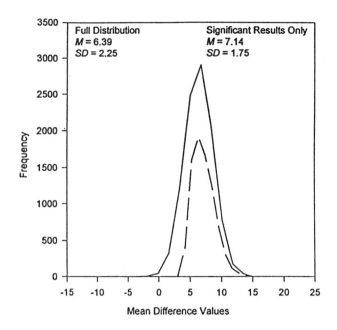

Figure 3. Frequency distributions of mean difference scores for the full distribution (solid line) and significant results only (dashed line) with 1 − β = .802.

sophical discussions as one method to reduce strictly mechanical application of statistics and research methodology by students and to stimulate critical analysis of research interpretation.

This computer program also works with fewer trials (e.g., 30) to simulate more realistic numbers of studies associated with a literature review of a specific research question. Additionally, this demonstration provides a transition to discuss not only philosophical issues of research methodology, but applied material such as (a) proposed methods to control and identify publication bias, (b) sample size and the probability of replication of results, and (c) the use of power analysis to determine appropriate sample sizes. By experiencing the consequences of excluding nonsignificant results from research interpretation, students will gain an invaluable lesson to aid research interpretation.

References

Berlin, J. A., Begg, C. B., & Louis, T. A. (1989). An assessment of publication bias using a sample of published clinical trials. *Journal of the American Statistical Association, 84*, 381–392.

Bozarth, J. D., & Roberts, R. R. (1972). Signifying significant significance. *American Psychologist, 27*, 774–775.

Cohen, J. (1988). *Statistical power analysis for the behavioral sciences* (2nd ed.). Hillsdale, NJ: Lawrence Erlbaum Associates, Inc.

Cohen, J. (1994). The earth is round (*p* < .05). *American Psychologist, 49*, 997–1003.

Dear, K. B. G., & Begg, C. (1992). An approach for assessing publication bias prior to performing a meta-analysis. *Statistical Science, 7*, 237–245.

Easterbrook, P. J., Berlin, J. A., Gopalan, R., & Matthews, D. R. (1991). Publication bias in clinical research. *The Lancet, 337*, 867–872.

Forsythe, G. E., Malcolm, M. A., & Moler, C. B. (1977). *Computer methods for mathematical computations.* Englewood Cliffs, NJ: Prentice Hall.

Graziano, A. M., & Raulin, M. L. (1989). *Research methods: A process of inquiry.* New York: Harper & Row.

Hedges, L. V. (1984). Estimation of effect size under nonrandom sampling: The effects of censoring studies yielding statistically insignificant mean differences. *Journal of Educational Statistics, 9*, 61–85.

Hopkins, K. D., & Glass, G. V. (1978). *Basic statistics for the behavioral sciences.* Englewood Cliffs, NJ: Prentice Hall.

Matlab 4.0 [Computer program]. (1995). Natick, MA: Math Works.

Oakes, M. (1986). *Statistical inference: A commentary for the social and behavioral sciences.* New York: Wiley.

Ray, W. J. (1993). *Methods toward a science of behavior* (4th ed.). Monterey, CA: Brooks/Cole.

Shaver, J. P. (1993). What statistical significance testing is, and what it is not. *Journal of Experimental Education, 61*, 293–316.

Sigmastat 1.0 [Computer program]. (1994). San Rafael, CA: Jandel Scientific.

Simes, R. J. (1986). Publication bias: The case for an international registry of clinical trials. *Journal of Clinical Oncology, 4*, 1529–1541.

Statistics Toolbox [Computer program]. (1996). Natick, MA: Math Works.

Sterling, T. C. (1959). Publication decisions and their possible effects on inferences drawn from tests of significance or vice versa. *Journal of the American Statistical Association, 54*, 30–34.

Tversky, A., & Kahneman, D. (1971). Belief in the law of small numbers. *Psychological Bulletin, 76*, 105–110.

Notes

1. This article is dedicated to the memory of the late Brian J. Riniolo, my brother.
2. Special thanks to John Jeka for his eloquent teaching of computer skills and to Jane Doussard-Roosevelt for her helpful suggestions in writing this manuscript.

Propagation of Action Potentials: An Active Participation Exercise

Gary Felsten

Students often perceive the physiological portions of introductory psychology courses to be difficult or even daunting. They encounter novel terminology, complex structures, and processes that are difficult to visualize. Transmission of information within and between neurons is a basic aspect of physiological psychology that is difficult for some students to understand because it involves changes across both time and space. Techniques that allow them to visualize the process aid comprehension. Computer animations of neural signaling are helpful, as are exercises that require active participation. For example, Reardon, Durso, and Wilson (1994) described an exercise that helps students visualize important aspects of synaptic transmission. Their exercise focuses on integration of excitatory and inhibitory postsynaptic potentials, temporal and spatial summation, and mechanisms of agonist and antagonist drugs at postsynaptic receptors. Their exercise does not demonstrate processes involved in the propagation of action potentials, which are described here. Instructors may use the two exercises together to provide a fairly complete demonstration of basic neural communication.

The exercise described here allows students to visualize events associated with propagation of action potentials along unmyelinated and myelinated axons. It requires active participation; each student is a segment of the axon. The exercise, which may be the neuronal version of the stadium "wave," is fun and well-suited to large classes, where it is possible to set up a race between action potentials in myelinated and unmyelinated axons. Students quickly learn why the race is unfair and the outcome is always predictable.

The Exercise

I present this exercise after discussing the structure and properties of the neuronal membrane and the ionic bases for the resting potential and the action potential. During the exercise, students line up side by side with about 0.3 m of space between them; each student constitutes a tiny segment of the axon. They relax with their hands at their sides and I explain that the position of each student's right hand represents the membrane potential in that segment of the axon. When the right hand is below the student's head, it signifies the membrane potential is negative; when the hand is above the head, it signifies the membrane potential is positive.

Resting Potential

The queue of students standing with their arms extended at their sides represents the axon of a neuron at rest. The position of their hands represents the resting membrane potential of about −70 millivolts (mV). Students discuss why the inside of the resting axon is negative relative to the outside, and we briefly review the distribution of sodium and potassium ions.

Graded Depolarization

Students describe what would happen if sodium gates opened in their segment of axon. They state that sodium ions would enter and the inside of the axon would become less negative (or more positive). They move their right hands upward a few inches and then back down to represent a small depolarization. Then they show a slightly larger depolarization by moving their hands upward a little further.

All-or-None Threshold

The level of their waists represents the threshold for generation of the action potential (about −55 mV). Any depolarization above that level triggers an all-or-none action potential. Students see that the threshold is more positive than the resting potential, but still quite negative.

The Action Potential and Its Ionic Basis

Students represent the action potential by quickly raising their right arms to their fullest natural extensions over their heads and then returning them to their resting positions. I ask what raising their arms represents (depolarization) and what the membrane potential is when their hands are at their highest levels (about +30 mV). I ask what happens to cause the depolarization (opening of sodium gates and entry of sodium ions into the axon) and why sodium ions enter (both concentration and electrical gradients favor it). I ask what lowering their hands represents (repolarization) and remind students that the membrane potential dips a little below the resting potential (hyperpolarization) during repolarization. I ask what causes the repolarization (opening of potassium gates and flow of potassium ions out of the axon), why potassium ions exit (both concentration and electrical gradients favor it), and why sodium ions don't continue to enter the axon if they are still more concentrated outside the axon (the inside is now positive and the sodium gates have closed). I also ask students to explain the absolute and relative refractory periods during the repolarization (sodium permeability is low and potassium permeability is high).

Propagation Along Unmyelinated Axons

I remind students that the spread of depolarization from one segment of the axon to the adjacent segment causes channels to open, which allows sodium ions to rush in, further depolarize the segment above threshold, and cause regeneration of the action potential. Students represent the spread of depolarization by gently tapping the next student on the shoulder. Beginning with the first student, who represents the axon hillock, students in turn raise and lower their right arms as described previously and tap the next student's shoulder as they lower their arms. As students are tapped on the shoulder, they move their arms to represent the action potential. Students easily see that the action potential is regenerated at successive segments as it propagates down an unmyelinated axon. Students take a few practice runs and then we time how long it takes for the action potential to propagate down the axon. The last student in line (who represents the axon terminal) may have a bucket of styrofoam balls (which represent neurotransmitters), which may be tossed when the action potential reaches the terminal.

Propagation Along Myelinated Axons

For this demonstration, approximately every fifth student represents a node of Ranvier, who will regenerate an action potential when tapped on the shoulder. The four students between each node are myelinated segments and will conduct the signal simply by tapping the next student on the shoulder. Students representing myelinated segments may be given white paper hats, such as those used by painters or workers in fast-food restaurants, to represent the myelin. Students take a few practice runs before we time propagation down a myelinated axon. It is easy to see how the signal moves quickly through myelinated segments before regeneration at the nodes. If the class is large enough, a race between action potentials in myelinated and unmyelinated axons clearly demonstrates the advantages of myelination.

Effects of Local Anesthetics

It is easy to demonstrate the effects of local anesthetics. A student midway along the line holds a large card with the name of an anesthetic, such as Novocain, printed on it. When that student is tapped on the shoulder, he or she does not generate the action potential and does not tap the next student on the shoulder. Propagation simply stops.

Advantages and Effectiveness of the Exercise

I obtained objective and subjective measures of the impact of this exercise on students in an introductory course, Psychology as a Biological Science, and an upper level course, Physiological Psychology. In the introductory course, I dismissed one half of the 28 students present early, after completion of the discussion on action potentials. The remaining students participated in the exercise, which lasted about 10 min. At the beginning of the next class, students completed a challenging, unannounced, 20-item, fill-in-the-blank quiz on action potentials. I did not use scores on this quiz in calculating course grades, but students did not know this when they completed the quiz. Among students who participated in the exercise, 6 were present for the quiz and averaged 72.5% correct ($SD = 15.1$) compared to 65.8% ($SD = 19.8$) for students dismissed early ($n = 13$) and 22.1% ($SD = 7.6$) for students absent for the discussion about action potentials ($n = 7$). ANOVA showed an overall main effect of group, $F(2, 23) = 20.3$, $p < .001$. Scheffé's test showed no significant difference between students who participated in the exercise and those dismissed early, but both groups scored higher than students who missed the discussion and exercise, $p < .05$. The distribution of grades among students who were present for the discussion provided some support for the effectiveness of the exercise. Of the three highest grades (90%), two were earned by students who participated in the exercise; of the three lowest grades (20% to 50%), all were earned by students who did not participate. At the end of class, I demonstrated the exercise to students who had not participated previously.

In the upper level course, all 12 students participated in the exercise at the conclusion of our discussion of action potentials. Two weeks later, they completed an examination on action potentials and on synaptic transmission, for which there was no interactive exercise. Students averaged 88.2% ($SD = 9.7$) correct on action potentials and 73.0% ($SD = 24.5$) correct on synaptic transmission, $t(11) = 2.31$, $p < .05$, two-tailed. Although I endeavored to make questions for both topics equally challenging, I cannot rule out the possibility that difficulty levels differed between topics.

Students in both classes completed anonymous surveys at least one class session after performing the exercise. They indicated on a scale of −3 (*strongly disagree*) to +3 (*strongly agree*) the extent to which they believed each of eight instructional tools was helpful, interesting, and fun for their "understanding of the generation and transmission of action potentials." The eight items were textbook explanations, textbook pictures, explanations by the instructor, pictures presented by the instructor, class discussion, questions from students, questions from the instructor, and the group exercise. These items evaluated what students believed contributed most to learning this challenging material and the impact of the action potential exercise relative to other pedagogical tools. The classes used different textbooks and the instructor used more comprehensive explanations in the upper level course.

Figure 1 shows mean ratings for textbook explanations, explanations by the instructor, and the action potential exercise. I combined the data for the groups after ANOVA; post hoc tests showed both groups had the same pattern of ratings for these three instructional tools. Overall differences for helpfulness, interest, and fun were all significant, $Fs(2, 134) \geq 14.0$, $ps < .001$. Scheffé's test showed instructor explanations and the action potential exercise did not differ on any of these dimensions, but students rated both higher

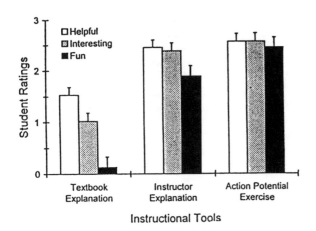

Figure 1. Mean student ratings (+*SE*) of instructional tools for understanding the action potential. Data were pooled from two courses because patterns of ratings did not differ. Scores could range from −3 (*strongly disagree*) to +3 (*strongly agree*).

than textbook explanations on all dimensions, *ps* < .05. Figure 1 clearly shows students perceived the interactive exercise as helpful and engaging.

Conclusion

This exercise is easy to do, requires little time, and was perceived by students to be among the most helpful, interesting, and fun approaches to learning about the propagation of action potentials. Objective tests provided some support for the efficacy of the exercise, but further testing with larger groups is warranted. The exercise is most appropriate for psychology courses that cover the biological bases of behavior, such as Introductory Psychology, Physiological Psychology, Sensation and Perception, and Brain and Behavior, and for biology courses that cover neural function. Educators may include this exercise in pedagogical discussions as an example of how participatory exercises engage students and help them learn difficult concepts and processes.

Reference

Reardon, R., Durso, F. T., & Wilson, D. A. (1994). Neural coding and synaptic transmission: Participation exercises for introductory psychology. *Teaching of Psychology, 21,* 96–99.

Some Simple Classroom Experiments on Cerebral Lateralization

Ernest D. Kemble
Terri Filipi
Linda Gravlin

Hemispheric specialization of function is a popular research area that is prominently featured in many introductory texts (e.g., Ruch, 1984; Wortman, Loftus, & Marshall, 1981). We recently completed a series of experiments on this topic for our undergraduate research methods course and found them to be very useful. This article briefly outlines the instructional advantages of this topic and describes two simple experiments that can be conducted readily in class-room settings.

A prominent feature of this area is high student interest. Throughout the experiments our students actively participated in discussions of the readings and experiments; several students remained after each class to continue discussions. At quarter's end, the students were asked to rate the intellectual stimulation of the topic on a scale of 1 (*least*) to 5 (*most*) as part of a standardized course evaluation. Seventeen of 19 students were present for the evaluation and all rated this project as a 4 (*N* = 9) or 5 (*N* = 8). This interest was also translated into some of the most thoughtful and thoroughly prepared laboratory reports we have seen in recent years.

The rapid development and popularity of this area has also produced a large and diverse literature including popularized nontechnical accounts (e.g., Bakan, 1971; Gazzaniga, 1967; Kimura, 1973), which sometimes claim far-reaching significance for the topic (e.g., Bogen, 1975; Jaynes, 1976; Ornstein, 1978); extensive scholarly reviews (Corballis & Beale, 1983; Gazzaniga, 1970; Hellige, 1983; Springer & Deutsch, 1981); and an extensive primary research literature (see, e.g., Corballis & Beale, 1983; Kinsbourne, 1982; Springer & Deutsch, 1981, for references). This extensive literature provides the instructor wide flexibility in both the range and depth of readings to be used. For more advanced students, the review of this area by Springer and Deutsch (1981) provides an excellent introduction. Finally, several approaches to hemispheric specialization are now available that are applicable to normal subjects and require only minimal equipment (see Springer & Deutsch, 1981, for review).

Preliminary Readings

Because most of our students were in their first or second year in college, we began with a series of nontechnical readings (Bakan, 1971; Gazzaniga, 1967; Sperry, 1964), some related supporting data (Geschwind & Levitsky, 1968; Wada & Rasmussen, 1960), and some suggested extensions of hemispheric asymmetry to other areas of human behavior (Bakan, 1971; Bogen, 1975; Ornstein, 1978; Witelson, 1977). These readings were supplemented by a brief overview of anatomical differences among sensory systems (particularly the pattern and degree of bilateral representation in the CNS) and discussions of major methodological issues raised by the readings (e.g., limitations of research on clinical populations, importance of stimulus and response variables, etc.). These assignments gave the students a brief overview of the area and some of its major methodological problems. Readings and discussion then focused on a number of experimental approaches to hemispheric specialization in normal subjects (Bakan, 1969; Kimura, 1961; Kinsbourne, 1972; Levy, 1969; Quinn, 1972). Because all sensory systems have at least some bilateral representation in the CNS, considerable discussion was devoted to the techniques and experimental controls necessary to restrict stimuli, or stimulus configurations, to a single hemisphere. The importance of methodology in changing fundamental views about hemispheric function is particularly well illustrated by the development of the "Z lens" (see Springer & Deutsch, 1981, pp. 38–40) and was included in this section. One week was devoted to the initial material. The students then read a series of primary research reports directly related to the experiments they were conducting. Classroom discussion focused on the methodological details of both the readings and our experiments.

Experiment 1. Tactile Letter and Number Identification

Because their commissures are intact, it is critical to restrict, or in some way favor, the sensory input of normal subjects to one hemisphere. In many ways, the tactile system mediating light touch is well-suited for this purpose. Because this system projects primarily (approximately 95%) to the contralateral hemisphere, tactile stimulation can be largely restricted to right or left hemisphere by stimulating the contralateral side of the body only. Because the left hemisphere seems to be most heavily involved in language processes, it seemed reasonable to expect that tactile identification of language-related stimuli (letters) should be superior with the right hand, whereas no hand difference should be found with other stimuli (numbers). This experiment compared the latencies for correctly identifying single letters or digits by touch with the right and left hands.

Materials and Procedure

The apparatus consisted of a plywood box (20 × 45 × 20 cm) open at each end and outfitted with a cloth curtain suspended over one end extending to the apparatus floor. The stimuli were 18 children's wooden alphabet blocks consisting of nine single letters (C,D,F,L,P,R,S,U,Y) and nine single digits (0,1,2,3,4,5,6,7,9). In choosing stimuli, letter (e.g., O,I) and number (e.g., 0,1) pairs having similar geo-

metric shapes were avoided. It is important that the outlines of the stimuli are sharp. If the letters and numbers are pressed rather than cut into the blocks, it may be necessary to increase their relief by carefully deepening their borders with a small electric drill. If the blocks contain a raised border, this should also be removed. Latencies for correct identification (multiple guesses were permitted) were timed by stopwatch.

Subjects were seated before the curtained end of the apparatus and the experimenter sat opposite the subject. Single blocks were placed on the floor of the apparatus and the subject was instructed to insert the right or left hand under the curtain, lightly trace the outlines of the stimulus with fingertips, and identify the stimulus. The stopwatch was started when the block was touched and stopped after a correct identification. Because this is a surprisingly difficult task, a cue card depicting all stimuli was placed before the subjects, who were always told whether the stimulus was a letter or a digit. Even so, identification latencies of 10–15 seconds were not uncommon. Because there are strong practice effects on this task, subjects were given eight warm-up trials (alternating hands, letters, and digits) followed by 12 letter and 12 digit trials. Letters and digits and right and left hands were alternated. At the conclusion of testing, four mean identification latencies were calculated for each subject (right hand, letter; right hand, digit; left hand, letter; left hand, digit). These four means were employed for statistical analyses (t tests, analyses of variance) of data from 9 male and 22 female students.

Results

Initial comparisons revealed no overall difference in the performance of preferred and nonpreferred hand on warm-up trials and no systematic change in identification latencies for letters or digits in the course of the experiment. Thus, the results were not biased by overall superiority in the performance of the preferred hand at the outset of the experiment or by practice effects ($p > .10$). Comparisons of right- and left-hand performance revealed that female students identified letters more quickly with the right hand (M = 8.74 sec) than with the left (M = 12.41 sec, $p < .05$), but with no hand difference in digit identification (right, M = 6.87 sec; left, M = 6.42 sec, $p > .10$). There were no hand differences among males in either letter (right, M = 10.61 sec; left, M = 11.19 sec, $p > .10$) or digit (right, M = 6.09 sec; left, M = 6.41 sec, $p > .10$) identification. Thus, the data support some left hemisphere specialization for language-related stimuli but also indicate that differences are sex-dependent under some testing conditions.

Experiment 2. Verbal Interference With a Manual Task

A related experimental approach, which also seems to reflect hemispheric specialization, requires subjects to balance a wooden dowel rod on the forefinger of the right and left hand while engaged in a verbal task, or while remaining silent (Kinsbourne & Cook, 1971; Johnson & Kozma, 1977). These investigators found that balancing durations with the right, but *not* the left hand were shortened by a verbal task.

They suggested that the massive and complex activity required of the left hemisphere by the verbal tasks competed with neural activity required for right-hand balancing. Since the right hemisphere is presumed to be less involved in language, the verbal task did not compete with left-hand balancing.

Materials and Procedure

This experiment requires only 4–6 wooden dowel rods (1.25 cm dia., 92 cm length), a stopwatch, and a list of verbal problems. Our verbal task consisted of a series of spelling problems (e.g, repeat the alphabet backwards, recite the alphabet forward giving every third letter, spell Afghanistan backwards). Because some subjects can balance the dowel for up to 600 sec. several pages of problems should be prepared.

The students were allowed to practice balancing the dowel for 5 min, alternating the right and left hands, and then received eight test trials (right hand = 4, left hand = 4). On each trial, the subject positioned the dowel on the right or left forefinger using the other hand. On command, the supporting hand was removed and the experimenter started a stopwatch, which was stopped when the dowel dropped or touched any other part of the subject's body. Half of the trials on each hand were conducted in silence and half with verbal tasks. The order in which conditions were presented was systematically varied across subjects. At the conclusion of testing, mean balancing durations for each hand under both silent and verbal conditions were calculated.

Results

The preferred hand ($M = 64.72$ sec) showed a marginally significant superiority in balancing duration to the non-preferred hand ($M = 49.57$ sec, $.05 < p < .10$) during silent trials. The durations for males were also significantly longer than for females with both the right (male, $M = 155.94$ sec; female, $M = 25.63$ sec, $p < .02$) and left hands (male, $M = 135.58$ sec; female, $M = 12.72$ sec, $p < .05$). Comparisons of balancing durations under silent and verbal conditions revealed that the verbal task impaired performance in both the left (silent, $M = 49.58$ sec; verbal, $M = 30.08$ sec, $p < .002$) and right hands (silent, $M = 64.72$ sec; verbal, $M = 32.2$ sec, $p < .001$). Although these comparisons suggest no lateralized effect on balancing, examination of the data shows that the right hand (37.2% decline) was more severely impaired than the left (11.9% decline, $p < .05$) by the verbal task. There was no sex difference in this effect ($p > .10$). Thus, while the left hemisphere does seem to be more importantly involved in this task, both hemispheres seem to participate in more complex verbal tasks. Clearly, referring to the left hemisphere as "the language hemisphere" is an oversimplification.

Discussion

In addition to the two experiments described here, we also completed a dichotic listening task similar to that reported by Kimura (1961). This experiment revealed right ear (left hemisphere) superiority in word recognition, which disappeared when subjects were instructed to pay attention to their right ear. Thus, demonstrations of hemispheric asymmetry may be partially dependent on the instructions given to subjects. These three experiments required less than 5 hours of laboratory time to complete and nicely illustrated the importance of a host of variables (e.g., sensory modality, task complexity, sex differences, measurement methods, and instructions) for research in this area. In the course of the experiments it became quite obvious to our students that the hemispheres interact with each other in subtle ways rather than simply dividing major functions. Although the dichotic listening task requires somewhat elaborate equipment that may not be available in many labs, a number of additional simple measures have been described (e.g., Johnson & Kozma, 1977; Kinsbourne, 1972; Kinsbourne & McMurray, 1975; Levy & Reid, 1976), which may lend themselves to similar manipulations and further classroom projects. The simplicity of these experiments and the high student interest they engender make this an excellent way to introduce students to physiological psychology and research methodology.

References

Bakan, P. (1969). Hypnotizability, laterality of eye movements and functional brain asymmetry. *Perceptual and Motor Skills, 28*, 927–932.

Bakan, P. (1971, April). The eyes have it. *Psychology Today*, pp. 64–67, 96.

Bogen, J. E. (1975). The other side of the brain. VII: Some educational aspects of hemispheric specialization. *UCLA Educator, 17*, 24–32.

Corballis, M. C., & Beale, I. L. (1983). *The ambivalent mind: The neuropsychology of left and right*. Chicago: Nelson-Hall.

Gazzaniga, M. (1967). The split brain in man. *Scientific American, 217*, 24–29.

Gazzaniga, M. S. (1970). *The bisected brain*. New York: Appleton-Century-Crofts.

Geschwind, N., & Levitsky, W. (1968). Human brain: Left–right asymmetries in temporal speech region. *Science, 161*, 186–187.

Hellige, J. B. (Ed.). (1983). *Cerebral hemisphere asymmetry: Method, theory, and application*. New York: Praeger.

Jaynes, J. (1976). *The origin of consciousness in the breakdown of the bicameral mind*. Boston: Houghton Mifflin.

Johnson, O., & Kozma, A. (1977). Effects of concurrent verbal and musical tasks on a unimanual skill. *Cortex, 13*, 11–16.

Kimura, D. (1961). Cerebral dominance and the perception of verbal stimuli. *Canadian Journal of Psychology, 15*, 166–171.

Kimura, D. (1973). The asymmetry of the human brain. *Scientific American, 228*, 70–78.

Kinsbourne, M. (1972). Eye and head turning indicates cerebral lateralization. *Science, 176*, 539–541.

Kinsbourne, M. (1982). Hemispheric specialization and the growth of human understanding. *American Psychologist, 37*, 411–420.

Kinsbourne, M., & Cook, J. (1971). Generalized and lateralized effects of concurrent verbalization on a unimanual skill. *Quarterly Journal of Experimental Psychology, 23*, 341–345.

Kinsbourne, M., & McMurray, J. (1975). The effect of cerebral dominance of time sharing between speaking and tapping by preschool children. *Child Development, 46*, 240–242.

Levy, J. (1969). Possible basis for the evolution of lateral specialization of the human brain. *Nature, 224*, 614–615.

Levy, J., & Reid, M. L. (1976). Variations in writing posture and cerebral organization. *Science, 194,* 337.

Ornstein, R. (1978). The split and the whole brain. *Human Nature, 1,* 76–83.

Quinn, P. (1972). Stuttering: Cerebral dominance and the dichotic word test. *Medical Journal of Australia, 2,* 639–643.

Ruch, J. C. (1984). *Psychology: The personal science.* Belmont, CA: Wadsworth.

Sperry, R. (1964). The great cerebral commissure. *Scientific American, 210,* 42–52.

Springer, S., & Deutsch, G. (1981). *Left brain, right brain.* San Francisco: Freeman.

Wada, J. A., & Rasmussen, T. (1960). Intracarotid injection of sodium amytal for the lateralization of cerebral speech dominance: Experimental and clinical observations. *Journal of Neurosurgery, 17,* 266–282.

Witelson, S. F. (1977). Developmental dyslexia: Two right hemispheres and none left. *Science, 195,* 309–311.

Wortman, C. B., Loftus, E. F., & Marshall, M. (1981). *Psychology.* New York: Knopf.

Classroom Demonstration of Behavioral Effects of the Split-Brain Operation

Edward J. Morris

Various lab assignments and computer simulations illustrate the effects of the surgical procedure referred to as the commissurotomy. Most introductory psychology textbooks include descriptions of patients' behavior after the split-brain operation, but most of the examples are anecdotal. No demonstration exists to illustrate to students the potential subjective experiences of such patients.

The following demonstration allows students to participate in an activity designed to simulate the difficulty split-brain patients experience with certain perceptuomotor tasks soon after surgery (Nebes & Sperry, 1971). Participants experience the potential frustration patients feel as well as demonstrate for observers deficits in information processing that these patients may exhibit.

Method

Two volunteers sit at a desk; they should attempt to sit in one chair. The volunteer sitting on the left of the chair represents the brain's left hemisphere and the other represents the brain's right hemisphere. The instructor should ensure that both participants are right-handed in order to demonstrate the better dexterity of the right hand. The instructor may also vary the procedure to use two left-handed volunteers in order to demonstrate the possible differences among left-handers who have more dexterity in their left hands but who may be similar to right-handers in having their language dominance in the left hemisphere.

Each student places the outer hand (left hand for the left subject and right hand for right subject) behind his or her back. Subjects place their inner hands on the desk, one crossing over the other. The two hands on the desk represent the split-brain patient's left and right hands. The instructor directs the participant representing the left hand to refrain from talking from this point on.

Activity 1

Place a shoe with a lace on the desk in front of the subjects. Direct them to tie the lace. The participants must use only the designated hands. The volunteer using the right hand may talk. The instructor may ask the observing students why only the volunteer using the right hand may talk and may remind the students at this point that the left hemisphere is typically the dominant hemisphere and usually holds the language centers. This discussion gives students an opportunity to draw for themselves the conclusion that the left hemisphere is the only hemisphere able to communicate verbally its experiences. The instructor may then direct the discussion toward the data concerning left-handedness.

The instructor then discusses the difficulty with which the volunteers tied the shoe and how practice might affect their performance. The instructor describes the initial lack of spontaneous activity and numbness in the left side of the body and apparent "blindness" in the left visual field of split-brain patients (Gazzaniga, 1967, 1987).

Activity 2

In this demonstration, the instructor simulates the apparent visual deficits observed among split-brain patients. The instructor directs the volunteer representing the right hemisphere to look to the left and the representative of the left hemisphere to look to the right. The instructor may use a cardboard partition to separate the lines of sight and flashcards or actual objects to introduce a stimulus to the right visual field. The instructor should then ask the volunteer representing the right hand to name the stimulus and choose the correct stimulus object from a selection of objects. The volunteer should correctly name the object and choose the stimulus object correctly, demonstrating the link

199

betiVeen the right visual field and the left hemisphere. The instructor then directs the volunteer representing the left hand to choose the presented object. The volunteer is likely to choose incorrectly or not at all, demonstrating the right hemisphere's lack of awareness of the right visual field.

The activity should be repeated with the stimulus presented to the left visual field. The left hand's ability to correctly choose from an array of objects containing the stimulus object demonstrates the connection between the right hemisphere and the left visual field. Next, the instructor should direct the volunteer representing the left hemisphere to name the stimulus object. The response will be incorrect, representing a guess by the left hemisphere.

In the discussion following this activity, the instructor may explain how this simulation demonstrates the apparent visual deficits observed in a specially contrived laboratory setting in which the gaze of the subject would be unnaturally restricted. In more normal settings, the subject would be able to scan both visual fields, allowing both hemispheres to receive the data presented to only one hemisphere in this demonstration.

Activity 3

The instructor blindfolds the volunteers and directs them to tie the shoe again. With visual cues absent, the volunteers are either unable to complete the task or find it very difficult. With each hemisphere attempting to complete the task independent of the other, the difficulty is soon apparent.

The instructor may ask students in the audience to speculate why the task is now more difficult. If the students do not spontaneously generate the idea that the volunteers could make the job more manageable by allowing the volunteer representing the right hand to talk the left hand through the task, then the instructor may direct the volunteers to do so. This activity helps the audience to infer that cooperation and coordination are possible, even when the subjects cannot see both hands.

Activity 4

While the subjects remain blindfolded, the instructor places a familiar object, such as a quarter, in the left hand. The instructor asks the left-hand volunteer if he or she can recognize the object, but the volunteer may respond only in a nonverbal manner. The instructor asks the speaker for the pair (i.e., the volunteer representing the right hand) to name the object. Very often the left-hand subjects will make a guess concerning the nature of the object. Given the circumstances, the guess may be accurate if the instructor selects an object readily available in the classroom setting.

During the ensuing discussion, the instructor may ask students how the left-hand volunteer's inability to name the object is similar to the experience of the split-brain patient. Again, the instructor elicits students' speculation about the relation between hemispheric language dominance and the experience of the split-brain patient.

Although the volunteer representing the left hand cannot communicate verbally, the instructor should encourage students to generate ideas concerning how the left hand might communicate its knowledge in other ways. For instance, the left-hand subject may pick the object from an array of objects placed in front of the volunteer pair upon removal of the blindfold.

Activity 5

For the final demonstration, the instructor places a retractable ball-point pen in the left hand and repeats the procedure for Activity 3. After the students speculate on the same conditions as in Activity 3, allow the left hand to retract the pen repeatedly. The instructor then encourages the volunteer using the right hand to try to name the object.

This activity allows students to generate hypotheses concerning the laterality of hearing. It also demonstrates the patient's reliance on all senses to make judgments and that the right hemisphere may be incapable of explaining the judgments. Consequently, the verbal hemisphere may not be capable of sufficiently explaining reactions or behavior, but may resort to rationalizations after the fact.

Instructors should encourage other students in the class to develop hypotheses concerning the behavior of the volunteers and suggest ways to test these hypotheses. The instructor would then be set to explain the laterality of the sensory organs.

Discussion

In these demonstrations, volunteers undergo the frustration split-brain patients may experience in a manner that loosely approximates actual conditions. When given time to practice, the volunteers learn to compensate for the handicaps involved with the condition. This learning process is similar to what split-brain patients experience after adaptation to the deficits. The restriction on the left-hand volunteer's speech makes the tasks more frustrating. This limitation simulates the split-brain patient's hemispheric dominance for language. Such insight into the subjective experience of the split-brain patient is impossible with computer simulations or textbook descriptions.

Before developing this demonstration, I used a class discussion and lecture to present the material and concepts involved in hemispheric dominance and the commissurotomy. This discussion preceded a computerized simulation that required students to conduct experiments with a simulated split-brain patient (Hay, 1985). After observing and participating in the classroom demonstration described in the present article, students report that the computer simulation is more understandable and meaningful.

Informal evaluation of the demonstration's effectiveness suggests that the students are more aware of brain functioning patterns demonstrated by the deficits resulting from the split-brain operation. Students ask more questions, and discussion is more spirited than in classes that do not see the demonstration, suggesting a greater level of interest.

In a survey of three introductory psychology classes, 85% *of 131 students rated these demonstrations as either helpful* or *very helpful* in understanding the information presented in class regarding the split-brain patient. More than 50% of the students rated the demonstrations as *more helpful* in understanding the related concepts than the computer simulation used in their laboratory assignments.

References

Gazzaniga, M. S. (1967). The split brain in man. *Scientific American, 217,* 24–29.

Gazzaniga, M. S. (1987). Perceptual and attentional processes following callosal section in humans. *Neuropsychologia, 25,* 119–133.

Hay, J. C. (1985). *Psychworld.* New York: McGraw-Hill.

Nebes, R. D., & Sperry, R. W. (1971). Hemispheric deconnection syndrome with cerebral birth injury in the dominant arm area. *Neuropsychologia, 9,* 247–259.

Note

I thank Vickie S. Morris, Barbara St. John, and three anonymous reviewers for their critical reading of an earlier draft of this article.

Neural Coding and Synaptic Transmission: Participation Exercises for Introductory Psychology

Richard Reardon
Francis T. Durso
Donald A. Wilson

Introductory Psychology students typically report that the material on physiological psychology is troublesome to master. Part of the problem may be instructors' difficulty in imparting an appreciation of the functioning of one neuron and how that neuron communicates with several other neurons.

There are few exercises that help students visualize and assimilate the fundamentals of neuroscience. Ackil (1986) described a trivia-type board game using physiological terms and concepts. This game may be helpful in motivating students to study, but it is not really a demonstration and thus does not permit students any experience of the workings of the neuron. Hamilton and Knox (1985) described a simulation of the major structures of the nervous system. This simulation captures the operation of the nervous system at a molar level; however, it does not help explain functioning at the neuronal level. Kasschau (1981) offered a simple and effective, but limited, demonstration of neuronal functioning, depicting the relative difference in speed between an action potential and synaptic transmission.

We report herein two additional exercises that involve students in a series of simulations of neuronal processes. The first exercise illustrates how excitatory and inhibitory postsynaptic potentials accumulate to produce an action potential. The second exercise, a follow-up to the first, illustrates chemical transmission at the synapse.

Neural Coding Exercise

Students simulate how the neuron accumulates and decodes inputs to produce an action potential. This exercise demonstrates spatial and temporal summation of graded excitatory and inhibitory postsynaptic potentials, the importance of firing rate, the all-or-none nature of the action potential, and the refractory period. In addition, students can gain an appreciation of the complexity of even the smallest neural network and begin to understand how noise in the system and perturbations at the neuronal level need not affect the output from a higher order system. We introduce the exercise soon after neural functioning has been presented in a regular class session.

We use the exercise in discussion sections (10 to 25 students), although it could also be performed in classes of 30 to 45. Some students' ability to view the proceedings may be restricted in classes larger than 45. The minimum time required is 8 to 10 min. The only materials needed are seven index cards; six cards have the letter *E* in one color ink, and the seventh card has an *I* in a contrasting color. We have found that the following sequence of four cases is optimal.

The Basic Simulation (Excitation Only)

One student acts as the receiving neuron and is stationed at the blackboard facing the class. Six other students, preferably in the front row of the class, represent six input paths. (These students are referred to as *inputs*.) The instructor gives each an *E* index card, thus all inputs in the basic simulation are excitatory. Each of the inputs is instructed to hold up his or her card for 3 s, with a 5-s interval between card flashes (i.e., each trial lasts 8 s; the instructor should stagger the starting times for each of the inputs by about 1 to 2 s). The receiving neuron fires whenever any three cards are visible at the same time; that is, the neuron reaches a firing threshold whenever three cards are simultaneously presented. To represent firing, the receiving neuron turns around and writes "I fire" on the blackboard. This turning away from the inputs mirrors a refractory period, during which time the neuron cannot respond to inputs. The receiving neuron is told to ignore a card that is in the process of going up or down, and the inputs are instructed to make their card presentations crisp. After 1 or 2 min, the instructor ends the simulation, and the class counts the number of times the receiving neuron fired.

Excitation and Inhibition

The second simulation illustrates what happens when inhibition is added. A seventh student with the *I* card joins the inputs of the basic simulation. Whenever the receiving neuron sees the *I* card, he or she must ignore one of the *E* cards that might be visible at the same time. Thus, the receiving neuron would not fire if three *E*s and one *I* were visible at the same moment. However, it would fire if four *E*s were present at the same time as the *I*. The decrease in firing rate should be quite noticeable.

Temporal Summation

Temporal summation refers to the ability of the neuron to make decisions about its own firing rate based on the rates of the incoming input signals. For this simulation, six inputs are all excitatory. Five of the inputs flash their cards for 3 s at 5-s intervals, as in the basic simulation. The sixth input flashes for 3 s with a 3-s interval between signals (each trial is 6 s for this input). The increase in firing rate over that of the basic simulation is fairly dramatic.

Spatial Summation

Spatial summation of graded postsynaptic potentials refers to the neuron's tendency to add together inputs arriving at different locations. Because graded potentials decrease in amplitude with distance, inputs closer to the cell body have a greater effect on the receiving neuron than those farther away. To simulate this, four of the six inputs are in the front of the classroom, and the remaining two are in the rear of the room, separated by several students. (Otherwise, this simulation is the same as the basic simulation in terms of input signal duration and interval.) The students should notice how much more difficult it is to detect the inputs in the rear of the room compared to those in the front. The neuron will occasionally miss one of these inputs, thus failing to reach threshold, resulting in a firing rate that is slower than that of the basic simulation.

As time permits, the instructor may lead the class through additional, more complex simulations. For example, in a variation of the excitation/inhibition simulation, the lone inhibitory input could be shown to have an even greater inhibitory effect by increasing its input rate. Or, a lone inhibitory input in the back of the room can be shown to have very little effect on the firing rate of the receiving neuron.

Effectiveness of the Exercise

To gauge the impact of this exercise on our students, we selected eight discussion sections from a single semester offering of our large Introductory Psychology course. Two instructors were involved; both were experienced graduate students who were responsible for four sections each. Each instructor supervised the simulations in two of their discussion sections and delivered a lecture of about 25 min on the action potential and neural coding to the other two sections. The lectures were generated from the instructor's manual of the text used for the course. One week later, the students in all eight sections who were present the previous week were given an 8-item, multiple-choice quiz on neurophysiology. These items were taken from the same item pool used in actual exams, but they did not duplicate items from the exams given that semester. Four of the items assessed general knowledge about the functions and parts of the neuron and about the action potential. They did not address neural coding. The remaining four items did attempt to tap students' understanding of excitation/inhibition, temporal summation, spatial summation, and firing rates.

The exercise groups performed better than the lecture groups on three of the four items that dealt with coding. The percentage correct for each group (exercise and lecture, respectively) for each item was Item 1, 32% and 26%; Item 2, 68% and 73%; Item 3, 80% and 63%; and Item 4, 71% and 60%. The overall percentages of correct items for each group were 63 for the exercise group and 55 for the lecture group. The total correct scores for the four items were analyzed with an unpaired two-group t test. The exercise groups ($M = 2.51$ or 63%) performed better than the lecture groups ($M = 2.21$ or 55%), $t(119) = 1.60$, $p < .06$, one-tailed. Differences between the exercise and lecture groups could have been due to variables other than the exercise–lecture manipulation (e.g., the exercise group may have simply been brighter than the lecture group). Therefore, we also performed a t test on the differences between the exercise and lecture groups on the items that were unrelated to coding. On the four such items, the mean correct score was 1.80 for the exercise groups and 1.87 for the lecture groups, not a significant difference, $t(119) = .36$, one-tailed. The data suggest that the exercise produces an effect that is at least as good as a lecture on neural coding (in a way that is probably more fun than a lecture).

Synaptic Transmission Follow-Up Exercise

Once students have a grasp of neural coding, we simulate synaptic transmission. In this exercise, which models the familiar children's game Musical Chairs, students take the role of various drugs and neurotransmitters. They simulate the action of the neurochemicals at the releaser sites of the originating axon and at the receptor sites of the receiving dendrite. Differences among drugs that block reuptake, occupy receptor sites, and mimic the neurotransmitter can be illustrated easily.

Basic Simulation

Place four chairs in the front of the class to represent origin sites of the releasing axon and an equal number of chairs facing them to represent the receptor sites on the receiving dendrite. In the basic simulation, students representing neurotransmitters sit in the axon chairs and, on a signal from the instructor, attempt to occupy the receptor chairs; they must sit completely in the receptor chairs and then attempt to return to the axon chairs (reuptake). The students remain seated except during the short time when they are moving between the two sites. In the basic simulation, attempts to occupy chairs will be successful; however, in later simulations, the presence of drugs might prevent or facilitate the occupation of either the receptor or releaser site. When all of the receptor chairs are occupied by a "neurotransmitter," or a substance that mimics a neurotransmitter, the neuron reaches its firing threshold.

In the basic simulation, the student experiences several basic features of synaptic transmission: (a) the origin of neurotransmitters in the sending neuron, (b) the release of neurotransmitters into the synaptic gap, (c) the stimulation of receptor sites by the neurotransmitters, and (d) the return of the neurotransmitters to the originating points. This last feature—reuptake—is often poorly communicated in introductory texts and lectures. In addition, when other chemicals enter the simulation, the student can gain an appreciation of basic neurotransmission and begin to understand how different drugs affect synaptic transmission. This physiological springboard helps the instructor explain both the effects of substance abuse in later chapters that cover drugs and behavior and the effects of antipsychotic medications when the course turns toward psychopathology and treatment. We offer three examples.

Mimicking the neurotransmitter. The stimulant drug nicotine has effects similar to the neurotransmitter acetylcholine. In the simulation, four students representing the drug nicotine and four students representing the neurotransmitter are available to sit in the receptor chairs. Initially, students representing the drug can stand behind the axon chairs. At the instructor's signal to release the neurotransmitter, both the neurotransmitter and the drug students will attempt to occupy the receptor site chairs, quickly filling them. With reuptake, the neurotransmitter students must return to the axon chairs, but the drug students will be present to continue occupation of the receptor chairs, that is, to continue stimulation.

Occupying receptor sites. The class of medications used to treat schizophrenia have their major effects by occupying the receptor sites that dopamine normally occupies. In schizophrenics, receptor sites are thought to be too sensitive to dopamine, thus, practically speaking, there is an excess of dopamine in these patients. By blocking the receptor sites, antipsychotic drugs prevent dopamine from contributing to the initiation of the postsynaptic potential. The blocking of dopamine, therefore, tends to relieve psychotic symptoms. In the simulation, at the instructor's signal, both the students representing neurotransmitter and those representing antipsychotic drugs are released into the synaptic gap to sit in the receptor chairs. To distinguish blocking agents (e.g., in this simulation) from the mimicking agents (e.g., as in the previous simulation), the blocking agents will begin the exercise behind the receptor chairs instead of behind the

axon chairs. Initially, the advantage will go to the neurotransmitter students, but as they return to the axon chairs, some receptor chairs will be occupied by the students who represent antipsychotic drugs, thus preventing the neurotransmitter students from sitting in a receptor chair following the next release of neurotransmitter. Neurotransmitter students who do not contact a receptor site because a receptor blocker is sitting in the receptor chair must return, through reuptake, to an axon chair to be released again. We usually mention the other ramifications of the dopamine phenomenon: Antipsychotic medications can block transmissions unrelated to the psychotic disturbance, resulting in Parkinson's-like symptoms; and patients with Parkinson's disease are often treated with the dopamine precursor, L-dopa.

Blocking reuptake. Some antidepressant drugs prevent the neurotransmitter norepinephrine from returning to the releasing axon, thus leaving more of the neurotransmitter in the synaptic gap. This effect is desirable because one of the biochemical problems in psychotic depression is not enough norepinephrine. In the simulation, four students representing antidepressant drugs occupy the releasing site chairs of norepinephrine after the latter have been released into the gap. The four students representing the neurotransmitter, because they must sit somewhere, will continue to occupy and reoccupy the receptor sites, increasing the neurotransmitter's impact on the receiving neuron.

Each simulation takes less than 3 to 4 min. During the first 2 to 3 min, student participants are assigned their roles; the remaining 1 min or so of actual simulation is sufficient to make the appropriate points. We have found that students participating in the exercise and those observing it are able to remember which students are neurotransmitters and which have some other role—the initial 2- to 3-min setup, if done carefully, tends to make this clear. However, some instructors may find it helpful to have students hold cards that identify the roles.

Beyond these basic simulations, the instructor can introduce complexity by combining drugs, placing inert substances into the system, considering the role of enzymatic degradation (e.g., by having some enzyme students "grab" neurotransmitter students, removing them from the synapse), and considering the more complex actions of some drugs. Cocaine, for example, stimulates the release of norepinephrine and inhibits its reuptake. Amphetamines stimulate the release of norepinephrine, mimic norepinephrine, and block reuptake.

Conclusion

The data we collected support our impressions that the neural-coding exercise improves students' understanding of the complexity of coding. Because the synaptic transmission follow-up exercise is used optionally, depending on time availability, we have no formal data on its effectiveness. However, anecdotal reports from our discussion instructors over several semesters suggest that it helps make concrete the often abstract presentations of synaptic transmission in textbooks.

For both exercises, students (and sometimes instructors) often report that they feel silly playing their roles. We tell them that feeling silly is appropriate and acceptable if an understanding of neural functioning results.

References

Ackil, J. E. (1986). PhysioPursuit: A trivia-type game for the classroom. *Teaching of Psychology, 13,* 91.

Hamilton, S. B., & Knox, T. A. (1985). The colossal neuron: Acting out physiological psychology. *Teaching of Psychology, 12,* 153–156.

Kasschau, R. A. (1981). Conduction of a neuronal impulse. In L. T. Benjamin, Jr. & K. D. Lowman (Eds.), *Activities handbook for the teaching of psychology* (pp. 207–208). Washington, DC: American Psychological Association.

Note

We thank Karen Bailey and Nick McDonald for allowing us to use students in their discussion sections to test our exercises and Terrie Thomas for her comments. Helpful suggestions by Ruth Ault and the reviewers are also gratefully acknowledged.

15. DEVELOPMENTAL PSYCHOLOGY

"Dear Mom and Dad": Using Personal Letters to Enhance Students' Understanding of Developmental Issues

Ellen N. Junn

When teaching courses on human development, I am invariably struck by the implicit, sometimes faulty, assumptions and analyses that students often rely on when confronted with developmental issues. First, the typical college student possesses only vague knowledge about children and their development. Second, students' perceptions of themselves as potential parents are often characterized by idealism and a false sense of having complete control over a child's developmental progress. At some levels, this sense of optimism is probably important and healthy for anyone caring for children, but it does not account for the many factors that interact in complex ways to affect development (Belsky, Lerner, & Spanier, 1980). Third, in courses dealing with human development, students often use their personal experiences as the sole criterion for evaluating research. For instance, when presented with a controversial topic, such as moral development, students often engage in heated debate over research findings, basing their arguments on nothing more than their own anecdotal experiences.

In an effort to address these issues, I designed a written exercise involving the writing of two semiautobiographical personal letters. A letter-writing assignment was chosen because it seemed particularly amenable to addressing a variety of developmental issues, and it is an innovative approach that has been used successfully by several researchers for purposes such as enhancing students' critical reading skills (Chamberlain & Burrough, 1985; Keller, 1982). This article describes the assignment, students' reactions to it, and the benefits of this technique.

The Assignment

Seventeen students enrolled in an upper division psychology course on parenting and family relations were given a detailed handout explaining the assignment. Students were told that the purpose of the assignment was to provide them with an opportunity to discuss various issues in developmental psychology from a personal, concrete perspective. Students were also told to draw from or incorporate relevant research in this assignment. Students were required to write two personal letters: (a) one to a future or actual child (son, daughter, or both) on the occasion of the child's 18th birthday and (b) one to both of the students' parents. In the handout, the instructor guaranteed confidentiality and assured students that the letters were not designed to demand disclosures of private or emotional family events. Instead, students were told to address a number of specific questions in each letter to the degree they felt most comfortable.

In the first letter to their child, students were told to cover the following areas: (a) When or why did you decide to have this child? (b) What specific qualities do you think are most important for a mother/father to have, and why? (c) What qualities do you personally possess that may help make you a successful parent? What qualities do you possess that may interfere with your ability to be a good parent? (d) Describe the qualities you hope your child will possess, and why. In doing so, address each of the following developmental areas and mention something specific you could do as a parent to foster growth in these areas: discipline, intellectual development, social and emotional development, sex-role development, moral development, and personality development. For this section, students were encouraged to use their knowledge of relevant research and theory in formulating concrete and reasonable ways of translating research findings into productive parenting practices with children. (e) Mention what you wish for your child in the future, and pass on any words of wisdom you might have acquired.

In the letter addressed to both of their parents, students were to cover four related areas: (a) Describe your general feelings about your present life and values and try to assess how much impact your parents had on you. (b) Describe three of the most important strengths of your mother and your father. Do you share these qualities? (c) Everyone has certain shortcomings; briefly describe a weakness or something that you would like to have changed in your parents. Do you share any of these qualities? (d) Given the following areas (discipline, intellectual development, social and emotional development, moral development, sex-role development, and personality development), choose one or two areas in which your mother and your father had the most influence on you, and explain how or why. (e) Thank your mother and father for something special.

Finally, in an optional third letter, students were told that they could send the instructions for the first letter (letter to your child) to their own mother or father and have them write the letter with the student in mind. In turn, students and parents could then exchange letters with one another.

Student Feedback

At the end of the course, 16 of the 17 students completed an anonymous questionnaire concerning their reactions to the assignment. Ratings for three questions were made on a 7-point scale, ranging from *strongly disagree* (1) to *strongly agree* (7). Student response to the assignment was very positive. The mean rating students gave for the value of the assignment in integrating course material with personal experience was 6.4 ($SD = .73$). Students also agreed that the assignment was relevant to the course ($M = 6.1$, $SD = 1.15$). Moreover, when asked how they felt about the exercise in general, almost all of the students (88%) felt either moderately or very positive about the assignment ($M = 6.4$, $SD = .89$); only two students (12%) felt neutral about the assignment. In fact, when polled on whether the assignment promoted learning, every student responded in the affirmative.

Several themes emerged from students' open-ended comments. Students were enthusiastic about the exercise, and some wrote the following statements: "it was a fantastic exercise," "loved everything about it," "invaluable," "it was like a rock thrown into still water—ripple effect—really made me think," and "it was very interesting, fun, and insightful." Students also agreed that they profited from this exercise, and one wrote that the assignment "has made it easier to relate to the issues in class." All students wrote that the exercise gave them valuable insights into their feelings about a whole range of issues—everything from simply sorting out feelings associated with the possibility of becoming a parent someday, to being flooded with special childhood memories, to renewing often unexpressed feelings of deep warmth and appreciation for their parents or children, and to gaining new insights into themselves and their parents. However, not all of the emotions associated with doing the exercise were positive. Two students wrote that the assignment was "difficult" or "stressful" because suppressed, sometimes hurtful childhood memories surfaced. These same students also stated that the exercise was nonetheless "very beneficial" and helped them sort out and express their feelings to their parents in a direct and constructive way. When asked if they intended to deliver the letter to their adult child someday, 75% of the students responded "yes," and the remaining 25% were unsure. The students who planned to give the letters to their children hoped that the letter would promote "insights" and "open closer communication" channels between parent and child. The responses for delivering their parent letters were more mixed: 63% responded "yes," 25% said "no," and 12% were unsure. The reason for not sending the letter to their parents was that these students were either "embarrassed" or "didn't want to hurt them." On the other hand, the primary reason cited for sending the letter to their parents was summed up by one student who stated, "I wanted to affirm [my parents] for their efforts and impact on my life." One student intended to try the optional third letter at a later date. Another student even intended to get her fiance to complete the assignment as well.

Finally, students were told that although the exercise was of a more personal nature, their performance on the assignment would be evaluated objectively in terms of how completely they addressed all parts of the letters and, in particular, how well they demonstrated an ability to integrate and incorporate developmental research and theory with their personal experiences. Because this assignment was the smaller of two writing assignments for the course

and because I was not certain of how students would respond to the assignment, I began by allocating this exercise a relatively small number of points (25 out of total of 325 points for the entire course). Student performance was evaluated by scoring each of the five parts of both letters as deserving anywhere from 0 to 6 points, depending on the specific area being addressed. Thus, in the first letter addressed to the students' child, the maximum number of points assigned for sections (a) through (e) were 1, 2, 2, 6, 1 points, respectively, with a maximum of 12 points for this first letter. The maximum number of points allocated for sections (a) through (e) in the second letter addressed to students' parents were 1, 4, 2, 3, 1, respectively, for a maximum of 11 points. An additional 2 points were allotted for overall clarity, writing style, and neatness. Students who completely addressed all areas of the letters and who clearly integrated research data and theory to support their conclusions were awarded the maximum number of points. The scores for the class ranged from 25 to 9, with a class average of 19.6 ($SD = 4.9$).

Discussion

This exercise achieved at least three objectives cited at the beginning of the article. First, in order to perform well on this assignment, students had to possess and display knowledge about children and their development.

Second, in completing the exercise, students became acutely aware of their implicit, often very unrealistic notions and attitudes regarding child development and parenting issues. For example, many students wrote the following comments: "It was astounding! It really made me reflect on my values and get a realistic view of parenting." "It made me think about what I expect of my children and it made me realize and reevaluate my expectations. I learned that my expectations for my children have to grow with them." "I learned that I had expectations for my future child that I never realized before." Upon returning the papers to students, I opened the discussion with the observation that although students expressed a general awareness that their expectations were often implicit and unrealistic, it was nonetheless highly instructive to contrast the tone of their letters to their child with the tone of the letters to their parents. Hence, the letters students addressed to their child were overwhelmingly positive, joyous, and replete with good intentions, whereas the letters to their parents were much more down-to-earth, concrete, and realistic in tone. Part of the reason for this difference is the fact that in writing to a future child, students often relied on their wishes and hopes for an "ideal" child as a future parent; whereas in writing to an actual parent, students resorted to writing about their concrete childhood experiences in a matter-of-fact, sometimes brutally honest manner without acknowledging the possibility that their parents once nursed or still possess similar idealistic expectations and hopes for them as children. This led to a fruitful discussion of the impact of expectations on development and the pitfalls of making attributions based on information that is related to the self versus related to another individual (e.g., Jones &

Nisbett, 1972; Nisbett & Ross, 1980). This awareness or egotism (e.g., Synder, Stephan, & Rosenfield, 1976) was cited by several students who wrote, "It let me come to terms with my children and what I want for them in their lives. I want them to know that I wasn't perfect and that I don't expect perfection from them." Another student expressed similar sentiments by writing, "It made you think of your past and future. Writing to my future child made me really think about how I was as a son. It also made me think about what to do if my children turn out like me."

Third, and perhaps most important, this exercise was designed to promote students' ability to understand, apply, and integrate current research and theory with their own lives in a productive and potentially useful way. Judging from the quality of the class discussions and the written comments of students, this assignment appears to have had some real impact in this area. For instance, one student wrote, "Most of us are always busy with our lives and trying to be a good mom or dad. But we don't sit down and think to learn about the research and theory out there that could be beneficial to us." Another student wrote, "This [assignment] really made me evaluate *how* to instill those qualities in my own child someday by becoming more aware of research." Finally, another student wrote, "By understanding the research, I learned that parenthood [and development] are very complex issues." All of these statements indicate that students are consciously and actively attempting to relate developmental research and theory to understand and perhaps even guide their own everyday experiences.

A similar letter-writing technique was discussed by Keller (1982) and Chamberlain and Burrough (1985). However, their methods were designed to enhance students' critical reading skills, and students were asked to critique a journal article in the form of a letter to a parent or a close friend. Thus, their students' letters were impersonal and not autobiographical. Other instructors have personalized assignments by having students keep journals or diaries (Baldwin, 1977; Hart, 1972; Hettich, 1976, 1980; Miller, 1979; Nin, 1969–1981; Ranier, 1978) or by presenting students with fictional or "live" case studies (Beckman, 1972; Gilliland, 1982; Graham & Cline, 1980; Hoover, 1980; McManus, 1986). However, all of these methods have various problems: Student journals tend to be difficult and time-consuming for instructors to monitor and evaluate; case studies are often limited in reflecting the complexities of real-life situations; and "live" case studies require instructors and students to arrange actual meetings with a "live" subject (see Graham & Cline, 1980; Hettich, 1980; McManus, 1986, for more on these points). My letter-writing technique is simple, straightforward, and avoids many of the pitfalls of the just-mentioned methods, yet it permits students to reap many of the rewards.

For example, in my letter-writing technique and others like it students are able to integrate abstract course concepts with their everyday lives (see Graham & Cline, 1980; Keller, 1982; Lott, 1978, for similar results), and this may stimulate critical thinking skills (Chamberlain & Burrough, 1985; Graham & Cline, 1980; Hettich, 1976, 1980; Keller, 1982). As other investigators have noted, one reason techniques such as these may be successful is that students enjoy the opportunity to express their own views and relate what they are learning to their own experiences (Beers, 1985; McKeachie, Lin, Moffett, & Daugherty, 1978; Polyson, 1985). In addition, techniques that rely on concrete or personal information increase student interest and motivation and may enhance retention of course information (Beckman, 1972; Beers, 1985; Hart, 1972; Kulik, Brown, Vestewig, & Wright, 1973; McManus, 1986). Furthermore, participants engaged in exercises that draw on personal experience also report greater self-understanding and personal growth (Baldwin, 1977; Jung, 1972; McManus, 1986; Miller, 1979; Milner, 1967; Nin, 1969–1981; Rogers, 1969). Other benefits include reducing plagiarism (Keller, 1982) and improving communication and writing skills (Beers, 1985; Blevins-Knabe, 1987; Britton, Burgess, Martin, McLeod, & Rosen, 1975; Staton, 1980).

Clearly, this personal letter-writing technique suggests many beneficial outcomes for student learning and represents a simple, engaging, and worthwhile assignment in the eyes of students. Instructors who wish to use this technique might heed a number of suggestions. Provide a detailed handout outlining the assignment's purpose and requirements and discuss these in class. In more intensive personal techniques, others have noted the need for instructors to demonstrate high levels of flexibility, sensitivity, and respect, particularly for the student who may find writing about personal experiences difficult (Polyson, 1985; Vande Kemp, 1981). Problems of this kind can probably be avoided if the instructor prepares well, remains flexible, and stresses that the assignment is meant to deepen understanding of developmental phenomena without being painful or intrusive. Evaluation of students' performance on this exercise is not difficult. Instructors could easily amend the exercise to incorporate more points. Instructors should also provide warm, meaningful, supportive, and sensitive feedback to students concerning their letters. An additional suggestion is to include comments on a separate page and avoid marking the original letter, because many students may wish to deliver their letters someday. Finally, this exercise can be a springboard for rich discussions involving a host of important topics, including the complexities of developmental interaction as well as other more specific empirical, theoretical, and methodological issues.

References

Baldwin, C. (1977). *One to one: Self-understanding through journal writing.* New York: Evans.

Beckman, M. D. (1972). Evaluating the case method. *Educational Forum, 36,* 489–497.

Beers, S. E. (1985). Use of a portfolio writing assignment in a course on developmental psychology. *Teaching of Psychology, 12,* 94–96.

Belsky, J., Lerner, R. M., & Spanier, G. B. (1980). *The child in the family.* Reading, MA: Addison-Wesley.

Blevins-Knabe, B. (1987). Writing to learn while learning to write. *Teaching of Psychology, 14,* 239–241.

Britton, J., Burgess, T., Martin, N., McLeod, A., & Rosen, N. (1975). *The development of writing abilities* (11–18). London: Macmillan.

Chamberlain, K., & Burrough, S. (1985). Techniques for teaching critical reading. *Teaching of Psychology, 12,* 213–215.

Gilliland, K. (1982). Use of drama students as "clients" in teaching abnormal psychology. *Teaching of Psychology, 9,* 120–121.

Graham, P. T., & Cline, P.C. (1980). The case method: A basic teaching approach. *Theory Into Practice, 19,* 112–116.

Hart, N. I. (1972). Using the personal journal in literature teaching. *Reading Improvement, 9,* 87–89.

Hettich, P. (1976). The journal: An autobiographical approach to Learning. *Teaching of Psychology, 3,* 60–63.

Hettich, P. (1980). The journal revisited. *Teaching of Psychology, 7,* 105–106.

Hoover, K. A. (1980). Analyzing reality: The case method. In K. A. Hoover (Ed.), *College teaching today: A handbook for postsecondary instruction* (pp. 199–223). Boston: Allyn & Bacon.

Jones, E. E., & Nisbett, R. E. (1972). The actor and the observer: Divergent perceptions of the causes of behavior. In E. E. Jones, D. E. Kanouse, H. H. Kelley, R. E. Nisbett, S. Valins, & B. Weiner (Eds.), *Attribution: Perceiving the causes of behavior* (pp. 79–94). Morristown, NJ: General Learning Press.

Jung, J. (1972). Autobiographies of college students as a teaching and research tool in the study of personality development. *American Psychologist, 27,* 779–783.

Keller, R. A. (1982). Teaching from the journals. *Teaching Sociology, 9,* 407–409.

Kulik, J. A., Brown, D. R., Vestewig, R. E., & Wright, J. (1973). *Undergraduate education in psychology.* Washington, DC: American Psychological Association.

Lott, J. (1978). Improving reading in the social studies: Classroom journals. *Social Education, 42*(1), 15–17.

McKeachie, W. J., Lin, Y-G., Moffett, M. M., & Daugherty, M. (1978). Effective teaching: Facilitative vs. directive style. *Teaching of Psychology, 5,* 193–194.

McManus, J. L. (1986). "Live" case study/journal record in adolescent psychology. *Teaching of Psychology, 13,* 70–74.

Miller, S. U. (1979). Keeping a psychological journal. *Gifted Child Quarterly, 23,* 168–175.

Milner, M. (1967). *On not being able to paint.* New York: International Universities Press.

Nin, A. (1969–1981). *The diary* (Vols. I–VII). New York: Harcourt Brace Jovanovich.

Nisbett, R. E., & Ross, L. (1980). *Human inference: Strategies and shortcomings of social judgment.* Engelwood Cliffs, NJ: Prentice-Hall.

Polyson, J. (1985). Students' peak experiences: A written exercise. *Teaching of Psychology, 12,* 211–213.

Ranier, T. (1978). *The new diary.* Los Angeles: Tarcher.

Rogers, C. R. (1969). *Freedom to learn.* Columbus, OH: Merrill.

Snyder, M. L., Stephan, W. G., & Rosenfield, D. (1976). Egotism and attribution. *Journal of Personality and Social Psychology, 35,* 656–666.

Staton, J. (1980). Writing and counseling: Using a dialogue journal. *Language Arts, 57,* 514–519.

Vande Kemp, H. (1981). Teaching psychology of the family: An experiential approach and a working bibliography. *Teaching of Psychology, 8,* 152–156.

Using Biographies of Adults Over 65 Years of Age to Understand Life-Span Developmental Psychology

Joan M. Neysmith-Roy
Carmel L. Kleisinger

Developmental psychology is informative in understanding not only the interrelations of the major life stages but also the process of learning. Individuals develop from concrete to abstract interaction with their worlds as life proceeds from infancy to adulthood, and the learning process, at any specific stage in life, is evidently facilitated by moving from direct experience to abstract concepts. Zuber-Skerritt (1992) described the learner as "not merely a passive consumer of accumulated knowledge, but an active producer and reproducer of knowledge and theory" (p. 55). Too frequently the undergraduate program demands that students in their early adult years absorb abstract concepts and relations without the benefit of the life experience from which the theories have evolved. Teachers can facilitate the learning process and provide a clearer understanding of the material being studied by sequencing material from the concrete to the abstract. In the process, students are encouraged to rely less on rote memory for accumulating knowledge and more on integrating experience with abstract learning for true understanding of the theory under consideration.

Clements (1995) found that integrating experiential-learning activities in the classroom increased interest in subject matter and understanding of course material but did not significantly affect average final grades. Clinchy (1995) demonstrated the use of interviews as a powerful tool that allows an individual to "actively construct, rather that passively receive, knowledge about developmental psychology" (p. 100). Furthermore, Rissland (1991) emphasized the use of examples or specific incidents as a means of applying knowledge and gaining more generalized principles. Pulos (1993) and O'Sullivan (1993) used activities and interactions with real people to help dispel misperceptions about particular groups or cultures. The project described herein is one such activity—an interview that provided specific examples to help students better understand Erikson's (1963) eight stages of human development.

For a semester course in Life-Span Developmental Psychology, the instructor wanted to help students synthesize and integrate information and ideas, grow personally, develop an informed appreciation of other cultures, and learn specific concepts and theories of the subject matter. Therefore, second-year undergraduates were given the choice of either completing a biographical project with a senior citizen in the community or writing a traditional term paper. Although both projects could lead to a better understanding of the interrelations of the major life stages, the instructor assumed that students working with a senior citizen to compose a life log would vicariously experience the major life stages of one specific individual. At the end of the semester, students who did the biographical project evaluated the extent to which class goals were met and suggested possible improvements.

Procedure

During the first 2 weeks of the semester, Erikson's (1963) eight stages of human development were explained in detail. During the seventh lecture (third week) of the semester, students received a two-page sheet that described the option of completing either the biographical project or the term paper. Both were explained briefly in writing and orally. Students were then given 1 week to make their choice. In the fourth week, they attended either a 1-hr class devoted to the biographical project or a 1-hr class on researching and writing a traditional term paper. Students who chose the biographical project were instructed to work with an older adult (over 65 years of age) to produce a log of his or her major life events, starting with the earliest memories and continuing to the present. The log was a biography of written and pictorial memories, organized by the student, from material gleaned from the interviews.

For this project, students received training in interviewing techniques and were assisted in developing a series of interview questions. For example, students asked their senior to talk about the period in life that the senior had found most exciting. After that specific story was told, the student worked forward and backward through the stages to gather the necessary material. Ethical issues and needs of the elderly were also stressed. Students learned various styles for developing a presentable life log as well as the difference between the requirements for the life log and the paper that accompanies it.

Students met with their senior citizen at least three times. In the first session, the student described the project and obtained a completed consent form. In a second meeting, the student interviewed the senior citizen to gather the important demographic and historical information and requested that the senior bring some photos to the third session. The third session was used to verify the information with the senior citizen and to integrate photos into the final version of the life log. Total interview time ranged from 4 to 6 hr over the three sessions.

Students also wrote a six- to eight-page paper describing how their individual worked through the major life stages. In this case study, students highlighted the tasks and developmental issues of each stage, discussing how earlier experiences may have influenced later stages. Students presented the logs to their senior citizens at the end of term. Many had photos taken of that presentation, which demonstrates the bond that developed between participants and students.

Table 1. Student Agreement With Positive and Negative Evaluation Statements

Statements	Agreement	
	n^*	%
Academically challenging	22	62.9
Interesting	32	91.4
A learning experience	30	85.7
Fun	29	82.8
Creatively challenging	26	74.3
Too time-consuming	1	2.8
Boring	0	0.0
Not beneficial	0	0.0
Not challenging enough	1	2.8
Too difficult	0	0.0

$^*N = 35.$

The life log was worth 10% of the total points in the course, and the accompanying paper was worth 20%. The logs were not corrected for minor errors because I did not want to deface them. However, major errors, such as frequent poor sentence structure, spelling errors, or serious grammatical mistakes, were returned to the student for correction. Grading the life log and the paper took longer than grading the traditional term paper, but the wealth of material from the life experiences of these senior citizens more than made up for the extra time. Each life log and paper combination took about one and a half times longer to correct than the traditional term paper.

Project Evaluation

Of the 54 people who completed the class, 35 chose to do the biographical project. These students were asked to evaluate the project after they had submitted it to me but before they knew their grade. First, students rated on a 5-point scale (ranging from 1 [strongly disagree] to 5 [strongly agree]) if the project was a valuable way to learn about life-span development. Twenty-four (68.6%) strongly agreed with the statement, 11 (31.4%) somewhat agreed, no one was neutral, and no one somewhat disagreed or strongly disagreed.

Next, students rated the statement, "This project was helpful in providing an understanding of how to apply developmental theory and integrate the different life stages to real people and situations," on the same 5-point scale. Twenty-two (62.9%) strongly agreed, 11 (31.4%) somewhat agreed, 2 (5.7%) were neutral, and no one either somewhat disagreed or strongly disagreed. Finally, students read a list of five positive and five negative reactions that they might have had concerning the project. They were asked to check any that applied to them. Table 1 summarizes the answers.

Six students added other comments. One emphasized that the project became a great positive experience not only for herself but the whole family, another stated that the project brought her closer to her grandmother and her mother's side of the family, one was pleased with being able to use psychological theories to evaluate a person's life experience, and two students mentioned that they now wanted to develop biographies with their own parents.

Students were then asked specifically if they would modify the requirements of the biographical project. Four (11.4%) would modify it, and 31 (88.6%) would not. As a result of implementing changes based on previous evaluations of the project, the percentage of students who would make the same choice next time changed from 75% in the first use of the project to 100% in the most recent semester. Of those who wrote the term paper and completed the evaluation form, 66.3% stated that they would prefer to do the term paper if given a choice again, whereas 34.6% stated that they would try the biographical project because "those who did that really enjoyed the experience." Finally, students were asked to give an overall rating on the assignment: 19 (54.3%) rated it excellent, 15 (42.9%) very good, 1 (2.9%) acceptable, and no one marked the project as fair or poor.

Discussion

Students who chose to do the biographical project, rather than the usual term paper, both enjoyed and learned from the experience. Many students remarked that they had learned about senior citizens' lives and had begun to feel both comfortable with the senior citizens and less afraid of their futures. They also mentioned that the project afforded creativity and integration of concrete experiences with theoretical ideas.

The senior citizens' reactions to the project were also very positive. Some commented as follows:

I was pleased to be asked to participate. Researching pictures and recalling events of my life was very exciting. I will treasure my life log and will share it with anyone who might be interested. For the student, I'm sure it will have been an interesting project, and it was a privilege to participate.

I enjoyed talking about my life. I think it's always helpful to look back. I also think it's important for young people to listen.

A humbling and learning experience for both of us. The organization of a personal biography is truly challenging.

The biographical project was well accepted by students and senior citizens, and it met three of the four goals for the class.

Synthesize and Integrate Information and Ideas

Many students commented on the value of using one specific life experience to get a practical glimpse of how Erikson's (1963) eight stages of human development interact and influence later stages. Some senior citizens had difficulty remembering details of the preschool years. Many of these individuals were able to rely on family stories or made contact with siblings and other relatives to obtain information to include in the life log. Two students were unable to get any early information on their senior citizen, so the life logs contained basic demographic information for the preschool period. For the paper section of the assignment, these two students explained the paucity of information and then

spoke of hypothetical possibilities drawn from both the limited demographic information and the social experiences of these senior citizens during the later stages.

Foster Personal Growth

Several students commented on how much they had learned about the life of a senior citizen. They became less afraid of their own aging process when they realized that the elderly do make contributions to their families and society. Students who interviewed their own relatives learned a lot about their own family's history. Some students said that the project gave them a tool to ask more in-depth questions of a family member. Most mentioned how much closer they felt to the senior citizen as a result of the interaction.

Appreciate Other Cultures

This particular goal was minimally met in the project. Rather than appreciating other cultures, students learned to appreciate stages in life that they had not yet encountered. After interviewing a female member of the gay community, one student wrote, "I feel I have a new mentor in my life. I see now that there is life for gays in our senior years. I was really becoming concerned for this issue until I did this project."

Learn Specific Concepts and Theories

This biographical project was only one section of the entire course, but students did learn about Freud, Erikson, Piaget, and other theorists in the process. They also learned the importance of obtaining consent before interviewing an individual as well as the harsh realities of ethical research when a participant withdraws before completing the project. Luckily, this happened to only one student, who found a replacement.

Potential problems in conducting this project can be avoided by taking a few precautions. The specific hour devoted to teaching students the skills needed for completing the project greatly enhanced the ease with which students completed the task. Moreover, the six lectures explaining Erikson's (1963) eight stages of human development and their interrelations prepared students to handle the demands of both the biographical project and the term paper. When this early introduction was omitted, students felt unprepared to work on their projects and term papers.

One of the instructor's major concerns was the possibility that students might not follow through with presenting the life log to the senior citizen. Many senior citizens had supplied treasured photographs that students needed to return. To ensure this, credit was not given for the project until students turned in a form, signed by the senior citizen, indicating receipt of the life log. An additional backup was to include participants' phone numbers on their consent forms.

References

Clements, A. D. (1995). Experiential-learning activities in undergraduate developmental psychology. *Teaching of Psychology, 22,* 115–118.

Clinchy, B. M. (1995). A connected approach to the teaching of developmental psychology. *Teaching of Psychology, 22,* 100–104.

Erikson, E. (1963). *Childhood and society.* New York: Norton.

O'Sullivan, M. J. (1993). Teaching undergraduate community psychology: Integrating the classroom and the surrounding community. *Teaching of Psychology, 20,* 80–83.

Pulos, S. (1993). Illustrating life-span development in physical competence. *Teaching of Psychology, 20,* 244–245.

Rissland, E. L. (1991). Example based reasoning. In J. F. Voss, D. N. Perkins, & J. W. Segal (Eds.), *Informal reasoning and education* (pp. 187–208). Hillsdale, NJ: Lawrence Erlbaum Associates, Inc.

Zuber-Skerritt, O. (1992). *Professional development in higher education.* London: Kogan Page.

Note

We thank our students for their enthusiasm and cooperation in evaluating the biographical project, and we thank Ruth Ault for her detailed assistance in preparing this article.

Create-a-Children's Game:
An Exercise for Developmental Psychology Classes

Georgia N. Nigro

Outside-the-classroom activities for developmental psychology courses are not difficult to devise when a ready source of willing children and parents exists. Developmental students can observe gender segregation firsthand, try out Piagetian conservation tasks, and ask adolescents about the moral dilemmas they have faced. Ready sources of children and parents may be harder to identify in small towns, the sites of many residential colleges. This exercise does not depend on a pool of participants; instead, it relies on students' knowledge of children's material world. Inspired by Berrenberg and Prosser's (1991) create-a-game exam technique for a history of psychology course, I developed a create-a-children's-game exercise for developmental psychology students. Although I used the exercise as a laboratory assignment, worth 15% of the final grade, it could easily serve as an exam exercise, as in Berrenberg and Prosser's case. After describing the assignment and examples of the games, I offer some thoughts about adapting the exercise to achieve other goals in the developmental psychology course.

Instructions and Grading

Students in my developmental psychology course complete two of three outside-the-classroom laboratory assignments, each worth 15% of their total grade. For the game assignment, students can work in groups of up to four individuals, so long as they understand that each individual will receive the same grade. Students have the assignment in hand for 1 month, a period that includes a 1-week recess. Instructions for the assignment are as follows:

> Create a new game for children. Include rules, game board, game pieces, or whatever is needed to play the game. Distinguish your game from others like it, and argue convincingly, based on what you have learned in developmental psychology, that children will like your game. Discuss briefly what it will do for children of a specific age range.

In class, I describe the criteria I use in grading: (a) logical consistency of the rules, (b) developmental appropriateness of the game, (c) completeness of the discussion distinguishing the game from others like it, (d) imaginativeness, and (e) artfulness of the materials. Excellence in one criterion can override weakness in another, I tell students.

More than two thirds of the class choose to complete this assignment, and the resulting distribution of grades is negatively skewed because most students meet the grading criteria handily. Logical inconsistencies are rare and usually occur in descriptions of multiple routes to winning. Developmental appropriateness of the games is exceptionally high; students seem particularly deft at appealing at once to the perceptual, cognitive, motoric, and socioemotional skills of the developing child. Due to packaging limitations, students are sometimes hampered in their ability to distinguish their games from others on the market, but they make strong efforts. Imaginativeness and artfulness of the games are very impressive. My later descriptions inadequately capture these qualities.

Examples of Games

Most of the games involve boards, although, as the later examples illustrate, students transform this basic component of games in interesting ways. Two examples follow.

1. *The Color Connection.* In this two-part game, players first create a game board by placing colored tiles on a flat surface according to the roll of a 12-sided color die and a

6-sided standard die. So, for example, if a player rolls 3 and blue, the player receives three blue tiles and places them on the surface so that one side of each touches the side of a previously laid tile. When all tiles have been played, each player places a white "home" base on top of his or her last laid tile, and the second part of the game begins. In this part, players travel the bases, either as a group trying to better its own best time or individually, against other players, traveling to and from each home base via the most direct route. A turn involves rolling the dice and traveling the number of tiles indicated, landing on the color rolled. The game is suitable for children aged 5 and older.

2. *Quinoovers*. In this game of questions and maneuvers, children begin at a starting line that is set up, along with a finish line, by the players themselves each time they play. An older child or adult serves as questioner and asks the first child in line a question drawn from a question deck (e.g., "Name a sport that begins with the letter B"). If the child answers correctly, the questioner then reads a motion drawn from the motion deck, such as, "Take two crab steps forward." These movements take the child closer to the finish line, and the first player to reach it wins. The game is suitable for children of many ages, depending on the level of the items in the question deck.

Student Response

Students are very enthusiastic about this assignment, as demonstrated by the large proportion of students who choose to complete it, the obvious effort that goes into their constructions, and the level of engagement with developmental issues exhibited in their discussions of the games. None of the games follows the formula that seems to operate in the marketplace today: Take the current commercially successful stars, inscribe them on a game board with a circuitous route, and apply the rules of chance to move the game pieces from start to finish. Students take the whole child into account; their games are more active, social, and cognitive than many commercially available ones.

Students have also registered their enthusiasm for this assignment by suggesting interesting elaborations and variations on it. One suggestion is to invite classrooms of children from local schools to visit campus so students can field test the games. In the process of discussing this suggestion, students in a recent term had a lively exchange about children's cheating—what to do about it, what developmental functions it serves, and individual differences in it. Another suggestion is to incorporate more discussion of games and toys into course lectures. I am particularly interested in the opportunities for multidisciplinary contributions. For example, Fine's (1987) ethnographic study of little league baseball, with its keen attention to the problems of doing fieldwork with children in natural settings, would fit well into a methodology lecture. Formanek-Brunell's (1992) social history of doll play in 19th-century America would challenge students' thinking about contemporary doll play. The value of these multidisciplinary contributions should be obvious: By sharing in the sensibilities of researchers from other disciplines, we stand a better chance of understanding children in time and place (Elder, Modell, & Parke, 1993). Games are a felicitous route to that understanding.

References

Berrenberg, J. L., & Prosser, A. (1991). The create-a-game exam: A method to facilitate student interest and learning. *Teaching of Psychology, 18,* 167–169.

Elder, G. H., Jr., Modell, J., & Parke, R. D. (1993). Studying children in a changing world. In G. H. Elder, Jr., J. Modell, & R. D. Parke (Eds.), *Children in time and place* (pp. 3–21). New York: Cambridge University Press.

Fine, G. A. (1987). *With the boys.* Chicago: University of Chicago Press.

Formanek-Brunell, M. (1992). Sugar and spite: The politics of doll play in nineteenth-century America. In E. West & P. Petrik (Eds.), *Small worlds: Children and adolescents in America, 1850–1950* (pp. 107–127). Lawrence: University Press of Kansas.

Note

I thank the students in my developmental psychology classes for sharing their fabulous ideas with me. I am especially grateful to those who gave me permission to describe their games in print.

Dr. Kohlberg Goes to Washington: Using Congressional Debates to Teach Moral Development

Johnna K. Shapiro

The study of moral development—of how children learn the meaning of right and wrong—is one of the largest areas of empirical research within the general area of social development (Flavell, 1985). In teaching about this topic, instructors often point out the threefold nature of morality: It depends on emotional development (in the form of ability to feel guilt or shame), social development (manifested by the recognition of the group and the importance of moral behavior for the group's existence), and cognitive development (especially the ability to take another's perspective).

One of the most prominent theories of moral development takes this cognitive–developmental perspective (Kohlberg, 1976). Kohlberg's theory emphasizes the reasoning behind an individual's moral choices, rather than the choices themselves. This reasoning is evaluated through the use of moral dilemmas, in which correct behavior is ambiguous and must be decided on and justified by the person being evaluated. For example, the classic Heinz dilemma (Rest, 1979) presents the story of a man whose wife is dying. She must receive a particular drug that is available from one pharmacist in the town. Heinz has only half the money that the pharmacist is charging and cannot persuade the pharmacist to lower the price. The dilemma is whether Heinz should steal the drug in order to save his wife. The evaluator is interested in why the individual believes that Heinz should or should not steal the drug; the decision itself (yes or no) is secondary. The structure, rather than the content, of moral decision making is of greatest interest to Kohlberg and allows discrimination among the different stages of moral development in the theory.

Students in introductory psychology and developmental psychology courses often have difficulty grasping the idea that the answer to a dilemma may be less important than the reasoning behind it. In addition, students often understand the abstract differences among stages of moral reasoning outlined by the theory but have trouble recognizing those differences when asked to go beyond stories, such as the Heinz dilemma, to real-world situations that are morally ambiguous. This classroom activity uses actual arguments from congressional debates to provide practice in applying the theory and to demonstrate that seemingly identical moral choices can often arise from different patterns of reasoning. The time involved can be as little as 15 min for a brief presentation to a full class period involving in-depth discussion of the debate topics and relevant issues.

The activity begins with the introduction of a topic that has been debated in Congress. Debates are easily accessed through electronic media (from the C–SPAN Network) or print media (from the *Congressional Record*). The topic should be one on which students are likely to have personal opinions. One topic used successfully was the debate on whether the United States should enter the conflict in the Arabian Gulf. (See appendix for examples on both sides of the Gulf War debate at all six stages.) Other examples include debates on abortion rights, gun control, or possible U.S. military interventions (e.g., in Bosnia or Haiti).

At least two arguments at each of the six stages of Kohlberg's (1976) theory should be chosen, one falling on each side of the debate. Students are presented with the arguments and challenged to use Kohlberg's description of the six stages of moral development to determine the stage of moral reasoning at which each anonymous legislator was operating. Students can also be asked to explain and/or defend their findings, either in groups of three or four students or with the entire class. If time is short, worksheets containing the arguments can be distributed for students to take home and bring back to class for discussion. If time allows, students can debate the topic among themselves before receiving the congressional arguments. Each student is asked

to write out (anonymously) his or her opinion and a brief statement of the reasoning behind that choice, as is done in Congress. After reading the various statements, the class can then determine the stage at which each anonymous student's reasoning would fall on the Kohlberg scale. As always, an instructor should consider the atmosphere within a given classroom before using this technique. Students should feel comfortable with one another before judging and being judged (even anonymously). An alternative method could include the students generating arguments for either side based on the six stages. This procedure would eliminate any possibility of students feeling embarrassed by reactions to their reasoning.

After the topic is discussed and the stages of congressional arguments determined, other potential discussion topics remain. Instructors can ask whether the technique is a fair and sensitive indicator of moral development and whether reasoning (i.e., cognition) is different from actions (i.e., behavior). Strengths and weaknesses of Kohlberg's (1976) theory can be discussed as well. For example, students can be asked to comment on whether the theory itself is biased toward particular kinds of reasoning and if the evaluation may be different, depending on one's culture or the topic being debated. If the sex of the legislator giving the argument is known, the problem of potential gender differences in moral reasoning can also be brought up, which would lead naturally into a discussion of the work of Gilligan (1982) and others. (Students can also be asked to determine the sex of the person making the argument, if possible, and to defend that person's decision using Gilligan's theory.)

This activity increases student interest in moral thinking and in the nuances of Kohlberg's (1976) theory. It involves students in a real-life moral dilemma, encourages discussion on the merits of a major developmental theory, and demonstrates the distinction between the content of a moral decision and the cognitive structure behind that content.

References

Flavell, J. H. (1985). *Cognitive development* (2nd ed.). Englewood Cliffs, NJ: Prentice Hall.

Gilligan, C. F. (1982). *In a different voice*. Cambridge, MA: Harvard University Press.

Kohlberg, L. (1976). Moral stages and moralization: The cognitive–developmental point of view. In T. Lickona (Ed.), *Moral development and behavior: Theory, research and social issues* (pp. 31–53). New York: Holt.

Rest, J. R. (1979). *Revised manual for the Defining Issues Test*. Minneapolis: Minnesota Moral Research Projects.

Appendix

To the best of my knowledge, the following are actual quotations taken from U.S. congressional debates on a resolution supporting the administration's policy on Iraq's invasion of Kuwait. The debates were broadcast on the C–SPAN network in December 1989. Accompanying each quotation is the related stage in Kohlberg's (1976) theory of moral development.

Arguments Against U.S. Involvement

"We shouldn't consider war . . ."

"because it would hurt our economy . . ." (Stage 1).

"because we'll have more money for domestic issues . . ." (Stage 2).

because we don't want to appear too militaristic . . ." (Stage 3).

because war is killing and killing is against the law . . ." (Stage 4).

"even though the situation is bad, war is damaging to people and property and society agrees *that* is bad . . ." (Stage 5).

"although atrocities have been committed, it would be an even greater atrocity to wage war . . ." (Stage 6).

Arguments For U.S. Involvement

"We should consider war . . ."

"because our oil is threatened . . ." (Stage 1).

"because we can gain security of the oil supply . . ." (Stage 2).

"because we don't want the world to see us as weak . . ." (Stage 3).

"because the U.N. has laid down written resolutions which should be upheld . . ." (Stage 4).

"the situation is extreme enough that society's rights are threatened and need to be defended . . ." (Stage 5).

"evil is on the march, and it would be morally wrong to allow it to continue . . ." (Stage 6).

The Garbage-Can Illusion as a Teaching Demonstration

Robert Cavalier
Richard Wesp

A variety of classroom demonstrations of illusions are available to stimulate student interest in perception. Cowan (1974) described how to create several illusions of movement by using an overhead projector. Fawl (1981) described an illusion that demonstrates the influence of size on the estimation of weight. Corey (1989) explained how to construct a moving cube illusion. Klopfer and Doherty (1992) described construction and classroom use of the Janus illusion.

Although these more traditional demonstrations and reproductions of geometrical illusions in most introductory textbooks are valuable, they fall short in illustrating to students how perceptual interpretations may routinely lead to perceptual distortions in everyday life. We have observed for several years that students overestimate the height of a classroom garbage can. This illusion is very powerful and dramatically illustrates the phenomenon of perceptual distortion. This article demonstrates the magnitude of this phenomenon and explains how it can be used as a classroom demonstration of illusions in everyday life.

Method

We asked a class of 31 introductory psychology students (15 women and 16 men) to write their name on a piece of paper. The instructor placed a classroom waste paper can (14.5 in. tall with a base 10 in. in diameter) on the desk in front of the class and stated, "I want you to estimate the height, in inches, of this can." While pointing first to the bottom and then to the top of the can, the instructor repeated the instructions by asking "How tall is the can from its base to its top? Write your estimate in inches on the piece of paper." Using a similar procedure, the instructor asked students to estimate the width of the bottom of the can and then collected the papers. Students asked the instructor to divulge the actual size of the can and expressed surprise and disbelief when they were told and then shown that the can was 14.5 in. tall. Next, the class discussed the power of the illusion and possible reasons for it.

Results

Of the 31 participants, 4 students (2 women and 2 men) underestimated the height of the can: Three estimated 14 in. and one estimated 13 in. The remaining 27 estimates ranged from 15 to 30 in. The mean estimate of 20.2 in. was significantly larger than the actual height of 14.5, $t(30) = 6.27$, $p < .001$. The mean estimate of the base was 10.1 in. and was not significantly different from the actual width of 10, $t(30) = .39$, $p < .10$.

In a later class, students were asked to rate the demonstration in terms of how much it increased their ability to understand the material covered. On a 7-point scale ranging from 1 (not at all) to 7 (very much), the average student rating was 5.8.

Discussion

Results indicate a robust and reliable overestimation of the height, but accurate judgments of the width, of the garbage can. Estimates averaged nearly 1½ times the actual height, and 87% of the students overestimated the height. The relative accuracy in predicting the width demonstrates that the overestimation of height is more than an inability to make size judgments. These results have been informally replicated several times. Student ratings suggest that they found this demonstration useful.

This error in the estimation of the height of an object that students see every class helps to demonstrate the ecological validity of the laboratory research presented in textbooks. Although textbooks describe other examples of real-life illusions (e.g., the moon illusion or why fog might distort a pilot's sense of depth), they do not provide students with immediate, concrete personal experience with an illusion (Kozub, 1991). Students are surprised at the size of their overestimation of this common object and this, we believe, generates an interest in the phenomenon. Thus, the demonstration reinforces the importance and relevance of an understanding of perceptual theories.

The illusion is reliable; the compelling question, as with many illusions, is why perceivers misjudge what they observe. We have considered many explanations for this overestimation. For example, one may argue that the demonstration is not truly an illusion or that it is simply an example of the vertical–horizontal illusion. Our students, colleagues, and reviewers of this article have offered many other explanations. The value of the demonstration is not that it answers questions but that it encourages discussion about the process of perception itself. Because the demonstration requires such little time and equipment, classroom-generated theories are easily tested, further emphasizing to students the empirical basis of psychology.

We have had students generate, discuss, and test several theories about the phenomenon. In a recent class, for example, a student noted the similarity between the garbage-can illusion and the horizontal–vertical illusion. The observation led to the hypothesis that the horizontal–vertical illusion "explained" the garbage-can illusion. This hypothesis allowed for discussion of the problem of assuming that two phenomena are caused by the same underlying process simply because they share a common attribute; in this case, both illusions involve the overestimation of height. Then, we considered ways of testing the hypothesis that the two illusions were based on a common process. In another class, students questioned whether the illusion might be found with other common objects, and they designed a simple study to test their idea. Thus, the garbage-can illusion offers several interesting possible explanations, many of which can be empirically tested. Its demonstration has been suc-

cessful in stimulating student interest and discussion about illusions and perception.

References

Corey, J. R. (1989). Constructing a moving cube illusion. *Teaching of Psychology, 16,* 139–140.

Cowan, T. M. (1974). Creating illusions of movement by an overhead projector. *Teaching of Psychology, 1,* 80–82.

Fawl, C. L. (1981). Size–weight illusion: A pound is a pound the world around? In L. T. Benjamin, Jr. & K. D. Lowman (Eds.), *Activities handbook for the teaching of psychology* (Vol. 1, pp. 44–46). Washington, DC: American Psychological Association.

Klopfer, D., & Doherty, M. E. (1992). The Janus illusion. *Teaching of Psychology, 19,* 37–40.

Kozub, F. J. (1991). Oh say, can you see? *Teaching of Psychology, 18,* 180–181.

Demonstrations of Color Perception and the Importance of Contours

David T. Horner

The Young-Helmholtz trichromatic theory and opponent-process theories of color vision provide different predictions for the perception of color afterimages. Trichromatic theory suggests afterimages result from selective bleaching of cone photopigments during adaptation to a color stimulus. Opponent-process theories suggest the visual system treats certain colors as opponent pairs and afterimages result from activation of opponent cells beyond the receptor level. The following techniques give students concrete examples of color perceptions that theories of color vision must explain. Further demonstrations emphasize the importance of contours (Marr, 1982; Marr & Hildreth, 1980).

Color Perception Demonstrations

Chromatic Adaptation

Presentation. Using a red permanent marker, color a solid square (15 cm × 15 cm) on an overhead transparency. Color over the square two more times to ensure a vivid stimulus. Place a small black dot on the square's center. Students should stare at the center of the square projected on a screen with room lights extinguished. Note the square's even coloring, then cover the transparency's right half with paper while students stare for 60 s. Students may blink, but should maintain their fixation point steadily. The square's uncovered left half provides a red adapting stimulus, whereas the

covered right half provides none. After 60 s, students maintain their fixation point as you remove the paper. The square's left half (*adapting stimulus*) appears much duller than the right half (*novel stimulus*).

Discussion. One explanation for the adapting stimulus appearing duller than the novel stimulus is that the adapting stimulus selectively bleaches the photopigments in particular receptors (Vimal, Pokorny, & Smith, 1987). This explanation is consistent with the Young-Helmholtz trichromatic theory of color perception. The absorption spectra for cone pigments (Bowmaker & Dartnall, 1980) show the receptors most affected by red light are the cone cells most sensitive to long wavelengths (L cones; 564 nm peak absorption). The L cones adapt more than the cones most sensitive to medium wavelengths (M cones; 534 nm peak absorption) or short wavelengths (S cones; 420 nm peak absorption). Presentation of the novel stimulus allows students to compare perception using adapted and unadapted receptors. In addition, the absorption spectra for the L and M cone pigments overlap relatively closely; this is an important point for the demonstration described in the next section.

Afterimage Using a Red Adapting Stimulus

Presentation. Students stare at the center of the red square (as previously described) for 60 s, to adapt primarily the L cones. After 60 s, replace the red square with a clear transparency (a white stimulus) with a small *x* in the center to facilitate fixation. When students fixate, a blue-green afterimage appears.

Discussion. One explanation for a blue-green afterimage is that it resulted from selective bleaching of the photopigments in L cones during adaptation. The absorption curve for L cones covers longer wavelengths than M cones, and L cones absorb more light during adaptation. The retinal area stimulated by long wavelengths during exposure to the red square subsequently responds to all wavelengths (a white stimulus). The L cones contributed less to the resulting afterimage because the white stimulus activated their photopigments less than the photopigments in the M and S cones. The white light stimulated primarily the relatively unadapted M and S cones and their combined action resulted in a blue-green afterimage. The next demonstration shows that selective bleaching may not completely explain afterimages.

Afterimage Using a Green Adapting Stimulus

Presentation. Create a square as in the first demonstration using a green permanent marker. Students stare at the center of the square for 60 s. Photopigments in the M cones bleach the most, but the L cone photopigments also bleach, as indicated by the absorption spectra. The stimulus has less effect on S cones. After 60 s, replace the green square with a clear transparency, and students perceive a red afterimage.

Discussion. Explanations based solely on photopigment bleaching predict a blue-violet afterimage: Adapting to green light causes bleaching in both the M and L cones but the S cones remain relatively unaffected. When all wavelengths subsequently stimulate the retinal region adapted to green light, the M and L cones contribute less to the resulting percept because their photopigments absorb less light than the S cones. Thus, trichromatic theory cannot explain all afterimage phenomena, indicating the need for an opponent-process theory such as that articulated by Ewald Hering (1878) and further developed by Hurvich and Jameson (1957). Afterimages are the complementary hue of the adapting stimulus and trichromatic theory fails to account for this fact.

Demonstrating the Importance of Contours

Disappearance of the Adapting Stimulus

Presentation. Create a square as in the first demonstration, but colored only once to create a less saturated red stimulus. Students stare at the center of the square, maintaining their fixation point for 90 s. If they hold their eyes steady, portions of the square disappear and reappear, and sometimes the entire stimulus fades.

Discussion. Holding the eyes steady stabilizes the retinal image, eliminating movement of contours and causing form perception to cease (Pritchard, Heron, & Hebb, 1960; Riggs, Ratliff, Cornsweet, & Cornsweet, 1953; Yarbus, 1967). If the eyes move, the stimulus reappears because some of its edges fall on previously unstimulated receptors, demonstrating the importance of retinal contour information and its change over time. The fact that the stimulus rarely disappears for a long time despite attempts to maintain constant fixation demonstrates the existence of involuntary eye movements (Ditchburn, 1981) that keep the retinal image moving. The low saturation of the stimulus also produces lower contrast, contributing to the loss of contour information. The next demonstration illustrates the role of involuntary eye movements in preserving contours.

Afterimage Using a Red Adapting Stimulus (Revisited)

Presentation. Students stare at the center of the red square described in the first demonstration for 60 s (white light from the overhead projector surrounds the square). Blue-green shimmering soon occurs around the edges of the square.

Discussion. Small involuntary eye movements that shift the square's image slightly on the retina cause the shimmering. The edge of the square's retinal image shifts off adapted receptors and white light hits those receptors, resulting in a blue-green afterimage, as predicted by trichromatic theory. Repeating the demonstration with a green adapting stimulus would also be of interest.

Conclusion

The first demonstration surprises students, evoking audible responses. In a large class, these responses are more noticeable and laughter quickly follows. Students react as if it were a magic trick and enjoy repeating it using any colored surface. Although there is no formal assessment of learning outcomes, students attend closely to explanations following the demonstration.

Students appreciate the sequencing of the color perception demonstrations, providing a particularly effective means of explaining color processing. The first demonstration illustrates selective bleaching of the L cones, which helps students understand what is happening to receptors during the second demonstration. The third demonstration allows students to compare the bleaching explanation and the opponent-process explanation. Furthermore, combining the afterimage demonstrations with presentation of absorption spectra is a useful technique for explaining afterimages.

Students often see shimmering and disappearing contours while viewing the color transparencies, and the contour demonstrations address such observations. The demonstrations also highlight the association between form perception and color vision, thus linking two important areas of research. Students gain an understanding of the complexities involved in visual perception.

The demonstrations have several practical advantages. They immediately capture student interest and actively involve students in visual observations. They are simple and require easily created overhead transparencies. Presentation times are short, but times for discussion vary depending on course goals. The demonstrations work well in small rooms and large lecture halls.

References

Bowmaker, J. K., & Dartnall, H. J. A. (1980). Visual pigments of rods and cones in a human retina. *Journal of Physiology, 298,* 501–511.

Ditchburn, R. W. (1981). Small involuntary eye movements: Solved and unsolved problems. In D. Fisher, R. A. Monty, & J. W. Senders (Eds.), *Eye movements: Cognition and visual perception* (pp. 227–235). Hillsdale, NJ: Lawrence Erlbaum Associates, Inc.

Hering, E. (1878). *Zur lehre vom lichtsinne* [Toward a theory of the light sense]. Vienna: Sohn.

Hurvich, L. M., & Jameson, D. (1957). An opponent process theory of color vision. *Psychological Review, 64,* 384–404.

Marr, D. (1982). *Vision.* San Francisco: Freeman.

Marr, D., & Hildreth, B. (1980). Theory of edge detection. *Proceedings of the Royal Society of London, 207B,* 187–207.

Pritchard, R. M., Heron, W., & Hebb, D. O. (1960). Visual perception approached by the method of stabilized images. *Canadian Journal of Psychology, 14,* 67–77.

Riggs, L. A., Ratliff, F., Cornsweet, J. C., & Cornsweet, T. N. (1953). The disappearance of steadily fixated visual test objects. *Journal of the Optical Society of America, 43,* 495–501.

Vimal, R. L. P., Pokorny, J., & Smith, V. C. (1987). Appearance of steadily viewed lights. *Vision Research, 27,* 1309–1318.

Yarbus, A. L. (1967). *Eye movements and vision.* New York: Plenum.

Note

An earlier version of this material was presented at the Council of Teachers of Undergraduate Psychology's Creative Classroom Session at the Midwestern Psychological Association meetings, Chicago, May 1995.

A Teaching Demonstration Involving Perceived Lunar Size

Mark A. Kunkel

The moon has been the object of considerable research in psychology. Previous investigations have tended to cluster along two pathways: (a) sensory–perceptual, in which the moon illusion (see Plug, 1981) has figured prominently, and (b) lunar–behavior relations deriving from the historical concept of lunacy (cf. Rotton & Kelly, 1985). Research in the former domain has demonstrated the perceptual tendency to overestimate the size of the moon and to assume that lunar size varies with its height in the night sky. Many explanations have been advanced for these perceptual errors, including adaptation (Gilinsky, 1980), the nature of received external reality (Ariotti, 1973; Ross & George, 1976), loom–zoom phenomena (Hershenson, 1982), multimechanism (Coren & Aks, 1990; McCready, 1986), specific distance (Baird & Wagner, 1982), terrestrial passage (Reed, 1984), vestibular influences (Carter, 1977), visual accommodation and oculomotor adjustment (Iavecchia, Iavecchia, & Roscoe, 1983), visual angle (Baird, Wagner, & Fulk, 1990), and visual contrast (Enright, 1989; Smith, Smith, Geist, & Zimmerman, 1978; Tsai, 1987). Investigations of the relation between the moon and behavior have mostly sprung from folklore hypotheses of lunar influence on accidents and disasters (Kelly, Saklofske, & Culver, 1990), crime and other antisocial events (Frey, Rotton, & Barry, 1979; Little, Bowers, & Little, 1987; Tasso & Miller, 1976), substance use (Sharfman, 1980), suicide (Garth & Lester, 1978), and mental illness (Blackman & Catalina, 1973; Campbell & Beets, 1978; Stone, 1976; Templer & Veleber, 1980; Weiskott & Tipton, 1975).

The relative abundance of moon-related research and students' firsthand experience with these phenomena lend themselves well to a teaching demonstration involving estimates of perceived lunar size. The simple yet psychometrically sound demonstration described herein takes approximately 20 min and is easily understood by students. The demonstration may be applied, depending on its placement within the course and instructor preference, to various topics in general psychology. Presented early in the course, the primary application of the demonstration is to philosophy of science, research methods, schools of psychology, and basic statistics, in which students may better appreciate the underlying assumptions of research and the way results are interpreted and explained. The demonstration can also be integrated into later discussions of sensation, perception, and mental illness.

Student preparation for the demonstration varies with its placement in the course. Presented early as part of a discussion of science in psychology or research methods, the demonstration will be enhanced by student familiarity with schools in psychology and basic statistical concepts of reliability and validity. Later application to perception could benefit from student appreciation for concepts, such as proximal and distal stimuli, developmental influences on perception, and perceptual error. The demonstration also has been used to introduce various models of mental illness and the way in which the models influence scale construction, diagnostic terminology, and interpretation of findings.

Students receive a form (see Appendix) on which they are asked to imagine themselves outside on a clear evening with a bright full moon. They are then directed to mentally select from a group of items one that will occlude or cover up the full moon when held in the outstretched hand. The range of objects was chosen based on previous investigations of estimated lunar size (Coren & Aks, 1990).

Students' responses are compiled through asking for raised hands for each item choice. Alternatively, student responses may be written on small slips of paper and passed forward. A frequency histogram is constructed of students' estimates. Should the demonstration be used early in the course, the status of the demonstration as a scientific experiment may be evaluated within the context of philosophy of science and scientific methods. The concepts of experimental control, reliability, and validity can also be evaluated as they relate to students' participation in the demonstration. The demonstration can be used in conjunction with a history and systems overview to illustrate a structural approach to research in psychology. Analytical introspection and subject adequacy can also be demonstrated. Measures of dispersion (e.g., range) and central tendency (e.g., mean, median, and mode) can be computed and compared to existing norms (see Table 1) in a treatment of introductory statistics.

The demonstration can also be used in a discussion of sensation and perception. The full moon occupies one degree (or 1/180th) of the night sky, irrespective of its altitude or the time of year, and can be occluded by a pea held at arm's length. As can be seen in Table 1, students tend to overestimate the size of objects required to occlude the moon; modal responses are between a quarter and a softball. The concepts of proximal versus distal stimuli, retinal size, contrast effects, and developmental influences of experience on perception can be brought to bear in interpreting the findings. Some of the references cited earlier are helpful in preparing such discussions, and students can be led to appreciate the fallacy of the "single right answer" in much of

psychological inquiry. Another advantage is that students can easily verify their findings during the next full moon.

Finally, the demonstration can also contribute to a discussion of abnormal psychology, psychological disorders, or mental illness. Following an overview of the historical concept of lunacy and present folklore hypotheses about the influences of the full moon on human behavior, the instructor could present the demonstration as a test of lunacy or susceptibility to lunar influence. If the instructor argues, for example, that those who overestimate the moon's size are thought to be more subject to its influence, students will be led to appreciate how theories of abnormal psychology are grounded in prior assumptions. The notion of lunacy leads naturally to a discussion of a precedent for supernatural influences on behavior. If so inclined, the instructor can follow the thread of moon–behavior research into other investigations in which no significant effect has been found (Rotton & Kelly, 1985), perhaps also mentioning other areas (e.g., parapsychological phenomena) in which psychological perspectives differ from popular wisdom. In addition to being interesting for students, the demonstration has also been found to enhance their receptivity to other psychological findings that call into question their own experience.

References

Ariotti, P. (1973). Benedetto Castelli and George Berkeley as anticipations of recent findings on the moon illusion. *Journal of the History of the Behavioral Sciences, 9*, 328–332.

Baird, J. C., & Wagner, M. (1982). The moon illusion: I. How high is the sky? *Journal of Experimental Psychology: General, 111*, 296–303.

Baird, J. C., Wagner, M., & Fulk, K. (1990). A simple but powerful theory of the moon illusion. *Journal of Experimental Psychology: Human Perception and Performance, 16*, 675–677.

Blackman, S., & Catalina, D. (1973). The moon and the emergency room. *Perceptual and Motor Skills, 37*, 624–626.

Campbell, D. E., & Beets, J. L. (1978). Lunacy and the moon. *Psychological Bulletin, 85*, 1123–1129.

Carter, D. S. (1977). The moon illusion: A test of the vestibular hypothesis under monocular viewing conditions. *Perceptual and Motor Skills, 45*, 1127–1130.

Coren, S., & Aks, D. J. (1990). Moon illusion in pictures: A multimechanism approach. *Journal of Experimental Psychology: Human Perception and Performance, 16*, 365–380.

Enright, J. T. (1989). Manipulating stereopsis and vergence in an outdoor setting: Moon, sky and horizon. *Vision Research, 29*, 1815–1824.

Frey, J., Rotton, J., & Barry, T. (1979). The effects of the full moon on behavior: Yet another failure to replicate. *Journal of Psychology, 103*, 159–162.

Garth, J. M., & Lester, D. (1978). The moon and suicide. *Psychological Reports, 43*, 678.

Gilinsky, A. S. (1980). The paradoxical moon illusions. *Perceptual and Motor Skills, 50*, 271–283.

Hershenson, M. (1982). Moon illusion and spiral aftereffect: Illusions due to the loom–zoom system? *Journal of Experimental Psychology: General, 111*, 423–440.

Iavecchia, J. H., Iavecchia, H. P., & Roscoe, S. N. (1983). The moon illusion revisited. *Aviation, Space and Environmental Medicine, 54*(1), 39–46.

Table 1. Introductory Psychology Students' Estimations of Object Size Required to Occlude Full Moon When Held at Arm's Length

Object	Frequency	%
BB	2	.5
Pea	12	3.0
Dime	30	7.6
Penny	16	4.1
Nickel	30	7.6
Quarter	70	17.8
Golf ball	34	8.6
Baseball	26	6.6
Softball	56	14.2
Small salad plate	34	8.6
Large dinner plate	30	7.6
Frisbee	28	7.1
Basketball	12	3.0
Beach ball	14	3.6

Note. M estimation = 7.76, SD = 3.11. N = 394.

Kelly, I. W., Saklofske, D. H., & Culver, R. (1990). Aircraft accidents and disasters and the full moon: No relationship. *Psychology, 27*(2), 30–33.

Little, G. L., Bowers, R., & Little, L. H. (1987). Geophysical variables and behavior: II. Lack of relationship between moon phase and incidents of disruptive behavior in inmates with psychiatric problems. *Perceptual and Motor Skills, 64,* 1212.

McCready, D. (1986). Moon illusions redescribed. *Perception and Psychophysics, 39*(1), 64–72.

Plug, C. (1981). The moon illusion: Annotated bibliography. *Reports from the Psychology Department: University of South Africa, 6,* 1–42.

Reed, C. F. (1984). Terrestrial passage theory of the moon illusion. *Journal of Experimental Psychology: General, 113,* 489–500.

Ross, H. E., & George, M. (1976). Did Ptolemy understand the moon illusion? *Perception, 5,* 377–385.

Rotton, J., & Kelly, I. W. (1985). Much ado about the full moon: A meta-analysis of lunar-lunacy research. *Psychological Bulletin, 97,* 286–306.

Sharfman, M. (1980). Drug overdose and the full moon. *Perceptual and Motor Skills, 50,* 124–126.

Smith, O. W., Smith, P. C., Geist, C. C., & Zimmerman, R. R. (1978). Apparent size contrasts of retinal images and size constancy as determinants of the moon illusion. *Perceptual and Motor Skills, 46,* 803–808.

Stone, M. H. (1976). Madness and the moon revisited. *Psychiatric Annals, 6,* 170–176.

Tasso, J., & Miller, E. (1976). The effects of the full moon on human behavior. *Journal of Psychology, 93*(1), 81–83.

Templer, D. I., & Veleber, D. M. (1980). The moon and madness: A comprehensive perspective. *Journal of Clinical Psychology, 36,* 865–868.

Tsai, L. S. (1987). An enlarging hole on the palm illusion and a theory of the moon on the horizon. *Perceptual and Motor Skills, 65,* 816–818.

Weiskott, G. W., & Tipton, G. B. (1975). Moon phases and state hospital admissions. *Psychological Reports, 37,* 486.

Appendix

Imagine that you are outside on a clear night in which there are no clouds, and there is a bright full moon. Pretend that on a table in front of you are objects that range in size from a BB to a beach ball as follows:

1. BB
2. Pea
3. Dime
4. Penny
5. Nickel
6. Quarter
7. Golf ball
8. Baseball
9. Softball
10. Small salad plate
11. Large dinner plate
12. Frisbee
13. Basketball
14. Beach ball

Please pretend that you are going to pick one of these things that WHEN HELD AT ARM'S LENGTH JUST COVERS UP THE MOON. Imagine that you are picking one that when you hold it in your hand will JUST BARELY COVER UP THE MOON so that you can no longer see it.

_____Put the number of the object you chose here.

17. LEARNING

Classical-Conditioning Demonstrations for Elementary and Advanced Courses

Charles I. Abramson
Tim Onstott
Shawn Edwards
Kathy Bowe

Given the number of articles devoted to demonstrating classical-conditioning principles, a regular reader of *Teaching of Psychology* may wonder why instructors are interested in yet another conditioning situation (one involving earthworms and houseflies, at that). As this article shows, the most straightforward answer is that invertebrates provide the best combination of accuracy, versatility, and cost-effectiveness of any classical-conditioning demonstration available.

Invertebrates offer many advantages for classroom demonstrations of conditioning at the introductory and advanced levels (Abramson, 1986, 1990). First, they are easy and inexpensive to procure and maintain. Earthworms, for example, can survive for weeks with minimal care. They can be ordered from commercial suppliers (or brought from home!) and turned loose when the demonstration is complete. Second, students can train their own animals in a variety of classical-conditioning situations that cost dollars rather than hundreds of dollars. The apparatus can often be manufactured from material available at a local hobby shop. Third, invertebrates can be used in conjunction with existing demonstrations or alone to illustrate, for instance, the importance of control groups, stimulus preexposure effects, and compound conditioning. Fourth, students gain an appreciation of the similarities and differences in behavior throughout a wide range of species. Fifth, advanced students can gain practical experience with such issues as developing taxonomies of learning, removing inconsistencies in the definition of learning phenomena, and explaining invertebrate learning in terms of cognitive concepts.

A number of inexpensive invertebrate preparations are available to demonstrate principles of classical conditioning. These demonstrations are versatile, provide hands-on experience, and permit sophisticated discussions of learning to be introduced at the introductory and advanced levels. Three classical-conditioning demonstrations using planarians, earthworms, and honeybees are illustrated in a manual designed for the laboratory classroom (Abramson, 1990). This article describes two new demonstrations that expand the range of classical-conditioning exercises reported in that manual. The principal difference between the experiments reported in the manual and those described herein is that they use less equipment and, in the case of the honeybee, are potentially less dangerous.

In the first demonstration, olfactory conditioning of contraction in the earthworm is described. This is followed by a description of olfactory conditioning of proboscis extension in the housefly. Both procedures produce robust conditioning within 30 min, equipment costs less than $50 for an entire year, and both procedures can be easily modified to investigate all of the training variables and methodological and conceptual issues known to influence classical conditioning.

Classical Conditioning in the Earthworm
(Lumbricus terrestris)

Abramson (1990) described a classical-conditioning experiment, first reported by Ratner and Miller (1959), to condition earthworms by pairing vibrations (the conditioned stimulus [CS]) and light (the unconditioned stimulus [US]). After approximately 60 pairings, the animal contracts to the vibration. This demonstration, although effective, requires constructing the various components of the conditioning apparatus and dark adapting the worms before use. Moreover, to keep the worms dark-adapted throughout the experiment, they must be run under red light. Training animals under such conditions is often impractical in student laboratories.

Earthworms, however, readily associate a floral odor, such as rose oil (the CS), with n-butanol (the US), which elicits a contraction. After as few as five pairings of the rose oil and n-butanol, the worm contracts to the scent of rose.

Materials

The conditioning chamber consists of a 22.9-cm × 8.1-cm × 5.4-cm drawer organizer manufactured by Rubbermaid (part number 2915 of the Keepers series) that can be found in most supermarkets for less than $2. To keep the worm moist during training, we line the floor of the chamber with a wet unscented paper towel cut to the dimensions of the chamber. It is important to use dechlorinated water to moisten the paper towel and to rinse any dirt off the worm.

The rose oil (23-ml bottle) can be obtained from any fragrance shop for about $5. Because 50 ml of n-butanol will last an entire semester, we obtain free samples from a chemistry department. Otherwise, a 500-ml bottle is available for less than $11 from chemical suppliers, such as Sigma Chemical Company (800–325–3010). n-Butanol is flammable, so one should handle it carefully and avoid prolonged inhalation and extensive contact with skin. To reduce the probability of an accident, we suggest that a teaching assistant (TA) or instructor prepare the two odor-delivery devices (i.e., the plastic syringes) for distribution to students. We find that 20-cc syringes are a convenient size and can be readily obtained at hobby shops or surplus suppliers; a package of two costs about $3. Wooden toothpicks, thumbtacks, millimeter rulers, and filter paper are also needed and can be purchased for about $3.

For instructors worried about the use of n-butanol, we suggest trying different USs, perhaps as part of a student project. Another suggestion, which needs experimental verification, is to try a strong puff of air delivered through a drinking straw. We must repeat that common sense is all that is necessary to work with n-butanol.

The earthworms can be obtained year round from local bait supply companies, but the results are more robust if the earthworms are purchased from a biological supply house, such as Connecticut Valley Biological Supply Company (800–628–7748) or Ward's (800–962–2660). We suspect that the robustness obtained with laboratory reared worms is due to the superior maintenance and rearing conditions associated with biological supply houses. Connecticut Valley sells 100 medium-size worms for about $28. The worms can be stored in a worm farm (less than $14) also available from Connecticut Valley. The worm farm is a self-contained unit that comes with food and bedding. Except for the worms, filter paper, and toothpicks, the supplies are reusable and should last several semesters.

Preparation and Procedure

In a small class, each student can condition his or her own worm; however, in larger classes, students can be divided into groups with each student responsible for a task (one delivers the CS, one delivers the US, one records the response, etc.). Students can alternate tasks on different trials so that each student has a chance to perform each task at least once. Prepare the CS delivery device by dipping a toothpick into the bottle of rose oil and smearing a drop on a piece of clean filter paper. Secure it to the tip of the syringe's plunger with an uncoated thumbtack. (Coated tacks tend to interact with the CS and US odors.) Follow the same procedure to prepare the US syringe, except replace the rose oil with n-butanol and use a new toothpick. To test whether the syringes have been prepared properly, depress one near your nose. You should smell an odor, and the thumbtack holding the filter paper should remain embedded in the plunger of the syringe.

Following this preparation, gently remove the earthworm from its home container and wash off any dirt with dechlorinated water. Place the clean worm in the conditioning chamber, and allow 5 min for the worm to adapt to its surroundings. To record conditioned (CR) and unconditioned

responses (UR), place the ruler inside the conditioning chamber. This procedure will help the student quantify the length of contraction. With a little practice, however, students become adept at estimating contraction length without the aid of a ruler. When the worm is in the chamber with the ruler, present the CS to the head of the earthworm for approximately 2 s by gently pushing down on the plunger of the syringe in one smooth stroke. The head of the worm can be easily identified because it is located on the end closest to the *saddle*. The saddle or clitellum is pinker and fatter than the rest of the worm and plays an important role in reproduction. Immediately follow the presentation of the CS with the presentation of the US for approximately 2 s. The shorter the CS–US interval, the better the conditioning. Following the presentation of the US, record on a data sheet the length of the contraction to both the CS and US. The UR of earthworms to n-butanol is typically a contraction of about 1.5 cm. The CR to the odor of rose is a contraction that ranges from .5 cm to 1 cm. Follow the US presentation with a 2-min intertrial interval. Students can perform 24 acquisition trials and 15 extinction trials in 2 hr. Following the experiment, the earthworms can be released outside.

Olfactory Conditioning in the Housefly
(*Musca domestica*)

One of the most powerful demonstrations of classical conditioning in invertebrates is conditioning honeybees to extend their proboscises—tubes through which liquids are sucked into the bees' mouths—upon receiving an odor (e.g., Smith, Abramson, & Tobin, 1991). An olfactory CS is paired with sucrose feeding (US). Olfactory conditioning has also been demonstrated in blowflies (Akahane & Amakawa, 1983) and houseflies (Fukushi, 1979).

The limitations of the honeybee demonstration are the necessity of procuring a source of honeybees and the need to handle them. There is also the danger of students getting stung through carelessness or by a bee that has escaped.

Fukushi (1973) described olfactory conditioning in houseflies by pairing the odor of acetic acid (CS) with a sucrose feeding (US). Following several CS–US pairings, the fly would extend its proboscis to the CS. To prepare the flies for training, Fukushi anesthetized them on ice for 1 hr and then mounted them dorsal-side down on a bed of clay by fastening staples over the wings. They remained in this state for 3 days to adjust to the conditioning situation before training. Our modification of the Fukushi procedure improves the method of fastening the flies so that it takes only a few seconds and eliminates the 3-day wait. Water-deprived flies can be captured in the morning and prepared in time for an afternoon class. Alternatively, they can be prepared the night before. As in all appetitive conditioning, animals must be temporarily deprived of food or water. In the fly exercise, drinking water can be removed from the home cage the day before the animals are to be captured.

Materials

Flies and a group cage can be obtained from Carolina Biological Supply Company (800–334–5551) for less than $45. An established culture yields enough flies for an entire year.

To mount the flies, one needs any odorless wax (e.g., an unscented candle), enough toothpicks or metal pins (e.g., insect pins or any pin at least 4 cm long) to mount one fly per pin, a small metal spatula or painting knife, a heat source for melting the wax (e.g., a hot plate or fondue pot), and a lit candle. With the exception of the hot plate, the total cost for these items is less than $5. To make the flies easy to handle, have ready test tubes, cotton balls, a test tube stand, and a container of ice. Also set aside a small cork or a piece of Styrofoam™ on which to hold the mounted flies. The dimensions are not critical so long as it is large enough to be stable.

The odor-delivery device for the CS is the same as the device used for the US in the earthworm demonstration. Also, for delivering the US, one will need more filter paper, tweezers, and a 50% (by weight) solution of sucrose (sugar) and water. A 100-ml bottle of acetic acid can be obtained from Sigma Chemical for about $15 and will last several semesters.

Preparation and Procedure

One can easily capture flies in their home cage by covering them with the open end of a test tube. When the fly crawls to the back of the tube, quickly plug the end with a bit of cotton. Withdraw the tube containing the fly from the cage, place it in the test tube holder, and repeat the procedure as many times as needed.

The next step is to prepare the pin on which the fly will be fastened. Heat the odorless wax until it liquefies. Dip the spatula into the hot wax until the tip has a bead of molten wax. Transfer this bead to the center of a metal pin by placing the spatula against the pin while turning the pin between the thumb and forefinger. When done properly, a small ball (1 mm in diameter) of wax forms on the center of the pin.

Preparing the CS delivery syringe is described in the earthworm demonstration. The CS is acetic acid; the US is sucrose solution. The US is made by heating sugar and water together until all sugar crystals dissolve. To mount the flies to the pins, render them unconscious by immersing the test tube in a container of ice. When the fly no longer moves, remove it from the test tube. Manipulate the fly so that its legs rest between your thumb and forefinger. With your hand, pass the pin over the candle flame, liquefying the wax until it forms a droplet. Press the droplet of wax on the thorax (i.e., the middle portion of the fly containing the legs) so that the pin is lateral to the anterior–posterior axis of the fly (i.e., the pin is perpendicular to the body of the fly). Hold the pin against the thorax for a few seconds to allow the connection to harden. This procedure sounds more complicated than it is; with a little practice, you can attach the fly to the pin in less than 5 s. Next, insert the pointed end of the pin into the Styrofoam™ block or cork, which will serve as the conditioning stand. The stand is secured to a desk or laboratory bench with double-sided tape or a bit of unscented clay. Insert the pin (with the fly attached) into the cork or Styrofoam™ block at a height that ensures the legs of the fly are firmly on a flat surface.

In a minute or so, the fly will regain consciousness. Administer the acetic acid CS for 2 s per trial using a smooth stroke of the syringe. To present the US, dip one end of a piece of filter paper in the sucrose solution, which is now at room temperature, and touch the front legs of the fly. Carefully present the sucrose US so that excess sucrose does not coat the conditioning stand. To avoid having the fly stand in the solution, wipe up any excess solution with a damp towel during the intertrial interval. The US should elicit extension of the proboscis in a hungry fly. Allow the animal to feed for approximately 2 s. Record the presence or absence of a CR and a UR during the 1-min intertrial interval. Present a minimum of 15 acquisition trials. After the demonstration, the flies can be released from the wax and set free. Alternatively, they can be placed in a freezer for several minutes and then discarded.

Discussion

We have used the earthworm and housefly demonstrations with positive results in such classes as introductory psychology, psychology of learning, and experimental psychology, in teaching workshops, and in secondary schools. Students enjoy the hands-on experience and often marvel at how readily these animals seem to learn. Moreover, graduate and undergraduate TAs can be trained easily to run the demonstrations in their own classrooms.

The worm and fly demonstrations can be modified to study habituation, sensitization, and pseudoconditioning. For example, pseudoconditioning can be studied in earthworms by preexposing groups of worms to different numbers of US presentations followed by a single CS-only test trial. (Note: The only time the animal ever receives the CS is during this one test trial.) The question of interest is whether the worms will contract to the CS even though the CS and US have not been paired. A similar experiment can be performed by giving flies several US presentations (sucrose feedings) and testing whether the proboscis extends to the CS even though the CS and US have not been paired. Habituation can be studied simply by using a diluted US and recording the number of contractions and proboscis extensions in worms and flies, respectively. To observe a sensitization response, use the habituation paradigm but interpolate trials in which the US is at full strength. Moreover, the earthworm procedure can be modified to study signaled avoidance (i.e., when the worm contracts to the CS, the US is not administered). This flexibility and the ease with which it can be done is not available in any existing vertebrate-based demonstrations. The CSs used in the demonstrations can be varied. Odors such as sweet pea, carnation, and rose work well with earthworms and probably will do so with flies. Because there are so few conditioning studies with earthworms and houseflies, the effectiveness of CSs, other than those in compound-conditioning situations mentioned herein, can be determined only by experiment. In our compound-conditioning experiments with earthworms, rose and sweet pea are used as CSs. Instructors who prefer to use nonneutral CSs may use diluted versions of USs. Keep in mind, however, that conditioning using nonnatural CSs may be better characterized as US–US conditioning (Abramson, 1994).

Class discussion of the laboratory exercise can focus on various topics. We have used the demonstrations to introduce to introductory and advanced students the concepts of pseudoconditioning; central excitatory state; the importance of having a neutral CS; the need for observation, instrumentation, and control groups; the importance of providing noncognitive explanations of animal behavior; the importance of developing classification systems in psychology; the effects of various training variables; and the generalization of conditioning across the animal kingdom. Abramson (1994) provided a detailed discussion of these issues and how they relate to teaching.

Another benefit not provided by any vertebrate-based demonstration of classical conditioning is the exciting and wide range of possible student projects. Having graded too many rat experiments, I am pleased when students turn in projects investigating the transfer of learning in bees and planarians; compound conditioning in earthworms; the effect of pesticides on conditioning in planarians, bees, and earthworms; and the effect of diet on conditioning in flies.

Evaluation

The effectiveness of using invertebrates was assessed by giving to 39 introductory and 23 experimental psychology students a brief questionnaire at the end of the semester. The questionnaire focused on their knowledge of the basic phenomena of classical conditioning and the affective quality of the demonstration experience. In a 1-hr session, students classically conditioned an earthworm and compared the experience with a commercially available computer simulation of the classical-conditioning process (CC.Dog, 1993).

In comparing the affective quality of the demonstration, more than 97% of the introductory and experimental students indicated that the worm demonstration gave them a better feel of what it is like to conduct a classical-conditioning experiment. In addition, more than 95% of the students thought that the time required to set up the demonstration did not distract them from understanding the basic principles of classical conditioning. Of the introductory students, 77% thought that conducting the demonstration helped them understand these principles, and 83% of the experimental students agreed. As to the importance of observation in classical conditioning, 90% of the students in both groups agreed that the worm demonstration was superior to the computer-based demonstration. The only situation in which the worm demonstration was not superior was in ease of use; more than 77% of the students in both groups indicated that the computer demonstration was easier to use.

Students reported that the worm demonstration was more effective than the computer in helping them understand the basic principles of classical conditioning. More than 70% of students in both groups indicated that the worm demonstration increased their understanding of CS–US intervals, stimulus duration effects, type of pairing, and the role of observation in the design and analysis of experiments. More than 90% of the students in both groups agreed that the worm demonstration was more effective in helping them understand the importance of central excitatory states, control groups, neutral versus nonneutral conditioned stimuli, and extinction. In addition, more than 90% of the students agreed that the worm demonstration gave them the best understanding of the classical-conditioning process.

Upon completing the survey, students were invited to write down any comments. These comments show, perhaps more than the survey, the importance of live-animal demonstrations. One experimental student wrote,

> It was easier to see the results on the computer, but I had a better understanding of what was going on by watching the animal respond. Using the animal lets you see differences between animals and problems that might occur. The computer was more like playing a game.

A second experimental student wrote, "With computers you might think you know what is going on, but when it comes time to prove it with real animals you know only what is on the screen." The comments made by introductory students were also positive toward the use of animals. One student wrote, "It was really cool to see it work on the worms. It helped me understand the concepts in a realistic way." A second student wrote, "In general, the animals are more interesting and more useful to learning. While the computer is easier to set up, the extra time on the animals is well worth it."

A formal evaluation of the housefly demonstration was not conducted. When demonstrating proboscis conditioning in our teaching laboratories, we use honeybees whenever possible. The rationale behind the fly preparation was to develop a laboratory experience that can be taken into secondary school classrooms where bees are not permitted and to provide college instructors with a proboscis-conditioning situation if bees are not available. It is interesting to note that 10- to 12-year-old children tend to prefer houseflies to earthworms, whereas the reverse is true for college students. When given a choice between the earthworm or fly demonstration, college students report that the large size of the worm is advantageous not only in conducting the experiment but also in recording CRs and URs. For example, the proboscis of a housefly, although readily observed, is small, and dexterity is required to feed a fly without covering it with sucrose. A student with a shaky hand, for instance, will have difficulty administering the US.

In these days of increased regulation of vertebrate animal colonies and dwindling departmental resources, the use of invertebrates in exercises of the type reported herein is an excellent way for students to gain hands-on laboratory experiences with minimal expense. With a few dollars and a little effort on the part of instructors, the hands-on approach to the study of behavior can once again form an integral part of the psychology curriculum.

References

Abramson, C. I. (1986). Invertebrates in the classroom. *Teaching of Psychology, 13*, 24–29.

Abramson, C. I. (1990). *Invertebrate learning: A laboratory manual and source book.* Washington, DC: American Psychological Association.

Abramson, C. I. (1994). *A primer of invertebrate learning: The behavioral perspective.* Washington, DC: American Psychological Association.

Akahane, R., & Amakawa, T. (1983). Stable and unstable phase of memory in classically conditioned fly, *Phormia regina*: Effects of nitrogen gas anaesthesia and cycloheximide injection. *Journal of Insect Physiology, 29,* 331–337.

CC.Dog [Computer software]. (1993). Orlando, FL: Crofter.

Fukushi, T. (1973). Olfactory conditioning in the housefly, *Musca domestica. Annotationes Zoologicae Japonenses, 46,* 135–143.

Fukushi, T. (1979). Properties of olfactory conditioning in the housefly, *Musca domestica. Journal of Insect Physiology, 25,* 155–159.

Ratner, S. C., & Miller, K. R. (1959). Classical conditioning in earthworms, *Lumbricus terrestris. Journal of Comparative and Physiological Psychology, 52,* 667–672.

Smith, B. H., Abramson, C. I., & Tobin, T. R. (1991). Conditional withholding of proboscis extension in honeybees (*Apis mellifera*) during discriminative punishment. *Journal of Comparative Psychology, 105,* 345–356.

Note

The work in this article was supported by funds from Oklahoma State University Center for Effective Instruction. We will happily assist instructors in forming their own invertebrate teaching laboratories.

Preparing for an Important Event: Demonstrating the Modern View of Classical Conditioning

Art Kohn
James W. Kalat

Are your students less impressed by classical conditioning than they should be? As instructors, we know that classical conditioning can profoundly shape our emotional and motivational lives. Despite our enthusiasm, however, many students remain unimpressed and wonder why we make a fuss about a dog learning to salivate to a bell.

One reason that students underestimate classical conditioning is that the conditioned response (CR) and unconditioned response (UR) are very similar in most of our classroom examples. This similarity may cause students to overlook the fact that the CR and UR serve different adaptive functions. For example, the CR and UR were identical in each of the creative demonstrations described in *Teaching of Psychology* (Cogan & Cogan, 1984; Gibb, 1983; Sparrow & Fernald, 1989; Vernoy, 1987). Cogan and Cogan (1984), for instance, signaled the students (the conditioned stimulus, CS) to place lemon powder (the unconditioned stimulus, US) in their mouths; in this demonstration, both the CR and UR were salivation. In Sparrow and Fernald's (1989) demonstration, the instructor flashed a light (the CS) and shortly after that produced a loud noise (the US); both the CR and the UR were a startle reaction. Likewise, the CR and the UR are similar in most of our standard textbook examples, including the salivary reflex, the eye blink response, and the Little Albert story.

Although these examples illustrate the essential procedures of classical conditioning, they suggest to students two conclusions that are not entirely correct: (a) the CR and UR are necessarily similar, and (b) the function of classical conditioning is simply to expedite a response so that it occurs before the US begins.

These notions are clearly inconsistent with the emerging view of classical conditioning that (a) the CR can be very different from the UR, and (b) the function of classical conditioning is to elicit a preparatory response (CR) that enables the subject to cope better with an impending event (Holland, 1984; Hollis, 1984; Rescorla, 1988; Zener, 1937). In this emerging view, the CR is a preparation for the US, whereas the UR is a reaction to it.

Several lines of research illustrate how the CR and UR can be quite different. For example, in the signaled-shock procedure, the rat's UR to a shock is to run around and squeal; its CR, however, is to freeze (Bindra & Palfai, 1967). The difference between the CR and UR is also apparent in Siegel's (1977, 1983) classical conditioning explanation of drug tolerance. In this procedure, the UR to an anesthetic drug is a reduced sensitivity to pain; the CR, however, involves mobilizing the body against the effects of the drug.

The following demonstration can help students better understand the contemporary view of classical conditioning. The demonstration can be performed quickly, requires little preparation or equipment, and conditions almost everyone in the classroom. Finally, the CR and UR are different, highlighting the preparatory nature of the CR.

The Demonstration

Before class, tape 5 to 10 balloons to a wall or to a table in front of the class. You should inflate them fully so that they produce a loud noise when they burst. Explain to the class that you are going to demonstrate classical conditioning and that, for the next few minutes, you want everyone to observe their own reactions closely.

Take a long needle, dart, or pin, show it to the class, loudly count "One, two, three," and break the first balloon.

Wait a few seconds, and then repeat this procedure with the next balloon and with two or more additional balloons. Be sure to vary the amount of time between balloon bursts so that you do not inadvertently induce temporal conditioning. (You may notice that students flinch less and less with each successive balloon.) When you get to the fifth or sixth balloon, say "One, two, three," lower the needle toward the balloon, but miss it. The balloon does not burst. How do the students react?

When we first tried this demonstration, we expected the students to flinch as a CR. In fact, nearly all of the students sat unmoved and expressionless. Had the demonstration failed?

Not at all. Wait a few seconds, perhaps pass the time by feigning your confusion over their lack of response, and discreetly slip the needle down to your side; then, without providing the "One, two, three" warning, burst a balloon. The students jump visibly; indeed, they will jump more than they had to any of the previous balloon bursts.

Following the demonstration, while everybody settles down, draw a graph on the board and label the x-axis *Trial Numbers* and the y-axis *Mean Size Startle Reaction*. Next, ask the students to recall the extent of their startle reaction on each trial including the ones when you did not pop the balloon and when you popped it without warning. In turn, plot the class's mean reaction on the chart. Results will show a steady decline in responding across trials, except that the last trial—the one with the unwarned burst—will involve the largest response of all.

Now, challenge your students to identify the CS, US, CR, and UR. Ordinarily, they have no trouble identifying the bang as the US and their flinching as the UR. Likewise, they will recognize that the CS is some combination of your counting "One, two, three" and the movement of your hand. However, they may have a bit of trouble identifying the CR; initially, some students may guess that the CR was also flinching, but point out that this cannot be the case because few students flinched when the CS was presented alone. If they continue to have trouble, point out that the CR is the response elicited by the CS. Ask them "What did you do when you heard me counting?" After a bit of introspection, they quickly realize that when they experienced the CS, their CR was not flinching; instead, it consisted of tightening their muscles in order to inhibit a flinch. To reinforce this interpretation, refer to your graph and point out that (a) across trials, their flinching decreased as they were better able to emit the preparatory muscle-clenching response; (b) they did not jump at all when they heard "One, two, three" alone; and (c) they jumped their highest during the last trial because, when you gave no warning, they had no chance to emit the preparatory CR.

Evaluation

To evaluate the validity of our observations, we recently conducted this demonstration in our class and carefully monitored the students' responses with a video camera.

Method

We performed the demonstration for 55 students in Introductory Psychology. Before the demonstration, we ar-

ranged a video camera facing the students which provided a clear record of their activities. The students appeared to habituate to the camera very quickly, and it seemed to have no effect on their subsequent behavior. With the camera rolling, the instructor popped five balloons, faked the popping of the sixth one, and after a brief delay, popped the last balloon without giving the "One, two, three" warning.

Later, two judges watched the tape and rated the extent of the class's startle reaction for each trial. Judges rated startle reactions on a scale ranging from *no reaction* (0) to *large reaction* (4). Both judges were blind to the purpose of the demonstration.

Results

As Figure 1 shows, the extent of the startle reactions was consistent with our expectations. The students emitted an intermediate-size startle reaction in Trials 1 and 2, a somewhat reduced reaction during Trials 3 and 4, and no reaction on Trial 5. Likewise during Trial 6, when only the CS was presented, subjects again showed no startle reaction. Finally, during Trial 7, when the US was presented without the CS, the subjects emitted the largest response. In rating the tape, the two judges showed a high interrater reliability, with a mean correlation of .853 and a Spearman–Brown correlation of .917.

Discussion

After completing the demonstration and emphasizing the preparatory role of the CR, you may wish to discuss alternative explanations of the results. The simplest alternative is that no conditioning occurred during the procedure and that the CS "One, two, three" had acquired its aversiveness before the demonstration. This seems unlikely, however, because the CS evoked little flinch inhibiting on Trial 1 and much more on successive trials, suggesting that some form of learning took place. Another explanation is that the subjects habituated to the loud noise during Trials 1 through 5; however, habituation cannot account for the very large startle response on the last trial.

A third explanation involves operant, rather than classical, conditioning. According to this interpretation, in the presence of the discriminative stimulus "One, two, three," the students began to emit the operant response of tensing

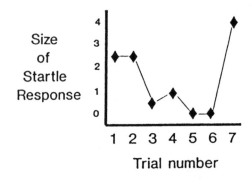

Figure 1. Mean startle reaction on successive trials of balloon popping. On Trial 6, we faked popping the balloon; on Trial 7, we popped the balloon without the "One, two, three" warning.

their muscles. In turn, this tensing response may have been reinforced by minimizing their startle response. We find it difficult to determine whether the tensing response is operant, classical, or a mixture of both; in class, therefore, we emphasize that operant and classical conditioning frequently overlap and are capable of evoking similar responses. Furthermore, we point out that, in some cases, such as autoshaping (Williams & Williams, 1969), both types of conditioning work together to sustain a pattern of behavior.

Finally, it also may be instructive to contrast the results of this demonstration with one described by Vernoy (1987). Vernoy used a long needle to pop a balloon held by the students themselves. The ensuing pop produced a noticeable startle reaction that was the UR. After popping 5 to 8 balloons, however, Vernoy held the balloon himself and inserted the needle in such a way that it did not pop the balloon; although there was no US, Vernoy reported that the students still showed a startle reaction, which was the CR. Why did the students startle in his demonstration and not in ours?

One explanation for the differing results is that the students in Vernoy's demonstration did not emit the flinching responses that Vernoy reported. We recently made several attempts to replicate Vernoy's procedure using a panel of judges to rate the extent of the students' startle responses. In each case, the judges reported no startle reaction when the balloon did not pop.

A second explanation for the difference is that the students in Vernoy's procedure may have experienced pseudo-conditioning. In pseudoconditioning, successive presentations of the US, especially of an aversive US, sensitizes subjects and thereby increases the probability of their emitting the UR following a neutral stimulus (Staddon & Ettinger, 1989). As Wickens and Wickens (1942) put it,

> if a series of fairly strong unconditioned stimuli is presented alone and that series is followed by a previously neutral stimulus, it is found that this previously neutral stimulus now produces a response similar to the one given to the unconditioned stimulus. (p. 518)

Thus, in Vernoy's procedure, the bangs may have sensitized the subjects such that the movement of the instructor's arm produced a startle reaction.

A more intriguing explanation for the differing results concerns the preparatory nature of classical conditioning. In Vernoy's procedure, the balloon was close to the students' faces. Perhaps the students learned the natural preparatory action (CR) of pulling back from the balloon as the needle approached it. In our demonstration, however, the students were seated farther away from the balloon; for them, the natural preparatory response (CR) may be to inhibit an embarrassing startle reaction.

The modern understanding of classical conditioning emphasizes that this primitive form of learning is broader and more intriguing than previously thought. Classical conditioning not only can produce anticipatory salivation, but also can evoke a range of adaptive responses that help people and animals prepare for important events. We believe that this modern view of classical conditioning will earn from students the respect it deserves.

References

Bindra, I., & Palfai, T. (1967). Nature of positive and negative incentive motivational effects on general activity. *Journal of Comparative and Physiological Psychology, 63,* 288–297.

Cogan, D., & Cogan, R. (1984). Classical salivary conditioning: An easy demonstration. *Teaching of Psychology, 11,* 170–171.

Gibb, G. D. (1983). Making classical conditioning understandable through a demonstration technique. *Teaching of Psychology 10,* 112–113.

Holland, P. (1984), Origins of behavior in Pavlovian conditioning. *Psychology of Learning and Motivation, 18,* 129–174.

Hollis, K. L. (1984), The biological function of Pavlovian conditioning: The best defense is a good offense. *Journal of Experimental Psychology: Animal Learning and Behavior, 10,* 413–425.

Rescorla, R. A. (1988). Pavlovian conditioning: It's not what you think it is. *American Psychologist, 44,* 151–160.

Siegel, S. (1977). Morphine tolerance as an associative process. *Journal of Experimental Psychology: Animal Behavior Processes, 3,* 1–13.

Siegel, S. (1983). Classical conditioning, drug tolerance, and drug dependence. *Research Advances in Alcohol and Drug Problems, 7,* 207–246.

Sparrow, J., & Fernald, P. (1989). Teaching and demonstrating classical conditioning. *Teaching of Psychology, 16,* 204–206.

Staddon, J. E. R., & Ettinger, R. H. (1989). *Learning: An introduction to the principles of adaptive behavior.* San Diego: Harcourt Brace Jovanovich.

Vernoy, M. W. (1987). Demonstrating classical conditioning in introductory psychology: Needles do not always make balloons pop! *Teaching of Psychology 14,* 176–177.

Wickens, D. D., & Wickens, C. D. (1942). Some factors related to pseudoconditioning. *Journal of Experimental Psychology 31,* 518–526.

Williams, D. R., & Williams, H. (1969). Auto-maintenance in the pigeon: Sustained pecking despite contingent nonreinforcement. *Journal of the Experimental Analysis of Behavior, 12,* 511–520.

Zener, K. (1937). The significance of behavior accompanying conditioned salivary secretions for theories of the conditioned response. *American Journal of Psychology, 50,* 384–403.

Note

We thank Neal Womack and Wendy Howard for helping to collect the data reported herein. We also thank Greg Kimble for his perceptive comments on a draft of this article and Wendy Kohn and Ruth Ault for their editorial assistance.

Demonstrating Classical Conditioning in Introductory Psychology: Needles Do Not Always Make Balloons Pop!

Mark W. Vernoy

When introducing students to psychology, I am constantly striving to make each topic come alive for them. One of the topics that is not only easy to demonstrate but is also capable of sparking a good deal of enthusiasm in students is classical conditioning. In my introductory psychology classes, I have tried several types of classical conditioning demonstrations. I have demonstrated the conditioned eyeblink, which never worked very well and was hard for the students in the back row to see. I have taught students how to condition their dogs to salivate to a tone (Pavlov, 1927), and brought my pet basset hound into class as living proof that dogs really can be taught to drool on command. (Most of my students thought this was disgusting, so I never did it again.) I even considered duplicating John B. Watson and Rosalie Rayner's (1920) Little Albert experiment, but the college child care center pointed out that the California child abuse laws specifically prohibit its replication. After several such failures and near misses, I finally found a classical conditioning demonstration that is effective, sanitary, and legal. This article describes that demonstration, which has proven to be not only effective but also fun for me and my students.

The premise of the demonstration is that nearly all of us have been classically conditioned to flinch or blink when we watch someone stab a balloon with a needle. In this conditioning situation, the neutral stimulus is the needle, the unconditioned stimulus is the noise produced by the popping balloon, and the unconditioned response is the startle response (a flinch or blink) produced by the loud noise. Eventually, the needle becomes the conditioned stimulus that produces the startle response when it is brought in contact with balloon. In this way, we have learned that needles always pop balloons. Or do they?

The equipment needed for this demonstration includes about 20 to 30 good quality, round balloons and a needle. Any sharp sewing needle will do, but for dramatic effect I use a foot-long needle that I borrow from a colleague who is an amateur magician. You can acquire these large needles at any good magic shop.

Before class, blow up about 30 balloons and transport them to the classroom in a large trash bag. When you are ready to begin the demonstration, randomly distribute 10 to 15 balloons to students in the classroom, then bring out the needle and pop about half of the balloons. (When popping the balloons, make sure students hold them away from their faces and the faces of other students.) Then, begin a discussion of classical conditioning and ask students to identify the unconditioned stimulus, the unconditioned response, and so on. Make sure to ask the students what makes them jump when the balloon pops, and persist until they produce the obvious answer: noise. Then, pop the remaining balloons.

Now the fun begins. Pick up one of the balloons from the trash bag and stick the needle into the balloon without popping it. As you might have guessed, there is a trick to this part of the demonstration. Piercing a balloon without popping it does not require a special balloon or a special needle; all that is necessary is to know where to stick the needle. In a blown-up balloon, there are usually two places where the rubber is relatively thick because of the small amount of tension on the skin of the balloon: the nipple and near the knot. Thus, if you pierce the balloon with a sharp needle in the thick area of the nipple, the balloon should not pop; if you pierce it with a foot-long needle, you should be able to insert it through the nipple and pull it out through the thick area near the knot, without popping the balloon.

After having been conditioned to the popping of balloons at the beginning of the demonstration, the students can be expected to flinch or blink when you insert the needle in the balloon. But the balloon does not pop. There is no unconditioned stimulus, but the students flinch anyhow. This generates a real enthusiasm for joining in on a discussion of the classical conditioning processes at work. In this discussion, encourage students to use classical conditioning terminology. (By the way, after the balloon is pierced, it loses air and soon becomes flat. You can let it go flat to show that you did indeed pierce it, or if you have a long needle you can run the needle through the balloon to show it was pierced, then end your act by throwing the balloon up into the air and popping it.)

References

Pavlov, I. P. (1927). *Conditioned reflexes*. New York: Dover.
Watson, J. B., & Rayner, R. (1920). Conditioned emotional reactions. *Journal of Experimental Psychology, 3*, 1–14.

Demonstrating the Influence of Cognition on Emotion and Behavior

Jerry L. Deffenbacher

Cognitive processes have long had an important place in psychology, and developments of the last 2 decades highlight the influence of cognition on many phenomena. Thus, exercises that demonstrate the influence of cognitive variables are very useful in psychology classes. This article describes such an exercise, along with an evaluation of its effectiveness and examples of its use.

Description of the Exercise

The exercise takes approximately 10 min, requires only a board or overhead, and uses an induced mood paradigm (e.g., Velten, 1969). The cognitive effects are not generated through repetition of affect-related words, but by having students visualize a life stressor while attending to self-dialogue provided by the instructor. The stressor involves the breakup of an important male–female relationship; it was chosen because of easy identification for most students and its relatively high rating on the Schedule of Recent Life Events (Holmes & Rahe, 1967).

Some instructors may begin the exercise with little introduction in order to reduce potential demand characteristics or because of other class goals. Other instructors may wish to introduce the topic of cognitive influences on emotion and behavior to set up the exercise. If an introduction is used, it will vary with the instructor, purposes, and topics, but generally will emphasize the influence of information processing on emotion and behavior. For example, in teaching abnormal psychology, I have introduced the topic as follows:

Many in class tend to think that life events "cause" us to feel and behave in certain ways. Our language strongly supports this notion. For example, "Psychology tests really depress me," "Speeches make me very anxious," or "My dad drives me crazy when he treats me like a child" [examples were chosen because of ease of identification and common experience in class]. The external events (psychology tests, speeches, and dad) are seen as causing the feelings of stress (depression, anxiety, and anger) and associated reactions. It is true that some reactions are caused fairly directly by an external stimulus such as a startle reaction to a loud, unpredicted noise or pain to a physical injury. For many important human emotions and behaviors, however, this commonsense notion is not valid.

Reactions are determined more by the beliefs we hold about the event than by the event itself. It is how we evaluate or cognitively appraise the situation that strongly influences our emotional and behavioral reactions.

If such materials were not desired before the exercise, they could be used as part of the debriefing and in linking the exercise to goals and objectives of the lecture.

Then the exercise is introduced. The initial goals are to outline the process and encourage student involvement. This introduction might be presented as follows:

In order to give you a personal sense of how attitudes or cognitions influence our experiences, I want to set up a brief experiment with you. In a minute I am going to ask you to close your eyes and imagine that you are a person who is facing a significant life stressor. As you imagine the situation, put yourself into that situation, like it is happening to you right now. As you do this, I am going to read you some thoughts you might be having. Let the thoughts sink in, and attend to the feelings and reactions they generate in you.

The stressor is then described. Students are asked to imagine that they are a 21-year-old whose boyfriend/girlfriend has just broken off an important, steady relationship of the last 2 years. Students are asked to close their eyes and be that person as they are read the first (depression) scenario (order of scenarios can be altered to fit class goals):

Ok, now get yourself comfortable, close your eyes, and imagine that you are that person . . . [give about 10 sec for this to be done]. . . . Remember, you are that 21-year-old whose boyfriend or girlfriend has just left you . . . [3 to 5 sec pause] . . . and you are thinking to yourself . . . [scenario is read in a slow manner using pacing and inflection to communicate a depressive tone]. . . . I gave him/her all my love, and he/she threw it all away. . . . My only real chance at love, and it's gone. . . . I'll never find anyone else. . . . But I must have his/her love, without it I'm nothing. . . . I can't live without him/her. . . . It's hopeless. . . . Life is empty, meaningless. . . . It's all my fault. . . . If only I had been able to love him/her more, this would not have happened. . . . But maybe he/she is better off without me. . . . Maybe, everyone is better off without me . . . [with the instructor's voice trailing off] . . .

Visualization and experiencing continue for about 15 sec, and then students are asked to open their eyes and write down their reactions. After students write down their reactions, the instructor asks students to report the reactions aloud. Commonly reported elements include depression, despair, extreme sadness, hopelessness, lost and alone, rejected, suicidal, and occasionally anxiety or anger. These reactions are written on the board or overhead as they are mentioned. As reports dwindle, the instructor notes the clustering around a theme of depression.

Then the class is asked to repeat the process as the second (anger) scenario is introduced:

Ok, now let's repeat the process. Settle yourself and close your eyes . . . [10 sec for students to do this]. . . . Now imagine that situation again . . . your boyfriend or girlfriend has just left you . . . [5-sec pause] . . . and you are thinking to yourself . . . [the remainder of this scenario is read in a brusque, fast-paced, angry tone]. . . . That creep! [instructor may fill in any negative label that feels comfortable]. . . . He/she can't do that to me! . . . . No one can do that to me and get away with it. . . . He/she can't leave me. . . . I'll show him/her. . . . By god, if I can't have him/her, no one can! . . .

Approximately 15 sec are given for visualization and development of reactions. Visualization is terminated by asking students to open their eyes and write down their experiences. After 20 to 30 sec, the students report their reactions to this scenario. Common reactions include anger, rage, revenge, vindictiveness, hostility, and homicidal feelings. The instructor writes these adjectives in an area separate from the descriptors of the prior scenario, and the theme of anger is pointed out. If desired, the instructor may note that some students appear to be trading the suicidal feelings of the prior example for homicidal feelings in this example. It may also be noted that, although the situation has not changed (the same person lost the same important relationship), the reactions have changed dramatically.

The class is asked to repeat the process a third time, and the realistic, negative emotion scenario is introduced in a normal tone and pace:

Once again, close your eyes and let yourself be that person . . . [10 sec]. . . . Remember, you are that 21-year-old, and your boyfriend or girlfriend has left you . . . and you are thinking to yourself. . . . I wish he/she hadn't broken off the relationship because I really love him/her . . . and I wish he/she felt the same about me as I feel about him/her . . . and wanted to work on our relationship. . . . I'm really sad that he/she is gone. . . . It's going to be very lonely without him/her. . . . While it hurts now, and probably will for some time to come, it's not the end of the world. . . . Maybe we'll work it out, and maybe we won't. . . . I sure hope we do, but if we don't, I'll survive. . . . In

time, I'll probably find other important relationships . . .

Again, approximately 15 sec are allowed for visualization before the instructor tells students to open their eyes and write down their reactions. In 20 to 30 sec the instructor inquires about reactions and writes these responses on the board or overhead so that students can see all three lists at once. Simultaneous access to all three lists makes contrasts among experiences easier. Reactions to the third scenario tend to be a mixture of negative emotions (sadness, loneliness, hurt, and mild depression) with coping feelings and orientations (realistic, able to go on, able to cope, not overwhelmed, optimistic, and hopeful). The instructor may want to reflect on the mixture of emotional and behavioral characteristics and contrast it with the two previous lists. Again, pointing out different reactions to the same stressor will be instructive.

At this point, students rate the intensity of their negative emotions produced by each scenario on a scale ranging from *none of the reaction or calm* (0) to *maximum amount of negative emotion or overwhelmed* (100). Experiences with each scenario are rated and written down. Then, while the instructor points to the first list and refers to the first (depressive) scenario, students give aloud a rating from 0 to 100 for their experience. Several scores are written on the board, and a rough modal score is noted. This process is repeated for each scenario. The instructor can refer to the range of scores to demonstrate individual differences in reactions, whereas reference to the mode suggests some commonality in strength of reactions. The results may be summarized by noting that reactions vary widely in type and intensity as a function of cognitive processing because the situation was unchanged throughout. This summary prompts further discussion that usually covers the purposes of the exercise.

Evaluation of the Exercise

The effectiveness of this exercise was evaluated in four undergraduate, summer-session classes (introductory psychology, theories of personality, abnormal psychology, and a seminar on stress management). The first three were taught by other faculty, and I taught the fourth. Instructors were given a draft of this article and asked to introduce the exercise at an appropriate point in their classes. They followed the instructions except that, prior to the exercise, students received a form on which to record their reactions and ratings (0 to 100) for each scenario. After each scenario was completed, students listed their reactions and recorded ratings before these were listed on the board. The anonymous recording sheets were turned in at the end of the exercise and discussion. Data from 5 students in introductory psychology, 3 each in personality and abnormal psychology, and 1 from stress management were discarded either because of the absence of a response to one scenario or a comment that reflected lack of involvement with the scenario (e.g., "That would never happen to me" or "I just couldn't get into that one"). Final sample sizes were 35 for introductory, 28 for personality, 37 for abnormal, and 38 for stress management.

Table 1. Intensity of Negative Emotions From the Exercise in Four Psychology Classes

	Cognitive Scenario					
	Depression		Anger		Realistic Negative	
Class	M	SD	M	SD	M	SD
Introductory	75.72	13.98	75.74	15.40	28.69	16.08
Personality	74.41	16.02	70.83	17.46	32.00	18.19
Abnormal	72.78	16.99	71.43	18.42	26.65	15.38
Stress Management	83.61	13.78	82.37	15.97	37.13	14.65

Data are summarized in Table 1. Univariate, repeated measures analyses of variance (ANOVAs) revealed significant differences across scenarios in introductory psychology, $F(2, 68) = 103.25$; personality theory, $F(2, 56) = 74.53$; abnormal psychology, $F(2, 72) = 144.21$; and stress management, $F(2, 74) = 147.17$; all $ps < .001$. Newman-Keuls post hoc tests ($ps < .001$) showed that the depression and anger scenarios produced significantly more intense ratings than the realistic negative scenario in all classes, but did not differ from one another in any class.

Although some demand characteristics may be present in the use of this exercise, data were collected anonymously, which should have reduced the influence of demand factors. This evaluation suggests that the exercise generated significant differences in reported type and intensity of reactions in a variety of undergraduate psychology classes and may, therefore, be used successfully in the manner described. In addition, all instructors reported that the exercise generated many questions and comments, further supporting the notion that students were actively involved with it.

Uses of the Exercise

This exercise can be used to introduce the topic of cognitive influences. For example, in introductory psychology and the psychology of motivation and emotion, it might be used to introduce the influence of cognitive factors on emotion, motivation, and behavior. It can demonstrate person factors in Person × Situation interactions in personality and social psychology classes. The importance of person factors is shown by pointing out that situational factors (loss of relationship) remain constant across the scenarios, but that reactions change dramatically as person factors (self-dialogue) change. It can help outline the importance of cognitive processes in coping with stress, adjustment, and psychopathology for introductory, adjustment, and abnormal psychology classes. It also can be used in discussions of cognitive processes in counseling and psychotherapy (e.g., in introductory, abnormal, adjustment, and clinical or counseling psychology courses) and to introduce cognitively oriented psychotherapies, such as rational emotive therapy (Ellis, 1962) or cognitive therapy (Beck, 1976).

The technique introduces general topics in an experiential way and provides examples of specific psychological concepts. For example, notions such as absolutistic thinking (Beck, 1976) or irrational beliefs (Ellis, 1962) may be demonstrated in thoughts such as "I have to have her love" from the first scenario. Other cognitive constructs, such as catastrophizing (e.g., "I can't live without him/her") and over-generalization ("I'll never find anyone else" or "Life is empty, meaningless"), can be introduced. If contrasting examples are desired, they can be drawn from the third scenario (e.g., "I wish she wanted to work on our relationship" as a preferential statement; "It's not the end of the world" as a realistic negative, noncatastrophizing characterization; and "While it hurts now, and probably will for some time to come" as a temporally discriminant thought). The specificity hypothesis (Beck, 1976; Greenberg & Beck, 1989), which suggests that different emotions are related to different information-processing patterns (e.g., depression to cognitions about loss), can be demonstrated. An additional scenario demonstrating anxiety specificity could be constructed by having students imagine that their friend has mentioned relationship problems and is coming over to discuss them. The person could be depicted as worrying in anticipation of a relationship breakup and might be thinking thoughts such as "What's wrong? I just know that I'm going to be dumped. What will I do? I can't take it." Different types of attributions (Abramson, Seligman, & Teasdale, 1978) may be illustrated. For example, "It's hopeless. Life is empty, meaningless" (global, stable, external attribution), "it's all my fault" (global, stable, internal attribution), and "if we don't, I'll survive. In time, I'll probably find other important relationships" (more specific, unstable, internal attribution) can be contrasted. Examples such as these allow the instructor to use the exercise for introducing specific concepts as well as general topics.

References

Abramson, L. Y., Seligman, M. E. P., & Teasdale, J. (1978). Learned helplessness in humans: Critique and reformulation. *Journal of Abnormal Psychology, 87*, 32–48.

Beck, A. T. (1976). *Cognitive therapy and the emotional disorders*. New York: International Universities Press.

Ellis, A. (1962). *Reason and emotion in psychotherapy*. New York: Stuart.

Greenberg, M. S., & Beck, A. T. (1989). Depression versus anxiety: A test of the content-specificity hypothesis. *Journal of Abnormal Psychology, 98*, 9–13.

Holmes, T. H., & Rahe, R. H. (1967). The social readjustment rating scale. *Journal of Psychosomatic Medicine, 11*, 213–218.

Velten, E. A. (1969). A laboratory task for the induction of mood states. *Behaviour Research and Therapy, 6*, 473–482.

Using a Videotape Clip to Demonstrate the Fallibility of Eyewitness Testimony

Nancy R. Gee
Jennifer L. Dyck

One of the most interesting topics in cognitive psychology is eyewitness testimony. Students readily see the application of what they are learning about cognition to the courtroom. Although everyday relevance makes learning about this topic appealing, it may also lead students to apply their intuitive, but often incorrect, beliefs about memory to understanding the research. A demonstration can help to connect their beliefs with the research and therefore change some of their inaccurate beliefs about memory for witnessed events.

There are several ways to demonstrate memory for witnessed events. First, an instructor can create a staged, live demonstration, in which an actor interrupts the class, and students then attempt to identify this person (Luus & Wells, 1994; Moye & Yarbrough, 1992). This demonstration can be effective, but it is often difficult to coordinate the actors. Other problems can include ethical concerns and students attempting to stop the staged crime in progress. Second, an instructor can create a videotape of a staged crime. Creating a videotape can be time consuming, but there are several such tapes available (Dragon, 1992; Ray, 1947).

The demonstration that we developed has several advantages over these videotapes. First, it is more current and, therefore, more appealing to students than the film described by Ray (1947). Second, the questionnaire for testing eyewitness memory is already developed, unlike that of Dragon (1992), who suggested that a corresponding questionnaire could be developed. Third, the videotape that we chose is available for rental at a local video store. Additionally, we have used this demonstration successfully over 20 times in either a cognitive psychology course or in the memory section of an introductory psychology course.

Method

Materials

The materials needed for this demonstration include a videotape copy of *RoboCop* (Davison & Verhoeven, 1987), which can be rented at any video store, the RoboCop quiz, and answers to the quiz.

The videotape clip of *RoboCop* (Davison & Verhoeven, 1987) that we chose involves a criminal robbing a gas station and RoboCop apprehending the criminal. The videotape clip starts approximately 49:41 min from the beginning of the movie and lasts 2:45 min, ending at 52:26 min. At the end of the scene as the criminal is escaping on his motorcycle, he runs into a parked car. We recommend stopping the videotape clip after it is apparent that the criminal will collide with a parked car, but just before he actually hits the car, because that part of the scene may be too violent for some students.

Although some students in the class may have previously seen the movie, they do not seem to remember much about it. Data supporting this claim come from a survey administered to students ($N = 48$) in an Introductory Psychology class after participating in the demonstration. The correlation between students' scores on the quiz and the number of times they had previously viewed the movie was not significant, $r(46) = .20$, $p < .05$.

The quiz consists of 15 multiple-choice questions about the videotape clip. A sample question, with the correct answer indicated by (*), is:

What did RoboCop do as soon as he discovered the robbery?
*a) sped his car up
 b) slowed his car down
 c) parked his car
 d) started shooting

Procedure

We typically show the videotape before raising the topic of eyewitness testimony and at least 15 min before giving the quiz. We have often shown it at the beginning of class, followed by unrelated lecture material for half of the class period. We have also shown it in the class session before discussing eyewitness testimony. Please note the warning at the beginning of the videotape. Do not charge your students admission and show only the specified segment of the videotape. We find that this demonstration is most effective when we give a plausible cover story for why we are showing the video clip. A sample cover story is that the videotape will wake them up and get their adrenaline flowing, so they can pay attention more fully during the remainder of the lecture. In the discussion after the quiz, it is important to fully debrief the students on the reason for showing the videotape clip.

Results and Discussion

Students can score their own quizzes. We find that most students answer more than half of the items correctly. In the survey of Introductory Psychology students mentioned previously, the mean number of correct responses on the quiz was 9.60 ($SD = 1.93$) out of 14 items. Students are generally surprised that they are not more accurate in answering the quiz. If they are particularly skeptical about some of the answers, we show the videotape clip a second time so that they can compare their answers to the videotape. This ability to replay the crime is an advantage of a videotape demonstration over a live demonstration. We use their performance on the quiz to lead into a discussion on the accuracy of real eyewitness identification. Many of the questions on the quiz concern peripheral details about the crime scene; Cutler, Penrod, and Martens (1987) found that attention to peripheral details is inversely related to identification accuracy. This is an interesting issue to discuss with the students.

We examined the effectiveness of this demonstration through a survey administered to the Introductory Psychology class. Students overwhelmingly found the demonstration helpful and enjoyable. For example, they gave the statement "I think today's demonstration made the concepts we covered much more clear than is typically true of this class," a mean of 5.94 ($SD = 0.86$) using a 7-point Likert scale ranging from 1 (*disagree completely*) to 7 (*agree completely*). Additionally, when asked "How helpful was today's demonstration in understanding eyewitness testimony?" students rated this question as 6.38 ($SD = 0.76$) on a 7-point Likert scale ranging from 1 (*not at all*) to 7 (*very much*). Students also gave positive written comments such as "I like it because it was fun and changed the pace of the class. It also opened our eyes to how 'bad' eyewitness testimony can be. I thought I would be a good eyewitness until I took the quiz. It really enforced the reading in the book." A second student added, "I like that it was a surprise, you know no one can cheat. I thought it was fun and a different way to explain."

Some students may express a sense of "unfairness" regarding the last question on the quiz because none of the multiple-choice answers are correct. The quiz includes this question to raise the issue of asking leading questions. Studies by Loftus and her colleagues (Loftus, 1979; Loftus & Hoffman, 1989; Loftus, Miller, & Burns, 1978) suggested that asking leading questions of an eyewitness can alter memory for that event.

Depending on the level and focus of the course, the instructor can introduce several other topics, such as the misinformation effect (Loftus & Hoffman, 1989; McCloskey & Zaragoza, 1985; Zaragoza, McCloskey, & Jamis, 1987), or use of the cognitive interview for eyewitnesses (Aschermann, Mantwill, & Kohnken, 1991; Bekerian & Dennett, 1993; Geiselman, Fisher, MacKinnon, & Holland, 1985; Geiselman & Padilla, 1988; Memon & Bull, 1991). Finally, articles in a recent *American Psychologist* (Bekerian, 1993; Egeth, 1993; Loftus, 1993; Wells, 1993; Yuille, 1993) issue summarize the current state of much research on eyewitness testimony and may be useful in preparing material for class discussion.

References

Aschermann, E., Mantwill, M., & Kohnken, G. (1991). An independent replication of the effectiveness of the cognitive interview. *Applied Cognitive Psychology, 5,* 489–495.

Bekerian, D. A. (1993). In search of the typical eyewitness. *American Psychologist, 48,* 574–576.

Bekerian, D. A., & Dennett, J. L. (1993). The cognitive interview technique: Reviving the issues. *Applied Cognitive Psychology, 7,* 275–297.

Cutler, B. L., Penrod, S. D., & Martens, T. K. (1987). The reliability of eyewitness identification. *Law and Human Behavior, 11,* 233–258.

Davison, J. (Executive Producer), & Verhoeven, P. (Director). (1987). *RoboCop* [Videotape]. (Available from Orion Home Video)

Dragon, W. (1992, May). *To be or not to be: Uses for a video-taped shooting in the classroom.* Paper presented at the Midwestern Psychological Association Meeting, Chicago.

Egeth, H. E. (1993). What do we not know about eyewitness identification? *American Psychologist, 48,* 577–580.

Geiselman, R. E., Fisher, R. P., MacKinnon, D. P., & Holland, H. L. (1985). Eyewitness memory enhancement in the police interview: Cognitive retrieval mnemonics versus hypnosis. *Journal of Applied Psychology, 70,* 401–412.

Geiselman, R. E., & Padilla, J. (1988). Cognitive interviewing with child witnesses. *Journal of Police Science and Administration, 16,* 236–242.

Loftus, E. F. (1979). *Eyewitness testimony.* Cambridge, MA: Harvard University Press.

Loftus, E. F. (1993). Psychologists in the eyewitness world. *American Psychologist, 48,* 550–552.

Loftus, E. F., & Hoffman, H. G. (1989). Misinformation and memory: The creation of new memories. *Journal of Experimental Psychology: General, 118,* 100–104.

Loftus, E. F., Miller, D. G., & Burns, H. J. (1978). Semantic integration of verbal information into visual memory. *Journal of Experimental Psychology: Human Learning and Memory, 4,* 19–31.

Luus, C. A. E., & Wells, G. L. (1994). The malleability of eyewitness confidence: Co-witness and perseverance effects. *Journal of Applied Psychology, 79,* 714–723.

McCloskey, H., & Zaragoza, M. S. (1985). Misleading postevent information and memory for events: Arguments and evidence against memory impairment hypotheses. *Journal of Experimental Psychology: General, 114,* 1–16.

Memon, A., & Bull, R. (1991). The cognitive interview: Its origins, empirical support, evaluation, and practical implications. *Journal of Community and Applied Social Psychology, 1,* 291–307.

Moye, T., & Yarbrough, N. (1992). *Instructor's resource manual to accompany Wortman/Loftus Psychology* (4th ed.). New York: McGraw-Hill.

Ray, W. S. (1947). An instructional film for use in the fidelity of report experiment. *The Journal of Psychology, 24,* 293–296.

Wells, G. L. (1993). What do we know about eyewitness identification? *American Psychologist, 48,* 553–571.

Yuille, J. C. (1993). We must study forensic eyewitnesses to know about them. *American Psychologist, 48,* 572–573.

Zaragoza, M. S., McCloskey, M., & Jamis, M. (1987). Misleading postevent information and recall of the original event: Further evidence against the memory impairment hypothesis. *Journal of Experimental Psychology: Learning, Memory, and Cognition, 13,* 36–44.

Memory and the Seven Dwarfs

Marianne Miserandino

Name the seven dwarfs. This deceptively simple task can be an engaging and effective way to illustrate basic principles of memory for students in introductory psychology or cognition classes. The task is appropriate for any class size and can be easily adapted to the level and interest of the class. This demonstration has been used in three different classes of introductory psychology at a small liberal arts college and at a community college. The entire demonstration takes approximately 15 to 20 min.

Theoretical Background

This demonstration is based on Meyer and Hilterbrand's (1984) study of recall and recognition of the names of the seven dwarfs. They found that subjects were more likely to recall the five rhyming names and to recall them in a cluster. They also found that recognition facilitated subjects' memory, indicating that the names were "available but not accessible" in memory (p. 54). These authors suggested that the results of their study can be used as a classroom demonstration of basic memory processes.

Part 1: Free Recall of the Seven Dwarfs

Instructions

Explain to the class that an interesting and effective way to learn about principles of memory is to examine their own thought processes as they perform a memory task. Instruct them to take out a blank sheet of paper and to write down all responses that come into their minds in the order they recall them. Because an important part of the demonstration is the process of recall, emphasize that their incorrect responses are just as important as their correct responses in illustrating how memory is organized. Their task is to name the seven dwarfs.

Discussion

Discuss the following topics with the class, cautioning them to limit their discussion to responses that they know are clearly wrong. Do not reveal correct dwarf names during this initial discussion. Students' responses will suggest many questions and ideas. Lead the discussion in the direction that best suits the class.

Difficulty or ease of the task. How difficult or easy did students find the task? Why? Many students claim that they were unable to name all seven dwarfs because of the lack of recent practice or the culture-bound nature of the task.

Others, such as Disney or trivia buffs, may have been more familiar with the dwarfs and found the task easy. Still others will claim that distractions, such as the weather or disruptions, precluded their success.

In an introductory class, 12 of 66 students correctly named all seven dwarfs. Four students did not correctly name any. Two of these students had not grown up in American culture: One was from Honduras, and the other was from Sri Lanka. There were 152 wrong guesses of 84 different names.

Tip-of-the-tongue phenomenon. Did students have the feeling that they knew a name but were unable to articulate it, like it was "on the tip-of-their-tongues"? If students volunteer that they did have this experience, ask them to describe as much as they can about the word: How many syllables does it have (six of the seven dwarf names have two syllables)?; What letter does it start with (s and d occur most frequently)?; What meaning or connotation does the word have (most of the names are vivid, state adjectives)? Generally, students will be quite accurate. Explain that this is called the *tip-of-the-tongue* (TOT) phenomenon, which occurs when the generation process does not produce a complete response but produces parts that must then be constructed into a whole (Glass & Holyoak, 1986).

Organization of memory by sound, letter, and meaning. Instruct students to study carefully the order in which they recalled the names, looking for any patterns. Memory is usually organized by sound, letter, or meaning, and this is illustrated by people's wrong answers in two ways. First, many of their wrong answers will be similar in sound, letter, and/or meaning to correct dwarf names. For example, 91% of the class's wrong guesses were two-syllabled names ending in a y-sound; 5 of the 7 correct names end in y and have two syllables.

Similarly, s and d each occurs as the initial letter of correct names twice. Wrong guesses beginning with the letter s occurred the most frequently (in 22% of the wrong guesses), and 14% began with the letter d.

Students also recalled words similar in meaning to actual dwarf names, such as Lazy (13.8%), Clumsy (12.3%), Droopy (7.7%), or Grouchy (6.1%). Also, many people recalled names from the correct superordinate category but named characters other than dwarfs—Snoopy (6%), Pokey (6%), Moe (5%), Curly (3%), and Charlie (1%)—and two other Disney characters—Goofy (9%) and Thumper (1%).

Second, organization by sound, letter, and meaning will typically cause subjects to recall names in a run or pattern of similar names. Runs occur when the generation of one correct item acts as a cue that facilitates recall of other items with similar sounds or meanings (Bousfield & Wicklund, 1969; Meyer & Hilterbrand, 1984). Virtually all of the students demonstrated runs in their recall of dwarf names. These runs occurred for both correct and incorrect names and varied in length from 2 to 15 names.

Recall versus recognition. Ask the class if they would be able to remember more names if this was a recognition task. Recall involves a two-step process: generation of possible targets and identification of genuine ones. Recognition is generally easier because the first step is given as part of the question; subjects need only decide if the given information is correct (Glass & Holyoak, 1986). Because the task is easier, the majority of students say they would prefer and do better on a recognition task.

Part 2: Recognition of the Seven Dwarfs

Instructions

Prepare a handout for the class by listing the following correct dwarf names and distractors on a page: Grouchy, Gabby, Fearful, Sleepy, Smiley, Jumpy, Hopeful, Shy, Droopy, Dopey, Sniffy, Wishful, Puffy, Dumpy, Sneezy, Lazy, Pop, Grumpy, Bashful, Cheerful, Teach, Shorty, Nifty, Happy, Doc, Wheezy, and Stubby. Instruct students to circle the names they recognize as correct dwarf names, cross out the ones they know are incorrect, and leave the others alone.

Discussion

Ask students if they were able to remember more of the dwarfs on this task and to explain why. Did they find this recognition task easier than the recall task? Some students may have found that the discussion of wrong answers cued the correct names or that the names on the paper itself cued their recall.

In the introductory class, the 12 students who correctly named all seven dwarfs in the recall task also correctly recognized all seven. Omitting these students, 91% of the others did better on the recognition task than they did on the recall task, 6% did the same, and 4% did worse.

Finally, give the class a list of the seven dwarfs. In order from most to least likely to be recalled, according to Meyer and Hilterbrand (1984), they are: Sleepy, Dopey, Grumpy, Sneezy, Happy, Doe, and Bashful. Meyer and Hilterbrand (1984) found that college students were more likely to recall the five rhyming names and to recall them in a run, an example of organization by sound. The subjects were least likely to remember Bashful, an example of organization—or absence of—by meaning.

Short-term memory (STM) and long-term memory (LTM). STM is transient memory that can hold information for only a few moments. It is often called *working memory,* because it holds information that is currently in use. LTM can hold information for a greater time—hours, days, and years (Anderson, 1985). Many experiments have been conducted to determine the capacity of STM. Despite much debate about how to measure the capacity of STM, most psychologists agree that it is approximately seven pieces of information, plus or minus two (Miller, 1956)—the same as the number of dwarfs. Through the use of chunking or other organizing schemata, however, the actual number of items recalled can be greater than 5 to 9. For many students, the recall task was a test of recall from LTM—assuming that the names were encoded there to begin with, raising more issues for discussion. But now, if they have been following the discussion, the names should be in STM.

Discussion of other memory processes. Many other issues can be discussed, depending on the level and interest of the class:
1. Choice of distractors for multiple-choice and other tests. The distractors used here came from the subject's wrong guesses in the Meyer and Hilterbrand study.
2. Judgment tasks. Have students classify their responses as positive hits, negative hits, false positives, and false negatives.
3. Measurement of the capacity of STM and LTM.
4. Iconic memory, echoic memory, and memory for other senses. Do they exist? Are they different? Do they have different capacities?

Part 3: Posttest Recall of The Seven Dwarfs

Complete the demonstration by having students turn the sheets over and recall the names of the seven dwarfs. Now everyone theoretically should be able to name all seven dwarfs—plus or minus two. Indeed, 95% of the students named 5 to 7 dwarfs this time, including 3 of the 4 students who were unable to name any the first time.

Student Evaluations

Students in the introductory psychology class were enthusiastic about this demonstration. On a scale ranging from *no, not at all* (1) to *yes, very much* (7), students gave a mean rating of 5.79 (SD = 1.15) to their enjoyment of the activity. An overwhelming 94% of the students rated the demonstration as a 5 or higher in helping them to understand the difference between recall and recognition (M = 5.96; SD = .99) and in illustrating the basic principles of memory (M = 5.73; SD = .92), and 75% rated it as a 5 or higher in helping them to understand how items are organized in memory (M = 5.22; SD = 1.23). Finally, 91% of the students found that, overall, it was useful or very useful (M = 5.69; SD = .95).

References

Anderson, J. R. (1985). *Cognitive psychology and its implications.* San Francisco: Freeman.

Bousfield, W. A., & Wicklund, D. A. (1969). Rhyme as a determinant of clustering. *Psychonomic Science, 16,* 183–184.

Glass, A. L., & Holyoak, K. J. (1986). *Cognition*. New York: Random House.

Meyer, G. E., & Hilterbrand, K. (1984). Does it pay to be "Bashful"?: The seven dwarfs and long-term memory. *American Journal of Psychology, 97,* 47–55.

Miller, G. A. (1956). The magical number seven, plus or minus two: Some limits on our capacity for processing information. *Psychological Review, 63,* 81–96.

Note

I thank Raymond J. Folven for piloting the demonstration with his Introductory Psychology students so that their data could be used in my analyses. I also thank Joseph J. Palladino, the reviewers, and Mary Murray for comments and suggestions on this article.

Mnemopoly: Board Games and Mnemonics

Lawrence M. Schoen

The topic of human memory, whether it occurs in an introductory class or an advanced course in cognitive psychology, fascinates students. Instructors can introduce different kinds of memory (e.g., working, implicit, episodic, and autobiographical), but the critical question is simply where to begin. To capture students' imagination regarding the power of memory, I recommend starting with mnemonics. The demonstration described herein begins with the introduction of simple techniques and builds to an effective mnemonic system that incorporates and illustrates the underlying principles of human memory.

Most students are familiar with some memory aids such as rhymes (e.g., Thirty days hath September . . .), acrostics (e.g., Roy G. Biv), or even a peg word system (e.g., One is a bun, two is a shoe . . .), but the more flexible and powerful mnemonic tricks are likely to be novel and intriguing to them. Higbee (1988) discussed four main principles common to successful mnemonic systems: meaningfulness, organization, association, and visualization. The effectiveness of any mnemonic system depends on how well these four principles facilitate encoding, storage, and retrieval of the information to be remembered.

Two powerful mnemonic systems are the *method of loci* and the *phonetic peg system*. The method of loci involves learning a series of places, such as the rooms in a house or the route one may take walking around campus. Each place is then paired with a piece of information one wishes to remember. Retrieval is accomplished by mentally retracing one's route, pausing at each locus to "pick up" the item that had been placed there, and then moving on to the next locus. The phonetic peg system uses a code in which numeric values are replaced by phonemes, each number referring to a specific set of sounds (e.g., 1 is the sound represented by the voiced plosive *d* or its voiceless twin *t*, and 5 is the sound of *l*), with vowels added as one chooses to produce a wide range of peg words. Thus, 15 may be *dial* or *tail* or *tile* (Higbee, 1988). One learns a list of peg words and, as with the method of loci, pairs each peg with an item to be remembered. Recall is accomplished by visualizing the peg corresponding to the item number and "seeing" its paired item.

Unfortunately, these systems do not always fit well with in-class instruction. Although one can visualize a path or series of places, my students find the method of loci daunting when the number of locations is more than 20. The method works best when one can actually move from locus to locus, seeing each scene and its relation to other scenes. When such a field trip is impractical, the classroom demonstration can fail if students have not acquired a full set of loci. The phonetic peg system's elaborate rules presuppose some knowledge of phonetics (e.g., minimally distinctive phoneme pairs, such as *d* and *t*, have the same numeric value). Psychology students cannot be expected to possess the required knowledge. More important, whether learning a series of places or a list of peg words, one must first commit the system to memory. A frequent student complaint is the circularity of needing a mnemonic system in order to acquire a mnemonic system!

One can, however, ease into a mnemonic system by way of simpler memory techniques, using mnemonics to teach mnemonics. Ideally, that mnemonic would maintain the power of the method of loci and the phonetic peg system, but it would be easier to acquire. Any highly structured, overlearned domain of knowledge can be used as loci or pegs to store memories, whether it be images of one's relatives (each pictured interacting in some way with the item to be recalled) or the mascot of each team in the National Football League. For a classroom demonstration, however, one needs a shared experience that has a well-organized structure. The board from the game Monopoly® by Parker Brothers satisfies these needs.

The Monopoly® board (or *Mnemopoly* as it was christened) is an effective mnemonic system because it has all four characteristics Higbee (1988) identified. The board is easy to visualize as it has four sets of 10 locations and a corner or railroad at every fifth space. The board may be organized in many ways: by fourths (each side of the board), by eighths (from corner to railroad or from railroad to corner), by color and groupings of properties (e.g., Baltic and Mediterranean are violet; Illinois, Indiana, and Kentucky are red), by the strategic play value of each subgrouping relative to other particulars on the board (e.g., individuals "getting out of jail" are apt to land on the purple properties, the orange properties, the Electric Company, or the Pennsylvania Railroad), and so forth. These provide ample opportunities for association and meaning.

Monopoly® has been a part of popular culture since 1935; over 100 million game sets have been sold in 33 countries and 23 languages (*The Story of the MONOPOLY® Game*, 1987). Thus, even if students vary in their degree of familiarity with the board's layout, they should be sufficiently acquainted with it to provide a common starting point for the demonstration.

Demonstration

Begin by introducing students to the basic principles of mnemonics, such as acrostics and rhymes, illustrating them with examples. Depending on financial resources, instructors can provide a copy of the game board to each student, distribute drawings of the board, or project a copy of the board overhead. Instruct students to develop their own mnemonic devices to learn the game board (see Table 1 for students' examples), telling them that the board will not be available during their retrieval attempt. Because the game board is so highly structured, and because students are already familiar with its elements, they generally require no more than 30 min to encode it. (Alternatively, students can skip memorizing the board, and it can remain available during retrieval, thus shortening the time for the demonstration.)

The instructor reads aloud a list of 40 words, going no slower than 10 s per item. Concrete and visualizable words are recommended, but abstract materials should also work. Instruct students to work their way around the board, imaging a combination of each location with the current item. Long before the full list has been read, students are apt to be anxious and convinced that they are not successfully encoding the words; provide some reassurance, encouraging them to continue the procedure and stay focused. After reading the entire list once, remove the reference boards and ask students to imagine the game board and move around it, writing

Table 1. Some Mnemonic Devices Students Created in Learning the Mnemopoly Board

Acrostics
Very amusing psychologists often ramble, yet grade better.
  (violet, aqua, purple, orange, red, yellow, green, and blue are the property colors)
Atlas ventured watery marshes grimly.
  (Atlantic, Ventnor, Water Works, Marvin Gardens, and Go-To-Jail are on the third side)
Rhymes
From the Reading to the Penn,
Next it's B & O,
Coming home it's Short Line then,
On the Rail Road
  (the four railroads)
The first chest floats upon the seas,
The next has oranges between.
The third side has none, if you please.
The final chest sits in the green.
  (the three community chests)

down the item they find at each square. After the recall task, have students explain how they encoded particular items.

Evaluation

To compare Mnemopoly with the method of loci and the phonetic peg system, I gave three groups of eight Introductory Psychology students instruction in one of the three systems for 20 min. Then, with their appropriate game boards, campus maps, or peg word lists for reference, they were presented 40 words and allowed 10 min to encode them. When all eight students in each group had encoded the entire set of 40 words, each reference board, map, or peg word list was removed. Students then attempted to recall the complete set of words, and they returned 1 week later to attempt a second recall. An analysis of variance of this 3 × 2 mixed design indicated significant main effects for both mnemonic system, $F(2, 21) = 125.3$, $p < .001$, and time, $F(1, 21) = 16.8$, $p < .001$, as well as a significant Mnemonic System × Time interaction, $F(2, 21) = 5.2$, $p < .02$. Simple effect tests indicated that, in both recall conditions, all three mnemonic groups differed significantly (see Table 2 for means and standard deviations). Within mnemonic groups, both the Mnemopoly and the phonetic peg systems decreased significantly over time, whereas the method of loci group did not, thus accounting for the interaction.

Discussion

Without exception, students are amazed at how list items seem to occur to them—instantly and effortlessly. The Mnemopoly system incorporates the best features of the other two systems, although possessing only 40 squares makes it, at least conceptually, less powerful and flexible than an expandable map or peg word list. The main strength of Mnemopoly lies in its relatively swift acquisition. Students' comments after completing the recall task using the method of loci or the phonetic peg system suggest that failures were most often due to an inability to remember the reference point (locus or peg) rather than the item they had associated with it. Thus, the 20-min time limit may have been inadequate for encoding 40 loci and surely was too brief to master the phonetic rules and acquire the 40 peg words. In contrast, students reported remembering the 40 Mnemopoly sites but forgetting (or failing to encode properly) the target associated with each place.

Table 2. Mean Number of Items Recalled for Three Mnemonic Systems

| | Time | | | |
| | Immediate | | 1-Week Delay | |
Mnemonic System	M	SD	M	SD
Mnemopoly	38.8	1.3	36.3	2.8
Method of loci	31.3	3.4	30.9	4.3
Phonetic peg	21.1	3.0	15.0	2.9

Note. Maximum score = 40.

Unlike the method of loci, which typically requires one to move through it serially until the desired item is reached (i.e., loci are generally not numbered), the inherent structure of the Mnemopoly board provides access to any of the loci, much as is possible with the phonetic peg system. Similarly, the Mnemopoly board allows a greater level of elaboration and richness to each square (as is found with the method of loci) than can be readily attained with the phonetic peg system. More than simply memorizing the board, students use the board's organization to encode relations among items to be remembered by storing them at related spaces on the board. Although the demonstration has students move sequentially around the board, the inherent structure would allow recall instructions such as "every third square" with little added difficulty.

A rich imagery structure is the hallmark of a successful mnemonic system. Students readily comprehend this point when they describe how they encoded particular items. For example, one student remembered the word *dinosaur* (17th on the list) by visualizing a brontosaurus dipping its head into a large chest and munching on the oranges it had found there. When asked why the chest had oranges, he explained that the 17th space was the second community chest, in the middle of the orange properties.

Demonstrating, learning, and testing the Mnemopoly system introduce numerous facets of memory. The instructor can discuss related processes, such as encoding, storage, and retrieval, as well as memory deficits, interference, and forgetting, with students who now have a greater interest in and a better understanding of these concepts.

References

Higbee, K. L. (1988). *Your memory* (2nd ed.). New York: Prentice Hall.

The story of the MONOPOLY® game. (1987). Beverly, MA: Parker Brothers.

Notes

1. An earlier version of this article was presented at the annual meeting of the Southern Society for Philosophy and Psychology, Louisville, KY, April 1990.
2. I thank Joseph J. Palladino, Ruth L. Ault, and six anonymous reviewers for their valuable comments and infinite patience. Thanks also to Beth Boring, Bruce Davis, Kim Heuberger, Merlin Mann, Beth Nelson, Trisha Southard, and Liana Urfer for their help in developing this new mnemonic system.

Exploring Mental Illness Through a Poetry-Writing Assignment

Joan C. Chrisler

Encouraging creative thinking and enhancing writing skills are important goals of teachers at all levels. In recent years, *Teaching of Psychology* has published numerous articles on how to incorporate writing assignments into psychology courses (e.g., Beers, 1985; Bennett, 1985; Klugh, 1983; Nodine, 1990). This article illustrates an atypical and challenging writing assignment for courses in introductory or abnormal psychology.

The aim of this assignment is to increase students' understanding of mental illness and their empathy toward the mentally ill. Popular culture frequently presents the mentally ill as objects of humor or derision; textbooks, with their dry language and reliance on the medical model, are more likely to portray the mentally ill as collections of symptoms than as people. The idea for this assignment arose as I was trying to think of a way to encourage students to identify with those who have psychological problems. I wanted a short writing assignment that would encourage students to reflect on what it might be like to experience mental illness. Poetry, with its emotional base, vivid imagery, and often fragmented language, seemed ideal.

Writing Assignment

Students are told 2 weeks before the assignment is due that they are to write a poem about the experience of mental illness. The format, length, and topic are left entirely up to them. They may choose to be concrete or abstract, serious or humorous, or personal or theoretical, and they may describe the experience using first- or third-person pronouns. The poems need not be written in a rhyming format. Anything goes!

The class generally seems shocked when they are told about the assignment, but after being assured that they will be judged primarily on content, rather than format or poetic language, they rise to the challenge. Because length is unimportant, one can count on receiving several haiku. Someone will always hand in "Roses are red; violets are blue. I'm schizophrenic and so am I." (This response is given a failing grade because, besides its lack of originality, it describes multiple personality and not schizophrenia.) However, most students take the assignment seriously and turn in work that shows that they have thought long and carefully about their topics. Most work is creative and interesting; some poems are so beautifully written that I refer them to the college literary magazine.

Students have responded to the assignment with varying degrees of enthusiasm. One student wrote about his negative emotional reaction to the assignment and titled it "Poemaphobia." (I gave him an A.) Many have told me that once they got over their amazement at being asked to write a poem for a psychology class they found the task to be both challenging and fun.

To earn an A, a poem must convey an excellent understanding (or be an excellent description) of anxiety, depression, psychosis, or some particular disorder (e.g., avoidant personality disorder). A B is given to a poem that conveys a good understanding or description of the experience of mental illness. Some latitude is available for the evaluation of writing ability. For example, an adequate description of avoidant personality would earn a grade of B; an adequate description that is also well written (e.g., the poem's lines contain the appropriate number of syllables for its rhyme scheme, and the poet's choice of words is good) would earn a B+. Oddly, despite the subjectivity involved in evaluating an assignment of this type, no students have ever complained about their grades.

For the past 2 years (after obtaining permission from the students—some give permission only if their work remains anonymous), I have posted the best work on a bulletin board in the psychology building. Much to the poets' delight, the display attracted students and faculty from all over campus.

I have used this assignment in three classes during the last few years and have been pleased with the results. I believe that the time students spend thinking about particular aspects of mental illness in preparation for this assignment results in better understanding and increased empathy for the mentally ill.

This is a versatile assignment for introductory and abnormal psychology classes. With a little ingenuity, it can be adapted for use in other courses. For example, students might write a poem about being elderly for a developmental psychology course, about the experience of chronic or terminal illness in a health psychology course, or about being the object of prejudice in a social psychology course. Readers are invited to try this assignment and judge its value for their classes.

References

Beers, S. E. (1985). Use of a portfolio writing assignment in a course on developmental psychology. *Teaching of Psychology, 12,* 94–96.

Bennett, S. M. (1985). Coordinated teaching of psychology and composition: A valuable strategy for students and instructors. *Teaching of Psychology, 12,* 26–27.

Klugh, H. E. (1983). Writing and speaking skills can be taught in psychology classes. *Teaching of Psychology, 10,* 170–171.

Nodine, B. F. (Ed.). (1990). Psychologists teach writing [Special issue]. *Teaching of Psychology, 17*(1).

Note

An earlier version of this article was presented at the annual meeting of the American Psychological Association, Boston, August 1990.

The Disordered Monologue: A Classroom Demonstration of the Symptoms of Schizophrenia

Timothy M. Osberg

One of the challenges in teaching students about schizophrenia is to provide vivid descriptions of its symptoms. Recent films depicting case examples of people with schizophrenia have helped. For example, *Madness* (a segment from PBS's *The Brain* series) and *Into Madness* (from HBO's *America Undercover* series) contain some compelling case examples of this disorder. A more powerful demonstration of the bizarre symptoms experienced by people with schizophrenia would be for the instructor to model the typical outward presentation of schizophrenia to the class. This article describes a classroom demonstration that simulates a verbal encounter with a person experiencing symptoms of schizophrenia. My goal was to achieve a portrayal that was sensitive and accurate.

Procedure

Modeling schizophrenia does not require an instructor to learn all the bizarre behavioral nuances that may accompany it. Demonstrating the bizarre quality of language and thought that might be observed in a person with schizophrenia suffices. Before discussing schizophrenia and without any prior warning, I launch into the following monologue:

Okay class, we've finished our discussion of mood disorders. Before I go on I'd like to tell you about some personal experiences I've been having lately. You see I've [pause] been involved in highly abstract [pause] type of contract [pause] which I might try to distract [pause] from your gaze [pause] if it were a new craze [pause] but the sun god has put me into it [pause] the planet of the lost star [pause] is before you now [pause] and so you'd better not try to be as if you were one with him [pause] because no one is one with him [pause] any one who tries to be one with him [pause] always fails because one and one makes three [pause] and that is the word for thee [pause] which must be like the tiger after his prey [pause] and the zommon is not common [pause] it is a zommon's zommon. [pause] But really class, [holding your head and pausing] what

do you think about what I'm thinking about right now? You can hear my thoughts can't you? I'm thinking I'm crazy and I know you [point to a student] put that thought in my mind. You put that thought there! Or could it be that the dentist did as I thought? She did! I thought she put that radio transmitter into my brain when I had the novocaine! She's making me think this way and she's stealing my thoughts!

You can read the monologue to students, but practicing it several times before class gives it a more spontaneous quality. Your affect during the monologue can also influence its impact. Persons with schizophrenia often show either inappropriate affect (e.g., laughing when talking about tragic things) or blunted affect (i.e., displaying no emotion at all). I suggest caution in how you modulate your affect during the monologue. Some instructors with a flair for the dramatic might want to heighten its impact by displaying the silly affect of the person with the disorganized subtype of schizophrenia. However, this runs the risk of offending students who may have a friend or family member who suffers from schizophrenia.

After the monologue and after students collect themselves (reactions range from laughter to incredulity), I explain that the speech was meant to demonstrate the language of a person with schizophrenia. I ask students to give their reactions to my speech. I ask them what they were thinking and if they felt uncomfortable. The answers to these questions prompt a discussion of how people with schizophrenia might feel about the way others react to them. The schizophrenic person might be sensitive to and hurt by the reactions of others. Other issues can also be examined. To what extent do the bizarre and seemingly meaningless ideas expressed have idiosyncratic meaning for the person? Might some of the delusions represent the person's primitive attempts to explain the symptoms he or she is beginning to experience? The monologue also helps to debunk the common misconception that schizophrenia means multiple personality.

While discussing the text's material on schizophrenia, I refer to the monologue because it contains simple examples

240

of the more common disturbances in the content and form of thought as spelled out in the *DSM–III–R* (American Psychiatric Association, 1987). Disturbances in the form of thought include *loose associations* (jumping from topic to unrelated topic), *neologisms* (creating new words), *perseveration* (repeatedly returning to the same topic), and *clanging* (rhyming and punning). Disorders of thought content include *thought broadcasting* (believing others can hear one's thoughts), *thought insertion* (feeling people are inserting thoughts into one's mind), *thought withdrawal* (believing someone is removing one's thoughts), and *delusions of being controlled* (by some external force). Examples of these phenomena in the monologue include:

clanging—abstract/contract/distract; gaze/craze; makes three and that is the word for thee
perseveration—no one is one . . . and any one who tries to be one . . . fails because one and one
neologism—zommon
loose association—included throughout
thought broadcasting—You can hear my thoughts can't you?
thought insertion—You put that thought there!
thought withdrawal—she's stealing my thoughts
delusions of being controlled—she put a radio transmitter in my brain

I reproduce the foregoing list as an overhead (the monologue itself can also be reproduced as an overhead and presented before this) and review each example as I discuss the common symptoms of schizophrenia described in the *DSM–III–R*.

Evaluation

On the four occasions I have used this demonstration, the students have been very engaged by it. Their reactions are enthusiastic and generate lively discussion. Students evaluated the demonstration after I used it in an abnormal psychology class (*N* = 27). An open-ended question asked students to describe their thoughts as I spoke the monologue. Also, students rated the demonstration on a scale ranging from *not very useful* (1) to *very useful* (4) and indicated their recommendations concerning whether I should use the demonstration in future classes on a scale marked *No*, *Maybe*, and *Yes, definitely*.

Students' open-ended comments included: "I was confused"; "I thought you were crazy"; "It made me nervous"; "I couldn't understand what was going on. I looked around to see everyone else's reactions"; "I would have felt uncomfortable if someone I met on the street talked like that instead of a classroom professor"; and "I thought for [a schizophrenic] to do this must take some higher thought processes—the way he rhymed, etc." In light of some of these comments, one reviewer of this article pointed out the possibility that a student with a friend or family member diagnosed as schizophrenic might react strongly to the demonstration. However, to date no student has been upset after the demonstration. To the contrary, on one occasion, a student with a family member diagnosed as schizophrenic approached me after class to praise the demonstration. She confided that the demonstration and discussion had helped her gain a better understanding of her relative's disorder. Nevertheless, you might want to prepare yourself to handle any concerns raised by students during or after class by assembling referral information for a local mental health clinic or mental health organization.

The mean rating of the usefulness of the demonstration was 3.7 (*SD* = .49), indicating that students thought it had considerable merit. In addition, 100% indicated *Yes, definitely* in response to my question about whether I should use the demonstration in future classes. Thus, students consider the monologue an engaging and useful demonstration. It takes only 10 to 15 min, including discussion, and offers an alternative to lengthy video portrayals or field trips for introductory psychology or abnormal psychology classes.

References

American Psychiatric Association. (1987). *Diagnostic and statistical manual of mental disorders* (3rd ed., rev.). Washington, DC: American Psychiatric Association.

Raymond, A., & Raymond, S. (Producers), & Raymond, S. (Director). (1989). *Into madness* [Film]. AR/SR Productions (HBO Presentation).

Sage, D. L., Jr. (Producer, Director). (1984). *Brain, Part 7: Madness* [Film]. New York: WNET.

Note

I thank Charles L. Brewer and three anonymous reviewers for their helpful comments on an earlier version of this article.

Defining Aggression: An Exercise for Classroom Discussion

Ludy T. Benjamin, Jr.

Aggression is a topic included in virtually every textbook on introductory psychology. Some books place aggression in the section on motivation and emotion while others cover it as part of social psychology. Most include it in reference to research on humans but discussion of some animal studies of aggression is also common. Treatment of related concepts such as violence, anger, frustration, and assertiveness are also common topics.

Whereas textbook coverage of aggression is almost guaranteed, a definition of the term is not. In a nonrandom sample of 10 introductory psychology books (selected from the author's bookcase), 5 provided an explicit definition of aggression but the others left the meaning embedded in a series of paragraphs and so required the reader to serve as lexicographer. Considering the complexity of the term *aggression*, it is not surprising that these authors might choose to avoid espousing a particular definition.

The exercise described in this paper uses aggression as an example of a typical construct in psychology, permeated with a host of subtle meanings and not so subtle disagreements that make it difficult to reach a consensual definition. One could use other constructs such as intelligence or self-esteem, but aggression was chosen because it generates considerable discussion among students. Anecdotal evidence for the fascination with this topic can be drawn from the prevalence of aggression as a theme in movies and television, the popularity of sports, and the interest many people show in reports of violent crime.

The activity described here can be used in a number of classes, including the course in introductory psychology and, in fact, anywhere you treat the topic of aggression. It should be used prior to any lecture on aggression and before the students have read their textbook coverage of the subject. This exercise works best in a class of 50 students or less, but by altering the data reporting procedures it can be used in much larger classes, although discussion obviously will suffer in large classes. The activity requires about 50 minutes but could be made shorter or longer depending on the preferences of the instructor. The instructor's role in this exercise is to serve as a tabulator of the data and as moderator of the discussion.

Procedure

At the beginning of the class, give each student a copy of a questionnaire containing the 25 numbered statements shown in Table 1. Instruct the students to "read each statement and decide whether or not you believe the situation described is one of aggression." Wording of this instruction is critical so as not to bias the responses. Avoid using phrases like "aggressive act" or "aggressive behavior" because one of the issues to be discussed is whether some overt behavior needs to occur in aggression. Ask the students to circle the number of each statement that describes aggression. Tell them they should respond according to their own beliefs and not how they think they should respond or how they think most people would respond. Compliance with this request can be enhanced by telling the students not to put their names on the questionnaires. Indeed, there is no reason in this exercise to know how a particular person responded. You may want to have the students indicate their sex on the questionnaire if you would be interested in look-

Table 1. Aggression Questionnaire

1. A spider eats a fly.
2. Two wolves fight for the leadership of the pack.
3. A soldier shoots an enemy at the front line.
4. The warden of a prison executes a convicted criminal.
5. A juvenile gang attacks members of another gang.
6. Two men fight for a piece of bread.
7. A man viciously kicks a cat.
8. A man, while cleaning a window, knocks over a flowerpot, which, in failing, injures a pedestrian.
9. A girl kicks a wastebasket.
10. Mr. X, a notorious gossip, speaks disparagingly of many people of his acquaintance.
11. A man mentally rehearses a murder he is about to commit.
12. An angry son purposely fails to write to his mother, who is expecting a letter and will be hurt if none arrives.
13. An enraged boy tries with all his might to inflict injury on his antagonist, a bigger boy, but is not successful in doing so. His efforts simply amuse the bigger boy.
14. A man daydreams of harming his antagonist, but has no hope of doing so.
15. A senator does not protest the escalation of bombing to which he is morally opposed.
16. A farmer beheads a chicken and prepares it for supper.
17. A hunter kills an animal and mounts it as a trophy.
18. A dog snarls at a mail carrier, but does not bite.
19. A physician gives a flu shot to a screaming child.
20. A boxer gives his opponent a bloody nose.
21. A Girl Scout tries to assist an elderly woman, but trips her by accident.
22. A bank robber is shot in the back while trying to escape.
23. A tennis player smashes his racket after missing a volley.
24. A person commits suicide.
25. A cat kills a mouse, parades around with it, and then discards it.

ing at potential sex differences in the definition of aggression. Such differences, if obtained, would undoubtedly add to the interest in the discussion.

Allow the students about 5 minutes to complete the questionnaire. Most, if not all, of the students will finish before that time, so you should be ready to proceed when the last person has finished. Collect the questionnaires, shuffle, and redistribute them to the class so that each student gets a copy. Most students will be given a questionnaire other than their own, but it is unimportant if they get their own copy back. This procedure allows students to report on the responses that may or may not be their own, thus eliminating a potential source of embarrassment.

Record the data on the board by asking students for a show of hands on each numbered item, with hands being raised if the item is circled on the questionnaire they are holding. It is important to know the exact size of the class in this exercise to know when you have unanimity. For example, with a class size of 34, total agreement would come from a score of 34, in which case every student agreed that the item described aggression. A score of zero would mean that no one thought the item described aggression. Such unanimity is rare and typically occurs only on those items in which there seems to be no intent to harm. Tabulating the data on the chalkboard can be accomplished quickly, usually in less than 5 minutes, so that the bulk of the class time can be devoted to discussion.

Class Discussion

Use the questionnaire results to get the students talking about how aggression is defined. You might begin with those items for which there is greatest agreement and proceed to those on which the class is evenly divided. Note that the 25 statements are quite diverse and are intended to span the gamut of issues relevant to consideration of aggression: harm to living versus nonliving things (9 and 23), accident versus intention (8 and 21), actual damage versus no physical damage (10, 13, and 18), self-defense (3, 13, and 14), duty or job responsibility (3, 4, 19, 20, and 22), predation and instinctual behavior (1, 2, and 25), survival (1, 6, and 16), acts involving animals other than humans (7, 16, 17, and 18), covert acts (11 and 14), inaction (12 and 15), self-injury (24), and killing for sport (17 and 25).

Attempt to get students to make these points by grouping the related items in the discussion. For example, items 16 and 17 make an interesting comparison. The latter is more often viewed as aggressive, and a similar pattern emerges in items 1 and 25. In both pairs, students distinguish between killing for food and killing for sport. Many will argue that food-seeking justifies the act and would not label it aggression. Debate on these items and many others is typically lively and opposing viewpoints are common. Should alternate views not be forthcoming on some issues, the instructor may wish to play the role of devil's advocate.

If there is time, or in a separate lecture in the next class period, you can present some of the definitions of aggression proposed by psychologists. Consider the following examples:

1. "Behavior intended to hurt another person" (Freedman, 1982, p. 259).
2. "Any behavior whose intent is to inflict harm or injury on another living being" (McGee & Wilson, 1984, p. 503).
3. "Hostile or forceful action intended to dominate or violate" (Lefrancois, 1982, p. 596).
4. "Behavior that is intended to injure another person (physically or verbally) or to destroy property" (Atkinson, Atkinson, & Hilgard, 1983, p. 321).
5. "A response that delivers noxious stimuli to another organism" (Buss, 1961, p. 3).

The first four definitions require intent, but the last one does not. The first one limits aggression to humans, while the second and fifth broaden it to include all living organisms. But what about kicking wastebaskets and smashing tennis rackets? That could be considered aggressive under the fourth definition. All definitions talk about behaviors, actions, or responses but leave one unclear as to whether inaction can be aggressive or not. Providing these definitions to students helps them to understand that, like them, psychologists also have some difficulty in agreeing on what does or does not constitute aggression.

Students in my class consistently have rated this activity high in terms of satisfaction and as an exercise in learning. Written comments indicate that a number of them believe that it serves to sharpen their critical thinking skills. A few miss the point and want to be told the "real" definition of aggression after the exercise is over, but that kind of reaction is quite rare.

Additional Suggestions

You can use this exercise as a basis for discussion or as a lecture on the causes of aggression: Is aggression instinctual?; Is aggression a natural reaction to conditions such as frustration, conflict, and pain?; Is aggression learned, and if so, how and from what sources? This last question presents a good opportunity to discuss aggression in the media, particularly television, and what effect it may have on the behavior of viewers (see Liebert, Sprafkin, & Davidson, 1982).

Other topics of interest include: aggression in athletics, competitiveness versus aggressiveness, assertiveness versus aggressiveness, the positive role of aggression, violent crime, the relation of prejudice to aggression, and methods for the control of aggression.

References

Atkinson, R. L., Atkinson, R. C., & Hilgard, E. R. (1983). *Introduction to psychology* (8th ed.). New York: Harcourt, Brace, Jovanovich.

Buss, A. (1961). *The psychology of aggression*. New York: John Wiley.

Freedman, J. L. (1982). *Introductory psychology* (2nd ed.). Reading, MA: Addison-Wesley.

Johnson, R. N. (1972). *Aggression in man and animals*. Philadelphia: W. B. Saunders.

Kaufmann, H. (1970). *Aggression and altruism*. New York: Holt, Rinehart and Winston.

Krech, D., Crutchfield, R. S., Livson, N., Wilson, W. A., & Parducci, A. (1982). *Elements of psychology* (4th ed.). New York: Alfred A. Knopf.

Lefrancois, G. R. (1982). *Psychology* (2nd ed.). Belmont, CA: Wadsworth.

Liebert, R. M., Sprafkin, J. N., & Davidson, E. S. (1982). *The early window: Effects of television on children and youth* (2nd ed.). New York: Pergamon.

McGee, M. G., & Wilson, D. W. (1984). *Psychology: Science and application*. St. Paul, MN: West Publishing.

Note

The items in Table 1 were taken from Johnson (1972), Kaufmann (1970), and Krech, Crutchfield, Livson, Wilson, & Parducci (1982). Some of their items were modified for use in this questionnaire.

The Power of Stereotypes: A Labeling Exercise

Susan B. Goldstein

The purpose of this exercise is to convey to participants the powerful cognitive, affective, and behavioral impact of stereotypes on the perceiver as well as the target. Research indicates that once strong stereotypes are activated, people are likely to attend to (Bodenhausen, 1988; Major, Cozarelli, Testa, & McFarlin, 1988) and recall (Stangor & McMillan, 1992; von Hippel, Sekaquaptewa, & Vargas, 1995) expectancy-confirming information. They are also likely to make stereotype-consistent attributions for the behavior of others (Hewstone, 1990). As targets of stereotypes, people may alter their behavior in anticipation of being perceived in a stereotypical manner (Steele & Aronson, 1995) or may even fulfill the stereotypical expectancies of others (Hilton & Darley, 1991; Jussim & Fleming, 1996). Both the outgroup members (Stephan & Stephan, 1993) and the ingroup members (e.g., Fichten, Robillard, Tagalakis, & Amsel, 1991) of stigmatized groups are likely to link particular affective reactions to group labels.

This exercise provides a set of stereotypes that guide the selective attention, recall, and attributions of participants as they interact with each other. It also demonstrates the impact of being stereotyped on the self-perception and behavior of the targeted individual.

The Labeling Exercise

Preparation

The labeling exercise takes approximately 1 hr to conduct. I have found it to be successful with classes as small as 10 and as large as 60. With some assistance it may be feasible to conduct the exercise with numbers larger than 60. The setting should be a room large enough to allow participants to move about easily. A circular arrangement of chairs works well because participants can interact easily as they move within the circle and then can return to their chairs during the debriefing and discussion phases.

The only material needed is adhesive (e.g., file folder) labels for each participant; each label indicates a different stereotypic trait descriptor. Examples include *good at math, childlike, violent, materialistic, musical, frail, artistic, uneducated, lazy, overemotional, athletic, dishonest, forgetful, unclean, cute, helpless, exotic, jovial,* and *quick tempered*. I find that using trait descriptors is preferable to using the names of specific target groups (e.g., Puerto Rican, disabled, African American). Asking participants to treat others according to group labels requires that they generate the accompanying stereotype, which they may be unable or unwilling to do. Further, the use of trait descriptors allows participants to focus on the stereotyping process rather than the accuracy of specific trait–group associations.

Procedure

Introduce the exercise. For participants without academic background on the psychology of stereotyping, a brief (10–15 min) explanation of theoretical perspectives may be useful. Duckitt (1992) and Hilton and von Hippel (1996) are helpful instructor resources. The former provides a comprehensive overview of major theoretical approaches, whereas the latter presents a review of the stereotyping literature with particular attention to cognitive and motivational aspects of stereotype formation and maintenance.

The instructor should tell participants that to learn more about how stereotypes work, they will be labeled. It is also important to explain that participation is voluntary, and that students who wish not to be labeled can play a useful role as observers. The facilitator may also wish to acknowledge that although some participants have had a great deal of experience being the target of stereotypes, this may still be a useful exploration of the process of stereotyping.

Distribute labels. Attach adhesive labels (to participants' forehead or back) so that they are not visible to the wearer. I deliberately emphasize the act of randomly distributing labels to minimize the effect of the specific assigned trait on the participant.

Assign the task. Tell participants to converse with one or two others on the topic of "future goals." Although other topics may be used, I have found that the discussion of future goals easily elicits reactions based on the trait descriptors and is appropriate for a variety of participant populations. As time allows, participants may shift conversation partners and hold brief discussions with several different people (cocktail party style). Instruct participants that throughout this process they are to treat others according to their label. For example, someone engaged in conversation with a participant labeled *uneducated* may intentionally use very simple words, or one may frequently remind the person labeled *forgetful* about the requirements of the task. This phase lasts approximately 15 min.

Debrief. I begin the debriefing session by reiterating that I distributed labels randomly and that the way participants were treated does not in any way reflect their actual characteristics. Although participants are generally anxious to see and remove their labels, I encourage them to keep their labels on initially as we debrief. Otherwise, participants tend to tailor their descriptions of their experiences to fit the label. With smaller groups, all participants can talk about their own behavior and the treatment they received during the exercise. With larger groups, some volunteers can discuss their experiences. Ask any observers to comment on their observations. Participants may then view their labels and debrief further if desired. This debriefing phase often focuses on the degree to which it is uncomfortable to knowingly stereotype others and the frustration experienced in being stereotyped oneself.

Discussion. This exercise raises several topics for discussion. First, participants usually notice the ease with which one can find stereotype-confirming information. When asked, they will generally say that it was easy for them to respond to others in a manner consistent with the trait descriptors. In exploring the nature of these stereotype-consistent responses, participants can be guided to recognize the role of selective attention and attribution.

Second, possible reactions to being labeled may be discussed. Participants tend to either expend a great deal of energy attempting to disprove the label or they behave in a manner that confirms the stereotype-based expectation. They may also acknowledge the difficulty of ignoring stereotypical treatment. Students can often provide vivid examples of the way they have altered their own behavior in anticipation of being stereotyped. A third topic for discussion focuses on positive stereotypes. Participants labeled with positive traits, such as *jovial* or *good at math* can be asked to reflect on their experiences. These reports generally indicate that positive stereotypes can be just as limiting and frustrating as negative ones.

A fourth issue deals with the social interaction of participants. If participants can describe a rough sociogram of the group as it occurred during the exercise, they may find that similarly labeled individuals (e.g., *childlike*, *frail*, and *slow*) clustered together. Participants can then speculate on the

reasons for such groupings and on implications for intergroup relations. A fifth topic for discussion is the significance of this exercise for prejudice reduction. Participants can be asked to think about what would have led them to reject the trait descriptors. This generally results in a discussion of efforts to attend to stereotype-disconfirming information.

Finally, it is counterproductive to leave students concerned about stereotyping to the extent that subsequent classroom discussion of group differences closes down. Participants can be asked to suggest ways to discuss issues of diversity without stereotyping. Some ideas include distinguishing between rigid stereotypes and generalizations, focusing on diversity within groups and the multiple group identities of each individual, emphasizing similarities across groups, and maintaining an awareness of stereotyping processes.

Participant Evaluations

A total of 75 participants evaluated this exercise immediately following its completion. These participants were enrolled in three separate Psychology of Prejudice classes of approximately 25 students each. None of these students elected to observe rather than participate in the exercise. Participants responded to five items on a 7-point scale ranging from 1 (*strongly disagree*) to 7 (*strongly agree*), with 4 (*not sure*) as the midpoint. Several students also responded to a request for written comments following the rating scales. Responses were quite positive, with participants indicating that they found the instructions clear ($M = 6.5$, $SD = 0.8$) and the activity interesting ($M = 6.4$, $SD = 0.9$). Participants also believed that the activity taught them something useful about prejudice ($M = 6.4$, $SD = 0.7$) and that it should be used in future classes ($M = 6.7$, $SD = 0.6$). Finally, participants generally felt comfortable participating in this activity ($M = 6.0$, $SD = 1.3$) although the rating for this item was somewhat lower and more variable than the other items. In each of the cases where students' scores indicated that they were uncomfortable participating, they also indicated that they felt the exercise should be used in future classes. I believe that the lower mean on this last item is indicative of the degree to which it is uncomfortable to become aware of one's stereotypes or to knowingly stereotype others. The participants' written comments support this interpretation. For example, typical comments were "It was uncomfortable to learn about my biases," and "It was difficult to treat people stereotypically, but [the exercise] was extremely helpful in learning about prejudice." I have found that former students refer to this exercise as a meaningful experience that provided them with a clearer understanding of the power of stereotypes in guiding their self-perceptions and their view and treatment of others.

References

Bodenhausen, G. V. (1988). Stereotypic biases in social decision making and memory: Testing process models for stereotypic use. *Journal of Personality and Social Psychology, 55,* 726–737.

Duckitt, J. (1992). Psychology and prejudice: A historical analysis and integrative framework. *American Psychologist, 47,* 1182–1193.

Fichten, C. S., Robillard, K., Tagalakis, V., & Amsel, R. (1991). Casual interaction between college students with various disabilities and their nondisabled peers—The internal dialog. *Rehabilitation Psychology, 36,* 3–20.

Hewstone, M. (1990). The "ultimate attribution error"?: A review of the literature on intergroup causal attribution. *European Journal of Social Psychology, 20,* 311–335.

Hilton, J. L., & Darley, J. M. (1991). The effects of interaction goals on person perception. *Advances in Experimental Social Psychology, 24,* 235–267.

Hilton, J. L., & von Hippel, W. (1996). Stereotypes. *Annual Review of Psychology, 47,* 237–271.

Jussim, L., & Fleming, C. (1996). Self-fulfilling prophecies and the maintenance of social stereotypes. In N. Macrae, M. Hewstone, & C. Stangor (Eds.), *The foundations of stereotypes and stereotyping* (pp. 161–192). New York: Guilford.

Major, B., Cozarelli, C., Testa, M., & McFarlin, D. B. (1988). Self-verification versus expectancy-confirmation in social interaction: The impact of self-focus. *Personality and Social Psychology Bulletin, 14,* 346–359.

Stangor, C., & McMillan, D. (1992). Memory for expectancy-congruent and expectancy-incongruent information: A review of the social and social developmental literatures. *Psychological Bulletin, 111,* 42–61.

Steele, C. M., & Aronson, J. (1995). Stereotype threat and the intellectual test performance of African-Americans. *Journal of Personality and Social Psychology, 69,* 797–811.

Stephan, W. G., & Stephan, C. W. (1993). Cognition and affect in stereotyping: Parallel interactive networks. In D. M. Mackie & D. L. Hamilton (Eds.), *Affect, cognition, and stereotyping: Interactive processes in group perception* (pp. 111–136). Orlando, FL: Academic.

von Hippel, W., Sekaquaptewa, D., & Vargas, P. (1995). On the role of encoding processes in stereotype maintenance. *Advances in Experimental Social Psychology, 27,* 177–254.

Notes

1. Portions of this article were presented at the Western Psychological Association Convention, April 1996, San Jose, CA.

2. I thank Ruth L. Ault and the anonymous reviewers for their comments on a draft of this article.

Unveiling Positions of Privilege: A Hands-On Approach to Understanding Racism

Sandra M. Lawrence

Teaching courses involving racism and other forms of oppression to White, middle-class undergraduates can be difficult for a host of reasons (Adams & Zhou-McGovern, 1994; Sleeter, 1994; Tatum, 1992, 1994). For one, White undergraduates tend to view racism as synonymous with personal prejudice (Wellman, 1993) and are less likely to consider racism as deeply rooted in systems of advantage. Teaching White, middle-class students about racism is further complicated because race- and class-privileged positions are often invisible to them, therefore White students do not see themselves as race privileged. They have been educated, both formally and informally, not to see color or, when they do, to minimize its importance (Helms, 1990, 1995; Katz, 1978). Making race more visible for students holding onto this "color-blind orientation" (Frankenberg, 1993) is an important step in helping students understand how racism functions in this society.

One successful classroom exercise that enables students to see the privileged positions of the White, middle class involves a collaborative activity of making mobiles. Schniedewind and Davidson (1983) designed this activity for elementary and middle school teachers who wanted to help their students understand how institutional racism, sexism, classism, and other forms of oppression lead to inequalities in resources. The creators also expected this activity to provide school-aged children with an opportunity to witness how individuals or groups who are targets of oppression are often blamed for the inequalities imposed on them.

As I read the description of this exercise, it was evident to me that this exercise could be a powerful means for revealing to White college students their "White privilege" (McIntosh, 1988), an abundance of advantages that they often have trouble seeing. The capacity to make the invisible visible is the primary reason I incorporated this exercise into my curriculum and have used it successfully for 4 years with sophomore, junior, and senior students in a Race, Class, Culture, and Gender course.

Method

For the mobile activity, 21 White, female students from predominantly middle-class backgrounds sat in groups of 4 (one group of 5) at five tables separated from one another. I began the class by asking students in each group to work collaboratively to compose a working definition of an abstract concept related to the course. One term that I often used is *multiculturalism* (others such as *social justice, equity,* and *tolerance* could also be used). While the group members exchanged ideas and took notes on their discussion, I placed a packet of materials for making a mobile on each table.

All five packets contained basic construction elements for making mobiles, but three of the packets contained more elaborate materials. For example, the packet with the least materials contained a 12-in. wooden dowel, one coat hanger, two pieces of construction paper, and a spool of thread. The packet with the most materials contained three dowels, two coat hangers, string, fishing line, precut wire, 10 pieces of colored paper, felt tip markers, crayons, pipe cleaners, streamers, scissors, ribbon, pom-poms, glue, and tape.[1]

I gave students 15 min to reach consensus on their definitions (even though they could have continued for longer); thereafter, I instructed them to work with their group members for 30 min to create a mobile representative of their definition using only the materials provided. At the conclusion of the mobile construction period, I asked students to demonstrate their finished products to the class. I asked the group with the most resources to present first, followed by the group with the least materials. Once students displayed their mobiles, I asked one open-ended question: "What was it like for you to participate in this exercise?" During the discussion, students remarked about the feelings and ideas that occurred to them during the exercise. As a follow-up assignment, I asked students to reflect in writing either about their experience during the class session or about their thoughts concerning one of the required readings dealing with racism.

Results and Discussion

From the beginning of the mobile task, groups with minimal materials were hampered and frustrated by limited resources. As they noticed the lavish materials of more privileged groups, they muttered about the "unfairness" of the exercise. In reflection papers, students wrote about their feelings trying to make do with their inadequate supplies although others had abundant materials. They also commented on their reluctance to display their projects knowing they could have created more artistic mobiles if they had received better resources. In describing their feelings, students in these disadvantaged groups remarked about being angry and "feeling robbed and cheated."

Once out of their "less privileged" roles, students learned more about the real privilege they do have. They had an opportunity to "stand in someone else's shoes" if only for a brief period and gain a new perspective. One student described in writing the impact the exercise had on her thinking about power and privilege:

> I came out of today's class thinking that it was, very possibly, the best class I have had so far at the college. I realized many things during this class. . . . Most important, I felt "underprivileged" for probably the first time in my life. . . . It showed me that American's underprivileged children DO feel cheated and DO notice that others have what they

don't have. I can see why what you are given DOES make a difference. . . . It was an immediate feeling like something had clicked in my head and I now had a new understanding.

This student, like others, realized that groups who get less are aware of the differential treatment they receive even if those in more privileged positions are oblivious to those differences. They also learned that power and privilege have a direct bearing on chances for academic success and social mobility.

Although all of the students in the less privileged groups recognized the inequality of materials during mobile construction, not one student in the privileged groups noticed that some groups had fewer materials. These students began to recognize that some groups were advantaged (and others were not) only during the discussion following the demonstration when less privileged groups shared their feelings. Only then did the students privileged with a colorful array of construction elements come to understand what had occurred, and they were shocked that they did not notice sooner. One privileged student wrote about how unaware she and her group members were to the unequal conditions in the room:

> It never occurred to me that there were differences in the materials that were distributed. . . . I was in the upper middle class group, completely unaware of my position or privilege, just because I was content with what I had. I had no desire to be interested in the other groups. I kept my blinders on to the inequalities.

Another member of a privileged group, "amazed at her obliviousness" to the differential treatment during the exercise, remarked about the shame she felt at the thoughts she entertained about her classmates' abilities. When the second group demonstrated their rather drab mobile, she found herself questioning the group's creativity:

> It actually occurred to me, "what was wrong with them that they didn't make a colorful collage?" I imagined that perhaps they weren't as creative as our group was, or they spent too much time planning what they were going to do, instead of actually doing it. . . . I was so ashamed that I thought that.

Other students in privileged groups found themselves thinking similar negative thoughts about their classmates' motivation, organizational skills, and ability to focus. Once out of their roles, they realized how their privileged status had kept them from seeing the reasons for their classmates' poor performance. They also recognized similarities in their assumptions and those commonly made in reference to the poor academic performance of some students of low income or of color, attributing differences in performance to deficiencies within students rather than to systems of inequality in operation (Darling-Hammond, 1995; Nieto, 1992).

By reflecting on their obliviousness and the invalid assumptions they were quick to make, students were able to understand their own race and class privilege. In fact, 15 of the 21 students who participated in the mobile exercise reported in their writings that the activity had a profound effect on their views of themselves and others. Students related in writing how the class session "surprised," "rattled," or "jolted" them into a greater understanding of the

---

[1]For those making these packets, be sure to prepare packets two and three with increasing amounts of "meager" materials. Packet four should contain scissors plus an assortment of "lavish" materials but not as many as packet five.

advantages they receive because of their positions in society. From this experience, students also learned that they needed to look beyond their assumptions and stereotypes to understand the differences in performance that many people targeted by race and class oppression display. Because race and class stratification are not often visible to those in privileged positions, they acknowledged their need to be more vigilant and ask questions of the institutional policies and practices in place, instead of focusing on those targeted by oppression and asking "what's wrong with them?"

Conclusions

Because attitudes and beliefs about race are deeply rooted and often long-standing, I would be remiss to claim that any single class activity, no matter how carefully designed or implemented, could change those attitudes. Research has demonstrated, however, that semester-long courses in the psychology of racism and antiracist education can be successful in both altering belief systems and changing racist behaviors (Lawrence & Bunche, 1996; Lawrence & Tatum, 1997; Tatum, 1992, 1994). Such courses combine readings, films, reflective writing, and experiential activities in ways that create dissonance (often painful) in students' knowledge and perceptions about themselves and society. Establishing trusting classroom environments that invite risk taking and provide ample opportunities to process emotional reactions that often accompany new ways of viewing the self and the world are essential.

Although one activity cannot effect change, it can initiate that process. Through this brief exercise, White, middle-class undergraduates had the opportunity to try on a new pair of spectacles, lenses that enabled them to see their privileged positions, while at the same time bringing their assumptions about those less privileged into clearer view, a requisite step in unlearning racism.

References

Adams, M., & Zhou-McGovern, Y. (1994, April). *The sociomoral development of undergraduates in a "social diversity" course: Theory, research, and instructional applications*. Paper presented at the meeting of the American Educational Research Association, New Orleans, LA.

Darling-Hammond, L. (1995). Inequality and access to knowledge. In J. A. Banks & C. A. McGee-Banks (Eds.), *Handbook of research on multicultural education* (pp. 465–483). New York: Macmillan.

Frankenberg, R. (1993). *White women, race matters: The social construction of whiteness*. Minneapolis: University of Minnesota Press.

Helms, J. E. (Ed.). (1990). *Black and White racial identity: Theory, research and practice*. Westport, CT: Greenwood.

Helms, J. E. (1995). An update of Helms's White and people of color racial identity models. In J. G. Ponterotto, J. M. Casas, L. P. Suzuki, & C. M. Alexander (Eds.), *Handbook of multicultural counseling* (pp. 181–197). Thousand Oaks, CA: Sage.

Katz, J. H. (1978). *White awareness: Handbook for anti-racism training*. Norman: University of Oklahoma Press.

Lawrence, S. M., & Bunche, T. (1996). Feeling and dealing: Teaching White students about racial privilege. *Teaching and Teacher Education, 12*, 531–542.

Lawrence, S. M., & Tatum, B. D. (1997). White educator as allies: Moving from awareness to action. In M. Fine, L. Weiss, L. Powell, & M. Wong (Eds.), *Off White: Readings on race, power, and society* (pp. 333–342). New York: Routledge.

McIntosh, P. (1988). *White privilege and male privilege: A personal account of coming to see correspondences through work in women's studies* (Working Paper No. 189). Wellesley, MA: Wellesley College Center for Research on Women.

Nieto, S. (1992). *Affirming diversity: The sociopolitical context of multicultural education*. New York: Longman.

Schniedewind, N., & Davidson, E. (1983). *Open minds to equality: A sourcebook of learning activities to promote race, sex, class, and age equity*. Englewood Cliffs, NJ: Prentice Hall.

Sleeter, C. A. (1994, Spring). White racism. *Multicultural Education*, 5–8.

Tatum, B. D. (1992). Talking about race, learning about racism: The application of racial identity development theory in the classroom. *Harvard Educational Review, 62*, 1–24.

Tatum, B. D. (1994). Teaching White students about racism: The search for White allies and the restoration of hope. *Teachers College Record, 95*, 462–476.

Wellman, D. (1993). *Portraits of White racism* (2nd ed.). New York: Cambridge University Press.

Freudian Principles in Everyday Life

Marianne Miserandino

Sigmund Freud was one of the great minds of the 19th century and one of the most influential theorists in the history of psychology. A testament to Freud's genius is that many of his theories, ideas, and terms have permeated European and American culture and are still evident 100 years later in modern America, for better or for worse (Torrey, 1992). But just as the proverbial fish is the last to know that the water is wet, it is often difficult for beginning psychology students to appreciate the genius of Freud when so much of his thought is already familiar to them.

A recent computer search of the Expanded Academic Index of bibliographic references and abstracts of more than

1,500 scholarly and general interest journals in the humanities, social sciences, general sciences, and current events from 1990 to 1993 led to references of psychoanalysis and culture, feminism, literature, motion pictures, philosophy, and religion. On the PsycLIT data base alone, between 1987 and 1993 Freud appeared in the title or abstract of more than 2,000 articles; the keyword *psychoanalytic* was used in more than 7,300 references. Beyond the obvious influences in literature and literary criticism, some of the more unusual references were psychosexual stages as reflected in the Masters of the Universe series of action figures (Ainslie, 1989); the family drama as reflected in the comic book characters Batman and Robin (Lang, 1990) and in the paintings of Mary Cassatt (Zerbe, 1987); pre-oedipal issues in Ingmar Bergman's film *Cries and Whispers* (Brattemo, 1990), Alfred Hitchcock's film *The Man Who Knew Too Much* (McEwen, 1987), and in the films *The Shining* (Cocks, 1987) and *Back to the Future* (Bick, 1990).

Students' familiarity with Freudian concepts may make it even more difficult for instructors to present the heavily theoretical psychoanalytic perspective. Yet, in the last 7 years *Teaching of Psychology* has published only two articles related specifically to Freudian principles. In the most recent one, Carlson (1989) noted how the psychoanalytic perspective is perhaps the most difficult of all personality systems to present, and she described a demonstration to compensate for the dearth of available exercises. Her "Psychosexual Pursuit" is an engaging board game in which players must complete their psychic development around the game board before depleting their supply of psychic energy ($100). Highlights of the game include rolling dice (the higher the roll, the greater overindulgence during a given stage), buying the use of a defense mechanism, and rolling doubles to get out of the latency stage.

Davidson (1987) described a project for an undergraduate laboratory in personality assessment on the anal personality type. Based on lectures and readings on Freudian principles, students develop hypotheses about the relation among the three anal traits of frugality, orderliness, and obstinacy and the various domains of expression for each. Students then construct and validate a questionnaire to measure the anal personality and, in the process, increase their understanding of Freudian concepts and questionnaire design.

In addition to reviewing the basic principles of Freudian theory, the exercise described herein is designed to help students see the range and variety of Freud's influence in American thinking today. Students indicate the strength of their agreement or disagreement with 15 statements chosen to represent the breadth of Freudian concepts (see Table 1). Statements are worded so that a Freudian psychologist would strongly agree with 9 and strongly disagree with 6 of them. Statements cover Freud's general theory of psychosexual development (Statement 1), as well as individual stages: oral (Statement 6); anal (Statement 9); phallic, with the oedipal complex (Statements 4 and 8) and the oedipal fixation of penis envy (Statements 10 and 12); and genital (Statements 2, 11, and 14). Other statements tap Freud's notion of the death instinct as manifested by aggression (Statements 3 and 7), repression (Statement 5), dream symbolism (Statement 13), and parapraxes or Freudian slips (Statement 15). All statements were designed to illustrate

Table 1. The 15 Freudian Principle Statements

[a]1. Events that occurred during childhood have no effect on one's personality in adulthood.
[a]2. Sexual adjustment is easy for most people.
3. Culture and society have evolved as ways to curb human beings' natural aggressiveness.
4. Little boys should not become too attached to their mothers.
5. It is possible to deliberately "forget" something too painful to remember.
6. People who chronically smoke, eat, or chew gum have some deep psychological problems.
[a]7. Competitive people are no more aggressive than noncompetitive people.
8. Fathers should remain somewhat aloof to their daughters.
[a]9. Toilet training is natural and not traumatic for most children.
10. The phallus is a symbol of power.
11. A man who dates a woman old enough to be his mother has problems.
12. There are some women who are best described as being "castrating bitches."
[a]13. Dreams merely replay events that occurred during the day and have no deep meaning.
14. There is something wrong with a woman who dates a man who is old enough to be her father.
[a]15. A student who wants to postpone an exam by saying "My grandmother lied . . . er, I mean died," should probably be allowed the postponement.

Note. Unless specified otherwise, these items are scored as follows: *strongly disagree* = 1, *disagree* = 2, *neutral* = 3, *agree* = 4, and *strongly agree* = 5. Add up the score for each question to yield a total score.
[a]These items are scored in reverse, *strongly disagree* = 5, *disagree* = 4, *neutral* = 3, *agree* = 2, and *strongly agree* = 1.

principles assimilated by popular culture and typically covered in an introductory psychology or personality textbook.

Procedure

Students respond to each statement by choosing one of the following responses: *strongly disagree, disagree, neutral, agree,* or *strongly agree.* Each response receives a score of 1 through 5 representing the extent of concurrence with the Freudian perspective. Respondents with a Freudian perspective would strongly agree with 9 of the items and strongly disagree with 6 (marked with asterisks in Table 1). Their total score, summed across the 15 items, should be near the maximum score of 75. Respondents who agree with the marked items and disagree with the unmarked items (the non-Freudian position) would get minimal points per item and should have a total score near 15.

Results

Three professors used this exercise in four different introductory psychology classes, including one graduate seminar. Scores from 78 undergraduates in three classes ranged from 39 to 56 (M = 47.6, SD = 4.3). Individual scores for graduate students (n = 12) in a counseling program, who were taking an introductory course in psychology because their undergraduate degrees were not in psychology, were not available. The class agreed or strongly agreed with Freudian notions

249

on an average of 6.5 of the statements. The student with the lowest score held a Freudian position for only 4 of the 15 questions, whereas the two highest scorers held Freudian positions for 12 questions.

Instructors in all of these classes used the exercise to introduce Freudian principles. Students then studied Freud's theories in more depth. One of the undergraduate instructors readministered the exercise to her class after they discussed Freud in class, thus using it as a test of attitude change after exposure to Freudian theories. Although the range of the 19 scores was greater on the posttest (41 to 61 compared to 41 to 56), the mean did not change significantly (pretest $M = 48.1$, $SD = 4.4$; posttest $M = 47.2$, $SD = 4.6$). The maximum attitude shift in both directions was 8 points.

Discussion

Discussion of students' responses should center on why they believe as they do. Where did they learn these ideas? What kind of evidence should be used to evaluate some of these statements? Would a person from another culture answer these questions differently? What other factors would affect people's responses? Were some of these statements true in the past but not true now? If so, why? What has changed? Were students surprised that some of the statements are associated with Freudian theory? Why? Can students identify the Freudian concept? Can students explain the reasoning behind each question?

One of the basic tenets of Freud's theory is that humans are driven by life instincts (e.g., sex) and by death instincts (e.g., aggression). If anxiety or social constraints prevent direct expression of sexuality or aggression, these impulses will be expressed indirectly or unconsciously. Thus, dreams and parapraxes are two ways of studying unconscious wishes or impulses. Similarly, Freud believed that the aggressive drive is often sublimated into competition and achievement.

Furthermore, Freud proposed that individuals pass through a series of psychosexual stages during which id impulses of a sexual nature must find satisfaction in a socially acceptable way. Unresolved conflicts between id impulses and society's restrictions during childhood affect one's personal adjustment in adulthood. For example, people who chronically smoke, eat, or chew gum—oral-incorporative personalities—are said to have had trouble with feeding and weaning early in the oral stage. Similarly, problems concerning toilet training during the anal stage may lead to the development of anal-expulsive or anal-retentive personalities in adulthood. Problems during the genital stage are often manifested in an Oedipus complex and castration anxiety in men or in an Electra complex and penis envy in women. Because of penis envy, women fixated at this stage, according to Freud, symbolically castrate men through embarrassment, deception, and derogation.

The discussion can address a possible double standard of acceptable behavior for men and women on questions about fathers and daughters (Statement 8) versus mothers and sons (Statement 4) or of dating an older person (Statements 11 and 14). Did anybody respond to these sets of statements differently? Why? What does this mean?

Student Evaluations

Student reactions to this exercise were positive. Using a 7-point scale ranging from *not at all* (1) to *very* (7), with *neutral* (3) as the midpoint, the graduate class ($n = 14$) found it particularly thought provoking ($M = 6.1$, $SD = .86$) and a useful way to introduce Freudian principles ($M = 6.3$, $SD = .91$). They also reported that the exercise made them realize the extent of Freud's influence on American culture ($M = 6.1$, $SD = 1.14$) and gave them an appreciation for the range and variety of Freud's theories ($M = 5.7$, $SD = 1.07$). In the three undergraduate classes, 67% of the 79 introductory psychology students found the exercise to be somewhat to very thought provoking, and 50% to 60% found the exercise helpful in making them realize the range, variety, and extent of Freud's influence. Most students (54%) agreed that overall the project was very useful.

Undergraduate students' written comments on the evaluation echoed these results: "It was helpful because it made you think about everyday affairs and people you know. A good way to begin to help people to understand Freud." "I didn't know Freud believed so many things on so many subjects." "Interesting how you put his theories into questions and scenarios of today's world." "Freud's theories are interesting but he tended to be quite an extremist. It seems society, especially the media, believes in Freud's concepts." Finally, Freud would certainly applaud the insight of one of the counseling graduate students who said "more in-depth [discussion of the] connection between questions and answers would be interesting."

By turning basic principles of Freudian psychology into statements that reflect current American views and values, an interesting and entertaining demonstration was created. This exercise helped students learn the basics of Freudian psychology and appreciate Freud's genius. A similar demonstration could be created for other personality theorists, such as Carl Jung, Melanie Klein, Erik Erikson, Karen Horney, or B. F. Skinner. The design of such a questionnaire is left to readers and their students.

References

Ainslie, R. C. (1989). Master of the universe: Children's toys as reflections on contemporary psychoanalytic theory. *Journal of the American Academy of Psychoanalysis, 17*, 579–595.

Bick, I. J. (1990). Outatime: Recreationism and the adolescent experience in *Back to the future. Psychoanalytic Review, 77*, 587–608.

Brattemo, C. E. (1990). Reality transformed to dream: Some comments on Ingmar Bergman's film *Cries and whispers* and the collapse of language. *Scandinavian Psychoanalytic Review, 13*, 47–61.

Carlson, J. F. (1989). Psychosexual pursuit: Enhancing learning of theoretical psychoanalytic constructs. *Teaching of Psychology, 16*, 82–84.

Cocks, G. (1987). The hinting: Holocaust imagery in Kubrick's *The shining. Psychohistory Review, 16*, 115–136.

Davidson, W. B. (1987). Undergraduate lab project in personality assessment: Measurement of anal character. *Teaching of Psychology, 14*, 101–103.

Lang, R. (1990). Batman and Robin: A family romance. *American Imago, 47*, 293–319.

McEwen, D. (1987). Hitchcock: An analytic movie review. *Psychoanalytic Review, 74*, 401–409.

Torrey, E. F. (1992). *Freudian fraud: The malignant effect of Freud's theory on American thought and culture.* New York: Harper-Collins.

Zerbe, K. J. (1987). Mother and child: A psychobiographical portrait of Mary Cassatt. *Psychoanalytic Review, 74*, 45–61.

Note

I thank Patricia Scully and Lester Sdorow for pretesting this exercise at Beaver College, and I thank Ruth Ault and three anonymous reviewers for comments and suggestions on a draft of this article.

251

Gender Bias in Leader Selection

Michelle R. Hebl

The pervasiveness of stereotypes and how they affect behavior are often not evident to students. Helping students see this relation is also not easily illustrated through textbooks or class discussions. The present exercise is designed to show the possible behavioral ramifications of gender stereotyping. Specifically, students experience firsthand gender stereotyping when they select leaders of small, mixed-sex groups.

Past research has indicated that men are significantly more likely to be chosen as leaders than women in initially leaderless, mixed-sex groups (Eagly & Karau, 1991). Gender stereotypes about leadership may have influenced these findings. For example, subjects endorsed the abilities to "separate feelings from ideas," "act as leaders," and "make decisions" as being much more descriptive of men than women (Broverman, Vogel, Broverman, Clarkson, & Rosenkrantz, 1972, p. 63). These and other stereotypically masculine items have been positively correlated with college students' perceptions of leaders (Lord, De Vader, & Alliger, 1986). Eagly and Mladinic (1989) proposed that gender stereotypes also are comprised of beliefs that men occupy advantaged social positions of power and status relative to women. Such views lead people to perceive men as more in control and more powerful than women, even when they are not. Indeed, research by Porter, Geis, and Jennings (1983) revealed that, given an ambiguous setting involving both men and women, independent raters perceive men to be in charge much more often than women.

Stereotypes about women may also enhance biases in leader selection (Geis, Brown, Jennings, & Corrado-Taylor, 1984; Nye & Forsyth, 1991). Geis, Brown, Jennings, and Porter (1984) suggested the most general stereotype about women is that they are not autonomous and are unqualified to assume achievement-oriented responsibilities in the world. However, women, relative to men, are believed to be more "talkative," "tactful," and "aware of others' feelings" (Broverman et al., 1972, p. 63), as well as more expressive and communal (Eagly & Mladinic, 1989). Thus, gender stereotyping may have a differential impact on leader selection when type of leadership is manipulated (Eagly & Karau, 1991). Whereas task-oriented competitive leaders focus on task contributions and productivity, social cooperative leaders focus on social contributions, prosocial behavior, and social climate. Male group members make more task-oriented contributions than do females (Wood, 1987), so group members may choose male leaders in task-oriented competitive situations. However, social leaders may focus on prosocial behaviors, so men may be selected as social leaders less often than they are selected as task-oriented competitive leaders.

The present demonstration illustrates the gender bias in leader selection. The type of group leadership (task-oriented competitive or social cooperative) is manipulated across groups.[1] Men were expected to emerge as leaders more often than women in task-oriented competitive groups but not in social cooperative groups.

Procedure

Students are divided into groups of four or six, each comprised of an equal number of men and women. Any students left over can be grouped together and their data later discarded or analyzed separately. If possible, students should not know other members of their group because previous direct experience may override the heuristics of gender stereotyping and weaken the effects of the demonstration.

The demonstration should be used before students read about gender stereotypes and group dynamics. The activity can be introduced as a psychology game. Distribute written instructions describing the group task to each member of each group; otherwise, the person receiving or reading the instructions may be chosen or accepted as the leader. The two sets of instructions are as follows:

Task-Oriented Competitive
You will be playing a board game with your group. The board game involves competition against another group, and you will focus on specific tasks. You should try your hardest to win the game. To do this, you should focus on the game's objectives as much as possible. To start, your group should first select a person who will be in charge of the group. After this leader is selected, specific instructions about the game will be given and you will start playing.

Social Cooperative
You will be playing a board game with your group. The board game does not involve winning but, instead, involves agreeing with each other, supporting one another, and setting aside differences in order to get along maximally with each other. To start, your

---

[1]It may be possible to differentiate a social orientation from cooperation and a task orientation from competition. Future research may address this issue by including social competitive instructions and task-oriented cooperative instructions in addition to the social cooperative and task-oriented competitive instructions described herein.

group should first select a person who will be in charge of the group. After this leader is selected, specific instructions about the game will be given and you will start playing.

Students take 2 min to read their instructions and select group leaders. Groups are not specifically instructed about how to select leaders. Any method of nomination and selection is acceptable as long as all group members ultimately agree on the leader.

After verifying that leaders for each group have been chosen, the instructor informs the groups that they will not play a game after all. Instead, the actual purpose of the activity was to examine leader selection and processes. The gender of each student chosen as task-oriented and social leaders is compiled. The instructor or a student volunteer can tally both the gender of the leader selected as well as the technique each group used in selecting its leader.

Results

This study examined leader selection in 103 groups of introductory psychology students, with two men and two women comprising each group. Students participated in one of eight sessions that varied from 30 to 250 members each. Fifty-one of the groups received the task-oriented competitive instructions, and 52 groups received the social cooperative instructions. The results, by gender and type of instruction, are displayed in Table 1.

A binomial test revealed that, as predicted, significantly more men than women were selected as leaders, $z = 2.66$, $p < .01$. Also as predicted, a chi-square test using the Yates correction revealed that, as the type of instruction differed, the gender of the leader selected also differed, $\chi^2(1, N = 103) = 8.93$, $p < .01$. This significant effect is largely attributable to the underselection of women for task-oriented group activities (11 observed and 18.8 expected) coupled with the overselection of women as leaders of social activity groups (27 observed and 19.2 expected).

Evaluation

To evaluate the impact of the demonstration, 71 students completed a questionnaire about the activity. They responded on a 7-point scale ranging from *not at all* (1) to *very much* (7). Items on the scale and mean ratings were as fol-

Table 1. Number of Leaders Selected by Gender and Instructions

Type of Instruction	Men	Women	Total
Task-oriented			
Observed	40	11	
Expected	32.2	18.8	
			51
Social			
Observed	25	27	
Expected	32.8	19.2	
			52
Total	65	38	103

lows: (a) This activity would be a valuable addition to a class discussion on stereotypes (M = 6.24). (b) This activity gave me a clear understanding of the influence of stereotypes on behavior (M = 5.97). (c) How aware of stereotypes' influence on leadership behavior are you as a result of this demonstration (M = 6.38)? (d) This activity would benefit other students in psychology (M = 6.06).

Students were also asked for additional comments about the activity. Only positive aspects of the exercise were mentioned, such as the following: (a) "This activity was a good way of meeting others and loosening up the classroom." (b) "Very interesting . . . surprising . . . opens many questions." (c) "It's interesting how gender subconsciously affects our decisions." (d) "After you explained it, it really made sense. I never thought about stereotypes in that way." (e) "Most people already realize that there are stereotypes, but this graphically demonstrates how prevalent they are." (f) "I was fooled. I really thought we were going to play a game and nominated our leader because he was the tallest and biggest member of the group, and he looked like he already had authority."

Discussion

Results revealed that, overall, leadership positions were most likely to be filled by men, but this finding was evident only under task-oriented competitive conditions in which the ratio of male to female leaders was nearly four to one. Eagly and Karau (1991) suggested that, as leadership goals change from a position that requires task-oriented behaviors to one requiring socially complex tasks or the maintenance of good interpersonal relationships and group harmony, slightly more women than men emerge as leaders. Although a comparable finding was not statistically significant in the present study, data from the social cooperative instructions were in that direction. The classroom activity produces reliable and provocative effects that should make students more cognizant of gender stereotypes and their effects on leader selection.

Class discussion after the activity could be stimulated by the following questions:

1. Discuss the selection procedure. Did men or women more commonly nominate themselves? Which gender was more commonly nominated by other group members? What were the common procedures used in selecting leaders? In the present study, students' descriptions of their selection process included (a) "He was chosen because he was the tallest . . . he looked like he should be in charge," (b) "I knew from the beginning he would be the leader—he just looked the part," and (c) "The two women in our group asked him to be the leader."

2. Discuss the stereotypes students use in selecting leaders. When and why are stereotypes about men and women likely to influence leader selection? Are these stereotypes used when the groups meet for longer periods of time?

3. Discuss possible causes for the bias against female leaders. In everyday life, we witness more men than women as leaders; how may that affect leader selection? Do women avoid leadership positions? When women become leaders, how are they typically viewed in comparison with men?

4. Examine the gender differences that result when the task becomes one in which a social leader is required. Why does the gender bias disappear?

One possible variation of this demonstration is to assign groups to either feminine or masculine sex-typed activities. For instance, one group may be told to choose a leader for their discussion of the use of cloth versus disposable diapers for babies. The other group's discussion topic may be the choice of repairing cars at home with the guidance of manuals and friends versus taking the car to a repair shop. The visibility of stereotypes should be demonstrated as women are selected more often when the task is feminine sex-typed and men when the task is masculine sex-typed. In both cases, gender stereotypes guide individuals in their selection of leaders.

References

Broverman, I. K., Vogel, S. R., Broverman, D. M., Clarkson, F. E., & Rosenkrantz, P. S. (1972). Sex-role stereotypes: A current appraisal. *Journal of Social Issues, 28*(2), 59–78.

Eagly, A. H., & Karau, S. J. (1991). Gender and the emergence of leaders. *Journal of Personality and Social Psychology, 60,* 685–710.

Eagly, A. H., & Mladinic, A. (1989). Gender stereotypes and attitudes toward women and men. *Personality and Social Psychology Bulletin, 15,* 543–558.

Geis, F. L., Brown, V., Jennings, J., & Corrado-Taylor, D. (1984). Sex versus status in sex-associated stereotypes. *Sex Roles, 11,* 771–785.

Geis, F. L., Brown, V., Jennings, J., & Porter, N. (1984). TV commercials as achievement scripts for women. *Sex Roles, 10,* 513–524.

Lord, R. G., De Vader, D. I., & Alliger, G. M. (1986). A meta-analysis of the relation between personality traits and leadership perceptions: An application of validity generalization procedures. *Journal of Applied Psychology, 71,* 402–410.

Nye, J. L., & Forsyth, D. R. (1991). The effects of prototype-based biases on leadership appraisals: A test of leadership categorization theory. *Small Group Research, 22,* 360–379.

Porter, N., Geis, F. L., & Jennings, J. W. (1983). Are women invisible as leaders? *Sex Roles, 9,* 1035–1049.

Wood, W. (1987). Meta-analytic review of sex differences in group performance. *Psychological Bulletin, 102,* 53–71.

Notes

1. An earlier version of this article was presented at the 16th annual National Institute on the Teaching of Psychology, St. Petersburg Beach, FL, January 1993.
2. I thank Ludy Benjamin, Jr., Deborah Kashy, and Wendy Wood for their assistance in preparing this article and Ruth Ault and three anonymous reviewers for their helpful comments on an earlier version.

Defining Normal Sexual Behavior: A Classroom Exercise

Mary E. Kite

Almost all textbooks on human sexuality include a chapter on typical versus atypical sexual behavior. Most attempt to address what, for college students, may be the most fundamental question: "Am I normal?" Yet defining normal sexual behavior is difficult because so many issues are involved and it is hard to avoid sounding judgmental. Moreover, "normality" is culture-specific and influenced by historical factors. A number of strategies can be used to address this issue. For example, some textbook authors describe sexual behavior as existing on a continuum between normal and abnormal, but point to the difficulty in demarcating aberrant and acceptable sexual activities (cf. Allgeier & Allgeier, 1988; Crooks & Baur, 1987). Another approach is to discuss different categories of normality (e.g., Hyde, 1986). Strong and Devault (1988) presented four such categories: (a) statistical, based on the number of people engaging in a given behavior; (b) biological, based on behaviors that correspond to biological function (e.g., reproduction); (c) psychological, based on the absence of anxiety, guilt, or frustration; and (d) moral, based on cultural or historical context.

Despite these expositions, individuals coming to terms with their own and others' sexuality often find this issue difficult to understand. This classroom activity helps students realize the problem with delineating boundaries for appropriate sexual behavior. By constructing their own definitions of normality, students can see that although they may feel a particular sexual behavior is unsuitable for them, deciding what is appropriate or inappropriate for others is extremely difficult.

Method

Students complete a 30-item questionnaire (see Table 1) concerning sexual behavior by deciding whether or not they consider each item normal. After completing the question-

Table 1. Questionnaire for Student Evaluation of Normal Sexual Behavior

Please rate whether or not each of the following activities represents normal sexual behavior by placing either a Y (yes) or N (no) in the blank.

_____ 1. Watching X-rated movies several times a week.
_____ 2. Having sex with more than one person at the same time.
_____ 3. Preferring oral sex over intercourse.
_____ 4. Having intercourse with a member of the same sex.
_____ 5. Fantasizing about having sex with a member of the same sex.
_____ 6. Fantasizing about a person other than one's partner during sexual intercourse.
_____ 7. Masturbating in front of a partner.
_____ 8. Having sex somewhere other than a bed (e.g., floor, shower, kitchen, outdoors).
_____ 9. Never engaging in masturbation.
_____ 10. Becoming excited by exposing oneself in public.
_____ 11. Being celibate.
_____ 12. Being unable to achieve orgasm.
_____ 13. Enjoying being physically restrained during sex (e.g., bondage).
_____ 14. Becoming aroused by voyeurism (e.g., Peeping Toms).
_____ 15. Playing with food (e.g., fruit and whipped cream) during sex.
_____ 16. Dressing in the clothing of the other sex.
_____ 17. Preferring that one's partner initiates sex.
_____ 18. Inflicting pain during sex.
_____ 19. Receiving pain during sex.
_____ 20. Using sex toys (e.g., a vibrator) during sex.
_____ 21. Having rape fantasies.
_____ 22. Masturbating after marriage.
_____ 23. Not being aroused by a nude member of the other sex.
_____ 24. Being aroused by receiving an obscene phone call.
_____ 25. Being aroused by making an obscene phone call.
_____ 26. Engaging in sex with animals.
_____ 27. Deriving sexual pleasure from seeing or touching dead bodies.
_____ 28. Becoming aroused by being urinated on.
_____ 29. Becoming aroused by soiling the clothing of the other sex.
_____ 30. Becoming aroused by viewing or touching feces.

naire, students are divided into groups and attempt to construct a definition of normal sexual behavior. Each group shares its definition with the class; the ensuing class discussion examines the similarities and differences among these definitions. I also compare the class-generated definitions with Strong and Devault's (1988) categories of normality.

Results and Discussion

Students in my classes always have difficulty reaching a group decision about what constitutes normal sexual behavior. The definitions they construct are generally vague and consist mainly of statements reflecting personal choice (i.e., psychological normality). The following examples represent typical responses: "Normal is hard to define! What one thinks is normal may be abnormal to others. We think it is what the couple feels comfortable with." "Normalness during sexuality can be anything that doesn't leave each individual with guilt feelings." "Whatever happens between men and women except same sex and animal involvement." "Sexual behavior deemed as normal to the person, but also to society."

My classroom discussions focus on the difficulty students have in making the ratings and their reluctance to single out any but the most extreme behaviors (e.g., sex with animals) as abnormal. I have used this activity with eight sexuality classes, and it has always been well received. Students find the project enlightening, especially when they discover that others are having difficulty with the assigned task. They often refer to the activity in later class discussions because the issues that it raises resurface throughout the course. It also gives them a chance to talk about sexual issues in an impersonal format, which can eliminate barriers to open discussion.

This activity can be modified in several ways. One possibility is to use a rating scale format whereby students rate each behavior on a continuum of normal to abnormal, using, for example, a 5-point rating scale. When using this method, I found that students rely heavily on the neutral (no opinion) point of the scale. Instructors may also wish to focus on whether certain behaviors are viewed as less normal for women than men. Two versions of the questionnaire can easily be constructed—one referring to men and one referring to women—with class members completing one or the other. Responses on these two versions and definitions derived from them can be compared. Even if students are reluctant to rate women and men differently, class discussion can focus on the sex differences in actual participation in such behaviors and how societal norms are more restrictive for women than for men. In addition, sophisticated students can examine the class data from this activity by computing descriptive statistics, chi-square analyses, or simple group comparisons. Discussion might also focus on how such a questionnaire is constructed, whether the questions asked were appropriate for the activity, and whether students are a representative sample. Ways in which the "study" could be improved in response to the criticisms can be examined.

This classroom activity demonstrates the difficulty in defining normal sexual behavior. In addition, it can provide students with a better understanding of questionnaire construction and survey analysis. Most important, it can facilitate discussion about a difficult topic. The issues surrounding normal sexual behavior are complex, but the described activity provides opportunity for exploration and understanding.

References

Allgeier, A. R., & Allgeier, E. R. (1988). _Sexual interactions_ (2nd ed.). Lexington, MA: Heath.

Crooks, R., & Baur, K. (1987). _Our sexuality_ (3rd ed.). Menlo Park, CA: Benjamin/Cummings.

Hyde, J. S. (1986). _Understanding human sexuality_ (3rd ed.). New York: McGraw-Hill.

Strong, B., & Devault, C. (1988). _Understanding our sexuality_ (2nd ed.). St. Paul, MN: West.

Notes

1. Portions of this article were presented at the meeting of the American Psychological Association, New Orleans, LA, August 1989.
2. I thank Ann Choate and Kim Duffey for their help in constructing questionnaire items and Bernie Whitley for comments on a draft of this article.

Using Science Fiction to Teach the Psychology of Sex and Gender

Hilary M. Lips

We are seldom aware of how our own gender and the very concept of gender shape our lives. It is difficult to take issue with Bem and Bem's (1970) argument that gender is in many ways a "nonconscious ideology" (p. 89). We are like the fish that are too surrounded by water to understand what it means to be wet. When teaching about the psychology of sex and gender, I use science fiction to increase students' awareness of this nonconscious ideology. In recent years, a host of feminist writers of science fiction have elaborated worlds in which new possibilities for gender and/or sex are explored (see Rose, 1988, for an overview). I use the worlds two of these writers have created to jolt my students into thinking about how much they take gender for granted and to help them imagine how things could be different.

The first world to which I introduce them is the one created by Ursula Le Guin (1969) in *The Left Hand of Darkness*. On the planet described by her narrator, people do not come in two sexes and there are no all-inclusive gender roles. Every individual is simply an individual, not a woman or a man. Individual's status changes only for a few days every month when they go into a period of sexual desire labeled *kemmer*. During that time, the individual "becomes" either a woman or a man in terms of sex organs and reproductive capacity and tries to connect sexually with another individual who is also in kemmer. If approached in an early stage of kemmer, an individual may respond by "becoming" a man if the first individual is a woman or a woman if the first individual is a man. An interesting aspect of the process is that, each month, individuals do not know whether they will become a man or a woman and have no control over this outcome. There are some fascinating implications to this potential to become, at random, either a woman or a man: A sexual liaison may result either in becoming pregnant, if the individual turns into a woman, or in inseminating the sexual partner, if the individual turns into a man. In Le Guin's world, a person who is the mother of several children may also be the father of several others!

Once my students have become familiar with the world fantasized in *The Left Hand of Darkness*, I ask the class of 50 to 60 students to meet in small groups (5 or 6 students) to discuss its implications for society. For the first 10 min, I provide no structure for the discussion except the question, "How would daily life be different in the word described by Le Guin?" After giving the groups this initial opportunity to define for themselves what aspects of life might be most affected by the absence of gender except in a limited sexual context, I feed some specific questions to the discussion groups: What would such an arrangement mean for the definition of family? Monogamy? Social attitudes toward contraception, abortion, day care? Rape? What about homosexuality? In non-kemmer situations, what would be the implications for ordinary social interaction of not having gender roles as cues

to behavior? One person in each group serves as notetaker. After 30 min, each group reports its conclusions to the class and a general class discussion follows.

Two major themes emerge regularly from the group discussions: (a) the pervasiveness with which gender is used in our society to frame expectations about individuals and their behavior, and (b) the extent to which family structure affects social life and the intergroup relationships between women and men. Students comment frequently on the near impossibility of imagining what social interactions would be like without gender cues. The exercise helps even those who think they are already "liberated" from the constricting notions of femininity and masculinity to see how these concepts still affect their own assumptions and behavior. Students' comments also often reveal an increased awareness that women's and men's biological contributions to reproduction need not necessarily lead to a particular type of family structure or power relationship between women and men. They speculate in their discussions about how "things might be different" if men could become pregnant; they often come to the conclusion that "things could be different," even with our current biological arrangement.

I use this exercise at the beginning of my undergraduate course in sex and gender, but it would be equally appropriate for units on gender in other courses. My students appear to enjoy the exercise, and it reminds all of us just how much our society is structured by sex- and gender-related expectations.

Another world from science fiction that I introduce in my course is the utopian portrait of a future society created by Marge Piercy (1976) in *Woman at the Edge of Time*. In Piercy's world, there are women and men, but their lives are structured in ways that minimize the impact of sex and gender on social relationships. Women do not go through pregnancy: Babies are grown in tenderly managed test-tube nurseries, each cared for by three chosen female and male "co-mothers," who nurture them until puberty. Male as well as female co-mothers breastfeed the babies. Rather than individual parents, society has major responsibility for the care of children, and at adolescence, children make a ritual break from their parents and gain a set of specially selected advisers. The picture she paints is idyllic; my students have an interesting time articulating their reactions to it. Many of them are not at all convinced of the desirability of her solutions to social problems.

My favorite aspect of Piercy's novel, however, is the language. In the world fantasized by Piercy, there are no masculine and feminine pronouns—there is only *per* (for person), as in "I want to talk to per, but per won't listen." I introduce the language aspect to the course when we discuss the role played by language in shaping children's attitudes about gender. We talk about the evidence that children are exposed to a constant stream of language using the masculine gender as normative and so learn to think of the typical person as being a man—a step toward adopting the cultural assumption that the man is normative and the woman atypical or deviant. Then I ask them to imagine whether we could have a workable language that did not include gendered words, such as *he, she, policeman, chairman,* and *waitress,* that are already being replaced by more neutral ones. Usually they feel it would be awkward and unworkable, but when they are exposed to Piercy's approach, they are often surprised at how quickly it becomes easy and natural to read language that is not filled with references to gender. Sometimes, as an exercise, we hold small-group discussions in which all personal pronouns must be replaced by *per.* As the exercise begins, I hear bursts of laughter from the groups as they struggle with the unfamiliar forms, but after a few minutes most of the groups settle into the new linguistic requirements with only occasional lapses. Student comments after the exercise often reflect, first, their surprise at their ability to adapt to a genderless language, and second, their observation that when using the neutral pronoun *per* they often forgot to think of the gender of the person being discussed.

Piercy's novel alters language in a number of ways, highlighting how language is shaped by cultural assumptions and by power relationships. The inhabitants of her utopia have no "family" names, and their first names are chosen or discovered rather than bestowed. She creates new words for new possibilities in relationships and renames familiar concepts and processes in order to make the reader think about them in a new way. This is typical of many writers of the new feminist science fiction (Wiemer, 1987) who, convinced that women's self-expression is constrained by a language that is shaped by and reflects traditional male–female power relationships, are struggling to create new forms of language. This whole enterprise presents psychology students with some interesting possibilities to consider and may ultimately motivate them to delve more deeply into not only the psychology of gender, but also the social psychology of language. Her approach enables me, for example, to ask my students to consider how a particular social relationship is legitimized by being assigned a universally recognized label: wife, husband, mother, father, stepfather. Are there, for instance, roles analogous to Piercy's "co-mothers" that go unrecognized in our society because of the lack of a label?

Because much science fiction now being produced is actually "social science" fiction, its usefulness in teaching psychology extends beyond the examples given here. Some other interesting examples of different visions of equality in male–female relationships can be found in Le Guin's (1974) *The Dispossessed* and Bryant's (1976) *The Kin of Ata Are Waiting for You.* A more detailed exploration of the relation between language and power is central to Elgin's (1984) *Native Tongue* and Staton's (1975) *From the Legend of Biel.* Gotlieb's (1976) *O Master Caliban!* delves into the relation between humans and ever more sophisticated computers. Sargent's (1976, 1978) *More Women of Wonder* and *The New Women of Wonder* contain many discussion-provoking short stories that challenge conventional notions about gender, including the work of James Tiptree, Jr., who is, in reality, psychologist Alice Sheldon. As stimuli for helping students notice and perhaps break free of their unacknowledged assumptions about people and behavior, these and other works of science fiction can be extremely useful.

References

Bem, S. L., & Bem, D. J. (1970). Case study of a nonconscious ideology: Training the woman to know her place. In D. J. Bem (Ed.), *Beliefs, attitudes, and human affairs* (pp. 89–99). Monterey, CA: Brooks/Cole.

Bryant, D. (1976). *The kin of Ata are waiting for you.* New York: Random House.

Elgin, S. H. (1984). *Native tongue.* New York: DAW Books.

Gotlieb, P. (1976). *O Master Caliban!* New York: Harper & Row.

Le Guin, U. (1969). *The left hand of darkness.* New York: Ace Books.

Le Guin, U. (1974). *The dispossessed.* New York: Harper & Row.

Piercy, M. (1976). *Woman at the edge of time.* New York: Fawcett Crest.

Rose, H. (1988). Dreaming the future. *Hypatia, 3*(1), 119–137.

Sargent, P. (1976). *More women of wonder.* New York: Vintage.

Sargent, P. (1978). *The new women of wonder.* New York: Vintage.

Staton, M. (1975). *From the legend of Biel.* New York: Ace Books.

Wiemer, A. J. (1987). Foreign l(anguish), mother tongue: Concepts of language in contemporary feminist science fiction. *Women's Studies, 14,* 163–173.

We Dream, You Do: "Great" Grandmothers Teach a Lesson in Women's Changing Roles

Elizabeth C. Vozzola

Students who came of age in the 1990s frequently harbor either misconceptions or outright biases against feminist psychology (Unger & Crawford, 1996). Thus, helping students understand that societal structures can and do put powerful constraints on the accomplishments and expectations of women is often one of the most difficult tasks facing an instructor teaching courses in gender or the psychology of women.

Teachers can foster a complex developmental understanding of societal biases and constraints by using a narrative approach to knowledge acquisition in conjunction with the empirical material summarized in most textbooks. Many psychology undergraduates find research using the scientific method "disappointingly reductionistic, meticulous, and abstract" (D. Fernald, 1996, p. 151). In contrast, humans appear to embrace stories or narratives precisely because they find stories satisfyingly complex, inexact, and concrete (Bruner, 1986; Epstein, 1994; Vitz, 1990). L. D. Fernald's (1987, 1989) research on the merits of narrative-assisted instruction lends empirical support to the appeal of narrative described by Bruner (1990) and Coles (1989).

The use of stories for teaching has roots in concepts of experiential learning described by Dewey (1963). The integration of experience and education finds application in teaching techniques such as collaborative learning (e.g., Brody, 1995), connected teaching (Clinchy, 1995), and active learning (e.g., Conner, 1996; Lawson, 1995; Perry, Huss, McAuliff, & Galas, 1996). When stories arise in a rich, real world context that engages both affect and cognition, narratives may present intellectual points particularly effectively and hence pull students into a greater appreciation of the empirical works they have been studying.

A Psychology of Women class at a women's liberal arts college envisioned, created, and carried out a project that allowed them to explore ideas about women's development within such a real world context. During a discussion of why age or cohort might sometimes prove an equally (or more) important explanatory variable than sex, several students volunteered "great" grandmothers to talk with the class. The students used an open discussion format to develop a set of interview questions designed to explore both life history background and cohort effects.

Seven students in the class nominated grandmothers who were willing to talk with the class. The instructor then mailed letters of invitation and the following student-designed questions to each of the invited grandmothers 2 weeks before the scheduled class:

1. What messages did your family and society give you as a girl about what a woman should be?
2. Did you have any particular role models?
3. What did you try to teach your daughter(s) and/or son(s) about what it meant to be a woman or a man?
4. Did you have the sense that expectations for the roles of women were similar or different for you and your daughter? (if you had one)
5. How do you perceive society's expectations for your granddaughter? What messages do you see the culture sending her about what it means to be a woman?
6. If you could choose, would you prefer to have grown up with the role expectations of your own generation, your children's generation, or your granddaughter's generation?

During the class, after I read a question, each grandmother responded in turn. Students, especially the granddaughters, frequently added comments or asked questions.

During the final half hour of class the students hosted an informal reception.

Student Responses

The students were surprised that all but one of the grandmothers, given the choice, would choose to grow up with the role expectations of her granddaughter's time. The heartfelt stories of dreams unfulfilled and opportunities not available wove an argument for the reality of gender bias more powerfully than any of the assigned readings.

During the following class, students responded to questions evaluating the experience and what they learned. There were no negative comments, and many students spoke of seeing for the first time how historical conditions set constraints on conceptions of self and achievement. The observation that the only grandmother who would not choose to live in modern times had led a relatively privileged life led into an interesting discussion on the interaction of cohort, gender, and social class.

Additional specific feedback came from a final journal assignment that asked each student to reflect on what important learning she would take away from the course. Sixteen of the 26 (61%) chose to write about "Great" Grandmothers' Night. The comments were uniformly positive.

> The most important and memorable experience for me was the "Great Grandmothers' Night." . . . I felt privileged to attend such a wonderful event. It was an informative evening filled with priceless experiences, advice, and wisdom. I learned so much about life and our changing society that evening. These women were inspirational.

> All at once I realized how fortunate I was to be born in a time where opportunity does exist and is actually obtainable. I also realized that it is up to the women of today to remove the barriers in society that make it so difficult to fit those opportunities in our everyday lives. There is still so much to do.

Conclusions

In a society that isolates adolescents from adults (Sprinthall & Collins, 1995), understanding the strong influence of historical norms and constraints on women may be hard to come by. Yet the content of any psychology of women or gender class is virtually meaningless without such historical perspective. The experience of using a life history interview and dialogue format suggests that the method holds great potential for fostering a complex understanding of the social and historical context of development.

The grandmothers experience did not include either a processing assignment or a formal evaluation. In the future, to ensure that students integrate the powerful emotional experience with critical thinking, they will first read Bruner's (1994) work on self-narrative. Following the interviews, they will write reaction papers (a) evaluating the strengths and weaknesses of interview data and generating ideas for improving the design in terms of participant selection, sample size, generalizability, and related issues of reliability and validity and (b) evaluating how the interview data support or dispute the empirical and theoretical course readings on gender bias and cohort effects. They will also complete a formal Likert measure rating the value of the assignment.

D. Fernald (1996) argued persuasively that narratives increase students' comprehension when they provide a meaningful context for instruction. He suggested that stories work their way not only into students' thinking but also into their feelings and dreams. The grandmothers' stories of Depression hardships and doors closed to women demonstrated how gender, history, culture, and class played out in real human lives. Enthusiastic student comments during the evening itself, during the class discussion the following week, and in reflection journals at the end of the course all suggest that the stories not only fostered a more complex developmental understanding of gender bias, but also worked their way into the students' feelings. "I keep reflecting on what Sarah's grandmother said, 'We dreamed, you do.' It makes me believe in myself whenever I think of that quote." Consistent with the feminist pedagogical goals of connected and collaborative learning and of valuing both affect and cognition (Belenky, Clinchy, Goldberger, & Tarult, 1986), grandmothers became teachers, and their lives became a lesson in women's changing roles.

References

Belenky, M. G., Clinchy, B. M., Goldberger, N. R., & Tarult, J. M. (1986). *Women's ways of knowing*. New York: Basic Books.

Brody, C. M. (1995). Collaborative or cooperative learning? Complementary practices for instructional reform. *Journal of Staff, Program, & Organizational Development, 12*, 133–143.

Bruner, J. (1986). *Actual minds, possible worlds*. Cambridge, MA: Harvard University Press.

Bruner, J. (1990). *Acts of meaning*. Cambridge, MA: Harvard University Press.

Bruner, J. (1994). The "remembered" self. In U. Neisser & R. Fivush (Eds.), *The remembering self: Construction and accuracy in the self narrative* (pp. 41–54). Cambridge, England: Cambridge University Press.

Clinchy, B. M. (1995). A connected approach to the teaching of developmental psychology. *Teaching of Psychology, 22*, 100–104.

Coles, R. (1989). *The call of stories*. Boston: Houghton-Mifflin.

Conner, D. B. (1996). From Monty Python to *Total Recall*: A feature film activity for the cognitive psychology course. *Teaching of Psychology, 23*, 33–35.

Dewey, J. (1963). *Experience and education*. New York: Collier Books.

Epstein, S. (1994). Integration of the cognitive and the psychodynamic unconscious. *American Psychologist, 49*, 709–724.

Fernald, D. (1996). Head and tales in introductory psychology. *Teaching of Psychology, 23*, 150–158.

Fernald, L. D. (1987). Of windmills and rope dancing: The instructional value of narrative structures. *Teaching of Psychology, 14*, 214–216.

Fernald, L. D. (1989). Tales in a textbook: Learning in the traditional and narrative modes. *Teaching of Psychology, 16*, 121–124.

Lawson, T. J. (1995). Active-learning exercises for consumer behavior courses. *Teaching of Psychology, 22*, 200–202.

Perry, N. W., Huss, M. T., McAuliff, B. D., & Galas, J. M. (1996). An active-learning approach to teaching the undergraduate psychology and law course. *Teaching of Psychology, 23*, 76–81.

Sprinthall, N. A., & Collins, W. S. (1995). *Adolescent psychology: A developmental perspective*. New York: McGraw-Hill.

Unger, R., & Crawford, M. (1996). *Women and gender: A feminist psychology*. New York: McGraw-Hill.

Vitz, P. C. (1990). The use of stories in moral development: New psychological reasons for an old educational method. *American Psychologist, 45*, 709–720.

Promoting Human Factors Psychology Thinking Through Design Assignments

David M. Carkenord

Sanders and McCormick (1993) stated that human factors psychology "seeks to change the things people use and the environments in which they use these things to better match the capabilities, limitations, and needs of people" (p. 4). Thus, a major goal of human factors psychology is the design of effective and user-friendly machines, tools, and systems. Teachers of undergraduate human factors psychology should foster in students a basic understanding of and appreciation for this primary theme. Promoting such understanding can be challenging, however, due in part to the limited work experiences of students and limited resources of the typical academic department. For example, it is difficult for students to reflect on the design of machines or equipment they have used in previous jobs due to their restricted work backgrounds. Also, it is seldom feasible for a department to purchase, for example, a data-entry keyboard specially designed to reduce cumulative trauma disorders in users. Hence, the challenge for instructors is getting students to identify with the concerns of human factors psychologists in a practical and interesting way.

One means of achieving such an end is to encourage students to begin thinking like human factors psychologists concerning the design of objects they encounter daily. As Norman (1988, 1992) suggested, many common, everyday things are designed with little regard for the capabilities and limitations of the human user. For example, Norman noted that, on most stove-top ranges, the correspondence between the burner controls and the burners themselves is often confusing. As another example, Norman explained that the buttons on most car radios are too small for easy use by the normal human finger. Given the prevalence of common things that have less than perfect designs, students can likely identify everyday objects in their lives that are poorly designed. In searching for such objects, students' cognitive frame of reference will move toward a human factors perspective.

Design Assignments

Overview

Students are instructed to identify some object they have encountered or use regularly that is not designed consistent with basic human factors principles. After identifying such an object, students propose some modification of the existing design that would make the object more user-friendly. Students submit a typed description of the identified design flaw and an explanation of how the flaw may be remedied. Students are encouraged to include diagrams to assist in explaining their design topic. The entire assignment is rarely more than one page. In a human factors course, the design ideas can be assigned once a week or once every 2 weeks.

Some Examples

Examining some specific examples submitted by students serves to highlight the type of thinking generated by these exercises. Many of their design ideas and solutions are specific to aspects of the local college campus (e.g., shower stalls in a dorm are too small and should be larger), but many others are more general in nature. For example:

1. An oven door that opens with a foot pedal rather than the conventional handle. This arrangement avoids the common heat-in-the-face problem and provides easier opening for elderly persons who may have trouble gripping the oven handle.
2. A countertop electric can opener that removes the top of a can and automatically stores the lid inside the opener to avoid the danger of a lid's sharp edges.
3. A button on a television set that, when depressed, would cause the television's remote control unit to emit a beep. This beep would allow the user to locate the remote if it becomes lost somewhere in the house.
4. An electric deicer on a retractable automobile radio antenna.
5. A running shoe with a replaceable sole would eliminate the need to replace the entire shoe when the sole is worn.
6. A small tab on each paper coffee filter in a pack to make removing just one filter easier.
7. Public telephones with card scanners so that one could simply "swipe" one's calling card and eliminate the need to enter the often lengthy card numbers.

Although these examples may not be mechanically or technically feasible to design and produce (or unknown to my students or me, they may be already available in some markets), they do highlight the fact that students have a wealth of innovative ideas and suggestions when offered the opportunity to think in human factors terms.

Class Discussion of Ideas

The assignments provide excellent material for class discussions. I read students' design ideas to the class and, if appropriate, try to replicate their diagram on the chalkboard. If anything is unclear about the design, the student designer explains the idea in more detail. On many occasions, students come to the chalkboard and produce their own drawing or diagram to make the design clearer. Another approach would be to have students present their own ideas directly to the class without the instructor's attempt to explain and interpret the ideas.

I challenge the class to provide feedback, both positive and negative, on the newly proposed design by posing such questions as the following: Would the new design effectively eliminate the original problem? How much would the new design cost? Would the new cost be justified? Would production of the new object be feasible? What unanticipated problems may the new design create? A discussion of such questions provides an excellent critical thinking exercise, and students' insights are often impressive. I am careful, however, to stress that although the class as a whole critiques a design, such critiques are not intended to insult the student designer. In fact, the give-and-take critique is one of the primary purposes of the assignments, making students realize that real-world human factors psychologists and engineers who design things are seldom able by themselves to view all possible outcomes of how their designs will interact with the human user. Thus, students come to realize that, even when purposefully thinking in human factors terms, all contingencies of a design are seldom identified.

Depending on the size of the class, the timing of the class discussion can be varied. With a large class (i.e., 25 students or more), I have collected all the assignments during one class period, identified the six or seven most thoughtful and innovative examples, and discussed those designs at the start of the next class period. With a small class, one can discuss all students' designs on the due date, but it may be advisable for instructors using the assignments for the first time to take time between the submission and discussion to identify some strengths and weaknesses of each design. This procedure enables the instructor to prepare questions, comments, and insights on each design before the discussion. Such preparation is especially helpful early in the course, when students are often uncertain about the type of class discussion and critique that is appropriate. As the course progresses, the instructor's previewing of the designs may become less important because students understand the discussion format.

Grading of Assignments

Students do not receive a formal letter grade on their design descriptions, but the assignments are a required part of the course, worth a small point value each. For assignments submitted on time, the student earns full credit. I do not attempt to assign points based on an evaluation of the soundness or practicality of the design suggestions due to the difficulty in making such a subjective decision.

Student Assessment of Assignments

I first used these assignments weekly in a class of approximately 25 students. Although I did not conduct an objective assessment of the assignments at that time, my feeling was that students viewed them very positively. Since then, however, students in a small class ($N = 8$) objectively evaluated the weekly assignments. They responded to four survey items, each on a 5-point scale ranging from *strongly disagree* (1) to *strongly agree* (5). Mean responses on the four items indicate very positive attitudes toward the assignments. Students reported that the assignments were an interesting part of the course ($M = 4.63$, $SD = 0.52$), helped them better understand human factors psychology ($M = 4.50$, $SD = 0.53$), helped them think like a human factors psychologist ($M = 4.38$, $SD = 0.74$), and made the content of the course more relevant to their daily lives ($M = 4.25$, $SD = 0.89$).

An open-ended item on the survey asked students to express any additional thoughts or opinions. Five of the eight students responded to this item, and all conveyed positive feedback. Some of the comments were "The design assignments add more interesting conversation in class," "I think the design projects add a lot to the class," and "Good idea!"

Discussion

Throughout the course, I stress that one of the major goals is to get students to view their world from a human factors perspective. At the onset, most students do not understand what this means, but eventually the majority of them do start to examine objects and situations from a human factors viewpoint. Toward the end of the semester, students often volunteer a human factors analysis on recent national or local news events. I believe the use of the assignments plays a major role in this perspective shift.

Use of the assignments is not limited to a human factors psychology course. Other courses that may cover the topic of human factors, such as industrial/organizational and introductory psychology, can also be enhanced by the assignments. Students may be required to develop only one or two ideas in these courses, but the goal of promoting human factors thinking will still be accomplished.

References

Norman, D. A. (1988). *The design of everyday things*. New York: Basic Books.

Norman, D. A. (1992). *Turn signals are the facial expressions of automobiles*. Reading, MA: Addison-Wesley.

Sanders, M. S., & McCormick, E. J. (1993). *Human factors in engineering and design* (7th ed.). New York: McGraw-Hill.

Note

I thank Diane Stubbins, Ruth L. Ault, Charles L. Brewer, and three anonymous reviewers for their helpful comments and suggestions on earlier drafts of this article.

Consumer Behavior Classroom Exercises That Really Work

Allan J. Kimmel

Because of its inherently interesting and relevant content, consumer behavior can be one of the more attractive courses in the psychology or business curriculum for both students and professors. The processes that guide consumer buying behavior and consumption provide insight into how consumers think and process information, reveal how things they own affect their lives and influence how they feel about themselves, and lead consumers to make more effective consumption decisions. Given its applied focus, the course is particularly suited for incorporating various experiential exercises, group activities, and cases to bring to life material presented in class lectures and readings.

In this article, I describe some exercises that work in my consumer behavior classes on a consistent basis, in the sense of generating student involvement in discussions, arousing interest in the material, stimulating critical thinking, and enhancing overall learning. I adapted these exercises from sources such as instructor's manuals (e.g., Shaw, 1995), journal articles (e.g., Lawson, 1995), and discussions with colleagues. English-speaking students in three French schools—diverse groups of Europeans, Asians, and Americans—offered helpful, informal feedback that enabled me to winnow out weaker exercises and strengthen those that served as useful learning experiences. Instructors can modify each example to suit the course focus (e.g., business or psychology) and student level.

Focus Group Simulation

This consumer research simulation demonstrates some difficulties inherent in the use of focus groups for marketing purposes as well as their potential for providing leads for quantitative investigations or real-world application. I precede the simulation with a brief lecture on the objectives and procedures for conducting a focus group. (Details pertaining to this qualitative research approach appear in Kinnear & Taylor, 1996.) The exercise can serve as an effective icebreaker if conducted early enough in the term.

About one week before the exercise, I inform students that they will play one of three roles during an interview simulation: either moderator, respondent, or observer. I recruit volunteers and solicit suggestions for discussion topics for which students have a clear interest (e.g., new products, marketing campaigns, campus-related issues). At the outset of the simulation I provide a separate role sheet to the moderator, respondents (approximately 6 to 8 volunteers for the group discussion), and observers (the remainder of the class) that describes their role in the simulation and the interview objectives.

The interview should last about 30 min. During a postinterview feedback stage, I ask the observers to identify the strengths and weaknesses of the moderator, discussion themes, and revealing comments. I follow the feedback stage with a full-class discussion dealing with ways to improve the group interview approach, its limitations, potential benefits, moderator strategies, and related issues. Due to moderator inexperience, time and physical constraints, and presence of critical observers, it is not surprising that the simulated interviews often are fraught with problems; however, failures tend to stimulate insightful feedback sessions and class discussions.

Variations of this exercise include having the class conduct separate focus groups simultaneously in adjoining rooms, videotaping the group sessions, and using more than one moderator to reduce the pressure that lone moderators might experience. To extend this exercise into a graded writing assignment, students can submit an individual report critically assessing the focus group as a marketing research tool or group reports for the "client" who hired their research team.

Satisfaction–Dissatisfaction Exercise

This exercise, suggested by Denis Hilton (personal communication, October 12, 1993), requires minimal preparation from the students as well as the instructor and is appropriate during course sections devoted to the consumer consumption experience or postacquisition phase of the consumer behavior process. The objective is to have students identify factors that relate to consumer satisfaction and dissatisfaction. I distribute an exercise sheet to half the class asking them to describe recently purchased products with which they were especially *satisfied*. I ask the rest of the class to describe products with which they were especially *dissatisfied*. I give the students a few minutes to think about each example and summarize what made them satisfied or dissatisfied. Students then circle the best example on their list; that is, the one associated with the most satisfaction or dissatisfaction.

Next, I ask students to state their circled product and to briefly explain why they found it especially satisfying or dissatisfying. As each student responds, I list on the blackboard the products and explanations (in brief) under columns marked "satisfiers" and "dissatisfiers." Once every student has responded, I instruct the class to review the product lists and try to determine how they differ. The task is to identify which product factor or related variable best distinguishes the products in the satisfier column from those in the dissatisfier column. Although there are exceptions, as when the same product appears in both lists, students tend to de-

262

vise some interesting hypotheses about the factors leading to consumer satisfaction and dissatisfaction. Some distinguishing factors my classes have noted are reflected in the following dichotomies: traditional–innovative, high–low involvement, necessities–luxuries, frequently–infrequently purchased, high–low expectations, good–bad value for money. Having recognized, for example, that involvement level appears to be a key distinguishing factor, the class can speculate as to why high (or low) involvement is more likely associated with consumer satisfaction than dissatisfaction and how this difference might influence consumers' postacquisition behavior.

Once there is general agreement about one or two product-related factors, I guide the class through a statistical comparison. Following a brief overview of the chi-square statistic, I draw a 2 (satisfaction–dissatisfaction) × 2 (level 1–level 2 of product factor) table on the blackboard and ask students to classify each listed product in the appropriate quadrant. Together, we calculate and interpret a chi-square value and discuss the implications of the results.

Stanton Chemical Company Marketing Dilemma Case

This case study, originally developed by Daniel L. Sherrell (cf. DeLozier, 1977), pertains to the topics of consumer perception, product positioning, and marketing ethics. The case describes the difficulties of the Stanton Chemical Company in marketing *Clo-White,* a liquid laundry bleach. Clo-White outperforms its competitors in cleaning ability and is odorless; however, consumers tend to purchase other brands because of their belief that a strong smell is associated with stronger cleaning ability. In fact, strong smell is an indication that bleach has lost some of its cleaning potential.

The case presents two alternative solutions to Stanton Chemical's dilemma: (a) inform and educate consumers about the association between strength and smell of bleach or (b) allow Clo-White to age and smell stronger, then promote it as a new and improved bleach. Also provided is a perceptual map positioning Clo-White and its chief competitors according to strength and price dimensions, along with some information about consumer market segments. I also attach a copy of the current American Marketing Association's (1972) ethics code.

Following a lecture on perceptual principles, I divide the class into four-person groups and instruct them to (a) list all the possible alternative strategies that Stanton Chemical might take to improve the market share of Clo-White; (b) describe the short- and long-term effects of each strategy; (c) select a preferred alternative, based on group consensus; and (d) evaluate the ethicality of each strategy. After about 30 min, each group describes the recommendation they would present to the company and the strategy's short- and long-term consequences. Typically, some groups agree about a recommended course of action, but inevitably there will be disagreement, which generally stimulates a lively discussion. At some point, the instructor should ask for suggestions as to how the company might carry out an educational campaign to inform consumers about the strength–smell association.

Overall, this case helps students appreciate the difficulty of educating consumers in ways that contradict strongly held perceptions and long-term beliefs. It also demonstrates how potentially profitable marketing actions are not necessarily the most ethical ones.

Multiattribute Attitude Model Exercise

I use this exercise, suggested by Stephen Holden (personal communication, November 2, 1994), to give students an opportunity to assess their product-related attitudes and to identify strategies for influencing consumer brand preferences. Following a brief overview of Fishbein's (1983) multiattribute attitude approach, students select an attitude object for which they have high involvement. I present a list of possible object categories, including such consumables as soft drinks, restaurants, cigarettes, and automobiles as well as less obvious "objects," such as politicians, dating partners, and schools.

Each student develops a calculation table on a sheet of paper. In the table's first column, they list between five and nine *salient attributes* that come to mind for the attitude object in question (such as "atmosphere" and "admission price" for the category of dance clubs). In the next column, they rate the *importance* that each attribute holds for them, using a scale ranging from 1 (*very little importance*) to 7 (*very much importance*). Next, they insert a "beliefs" heading to the right of the importance column, below which they list from three to five "brands" within the product or service category selected (e.g., the names of competing dance clubs). Students then list *belief* ratings, according to the extent they believe each brand possesses a satisfactory level of each listed attribute, using a scale from 1 (*poor or very unlikely to have*) to 7 (*good or very likely to have*). For the dance club example, a student may believe that a particular club has a good atmosphere but that the admission price is rather expensive and thus assigns values of 7 and 2, respectively. I have students calculate attitude scores for each brand by summing the Belief × Importance ratings across attributes. Before or after the calculations, the instructor can have students rank the brands according to their actual preferences. Students can then compare their preference rankings with their multiattribute scores and diagnose any discrepancies. I solicit students' reactions to the analysis, including considering possible limitations to the model.

Finally, I have students form small groups to discuss the strategic marketing implications of the Fishbein (1983) model. Their goal is to develop up to five marketing strategies to present to the class. The ensuing full-class discussion focuses on applications of the multiattribute model, such as strengthening perceived product–attribute linkages (cf. Solomon, 1996, pp. 179–180). By highlighting the personal and professional relevance of the multiattribute approach, this exercise does an excellent job of stimulating class involvement and facilitating learning of the material.

The Procter and Gamble Rumor Case

This case provides a unique way of involving students in the topic of personal influence by focusing on rumors about companies and their products. In advance of this exercise, the class reads a brief article on the nature of rumor (Rosnow & Kimmel, 1979) and a four-page case write-up developed by the author focusing on Procter and Gamble's (P & G) problems in fighting false rumors. (Koenig, 1985, described P & G's alleged Satanic conspiracy and other marketplace rumors in detail.)

In small groups, students develop strategies for fighting negative marketplace rumors by addressing questions presented at the end of the case. Specifically, the questions instruct the groups to (a) consider strategies that business enterprises might take to combat a rumor, along with risks associated with each, and (b) evaluate P & G's tactics in responding to the rumors that plagued the company for so many years. The final question asks group members to play the role of rumor consultants for another company recently targeted by false rumors and to recommend an action plan for controlling them and preventing their reoccurrence. (For example, in one version I had students consider false claims that the Snapple Beverage Corporation supported the Ku Klux Klan and antiabortion groups.) Each group presents its rumor-fighting strategy to the class and briefly applies it to the situation described in the final case question.

Throughout the discussion, I challenge students to specify how their approach ties in to what is known about the psychology of *rumormongering* (i.e., the variables known to perpetuate rumors) and the difficulties inherent in marketers' attempts to control personal influence among consumers (so-called word-of-mouth). To conclude the exercise, I describe Esposito and Rosnow's (1983) five-step plan for responding to rumors (from verifying the facts to waging an all-out offensive). Thus, students can compare their action plans with those recommended by experts.

Conclusions

I include up to 10 exercises in my consumer behavior classes, although the combination that I select varies each term. The 5 exercises described here are the ones I have used every time I have offered the course, a sign that they continually have met with success. For each of these exercises—but not with others I have tried—student participation is exceptionally high, with nearly every student having some input in either the small-group or full-class discussions. Recently, Meyers (1997) described the potential problem of social loafing in small-group activities; my recommended exercises are not entirely immune from this problem. However, I have found that the percentage of students who do not participate in the small-group discussions during the exercises decreases substantially when the group size is small (i.e., no more than four students to a group) and I appear attentive to their progress.

An interesting cross-cultural observation is that my European students generally are less likely to view social loafing in academic coursework as unacceptable than are my non-European students. The European social norm appears to be that if some group members do not contribute their fair share of the work, it is their fellow group members' responsibility to "pick up the slack." In essence, the group serves as a mutually supportive unit, recognizing that members may have personal or professional burdens that may undermine their contribution. In this light, the observation that social loafing is minimal for the five described exercises further attests to their utility.

My European students are more than willing to give critical feedback when they believe that an assignment or exercise is not a worthwhile or engaging learning experience. Although I have received critical suggestions about how to modify the five exercises, the overall feedback from my classes has been overwhelmingly positive. Students remain beyond the 3-hr class period to continue their discussions, refer to points made during the exercises in their writing assignments, discuss the exercises in the campus café or pub after class, and send additional comments to me via e-mail.

To more systematically assess the exercises, I obtained evaluations from one of my consumer behavior classes ($N = 26$). Students rated each exercise on a scale ranging from 1 (*strongly disagree*) to 7 (*strongly agree*) according to the extent to which it was a worthwhile use of class time, stimulated thinking about relevant course material, enhanced learning of course material, and should continue to be used in the course. All of the mean ratings fell within a range of 5.0 to 6.0 (see Table 1).

Consistent with other reports of successful class exercises (Meyers, 1997), those described here require some advance preparation of students before they are carried out. I have had success with the exercises without incorporating an evaluation component or assigning specific roles to individ-

Table 1. Means and Standard Deviations of Evaluations of the Class Exercises

Case	N[a]	Worthwhile Use of Time		Stimulated Thinking		Enhanced Learning		Continue to Use	
		M	SD	M	SD	M	SD	M	SD
Focus group									
Satisfaction	24	5.8	.90	5.2	1.01	5.1	.86	5.9	.75
Dissatisfaction	25	5.5	.86	5.1	1.16	5.0	1.30	5.2	1.29
Stanton Chemical	24	5.9	.83	5.4	.83	5.5	1.07	5.2	.83
Attitude	21	5.6	1.09	5.6	1.50	5.2	1.19	5.6	1.28
Rumor	26	5.8	1.12	5.7	1.20	5.8	1.26	6.0	1.18

Note. Based on a scale ranging from 1 (*strongly disagree*) to 7 (*strongly agree*).
[a]Unequal *N*s reflect the fact that some students were absent during the exercise.

ual students in their small-group work, which may be more a function of the cultural context than an inherent aspect of the exercises themselves.

The exercises are adaptable for use in other psychology and business courses, including research methods (e.g., the focus group and satisfaction–dissatisfaction exercises), social psychology (e.g., the multiattribute attitude model and rumor exercises), marketing (e.g., the Stanton Chemical and rumor exercises), and business ethics (e.g., the Stanton Chemical case). Finally, I have found these exercises to be equally successful with students of varying abilities, skills, and backgrounds and in academic programs with varying objectives (e.g., an undergraduate business major, a certificate program in international marketing, and a Master's program in luxury brand management).

References

American Marketing Association. (1972). *Code of ethics*. Chicago: Author.

DeLozier, M. W. (Ed.). (1977). *Consumer behavior dynamics: A casebook*. Columbus, OH: Merrill.

Esposito, J. L., & Rosnow, R. L. (1983). Corporate rumors: How they start and how to stop them. *Management Review, 72*, 44–49.

Fishbein, M. (1983). An investigation of the relationships between beliefs about an object and the attitude toward that object. *Human Relations, 16*, 233–240.

Kinnear, T., & Taylor, J. (1996). *Marketing research: An applied approach* (5th ed.). New York: McGraw-Hill.

Koenig, F. (1985). *Rumor in the marketplace: The social psychology of commercial hearsay*. Dover, MA: Auburn House.

Lawson, T. J. (1995). Active-learning exercises for consumer behavior courses. *Teaching of Psychology, 22*, 200–202.

Meyers, S. A. (1997). Increasing student participation and productivity in small-group activities for psychology classes. *Teaching of Psychology, 24*, 105–115.

Rosnow, R. L., & Kimmel, A. J. (1979, June). Lives of a rumor. *Psychology Today*, 88–92.

Shaw, R. (1995). *Instructor's resource manual with transparency masters and video guide*. Englewood Cliffs, NJ: Prentice-Hall.

Solomon, M. R. (1996). *Consumer behavior* (3rd ed.). Englewood Cliffs, NJ: Prentice-Hall.

SUBJECT INDEX

A

Abnormal psychology, 174–176; mental illness through poetry, 239–240; schizophrenia, 240–241
Achievement, 94–95
Action potential, 194–196
Active learning, 19–23
African Americans, 104–112
Afterimages, 21, 216–217
Aggression, 242–244
Animal, cross-species comparisons, 46; learning, 44–45, 163–168
Applied psychology course, 27–30
Attitude change, 79–82
Autobiographies, 21, 73
Avoidance conditioning, 165–166

B

Biography and life-span development, 208–211
Brain, action potential, 194–196; lateralization, 196–199; neural coding, 201–204; split, 199–201; synaptic transmission, 201–204

C

Case studies, 38, 86–87; novels as, 130–131
Central Limit Theorem, 190–193
Cerebral lateralization, 196–199
Class participation, 57–59
Classical conditioning, 119, 165; demonstrations, 221–225, 225–227, 228
Clinical psychology, see Abnormal psychology
Clustering technique in writing, 87–89
Cognition, and emotion, 229–231; eyewitness testimony, 232–233; metacognition, 113
Cognitive development, 42–43, 45–46
Cognitive disequilibrium, 82–84
Collaborative learning, see Cooperative learning
Color perception, 216–218
Combinatorial logic, 35–37
Comparative psychology, 46
Computers, and problem solving, 113–115; assisted instruction, 154–160; psychology activities, 143–145; visual displays for class, 146–150; web-assisted class, 150–153
Consumer behavior, 262–265
Contours, 216–218
Cooperative learning, 82–84, 84–85
Coping, 94–95
Critical thinking, and case studies, 86–87; and cooperative learning, 82–84; immersion approach, 115–121; questioning approach, 122–126; and writing, 116–129, 137–139
Critiquing journal articles, 131–133

D

Debates, 78–82
Developmental psychology, 205–208; children's games, 211–212; life-span, 208–211; moral development, 212–214
Diaries, 29
Discussion, 20–23, 120; and aggression, 242–244; and newspaper coverage of psychology, 180–181; and writing, 87–89
Distance learning, 14–17
Diversity, African Americans, 104–112; aging, 208–211; cultural relativism, 92–98; disability, 174–176; gender bias, 252–254, heterosexism, 98–103; international students, 90–91

E

Emotion, 93–94; and cognition, 229–231
Essay, questions, 134–137; tests, 55
Ethics, research, 38–41
Evolutionary theory, 42–49
Examinations, 50–54; create-a-game exam, 71–72; essay tests, 55
Eyewitness testimony, 232–233

F

Focus group simulation, 262–265
Freudian theory, 43; in everyday life, 248–251

G

Garbage-can illusion, 215–216
Gender, bias, 252–254; and science fiction, 256–257; women's changing roles, 257–259
Grading, 54–57, 120–121; class participation, 57–59; posters, 170
Group work, 20–21, 82–84, 84–85; African American content, 109–110; developmental psychology, 211–212; and racism, 246–248

H

Handedness, 188–190
History of psychology, 24–27; game, 71; presentism in, 25
Homosexuality, 87–88, 98–104
Human factors, 260–261
Humanistic psychology, 43–44

I, J

Icebreaker activity, 173–174
Imagination, 114

Industrial/Organizational psychology, 260–261, 262–265
Inquiry teaching, 34–37
International students, 90–91
Introductory psychology course, African American content in, 104–112; assignments, 9; content, 5–13; computer-assisted instruction, 154–160; discussion groups, 20–23; distance learning, 14–17; goals, 5–13; history of psychology in, 24–27; instructors, 7; large classes, 17–23; movies in, 177–179; research ethics in, 38–41; student expectations, 9–12, 68–70; team teaching, 31–32; writing in, 54–57
Invertebrates, 163–168
Journal articles, motivating students to read, 75–77

L

Large classes, 17–23; icebreaker, 173–174
Leader selection, 252–254
Lecture method, 17–23, 36
Letters, writing personal, 205–208
Library research skills, 35–37
Life-span developmental psychology, 208–211
Locus of control, 95–96
Lunar size, 218–220

M

Maslow's, Abraham, theory, 43–44
Mean, 182–185
Memory, 234–236; mnemonics, 22, 32–34, 236–238; Tip-of-the-Tongue phenomenon, 234
Metacognition, 113
Mnemonics, 22, 32–34, 236–238
Moral development, 212–214
Motivation, 93–94; of students, 67–68, 73–75, 75–77
Movies, popular, 177–179

N

Names, learning students', 18–19, 32–34
Neural coding, 201–204
Newspaper, accounts of psychology, 180–182
Novels, as case studies, 130–131

O

Observer bias, 185–188
Olfactory conditioning, 222–225
Operant conditioning, 165

P, Q

Papers, short, 55–56
Perception, color, 216–218; contours, 216–218; demonstrations, 21–22; and disability, 174–176; garbage-can illusion, 215–216; lunar size estimation, 218–220
Personality theory, 43–44, 92–93, 119
Personalizing courses, 18–23
Piaget's theory, 42–43

Poetry and mental illness, 239–240
Poster sessions, 168–171
Prejudice, gender bias, 252–254; racial, 246–248; stereotypes, 244–246
Press coverage of psychological research, 180–182
Problem-solving skills, 113–115
Projects, 171–173
Psychology portfolio, 137–139
Publication bias, 190–193
Questioning and critical thinking, 122–126, 127

R

Racism, 246–248
Rap singing, 173–174
Reading, 75–77; novels, 130–131
Relationships, 94
Research methods, 188–190; lunar size activity, 218–220
Riddles, 113–115
Rogers', Carl, theory, 43–44

S

Sampling distribution, 182–185
Schizophrenia, 240–241
Science fair, 171–173
Science fiction, 256–257
Self, 93; awareness, 96
Semantic Profile Technique, 64–66
Sexual behavior, 254–255
Social psychology, 44; stereotypes, 244–246
Spatial summation, 202
Specific-process theories, 44–46
Split brain procedure, 199–201
Statistics, 182–185; Central Limit Theorem, 190–193; significance testing, 190–193
Stereotypes, 244–246
Students, autobiographies, 21, 73; course expectations, 9–12, 62–64; impressions of courses, 64–66; learning names of, 18–19, 32–34; participation in class, 57–59; ratings of textbooks, 3–4; time management, 59–61; what motivates them, 67–68
Study, techniques that foster thinking, 118; skills, 59–61
Summation, spatial, 202; temporal, 202
Synaptic transmission, 201–204

T

Teaching assistants, 20–21
Team teaching, 31–32
Temporal summation, 202
Textbooks, and African American content, 105; and homosexuality, 99–101; selection of, 3–5
Tip-of-the-Tongue Phenomenon, 234
Touch, 196

U, V

Undergraduates, as teaching assistants, 21, 55–57
Verbal interference, 196–197
Video teaching, 14–17
Visualization, 114, 229–231

W

Web pages, 150–153
Women, changing roles, 257–259; gender bias, 252–254
Writing, activities, 19–20; clustering technique, 87–89; and critical thinking, 126–129; critiquing journal articles, 131–133; developmental psychology, 205–208; to discuss, 87–89; effective feedback, 139–142; grading of, 54–57; improving student skills, 134–137; and movies, 177–179; poetry as a way to explore mental illness, 239–240; about psychology, 137–139

APPENDIX

Structure of the Introductory Course
Chatman and Goetz, 1985, *12*, 150–152.
Miller and Gentile, 1998, *25*, 89–96.

Approaches to the Introductory Course: Techniques
Andrews, Gosse Gaulton, and Maddigan, 1999, *26*, 115–118.
Benjamin, 1991, *18*, 68–74.
Goodwin, 1997, *24*, 218–221.
Grasha, 1998, *25*, 85–88.
Morlock, Gaeddert, McCormick, Merrens, Shaffer, and Zandi, 1988, *15*, 144–145.
Smith, 1985, *12*, 156–158.
Zachry, 1985, *12*, 129–131.

Approaches to the Introductory Course: Content
Fisher and Kuther, 1997, *24*, 172–175.
Gray, 1996, *23*, 207–214.

Examinations and Grading
Baich, 1998, *25*, 181–185.
Madigan and Brosamer, 1991, *15*, 91–94.
Melvin, 1988, *15*, 137–139.
Sweidel, 1996, *23*, 246–248.

Students' Interests, Perceptions, and Motives
Becker, Davis, Neal, and Grover, 1990, *17*, 159–162.
Davidson, House, and Harm, 1993, *20*, 223–225.
Sass, 1989, *16*, 86–88.
Zanich and Grover, 1988, *16*, 72–74.

Enhancing Student Interest
Berrenberg and Prosser, 1991, *18*, 167–169.
Buskist and Wylie, 1998, *25*, 203–205.
Carkenord, 1994, *21*, 162–164.

Discussion Exercises and Group Activities
Budesheim, 1999, *26*, 106–110.
Cooper, 1995, *22*, 7–9.
Giordano and Hammer, 1999, *26*, 42–44.
McDade, 1995, *22*, 9–10.
Ventis, 1990, *17*, 42–44.

Diversity in the Introductory Classroom
Collingridge, 1999, *26*, 126–128.
Enns, 1994, *21*, 205–211.
Simoni, 1996, *23*, 220–226.
Whitten, 1993, *20*, 13–21.

Teaching Critical Thinking
Doolittle, 1995, *22*, 33–36.
Gray, 1993, *20*, 68–74.
King, 1995, *22*, 13–17.
Wade, 1995, *22*, 24–28.

Writing to Learn, Learning to Write
Chrisler, 1990, *17*, 55–57.
Gareis, 1995, *22*, 233–235.
Madigan and Brosamer, 1990, *17*, 27–30.
Rickabaugh, 1993, *20*, 170–172.

Willingham, 1990, *17*, 10–13.

Computers in the Introductory Course
Brothen, 1997, *24*, 213–216.
Seaman, 1998, *25*, 141–145.
Slattery, 1998, *25*, 152–155.
Worthington, Welsh, Archer, Mindes, and Forsyth, 1996, *23*, 175–181.

General
Abramson, 1986, *13*, 24–29.
Baird, 1991, *18*, 27–29.
Fish and Fraser, 1993, *20*, 231–233.
Harcum, 1991, *18*, 181–182.
Wurst and Wolford, 1994, *21*, 233–235.
Hemenover, Caster, and Mizumoto, 1999, *26*, 196–198.

Research Methods and Statistics
Connor-Greene, 1993, *20*, 167–169.
Dyck and Gee, 1998, *25*, 192–195.
Goldstein, Hopkins, and Strube, 1994, *21*, 154–157.
Johnson, 1996, *23*, 168–170.
Riniolo, 1997, *24*, 279–282.

Biopsychology
Felsten, 1998, *25*, 109–111.
Kemble, Filipi, and Gravlin, 1985, *12*, 81–83.
Morris, 1991, *18*, 226–228.
Reardon, Durso, and Wilson, 1994, *21*, 96–99.

Developmental Psychology
Junn, 1989, *16*, 135–139.
Neysmith-Roy and Kleisinger, 1997, *24*, 116–118.
Nigro, 1994, *21*, 243–245.
Shapiro, 1995, *22*, 245–247.

Sensation and Perception
Cavalier and Wesp, 1997, *24*, 125–127.
Horner, 1997, *24*, 267–268.
Kunkel, 1993, *20*, 178–180.

Learning
Abramson, Onstott, Edwards, and Bowe, 1996, *23*, 26–30.
Kohn and Kalat, 1992, *19*, 100–102.
Vemoy, 1987, *14*, 176–177.

Memory and Cognition
Deffenbacher, 1990, *17*, 182–185.
Gee and Dyck, 1998, *25*, 138–140.
Miserandino, 1991, *18*, 169–171.
Schoen, 1996, *23*, 30–32.

Psychological Disorders
Chrisler, 1992, *19*, 173–174.
Osberg, 1992, *19*, 47–48.

Social Psychology and Personality
Benjamin, 1985, *12*, 40–42.

Goldstein, 1997, *24*, 256–258.
Lawrence, 1998, *25*, 198–200.
Miserandino, 1994, *21*, 93–95.

Sex and Gender
Hebl, 1995, *22*, 186–188.
Kite, 1990, *17*, 118–119.

Lips, 1990, *17*, 197–198.
Vozzola, 1998, *25*, 289–291.

Industrial/Organizational Psychology
Carkenord, 1994, *21*, 235–237.
Kimmel, 1999, *26*, 203–206.

3965